HELP FOR

DEPRESSED MOTHERS

by

Barbara Ciaramitaro

Foreword by
Virginia Larsen, M.D.

The Chas. Franklin Press
18409-90th Avenue W. • Edmonds, WA 98020

i

First Edition Copyright © 1978 by Barbara Ciaramitaro

Second Edition, Revised and Expanded Copyright © 1982
by Barbara Ciaramitaro

Cover Illustration: Marina Horosko

ISBN: 0-9603516-3-9

Library of Congress Catalogue Number: 81-70362

Printed in the United States of America

DEDICATIONS

This book is dedicated to the women who shared their experience of depression after childbirth with me. Their encouragement and help were essential to my success.

I would also like to dedicate this book to my husband Jim who stood by me through it all, my son James who is growing into a fine person in spite of a difficult start, and Dr. N.J.G. who helped me unravel my past so that I could write my own future.

ACKNOWLEDGMENTS

The ideas of a number of writers have been incorporated into the Self-Help Workbook portion of this book without mention of their names. Where I have been consciously aware of such adaptations from other works I have noted my gratitude to the originators in Chapter 14 where I recommend their books among others for further reading.

However, hundreds of authors have shaped the very pattern of my thinking without my being consciously aware of the specific debt I owe to each of them. To them I can only say what every mother knows, "Imitation is the highest compliment."

FOREWORD

This book is an important contribution to new mothers who are depressed and is written by an understanding author who has developed very practical steps toward recovery. Ciaramitaro examines the feelings and problems of new parents who find the care of their babies depressing and/or overwhelming. These experiences and concerns faced by many new parents are also of interest to obstetricians and expectant parent educators, as well as many grandparents. All will find HELP FOR DEPRESSED MOTHERS combines useful research findings with the successful experience of new mothers who have experienced depressive reactions.

Virginia L. Larsen, M.D.

Dr. Virginia L. Larsen is currently Medical Director of the Truman Restorative Center in St. Louis, Missouri. During the 1960's she carried out original research in the area of postpartum depression while Chief of Medicine at the Mental Health Research Institute, Ft. Steilacoom, Washington.

TABLE OF CONTENTS

Foreword by Virginia L. Larsen

PART I: THE SELF-HELP WORKBOOK FOR DEPRESSED MOTHERS

Preface
How to Get the Most Help from Reading This Book

1.	You Are Not Alone	1
2.	How You Got This Way	4
3.	Rest for You and for Baby, Too	8
4.	Refueling Your Nervous System	11
5.	Eat Well to Get Well	16
6.	Activity Brings Energy	20
7.	How Your Doctor Can Help	26
8.	When to Call In the Professionals	29
9.	Look for Love Where It Can Be Found	35
10.	Mothering Yourself	38
11.	Mothering Your Child	42
12.	A Mother's Work	48
13.	Your Complete Program	53
14.	Books to Grow By	58

PART II: LETTERS FROM FORMERLY-DEPRESSED MOTHERS

Preface		67
15.	Anti-depressants Help Joanne	68
16.	Even Nurses Are Not Immune	71
17.	Lisa Takes the Long Road Back	76
18.	Rest in Bed Was Not Enough	82
19.	Abortion—A Realistic Alternative	86
20.	"I Need My Work to Be Happy and Growing"	88
21.	Ignorance—My Own and My Doctors'	94

PART III: UNDERSTANDING POSTPARTUM DEPRESSION

Preface	103

22. Depression—Still a Mystery 105
23. What the Researchers Say About Depression 110
24. Who Gets Depressed After Childbirth? 117
25. What Causes Postpartum Depression? 121
26. The Personal and Social Effects of Postpartum
    Depression 129
27. Prevention and Cure 135

PART IV: APPENDICES

Appendix I 145
Appendix II 147
Footnotes 149

PART I:

THE SELF-HELP WORKBOOK
FOR
DEPRESSED MOTHERS

PREFACE

This book is written by, for and about depressed mothers. It is written for you. It brings hope for complete recovery and a fuller life to women who are experiencing a serious depression following the birth of their child.

You will learn from the real-life accounts of women who have felt just as you now feel—alone, trapped, tearful, hopeless and ashamed. You will see how it was possible for them to turn the tide of their feelings into new and more helpful directions and to create for themselves and their families a better life than before.

Not all at once by an act of will . . . no. For many it took years of difficult struggle. But there are new techniques—new knowledge and insight—that can make it a shorter and easier struggle for you today.

Having gone through such a depression and struggle for recovery myself, I know what you are going through and I know the road to health and happiness. My story will take its place among the others and will help you find your way to a satisfying, fulfilling life.

ATTENTION: PLEASE READ

This book will be valuable to any woman who is now suffering or has in the past suffered from depression. If, however, there are feelings of suicide or abuse toward children, this book is not enough. PLEASE CONSULT YOUR DOCTOR IMMEDIATELY.

HOW TO GET THE MOST HELP FROM READING THIS BOOK

The chapters in this book contain medicine for the body, mind and soul. To get the full benefit from reading this book, the contents of each chapter must be carefully read and slowly digested in order to set free the flow of energy that can heal and restore you.

I therefore suggest that you read only one chapter each day. When you are finished with the chapter of the day, close the book and close your eyes. You have received an important message. Give it time to sink deeply into your consciousness. Welcome it into yourself.

Whenever possible you may reread the chapter through the day. Before the day is over you will act on that chapter's message and will be one step closer to health and happiness.

CHAPTER 1
YOU ARE NOT ALONE

The most important message of this book is that you are not alone. You are not some terrible freak of nature—the only woman to feel so miserable and unhappy at the very moment you expected to feel totally fulfilled. Each and every year thousands of women return home with their newborn babies and sink into a terrible depression—a deep black pit from which even the sky seems always gray.

I didn't know this when I became depressed 14 years ago. I had heard of the after-baby blues, that little let-down feeling that sometimes makes mothers tearful for a week or two after giving birth. I kept hoping that was all I was experiencing until I realized that my son was 6 months old, and I was so depressed I had fantasies of killing myself or him or both of us.

Then I sought psychiatric help. But in the three years I talked twice a week to a psychiatrist, I never once heard the comforting truth that I was but one of thousands of women each year who went into a serious depression after giving birth. No. Though my doctor treated me with respect, I nevertheless considered myself sick, weak, abnormal, different.

I was ashamed of my failure to be the successful, blissful new mother. I didn't tell my own parents anything about my depression for a whole year after I had started seeing a psychiatrist. Only my husband and one woman friend who cared for my son during my appointments knew anything about my depression—I was that ashamed.

After three years of psychotherapy I was pronounced cured, and I left the familiar psychiatrist's office with fear and trembling that a weak person like myself might not be able to manage life alone—that I might once more become depressed and have to return to therapy.

To fill the gap that leaving therapy made in my week I enrolled in a class at a nearby university—a psychology class, of course. For the class I had to write a paper on some adjustment problem. I decided to research the problem of adjusting to motherhood since it was one that I had experienced.

Only then, as I pondered through books in the back aisles of the university library, did I come across that remarkable but little-known bit of knowledge: In this country alone more than 4000 mothers each year are hospitalized with severe psychiatric disturbances within 6 months of giving birth. In addition, more than 100,000 women each year are treated in clinics and as private patients for depression following childbirth or struggle along alone at home because they are too ashamed of their feelings to seek help.

A light was turned on in my head, a great sigh of relief swept through my body. I was not alone. I was not a freak. I was no more different than thousands of other women who experience the same thing each year.

I was one of the lucky ones—I had recovered. I wondered how many women were so overwhelmed by the feeling that something was inherently wrong with them that they could not even begin to try to get better. I wanted to shout my discovery from the rooftops.

I wrote the paper for my psychology class, then rewrote it as an article and sent it in to the Writer's Digest Creative Writing Contest for 1971. It won 44th prize out of 2,000 entries. Thus encouraged, I sent the article out to magazines only to have it rejected by the editors.

Sadly, I put the article aside and went on about the business of living. I wrote other articles on other subjects and had several of them published over the years, but I never forgot about the thousands of women who were suffering as I had suffered and who were feeling all alone.

Then one day I read an ad about a man who had published his own book. Inspired by Jerry Buchanan's story, I resolved to do the same. I got out my old article manuscript and spent a year bringing my research up to date and gathering the stories of other women who had also experienced depression after childbirth. Then I wrote the first edition of this book and published it myself.

It was an ambitious plan for someone who had once been too depressed to pick up her son's scattered toys or wash the pile of dirty dishes in the sink. But the fact that you are reading this today shows that I succeeded. And you will succeed, too. You will succeed at doing things you have not yet dreamed of, because you are *not* alone.

Others have traveled this road before you. It is a rough and difficult road, but you will learn from them how best to travel it. You can have confidence that you will make it through, because they have made it and are calling back to you that the best is yet to come. Soon you will be one of them, reaching back with new strength and wisdom to help other women who are still depressed. And with such help each new generation of women will find the road smoother and easier to travel with confidence.

Having read this far, you have received the most important piece of information in this book. It is enough for one day. Please close the book and close your eyes. Let the full meaning of this chapter sink deep down inside of you. . . .

You are not alone.

CHAPTER 2

HOW YOU GOT THIS WAY

In chapter 1 you learned the most important thing this book has to tell you: that you are not alone in your depression following childbirth. Hundreds of thousands of women have felt what you are now feeling. Most have recovered to lead a happier life than before their depression. With the help of their advice and my own in this book you, too, can regain your health and happiness.

Chapters 3-13 of this part of the book contain a complete up-from-depression treatment program specially designed for you, the mother of a newborn infant. As you follow it step by step you will see that you can control the gloomy feelings that now seem to be controlling you. Again, *not* by force of will, but by understanding the physical as well as the psychological causes for your depression. This understanding will enable you to provide both your body and your mind with what is needed for your recovery.

Researchers are still trying to trace the exact sequence of events that lead to postpartum depression. One thing of which they are increasingly certain is that there are *physical* factors involved as well as psychological factors.

A pregnant woman goes through a great many physical changes over a period of nine months. These changes and their effects are reversed in a matter of hours or days after child-birth. Such an abrupt disruption of the body's processes places a considerable stress on the woman's body. With little time to recover the woman returns home to assume full responsibility for her infant's welfare. Round-the-clock feedings deprive her of much-needed sleep—another stress on her system.

Family routines are constantly interrupted as mother is called away by the baby's cries. Relationships become strained in the midst of the disorganization. Older children may require extra reassurance and attention. If this is a first child, the husband and wife have to do a lot of readjusting of their relationship to grow into their new responsibilities as father and mother, too. Thus psychological stresses are added to the physical ones.

Too many changes coming into your life in too short a time can exhaust your body's capacity to adjust. The capacity to adjust to stress is a physical thing. It has definite limitations related to the chemical processes which are involved in coping with stress.

Every thought and feeling you have is communicated to your body through the release of chemicals into your bloodstream. You can prove that to yourself right now.

Think of something which makes you feel afraid—perhaps a spider, a snake, or a snarling dog. Try to picture it so clearly that it seems to be actually there in front of you. Now notice your body's reaction to this thought. Your heart is beating faster; your breath is shallow; your muscles are tensed as if to run; your mouth feels dry. There is a knot in your stomach and a catch in your throat. Your skin feels cold and clammy.

All of these are physical reactions to a mere thought. When your brain visualizes something that it considers dangerous it sets off the production of hormones which prepare you to either fight this danger or run away from it. Those hormones race to every part of your body to produce the physical effects you just noticed. This is known as the "fight or flight" response and is your body's usual reaction to stress.

Now remind yourself that there is no real danger, that you were just fantasizing or imagining the spider or snake or dog. Imagine being wrapped in a warm, soft comforter or being cuddled by someone you care about. Soon your brain communicates this message to your body also. Your heart stops pounding; your breathing deepens with a sigh of relief; your muscles relax and you are able to swallow again. Soon you feel warm and safe inside.

When you are exposed to too many stresses in too short a time your body is in a constant state of alarm. Your brain's supply of chemical messengers becomes exhausted. Your thinking processes slow down, and you feel sluggish and confused. If the high level of stress continues you may reach your physical limit for adjusting to change. You become depressed.

Some researchers feel that we inherit our physical limit for coping with stress just as we inherit a limit on how tall we will grow. Others feel that our capacity for adjusting to change may become limited if we experience serious deprivations during childhood—particularly the early loss of a parent through death or divorce.

The fact that you are now depressed shows that you have reached your outer limit in dealing with stress. Your body has exhausted its usual stores of the chemicals that help it stay on an even keel in the midst of stress.

The depression you are feeling is a physical thing. It is your body's way of protecting you from further stressful demands. You are not going crazy. You are not imagining these strange physical and emotional feelings. You are not a failure as a woman or as a mother although that frightening thought may be one of your stresses right now. You have just reached a physical limit to your capacity to accept more changes in your life.

Now you will realize why it is especially important that you *make no further major changes in your life until you have fully recovered from your depression.*

This is no time to move to a new neighborhood or get a divorce. It is certainly the worst possible time to become pregnant with another child. While these changes in your life may seem to be desirable or even urgent, you must not make them while you are depressed. There will be plenty of time after you are well to plan and carry out any necessary changes in your life.

Now you must give your body a chance to recover its strength and rebuild its chemical resources for dealing with change and the stress change brings. Just as your brain sends messages to your body, so also your body sends messages to your brain. As you act in ways that restore strength and health to your body, your brain will receive the message that things are getting better, and, as soon as it is possible, it will recover from its state of chronic alarm.

Until then, whenever you become afraid that something terrible is happening to your body or mind you must sit down, relax as much as possible and accept each sensation as it comes. Describe your feelings calmly to yourself. "Yes, there is that weak feeling washing over me, that tightness in my arms and chest, that pounding heart. This is *not* a heart attack I am feeling, but it is definitely physical. My hormones are over-reacting to the stress I'm under. I must relax and let the feelings flow through me and out of me. As I get stronger these feelings will pass."

Being depressed is like stepping unexpectedly into quicksand. You feel yourself being sucked down quickly and helplessly. Your impulse is to panic and struggle against the grip of these gloomy feelings. But fearing the way you feel and trying to fight off your depression will only weaken you all the more.

Quicksand is mostly water. The way to keep it from sucking you under is to lay out flat on your back on its surface as though you were floating in a pool. In the same way, to keep on top of your depression, you must learn to relax in the face of it—to accept it as normal under the circumstances, to realize that you can and will get better as your body recovers its strength.

Close your eyes now and close this book. Repeat to yourself: "I have been through a lot of changes lately. My body needs time to catch up. I will give it all the time and care it needs."

CHAPTER 3
REST FOR YOU AND FOR BABY, TOO

After reading the first two chapters you see your depression in a new way. Even though these gloomy thoughts and frightening feelings seem strange to you, you now realize that they are commonly experienced by women after childbirth. They are the natural consequence of having exhausted your body's capacity to adjust to change.

You already know one thing you can do to hasten your recovery: you can avoid making any further major changes in your life while you are depressed. Now you are ready to learn a special way of relaxing and resting that will help you through the months when night-time feedings will disturb your sleep.

No one is more regularly deprived of a peaceful night's sleep than the mother of a newborn baby. Scientists who have studied our need for sleep tell us that regular disturbance of sleep (more than two nights in a row) leads to increased irritability and difficulty in concentrating. They also find that when you are under a lot of stress or are learning new skills you need even more sleep than usual.

Few mothers of newborns can afford to hire a night nurse to care for the baby while they get a full night's sleep (a worthwhile investment if you can afford it, by the way). But there is a way to relax so deeply in 20-minute periods throughout the day that many of the effects of sleeplessness can be overcome.

This form of relaxation is simple, but it must be perfected by regular practice several times a day every day for a number of weeks to give you its full benefits. Do not abandon its use until you have practiced it at least three times a day for a whole month. By then you will find it so valuable that you will gladly make it a part of your daily schedule.

Each time the baby goes to sleep take 20 minutes to practice this relaxation technique. Not only will you benefit, but your quiet occupation will allow your baby to reach a deeper state of sleep that will not be easily disturbed by noises made while doing other necessary chores once your relaxation period is over.

Go to your bedroom. Smooth the bedcovers and close the drapes. Lie down on your back with a pillow beneath your head. Grasp the bottom two corners of your pillow and tug them firmly until they rest on your shoulders. This will support your neck in a comfortable position.

If there is a second pillow handy place it under your knees. Having your legs slightly bent will ease any strain on your lower back. Now bend your elbows and rest your hands on your abdomen just below your ribs. Your body is now in a position of optimum comfort.

Close your eyes gently. Relax every part of your body. Be sure your jaws are relaxed, not clenched together. Loosen your tongue from the roof of your mouth and let it lie limply behind your lower teeth. Talk to each part of your body in your mind and tell it to relax, to let go of all tension: "Arms, relax. Let go, let go. Legs, relax. More, let go. Feet relax, feel limp, let go. Forehead, relax, let go."

When every part of you is relaxed, become aware of your breathing. Each time you breathe out say the word "one" in your mind. Women with visually-oriented minds may find it helpful to imagine a single bloom of their favorite flower or a dancing candle flame.

Other thoughts will pop up uninvited. Simply let them pass. Attach no importance to them. Don't follow them or allow your body to react to them. Just focus your attention on the word "One" or your chosen visual image each time you exhale. Do not try to fight off these intruding thoughts. Such an effort will make you tense and detract from the benefits to be had from this time of relaxation. As you practice day after day your mind will grow more calm and will, of its own accord, stray less often. Until then just bring it back gently to your chosen word or picture each time you notice it has wandered off.

You can open your eyes to check the clock when you wish. Do not stay in this state of relaxation for less than 10 minutes nor more than half an hour. Build up to 20 minutes three times a day.

Due to the disturbance of your night-time sleep and your greater need for rest, you may fall asleep after you have relaxed fully. If this sleep revives you and gives you a feeling of well-being so much the better. However, if you wake from such day-time sleep feeling groggy and worse than ever you may want to practice your deep relaxation in a comfortable chair rather than in bed.

Make sure both feet rest flat on the ground (if you are short like me put a telephone book or Sear's catalog under your feet). The small of your back should rest against the back of the chair. If it does not, tuck a small pillow behind you. A chair with arms may be most comfortable, but if you don't have one rest your hands on each thigh.

Now close your eyes and follow the same directions as given above. Mentally speak to each part of your body telling it to relax, then follow your breathing saying "One" or visualizing a picture in your mind each time you breathe out. Let other thoughts come and go. Watch them like guppies swimming in an aquarium. You are separate from these thoughts. They have no claim on you. They go on their own way while you relax. Relax.

CHAPTER 4

REFUELING YOUR NERVOUS SYSTEM

You are now practicing the deepest known form of relaxation three or more times each day. This practice may seem senseless at first, but its effect is cumulative. The more you practice the more quickly you will be able to reach the desired state of inner rest. As you spend more of your practice time actually resting instead of just attempting to reach that state of relaxation, you will notice an increase in the benefits you will receive from these brief periods throughout the day.

But it takes more than rest to rebuild your body's health and improve your mental state. What was it you learned back in grade school? Yes, it is still the same: diet, exercise, fresh air and plenty of rest.

If you are like me, you winced when you read the words diet and exercise. I gained so much weight on my short frame during the first five months of my pregnancy that my doctor had me on a diet all through the last four months. Nevertheless I looked and felt like a sluggish blimp when I returned home from the hospital.

Not only that, but I was also sick of cottage cheese and celery, and I craved the sweets I had already so long denied myself. As I became more and more depressed, I compensated for the empty feeling inside by stuffing down more and more of the forbidden goodies.

As for exercise, I had never enjoyed it though I guiltily forced myself through a workout whenever I became too ashamed of my appearance. Such efforts didn't last long nor did they make me feel much better about myself.

Not all women react in the same way when they get depressed. Many lose interest in food altogether. They quickly lose the extra weight from their pregnancy, but they don't stop there. They barely pick at their meals, sometimes feeling nauseous at the mere sight of food. Their strength dwindles yet they cannot eat the substantial meals that would build their strength. If they are nursing their baby, their milk supply dries up for lack of nutrients and this may add to their sense of failure as mothers.

Whether you are eating too much or too little or just the wrong foods, you can greatly increase your body's capacity for stress by improving your diet. Do not concern yourself with losing or gaining weight at this point. Instead concentrate on improving your health in every way possible.

The many changes your body has been through has placed a stress on your nervous system causing it to use up your natural reserves of vitamins and minerals. Many women reach an anemic state while still pregnant, and 20% of all women are anemic 4 days after giving birth. Whether or not you are actually anemic, you need to replace your body's stores of vitamins and minerals if you are to resist infections and regain your steady nerves.

To do this you will need to take a high-potency multiple vitamin every day for at least a year after giving birth. Such a high-potency vitamin and mineral supplement should contain:

Vitamins:

A	10,000	I.U.
D	400	I.U.
E	100-400	I.U.
C	250	mg.
B_1 (thiamin)	30	mg.
B_2 (riboflavin)	30	mg.
B_6 (pyridoxin)	30	mg.
B_{12} (cyanocobalamin)	25	mcg.
Niacinamide	100	mg.
Pantothenic Acid	100	mg.

Minerals:

Calcium	500-1000 mg.
Magnesium	250-500 mg.
Iron	15 mg.
Zinc	15 mg.
Manganese	5 mg.

Unfortunately you are not likely to find a multiple vitamin with these doses at your grocery or drug store. The usual one-a-day vitamins may be adequate to maintain good health under normal conditions combined with reasonably good eating habits. They are *not* adequate, however, for someone whose natural stores of nutrients has been depleted and who is experiencing depression as a reaction to stress. In short, they are not adequate to meet your present needs.

To find a vitamin formula as close to the one above as possible you will probably need to go to a health food store. Check your Yellow Pages for the one nearest to you. Even at a health food store you will need to carefully compare labels to find a suitable supplement—the storekeeper can help you. Be sure to notice how many tablets you will need to take each day to get the amounts of each vitamin and mineral listed in the formula. Also compare costs. You may need to buy two separate supplements—one for the vitamins and the other for the minerals.

Some vitamins are more helpful for dealing with stress than others. While the above-mentioned supplement contains a basic amount of these stress vitamins you may also want to take additional amounts of just these particular vitamins.

Here's why. The many B vitamins and vitamin C are water soluble—they cannot be stored in your body even under the best health conditions. They are very important to your body during times of stress, but your body has a hard time absorbing them at the very times it needs them most. So it is best to spread out your intake of vitamins B and C, taking a little at each meal and at bedtime rather than taking them all at once with your daily multiple.

To allow this a number of vitamin manufacturers have

come out with special stress formula vitamins. Such a formula should contain:

B$_1$ (thiamin)	10 mg.
B$_2$ (riboflavin)	10 mg.
B$_6$ (pyridoxin)	10 mg.
Niacinamide (nicotinic acid)	100 mg.
Pantothenic Acid (calcium pantothenate)	100 mg.
Vitamin C (ascorbic acid)	500 mg.

You will find several similar formulas to choose from at your health food store. Remember that this stress formula is to be taken *in addition to* your multiple. It is not an adequate vitamin supplement for your needs by itself.

Some researchers find that one mineral may also be particularly important for women who have just had a child. That mineral is zinc. If you had a lot of stretch marks during your pregnancy and if your skin is unusually oily now, you may well have a zinc deficiency which is contributing to your fatigue. If the multiple you have chosen does not have at least 15 mg. of zinc (and most don't), you may want to get a zinc supplement tablet of 30 mg. per tablet. Take one each day for a month and watch your skin improve and your energy pick up.

"How can I possibly afford to take so many vitamins?" you may ask. I know vitamins are expensive, but I also know that you could be letting yourself in for even more expensive doctor bills if you neglect to buy and take these vitamins. During my depression I was repeatedly rushing to my doctor for painful bladder infections, and I suffered such a severe case of the flu that I thought I was dying. It wasn't until I learned about nutrition and started taking vitamins, especially the B vitamins, that I was able to resist these infections.

A mother who is in poor health is on her way to becoming a poor mother. You must take good care of yourself if you are to be able to take good care of your baby.

If you are nursing, your baby will benefit directly from your vitamin intake and will be healthier and calmer for it. But whether nursing or not, your baby gets his or her sense of well-being from you. You have to be well to do well by your baby.

Go to a health food store. Buy a good multiple, a stress supplement and a zinc supplement and start taking those vitamins and minerals today.

CHAPTER 5
EAT WELL TO GET WELL

You are now doing two things daily to recover your physical strength and your mental sense of well-being. You are practicing a highly efficient form of relaxation every time your baby goes to sleep and you are taking a high-potency multiple and stress vitamins to replace your body's depleted store of nutrients.

Whatever you do, you must not completely skip any meal, not even breakfast. If you cannot bring yourself to eat anything else, get out your multiple vitamin and your stress formula vitamin and sit down at the kitchen table with a glass of milk or juice. (I find juices much more drinkable if I dilute them half and half with water. Also make sure that this is real juice and not a juice drink.)

Sip a little milk or juice slowly; take your vitamins, then finish your milk or juice. You have now received a powerful nutritional boost whether or not you are able to eat another mouthful.

If you have suffered from nausea or lack of interest in food, these nutrients will begin to restore your normal desire to eat in a few day's time. If you are overeating or eating all the wrong foods, these nutrients will allow your body to burn the calories in your food more efficiently giving you more energy and a more satisfied feeling from each meal with less fat storage from unused calories.

If you have not yet gotten to a health food store to buy your vitamins, please close this book and go or make arrangements to have someone take you. These vitamins are an essential part of this health-building, up-from-depression program. You must have them today.

While you are at the health food store you will notice many foods you may not have heard of before. Take time to browse up and down the shelves, read labels and look through the books on nutrition. You need not buy anything else besides your vitamins today, but as your eating habits change (and they will) you may find yourself doing more and more of your grocery shopping in health food stores.

I do not recommend making any drastic changes in your diet while you are depressed. By all means, avoid going on any kind of a crash diet even if you are greatly overweight. A diet would only be one more change, one more stress on a body that is already at the limits of its capacity to deal with stress. However, your health will benefit from a very slow, gradual turn toward a well-rounded diet with plenty of protein and natural bulk.

Oddly enough, whether you are underweight or overweight you will benefit from eating as many as six tiny meals per day rather than one to three large meals. You will find that your energy level will stay more constant through the day without great lifts and drops if you spread your food intake over many small meals.

Make sure that each of your tiny meals contains some protein—a small portion of meat or fish, one egg, some cheese, cottage cheese, yogurt or milk. I especially recommend protein foods which are high in tryptophan—trout, tuna, swordfish, beef flank steak, top round beef steak, fresh cooked ham (not cured ham), fried calf liver and raw pumpkin seeds (available at your health food store without the shell and salt). Tryptophan is an amino acid which has been found helpful in treating depression.

Every meal should also contain some fresh, raw fruit or vegetable—apple slices, a tomato or carrot, a piece of melon, an orange, strawberries, a plum, etc. This can occasionally be replaced by real fruit juice (not a juice drink) or a cooked vegetable.

Gradually shift to breads with more whole grain content—cracked wheat, whole wheat, rye or pumpernickel. After months of experimenting you may even develop a taste for rye with caraway or dill seeds, bran muffins, and wheat berry or seven grain bread. The more whole grain bulk your bread contains, the more satisfying each piece will be and the less problem you will have with constipation. A single piece of such bread at no more than 2 or 3 of your six tiny meals will be sufficient. This can be replaced by a bowl of shredded wheat, granola, oatmeal or one of the cereals high in bran, if you wish.

If you are a coffee drinker, try the decaffeinated brands. Caffeine places an extra strain on your nervous system that may add to your fatigue and depression. You might also enjoy trying some of the fragrant fruit or mint teas. They are much more soothing than black tea and will give you a greater variety to choose from.

In summary, eat as close to nature as possible. When shopping, spend most of your time going around the perimeter of the store—to the produce, dairy and meat departments—with only a quick dip into the proper aisles for whole-grain bread, non-sugared cereal, rice, beans, split peas or juice. You'll also be amazed at how much your grocery bill will go down as you eat fewer processed foods.

Remember—do *not* be forceful, rigid or sudden in your application of these diet principles. Food has many emotional meanings—it often provides the positive effects of much-needed mothering for depressed people. You will learn better ways of mothering yourself in a later chapter, but this is no time to deprive yourself of what simple pleasures and comforts you may have turned to in your distress.

It is enough that you take your vitamins faithfully and and slowly add one or two of the healthier foods (especially more protein foods) to your shopping list each week. Think of these diet changes as something nice you are doing for yourself. If you try something and find you don't like it, don't force yourself to eat it. Give it away to someone who does like it if you can and try something else.

But never give up completely on sampling healthy foods. Yogurt is a high protein food that takes a little getting used to because of tartness. Start with the new fruit-flavored frozen yogurt desserts. They have only half the calories of ice cream and are much better for you. In time you will even learn to enjoy plain yogurt topped with fruits and nuts or used in place of mayonnaise on salads and sandwiches. Tastes keep growing and changing if you give them a chance.

Good eating habits and good health go hand in hand.

CHAPTER 6
ACTIVITY BRINGS ENERGY

So far this book has not made too great a demand on your energy. You've been asked to read and absorb one short chapter in this book each day, to practice the most efficient known form of relaxation at least three times each day, to go to a health food store for two vitamin supplements and to take these vitamins faithfully each day. You've been asked to consider and only gradually adopt some principles of good nutrition. And most important of all you've been asked to adopt a new attitude toward yourself and your depression.

Following this program faithfully and letting the necessary time for healing pass will result in a gradual lifting of your depression and an increased flow of energy. You are probably not feeling anything like a flow of energy yet. That is still to come, but you will find that your energy will return to you all the sooner if you engage calmly and regularly in some form of exercise.

"Exercise!" you say. "Why I can hardly drag myself through the necessary chores of each day. I can barely force myself out of the chair to answer my baby's cries, and just as soon as I can I sink back into the chair exhausted. The housework never gets done, yet I am always so weak and tired. How could I possibly manage to exercise?"

This problem of inactivity is common to depression. You feel fatigued and gloomy. You feel that life isn't worth living, and so nothing seems worth the effort it costs to do it. You cut back further and further on the demands you make on yourself neglecting the housework and even your appearance. This brings on such guilt that you don't dare spend any energy you do have on the things you once did for recreation—bowling, roller skating, swimming, bike riding, etc. The more you cut back on doing things, the less you seem able to do.

Some women go through a stage of trying to fight off depression by being even more active than they were before their pregnancy. They throw themselves into their housework driving themselves mercilessly to meet a standard of perfection. They grimly set about following rigorous exercise programs to force their bodies back into condition. In the end they collapse, having succeeded only in further exhausting their body and perhaps being forced to halt by the onset of a serious illness or a complete "nervous breakdown."

Obviously I do not recommend this kind of exhausting exercise. Nevertheless some amount of aerobic (deep-breathing) exercise each day will increase your energy by improving the efficiency of your body's use of the food you eat. The important thing to keep in mind is that this exercise should be moderate and only slowly increased as your strength increases.

New mothers are often tied down to the house by their baby's demands. It is difficult to find time for a daily game of tennis or a swim. You may not even feel free to jog around the block. Nevertheless there is a simple form of aerobic exercise that you can practice in your own home if need be or just outside the back door. It requires nothing but comfortable clothing and a piece of rope for jumping.

That's right. I'm going to recommend that you take up jumping rope each day. You will decide how many jumps to make. Here's how. Get a piece of flexible clothes' line (not the plastic-coated kind). The rope should be long enough so that when you stand on the center of it the two ends reach up to your armpits.

Now jump the rope counting your jumps until you feel your breath coming faster than usual. When you feel somewhat breathless, stop and walk around until your breathing returns to normal. Then jump rope again until you are just beginning to be winded. That's all for today.

If you like you can write down how many jumps you did today as a guideline for tomorrow. The best time to jump rope (or do any other exercise) is two hours after a meal. Jump just enough to get winded twice, but jump every day.

The *every day* is important. Your body can increase its energy output only if the demand you place on it is a regular and predictable one that is within its capacity. If you miss jumping for as few as three days in a row you will notice a marked cutback in the number of jumps you are able to do before becoming breathless. Don't let this discourage you, but slowly build up your capacity again through persistent *daily* practice.

You may start by making 50 jumps, then walk around until your breath returns to normal and make 50 more jumps. Don't worry about getting tangled up in the rope. Everyone does. Just untangle yourself calmly and start in again. After a week or two you can make three sets of 50 jumps with a rest between each set. Keep adding on sets of 50 as you become more fit. When you can do 500 jumps in 5 minutes with no rests you will be in top physical shape. But take it slowly, a jump at a time.

If you jumped rope as a kid, you may remember there are a number of ways to cut the monotony of merely jumping. After a couple of days of practice to regain your coordination you might want to try jumping first with one foot, then with the other. Or crossing your arms in front of you with every other jump. Or jumping backwards for a time.

You can also jump rope to music. Some women have made up graceful and attractive jumping routines that look like a choreographed dance. Try to remember some of the old rope jumping rhymes you chanted as a child.

After a couple of weeks of daily rope jumping you will be in good enough condition to add more physical activity to your day's routine. Once a day pack the baby into a stroller or backpack seat and set off on foot. Take it easy and stroll to a store or park or just around the block. The walking will do you good, and the fresh air and sunshine will benefit both you and the baby.

If possible walk to a place where you can sit and watch people—a park or shopping center will do fine. Loneliness is one of the worst problems a new mother faces. It is important to get out and see other people in motion at least once each day. Buy a frosty glass of lemonade and sip it slowly watching the customers go in and out. Listen to scraps of conversation. Smile and nod at the people who stop to see the baby.

These trips will give you more perspective on yourself and your situation. They will also give you a reason to keep your appearance up to minimal standards. A bath and shampoo twice a week and combing your hair and brushing your teeth every day really are important. They will lift your spirits and make it possible for you to act on any opportunities that do arise for going out of the house.

Getting out of the house every day and preferably under your own steam (walking, biking or driving) is an essential part of your recovery. You are still a part of the larger world and will return to it more and more as your baby gets older. Don't lose touch. Call old friends or a sister or Mom and arrange to go shopping together or go to an afternoon matinee. Or join a class at the local Y—they often provide baby-sitting and you'll meet other friendly, helpful women there.

If you find yourself panicking when you go out of the house just use the same relaxation-and-describing-the-sensations-to-yourself technique (see chapter 2) outdoors that you use at home. Recognize that these anxiety attacks are a normal part of your depression brought on by trigger-sensitive hormone production. As you recover, these episodes will lessen and then disappear.

Back at home after your daily excursion there will be many chores to do. You will find that a change of activity whenever you get tired will be just as restful as plopping into a chair and staring at the mess. Don't bustle about taking on more than you can handle, but slowly and methodically do as much as you can on each job. When you tire of doing a standing job, do a sitting one. When you tire of doing indoor jobs, do an outdoor one.

Housework always expands to fill the time you spend at home and is never wholly done. Be sure you have tools adequate to the job—a first-rate vacuum if the floors are carpeted, a floor-scrubber if you have large areas of linoleum. Remember that no one notices a clean house—it looks just as it should and so is taken for granted. But everyone notices if your house is a mess.

Stand at the front door as if you were a guest coming to your own home for the first time. What will strike your eye and provoke your disapproval are all the toys on the floor and couch, dirty dishes and glasses from last night's snacks, filled ashtrays, shoes and clothes lying about, etc. Picking up is the most important household job you do each day.

If you can't face finding a place to put each piece of that assorted junk, get a bag or box and put everything into that and out of sight for now. You can sort through the bag or box in odd moments during the day—just see that you have emptied it before you go to bed so it will be free to use the next day.

Be sure to pick up everything loose in the frontroom just before your husband is due to arrive home from work. Aside from fixing the evening meal, this is the one job that will avoid the most conflict.

You may have very good reasons for wanting to get back at your husband by leaving the house a mess. You may feel that it is his fault you are stuck at home alone with the baby in the first place. But let's face it—an angry, unhappy husband is just one more stress on your system each day. Avoid it if you can.

If you are like me, you may find the very thought of preparing dinner late in the afternoon is just more than you can bear. By then your energy and spirits have reached an all-time low. The thing to do is to get a crock-pot and learn to use it. You can prepare your dinner in the morning, put it in the pot to slow cook all day, and forget about it. When you dish it out in the evening you'll almost feel as if someone else prepared it for you.

By all means use paper disposable diapers on the baby. I found they prevented diaper rash, and the tape closures eliminate worries of baby getting stuck with a pin. I sure wish someone would discover an easier way to sterilize bottles during those first weeks, but the disposable plastic-bag type bottles

24

work fine once you can use them and save a lot of bottle washing.

Use every convenient short-cut you can afford and get help with the housecleaning or baby or both at least once a week. If you can't afford paid help, exchange services with a friend or neighbor who also has a baby.

You may find that your husband is more willing to help you with the housework than he appears. Just don't make him defensive by complaining about his messy habits and how little help he is giving you. Instead start to do a job yourself; think of a way that four hands can do it more easily than two; then ask him to hold the other end of the sheet you are folding or to start the dish water while you clear the table.

Keep your requests specific and don't accompany them with whining about how tired you are and how much you've already done today. You don't need an excuse for wanting some help with household tasks.

Remember that his lack of experience in doing the laundry, dishes, etc. will make your husband feel awkward at first, and he will be easily scared off if you criticize his performance. If you can muster the patience to teach him you will find that your husband can be a true help-mate.

If just reading this chapter has made you tired, close your eyes and close this book. Repeat to yourself: "As I recover my health I will feel energy enough to add these exercises and activities to my daily schedule. For now I will rest and take my vitamins. I will jump rope each day to get my energy flowing, and in time I will be able to do all that needs to be done."

CHAPTER 7
HOW YOUR DOCTOR CAN HELP

In chapters 3, 4, 5 and 6 I have outlined a complete do-it-yourself program for recovering and maintaining physical health. It includes a healthy diet, vitamin and mineral supplements, rest, exercise and fresh air. For most instances of stress-caused depression it will bring about considerable improvement.

In addition to the usual stresses born by every mother of a newborn infant, some mothers carry the additional burden of infections, hemorrhaging, recovering from a cesarean birth, low thyroid. Others may suffer from hypoglycema (chronic low blood sugar levels), allergies, drug side effects or anemia. These additional stresses often produce symptoms of fatigue, confusion and tearfulness which closely resemble depression. In fact, in some cases, the "emotional" symptoms so predominate that the woman's physician may fail to test for these physical causes and may simply recommend psychotherapy.

Dr. Norman Geschwind, of the Harvard Medical School, estimates that as many as 40% of the people in mental institutions are actually suffering from a physical illness which was not detected by their doctor or phychiatrist. Their emotional symptoms are not relieved by the usual therapy techniques for the mentally ill. It is not until the underlying illness or deficiency is diagnosed and remedied that the way is cleared to recover.

These illnesses may have been stress-caused in the first place, but now they rquire medical intervention. They are readily curable—through diet, vitamin or mineral replacement, thyroid extracts, antibiotics or other known medical treatments. However, they must first be tested for and diagnosed by a competent doctor.

One of the women who wrote to me about her depression was particularly emphatic in her recommendation that a depressed woman get a complete physical examination from a doctor she can trust. Let me tell you her story.

Helen is a pleasant grandmother today, the wife of a retired farmer in the Midwest. She suffered her first depression after the birth of her first child some 45 years ago. A psychiatrist treated her at home with capsules, the content of which she did not know except that they were for her "glands."

After the birth of her second child she again became depressed. This time she was hospitalized for four months. She recovered and stayed on an even keel for 10 years after which she suffered three more depressions and hospitalizations in the course of having a third child.

While still in the hospital for her fifth depression in 1947, Helen told her doctor she would not return home until he found out the cause of all her suffering. He sent her to a clinic for some tests and discovered that she had a very low thyroid level. With daily thyroid extract tablets to correct for this deficiency Helen has been free of depression for the past 30 years.

"I know now," she writes, "I should have taken thyroid extract pills every day since my recovery from the first nervous breakdown. Today doctors are more alert. Yet four nervous breakdowns may have been averted, money saved, and endless anxiety. What a waste of too much, too many times!"

The stress involved in pregnancy, childbirth and child care may have been what exhausted Helen's ability to produce enough thyroid hormone. The lack of sufficient thyroid then produced frightening emotional symptoms that repeatedly caused her to be hospitalized for depression. However, it was not until her thyroid deficiency itself was remedied that it became possible for Helen to fully regain her health and self-confidence.

Take Helen's advice: "A depressed mother, especially one troubled with anxiety over practically nothing at all, overweight, too tired, can't sleep, etc., should go to her doctor for a *thorough physical examination.* If her doctor doesn't give one, she should ask for a metabolism test, given now by examination of blood taken from the arm. Thyroid deficiency may or may not be the cause, but in any case he will find out what is. A physical reason, usually."

I know this will be hard advice for you to act on. Women who have just been through childbirth in a hospital have often seen their doctor at his worst and least helpful. Nevertheless, only a doctor can order the tests you need to uncover illnesses such as these which may be an additional stress to your system at this time.

If you don't like or trust your present doctor, call the best hospital in town (often associated with a medical school) and ask for the names of several doctors who deal with metabolic disorders. Or call the local chapter of National Organization of Women (listed in your phone book) and ask for the names of several doctors recommended by other women. Select one of the names, make an appointment, and go to see him or her.

You must take good care of your body if you want to reach your mind. The message you will be giving your mind is this: "I am an important and worthwhile person. I will treat myself with respect and care. I will not allow myself to suffer unnecessarily when I may be able to prevent it with a physical examination. I will make that appointment today."

CHAPTER 8

WHEN TO CALL IN THE PROFESSIONALS

If you are following the up-from-depression program outlined in the first part of this book you are now doing these seven things:

1. Whenever you think to yourself "I am a terrible freak," you are reminding yourself that thousands of other women are depressed right now following the birth of their child.
2. Whenever you feel flashes of panic, fear or weakness, you are telling yourself that these are real feelings produced by the hormones your body makes when you are under too much stress. You accept and bear with these sensations with the certain knowledge that they will pass as you relax and recover.
3. Each time the baby goes to sleep you are practicing the deep form of relaxation outlined in chapter 3.
4. You are taking a high-potency multiple vitamin and mineral tablet each day and a stress formula vitamin with each meal and at bedtime.
5. You are experimenting with healthier foods and are including some protein food at each meal and snack throughout the day.
6. You are jumping rope (or jogging or fast-dancing) each day enough to make your breathing quicken and deepen twice.
7. You have made an appointment with a doctor you respect and trust for a complete physical examination.

If you have read this far and have done none of these things in a consistent daily way, it is time for you to come to grips with the fact that your depression is too deep-seated and has already lasted too long for you to remedy it by yourself. It is time to get professional help wih your depression.

In time your untreated depression itself becomes a stress on your body and mind. It drains your self-confidence and lowers your self-esteem. In desperation you may look around for someone to blame for your misery. You may end up getting an unnecessary divorce or abusing your child. If you turn this vengence in on yourself you may become an alcoholic or get addicted to drugs or attempt suicide. The longer you have been depressed the more important it is that you get professional help with your depression.

There is a time and a place for psychiatrists and other mental health workers in the treatment of depression. Although not a one of them can wave a magic wand over you and restore you to your former self, they can be a definite and sometimes life-saving help to a depressed woman.

If you are so depressed that you cannot begin to follow the program outlined so far, you must gather enough strength to tell your husband or mother or friend that you need help. Ask them to make an appointment for you at your county Mental Health Services Department. If they argue with you, don't argue back. Simply repeat your request as calmly and firmly as you can.

Most often this approach will get you the help you so desperately need just as effectively as "acting crazy" or attempting suicide and with far less pain and suffering all around. The people around you will take your need seriously if you take it seriously and seek out the help you need. The Mental Health Services Department will refer you to the psychiatrist or other mental health worker who can give you the kind of help you need at a price you can afford. Here is a brief summary of the kinds of help available.

Drug Therapy

Today physicians can prescribe anti-depressant drugs which will raise your spirits enough to allow you to help yourself. The tricyclic anti-depressants don't create an immediate and artificial "high" which will only wear off and plunge you lower than before. In fact you sometimes have to take them for 3 or 4 weeks before their effect becomes obvious. They work slowly and, for most people, surely like a vitamin or hormone therapy to restore your capacity to meet each day's demands. Once you are feeling better you may need to continue taking the anti-depressant for a month or two to avoid a relapse. They are not addicting.

Hospitalization

Modern anti-depressant drugs have made it possible for most depressed people to be treated while remaining in their homes. However, if your home situation is so stressful that recovery is simply impossible in those surroundings or if there seems to be an immediate danger that you will try to commit suicide, you may be hospitalized. In most states you must give consent to this—you cannot be hospitalized against your will.

Hospitalization does not mark you forever as a crazy, a lunatic. Attitudes toward mental illness are changing as people become more honest about their experiences and as more and more evidence is gathered to prove that "mental" illnesses are physically caused.

Supportive Therapy

"Is this the only time to seek out a psychiatrist—when you are too ill to help yourself?" you ask. No, there are other times when a psychiatrist's skills may be helpful as well. One such time is when your depression is just beginning to lift.

This can be a difficult time since you find yourself more excitable and more able to actually carry out some of the awful things you may have fantasized while in the depths of depression. You may not trust your own judgment yet, and rightly so. This is a good time to have a psychiatrist or psychologist to talk things out with a couple of times a week.

Group Therapy

Also, once you are beginning to recover you may gain much reassurance by meeting regularly with a group of people who are trying to understand their feelings under the guidance of a psychiatrist or psychologist. Such group therapy can give you a place to talk out your fears and feelings of guilt with people who understand and can offer you insights based on their own experience. Such acceptance by others who have had similar feelings will help to restore your self-confidence and self-esteem.

Analytic Therapy

There is another time when psychiatric help is necessary. If you lost a parent through death, divorce or adoption when you were a child or if you had a cold or abusive parent, you have very likely been operating most of your life under the burden of an emotional stress. This chronic emotional stress kept you in a weakened condition. When the physical stresses of pregnancy, childbirth and infant care were added you collapsed.

You can recover from your present depression without getting into this old emotional stress from your childhood. However, if you do so, this underlying strain will continue to weaken your grip on life and will make it likely that you will again become depressed whenever severe current stresses are added on top of this chronic stress.

Your present depression gives you an excellent opportunity to get psychiatric help in dealing with these old wounds, and so to emerge from this depression a stronger and more free person than you were before.

I myself spent three years talking out my present and past problems with a psychiatrist. I had lost my father through divorce when I was 4 years old and had lost much of my mother's attention as well since she had to go to work to support my sister and I. These old griefs plus a more recent trauma of having been raped when I was a teenager needed much work to set right.

I am now convinced that this analytically-oriented psychotherapy could have been much shorter had my psychiatrist and I known what is now known about the physical components of depression. Nevertheless, the results have been more than worth the three years of probing into my unconscious and the expense of a psychiatrist's help.

Joint Therapy

One other type of therapy that is often helpful to depressed mothers is joint therapy with their husbands. While you are suffering the greater physical and emotional effects from the changes you have been through, you must realize that your husband has also been under stress.

During your pregnancy he worried about how he would manage to pay the doctor bills, about your health and safety, and about his own ability to be a good father. Your depression at a time when he has been counting on you to take care of the baby increases this stress. Your irritability and tearfulness may also be making him wonder how he is failing you as a husband.

To keep from blaming himself and becoming overwhelmed and depressed himself, he may become critical of you or alternate between blaming you and trying to comfort you—all to no avail. If he becomes hostile in response to your depression or simply stays away from you as much as possible, you will experience more stress and may feel that your marriage is doomed.

Joint therapy with a skilled psychologist or social worker recommended by your county's Mental Health Services Department can help the two of you make the necessary adjustments in your relationship to each other. Your husband will need to take over some of the housekeeping and child care chores as you are physically unable to do it all. He will need encouragement in the face of this unexpected turn of events. He will also need to learn how to give you the emotional support you need while you are recovering.

It is very common for a depressed person to lose all interest in sex. Making love takes energy, and energy is something you have very little of right now. As you recover your health your sexual interest in your husband will revive. If you both understand this, you can learn to be patient with your present incapacity and confident about your future together.

Again and again women who have written to me about their depressions after childbirth have emphasized how important their husband's response to their depression was in helping or hindering their recovery. You may have married your husband under the illusion that he was a pillar of strength who knew the best solution to every problem you would ever face together. Such men exist only in fairy tales. To help you now your husband needs the guidance of an experienced psychologist as much as you do. Your relationship cannot help but be strengthened as you go together to learn how to work out this problem.

In summary, I recommend calling on the mental health professionals when:

1. you are too depressed to function at all in behalf of your own recovery,
2. you are beginning to regain a little energy and are frightened that you may use it to harm yourself or others,
3. You have suffered the loss of a parent in childhood or had a distant or hostile parent, or
4. you and your husband need help in knowing how to cope with this problem in your marriage.

Now close this book and close your eyes. Say to yourself: "I am doing all that I am able to do for myself right now. Depression is a serious illness and one that I don't have any experience in handling. I will get whatever help I need to make a full recovery in the shortest possible time."

CHAPTER 9
LOOK FOR LOVE WHERE IT CAN BE FOUND

You now have an appointment with a good doctor for a complete physical examination and an appointment with a counselor at the county Mental Health Services Department to discuss what kinds of psychological help you may need. Don't let these appointments lull you into forgetting your vitamins and rope jumping and relaxation practice.

Your doctor and psychiatrist can offer you valuable help toward recovery, but all their help will do you little good if you do not give your body the care it needs to regain its strength. No pill can replace rest, good food and activity. No amount of sensible advice will do you any good if you lack the energy to carry it out.

Remember that your depression is a *physical* illness. It is your body that lacks energy and strength. It is your body that sends out floods of adrenalin in reaction to the slightest problem or effort making your heart pound, your muscles stiffen, your mouth dry, your stomach churn, etc.

For too long we have been fooled by the emotional symptoms of depression (crying, despair, confusion). We have felt that depression was a mental illness and have neglected the treatment of the physical, stress-induced weakness of a depressed person.

Now each day brings us closer to understanding the role that the body plays in depression. By meeting the body's need for extra rest, better nutrition and a gradually increasing amount of activity we can recover from depression faster and more surely than ever before.

At the same time, there is no need to go to the opposite extreme and completely ignore the emotional needs which accompany depression. Again and again women who had been depressed after childbirth told me that they had felt in need of mothering for themselves. They certainly didn't feel capable of mothering their infants while their own need for mothering was so great. Some of these women actually received help from their own mother or their husband's mother. Receiving this loving help usually led to a rapid recovery and much gratitude.

It is only in recent years that women have been alone during childbirth and that first year of caring for an infant. Not so very long ago babies were delivered at home by midwives who had had children of their own. Women were often cared for by their mothers for weeks after the baby was born. A new closeness between mother and daughter was felt—a new bond born of the common experience of giving birth.

Today's woman is not so fortunate. Her mother may be working or living far away at the time she gives birth. If her mother comes at all, far too often it is only to visit, not to help. A woman may feel that she is expected to be independent and not ask for help. Her mother may feel she would be imposing or would be considered over-solicitous if she offered help. Or her mother may have a life of her own and not wish to be bothered any longer by her grown children's needs.

The need to be mothered is one we all feel throughout our lives. The need is strongest when we feel weakest and most child-like. Women who received little mothering as children will feel the need for mothering most of all. If there is a possibility of receiving such mothering now, make bold to ask for it. You may be amazed and gratified at the response.

But not all mothers are any more able to offer you love now than they were when you were a child. Such cold and distant mothers are protecting themselves from experiencing the deep hurts and angers from their own childhood. They have little love to offer because they received too little love from their own parents.

It is also possible that your mother was herself depressed after your birth. What you experienced as her lack of love for you may only have been her lack of energy with which to respond to your needs.

Her rejection is not now, nor has it ever been, a reflection on *your* worth as a person. She has done what she was able to do for you and can do no more.

What then can you do about your own need to be mothered now? First, you can properly mourn the love you failed to receive as a child. Not only with tears but with anger as well.

Choose a time when you are alone in the house if you can. Go to your bedroom and lay on the bed. Hit the mattress with your fists and kick it with your legs. Cry and scream out, "Why? Why? Why?" Cry and yell as much as it takes to fully vent your feelings. Then rest. Wrap up in a comforter and/or rock yourself in a rocking chair.

You may need to do this many times. Few people were allowed as children to express such grief and frustration. Under threat of punishment they choked back their tears and anger. But the despair and anger lived on in them and lessened their joy in life.

Now is the time to be a good mother to yourself. Let yourself get out all the bottled up feelings inside. No one will be hurt by it. No one will think you are an awful person for having such feelings.

It is a terrible thing to be weak and alone and to have no one to love and care for you. Though your mother may have been in the same house with you, her own problems kept her from really being "there" for you when you needed her. The loss of a mother's love is the worst possible loss. Mourn it deeply and fully as it deserves.

When that is done you must say to yourself, "I lost my mother's love long ago through no fault of my own. Now I must be my own mother. I must seek out love where it *can* be found— from my husband, from friends. I must also give myself love."

This book will help you learn how to mother yourself. Only when you can mother yourself will you know how to mother your child. Don't let *your* present problems force *your* child to grow up without a mother's love.

CHAPTER 10

MOTHERING YOURSELF

It is not easy to reconcile yourself once and for all to the loss of your mother's love. When you were a child you may have felt that your mother would love you if only you were good enough or pretty enough or successful enough at school or popular enough to suit her standards. Such reasoning gave you something to hang on to—a hope for the future, a reason to go on living.

As you grew up you may have continued to feel that you could somehow win the love you craved from your mother. You may have felt that giving her a grandchild would be sure to win her love.

What you must realize now is that your mother's love never did depend on you—on what you were or what you did. She gave you what love she was able to give. She could not have given any child more.

You may feel that that isn't so, that your mother did love a brother or sister more than you. But if you are able to talk honestly with that brother or sister today you will find out that he or she also felt unloved. A mother with problems left over from her own childhood is simply incapable of giving a full measure of love to any of her own children.

There is no way of returning to your childhood and having it come out right this time. You must recognize that you have lost your mother's love and will never be able to regain it. Feel that loss as deeply as you are able. Mourn it fully and physically. Only when you have released these feelings once and for all will you be free to meet your present needs as an adult and as a mother to your child.

"But how can a woman mother herself?" you ask. We usually think of love as an emotion, a sentiment that can be put into words. Yet every child knows that hearing the words, "Of course I love you," is not enough to make you really feel loved. In the depths of your depression you know that hearing these words from your husband (or even from your mother) means little to you. You do not *feel* loved.

And what would make you feel loved? Love is first and foremost a physical thing. It is the warmth and closeness of being held. You may have found that in your depression you sometimes wrap your arms around yourself or wrap yourself up tightly in a blanket. Such a feeling of being held gives you a measure of security, makes you feel loved.

You can ask your husband to hold you. Tell him exactly how you would like to be held. Tell him how to cuddle you and make you feel secure. Most husbands will be glad to help when they know just what is needed. There is no adequate substitute for the skin contact, the touching and warmth of being held. This was your first experience of love and is what you long for most when you feel a need for love.

Next to being held, we feel most loved when we are being fed and cared for bodily. Following the program of rest, nutrition and activity outlined in the first part of this book is a way of mothering yourself, and I hope you are keeping up with these ways of caring for yourself every day.

We also feel loved when we receive the help we need when we face a job that seems too difficult for us to do alone. You can give yourself that kind of mother's love as well. By finding a doctor you can trust and a counselor you can confide in you are giving yourself the help you need now to face the job of recovering from your depression.

The household chores and caring for the baby are also jobs that are overwhelmingly difficult for a depressed woman. You can mother yourself by getting help with those jobs, whether from a paid nurse or maid or from an exchange of labor with another mother or from doing these jobs together with your husband.

Avoiding people who make us feel badly for whatever reason is another way to help ourselves feel loved. When we are with some people we may feel uncomfortable, angry, guilty, worried or afraid. We may feel obliged to spend time with these people because they are related to us or are old friends or are our neighbors. However, at this time you don't owe these people anything, even if they are closely related to you. You *do* owe it to yourself to get well, and you can do that best by fulfilling your own emotional and physical needs. Simply tell such people firmly that you are not feeling well enough to spend any time with them. Then put them completely out of your mind.

We also feel loved when we are rewarded for doing things well. You can mother yourself in this way, too. When you finish any job, however small, tell yourself, "I did that well. I'm good at that." You can even physically pat yourself on the back as you praise yourself. You may feel silly, but you'll find it really does help you to feel loved. Remember, love is physical.

Whenever someone else gives you a compliment, you must repeat it to yourself like this, "He really likes the way I look right now (or the dinner I cooked for him)." Other people's compliments can only reach our ears. It is up to us to see that those words of praise reach all the way to our hearts to make us feel loved.

Finally we feel loved when we can ask freely for what we want, knowing that a way will be found for us to get it. You can love yourself by writing down the things and experiences that you want and asking yourself, "Now how can I get a good camera to take pictures of the baby?" or "How can I get out of the house and away from the baby a couple of hours each week?" You will find ways to do the things you want to do and have the things you want to have, and you will feel loved.

Summary

You can love yourself by:

1. allowing yourself to express all the anger and grief that has been locked up inside of you,
2. holding yourself and asking others to hold you,
3. caring for your body in the best possible way,

40

4. getting help with jobs that are too difficult to do alone,
5. praising your accomplishments and taking other's compliments deep into yourself, and
6. finding ways to do what you want to do and have what you want to have.
5. avoiding people who make you feel badly,
6. praising your accomplishments and taking other's compliments deep into yourself, and
7. finding ways to do what you want to do and have what you want to have.

CHAPTER 11

MOTHERING YOUR CHILD

In several places throughout this book I have promised you that once you knew how best to care for yourself you would know how to care for your baby. Now is the time to make good on that promise.

Your baby has the same needs you have. He or she needs nourishing food and drink, exercise, fresh air, plenty of rest and a mother's love.

There is a lot of confusion in people's minds about mother love. Most people believe that mother's love is instinctive, that it just pops into each mother's heart at the moment her baby is born (or even before) and tells her how to fill the baby's every need. It follows that a mother who does not feel herself overflowing with love for her newborn child must have something wrong with her.

All of this shows a popular misunderstanding of just what instinct is. An instinct is a pre-programmed response to certain very specific life conditions. The natural process of birth sensitizes both mother and baby. It prepares each of them to form a deep bond of love with the other through their *immediate reunion* as the baby is put to the mother's breast after emerging from her womb. So nature planned it.

But medical practice of the last 100 years or so has thwarted nature in carrying out this plan. Ever since men started delivering babies it became undignified for the deliverer to kneel at the mother's feet while she squatted in an upright position and pushed down with all her might to move the baby out into the world. How much more convenient for the doctor if mother were strapped onto a table with her legs in the air so that the doctor could stand up and pull the baby out with forceps while mother was drugged into oblivion.

The experience of birth should sensitize the mother to her infant. Instead she is anesthetized to the point that she cannot even feel parts or all of her own body during delivery. The infant, too, is affected by the anesthesia and must be smacked to wake it up to its necessity to breathe.

Then baby is washed, weighed, measured and wrapped in a blanket and taken to the nursery. Often the mother is not even allowed to touch her own baby in the delivery room at that very moment when nature has prepared her to be most receptive to her baby.

Mother may only be given her baby three or four times daily on a clocked schedule (for the nurses' convenience). Even if she is breastfeeding, the baby often will not be brought to her whenever it cries in hunger. No, baby will be given a bottle of sugar water in the nursery and will be brought to mother only when the clock says it is feeding time, even if the baby is then asleep. Little wonder that few mothers and babies form a close loving bond in the hospital.

Instincts just don't work if the conditions which nature planned for their appearance simply don't exist. While some hospitals are beginning to make necessary changes, there is still often little chance for instinctive mother love to be aroused in the typical modern hospital birth.

Jean, one of the women who wrote to me about her depression, expressed very well the feelings of the mother having a baby under such conditions. She wrote: "Birth is meant to be the crowning fulfillment of life, the most beautiful, God-like ecstatic experience life has to offer. Nature makes it so; Man has made it a mess.

"When my first babies (twins) were born, 35 years ago, they strapped your legs *up* in stirrups for the doctor's convenience—he didn't even have to bend down. Just as I felt this overpowering urge to push, they strapped me down. It would be like, if it were somehow possible, at the very instant you felt the beginning of an orgasm, somebody immobilized you and prevented you from having the orgasm. I was so frustrated, I did not have another baby for eight years. I became pregnant once and had a spontaneous abortion. Emotionally and psychologically, I felt I could never go through such frustration again."

She goes on to tell how the separation from her babies brought on her depression. "Premature twins, I was not even allowed to see them for days. After having had them 24 hours a day, the feeling of them in my own body, I was bereft with the terrible lost feeling. The hospital insisted I have a nurse come home with me and the nurse wouldn't even let me in the room they were in in their little breadboxes (incubators). I cried and cried and cried. *My* babies *stolen* from me without my consent."

Jean later had three more children, two of them when she was in her 40's, with no further depressions. She feels that having her later children by the Grantley Dick Reed method of natural childbirth and breastfeeding them prevented her from getting depressed after their births.

Many mothers who experience depression after childbirth wonder if they should ever have another child. Some women have been depressed after each of their babies and others, like Jean, have not. Twenty-50% of those women who have once had a postpartum depression will experience it again after later births.

If your depression came after the birth of your first child, don't be afraid to have an only child. Contrary to popular opinion, only children have the best of all worlds—the full love and attention of both parents and plenty of neighborhood playmates. Only children haven't been any lonelier than other children since most families left their farms and moved into the cities and suburbs. The parents of an only child also have the best of all worlds—an intelligent, creative child (usually) and a maximum amount of freedom and mobility. I myself chose to have an only child.

If you do want another child, wait at least three years. This gives you a chance to completely recover from your depression and to regain your resistance to stress. Follow the relaxation, vitamin, diet and activity recommendations in chapters 3, 4, 5,

44

and 6 right from the moment you decide to have another child until that child is at least one year old. Be sure you don't make any other major changes in your life at the same time you will be pregnant and for a year after childbirth. No move to a new home and certainly no divorce.

Seek out a doctor or midwife (yes, there are licensed midwives in a few parts of the country again today) who is sympathetic to the natural childbirth method and breastfeeding. Enroll in childbirth preparation classes *along with your husband* who should be allowed to stay with you through the birth.

Attend meetings of your local La Leche League during your pregnancy and while breastfeeding your baby for help and encouragement from other mothers who are breastfeeding their babies. Make sure the hospital you are going to has rooming in—where the baby is allowed to stay in the same room with the mother. All of this will provide the best possible chance of awakening whatever instinctive love may still be available to human mothers.

Can I guarantee that such a well-planned birth experience will mean you will not be depressed afterwards? No, I'm afraid I can't. One of the women who wrote to me, I'll call her Susan, had what seemed to be a perfect birth experience: short labor, natural birth, husband present, rooming in, breastfeeding and help from parents when she returned home.

Yet, after 4 months, Susan became "anxious over every little thing" and "began to feel that (her daughter) was a very demanding baby (she was nursing every 2 hours) and I started to feel tied down and a bit resentful." Susan's feelings intensified after she had an auto accident in which she was at fault (an added stress to her system). She lost much of her self-confidence and felt that the accident "reflected on my ability as a wife, mother and person in general."

For months Susan's depression ran its natural course into the deepest despondency. "When I realized that I was losing weight, not eating most meals, not sleeping, heart pounding all the time, 'panic flashes' which felt like adrenalin rushes in my head every time I thought about what was happening, I knew I needed help."

Susan went to the county Mental Health Clinic and spent 2 months in therapy by herself twice a week, then 2 more months in joint therapy with her husband. "We did lots of role-playing and acting out situations and I now feel much more sure of myself." After a three week vacation at a retreat and a visit to her sister, Susan came home rested and fully recovered.

"The whole thing really lasted about 6 months and I was so ecstatic when it was over. Feeling good again made me exhilarated—I could eat again, wanted to cook, play tennis, make love, see people, and just function normally. It was like a weight lifted off my head. One never appreciates feeling good until one has felt rotten for a while."

Susan plans to have another child but is wisely waiting for a couple of years. In the meantime she is working part-time as a craftsman—something she was never trained to do—and she loves it. "Part of what therapy helped me with was this career decision," she writes. We will talk more about mothers working in the next chapter.

We have come far afield in our discussion of mothering your baby. It is not my intention here to give you detailed instructions on caring for your baby's physical needs. You have surely received such information from your doctor or any one of a number of baby care books.

What I want you to understand on the deepest possible level is that you are not to blame for not feeling a gut-level, instinctive love for your child from the moment of its birth. It is not at all unusual for a new mother to have grave doubts about her ability to properly care for her infant. Nor is it unnatural to feel a certain amount of resentment at the loss of your freedom caused by the constant care of your baby.

As you practice the techniques for showing love to yourself given in chapter 10 you will find that you can show love for your child in the same ways. As you may recall, these seven ways to show love are:

1. Allow your baby to express angry or sad feelings. (Never punish your child for crying or say, "Hush, now. That

didn't really hurt." Of course it hurt or he or she wouldn't be crying.)

2. Hold your baby in a relaxed way as much as it wants to be held. (No, you won't spoil him or her. It is the child who does not get enough of the love it needs who will always be demanding everything else in sight.)

3. Give your baby the best possible food and drink, plenty of opportunity for activity (that means time out of the crib and playpen), some fresh air each day, and lots of undisturbed rest.

4. Help your baby do the things it wants to do that are too difficult for it to do alone.

5. Allow your baby to avoid those people who upset it. Don't force your baby to smile at, kiss or stay by people that he or she would rather stay away from.

6. Be generous in your praise of every good thing your baby does.

7. As your child gets old enough to tell you what he or she wants to have or do, take his or her desires seriously and try to find a way for the child to make, earn or do these things. (Notice I didn't say you should *give* your child everything he or she wants—it is far more valuable for you to show him or her how to make things or earn money by doing household chores in order to buy them.)

The more loving things you are able to do for your child the more your feeling of love for him or her will grow.

CHAPTER 12
A MOTHER'S WORK

There is worthwhile work to be done all around us—in the home and yard, in the job market, in volunteer organizations, in arts or crafts, or in your own business. Few things are as important to a woman's self-image and self-esteem as the work she does each day. You deserve to have work that you enjoy and are good at—work that is personally rewarding and motivating.

As your depression lifts and your energy begins to return, it will become important for you to choose the kinds of work that will best restore your sense of competence and self-worth. For help in deciding whether a paid or volunteer job outside of the home may be the kind of work you need, answer the following questions:

1. Were you employed either part-time or full-time during the early months of your pregnancy? _____Yes _____No

2. Did your contacts with other people occur primarily through your work? _____Yes _____No

3 Do your parents place great importance upon holding a job and being self-supporting? _____Yes _____No

4. When you were a child, did you imagine yourself growing up to be something other than a homemaker and mother? _____Yes _____No

5. Does your husband place great importance upon holding a job and being self-supporting? _____Yes _____No

6. Are you severely restricted by lack of money when you are not holding a paid job?   _____Yes _____No

7. Do you feel more free to spend money you have earned yourself?   _____Yes _____No

8. Have you found that you do not enjoy and/or are not good at the traditional homemaking skills?   _____Yes _____No

9. Do you feel more organized, efficient and competent when you have a job?   _____Yes _____No

10. Do you feel that people who work outside of their homes are given more respect than people who work at home?   _____Yes _____No

11. Do you resent your husband's freedom to leave home every day to go to work?   _____Yes _____No

If you answered *yes* to seven or more of these questions, it is likely that you would be happier working outside of the home on a regular basis. If you answered *Yes* to questions 6 and 7, a paid job would meet your needs better than volunteer work.

It is no longer necessary to become a full-time homemaker just because you have had a baby. More than half of all mothers of pre-schoolers now work outside of the home.

Mothers find that their children adjust most easily to their work schedules if they start working as soon as possible after the baby's birth. Involving yourself and your child in a babysitting co-op or some other babysitting service from birth can make it easier for your child to cope with your going outside of the home to work. Even mothers who are breastfeeding their babies find they can be away from home part of each day if they express some milk into a bottle before they leave.

Whether or not their mothers work, all children between the ages of 16 and 32 months go through a time of being anxious when their parents leave them. Keeping your schedule as regular as possible will make it easier for your child to learn that you can be trusted to return home. Your own confidence that you are doing the right thing will help your child to have confidence in you and to accept your going off to work.

If you decide to work outside the home, it may be more harmful than helpful to wait until your child is two or three years old. A child who has had such a long period of depending on you and you alone for care and companionship may feel cheated and resentful when you decide to leave home each day.

The second best time for starting to work outside the home will not come until your child is in kindergarten or first grade. However, that may well be too long for you to wait. So don't put off this important part of your full recovery program. Begin immediately to find a reliable person to care for your child on a regular basis, and, when your depression has been lifted for a month or two, seek out a part-time job or regular volunteer activity.

A part-time job or volunteer activity gets you out with other people every day. It gives you an identity of your own that doesn't depend on your role as a wife and mother. And, if you choose paid rather than volunteer work, it also gives you money for clothes, transportation and a babysitter's services.

Working outside the home gives you something around which to organize your household chores. Housework and child care are highly fragmented and disorganized activities. They can make a woman feel that *she* is disorganized—out of focus, lacking goals and direction. Having an outside job or regular volunteer activity to go to forces an order, a schedule on your day.

"Why only a part-time job? Why not work full time?" you may ask. Unless you already have a professional degree and can earn enough to pay a full-time housekeeper, you are likely to find yourself overtired and overworked in a full-time job.

Why? The fact that housework and childcare have traditionally been "women's work" means that the working mother often finds herself cooking dinner, washing dishes and giving the kids their baths in the evening while her husband relaxes after his day's work. Even in more liberated families where the husband pitches in to help with the housework it is generally up to the

50

woman to plan menus, assign tasks, keep track of where everything is kept and direct her child's growth and education. Such concerns leave her little time and mental energy to advance her own career.

A part-time job or volunteer activity in a field that interests you can keep your job skills current and your self-respect intact until your child is in school and able to take on a few household chores. That may be the time to go back to college full time, to move into a full-time job, or to try freelancing from home if you are so inclined.

When looking for a part-time job, paid or volunteer, take into account the time of day that you feel most restless, most eager to get out of the house. For me that is in the morning, so I look for a part-time job from 9 a.m. - 1 p.m. Slow starters often prefer to spend the morning at home and work in the afternoon.

Evening work has the advantage of giving your husband several hours a day alone with his child while saving you the expense of a babysitter. However, don't attempt evening work unless you are just naturally alert and lively in the evening. A morning person will find evening work too heavy a drain on her energy.

Finding a loving and responsible person to care for your baby while you work, whether you work in your own home or outside of your home, will greatly ease your mind and will broaden your baby's world. A relative, friend, neighbor, or former co-worker or schoolmate with one or more pre-schoolers may be willing to care for your baby for pay or to trade child-care times with you so that you can both work part-time. Other possibilities include day care centers, referral through your church, or through childbirth educators or La Leche League members in your area to a willing stay-at-home mother, or programs in child care run by local colleges or community colleges.

The responsibility of raising a child is sometimes a heavy one. It may be helpful to remember that no one, not even the best mother, can meet her child's every need. We each grow up with some of our needs unmet by our parents, and it is good that we do. For it is these unmet needs that drive us to seek out the company and wisdom of other people—to gain friends, listen to teachers and counselors, and eventually to fall in love with someone outside our own small family.

Your job is not to meet your child's every need, but to give him or her 1) the nurturing love that will allow healthy growth, and 2) the freedom to seek from others those things which you may not be able to give.

Much needs to be learned to be a good mother, but you start with being a mother who feels good. You can only feel good when you are giving your body the care it needs, when you are mothering yourself as well as your baby, and when you are earning your own self-respect through paid or volunteer work, whether inside or outside the home, that is personally satisfying and rewarding.

CHAPTER 13
YOUR COMPLETE PROGRAM

Your complete up-from-depression program now consists of
1. changing your own attitude toward your depressed self,
2. taking good care of your body,
3. getting professional help in assessing your physical and psychological needs,
4. venting the sad and angry feelings that will rise to the surface as you begin to regain energy,
5. learning to mother yourself and your baby, and
6. restoring your self-respect with work you enjoy and are good at when your depression has lifted.

In this chapter I will summarize each aspect of this program. If you have skipped ahead to read this chapter first it will serve as a preview of the special techniques taught in this Self-Help Workbook. If you have read each chapter as it came, one each day, and faithfully followed the suggestions in each one, then this chapter will serve as a convenient review and summary.

You will be able to turn directly to this chapter each day through the remainder of your recovery period to make sure that you are doing everything that can be done to speed your full return to health and happiness. I suggest that you reread this chapter every day to keep yourself moving in a positive, helpful direction. Just keep a bookmark at this page for quick and easy reference.

1. *Changing Your Attitude*

As children we absorbed our society's fear of mental illness and scorn toward those who have emotional problems. If we now turn these outmoded social judgments in upon ourselves, we will do ourselves much unnecessary harm.

More and more evidence is being uncovered that shows depression to be physically caused. There can be no more blame for being depressed than for being diabetic.

Thousands of women experience depression after childbirth each year. We must take comfort from the fact that the vast majority of these women recover. Their experiences have contributed to a growing knowledge of why such depressions occur and what can be done to speed your recovery.

2. *Your Body's Needs*

Depression is the name we give to abnormally low physical and emotional energy. To treat it we must care for the body's need for rest, proper nutrition and exercise.

At least three times a day (perhaps each time the baby goes to sleep) practice the deep relaxation method taught in chapter 3. In these 20 minute periods of rest your body will regain some of the vitality it is losing as your sleep is disturbed through the night.

Take a high-potency vitamin and mineral supplement every day (see chapter 4 for the best formula). Also take a stress formula vitamin three or four times a day.

Slowly incorporate more protein foods into six tiny meals each day. Add more fresh fruits and vegetables to your diet, and gradually switch from white bread to whole-grain wheat and rye breads. Eat nuts, sunflower seeds and fresh fruit for snacks.

A moderate amount of exercise each day will help your body get more energy from the food you eat. Jump rope, jog or fast dance for a few minutes every day. After a couple of weeks add a daily walk outdoors with your baby. Keep housework to the minimum—picking up the frontroom, making dinner and washing dishes. Get help with the rest of the housework.

3. *Doctors and Psychiatrists*

Emotional symptoms can be caused by a number of known illnesses and deficiencies: anemia (caused by various vitamin and mineral deficiencies), hypoglycemia (chronic low blood sugar), infections accompanied by delirium, internal hemorrhaging, allergies, drugs such as birth control pills, and thyroid deficiency. Get a complete physical examination from a doctor you can trust to explore these possibilities.

You need the help of a psychiatrist or other mental health worker if:

    a. you cannot do anything on behalf of your own recovery,

    b. your depression has led you to become dependent on alcohol or drugs or has caused you to attempt suicide or to abuse your child,

    c. you are afraid that you might harm yourself or others as your energy returns,

    d. you lost a parent through death or divorce when you were a young child or you had a cold or abusive parent, or

    e. you and your husband need help in coping with the problems that parenthood and your depression have made in your marriage.

Call your county Mental Health Services Department for an appointment to discuss your need for psychological help.

4. *Getting the Sadness and Anger Out*

Arrange to have 15 or 20 minutes alone in the house at least once a week and use them to pound and kick your mattress while screaming "Why? Why? Why?" or "No! No! No!". We have all had occasions to be sad or angry in our lives. Your present condition will bring these old experiences back to mind. Don't be afraid of the feelings these memories evoke, but give them full physical vent. Doing so will release the energy that was bound up in trying to forget them. That energy is needed by you now. Set it free.

5. *Mothering Yourself and Your Baby*

Every depressed mother feels a need for the kind of acceptance, love and reassurance that we call mothering. If your mother is able to give you this love, by all means tell her of your need for her special attention. However, you can also learn to mother yourself, even if no one else has ever mothered you much.

The first thing to remember is that love is a physical thing—it must be felt. Here are some ways you can make yourself feel loved:

    a. allow yourself to express your angry and sad feelings as well as your happy ones,

    b. wrap your arms or a warm blanket around yourself and ask others to hold you,

    c. care for your body's needs,

    d. get help with jobs that are too difficult to do alone,

    e. avoiding people who make you feel badly,

    f. praise your own accomplishments to yourself and take other's compliments deep into yourself, and

    g. find direct ways to do what you want to do and to have what you want to have.

You can give love to your baby by allowing him or her to express anger and grief as well as pleasure, by holding him or her often in a relaxed way, by caring for his or her physical needs, by helping him or her do the things he or she wants to do, by allowing him or her to avoid people who upset him or her, and by praising his or her accomplishments.

The more love you give yourself, the more love you will have to give to your baby.

6. *Work for Your Own Respect*

Engaging in work that you personally value and find rewarding is an important part of recovering your confidence and self-esteem. Whether you choose to work in your own home or outside your home, for pay or as a volunteer, you will be helped by finding a reliable person to care for your baby for the part of each day that you are working. Your baby's world will also become that much larger and richer.

This program is the most complete, detailed up-from-depression program available to the depressed mother today. It is based on my own experience, the experience of many other women who have written to me about their depressions (some of their letters are in Part II of this book), and on extensive research done in every health-related area over the past 14 years.

In the last chapter of this Self-Help Workbook I will list the many books that have helped me to prepare this program. You can get well without reading another thing if you faithfully follow every part of this program. But if your painful experience makes you want to learn more about depression—its causes, cure and prevention—then you will find the next chapter a good guide to further reading.

CHAPTER 14

BOOKS TO GROW BY

This is the only chapter in the Self-Help Workbook that you can take or leave as you wish. It is not essential to your recovery as are the other chapters. However, if you are an avid reader as I am you will find here many books which will expand your insight into your depression and your recovery and growth process.

But first a caution. The thoughts and feelings that will come into your mind during your depression and recovery are very painful ones. Depression has a way of reopening every old wound you thought had long since healed. It is of great importance that you allow and accept this great outpouring of anguished feelings and thoughts, that you learn to relax in the face of all that has ever seemed unacceptable to you.

This consciousness of your own thoughts and feelings *is* essential to your recovery, whereas reading about depression and health *is not* essential to your recovery. You must be careful, therefore, not to read so voraciously that you drown out your own thoughts and feelings with the words of others.

I call this "word stuffing". It is a great temptation—one to which I succumbed during my own depression—to read one book after another, hardly pausing between them, in a desperate search for an answer that can only rise from within you.

For that reason I recommend that you read only one chapter each day from this workbook *and act on the message* of that one chapter. If you have irresistibly raced through this workbook up to this point, it is still not too late. Close this book now and resolve to not read another word of anything for the remainder of today.

Tomorrow start again with chapter one of the Self-Help Workbook. Read only that one chapter and draw its message deep inside of you. Do not read from any other books or magazines until you have reread each of the 14 chapters in this way.

That will take you two weeks. If you *act* on the message of each chapter, building a pattern of habits into each day that will lead to a sure recovery, you will already feel better when you come again to these words. And you can congratulate yourself heartily on gaining a new, disciplined approach to your reading.

Continue on in the same way through Part II of this book if you wish or through any of the books listed in this chapter. Read only one book at a time and only one chapter of that book each day. You will be amazed, as time passes, how many books you can read in this way and how much more you gain from what you read.

When your depression has been fully lifted for at least 6 months, you can allow yourself to read a magazine article or a chapter from a second book each day in addition to the single chapter from your main book. This second book could well be a fiction. Read it, too, only a single chapter each day to get the most benefit from its story. In a year's time you will have read at least 18 books in this way and will have learned far more from them than you have ever learned from your reading before. Try it and see.

I. *Books About Depression and Stress*

The book you are holding right now is the first whole book written about postpartum depression. A British publisher has now brought out a paperback book entitled *Postnatal Depression* by Vivienne Welburn. It is available for $5.25 postpaid from Birth Books, P.O. Box 836, Peterborough, Ontario, Canada K9J 7A2. Two other books, also written by women, have single chapters dealing with depression after childbirth. They are *Our Bodies, Our Selves* by the Boston Women's Collective and *Women's Bodies, Women's Lives* by Ruth Halcomb. Both are available in paperback or at your public library.

There is an autobiography written by a woman who recovered

from a serious postpartum depression. I have not been able to locate a copy, but pass its title on to you: *My Fight for Sanity* by Judith Kruger. For more first-hand accounts of women's depressions after childbirth, see the section in this book titled "Letters from Formerly-Depressed Mothers."

A book which helped me to understand and live with my panic flashes during my own depression and recovery period is *Hope and Help for Your Nerves* by Claire Weeks, M.D. These recent books on depression may also help you: *The Book of Hope: How Women Can Overcome Depression* by Helen A. DeRosis, M.D., and Victoria Pellegrino; *Control Your Depression* by Peter M. Lewinsohn; *Feeling Good: The New Mood Therapy* by David D. Burns, M.D.; and *Unfinished Business; Pressure Points in the Lives of Women* by Maggie Scarf.

A further understanding of stress and its physical consequences can be gained from *The Stress of Life* by Hans Selye.

II. *Books About Health and Nutrition*

The two best books I have found on relaxation are *Release from Nervous Tension* by David Harold Fink, M.D., and *The Relaxation Response* by Herbert Benson, M.D. My own chapter on relaxation combines the techniques of these two doctors.

On the importance of good nutrition and vitamin supplementation, read *The Doctor's Book of Vitamin Therapy* by Harold Rosenberg, M.D., and A.N. Feldzamen, Ph.D.; *Psychodietetics: Food as the Key to Emotional Health* by E. Cheraskin, M.D., D.M.D., and W.M. Ringsdorf, Jr., D.M.D., M.S.; and *Mega- Nutrition: The New Prescription for Maximum Health, Energy and Longevity* by Richard A. Kunin, M.D. Good nutrition is important for your baby, too. For help with this, read: *Foods for Healthy Kids* and *Improving Your Child's Behavior Chemistry* by Lendon H. Smith, M.D.

Believe it or not, there is even a book on jumping rope: *The Perfect Exercise: The Hop, Skip and Jump Way to Health* by Curtis Mitchell. And for baby's exercise, there's *The Baby Exercise Book* by Dr. Janine Levy and *Games Babies Play and More Games Babies Play* by Julie Hagstrom and Joan Morrill.

A guide to how low thyroid function can affect your health and happiness is contained in *Hypothyroidism: The Unsuspected Illness* by Broda O. Barnes, M.D., and Lawrence Galton. This book also contains an easy test for low thyroid function that you can do yourself, then tell your doctor about.

For a better over-all understanding of your body's needs, read *Our Bodies, Our Selves* and *Women's Bodies, Women's Lives* already recommended or try *Wellness Workbook* by Regina Sara Ryan and John W. Travis, M.D., for an action-oriented, up-to-date approach to preventing illness.

III. *Books About Psychotherapy*

Here is a book on depression that describes the various therapies available and gives valuable advice to your husband, parents and friends as well as to you: *Up From Depression* by Leonard Cammer, M.D.

I also recommend *Notes of a Feminist Therapist* by Elizabeth Friar Williams for insight into women's emotional problems and an idea of what a female therapist may be able to offer you.

A more comprehensive and up-to-date book on therapies available is *Speaking Out: Therapists and Patients—How They Cure and Cope with Mental Illness Today* by Barbara Field Benziger. It is a little heavily weighted with information on mental hospitals as its author experienced several hospitalizations for depression. For social and psychological therapies available today, read *A Complete Guide to Therapy: From Psychoanalysis to Behavior Modification* by Joel Kovel, MD.

For interesting reading on psychoanalysis try *Listening with the Third Ear* by Theodor Reik for the analysts's side and Lucy Freeman's *Fight Against Fear* for the patient's side.

IV. *Books About Expressing Your Feelings*

Some important new books are out in paperback to help you learn to express your feelings and needs: *When I Say No, I Feel Guilty* by Manuel J. Smith; *Don't Say Yes When You Want to Say No* by Herbert Fensterheim, Ph.D., and Jean Baer; *Self-Assertion for Women* by Pamela E. Butler; and *How to be an*

Assertive (Not Aggressive) Woman by Jean Baer. Once you are well you may want to take one of the courses in Assertiveness Training being offered nearly everywhere to help you learn to feel good about speaking up for what you want and need.

The exercise described in this book for venting anger and grief came from Alexander Lowen's *Depression and the Body.*

V. *Books About Mothering*

There has been an explosion of great new books on the market about mothering yourself and mothering your baby. I highly recommend *The Growth and Development of Mothers* by Angela Barron McBride. You may also want to read *How to Be a Mother and a Person Too* by Shirley L. Radl and *Mother Care: Helping Yourself Through the Emotional and Physical Tansitions of New Motherhood* by Lynn DelliQuadri, M.S.W., and Kati Breckenridge, Ph.D.

Remember that we must *learn* how to be good mothers, good parents. Some books that can help are: *Best Practical Parenting Tips* by Vicki Lansky; *Now That You've Had Your Baby* by Gideon G. Panter, M.D.; *Right from the Start* by Gail Sforza Brewer and Janice Presser Greene; *How to Parent, How to Father* (yes, this one is for *you,* too) and *How to Discipline with Love* all by Dr. Fitzhugh Dodson; *Positive Parenting* by Alvin Eden, M.D.; *The Roots of Love* by Helene S. Arnstein; and *Your Child's Self-Esteem* by Dorothy Corkille Briggs, in addition to those recommended in the Books About Health and Nutrition section.

The Joy of the Only Child by Ellen Peck helped me to set aside the socially-induced guilt for having an only child and to see my family's size and life-style as the positive and happy thing it is. However, if after reading Peck's book you still decide to have another child, be sure to read the books on the Lamaze, Leboyer or Grantley Dick-Read method of natural childbirth or *Have It Your Way* by Vicki E. Walton. For those who have had a cesarean birth or may need to have one next time, read *The Cesarean (R)Evolution* by Linda Meyer. It has an excellent chapter for the cesarean woman suffering postpartum depression. Also order *Breastfeeding: A Loving Start* (vol. 1 & 2) available at

$2.50 each from La Leche League International, Inc., 9616 Minneapolis Ave., Franklin Park, IL 60131.

I am indebted to Alexander Lowen's *Depression and the Body* for insight into the fact that love is physical and must be experienced physically. For further understanding of that idea read *Touching* by Ashley Montague.

VI. *Books About Working*

An up-to-date guide for women of all ages who want to get a job is *Woman's Work Book* by Karin Abarbanel and Gonnie McClung Siegel. Also read *How to Have a Child and Keep Your Job* by Jane Price. Your state Employment Service may offer courses in how to write a resume, present your qualifications at an interview and find a job.

Working Mothers by Jean Curtis is a practical book filled with advice gathered in 200 interviews with working mothers. I am indebted to the author for information on the best times for a mother to return to work and on the special psychological burden of feeling solely responsible for the housework, cooking and child care that working mothers continue to bear.

I am also grateful to Elizabeth Friar Williams who, in her book *Notes of a Feminist Therapist,* gave me insight into the harmful emotional effects of feeling disorganized.

For help in finding reliable child care, read *Who Cares for the Baby: Choices in Child Care* by G. Glickman and N. Bass Springer.

VII. *More Interesting Reading*

For an interesting approach to understanding yourself and other people, read *Scripts People Live* by Claude Steiner. *I'm Running Away From Home, But I'm Not Allowed to Cross the Street* by Gabrielle Burton is a light-hearted look at what the Women's Liberation Movement means to this mother of five girls. *Free to Act: How to Star in Your Own Life* by Warren Robertson includes a unique and successful approach to overcoming depression.

Passages by Gail Sheehy is an overly-long, but highly readable book on the stages of growth *adults* pass through. Read it together with your husband. It can help you both to assess where you are and where you are headed. It will help you see both the importance and the temporary-ness of the crises in your life.

You will find many of these books in your public library (a good place to walk to with your baby). Browse through the books numbered 612 - 618.97 for books on physical and mental health, 649 for books on being a good parent, and 150 - 158.7 for books on psychology. If your library doesn't have the book you want, ask the librarian if she can order it for you from another library.

You will also find many of these books in paperback at your bookstore. The salesclerk can order a book for you directly from the publisher if it is not in stock.

Remember that these books can best help if you read them slowly to give yourself time to fully absorb what they say and to put it into practice.

PART II:

LETTERS FROM
FORMERLY-DEPRESSED
MOTHERS

PREFACE

When I first got the idea of writing a book on postpartum depression I knew it was a bigger job than I could manage alone. So I asked for help. I wrote a 100-word ad asking women who had been depressed after childbirth to tell me about their experiences.

The ad ran in the Easy Access column of the now-defunct *Harper's Weekly* on August 23, 1976. Within weeks letters began coming in from women in all parts of the United States and one from Canada. Each woman was eager to share her own story and to give helpful advice to other women going through a similar depression.

Their case histories broadened my viewpoint. Their enthusiastic response and encouragement made me realize just how much this book is needed. Anecdotes from their letters have added much of value to the Self-Help Workbook.

However, some of these women wrote so articulately about their feelings and had so much of value to say that I wished there was some way they could talk directly to you. So I asked their permission to include their letters whole in this book. Every woman who was asked gladly agreed and most gave me permission to include their real names. Their courage emboldened me to add my own story to theirs.

CHAPTER 15
ANTI-DEPRESSANTS HELP JOANNE

Dear Barbara:

Your clipping from HARPER'S WEEKLY has been hidden on my desk for the past couple of months, and I hope my letter is not too late to be of some help in your project. I am the mother of six children, ages 12-20, presently on sabbatical leave from my job as an English instructor at Tacoma Community College, also a writer, editor, and divorced.

Yes, I experienced depression after the birth of each of my children, and since I had six children and two miscarriages (minor) in eight years, I'm not sure that I ever got out of it completely. After the birth of my oldest child I was extremely depressed, but everyone told me it was "just natural" and I had to bear with it. My husband was overseas at that time; as I recall, it was a pretty black period. When I learned I was pregnant with my fifth child, I was also extremely depressed; my doctor got me through that pregnancy with plenty of tranquillizers, though I did not function well, but when that baby was nine months old I had a breakdown, was hospitalized briefly because the doctor and I both thought I was suicidal, and then went through several years of psychotherapy—about three years, and then off and on—and had my sixth baby.

I was treated by a psychiatrist after the breakdown, who gave me anti-depressants and mild tranquillizers, and I went weekly to his office for psychotherapy. When I became pregnant again, medication was removed and the depression became worse. After the baby was born, I was allowed to take a mild tranquillizer but did not require anti-depressants.

I had no relatives living near us and cared for my children

alone. My husband helped, but in his new job in Tacoma (after the third child was born) he travelled frequently, so I had almost total responsibility for the young children and the new babies.

I did not have a job after my marriage until 1965, when my last baby was a year old, and I determined to go to graduate school and obtain a master's degree so I could teach. I did this because I felt I had to do something with my life (I felt completely worthless as a mother, though I don't think now that I was); so really, I went back to college and later began to teach in order to avoid another breakdown. I was still having difficulty when I was a teaching assistant in 1965—mind blanking out completely, periods of extreme depression, etc.—but managed to keep on going. I hired someone to stay with the children at home for half a day while I was gone.

There is another factor which apparently no one perceived but which came out later: I am a person who appears to be chronically depressed. In the old days, they would have called it "melancholia." Doctors thought they were treating me for post-partum depression, but six years after my last child was born I came very near to another breakdown (1970) and began seeing a psychiatrist (this time a different one) again. Through him I have learned that apparently there is a biochemical basis for my depression, and I have been told I will have to take a low-maintenance dosage of anti-depressants for the rest of my life.

In both instances, weekly psychotherapy went on for about two years, and less often after that. I do not require psychotherapy now, and I never had to have shock treatments, which many depressed patients have.

I would advise a depressed mother, first of all, to have an understanding and sympathetic physician, and if necessary to be willing to undergo short-term psychotherapy or even group therapy through a community health clinic. The one thing she should not be left alone to do is to sit by herself—which is probably what she will want to do. If the depression is mild, it will not last long, and reinforcement through friends and/or other women who have had similar problems will help her. If the depression is more severe, she may require medical treatment, and she may discover, as I did, that she is a person already predisposed to depression, so that she suffers post-partum depression more intensely.

She needs love, support, and some kind of professional guidance if the depression is intense or lasts very long.

If there's anything one can say to a depressed mother, it might be that she *can* overcome it, no matter how difficult. My first depression occurred after the birth of my oldest son in 1956, and I am still fighting it, but I have managed to raise my family in spite of a bitter divorce, begin a second career as a writer, and I hope for better things to come.

With very best wishes,
Joanne H. McCarthy

CHAPTER 16

EVEN NURSES ARE NOT IMMUNE

Dear Barbara,

As a nurse, I had taken care of babies in Pediatrics. I had worked in the obstetrical wards. I felt capable and competent to become a mother, and what could be easier than to care for just one. After what I'd been through, I figured it would be a snap. Was I wrong.

I was all smiles leaving the hospital with my new little daughter, Janet. Six weeks later, I was a nervous, jangled mess. What I hadn't figured on was the 24 hour duty with no relief, days off or pay. I was dragging from lack of sleep, my nerves were ready to snap at the slightest sound, and I felt overwhelmed, misunderstood and weighted with a sense of despair that I could not shake.

I tried to "nurse" it away by reading the books. After all, that was the way I solved my problems in my profession. The books had all the answers. But nowhere, in 1954, could I find the answer to what I was going through. I knew I was behaving irrationally—blowing up at my well-meaning mother, and my bewildered husband.

I was desperately trying to hide the fact that I resented my beautiful child. She just took too much of my time. If the time I spent had brought results, I wouldn't have minded so much. But Janet had colic and screamed every evening from 4 to 10. No amounts of rocking, soothing, singing, etc. had any effect. She usually fell into an exhausted sleep after yelling for hours.

I tried warm water, rubbing her tummy, turning her over my knee, head down, head up, you name it. I got so I dreaded the evenings. I dreaded each day. My fears were that life would continue this way until I would do something desperate.

I had no smart colleague to give the right hints. Most of my friends were not married and had no small children. I tried calling the doctor. He laughed when I told him what was happening. I resented his laughing as if this dilemma was so trivial. He recommended phenobarbital drops for the baby. This medication is sleep-producing and relaxes the smooth muscle of the stomach and intestines. Because he offered me no other recourse I accepted the treatment for Janet. It did help, but I felt so guilty. It was so unnatural. It was like giving up and letting the computer write your poem.

I felt incompetent where I should have been competent. I had lost all objectivity. I felt chained to the house and the baby's routine. Where was the joy I was supposed to feel? My mother enjoyed the baby; my husband enjoyed her; but I felt like a dairy cow.

It was true that there were times of great satisfaction in those early months. Breastfeeding was not encouraged in those days, but I breast fed because I had learned how good it was for the baby. What the books didn't tell me was how good it felt to feed my baby from my body, and how this synergistic relationship helped cushion the shock of motherhood.

I realized I missed being at work with my peers. There was no one to talk to. When adults came over I had to leave to take care of the baby. Then I got pregnant again. I had two babies in 13 months. I ran to the obstetrician and burst into tears when he put his arm around me. I needed somebody to understand. I was not "big nurse" anymore. I was scared. I had the responsibility of two lives in my care, and I resented it.

But the pediatrician was still expectant of "nurse-like" behavior. When I asked questions he thought I should already know, he teased me or said, "Didn't your training cover that situation?" I got so that I was afraid to ask questions. Or, I would look up the nursing literature and, armed with the latest information on some problem, I would try to appear informed and intelligent as I asked my question.

What I really wanted the doctor to do was to tell me that I

could live through my child's two-year-old stage without becoming psychotic. I wanted him to spend as much time with me as he did with other new mothers. But, I was shunted aside and given over-the-shoulder instructions. I only saw him when my child was sick. I used the well-baby clinic for my child's innoculations, but the few times I asked for some advice on some aspect of child care, I felt stupid for asking. I had already been trained not to ask, and I muddled through by myself.

When Janet was seven, and the whole family had the flu, she woke up in the middle of the night crying that her back hurt. In those days, polio still was a feared disease. Janet was unable to touch her chin to her chest. This rigidity frightened me. I had to have some advice. Against all I had been learning I called the pediatrician at 2 a.m. I described the symptoms—which were indicative of polio. He said, "It's 2 a.m.—you describe a symptom that is very common in flu." I stammered something about being sorry I bothered him, and hung up.

I was a hysterical mother, probably much worse for my knowledge, in that it identified symptoms of diseases no one else would think of. I sunk into depression. I also had the flu and was pregnant with my third child.

Janet did not get better. I nursed her vainly for 2½ weeks as she got paler and weaker. But I was afraid to call the doctor again. Finally, my conscience overcame my fear of humiliation, and I asked him to make a house call. After his examination, he said with some surprise, "This child has pneumonia. Why didn't you call me before this?" I was speechless. If somebody had handed me cyanide tea at that moment I would have drunk it.

My worst moments were after the birth of the second child. I remember long days of lethargy when all I could do was make breakfast and slap some hamburger on the stove for dinner. Beds remained unmade, diaper pails overflowed. Janet was always pulling on my arm and whining. I would sit in a rocker and rock baby Michael for hours, sometimes falling asleep with him.

My mind was fuzzy. I couldn't remember things. I cried easily. I resented my husband going to work. I gained weight and spent some days in my nightgown and robe until he returned that evening.

The person I most clung to was my mother. She worked then, but she saw that I was in terrible shape, and so she'd come over every afternoon after work just to take the baby from my arms for an hour or so. I began to look forward to her coming. It was someone from the outside world entering my dismal milieu, someone who whispered that "This too will pass." Someone who understood how I felt.

She pitched in to help me recondition myself. I was able to slip out to a class, to a movie, even though my husband, who worked two jobs, was sleeping. She brought surprise foods I liked so I didn't have to cook some days. She took the children away for a weekend so my husband and I could be together.

I remember her at that time stroking my forehead while I lay in a blue funk, feeling sorry for myself. "Being a mother is the most rewarding, yet probably the most demanding job you will ever do. It tests you down to your core. But look at what you have. Look at the healthy and beautiful children you have produced. Remember, this family is your nucleus. You can make it a happy place. When Janet comes in with her little games, like when she was being toilet trained and filled her pants with rocks to fool you, I saw the look on your face. These precious moments are yours because you are here with them."

I kissed her and we hugged. I never really knew my mother until I became a mother. We had broken new paths to each other.

Although my husband expected me to "shape up" automatically, he was supportive in that he wanted to spend more time with me. So we'd find precious moments stolen from our separate worlds—his the working world, and mine the nursery. I remember him on Janet's first Thanksgiving with her in his lap. He had just given her a wing bone with some soft meat still attached to it. She was sucking it loudly, and he looked up at me and grinned. These looks, above our child's head—the pride and happiness he felt in our little family—helped to dispel the dreadful, energy-sucking miasma I felt at other times.

"Time," my mother had promised, "time will bail you out."
And, of course, it did.

Sincerely yours,
Ruth Wire

CHAPTER 17

LISA TAKES THE LONG ROAD BACK

Dear Ms. Ciaramitaro,

I was twenty when I had my daughter, and it was as if something that happened on the delivery table just set off craziness. I felt that the nurses were talking about me, and I was so depressed that my doctor put me on what he called "see-the-world-through-colored-glasses pills." The only trouble with them was that I had difficulty sleeping, even at night; consequently, when I got home I was exhausted and in no condition to cope with a baby.

I refused to continue taking the pills when I got home, even though they made me smile at people in spite of myself; I felt that was too artificial. Maybe I should've continued taking them for about a month in smaller doses, or perhaps I could have taken anti-depressants; but no one suggested them and I knew nothing about them.

When I got home the enormity of the responsibility hit me with a dull thud, and I lay awake all night feeling close to insanity. I almost wished I would go off the deep end to excuse me from everything, and I tried to induce a state of catatonia.

Over the next few years I was frequently depressed, crying for no apparent reason, having periods of days when I could hardly do anything. Sometimes I was nervous about going out of the house, and I hated to eat in restaurants because I felt that people were watching me. Sometimes I would scream at my daugher, and sometimes I would hit her, though never hard enough to make a mark.

At times I would rage at my husband and throw things at him. Once I chopped off my hair erratically. and another time I ripped up some of my clothes. My husband, of course, was bewildered and showed increasing shades of disgust. He was totally helpless and I'm not sure he cared except that it was all a big nuisance to him.

Shortly after my daughter was born I had contacted a psychologist I had seen briefly before I was married, and she referred me to a psychiatrist who would decide whether I needed hospitalization. No matter how miserable I was, I felt I couldn't leave the situation; so I gave him a "snow job."

When Pam was almost two I went to an internist for a complete physical because I was always tired. He gave me expensive tranquilizers and anti-depressants, but together they made me even more lethargic. Then one day, in an effort to escape things for awhile, I took a handful of pills. I just wanted to sleep, but on our doctor's advice I was committed to the psychiatric ward of a general hospital—really a very nice place. But it was almost Christmas, and after two weeks I was anxious —not eager—to get home.

On and off I wanted to get therapy, but when I was all right I felt I didn't need it anymore, and when I was down I didn't have the motivation to make the required phone calls. Besides, we were poor and I didn't think we could afford it.

When the following Christmas approached, though, and I began to show signs of the depression, we talked about calling a clinic. John did it for me, and I followed through with a visit. But too late. Before the next meeting we went to a party, where I felt like I would suffocate, though outwardly I looked like I was having fun.

I lay awake all night once again, imagining all the things I had done wrong. Emotional pain wracked my body. I was plain and simply in a different world from those around me at that time. When, near dawn, I tried to rouse my husband for comfort, he just rolled over and went back to sleep. I began taking pills again and kept taking them, this time with a more serious intent. I guess I hated myself so much I wanted to destroy what was me.

This time I ended up in a good psychiatric hospital, where I stayed for three months. I just didn't want to leave. There I was taken care of rather than having to take care of others.

After three months I was no better and our money had run out, so I was sent to a state hospital. I quickly became worse than before I was hospitalized initially.

In the meantime my husband asked for a divorce, and I got so bad that I had shock treatments. They did some little good, I think, in getting me to the point where something else could be done for me. That something was mostly occupational and work therapy, and, of course, simply the hospital milieu, which improved somewhat on an open ward.

I was fortunate in getting a job in the medical library, and that, along with time, helped. Also a place called Council House which took us out of the hospital to do volunteer work in groups for places like the Red Cross and, of all places, Americans for Democratic Action.

I went mostly to ADA because they always requested me. I did good work for them, and because they treated me like any old person and gave me responsibility I became a little more sure of my place in the world as a former mental patient.

Fifteen months after I entered the first hospital I was back in the world, with nothing. My husband was re-marrying and keeping our daughter, which I agreed to because I wasn't even sure I could take care of myself.

And, indeed, it was a struggle. The only thing that had gotten me out of the hospital was the promise of free schooling through the Bureau of Vocational Rehabilitation. It gave me an identity, a little better self-image, and something to do that was less threatening than a job.

But my lows now were even worse than they had been before, because now I was overwhelmed with a tremendous loss. My husband wouldn't even let me see our daughter, and I wasn't well enough to go to court.

Twice I took overdoses of pills serious enough to require the stomach pump; the second time I was in a coma for five days. While in the coma I think I may have had some kind of a conversion, because that seemed to be the turning point. I decided that if I couldn't succeed in killing myself then I'd damn well better learn not to be so miserable.

Two other events made a difference, too: I got seriously involved with a man, which, while a questionable relationship, gave some stability to my life after two years of no serious relationships; and I got a *good* therapist (a psychiatric social worker).

In the intervening years I'd gone through group therapy (besides what we had at the hospital) and two individual therapists, but they had perhaps only made the situation worse because the coldness of the therapists only made me feel yet more alienated. My hospital experiences had already made me cynical and bitter because so many of the people obviously didn't give a damn and in many cases probably lived off other peoples' misery.

But this woman *cared*. And she knew what she was doing. After two years with her I moved on to group therapy, this time with two more good people. And finally, six months with a behaviour therapist.

I was lucky, you know. Many people are still on the treadmill.

I'm about to finish graduate school, and although there have been some rough times since my last suicide attempt five years ago, I haven't been hospitalized again. I face the working world with some trepidation but some faith that even if it's rough I'll make it.

Sometimes I get depressed because I feel my life doesn't amount to much. I'm thirty-three and live alone and what do I have to show for thirty-three years of living? Few accomplishments, and unlike most women my age not even a family.

Yet there are times when I consider it a great adventure, and I suspect that once I start working I'll feel a little better about myself.

Now: what would I advise a depressed mother to do? Whatever she can to improve her self-image. School or whatever it takes.

She should not be ashamed to ask for help from any quarter.

Despite my bad experiences, I highly recommend therapy. I think it literally saved my life, and it put me back together to where I never have been in my life. There are clinics available almost everywhere now that charge little or nothing. If one therapist doesn't suit her, she shouldn't be afraid to ask for another. Sometimes personalities just don't click.

After my hospitalization I found a book called *My Fight for Sanity* by Judith Kruger, and it was great to be able to relate my experiences to someone else's. Too bad I hadn't found it earlier, because, before my hospital experience, I felt like I was the only one who had such weird feelings. There are lots of books about people's experiences with depression, I've subsequently found.

And then there is Recovery, Incorporated. Although it was designed for former patients, anyone can join it. I never did, even though I always meant to. I'm sorry now I didn't, because it may have greatly helped the healing process and hastened it.

I would even advise hospitalization if push comes to shove. It can help greatly being relieved of a situation for a while, along with the (hopefully) therapeutic milieu.

But above all, she must help her family to understand. No pouting, ranting or raving. She must tell them just how she feels, if only to say, "I can't handle it." If she has to, she should get books from the library that help families to deal with mentally ill members.

If she has a therapist, she should have the therapist talk with her husband to explain how to deal with her. If my husband hadn't been so helpless, I think I would have been a lot further ahead. That's the striking difference between Judith Kruger's experiences and my own.

Incidentally, although I haven't had more children, I'd like to very much when I feel I've established myself. Yet I'm very much afraid to for fear I'd go crazy on the delivery table again. That's an awfully high price to pay for motherhood. Will all my therapy make a difference the next time? Who can say, and so I may end up adopting if I continue to feel fearful.

I wish you much success with your book, and I hope it will

be well publicized. This is a group badly in need of help, if not simply relief from the terrible burden of feeling all alone with their problems.

Perhaps I gave you far more than you really needed, but I hope at least some of my experiences can be helpful to others.

Sincerely,
Lisa Miller

CHAPTER 18
REST IN BED WAS NOT ENOUGH

Dear Barbara,

I truly appreciate your interest in the depressed mother. It gives me a chance to spread what I learned after the most incredibly horrible experience of my life. After my second child was born I suffered a terrible crash which started three months after the birth. Up to that point I was very content and happy, but overworked from taking care of my two-year old all day and staying up nights to breastfeed my new son.

I was caught up in the health foods movement and under the impression that if I ate right I could adequately feed my son and plow fields at the same time. I greatly scorned self-pampering pregnant mothers as new-breed weak mothers who didn't care enough to prepare their own baby foods, etc., but were more interested in showers, etc.

Being in a different country and not knowing many people I had no help with my children. My closest neighbors, of which there are two, are the type who pretend life with their children is a smoothly rolling stream. It is obvious that this is not the case. However, I feel that they are victims of the "Motherhood is wonderful" bit that keeps women somewhat oppressed. We have a good relationship as friends, but they simply turn off the switch when it comes to family problems.

I was myself much the same until one day I went to get out of bed and I couldn't stand up. I was sure I had a virus, because I couldn't believe that my health could fail under the bombardment of all those vitamins I was taking. I stayed mostly bedridden for a month before going to a Doctor out of desperation.

I also was very wary of Doctors and still am. My Doctor

was right when he said that I needed sleep but crazy to give me seconal. He did not advise me to stop nursing my child which I did anyway to protect him from the barbituates. I knew when I got sick that I needed sleep and should stop nursing anyway, however my pride and good intentions kept me going. I couldn't understand why I was failing.

The barbituates were the clincher. At first I felt great when I took them. I was taking a combination of two eventually to keep it up. It was against my beliefs but it kept me going. Soon the effects wore off, and I was horribly sick all day. My mind was in a constant fog and my body felt heavier than lead. I was incredibly weak and shaky and, worst of all, I didn't know what was happening. I cried continually. A steady stream of silent tears.

Finally my Doctor told me to see a shrink and cut off my pills. This was after a month of dependence. I probably would have gone to one had I not been so sure that my problem simply required rest. Instead I finally called my Mother and cried over the phone to her which was not at all normal. She hung up and drove 750 miles through the night to be with me the next morning.

That one gesture of love and support was the turning point in my illness. She got me to a Doctor who gave me tranquilizers to ease my pains from the barbituates. I then fought a day and night battle trying to get sleep normally again. My morale was higher because I had help, although nothing can totally alleviate the mother's mind. I still ran myself ragged. Not stopping until I was on the edge of fainting.

Up to the point that my mother arrived on the scene I had been feeling increasingly like a failure as a mother and wife, not to mention a failure to myself, and there were times when the thought of death was euphoric. It never occurred to me that perhaps I had too much to handle until my Mother pointed out to me all the changes I had been through and the difficulties of young children anyway.

I should explain at this point that I had come from an upper middle-class suburb of Chicago to live with my husband in

Canada. I was 18 and got pregnant then married. We moved to the country where we used wood stoves and had frozen water in the winter, etc. A total life change. I got pregnant and had another child when I was 20. All of this was new to me. I hardly knew what a baby looked like until I had one and I had few people to discuss it with.

I was enjoying my life and hated myself for not being able to cope with it. My husband stayed home with me when I was sick for two months until the money ran out. I tried to brave it alone, but forget it. When I found myself wanting to get committed anywhere I called Mom.

It took me two years to get my strength back so that I could do more than the basic daily required functions for me and my children. Within the last 6 months I have regained enough strength to carry on almost as normal. I still take mild tranquilizers, but they are not addictive. Although I hate taking the pills they give me peace in place of illness and are aiding my recovery by relieving physical and mental duress.

My mother left me after two months and all my relatives gave me lots of support to carry on from phone calls, letters and visits. All that love was the best medicine there is.

I got it together enough to go to a University one year after I first got sick. It was good for my psyche to be among the living again, but too hard to keep up.

Which brings me to the moral of the story. My greatest learning experience from all this was that if you are unable to cope get help immediately. If you wait until you are sick the mental consequences can be overwhelming. Do not let false notions direct you. Listen to what your body and mind are telling you. The only rest you will get when you have small children is when you are completely away from them. Don't let pride keep you from admitting your inability to handle the situation.

Talk about your problems and try to bring other women out of themselves in an effort to strengthen woman unity. I finally met a woman my own age who had children and many of the same problems I had. We were able to discuss all of our problems openly and the affects were very positive.

The thought of another child terrifies me because I know I am not ready for it. If I did get pregnant I would make sure that I had help in the home for as long as I needed it. I would spend my pregnancy going to a psychiatrist to help me sort out the entire situation.

I am very tired all the time though I am supposed to be in fine health. Nerves can do this and many young mothers feel the same way. If they find that they cannot work a full day and take care of small children at the same time then they could make a settlement with themselves that they will just wait it out until the children are a bit older and meanwhile do something to keep them in contact and feeling good about themselves.

It is harder for some than others because of social pressures and the incredibly pitiful malice between working and non-working mothers. Women have to realize that they are being torn in opposite directions in all realms of their role. One must sift through and find what is right for oneself and not begrudge another who approaches the situation differently.

This is a very broad topic that you are undertaking to make sense of. It is very encouraging to see the effort because depression of the mother affects the entire family and leaves its mark on young children, thereby affecting society on several levels. I hope this somewhat incohesive letter makes sense to you and will give you a little more insight. We definitely need Doctors that realize the severity of the housewives' complaints instead of brushing them aside with a pat on the head and a tranquilizer.

Thank you for your effort.

Sincerely yours,
Julie Blunden

CHAPTER 19

ABORTION—A REALISTIC ALTERNATIVE

Dear Barbara Ciaramitaro,

I'd like to tell you about my experiences so that other women may benefit.

The births of the first two children—Curt, September, 1944, and Tesa (a girl), January, 1946—were not followed by depression.

Depression after the third—Tomi (son), July, 1948—began as soon as I stopped nursing him. (Did the induction of his birth by an inept physician play a part in causing the depression? I don't know.)

After the birth of the fourth—Tuck (boy), October 1950—depression started immediately. My doctor forbade nursing Tuck. I was exhausted by the time I gave birth to him: his birth was the fourth in six years, and I had been anemic since about the fifth month of pregnancy.

The best I can do to describe the symptoms is to call them, altogether, "psychosomatic flu." I lived on aspirin. I lost self-confidence. I was able to do only what absolutely had to be done.

The term, post partum depression, was not yet in full use when Tomi was born. The doctor to whom I went then advised me to do the housework I hated most when I felt most down. I hate all housework; but I followed his advice, and that *did* help.

After the birth of Tuck, I was so exhausted—and low in money—that the infant's four-year-old sister helped me.

I was not suicidal. I was so distracted I wasn't able to think enough to come to that decision; I was just holding on.

I did not work regularly before or after either birth. I was doing free-lance copy editing and proofreading off and on during those times; I dealt with publishers by mail.

I wonder if my advice would help. I don't know, for I wasn't able to use it myself. I'd say the mother should ask her husband for help with care of the baby and the other children and with cooking and housework. (Better: the husband should offer help.)

Only recently, after divorce, have I realized that my husband treated me as if we were living in Japan. He's a nisei (born here to Japanese immigrants); I'm caucasian. He had been raised according to Japanese custom: wife/mother at the bottom of the totem pole. I don't think he realized he was not so westernized as he thought he was.

I *think* the way I finally averted the depression is legal in this country now; the abortion I needed would not have been legal in 1954. I was fortunate in being in Copenhagen then; my husband, a member of the faculty of Columbia University, was on sabbatical.

The best decision probably is not to conceive; if conception occurs, have an abortion as soon as possible. The aftereffect of mine was not unusual: my body felt as if I had just given birth. Psychologically, the relief was immeasurable. The depressions were pure hell.

They'd better not amend the Constitution to forbid abortion. You may use what I have written—and my name.

Sally R. Hayashi

CHAPTER 20

"I NEED MY WORK TO BE HAPPY
AND GROWING"

Dear Barbara,

I'm so happy that you are embarking on a project to try to help women with their post-partum depressions. When my daughter, now $8\frac{1}{2}$ months, was born, I had very little help in the form of knowing about the experiences of other women, something that I feel would have helped me a great deal. Many of the books that I was reading during Johanna's early weeks were written by men and usually wrote the entire experience off completely in a few paragraphs as a case of "the blues."

I found the most helpful treatment to be in *Our Bodies, Our Selves* (Boston Women's Health Book Collective, Simon and Schuster) since not only did the book attack depression from both an emotional and physiological viewpoint (thus making me feel that there was something organic going on), but also gave the accounts of other mothers. I wished at that time that I could have read more and more.

Johanna is our first child. I have an absolutely loving husband, and his mother, who stayed with us for $2\frac{1}{2}$ weeks, is one of the most supportive women that I know, someone who knows how to give a lot of herself while still giving you emotional and physical space.

Johanna was a very non-fussy young infant, as babies go, at that age. Yet from the night that I returned home from the hospital (when I was so very engorged and hurting with hemorrhoids and episiotomy stitches) until about $2\frac{1}{2}$ weeks later, I was overcome with a deep, deep fear. I cried every evening, starting at about 6:00.

My mother-in-law offered encouragement, yet she never

went through the same thing and is one of the most serene and internally peaceful people I know, so I felt like such a looney compared to her. I clung to my husband, literally, every night until the fear subsided. He never judged me, never made me feel as if he resented this onrush of dependency. He was just there when I needed him. Yet I hated myself for my "reversion" to more dependent times in my life.

I never felt suicidal at that time. I just was filled with fear and felt like I was "strange," "weird," "going nuts," not in control of my own feelings and emotions. I began to understand that part of what I was afraid of was the complete responsibility I had for this utterly helpless child—care, nutrition, sleep, peacefulness.

I had my husband's support, yet I realize now that I really wanted and needed him to take a more active part in caring for her—feeding (difficult since I was nursing), reading about her development stages (so that I wouldn't be the only one who knew how to best prepare for her developing mental and physical abilities as well as her emotional needs), and general care—something that we're still in the process of working out to this day.

Since Johanna was born in the winter and couldn't go out for the first three weeks of her life, I felt that I was unable to see my therapist during that time. I realize now that my need to see him should have been honored and respected, by *me*, and that I should have found someone to care for her while I continued to see him.

My depression lifted, ironically enough, the day that my mother-in-law left. Perhaps not so "ironically," since for the first time I was able to resume some of the activities that I had abandoned beginning about one month before my delivery (I had had some late bleeding and had to stay in bed for most of the day). For the first time I was able to see that I *could* handle caring for a child, doing the laundry, shopping, etc.

Eight months later now I seem to be going through another stage of depression, brought on more by feelings arising out of my current and very early relationship with my mother than by having the baby, but compounded by the fact that *I'm* now a mother and 1) have an increased sensitivity toward the mother/ daughter relationship and 2) am feeling trapped by my mother role.

I'm trapped physically since I am still not able to go back to work (I am a graphic artist and quit a regular job to work freelance during my pregnancy and then was not able to look for clients once Johanna was born) since I want to continue nursing for another few months and then don't want to wean and go back to work at the same time (since I want to be sensitive not to hit Johanna with two "separations" at once.)

I find myself very resentful of and angry at my husband's job and his mobility. I also find myself trapped emotionally by still being the primary caretaker who's responsible almost totally (as I said before, we are in the process of working this out) for the physical, mental and emotional growth of my child.

My suggestion for a depressed mother would be not to isolate herself. To get as much support and help from a therapist and *other mothers*. To share openly her fears and other feelings about being a mother.

Hopefully she and her husband could work out an arrangement whereby he spells her several times a week so that she has time to herself. Better yet, perhaps they could plan for this baby in such a way that his job allows him to share equally in caring for her/him (something that is almost impossible to do in our society), or perhaps their living situation could open up at the time of childbirth so that they are living very close to other good friends or (helpful) family members.

I've felt for some time now that while the pre-child years of marriage or living together could involve a very close, intimate, almost exclusive living arrangement, that once children are born, good friends should make it a point to live near one another and share in the physical and emotional support of child bearing and raising.

Lastly I remember being struck by something that I read in *Our Bodies, Our Selves* which counseled mothers to stop waiting for their former, "normal" lives to return. That that life

90

would never come again and that it was time to start to build a new life. That was a shock and a rude awakening for me to realize that my old life was gone and would never return, that my days of absolute freedom and sporadic selfishness were over. Yet I feel a more whole person now, more real. And I love Johanna so very much. As Jane Lazarre said in a *Voice* article, "There's no doubt in my mind now that I could die for my child, but he has destroyed my life."

I'm now trying to find a new one that makes sense to me, that incorporates both my needs and Johanna's, that recognizes the creativity that is involved in mothering, and that gives me outlets for other forms of creativity as well.

Sincererly,
Ilene Zetterberg

When I wrote to Ilene asking for permission to include her letter in this book, she readily agreed and sent me this sequel to her story:

Through therapy and lots of support and help from my husband and close friends, many things are beginning to fall into place for me. The main theme for me has been my need to let go—not to take on the entire responsibility for Johanna but to entrust her care to others from time to time. I feel now that had I been able to do this at the beginning, that my depression *might* not have been so severe. I underscore "might" since there were —and are—so many facets to those feelings.

This isn't just a physical letting go as in getting baby sitters that I'm talking about—for me it's an emotional one as well; that is, trusting that the world is a good place for my child to explore and grow in (a world view that I did *not* get from my family) and that she—and I—needn't be afraid. That I don't have to take on the responsibility for making sure that "nothing bad" happens to her, a responsibility that proved to be so awesome for me that I literally stopped sleeping at about the time that I wrote to you.

Of course the feelings brought out at that time are far more complex than I'm presenting now, tying directly into my relationship with my mother and the fears that have grown in me since I was *very* young. Yet I'm convinced that the birth of my daughter was the instigating factor which brought these fears to a head.

A year ago I knew somewhere inside me that if and when I ever got through the nightmare that was engulfing me I would finally be on my way to accepting myself at last and quieting those fears. I'm there now—on my way—and it's such a luxury and relief to be on the other side of it and to see how helpful the crisis actually was in getting there.

I made the physical separation from Johanna first; at the beginning, babysitters for 3 hours/day, a couple of days a week. I remember just sitting and drinking tea that first time—all alone—and loving the aloneness. Then a friend knew someone who needed a graphic artist to do some work and I began working again, slowly. Soon after that a friend had a baby and I silk screened a t-shirt as a present and thought it was so much fun that I began doing more and more.

As new designs came to me and orders for more shirts, I luckily found a lovely woman who now cares for Johanna 6 hours/day. There's another child there—a bit aggressive and troubled at times—who was hitting Johanna as I left her that first day. Of course I came home and cried on and off for two hours as I printed my shirts, but after two days, Johanna not only didn't cry when I left, but couldn't wait to go to Terry's in the morning.

Now six hours isn't nearly enough time to do all I need to do, but Johanna is still young and I'd like to spend a few hours a day with her. I've found that I need my work to be happy and growing—something I had such a difficult time admitting to myself for fear of not being a "good mother."

I also need and love Johanna—and can give so much more to her now that there's a certain part of each day that I can count on for myself. I trust Terry (her babysitter)—her values, decision-making, care—completely and that's an important part of this.

Very rarely do I think of Johanna during the day. Now I'm

talking about the mental separation that I mentioned earlier. When I think that this is the same woman who called her husband from every phone booth when she dared to take a walk a couple of months after her daughter was born, I am amazed at the changes that have taken place.

I feel that I've learned so much from all of this. When I look at Johanna and see how independent she can be, how trusting, loving and open she is, how much she loves to run off and explore, I feel so grateful that I was and am able to be working these things through with a loving and caring husband, therapist and friends.

I'm learning more and more to trust myself, to separate other people's issues from my own, to draw limits, and not to take on the responsibility for other people's feelings. All of this ties in with those first weeks of depression and the crisis that occurred those 7 months later, when I couldn't do any of those things.

I hope that new mothers will talk more and more about their feelings, will be honest about them and will rid themselves of the guilt surrounding trying to be the "perfect mother," whatever that is. I'm finally enjoying being a mother so much that I'm actually thinking quite a lot about having another child—something I theoretically thought would be a "good thing to do" but didn't know how in the world I'd ever be able to go through again. I now look forward to having a baby in a year or so and to the changes in me that this year of growth has brought.

Sincerely,
Ilene

CHAPTER 21

IGNORANCE—MY OWN AND MY DOCTORS'

Dear Reader,

I married at the end of my sophomore year of college. Jim and I had been dating for for three years. A week before the wedding I went to my parents' doctor and asked to be put on the birth control pill. The doctor told me I would have to wait until my next period was over and could use some other means of contraception until then and for one month afterwards. I asked what else I could use, and he vaguely replied, "There are a number of other things. Just use something else," and dismissed me.

My college courses hadn't prepared me for this. My working class mother and mother-in-law were no more helpful. So I started using a contraceptive foam advertised in the women's magazines. In the meantime I was reading all the controversial articles on whether or not the Pill caused cancer, blood clots and other fatal diseases in the women who took it.

At the end of a month of marriage my period came right on schedule, so I decided to continue using the foam for a contraceptive. This spared me another embarrassing visit to my parents' doctor and, I felt at the time, spared me the greater risk to my health involved in taking The Pill.

My period did not come at the end of the second month I was married, and I knew immediately that I was pregnant as my periods had always been very regular.

I wasn't sure how to react. Jim and I briefly discussed abortion, but abortion was only then becoming legal in New York and California and was not widely accepted. We felt our families would be appalled if we aborted their grandchild. An abortion would have taken more money than we had, a great deal of determined action and many risks on our part. We discarded the idea and let the pregnancy progress.

As I began telling people I was pregnant they all responded with, "Isn't that wonderful!" I agreed that it was. It seemed the thing to do, and by the end of the pregnancy I had convinced myself (I thought) that I really wanted this baby. I revelled in all the attention I was getting.

I continued to go to college and work part-time in the college library up to the seventh month of pregnancy when the college's rules required me to quit work. Without a paycheck coming in I couldn't afford to take any more classes, and I walked around the campus numbly—hardly able to comprehend that they could really deny me access to the remainder of my college education just because I was seven months pregnant.

At home I readied a nursery and put a fresh coat of paint on an old crib that my husband had once slept in. I read all the childbirth and childraising books I could get my hands on.

I continued to see my parents' doctor during my pregnancy. He had also greeted the news with "Isn't that wonderful!" as though I had never asked him for contraceptive help. I was too "nice" and cowed by authority to disagree with him even in my own mind.

He asked me what kind of anesthetic I would like during delivery, and I said I wanted to have the baby naturally and to breastfeed him. He said he had seen one such birth and was all in favor of it. He also said an obstetrician would be doing the actual delivery.

And so it was that eight hours into labor on May 17, 1967, I met for the first time the man who was to deliver my baby. He asked me what kind of anesthetic my doctor and I had agreed on. I told him I wanted to have the baby naturally. He flew into a rage then and there. He said that natural childbirth was primitive, medieval and that he refused to deliver a baby without anesthetics.

I was amazed. I had assumed my doctor had checked with this obstetrician before encouraging me to believe that I could have my baby naturally. I was certainly in no position to argue at this point—eight hours into labor.

I said, "Do what you think is best, but I want to be awake when the baby is born." He calmed down and said, "Yes, yes, of course. That's what you *really* wanted, isn't it?" and walked out.

An hour or so later I was wheeled to the delivery room, and my husband's visits were cut off. I waited and waited, stifling the moan that rose in my throat with each contraction. A nurse walked through from time to time but didn't even examine me to see if I was ready to deliver. I lay there nearly two hours.

Then the anesthesiologist arrived, and suddenly there was lots of activity. A needle was poked into my lower spine. My legs were strapped up into stirrups. I had to keep my hands under a sheet. The lower half of my body went numb. I felt my body jerked down the table and saw the blood spatter as the doctor did an episiotomy.

The doctor told me to push, but I couldn't tell whether I was doing so or not. There was no feedback from my muscles. I heard a thin wail as my son's head appeared. The doctor pulled him out with forceps.

Soon his whole body was out and held upside down in the air. A nurse was flicking the bottom of his feet with her finger nail to make him cry more. I was anguished to see my baby hurt and made to cry. I felt helpless, all trussed up and numb. They told me his crying would send more oxygen throughout his body.

They measured him and did other things I couldn't see while I was being stitched up. Finally they rolled me onto a cart and pushed my son's clear-sided bassinet up alongside me. He was wrapped up tightly in a blue flannel blanket. I wasn't allowed to touch him.

They took him to the nursery and me to a 4-bed room. My husband and parents saw us both briefly as we were rolled past them. In spite of all I had been through, at that moment I felt absolutely euphoric. Jim said I looked like a triumphant Egyptian queen being carried in a procession.

In my room I was given a shot of sedative and went to sleep for a couple of hours. When I woke the nurse brought me tea and toast but still no baby. About 12 hours after the birth my son was brought to me for his first feeding. He was sound asleep. The nurse woke him by flicking the bottoms of his feet. I stifled my protest.

As soon as she left he fell right back asleep in my arms. I was holding him for the first time. I unwrapped him and touched his tiny hands and stroked his nearly-bald head. He certainly wasn't getting any nourishment that way. I stroked his cheeks and chin and lips trying to wake him gently. He slept on.

In 20 minutes the nurse came to take him away. "How did it go?" she asked. I shrugged and said, "He went to sleep."

My stitches hurt. My milk came in making my breasts hard and hot. Every 4 hours during the day my son was brought to me for 20 minutes. He was usually asleep. They were giving him bottles of sugar water in the nursery when he woke and cried for food. I couldn't rouse his interest in my breast.

The doctor came in on the second day and said the nurses had told him I didn't have a properly shaped nipple, and the baby couldn't breastfeed from me. He asked me to show him my breast which I did, and he said he was switching the baby over to formula and would give me dry-up pills.

I cried.

The next day I was sent home, but my son was kept at the hospital. He had jaundice, they said, and wasn't gaining weight properly due to my faulty attempt to breastfeed him. My husband came for me, and I broke the news to him.

The next two days were an agony of pain from my stitches and my milk-gorged breasts and my deprived arms and heart. My last memory of my son was hearing him scream when they circumsized him. They had told me he wouldn't even feel it, and it would be best for him to be circumsized like his father. I had signed the necessary papers and now felt I had again betrayed him.

Finally Jay was released from the hospital. That evening

Jim held his child for the first time. He hardly knew what to do with him and quickly handed him back to me. I didn't know what to do with him either, but I was the woman, the mother.

My milk was dried up now, and I continued Jay on his formula. He was colicky and cried for hours. It was an unbearably hot summer. Jay hardly ever slept. When I had done all I could for him I just sat down on the floor with him in my lap and cried along with him.

He screamed when I bathed him. He threw up all down my back when I burped him. I was up half the night with him and had no energy to make love with Jim. I resented Jim's attempts to force me, then finally submitted telling him I was just a hole in the wall to him.

I fell further and further behind in the housework. I could hardly manage to keep formula mixed, bottles sterilized, diapers washed, crib sheets changed. I smelled of urine and throw up from my contacts with the baby and didn't have the strength to bathe. What would be the use? The baby would just throw up on me again the next time I burped him. I called the doctor but got no help. Jay would outgrow it, I was told.

My life seemed a nightmare. I was so far removed from the college coed working her way through school that I had been only a few short months ago. The years stretched out bleakly ahead of me. There would be no degree, no professional career. Nothing but four walls and a crying kid.

All because I was a woman. My husband now had a child, too, but his life was unchanged. I envied him as he went off to his classes and job each day. Of course he should be the one to finish school. After all he could earn more now and after graduation than I could. And why was that? Because I was a woman.

Jim and I used to do everything together—go to school, go to work, cook, do the housework. We were equals, but having a child changed all that. Now our differing lives drove us apart. He couldn't begin to understand what I was going through, and he despaired of ever getting enough quiet to do his studying in the evening. He had no time left over for the baby or for me, except in bed. In fact the baby's crying and my crying were a terrible burden to him.

Finally I felt like I was cracking up. I couldn't concentrate, couldn't do the simplest daily tasks. I just barely found the strength to answer the baby's cries. I began to have terrible fantasies of bashing the baby's head against the wall or dropping him out the second story window. I felt trapped, helpless, in agony and ashamed.

I prayed as I had never prayed before, but there was no answer. I became convinced that there was no one out there to listen. I wanted to die. I felt the world was such a horrible place that the best thing I could do was kill my husband, my baby and myself—to put us all out of our misery. But I didn't have the strength.

I convinced Jim that I needed help. He made several calls and was referred to the Adult Psychiatric Institute. There resident psychiatrists were being trained, and people with low incomes could pay a nominal amount for help. After two interviews I was assigned to a psychiatrist for analytically-oriented psychotherapy.

After the first few sessions I seemed to run out of things to say. I spent many therapy hours in agonized silence. I felt as heavy as lead, unable to move or speak. My tongue felt thick in my mouth. When, with tremendous effort, I was able to say something the words came out slowly, syllable by syllable. Then I collapsed back into dark silence. Afterwards I would cry for hours—even out on the streets on my way home.

My therapist patiently waited for me to learn to trust him. After a while we discovered that I spoke more freely if I sat with my back to him, and my dreams became a means of communicating more than I consciously knew or felt or remembered.

I hadn't told anyone about my depression; I was too ashamed. After a year of therapy I was able to tell my parents what was happening. To my surprise they didn't reject me as the freak I thought I was.

I learned to drive, took swimming lessons at the "Y", got

out and away from the baby one day each week while Jim took care of Jay.

It was a hard time for Jim and I, but he stood by me even though he didn't understand what had gone wrong and why. As I began to recover, my sexual desire for him slowly returned, to his great joy.

Therapy gave me perspective, insight into my past and feelings, and some new skills for coping. It was a good start, but I still had many more things to learn. After three years of 2 or 3 visits per week I started talking about terminating therapy and going back to college. To my surprise my therapist agreed.

My doctor had allowed me to go on The Pill after Jay's birth. I never had another child, but devoted myself to being the best possible mother to Jay. I had paid dearly for my own ignorance and the ignorance of my doctors. What you don't know can hurt you most of all.

However, my depression was not the end of my life. In some ways it was only the beginning. I have had a number of good years since then, and I am convinced that the best years of my life are yet to come. I am sure you will find that true for yourself as well.

Best Wishes to You,
Barbara Ciaramitaro

PART III:

UNDERSTANDING
POSTPARTUM DEPRESSION

PREFACE

This section of the book has been written fc
sionals who are in a position to help and cou
mothers and for those women who have recovere   ~~~~
partum depression but still wonder what hit them and why. It is
not meant to be read by women who are presently depressed.

The research and statistics presented here have not been
gathered together in any other place, to the best of my knowledge. Each item has been carefully documented (where possible) and footnoted. Footnotes are numbered in parentheses,
like this (3), for ease in typesetting. All notes can be found at
the end of the book. They can also be used as a guide to further
reading.

There is a great need for more research in all the areas
covered in this part of the book. Until such research is conducted all statements about depression—its causes and effects,
its prevention and its cure—must be considered working hy-
potheses.

It is my hope that this book will help stir up the interest and
support necessary for such research to be undertaken.

CHAPTER 22
DEPRESSION—STILL A MYSTERY

Depression is the most widely experienced form of mental illness. The World Health Organization estimates that nearly 3% of the world population, or 100 million people, suffer from clinically significant depression—and the problem is growing.

In the United States 4 to 8 million people each year are seriously enough depressed to seek medical help and 250,000 of them are hospitalized for treatment (National Institute of Mental Health statistics). Approximately 15% of all U.S. citizens can expect to experience a serious depression at some time in their lives, and the possibility is twice as high for women (1 out of 6) as for men (1 out of 12).

Depression can occur at any age from infancy to senescence. It resembles the normal process of mourning the loss of a loved one.

The symptoms of depression commonly include:

fatigue
difficulty in concentrating
insomnia
weight loss
gloomy thoughts
tearfulness

Also present in most cases are:

a feeling of hopelessness
a loss of interest in sex
social withdrawal
a lack of pleasure in activities previously enjoyed

anxiety attacks

a feeling of guilt

Depression is a self-limiting disease. Roughly 70% of all people affected by it will recover, most of them within 6 months of onset. This recovery rate is the same whether or not a person receives treatment. Of the remaining 30%, half are permanently disabled and half commit suicide. Depression precedes 80% of all suicides.

What causes depression? We don't really know. There is no single known factor which is present in all cases of depression and which does not occur in persons who are not depressed. Hence there presently appears to be no simple, causal explanation.

The need for more research and better funding is urgent. In 1976 Congress appropriated $744 million for cancer research which may help $1\frac{1}{2}$ million Americans each year. Only a little more than $5 million went into research on the causes of depression although 4 to 8 million Americans become depressed each year and our suicide rate among young people has tripled in the past 20 years.

Numerous theories are being advanced and tested by researchers. Due to the lack of funding much of the data gathered is inadequate and contradictory. One thing appears certain: there are physical as well as psychological factors involved in depression.

Perhaps the ferment and uncertainty is a healthy sign. Thirty years ago everyone thought they knew what caused depression. Depression was a mental or emotional illness brought about by a childhood loss or trauma. The Freudian psychoanalytic therapy designed to remedy this illness did seem to help some people, failed to help others and was simply unavailable to most sufferers due to its high cost and the small number of qualified therapists.

Then in the 1950's it was discovered that depression could be drug induced. Treating high blood pressure patients with a drug named reserpine resulted in depressive symptoms including suicidal tendencies in 15% of the patients so treated. (1) Is it coincidental that the incidence of depression in the U.S. population at large is also 15%? How can a drug introduced into the body produce a mental or emotional illness?

To understand how reserpine induces depression we must know something about how the brain works. The brain contains millions of nerve cells or neurons. Each "neuron looks some-thing like a hand, with thin threadlike fingers, known as den-drites, plus a palm, or cell body, and a long slender thumb, called the axon. Every neuron connects to thousands of others, not by touching, but by coming close at areas known as synapses. A nerve signal, in the form of an electric blip, starts at the dendrite and races to the axon, where it causes [a chemical known as] the neurotransmitter to squirt across the synapse, triggering the whole process in the next neuron." (2)

There are two groups of neurotransmitters:
the catecholamines: epinephrine (adrenalin)
                norepinephrine
                dopamine
the indole amines: serotonin
                histamine (3)

Reserpine is known to deplete the amount of the neuro-transmitter called norepinephrine to be found in the spaces be-tween the nerve cells. When the level of available norepine-phrine was restored to normal in various animal and human experiments the depressive effects of reserpine were reversed or averted.

Thus a new theory of depression causation was born. J. J. Schildkraut hypothesized that " . . . depressions are associated with an absolute or relative deficiency of catecholamines . . . " (4)

This biochemical theory of depression causation has led to widespread use of two classes of drugs: the MAO inhibitors and the tricyclic antidepressants. While the two types of drugs work differently they both seem to make more norepinephrine available for use in the synapses between the nerve cells. Most clinicians feel that the use of these drugs results in rapid symptom relief in most patients after the first 2-3 weeks of use.

However, an important question is, as yet, unanswered by the biochemical or catecholamine theory of depression. What causes normal, healthy individuals who are not being treated with reserpine to deplete their stores of neurotransmitters?

Some possible answers are to be found in four areas of research: genetics, nutrition, stress, and sleep deprivation.

One possibility is that some individuals inherit a faulty mechanism for the production of one or more of the neurotransmitters. Under normal conditions this faulty production may be sufficient to meet the demands placed upon it. However, an unusually high demand (eg. during sickness or when one is under emotional stress) could produce a state of deficiency and depression.

Another possibility involves deficiencies of a different kind. The neurotransmitters are also known as biogenic amines because they are manufactured within the nerve cells of the brain from amino acids which are obtained in protein foods. The process of manufacture involves the conversion of the amino acids by means of various enzymes which require vitamins and minerals to function. Hence deficiencies in vitamins, minerals or proteins in one's diet might lead to a breakdown or insufficiency of biogenic amine production with a resultant depression.

A third possibility is that depression is a stress-induced malfunction. Stress is any life event or change which requires a person to adjust, adapt or cope in new ways. Such coping calls on the reserve capacities of the body, the little-used back-up systems for greater-than-usual production of neurotransmitters. Such secondary systems may be more prone to malfunction resulting in deficiencies and depression.

Sleep deprivation is one such stress—one that may be particularly *apropos* in a discussion of postpartum depression as we shall see. A persistant loss of sleep builds up a pressure within the brain to compensate with increased sleep. The chemicals involved in producing the various stages of sleep are the same biogenic amines that seem to be involved in depression.

It can easily be seen that these four possibilities are closely related and interdependent. While research goes on in each area separately, depression may be the ground of a vital synthesis of theories and findings.

In the next chapter we will take a closer look at what the researchers are saying about each of these possibilities.

CHAPTER 23
WHAT THE RESEARCHERS SAY ABOUT DEPRESSION

I. GENETICS

George Winokur, Professor of Psychiatry at Washington University School of Medicine in St. Louis, has done extensive research in an attempt to establish a genetic cause of or predisposition toward depression. (1) His data leads him to believe that there are at least three distinct types of depression:

1. manic-depression, in which the man or woman experiences episodes of euphoria and hyperactivity as well as episodes of deep despair;
2. depression spectrum disease, in which the female members of the family are predisposed to have a depression before the age of 40 whereas the males are often alcoholic or aggressively anti-social; and
3. primary depression, in which the person experiences no other form of psychiatric illness prior to a depression which typically has its onset after the age of 40.

The evidence for a genetic predisposition appears strongest in the manic-depressive syndrome, and treatment with lithium where possible seems to prevent or moderate both the unnatural euphoria and the depression.

There is also considerable evidence to support the existence of a depression spectrum disease. Alcoholic or sociopathic fathers, brothers or sons occur much more frequently than the norm in the families of women who become depressed before the age of 40. (2)

Nearly all women who experience a postpartum depression would fit into one of these two groups, and Winokur's findings on the occurrence of postpartum depression in families demonstrating a history of manic-depression or depression spectrum disease will be discussed in Chapter 25.

Joseph Mendels believes that the twin studies and family history studies which he summarizes in his book *Concepts of Depression* indicate "that there is some genetic factor that plays a part in the development of depression. However, it may be that this is neither a necessary nor a sufficient cause in itself. It is also possible that there may be more than one genetic mechanism leading to depression." (3)

II. NUTRITION

Psychiatric researchers who are studying nutrition as an aspect of mental illness have been focussing their efforts on understanding and treating schizophrenics. However, a few crumbs from their table do relate to depression and more work in this area certainly appears to be warranted.

It was only 40 years ago (in 1937) that it was discovered that many chronic inmates of our psychiatric hospitals were suffering from pellagra, a niacin (vitamin B_3) deficiency. When niacin was added to their diets they were able to return home and resume their normal lives. Nevertheless it remains rare today that a psychiatrist tests his patients upon admittance for any nutritional deficiencies.

Nutritionists are discovering that many people have an inherited or acquired need for much higher levels of certain vitamins and minerals than they receive in a conventional diet. If such needs are not met these people will show deficiency symptoms, many of which can be mistaken for psychiatric symptoms particularly if the deficiency is in the B vitamins or calcium or magnesium.

In addition to specific deficiency symptoms, an inadequate diet is a stress on the system which may lead to the development of functional hypoglycemia, a metabolism disorder, in those who are genetically predisposed. Dr. Carl C. Pfeiffer, director of Princeton's Brain Bio Center, writes that " . . . functional hypoglycemia (FH) . . . has been pinpointed as the cause of many everyday emotional problems such as fatigue, depression and irritability . . . (4) FH can cause abrupt mood swings and even mimic serious mental illness. It is often misdiagnosed as a psychiatric disturbance because of the psychopathological symptoms (5) . . . [which] include confusion, absent-mindedness, indecisiveness, loss of memory and/or concentration, irritability, moodiness, restlessness, insomnia, fears, nightmares, paranoia, anxiety and depression." (6)

An excess of certain heavy metals in the bloodstream can also cause symptoms which may seem psychological. We have long known about the "Mad Hatter" syndrome in those who work with mercury fumes and the emotional symptoms of mild lead poisoning. Researchers in biochemical aspects of schizophrenia feel that excess copper in the bloodstream may bring on active episodes of mental illness. There is particular evidence for such a connection in postpartum depression and psychosis as will be shown in Chapter 25.

While nutritional research into mental illness is often treated as the unwelcome step-child of more legitimate research, it is in reality a single aspect of stress as a causative factor in depression.

III. STRESS

We have known for many years that stress causes chemical and hormonal changes throughout the body. Hans Selye's pioneering work on stress identified what he called a "general adaptation syndrome or G.A.S." which is the body's natural response to stress of whatever kind (physical or psychological).

Selye writes: "It had long been known that . . . physical stressors could cause an initial excitement which was followed by a secondary phase of depression. It is interesting to learn that identifiable chemical compounds [adrenalines or corticoids], produced during the acute alarm-reaction phase of the G.A.S., possess this property of first keying up for action and then causing a depression." (7)

More recent work by Thomas H. Holmes and Minoru Masuda (8) has produced the Social Readjustment Rating Scale which consists of 43 life events requiring a change in one's day-to-day routine. Each event is given a certain value in Life Change Units (LCU's) in accordance with how stressful it was perceived as being by many experimental populations. It was found that clusters of these life events often precede the onset of physical and psychological illnesses.

"It has been adduced from these studies that this clustering of social, or life, events achieves etiological [causal] significance as a necessary, but not sufficient, cause of illness and accounts in part for the time of onset of disease." (9)

Holmes and Masuda offer this explanation of their findings: "It is postulated that life-change events, by evoking adaptive efforts by the human organism that are faulty in kind and duration, lower 'bodily resistance' and enhance the probability of disease occurrence." (10)

Eugene S. Paykel, of Yale University, conducted a study of 185 depressed patients interviewed after recovery and 185 controls from the general population corrected for age, sex, race, class and marital status. He reports: "Major differences were found between depressives and controls in the [life] events reported. There was a general excess of events in the depressed patients, who reported almost 3 times as many events as the controls. . . . (11) Many subjects reported a cluster of events that, on detailed scrutiny of narrative summaries, suggested a cumulative model of stress." (12)

Frederick K. Goodwin and William E. Bunney, Jr., both of the National Institute of Mental Health, offer an explanation that combines genetic predisposition with stress precipitation of depression: "Suppose that an individual with a strong family history of affective [mood] illness has a genetically transmitted defect in one of the systems that subserve the increase in the neurotransmitter amines that normally occurs in response to stress. In such an individual under chronic, or recurrent, stress, the stores of the critical neurotransmitter amines could eventually become depleted; and according to the amine hypothesis, this would lead to a clinical state of . . . depression." (13)

It is possible that the stress causation theory of depression could subsume the more traditional psychoanalytic theories of depression. Psychological events such as loss of a loved one or trauma experienced at any time of life have a very high Life Change Unit rating. They are among life's most stressful events. Also chronic neurotic patterns of thought and action caused by faulty reactions to childhood events would serve as long-term stressors that weaken one's capacity to respond adequately to current life events.

Christoph M. Heinicke writes, "A review of systematic studies that relate parental-deprivation experiences to the onset of depression reveals (i) that the greater incidence of adult psychiatric disturbance in general is associated with the childhood experience of parental death or extensive separation from the parent owing to divorce or marital separation; (ii) that a greater incidence of depression is associated with the childhood experience of parental death; (iii) that the patients who suffer from a severe, as opposed to mild, form of depression have frequently experienced parental death in childhood or an inadequate parent-child relationship, or both; (iv) that the patients who attempt suicide have more frequently experienced parental death in childhood; and (v) that the incidence of parental death in the 0-5 and 10-14 intervals is higher for depressed patients." (14)

IV. SLEEP DEPRIVATION

Sleep deprivation is another stressor that may be relevant to an understanding of depression, particularly postpartum depression. Many researchers have noted that depressed patients show a characteristic pattern of disturbed sleep.

Frederick Snyder asserts: "The important point about the sleep of depressed patients in the midst of actual psychoses is that it is, indeed, extremely troubled . . . Total sleep is diminished, sleep stages 3 and 4 (deep sleep) are particularly scarce; the night is broken by more or less frequent and prolonged awakenings; and the proportion of REM [dream] sleep within this fragmented sleep is usually, though not invariably, somewhat low." (15)

"In all cases, periods of greatest psychopathological dis-

114

turbance have been associated with reductions of total sleep and especially with low levels of REM sleep, while periods of sustained improvement have been reflected in, and in some cases clearly anticipated by, striking increases in REM sleep to above normal levels." (16)

Joseph Becker explains that REM (rapid eye movement, or dream) sleep is strongly influenced by catecholamine metabolism which includes norepinephrine, and the deep sleep of stage 3 and 4 is strongly affected by serotonin metabolism. (17)

For this reason some researchers have hypothesized that sleep deprivation may deplete these neurotransmitter amines leading to depression. Laverne C. Johnson comments: "While I have emphasized that a prolonged psychotic state does not inevitably follow prolonged sleep loss [100-200 hours], behavioral changes during sleep loss are often dramatic and incapacitating. The most-often reported changes are increasing fatigue, irritability, feelings of persecution, inability to concentrate, and periods of misperception and disorientation." (18)

Several pages later she concludes that "many who complain of fatigue, musculo-skeletal symptoms, headaches, visual disturbances, poor concentration, apathy, and depression may be suffering from subclinical sleep deprivation." (19)

SUMMARY

While this research says much that is true and useful about depression, nowhere does it prove conclusively what causes depression. Some support is given to the brain amine deficiency theory, but it is also known that drugs which replace the amine levels within a few short hours nevertheless take 2-3 weeks to lift the depression. In other words the problem may be more subtle or complex than a simple amine deficiency, however that deficiency is brought about.

As Eugene S. Paykel says, " . . . It is hard to escape the conclusion that depression is a final common pathway toward which a number of causes converge. The causes include not only separations, recent and past, and a variety of other events, but also genetic endowment, personality, and susceptibilities that depend on previous experience and individual perceptions of events. Any artificial mind-body dualism must be avoided; the psychological events presumably have their biological substrates and act through neuropharmacological mechanisms and metabolic pools, which may also be subject to their own disturbances and to cyclic fluctuations." (20)

Only additional costly research can give us the answers we need to prevent and quickly treat depression.

CHAPTER 24

WHO GETS DEPRESSED AFTER CHILDBIRTH?

A depression after childbirth can happen to any woman who gives birth to one or more children. The anecdotes and letters in the first two parts of this book show that such a depression can occur in rich and poor, in housewives and career women, in new mothers and experienced mothers, in the mainstream culture of suburbia and in the alternative back-to-the-land culture. No woman can consider herself excluded by virtue of lifestyle, health, education, social class, or the number of children she has previously delivered without depression.

How common is it for a woman to experience depression after childbirth? That depends on how serious a depression you mean. Clinicians generally recognize three distinct levels of postpartum depression:

1. the after-baby blues
2. a mild to moderate postpartum depression
3. postpartum psychosis

The after-baby blues is a let-down, tearful, irritable feeling which occurs 2-10 days after childbirth and generally corrects itself.

A postpartum depression has all the classical symptoms of any other depression listed in Chapter 22. It generally sets in before the 6th month after birth and lasts anywhere from several months to a year or more.

Postpartum psychosis is a severe psychiatric illness which requires hospitalization within 6 months after childbirth. It may be diagnosed as delirium, a manic episode, depression or schizophrenia.

I. *The After-Baby Blues*

From 50-80% of all women giving birth in U.S. hospitals experience the after-baby blues. (1) Usual symptoms include lack of energy, episodes of crying, anxiety and fear, confusion, headaches, worry about physical symptoms and attractiveness, occasional insomnia, and a negative attitude toward the husband. (2)

The after-baby blues are generally thought to be caused by the rapid drop in the level of two hormones, estrogen and progesterone, following childbirth. However, some doctors who have visited maternity hospitals in other parts of the world feel that there is a higher incidence of the blues in the U.S. because of our hospital procedures.

Marshall H. Klaus and John H. Kennell, Professors of Pediatrics at Case Western Reserve University School of Medicine, report: " . . . Our observations lead us to speculate that mother-infant separation, the assignment of the caretaking responsibilities to 'experts,' the concerns about the ability to care for the newborn at home, and the limiting of visitors are major factors" (3) in the incidence of the after-baby blues.

Recovery from the after-baby blues is generally considered to be 100%, and no treatment of this condition is considered necessary.

II. *Postpartum Depression*

The incidence of postpartum depression in the mild to moderate range is variously estimated at 3-23% of all births. (4) Over 3,000,000 American women give birth each year. That means that from 90,000 to 690,000 women become depressed each year after giving birth. Another way of stating it is that up to 1 out of 5 mothers undertake the care of their newborn infants while mildly to moderately depressed.

Most of these women receive little or no treatment for their depression either because they are too ashamed to admit to their "unnatural" feelings or because their doctors minimize the importance of their complaints. It is primarily for these women that this book has been written.

III. *Postpartum Psychosis*

The incidence of severe mental illness requiring hospitalization in postpartum women is comparatively small: 1-2.7 in 1000 births. (5) Even so 3,000 to 9,000 women are hospitalized within 6 months of giving birth in this country alone each year. From 6% to 12½% of all psychiatric hospital admissions of women occur during the postpartum period. (6)

"About 20 percent of patients with postpartum psychosis recover within a month. In 40 percent recovery takes longer than six months, and about 15 percent remain chronically ill. For about half of the patients it will remain an isolated event in their lives; the incidence of recurrence in subsequent pregnancies is about 1 in 7 women." (7)

WHO IS AT RISK?

While no woman can consider herself totally immune to postpartum depression, it is true that some women run a higher risk than others. Much more research is needed before we will be able to predict with certainty which women will suffer a postpartum depression. However, doctors and researchers have noted a number of factors which indicate a higher than normal risk.

HIGH RISK FACTORS

1. a postpartum depression after a previous birth
2. a previous manic, depressive or schizophrenic episode
3. parents or siblings who have had manic, depressive or schizophrenic episodes
4. an alcoholic or aggressively anti-social father
5. the loss of a parent through death or divorce during childhood
6. an unhappy childhood due to a cold or abusive parent
7. a neurotic personality structure
8. an unwanted pregnancy
9. a long or difficult labor or complicated birth
10. having a premature, ill or defective baby

A woman who is aware of having more than one of these high risk factors in her background should certainly consider the possibility of not having a child (or more children). Should she get pregnant unexpectedly she should certainly consider an abortion. If she decides to have a child she should be particularly careful to receive adequate nutrition and rest during the pregnancy, the best medical care, and household help and emotional support during the first year after giving birth.

Doctors can use these high risk factors in developing a questionnaire to use with all pregnant mothers in their care to help them predict which women will need extra attention and support throughout their pregnancy, delivery and postpartum period. They can also take such factors into account when counseling female patients on birth control and abortion.

EARLY PREDICTIVE SIGNS

While some women are depressed right from the day of delivery, most become depressed after returning home, during the first 3-6 months after giving birth. Dr. Virginia Larsen, principal investigator of a study of 200 military couples over a three-year period at Ft. Steilacoom in Washington, found several early signs predicting postpartum problems could be identified.

These signs included:

1. Someone other than the husband took the mother in labor to the hospital.

2. The father did not share the news of the baby's birth with any relative.

3. The mother was over-stressed by visitors after she came home with the new baby.

4. The mother had nightmares after delivery. . . .

5. The mother felt 'blue' and upset but was unable to express or work out her feelings.

6. The mother held her baby away from her body.

7. The new baby was referred to as 'it' or by a negative term such as 'the Monster.'*

Sensitivity to such early signs in addition to the high-risk factors previously mentioned and over-all stress levels in the life of the patient could lead to early intervention and support thus preventing a full-blown depression.

*Larsen, Virginia L., M.D., et al., *Attitudes and Stresses Affecting Perinatal Adjustment.* p. 24. Final Report under National Institute of Mental Health Grant MH-01381-01-02 covering Sept. 1, 1963 - Aug. 31, 1966.

120

CHAPTER 25
WHAT CAUSES POSTPARTUM DEPRESSION?

We are no more certain of what causes postpartum depression than we are of what causes any other depression. However, there are a number of factors unique to postpartum depression that deserve special attention in this chapter. Among them are genetic weakness and psychological predisposition combined with such physical and psychological stresses as hormonal changes, dietary inadequacy, sleep deprivation, social role expectations, and hospital procedures.

GENETIC FACTORS

George Winokur, together with Theodor Reich, studied the incidence of postpartum depression in women with manic-depressive histories. Of those 20 women studied who had had a diagnosed manic episode leading to hospitalization and who also had children, 40% had suffered a depression or mania after the birth of one or more of their children. (1) This is from 2 to 10 times the expected frequency in the general population of women.

Winokur also found that manic-depressive women "are more likely to fall ill during the postpartum period than at other times in their lives after age 15." (2) In 27% of those women with children who had ever had a manic or depressive episode, a postpartum illness was the first such episode in their lives. (3) He also found that "having had a single postpartum episode seems to predispose the patients to further postpartum episodes." (4)

A lesser (though still higher than normal) risk of postpartum depression is indicated in the case of women with family histories of depression spectrum disease (depressed mothers and sisters of alcoholic or aggressively anti-social fathers and brothers). (5)

PSYCHOLOGICAL PREDISPOSITION

As in depression in general, the loss of a parent through death or divorce during childhood has been found to be a predisposing factor in postpartum depression. (6) One can also interpret the greater incidence of postpartum depression found in women whose parents were manic, depressed or alcoholic in psychological (rather than genetic) terms. Such emotionally handicapped parents were not likely to have offered a wholesome atmosphere for their daughter's personality development.

One study found the incidence of postpartum depression to be related to hostile attitudes toward one's mother in 16% of the cases studied. (7) Other studies offer a possible explanation for this finding. They show that a woman's expectations of what childbirth will be like are still determined by what her mother has told her. (8) If her own experience of childbirth is more difficult than her mother led her to expect she may feel hostile toward her mother.

Stuart S. Asch and Lowell J. Rubin (9) "emphasize that postpartum depressions frequently occur in women whose own mothers were depressed following their birth . . . The recurrence of serious postpartum reactions in successive generations is quite marked."

They do not draw any genetic conclusions from this, however. Instead they present three cases in which a postpartum psychosis occurred in a person who had not borne a child—a 52 year-old woman after the birth of her first grandchild, a woman who adopted a newborn boy, and a new father.

They conclude: "Our case material adds to the literature that implicates in postpartum reactions the early mothering experience of the new parent, the vicissitudes of her separation and individuation from her mother, her sibling experience, and the nature of the oedipal resolution. These observations support the conclusion that postpartum reactions are primarily psychogenic, since we have described reactions in subjects whose hormonal and physiological changes were not involved because they were not parturients." (10)

PHYSICAL STRESS

Pregnancy and childbirth are physical stresses in and of themselves. In the early months of pregnancy the mother-to-be may have morning sickness and anxiety, clear indicators of the hormonal changes occurring within. As an adjustment is made to the increasing levels of estrogen and progesterone these symptoms subside and may be replaced by elation. (11)

Toward the end of pregnancy a woman is carrying an extra 25 to 40 pounds of weight with her wherever she goes. She naturally feels fatigued, and the downward pressure on her bladder leads to frequent urination disturbing her sleep at night.

Few would deny that the contractions of labor and the anesthesia and episiotomy generally experienced during delivery are stressors. Those women whose labor was prolonged suffer postpartum depression at a significantly higher rate. (12)

Then the estrogen and progesterone levels, whose increase was gradually adjusted to during the first three months of pregnancy, plunge back to pre-pregnancy levels in a matter of days. Blood volume is reduced by 30% following childbirth, and 20% of the new mothers are anemic on the fourth day after delivery. (13)

"Under no other circumstances does such marked and rapid tissue breakdown (catabolism) take place without a departure from a condition of health," says N. Eastman in his text titled *Williams Obstetrics.*

These are the usual stresses experienced by all childbearing women. However, in addition, some women experience complications of the pregnancy or delivery. This increased amount of stress is associated with an increased incidence of postpartum depression. (14)

DIETARY INADEQUACY

A woman's nutritional requirements are greatly increased during pregnancy and lactation (breastfeeding). She is eating for two and can easily become deficient in vitamins and minerals if she eats unwisely or neglects to take the prescribed supplements.

These deficiencies do not disappear of their own accord merely because the child has been born. Their symptoms must be properly recognized and remedied. As stated in Chapter 23, many of the deficiency symptoms—particularly of the B vitamins and calcium and magnesium—resemble psychological or emotional problems.

"The stress of pregnancy and childbirth often precipitates FH [functional hypoglycemia or low blood sugar] in those women susceptible by constitution and dietary history," writes Dr. Carl C. Pfeiffer, "resulting in a long-lasting period of postpartum difficulties." (15)

In addition to the possibility of vitamin or mineral deficiencies and the onset of functional hypoglycemia, there is a third nutrition-related stress unique to pregnant women and users of estrogen-containing birth control pills. Dr. Pfeiffer notes that the rise in estrogen levels causes a similar rise in serum copper. Such elevated copper levels have been implicated in bringing on active schizophrenic episodes.

It takes two to three months for the elevated copper levels of pregnancy to return to normal after delivery. "This high copper level may be a factor in causing postpartum depression and psychosis," Dr. Pfeiffer states, "more data are needed in this area." (16) Zinc supplementation is said to aid in reducing the copper level to normal.

SLEEP DEPRIVATION

Few people are as regularly deprived of a normal night's sleep as the new mother. A number of studies show that sleep has already decreased to a significant level by late pregnancy, perhaps due to physical discomforts and anxieties about the approaching birth.

Labor is notorious for starting at night shortly after the woman has gone to bed. It may continue for 12, 24 or more hours. The birth itself is often accompanied by a heady euphoria

124

which precludes more than an hour or two of sleep even with sedation. Then the strange hospital bed, the hall lights on all night, the discomforts of the episiotomy and milk letdown all contribute to sleep deprivation.

Finally the mother returns home with her infant but must usually assume all responsibility for the night feedings which some infants require for months. The mother, ever listening for her baby's cry even while asleep, will have a lowered waking threshold. (17) Her sleep pattern closely resembles that of the typical depressed patient.

Could such patterning result in her increased susceptibility to depression during the postpartum period? We know that sleep loss causes a chemical pressure in the brain for more sleep. The chemicals involved are the same biogenic amines being studied for their possible role in depression.

In one study of 91 mothers sleep loss was found to contribute most strongly to the occurrence of postpartum depression. (18) This study concludes, "In general, the more stresses in any realm of her world and the less opportunity for recuperative sleep, the greater the likelihood that a new mother will experience depressed moods in the postpartum weeks."

CUMULATIVE STRESS

You will recall from Chapter 23 that researchers have found a clustering of life changes in the year preceding physical and psychological illnesses. Such a clustering also tends to precede pregnancy. (19) Often the year before a child's birth may see the parents marrying, moving to a new home, completing or dropping out of an educational program, starting, changing or quitting jobs.

The birth itself is, of course, a major life change event. It is followed, particularly in the case of first-time parents, by a new assessment of the husband-wife relationship, the learning of the new social role of parent, and possibly by financial difficulties. The very number of changes to be absorbed in a limited period of time and with such weighty consequences may well be a factor in postpartum depression.

Even more common than depression after the first child is depression after the third child. Research is needed to determine if this is a consquence of the too-close spacing of children, another form of cumulative stress.

SOCIAL ROLE EXPECTATIONS

Our society makes several assumptions about women:

1. A woman's biological destiny and ultimate fulfillment lie in bearing a child.
2. A woman marries in order to gain the safety and security necessary to the bearing of a child.
3. Once the child is born, a woman's "maternal instinct" will enable her to fulfill the infant's every need.
4. Any woman who does not want to marry, or once married does not want to have a child, or, having borne a child, does not automatically know how to love and care for it is "unnatural," a failure as a woman.

These assumptions have long supported the existence of male privilege. Mentors have regularly bypassed their bright female students to cultivate a male disciple in the belief that women are only in school to meet the right man to father their children. Bosses have refused female applicants for management jobs because they will presumably leave the firm to marry and raise a family.

Thus locked out of academic and business achievement, women often do turn to the bearing and raising of children as the only means available to them to gain status and recognition in our society. As they do so our society's assumptions about women are confirmed as true. In short, these assumptions are self-fulfilling prophecies.

Feminists have long recognized how discrimination against women in our schools and in the job market has led to the stunting and wasting of women's talents. Some have conjectured that twice as many women as men suffer from depression because of the frustration resulting from sexual discrimination.

The woman who suffers depression after childbirth is often a woman who is in conflict within herself over society's expecta-

126

tions of her and her own feelings about herself. Her pregnancy may have been unwanted, but she quickly finds that everyone else thinks it is wonderful—a sign that she is a "real" woman after all. When she finds after delivery that she feels no immediate surge of motherly love, no innate sure knowledge of what her baby needs, she may feel that her own and everybody else's suspicions about her are confirmed—she is a freak, a failure as a woman.

It is time that we debunked the notion that women, and only women, know instinctively how best to care for children. Nuturing a child is a complex, learned behavior. (20) To do a good job of it a person needs a considerable body of knowledge and the skill that comes only from extensive practice.

Few women, in this age of isolated nuclear families, have any significant contact with infants before they bear their first child. (21) It is unrealistic to expect that such a woman, without training or social support, will confidently care for her child and feel fulfilled while doing it.

Wherever expectations differ dramatically from the realistic experience commonly encountered we have a breeding ground for depression. Nowhere in our society is there a greater gap between expectation and reality than in the realm of childbirth and childraising.

HOSPITAL PROCEDURES

"Because maternity hospitals follow the medical model of active intervention to cure disease, childbirth is often treated as an illness and the laboring woman forced into a role of passive, helpless sick person—rather than active, childbearing parent-to-be. Decisions are made, treatments and interventions are undertaken which may affect her life and the life of her unborn child for years to come; yet she is often not given sufficient information or encouragement to participate actively in her own childbearing experience. Should complications or difficulties occur, or the birth experience be less than satisfactory, the mother is all too often left with a sense of guilt, frustration and rage at not having been more assertive and involved in her own care and that of her baby. This reaction, and the often prolonged depression which accompanies it, affects numerous mothers, among whom these experiences are often vivid years after their children are born." (22)

SUMMARY

While the symptoms of postpartum depression do not differ significantly from those of depression in general, nevertheless a close look at the causative factors uncovers certain features unique to the childbearing experience. These features may be helpful to researchers in coming to a better understanding of depression. They are also useful in the tailoring of a treatment and preventive program to this specific group of depressed patients.

CHAPTER 26

THE PERSONAL AND SOCIAL EFFECTS
OF POSTPARTUM DEPRESSION

The personal suffering of a woman having a postpartum depression is very real. It is not imaginary—"all in her head." Regardless of whether the causes are eventually determined to be physical or psychological or a combination of the two, her experience is a painful one.

At the very least she will suffer a loss of confidence and self-esteem which will continue to plague her for years after her depression has lifted. At worst her inner suffering may drive her to the irrevocable act of suicide.

"People suffering from neurotic or psychotic depression are definite suicide risks," Dr. Solomon H. Snyder writes. "The likelihood that a depressed person will commit suicide is twenty-five times the likelihood for the normal population." (1)

Nor are these two extremes the only personal effects common to those having a postpartum depression. Many women undergo years of expensive treatment, perhaps even long-term hospitalization, to recover their health. Often they suffer from the stigma attached to the menally ill in our society.

Other women treat themselves. They turn to alcohol or become addicted to sleeping pills, pep pills or other drugs in an attempt to ease or escape their suffering. This complicates diagnosis, treatment and recovery. A woman who has been a closet alcoholic for 10 years may no longer be recognizable as the sufferer of a postpartum depression.

These severe personal consequences are not necessitated by the postpartum depression itself, but result from the lack of early and adequate treatment of the depression. As more women and more doctors become aware of the problem, programs will be devised to prevent postpartum depression or, at the least, to promptly notice and treat its occurrence.

MARITAL RELATIONSHIP

While the woman's suffering is paramount in the discussion of effects of postpartum depression, it is true that the effects are also more widely felt. Her husband finds that his dream of a happy family life has turned into a nightmare. His wife's unhappiness in the home makes him into an ogre, an oppressor. She may openly accuse him of having gotten her pregnant merely to gain a household servant to relieve him of his half of the chores and cooking.

She is almost surely experiencing a lack of sexual interest in him. He expected to have to share her with the baby; he didn't expect to have to give her up entirely.

Her illness makes her withdraw from all social contact, and in most circles this severely limits his social life as well. He certainly doesn't feel free to invite his boss home for dinner.

His sleep and leisure time are being disturbed by the baby's crying, too. He needs his rest so he can continue to hold up his end of the partnership—working for a living. Why can't she hold up her end—keeping him and the baby happy and doing the cooking and cleaning?

If his depressed wife blames the baby for her trouble, how can he learn to love his child and enjoy its company without feeling disloyal to her? If she becomes actively abusive toward the baby, he may become so as well in a last bid for solidarity with her.

The husband's dilemma is a difficult one. He is handicapped, as is his wife, by lack of knowledge of postpartum depression. He may take the easy way out and blame the whole mess on her. Such scapegoating demeans him and stops his growth as a husband and father. However, once he has taken this position he may harden himself against her need for his support and separate from or divorce her.

Again and again the women who wrote to me about their postpartum depressions emphasized how important their husband's reaction was in helping or hindering their recovery. It seems that any adequate treatment program must include educating and supporting the husband as well as the depressed woman herself.

BEHAVIORAL PROBLEMS IN THE CHILD

Nor does the effect of a postpartum depression end with the added strain on the husband and marital relationship. Most deeply affected of all, of course, is the newborn infant who experiences the mother's depression as lack of love and care.

There is mounting evidence that postpartum depression in the mother is a contributing factor to a number of childhood problems. Myrna Weissman and Eugene Paykel, in their study of 35 depressed women with children, write, " . . . The acute symptoms of depression conflict with the demands of being a mother and produce a widespread negative impact on the children . . . Depressive symptoms put the mother in an untenable position of having to give when she needs to get. The need of the depressed mother for help, guidance, and affection is frustrated by similar demands made upon her by her children . . . " (2)

In a study of 19 mothers of severely disturbed 4-6 year old children, Gartner and Goldstein (3) found that 68% of the mothers had suffered a prolonged depression in the child's first year and 78% reported serious marital conflicts.

"We hypothesize that depression in a mother during the crucial first year of the child's life may result in her psychological unavailability to her infant. The resultant affectional deprivation may then be expressed in a variety of ways, depending on the degree of deprivation, the temperament of the child and the extent to which other family members compensate for the deficiency." (4)

HYPERACTIVITY

Depression in the mother has also been found to be related to hyperkinesis (hyperactivity) in the child. (5) In this, human infants seem to resemble primate infants. When the mother of a pigtail monkey is separated from her infant, the little monkey will screech and race around randomly in search of her. (6) After 24-36 hours of such agitated behavior it will huddle into a corner in an obvious posture of grief and depression.

Does the psychological distance between a depressed human mother and her infant evoke the same response—hyperactivity in less severe cases and depression in more severe cases of maternal deprivation? Or could both the mother's depression and the infant's hyperactivity have a common cause, perhaps metabolic?

Dr. Carl C. Pfeiffer notes that human and animal infants are born with liver concentrations of copper that are seven times higher than adult levels. It takes 5 to 15 years for the copper to decrease to adult levels. "Since copper is a stimulant to the brain, this excess copper may be a factor in the hyperactivity of children which ameliorates with age and slow elimination of the copper burden." (7) In Chapter 25 we learned that the new mother also has a higher than normal copper level which may contribute to her postpartum problems. We know so much and so little.

CHILD BATTERING

The greater incidence of hyperactivity and behavioral and learning problems among children of depressed mothers bears witness to the psychological suffering and deprivation experienced by these children. But severe physical suffering may be visited upon them as well.

"Steele and Pollock (8) noted that the majority of child batterers have been depressed. According to various statistics, from 23 to 56 percent of battered children are between 10 months and 1 year old when the act is first reported. (9) It thus seems reasonable to assume that the majority of child battering begins even earlier—in the postpartum period . . . Kempe and Helfer (10) estimate the child battering rate at 250 to 370 per million of the population; there were approximately 60,000 reported cases in the United States in 1970 alone." (11)

Weissman and Paykel also assert, "The patient who is withdrawn and weepy with a doctor can be irritable and hostile to her children." (12)

Researchers are finding that the turning of a mother against her infant may begin in the separation of the mother and infant immediately after delivery in the typical U.S. hospital. Marshall H. Klaus and John H. Kennell, in their book *Maternal-infant bonding*, summarize the evidence that a special sensitivity period occurs in both mother and infant in the hour after delivery which facilitates the natural formation of a bond of loving attachment between the two.

If the infant is separated from its mother during this crucial time and for much of the time in the days following delivery the affectional bond may not be formed. This is particularly frequent in cases where the infant is premature or must for some other reason be kept completely separate from the mother for days or weeks.

"Relatively mild illnesses in the newborn . . . appear to affect the relationship between mother and infant. The mother's behavior is often disturbed during the first year or more of the infant's life, even though his problems are completely resolved prior to discharge, and often within a few hours. This is one of our principles of attachment—that early events have long-lasting effects." (13)

"Careful studies show an increase in the incidence of battering as well as failure to thrive without organic cause among premature infants and those hospitalized for other reasons during the newborn period when they are compared with infants not separated from their mothers." (14)

INFANTICIDE

In rare cases the mother's lack of attachment to the baby and her resentment of the baby's demands leads her to kill the infant. In a study of 20 women who attempted infanticide, it was found that 6 had also attempted suicide and 5 had tried to kill their husbands. (15) The average age of the infants involved was 16 months.

Since roughly 80% of all postpartum depressions begin within 2 months of the infant's birth (16), it is likely that these women had been severely depressed for a year or more before their attempt to kill their infants. Why wasn't their condition recognized? Why didn't they receive help long before they took such desperate measures to be rid of their misery?

SUMMARY

It is obvious that postpartum depression in the mother has a severe impact on the entire family unit. The fact that 90,000 to 690,000 families are so affected each year adds up to a tremendous impact on our whole society.

How many divorces could be avoided, how many homes kept together by timely recognition and treatment of a mother's depression? How many children could be spared the scars of parental neglect and abuse? How many women could avoid long years of hospitalization or alcoholism or drug addiction? It is time we found out. Postpartum depression is not only a women's problem—it is a social problem as well.

CHAPTER 27

PREVENTION AND CURE

The dire personal and social consequences of postpartum depression make its prevention a matter of top priority. At least one of the factors which makes for a high risk of postpartum depression is wholly preventable today, that is having an unwanted child.

BIRTH CONTROL AND ABORTION

There is no reason today why a woman of whatever age should have an unwanted child. No reason except our laxity about providing every child with an adequate sex education before the age of puberty and our reluctance to make birth control methods and abortion readily available to every woman of child-bearing age.

We cannot afford to let these emotional holdovers from the Victorian era rule our schools, counselors, doctors and clinics at the expense of women's mental health. We must redouble our efforts, in the light of our deeper understanding of the effects of postpartum depression, to make every child a wanted child. An unwanted child with a depressed mother has little chance for a satisfying life.

It is not only the ignorant teen-age mother who is likely to be bearing an unwanted child. It is also the woman whose birth control method has proven inadequate or the working class mother of three pre-schoolers who is too embarrassed to tell her doctor that she doesn't know how to stop her productivity. Or the older woman who thought she was safely past the menopause. In short, it can be any woman who is pregnant.

A doctor who is asked to perform a pregnancy test must take

it upon himself or herself to find out whether this pregnancy is a desired one. If the pregnancy is not wanted, abortion counseling should be offered. A doctor who is approached for an abortion should be certain his or her patient leaves with an adequate method of birth control for the future and full knowledge of how to use it. A doctor who delivers a baby must then immediately counsel the mother on the advisability of spacing her children and help her choose a birth control method to make that possible.

A doctor treating a woman for depression or other mental illness should make sure that the woman is properly using an adequate method of birth control. That abortion is an effective therapeutic measure for pregnant women with emotional problems has been shown repeatedly in this country (1) and abroad.

No doctor should ever assume that any woman patient knows all she needs to know about sex, birth control and abortion.

SOCIAL PREVENTIVE MEASURES

It is only when motherhood is but one choice among many satisfying alternatives open to a woman that every child will be a wanted child. Those discriminatory practices which limit a woman's education and job advancement must be eliminated. Those social pressures which tend to force a woman into early marriage quickly followed by motherhood must be counteracted.

School counselors must make it clear to parents that their daughter's educational preparation for the working world is every bit as important as their son's. Young women must insist on a moratorium—a time during their late teens and early twenties for exploring their own capabilities for making their way in the world without pressure to commit themselves to one man or one role.

Dr. Frederic F. Flach writes in *The Secret Strength of Depression:* "By encouraging women to better define themselves as individuals before getting married and to preserve that identity within the framework of marriage—to enter an I-Thou relationship without losing the 'I' in the process—women's liberation is offering a sensible way to avoid chronic depression. In this way, a woman will not only have more respect for herself and will have cultivated more avenues for self-expression and fulfillment, but she will also be less dependent on her role of wife and mother and on her youthfulness to provide her with a sense of identity and purpose." (2)

Every effort must also be made to prevent a woman who has borne a child from being forced into a stereotyped social role from which there are no acceptable deviations. This will require that a greater responsibility for direct child care be assumed by the father. It will also require more flexibility in the working hours of both men and women.

Adequate day care centers and drop-in child care facilities must be available to every mother regardless of her ability to pay for such services. Such drop-in centers have saved many a child from being ruthlessly battered by a woman driven beyond control by isolation and total responsibility for her infant while she is herself depressed.

REDUCING STRESS IN THE BIRTH EXPERIENCE

Both obstetricians and women planning to have a child should be aware of the indicators of high risk of postpartum depression listed in Chapter 24. A woman who has more than one high risk indicator in her personal or family background must be carefully guided and supported through her pregnancy, delivery and postpartum period. Extra care must be taken to prevent her from becoming deficient in nutrients or deprived of adequate sleep.

All personnel in the maternity wards of our hospitals must be made aware of signs of postpartum depression so they can help in the early identification of this problem. Women who have a long or difficult labor and delivery must be carefully watched. Women who have premature or jaundiced or otherwise ill babies must be given additional support and reassurance, including follow-up visits once they have returned home.

Klaus and Kennell (3) recommend a number of changes in hospital procedure to assist the formation of a strong affectional bond between the mother and her infant:

1. One person (preferably the husband) should be allowed to stay with the mother throughout the labor and delivery.

2. Immediately after the birth (and before drops are put into the baby's eyes) the baby should spend 30 to 45 minutes in the private and uninterrupted company of its mother and father. Eye-to-eye and skin-to-skin contact should be encouraged. It is important that the baby be alert enough to respond to the parents' overtures.

3. The mother should have the baby for several hours each day while in the hospital and should assume full responsibility for its care during those hours.

4. The husband and older children should be allowed to visit the mother while she has the baby with her.

Muriel Sugarman (4) warns that the depressing effect of an anesthetic on both the mother's and infant's nervous system decreases their responsiveness to each other at that very moment when attachment can be most easily achieved—immediately after birth. She feels that a natural childbirth is advisable for this reason.

Reva Rubin, Professor and Director of Graduate Programs in Maternity Nursing at the University of Pittsburg, emphasizes the importance of the way the mother is herself handled during the process of labor and delivery. "Mothers who have had a very recent experience of appropriate and meaningful bodily touch from a ministering person, as during labor, delivery, or the postpartum period use their own hands more effectively . . . Conversely if the mother's most recent experiences of contact in relation to her own body has been of a remote and impersonal nature, she seems to stay longer at this stage in her own activities with the baby." (5)

All of these conditions can be met more fully and naturally in a home birth supervised by a competent midwife. Such a lessening in the disruption of the mother's and the family's life lowers the level of stress experienced by both mother and infant during childbirth.

Dr. Cyril G. Barnes of the Institute of Obstetrics and Gynecology at the University of London observes that "major psychiatric illness seems to occur more commonly in women delivered in hospital than in those having their children in their own home." (6)

Finally there is evidence that even those mothers who have severe psychiatric disturbance following childbirth benefit from having the baby admitted to the psychiatric hospital with them. Such joint admissions of mother and infant were found "to reorient [the mothers] to reality and diminish their feelings of worthlessness and loneliness. Above all, it enables them to test out their mothering capacities in a supportive, structured setting, and to gain more confidence about their ability to care for the child and manage their other responsibilities at home." (7)

In short we must carefully evaluate the overall effect of our interventions in the natural process of childbirth, particularly where those interventions separate the mother and infant. We must make every attempt to provide a favorable environment for the development of a healthy parent-child relationship.

These preventive measures and perhaps others that further research will bring to light can significantly reduce the number of women who become depressed after childbirth each year. However, it may be that there are genetic factors and factors inherent in the physiological process of giving birth itself which will make postpartum depression a continuing occurrence. We must continue research into the cause of depression in general and postpartum depression in particular. At the same time we must apply what we do know—*all* of what we know—to the treatment of women who are already depressed.

WHO CURED WHOM?

While there is not a single causative theory of depression which has been proven beyond a doubt, clinical experience seems to show that a number of treatments are of some help to depressed patients. Among these are psychotherapy, tricyclic antidepressant drugs, and, in severe cases, electroshock (ECT) therapy.

The fact that 70% of all depressed patients recover with or without treatment poses a difficult problem for clinicians: Are their results brought about by the treatment they employed or by natural restorative processes in the patient?

Any psychotherapist who sees that 70% of his depressed patients improve and recover while receiving therapy from him is likely to become convinced that depression is psychologically caused (psychogenic) and must be psychologically cured. Likewise, the psychiatrist using drugs or electroshock treatment with his patients will feel strongly that his experience confirms a biochemical or some other physical cause for depression.

The danger in this situation is that it creates factions within the mental health community—factions which only seem able to unite in excluding the proponents of still another causative theory and its implicit cure, eg. the nutritional or orthomolecular hypothesis. Such political infighting has been a serious obstacle to the uncovering of medical knowledge and its ready application in all eras of medical history. We cannot afford to let it get in the way of understanding depression.

USING ALL OF WHAT WE KNOW

Both clinicians and researchers alike must keep an open mind as befits the state of our present ignorance in this area of mental health. At the same time depressed patients have a right to professional counsel and treatment. As anyone who has read Part I of this book must conclude, my own feeling is that, for the present at least, we must attempt to treat the whole person— both body and mind.

Myrna Weissman and Eugene Paykel come to a somewhat similar conclusion after their extensive study of 40 depressed women compared to 40 normal women. They write in *The Depressed Woman*, "There is little doubt that drugs have increased the possibility of rapid symptom-relief in depression. It is also clear from this research that the disruptions associated with the disorder do not entirely remit with symptom reduction and that the clinician's planning of treatment should include an awareness and a sensitivity to these social disruptions [increased friction with others and an inability to communicate openly and freely]. Overall, these findings point to the importance of social adjustment as a target area for psychotherapy and as a measure of its efficacy." (8)

DEPRESSION AS A VITAL SIGN

One possible medical analogy for depression might be that of blood pressure. (9) Everyone has a blood pressure, of course, and that pressure varies at different times of day and under different levels of stress. There is a wide range of blood pressure readings which are considered normal. However, there are extremes at both the high end of the scale and at the low end of the scale which are considered abnormal.

A businessman found to have high blood pressure (hypertension) is likely to be treated with a combination of drugs, diet and a careful look at his habits of exercise and the level of stress in his life. If chronic emotional stress is considered a contributing factor to his hypertension he may be advised to get psychological help.

In the same way, everyone has a predominating mood which varies depending on how one experiences life's events from moment to moment and day to day. There is a wide range of mood levels which are considered normal—from ebullience to grief—under varying life situations. However, there are also two mood extremes which are considered abnormal—mania at the high end of the scale and depression at the low end.

A woman experiencing a seriously low mood level over a period of weeks following childbirth is just as much in need of treatment as the man in the blood pressure example. Such treatment should consist of determining what physical conditions may be contributing to her low mood state as well as examining what psychological factors are involved in this particular case.

Then a treatment plan should be undertaken which includes anti-depressant drugs, nutritional supplementation, an exercise program, and psychotherapy for social and neurotic problems, just as is done for the patient with hypertension.

The needs for the future are clear:

1. more research on every aspect of depression and postpartum depression;

2. more education of women, their husbands and their doctors;
3. more preventive measures applied more consistently; and
4. more comprehensive treatment programs designed to speed a full recovery from postpartum depression.

PART IV:

APPENDICES

APPENDIX I
Drugs Which Can Have Depression
As A Side Effect

The following drugs have been known to occasionally have depression as a side effect. Persons treating a depressed woman would do well to inquire whether she is taking any of these medications.

Drugs Prescribed For:
Urinary infections:
Azo Gantrisin (sulfisoxazole and phenazopyridine hydrochloride)
Bactrim (trimethoprim and sulfamethoxazole)
Gantanol (sulfamethoxazole)
Gantrisin (sulfisoxazole)

Oral contraceptives:
Demulen (ethynodiol, diacetate and ethinyl estradiol)
Norinyl (norethindrone and mestranol)
Norlestrin (norethindrone acetate and ethinyl estradiol)
Oracon
Ortho-Novum (norethindrone and mestranol)
Ovral (norgestrel and ethinyl estradiol)
Ovulen (ethynodiol diacetate and mestranol)

Tranquilizer:
Tranxene (clorazepate dipotassium)
Valium (diazepam)

Appetite suppressant:
Tenuate (diethylpropion hydrochloride)

Anti-diarrheal:
Lomotil (diphenoxylate hydrochloride and atropine sulfate)

Anti-emetic (prevents vomiting):
Tigan (trimethobenzamide hydrochloride)

Sedative:
Phenobarbital (SK-phenobarbital solfoton)

Menstrual irregularity or pain:
Provera (medroxyprogesterone acetate)

Anti-arrhythmic agent (heartbeat irregularity):
Pronestyl (procainamide hydrochloride)

Anti-hypertensive (high blood pressure):
Aldomet (methyldopa)
Aldoril (methyldopa and hydrochlorothiazide)
Apresoline (hydralazine hydrochloride)
Diupres (chlorothiazide and reserpine)
Hydropres (hydrochlorthiazide and reserpine)
Inderal (propranolol hydrochloride)
Regroton (chlorthalidone and reserpine)
Reserpine
Salutensin
Ser-Ap-Es (reserpine, hydralazine hydrochloride, & hydro-
chlorothiazide)

Anti-inflammatory;
Indocine (indomethacin)
Medrol Tablets (methylprednisolone)
Naprosyn (naproxen)
Prednisone (deltasone, meticorten, orasone, sterapred)

This information was gathered from **The Complete Book of Symptoms and What They Can Mean** by Lawrence Galton. p. 393. New York: Simon and Schuster. c. 1978. and from **150 Commonly Prescribed Drugs: A Guide to Their Uses and Side Effects** by Edward R. Brace and Arthur Hull Hayes, Jr., M.D., Chicago: World Book-Childcraft International, Inc. c. 1980.

APPENDIX II
Postpartum Support Groups

There is a real need for a support system for new parents. Young couples, often isolated from their parents and totally inexperienced in caring for babies and children, need some place to turn for educational materials, advice from experienced parents and professionals, and emotional support.

Fortunately, a few such postpartum support programs are underway. They can serve as models for a nationwide network offering help to every parent of a young child.

One such program is called COPE, Coping with the Overall Pregnancy/Parenting Experience. COPE offers individual counseling, support groups, programs in perinatal psychology for hospitals and agencies, workshops, seminars for professionals, a telephone crisis intervention service, and training for COPE group leaders. For more information, send a postpaid, self-addressed envelope along with your request to COPE Groups, 37 Clarendon Street, Boston, MA 02116.

Our Canadian neighbors have developed a program specifically designed to aid mothers who are depressed after giving birth. It includes a telephone counseling service, weekly group meetings with other depressed mothers and with volunteers who have recovered from a postpartum depression, monthly meetings for fathers, and family counseling. There are no fees for this service. For more information send a self-addressed envelope along with your request to Post-Partum Counselling, 1946 West Broadway, Vancouver, B.C., Canada V6J 1X2.

Support groups are also available for women who have had cesarean births. By contacting one of the larger groups you can locate a group operating in your area. For referral write or call:

The Cesarean Birth Association
125 N. 12th Street
New Hyde Park, N.Y. 11040
(212) 523-8991

Cesarean Birth Council
P.O. Box 6081
San Jose, CA 95150
(415) 345-9928

The Cesarean Connection
P.O. Box 11
Westmont, IL 60559

C/SEC Inc.
66 Christopher Rd.
Waltham, MA 02154
(617) 547-7188

A list of many cesarean support groups throughout the United States, Canada and Australia may also be found in Appendix III of **The Cesarean (R)evolution: A Handbook for Parents and Professionals** by Linda D. Meyer.

There are other small support groups springing up around the country, many of which grow out of childbirth education classes. The need is enormous and presents an important challenge to professionals and to our whole society.

FOOTNOTES

CHAPTER 22

(1) Becker, Joseph. *Depression: Theory and Research.* New York: John Wiley & Sons. 1974. pp. 180-181.

(2) Description of nerve cells taken verbatim from Shafer, Richard A. "Mastering the Mind: Advances in Chemistry Are Starting to Unlock Mysteries of the Brain," *Wall Street Journal*, Aug. 12, 1977.

(3) Mendels, Joseph. *Concepts of Depression.* New York: John Wiley & Sons, Inc. c.1970. p.77.

(4) Schildkraut, J. J. The catecholamine hypothesis of affective disorders: A review of supporting evidence. *American Journal of Psychiatry*, 1965, vol. 122, p. 509.

CHAPTER 23

(1) Winokur, George. "Genetic Aspects of Depression" in *Separation and Depression: Clinical and Research Aspects*, edited by John Paul Scott and Edward C. Senay. Washington, D.C.: Publication No. 94 of the American Association for the Advancement of Science, 1973, pp. 125-137.

(2) Winokur, George. "Depression spectrum disease: Description and family study," *Comprehensive Psychiatry*, 1972 (Jan), vol. 13, pp. 3-8; and Winokur, George. "The Iowa 500: Familial and clinical findings favor two kinds of depressive illness," *Comprehensive Psychiatry*, 1973 (Mar), vol. 14, pp. 99-106.

(3) Mendels, *op. cit.*, p. 93.

(4) Pfeiffer, Carl C., M.D., Ph.D. *Mental and Elemental Nutrients.* New Canaan, Conn.: Keats Publishing, Inc. c. 1975. p. 380.

(5) Ibid., p. 383.

(6) Ibid., p. 385.

(7) Selye, Hans. *The Stress of Life.* New York: McGraw-Hill Book Company, Inc. c.1956. p. 264.

(8) Holmes, Thomas H. and Masuda, Minoru. "Life Changes and Illness Susceptibility" in *Separation and Depression*, op. cit., pp. 161-186.

(9) Ibid., p. 165.

(10) Ibid., p. 182.

(11) Paykel, Eugene S. "Life Events and Acute Depressions" in *Separation and Depression, op. cit.*, p. 221.

(12) Ibid., p. 224.

(13) Goodwin, Frederick K. and Bunney, William E., Jr. "Psychological Aspects of Stress and Affective Illness" in *Separation and Depression, op. cit.*, p. 106.

(14) Heinicke, Christoph M. "Parental Deprivation in Early Child-

hood" in *Separation and Depression, op. cit.*, pp. 157-158.

(15) Snyder, Frederick, M.D. "Sleep Disturbance in Relation to Acute Psychosis" in *Sleep Physiology and Pathology: A Symposium*, edited by Anthony Kales, M.D. Philadelphia: J. B. Lippincott Company. c.1969. pp. 173-174.

(16) Ibid., pp. 178-179.

(17) Becker, *op. cit.*, p. 187.

(18) Johnson, Laverne C., Ph.D. "Psychological and Physiological Changes Following Total Sleep Deprivation" in *Sleep Physiology and Pathology, op. cit.*, pp. 208-209.

(19) Ibid., p. 218.

(20) Paykel, *op. cit.*, p. 234.

CHAPTER 24

(1) Hamilton, James Alexander, M.D., Ph.D. *Postpartum Psychiatric Problems*. St. Louis: The C. V. Mosby Company. 1962. p. 107.

(2) Ibid., p. 109.

(3) Klaus, Marshall H., M.D., and Kennell, John H., M.D. *Maternal-infant bonding*. St. Louis: The C. V. Mosby Company. c.1976. pp. 93-94.

(4) Ritchie, C. Ann, R.N., M.N. "Depression Following Childbirth," *Nurse Practitioner*, vol. 2, no. 4, p. 14.

(5) Hamilton, *op. cit.*, p. 13 for 1 in 1000 births. Barzilai, Sh. and Davies, A.M. Postpartum mental disorders in Jerusalem: Survey of hospitalized cases 1964-1967, *British Journal of Social Psychiatry and Community Health*, 1972, vol. 6, pp. 80-89 for 2.7 in 1,000 births.

(6) Hamilton, *op. cit.*, p. 23 for 6-8%; the 12½% figure comes from a study cited in *Our Bodies, Ourselves: A Book By and For Women* by the Boston Women's Health Book Collective, 2nd edition, Simon & Schuster, Inc. c.1971, 1973, 1975.

(7) Miller, Mary Ann, R.N., M.S.N. and Brooten, Dorothy, R.N., M.S.N. *The Childbearing Family: A Nursing Perspective*. Boston: Little, Brown & Co. c.1977. p. 418.

CHAPTER 25

(1) Reich, Theodor and Winokur, George. Postpartum psychosis in patients with manic depressive disease. *Journal of Nervous and Mental Disease*, 1970 (Jul), vol. 151, p. 63.

(2) Ibid., p. 64.

(3) Ibid.

(4) Ibid. p. 67.

(5) Baker, Max; Dorzab, Joe; Winokur, George, and Cadoret, Remi. Depressive disease: The effect of the postpartum state. *Biological*

Psychiatry, 1971, vol. 3, pp. 357-365 as summarized in *Psychological Abstracts* 48: 1312.

(6) Gordon, R. E., and Gordon, K. K. Factors in postpartum emotional adjustment. *American Journal of Orthopsychiatry*, 1967, vol. 37, pp. 359-360.

(7) Heitler, Susan, Ph.D. "Postpartum Depression: A Multi-Dimensional Study" as summarized in *Dissertation Abstracts International*, vol. 36, pp. 5792-5793.

(8) Levy, Judith M. and McGee, Richard K. Childbirth as a crisis. *Journal of Personality and Social Psychology*, 1975 (Jan), vol. 31, pp. 171-179.

(9) Asch, Stuart S. and Rubin, Lowell J. Postpartum reactions: Some unrecognized variations. *American Journal of Psychiatry*, 1974 (Aug), vol. 131, p. 872.

(10) Ibid., p. 874.

(11) Dalton, Katharina. Prospective study into puerperal depression. *British Journal of Psychiatry*, 1971 (Jun), vol. 118, pp. 689-692 as reported in *Psychological Abstracts* 47: 6317.

(12) Heitler, *op. cit.*, p. 5792-5793.

(13) From a study cited in *Our Bodies, Ourselves, op. cit.*

(14) Heitler, *op. cit.*, pp. 5792-5793.

(15) Pfeiffer, *op. cit.*, p. 388.

(16) Ibid., p. 327

(17) Poitras, R. et. al. Auditory discrimination during REM and non-REM sleep in women before and after delivery. *Canadian Psychiatric Association Journal*, 1973 (Dec), vol. 18, pp. 519-526 as summarized in *Psychological Abstracts* 52: 4329.

(18) Heitler, *op. cit.*, p. 5792-5793.

(19) Holmes, *op. cit.*, p. 173.

(20) Rubin, Reva. Basic maternal behavior. *Nursing Outlook*, 1963 (Nov), vol. 9, p. 684.

(21) Klaus, *op. cit.*, p. 40—comment by T. B. Brazelton.

(22) Sugarman, Muriel, M.D. Paranatal influences on maternal-infant attachment. *American Journal of Orthopsychiatry*, vol. 47, no. 3, July, 1977, p. 415.

CHAPTER 26

(1) Snyder, Solomon H., M.D. *The Troubled Mind: A Guide to Release from Distress*. New York: McGraw Hill Book Company. c.1976. pp. 107-108.

(2) Weissman, Myrna M. and Paykel, Eugene S. *The Depressed Woman*. Chicago: The University of Chicago Press. c.1974. p. 121.

(3) Gartner, Dorothy and Goldstein, Harris S. Some characteristics

of mothers of severely disturbed children in a therapeutic nursery. *Psychological Reports,* 1972 (Jun), vol. 30, p. 901-902.

(4) Ibid., p. 902.

(5) Zrull, Joel P., McDermott, John F. and Poznanski, Elva. Hyperkinetic syndrome: The role of depression. *Child Psychiatry and Human Development,* 1970 (Fal), vol. 1, pp. 33-40 as summarized in *Psychological Abstracts* 49: 4913.

(6) Kaufman, Charles. "Mother-Infant Separation in Monkeys" in *Separation and Depression, op. cit.,* pp. 34-35.

(7) Pfeiffer, *op. cit.,* p. 326.

(8) Steele, B. and Pollock, C. Psychiatric study of parents who abuse infants and small children, in *The Battered Child,* edited by R. Helfer and C. Kempe. Chicago: University of Chicago Press, 1968, pp. 103-147.

(9) Gil, D. and Elmer, E. Incidence of child abuse and demographic characteristics of persons involved. Ibid., pp. 19-39 and Elmer, E. *Children in Jeopardy.* Pittsburg Press, 1967. p. 46.

(10) Kempe, C. and Helfer, R. *Helping the Battered Child and His Family.* Philadelphia: J. B. Lippincott Co., 1972.

(11) Asch, *op. cit.,* p. 871.

(12) Weissman, *op. cit.,* pp. 223-224.

(13) Klaus, *op. cit.,* p. 52.

(14) Ibid., p. 2.

(15) Lukianowicz, N. Attempted infanticide. *Psychiatrica Clinica,* 1972, vol. 5, pp. 1-16 as summarized in *Psychological Abstracts* 49: 9400.

(16) Reich and Winokur, *op. cit.,* p. 65.

CHAPTER 27

(1) Ford, Charles V., Castenuovo-Tedesco, Pietro and Long, Kahlila D. Abortion: Is it a therapeutic procedure in psychiatry? *JAMA: Journal of the American Medical Association,* 1971 (Nov), vol. 218, pp. 1173-1178.

(2) Flach, Frederic F., M.D. *The Secret Strength of Depression.* New York: J. B. Lippincott Co. c.1974. p. 267.

(3) Klaus, *op. cit.,* pp. 87-96.

(4) Sugarman, *op. cit.,* pp. 410-411.

(5) Rubin, Reva, M.N., M.S. Maternal Touch. *Nursing Outlook,* Nov., 1963, p. 830.

(6) Barnes, Cyril G. *Medical Disorders in Obstetric Practice.* Oxford: Blackwell Scientific Publications, Third Edition. 1970, p. 329.

(7) Luepker, Ellen T. Joint admission and evaluation of postpartum psychiatric patients and their infants. *Hosptial and Community Psychiatry,* 1972 (Sep), vol. 23, p. 286.

(8) Weissman, *op. cit.*, p. 199.

(9) Louise Hopkins, a psychiatric social worker and psychology instructor, planted the idea of this analogy in my mind during a discussion I had with her in the Summer of 1977.

The following publications may also be ordered from The Chas. Franklin Press:

The Cesarean (R)evolution, a patient advocacy handbook for parents and professionals, by Linda D. Meyer, $7.95
Special Delivery: A Book for Kids About Cesarean and Vaginal Birth by Baker and Montey, $6.95
How to Prevent a Cesarean Section by Linda D. Meyer, $3.00
Preventing Depression by Barbara Ciaramitaro, $3.00
Help for Depressed Mothers by Barbara Ciaramitaro, $8.95.

You may send your order with a check to:

The Chas Franklin Press
18409-90th Avenue W. · Edmonds, WA 98020

$\mathcal{The}$ Whole Family Newsletter

Dedicated to:
- growth and nurturing of Whole children
- personal growth
- marital enrichment/creative separation
- personal economic stability in an uncertain economy (tips on making and saving money!)

Samples of feature articles:
- How to conquer depression
- How to protect your child from sexual assault
- How to avoid a cesarean section
- How to find your niche in life
- How to nurture your child's self-esteem
- How to be a stay-at-home Mom and have a stimulating career too!
- A self-guided marital enrichment program
- How to make changes in your child's school
- Readers' forum

This is a warm, down-to-earth newsletter you'll surely enjoy because it is researched, written and published by other mothers who share **your** concerns!

The Whole Family Newsletter runs six pages bi-monthly at a cost of $10.00 per year. If after receiving your first copy you are dissatisfied, your money will be returned.

Send now for your subscription or sample.

Please send me:

☐ Sample. I've enclosed 25¢ and a stamped, self-addressed envelope.
☐ Subscription. I've enclosed $_____

Name _____

Address _____

City _____ State _____ Zip _____

Send order to The Whole Family Newsletter
4212 - 222nd S.W., Mountlake Terrace, WA 98043

CONTENTS

W9-DHJ-888

TRAVELING UPCLOSE   *vi*
INTRODUCTION   *viii*

I. BASICS *1*

Air Travel	1	Packing for New York	14
Airports & Transfers	3	Passports & Visas	15
Bus Travel	4	Public Rest Rooms	15
Car Rental	6	Safety	16
Consumer Protection	7	Students	16
Currency Exchanges	7	Subway Travel	17
Customs & Duties	7	Taxis & Car Services	18
Disabilities & Accessibility	8	Telephones	18
Discounts & Deals	9	Tipping	19
Drinking	10	Tour Operators	19
Driving	10	Train Travel	20
Emergencies & Consulates	10	Transportation	21
Gay & Lesbian Travel	11	Travel Agencies	21
Holidays	11	Travel Gear	21
Insurance	12	U.S. Government	21
Laundry	12	Visitor Information	22
Media	12	Volunteering	22
Money	14	When to Go	22

2. EXPLORING NEW YORK CITY *26*

➤ Map of the Five Boroughs	28–29	➤ Map of Manhattan Neighborhoods	47
Major Attractions	31	➤ Map of Upper West Side	48
➤ Map of Central Park (South)	36	➤ Map of Columbia University	
➤ Map of Central Park (North)	37	and Morningside Heights	52
Manhattan Neighborhoods	46	➤ Map of Harlem	55

➤ Map of Washington Heights   58
➤ Map of Upper East Side
   and Museum Mile   60
➤ Map of Midtown   66–67
➤ Map of Chelsea   72
➤ Map of Gramercy and Union Square   74
➤ Map of West Village   76
➤ Map of East Village and Alphabet City   81
➤ Map of the Lower East Side, Little Italy,
   and Chinatown   86–87
➤ Map of SoHo and TriBeCa   89

➤ Map of Lower Manhattan   92–93
The Outer Boroughs   98
➤ Map of Brooklyn Heights, Cobble Hill,
   and Carroll Gardens   100
➤ Map of Park Slope and Prospect Park   103
➤ Map of Astoria   107
➤ Map of North Bronx   109
➤ Map of Staten Island   111
Museums and Galleries   113
Parks and Gardens   127
Cheap Thrills   135

3. WHERE TO SLEEP 138

Hotels   138
➤ Map of Uptown Lodging   140
➤ Map of Midtown and Downtown
   Lodging   142–143

Bed-and-Breakfasts   146
Hostels and YMCAs   148
University Housing   150

4. FOOD 151

Manhattan Restaurants   152
Outer Borough Restaurants   176
Cafes and Coffee Bars   181

Markets and Specialty Shops   184
Greenmarkets   185
Reference Listings   187

5. SHOPPING 192

Department Stores   193
Clothes   194
Books   197
Records, Tapes, and CDs   199

Household Furnishings   200
Specialty Stores   201
Flea Markets   202

6. AFTER DARK 203

Bars   203
Comedy   211

Dance Clubs   213
Live Music   214

7. THE ARTS 218

Arts Centers   219
Dance   222
Movies and Video   223
Music   224

Opera   226
Spoken Word   227
Summer Arts   228
Theater   229

Fodor's UP CLOSE

NEW YORK CITY

the complete guide, thoroughly up-to-date

SAVVY TRAVELING: WHERE TO SPEND, HOW TO SAVE

packed with details that will make your trip

CULTURAL TIPS: ESSENTIAL LOCAL DO'S AND TABOOS

must-see sights, on and off the beaten path

INSIDER SECRETS: WHAT'S HIP AND WHAT TO SKIP

the buzz on restaurants, the lowdown on lodgings

FIND YOUR WAY WITH CLEAR AND EASY-TO-USE MAPS

Previously published as *The Berkeley Guide to New York City*

FODOR'S TRAVEL PUBLICATIONS, INC.

NEW YORK • TORONTO • LONDON • SYDNEY • AUCKLAND

www.fodors.com/

FODOR'S UPCLOSE™ NEW YORK CITY

Editor: Caroline V. Haberfeld

Editorial Production: Janet Foley

Maps: David Lindroth Inc., Eureka Cartography, *cartographers*; Robert Blake, *map editor*

Design: Fabrizio La Rocca, *creative director*; Allison Saltzman, *cover and text design*; Jolie Novak, *photo editor*

Production/Manufacturing: Robert B. Shields

Cover Photograph: Berenholtz/The Stock Market

8. SPORTS AND OUTDOOR ACTIVITIES *233*

Gyms and Rec Centers   *233*   Spectator Sports   *239*
Participant Sports   *234*

INDEX   *241*

TRAVELING
UPCLOSE

T ake the subway. Stay in a B&B. Try a hostel. Relax at an outdoor concert. Picnic in Central Park. Prowl the flea markets. Go to a festival. Memorize the symphony of the streets. And if you want to experience the heart and soul of New York City, whatever you do, don't spend too much money. The deep and rich experience of New York City that every true traveler yearns for is one of the things in life that money can't buy. In fact, if you have it, don't use it. Traveling lavishly is the surest way to turn yourself into a sideline traveler. Restaurants with white-glove service are great—sometimes—but they're usually not the best place to find the perfect knish or slice of pizza. Doormen at plush hotels have their place, but not when your look-alike room could be anywhere from Dusseldorf to Detroit. Better to stay in a more intimate place that truly gives you the atmosphere you traveled so far to experience. Don't just stand and watch—jump into the spirit of what's around you.

If you want to see New York City up close and savor the essence of the city and its people in all their charming, stylish, sometimes infuriatingly arrogant glory, this book is for you. We'll show you the local culture, the offbeat sights, the bars and cafés where tourists rarely tread, and the B&Bs and other hostelries where you'll meet fellow travelers—places where the locals would send their friends. And because you'll probably want to see the famous places if you haven't already been there, we give you tips on losing the crowds, plus the quirky and obscure facts you want as well as the basics everyone needs.

OUR GANG

Who's are we? We're artists and poets, slackers and straight arrows, and travel writers and journalists, who in our less hedonistic moments report on local news and spin out an occasional opinion piece. What we share is a certain footloose spirit and a passion for the Big Apple, which we celebrate in this guidebook. Shamelessly, we've revealed all of our favorite places and our deepest, darkest travel secrets, all so that you can learn from our past mistakes and experience the best part of New York to the fullest. If you can't take your best friend on the road, or if your best friend is hopeless with directions, stick with us.

Brooklyn updater **Matthew Lore** has lived in Park Slope for three years. Most mornings before turning up as an editor at Fodor's, he runs in Prospect Park, the neighborhood's treasured green oasis. He can frequently be found on Saturday mornings browsing among the veggies and plants at the Grand Army Plaza Greenmarket.

David Low, is a native New Yorker (born in Queens) who makes his living as a fiction writer and book editor. He also revised the Arts chapter and the Chelsea, Greenwich Village, SoHo, TriBeCa, Little Italy, and Chinatown exploring tours. He has had an obsessive interest in theater, movies, and other performing arts in the city since he saw his first Broadway play, *Baker Street,* a musical about Sherlock Holmes. He lives around the corner from the Strand Book Store, where he has spent many hours searching for bargains.

Amy McConnell, who worked on the lodging chapter and the Outer Boroughs section of exploring, will always remember the summer she spent uncovering the hidden charms of the Bronx, Queens, and Staten Island. After walking the length of the Bronx's Grand Concourse on scorching hot summer days, discovering ethnic cultures that she'd never heard of in Queens, and discussing secessionist politics with folks in Staten Island, she's developed a protective fondness for New York City's forgotten boroughs. Now she just has to win over her Manhattan-centric friends.

After two years of living on the Upper East Side, **Jennifer Paull** used her assignment to discover miles of museum galleries and new varieties of Hungarian sausage. The shopping chapter then took her all over town, from four-digit price tags to 40used books. She would like to thank Charlie for being a bad influence in Barneys.

Helayne Schiff lives and plays in Lower Manhattan. When she's not writing, performing, or updating for Fodor's, she can be seen anywhere below 23rd Street in search of the latest and greatest 'things to do' in downtown New York.

Covering the after-hours hot spots and the Upper West Side, Harlem, and the far north of Manhattan was native Californian **Mira Schwirtz.** She quickly learned to appreciate the pleasures of a cup of Cuban coffee in a Washington Heights greasy spoon, the go-go glitter of a TriBeCa dance club, the magnetic energy of a Harlem street, and the meditative beauty of Central Park, and very quickly went straight to New York's soul.

Tom Steele, who covered Manhattan restaurants, ate and wrote his way around town from the side streets of SoHo to the avenues of Midtown. Currently, he is the food editor of *Manhattan Spirit* and *Our Town.* His favorite restaurant at the moment is Gramercy Tavern. When he's not scouring the city for a good meal, he continues his work writing a viciously anti-food-police cookbook.

A SEND-OFF

Always call ahead. We knock ourselves out to check all the facts, but everything changes all the time, in ways that none of us can ever fully anticipate. Whenever you're making a special trip to a special place, as opposed to merely wandering, always call ahead. Trust us on this.

And then, if something doesn't go quite right, as inevitably happens with even the best-laid plans, stay cool. Missed your train? Stuck in the airport? Use the time to study the people. Strike up a conversation with a stranger. Study the newsstands or flip through the local press. Take a walk. Find the silver lining in the clouds, whatever it is. And do send us a postcard to tell us what went wrong and what went right. You can e-mail us at: editors@fodors.com (specify the name of the book on the subject line) or write the New York City editor at Fodor's upCLOSE, 201 East 50th Street, New York, NY 10022. We'll put your ideas to good use and let other travelers benefit from your experiences. In the meantime, bon voyage!

INTRODUCTION

I n recent years, the city of New York has been hanging banners around town proclaiming that it's the Capital of the World. And despite the claims to fame of other cities—Tokyo has more banks, Seattle has more musicians, Vancouver is the new darling among moviemakers, and Kuala Lumpur, Malaysia, now has the world's tallest skyscraper—New York can still lay claim to the most grand-championship titles. It's home to the United Nations and is a longtime nucleus of such varied fields as advertising, art, publishing, classical music, fashion, cuisine, finance, law, and headline-grabbing corporate takeovers. Though naysayers the world over have been predicting New York's demise for decades, it still seems you can't turn on the TV or read a magazine without getting the impression that at least half of everything in the United States happens in New York. And if you were to ask someone in Bangkok or Berlin or Bujumbura to sketch an American city, it's at least even money that the Empire State Building or the Statue of Liberty would appear in the picture.

Which leads to another thing New York City is the capital of: attitude. True, Parisians are probably equally, um, brusque, but you'll find few other places on earth where people so clearly bear the imprint of their hometown. After a few days walking Manhattan streets you'll really know your New Yorkers. Be they foppish like Eustace Tilley, Rea Irvin's famed *New Yorker* cartoon cover model, or tough and street savvy as DeNiro in *Taxi Driver,* whether they're newly immigrated cabbies or megalomaniac financiers, all seem to possess a real whoop-de-do enthusiasm (and wardrobe heavy on black clothes) for living here. Maybe it's survivor's mentality: The journalist Edward Hoagland once jokingly noted that annually the city's 7.3 million residents probably "see more death than most soldiers do."

Whatever the reason for the in-your-face attitude of New Yorkers, you'll have plenty of opportunities to mix and mingle with (or at least stand behind velvet ropes and stare at) this peculiar breed of urban dweller. For this is one of few American cities where people prefer to walk rather than drive (not surprising, given that traffic crossing Midtown averages 5.3 mi an hour), where face-to-face interaction has not been obliterated by cruise control and carpool lanes. New York sidewalks attract around 10,000 pedestrians per hour, making them some of the busiest on earth. By all means, take advantage of its 722 mi of convenient subway lines while you're visiting, but don't forget to get out and walk a few blocks; it's the best way to discover the city's 400 art galleries, 17,000 restaurants, 150 museums, and 200 skyscrapers—as long as you don't mind dodging the piles of doggie doo and, in the winter, crusty, black drifts of snow.

But long before these subways and skyscrapers were even a glimmer in New Yorkers' eyes, before the city became "the nation's thyroid gland," as Christopher Morley once described it, New York City was the tiny town of New Amsterdam, settled at the southern tip of Manhattan by the Dutch in 1624. In an astounding episode of flimflammery, the settlers had purchased Manhattan from the Indians for trinkets worth $24. This 22-square-mi island with the bargain-basement price exhibited an "anything goes" vibe from the get-go. When a missionary visited in 1643, he found an already cosmopolitan community of 500 settlers speaking 18 different languages. From its very inception, it was clear that New York would never become another lost-in-the-woods Roanoke.

Except for a decade or so break for the Revolutionary War (we won), the city, blessed with a commodious natural harbor, expanded into the corners of Manhattan Island and inched outward to swallow Brooklyn, the Bronx, Queens, and Staten Island. Canals and railroads built in the first half of the 19th century brought trade—and money—by the bushel, and the city soon became the largest and richest in the hemisphere, eclipsing its old rival, Philadelphia. But it was wasn't until the second half of the 1800s that the city really started to percolate. With America as a whole, and New York in particular, shining as a beacon of prosperity for the rest of the world (Europe was suffering through a devastating famine), immigrants poured in, and then poured in some more. The melting pot that we alternately glorify and curse today took shape as some 16 million Italian, African, Irish, Jewish, and German immigrants arrived over the next six decades. All told, over 120 different nationalities now live here, including a new wave of immigrants from Central America and Southeast Asia, and each has left their mark on the city, whether it's an innovative cuisine or a special festival.

Ironically, as the teeming masses fled Europe for New York in the 19th century, the city's wealthiest residents were striving to re-create the splendor of a European capital right here at home. The upper crust made no secret of their envy of Paris when they lobbied city officials to create Central Park in the 1850s. Throughout the century, city planning and private philanthropy gave birth to powerhouse institutions like the Metro-

> *No one knows for sure, but the name Manhattan may have come from the Munsee Indian word "manahactanienk," meaning "place of general inebriation."*

politan Opera, the Metropolitan Museum of Art, the New York Public Library, and the American Museum of Natural History. This self-aggrandizing spirit continued through the next century, producing, among other things, the Museum of Modern Art, the Studio Museum in Harlem, and Lincoln Center for the Performing Arts. Of course, you can't have world-class cultural institutions without world-famous artists, writers, and performers. The city's literary giants include Walt Whitman and Herman Melville in the 19th century; Marianne Moore, e.e. cummings, and Dorothy Parker in the 1920s; and Ralph Ellison, Carson McCullers, and Allen Ginsberg at mid-century. New York was the spot where "modern art" from Europe was introduced to an outraged public in 1913, and it's been synonymous with the avant-garde ever since—from abstract expressionists like Franz Kline to the pop art masters of the 1960s. Georgia O'Keeffe, Jackson Pollock, Mark Rothko, Agnes Martin, and Andy Warhol have all called the city home.

As much as New York can trumpet its economic, social, and cultural success, it also boasts an impressive array of things that don't work quite as well: It's crowded, dirty, expensive as hell, and yes, occasionally dangerous. Newt Gingrich rightfully received flak for dissing New York as a "culture of waste" in 1995, but the fact is, organized crime, bloated bureaucracy, mounting debt, and crumbling infrastructure *are* ongoing problems here. Add to that the crash of the go-go '80s—which clipped the wings of many a high-rolling Wall Streeter—and the subsequent recession of the early '90s—which sent many big corporations scurrying for low-rent New Jersey—and you'll see why many people seem ready to kick New York in the kidneys and turn out the lights. But do you really think it'd be that easy? As the millennium approaches, the city seems to be once again springing back to life and cleaning up its act: FBI records show that violent crime rates in NYC fell dramatically from 1988 to 1998. Notoriously sleazy XXX-filled Times Square is being cleaned up and turned over to Disney; parks like Bryant and Tompkins Square have been reclaimed from drug peddlers; and farmers' markets and neighborhood cafés are flourishing. Better still, the city's transportation department swears it's got a handle on the 60,000 or so potholes that show up annually, and they've just finished adding air-conditioning to 99% of the city's subway cars. Whether or not you agree that New York deserves to be called Capital of the World, you can't dispute that it's one hell of a town.

BASICS

contacts and savvy tips to make your trip hassle-free

I f you've ever traveled with anyone before, you know that there are two types of people in the world—the planners and the nonplanners. Travel brings out the worst in both groups. Left to their own devices, the planners will have you goose-stepping from attraction to attraction on a cultural blitzkrieg, while the nonplanners will invariably miss the flight, the bus, and maybe even the point. This chapter offers you a middle ground; we hope it provides enough information to help you plan your trip to New York without nailing you down. Keep flexible and remember that the most hair-pulling situations turn into the best travel stories back home.

AIR TRAVEL

MAJOR AIRLINE OR LOW-COST CARRIER?

Money talks. Most people choose a flight based on price, but there are actually other issues to consider. Major airlines offer the greatest number of departures; smaller airlines—including regional, low-cost, and no-frill airlines—usually have a more limited number of flights daily. Major airlines have frequent-flyer partners, which allow you to credit mileage earned on one airline to your account with another. Low-cost airlines offer a definite price advantage and fewer restrictions, such as advance-purchase requirements. Safety-wise, low-cost carriers as a group have a good history, but **check the safety record before booking** any low-cost carrier; call the Federal Aviation Administration's Consumer Hotline (*see* Airline Complaints, *below*).

MAJOR AIRLINES • Within the United States: **American** (tel. 800/433–7300). **America West** (tel. 800/235–9292). **Continental** (tel. 800/525–0280). **Delta** (tel. 800/221–1212). **Northwest** (tel. 800/225–2525). **TWA** (tel. 800/221–2000). **United** (tel. 800/241–6522). **US Airways** (tel. 800/428–4322). From Canada: **Air Canada** (tel. 800/776–3000). **Delta** and **US Airways** also serve New York from Canada. From the United Kingdom: **Air India** (tel. 0181/745–1000). **American** (tel. 0345/789–789). **British Airways** (tel. 0345/222–111). **Continental** (tel. 0800/776–464). **El Al** (tel. 0171/957–4100). **Kuwait Airways** (tel. 0171/412–0007). **United** (tel. 0800/888–555). **Virgin Atlantic** (tel. 01293/747–747). From Down Under: **Qantas** (tel. 800/227–4500 in the U.S., 02/9957–0111 in Australia). **United** has service from Australia and New Zealand to all three airports in the NYC area.

SMALLER AIRLINES • **Carnival Air Lines** (tel. 800/824–7386). **Midway** (tel. 800/446–4392). **Midwest Express** (tel. 800/452–2022).

DON'T STOP UNLESS YOU MUST

When you book, **look for nonstop flights** and **remember that "direct" flights stop at least once.** Try to **avoid connecting flights,** which require a change of plane. Two airlines may jointly operate a connecting flight, so ask if your airline operates every segment—you may find that your preferred carrier flies you only part of the way.

USE AN AGENT

Travel agents, particularly those who specialize in finding the lowest fares (*see* Discounts & Deals, *below*), can sometimes be helpful when booking a plane ticket. When you're quoted a price, **ask if the price is likely to get any lower.** Good agents know the seasonal fluctuations of airfares and can usually anticipate a sale or fare war. However, you take a risk when you wait: The fare could go *up* as seats become scarce, and you may wait so long that your preferred flight sells out. A wait-and-see strategy works best if your plans are flexible, but if you're committed to certain dates, don't delay.

GET THE LOWEST FARE

The least-expensive airfares to New York are priced for round-trip travel. Major airlines usually require that you **book in advance and buy the ticket within 24 hours,** and you may have to stay over a Saturday night. It's smart to **call a number of airlines, and when you are quoted a good price, book it on the spot**—the same fare may not be available on the same flight the next day. Airlines generally allow you to change your return date for a fee of $25–$50. If you don't use your ticket you can apply the cost toward the purchase of a new ticket, again for a small charge. However, most low-fare tickets are nonrefundable. To get the lowest airfare, **check different routings.** If your destination or home city has more than one gateway, compare prices to and from different airports. Flexibility is the key to getting a serious bargain on airfare. If you can play around with your departure date, destination, and return date, you will probably save money. Ask which days of the week are the cheapest to fly on—weekends are often the most expensive. Even the time of day you fly can make a big difference in the cost of your ticket. Also look into discounts available through student-and budget-travel organizations (*see* Students, *below*).

To save money on round-trip flights originating in the United Kingdom, **look into an APEX or Super-PEX ticket.** APEX tickets must be booked in advance and have certain restrictions. Super-PEX tickets can be purchased at the airport on the day of departure—subject to availability.

LOCAL RESOURCES • If you're in New York and shopping for a ticket out, you'll find dozens of companies advertising unbelievably cheap flights in the *Village Voice* and in the Sunday travel section of the *New York Times.* Most are legit, but call around, and check with the **Better Business Bureau** (tel. 212/533–6200) before you purchase. A couple to try: **Travel Abroad, Inc.** (47 W. 34th St., at Broadway, Suite 535, tel. 212/564–8989) or **ABS Travel, Inc.** (347 5th Ave., between 33rd and 34th Sts., tel. 212/447–1717).

CHECK WITH CONSOLIDATORS

Consolidators, also sometimes known as bucket shops, buy tickets for scheduled flights at reduced rates from the airlines then sell them at prices that beat the best fare available directly from the airlines, usually without advance restrictions. Sometimes you can even get your money back if you need to return the ticket. Carefully read the fine print detailing penalties for changes and cancellations, **confirm your consolidator reservation with the airline,** and be sure to check restrictions, refund possibilities, and payment conditions.

CONSOLIDATORS • **Airfare Busters** (5100 Westheimer, Suite 550, Houston, TX 77056, tel. 713/961–5109 or 800/232–8783, fax 713/961–3385). **Globe Travel** (507 5th Ave., Suite 606, New York, NY 10017, tel. 212/843–9885 or 800/969–4562, fax 212/843–9889). **United States Air Consolidators Association** (925 L St., Suite 220, Sacramento, CA 95814, tel. 916/441–4166, fax 916/441–3520). **UniTravel** (1177 N. Warson Rd., St. Louis, MO 63132, tel. 314/569–2501 or 800/325–2222, fax 314/569–2503). **Up & Away Travel** (347 5th Ave., Suite 202, New York, NY 10016, tel. 212/889–2345 or 800/275–8001, fax 212/889–2350).

AVOID GETTING BUMPED

Airlines routinely overbook planes, knowing that not everyone with a ticket will show up, but sometimes everyone does. When that happens, airlines ask for volunteers to give up their seats. In return these volunteers usually get a certificate for a free flight and are rebooked on the next flight out. Not bad. If there are not enough volunteers the airline must choose who will be denied boarding. The first to get bumped are passengers who checked in late and those flying on discounted tickets, **so get to the gate and check in as early as possible,** especially during peak periods.

Always **bring a photo ID to the airport.** You may be asked to show it before you are allowed to check in.

ENJOY THE FLIGHT

For better service, **fly smaller or regional carriers,** which often have higher passenger-satisfaction ratings. Sometimes you'll find leather seats, more legroom, and better food.

For more legroom, **request an emergency-aisle seat**; don't, however, sit in the row in front of the emergency row or in front of a bulkhead, where seats may not recline.

If you have particular dietary needs, **ask for special meals when booking.** These can be vegetarian, low-cholesterol, or kosher, for example.

To avoid jet lag try to maintain a normal routine while traveling. At night **get some sleep.** By day **eat light meals, drink water (not alcohol),** and **move about the cabin** to stretch your legs.

COMPLAIN IF NECESSARY

If your baggage goes astray or your flight goes awry, complain right away. Most carriers require that you file a claim immediately.

AIRLINE COMPLAINTS • U.S. Department of Transportation **Aviation Consumer Protection Division** (C-75, Washington, DC 20590, tel. 202/366–2220). **Federal Aviation Administration (FAA) Consumer Hotline** (tel. 800/322–7873).

AIRPORTS & TRANSFERS

Three major airports—**John F. Kennedy International, La Guardia,** and **Newark International**—serve New York City, though Newark is actually in the state of New Jersey.

John F. Kennedy International is the largest of New York's three airports, with five terminals located about 15 mi southeast of Manhattan, in Queens. There's a currency-exchange booth on the second floor of the JFK International building and one in the Delta terminal. Luggage storage (tel. 718/656–8617) facilities are in the International building (Building 4E/4W), between Gates 10 and 11 and between 33 and 34. Rates are $3.50–$5 per bag, per day. There are information booths in the east and west wings of the International building, on the first floor. Each terminal has its own parking lot. Six lots are for long-term parking with a 30-day maximum stay at a cost of $6 per day.

La Guardia Airport is the smallest New York airport, 8 mi northeast of Manhattan, in Flushing, Queens. There are currency-exchange windows on the upper level between the American and United terminals, and at the US Airways terminal. Luggage storage (tel. 718/478–1690) facilities are in the US Airways terminal on the departure level next to the food court and in the main terminal between the American and United ticket counters. Rates are $1.50–$3.50 per bag, per day. Parking costs $4 for the first four hours and $2 per hour after that, maxing out at $18 per day. There is no long-term parking at La Guardia.

Newark International Airport is about 16 mi southwest of New York City, in New Jersey. Newark has half a dozen currency-exchange windows; those in Terminal A are open daily 7 AM–8:30 PM, those in Terminal B, daily 7 AM–9 PM. Terminal B has a buy-back counter on the arrivals level between doors five and six (open daily noon–8) and a regular exchange counter on the concourse level. Terminal C also has an exchange center on the concourse level next to the bank and one on the ticketing level by door four; both are open daily 7 AM–8:30 PM. Luggage storage (tel. 201/961–4720) at Newark is at Terminal B on the ground-floor level, open daily 7 AM–9 PM. Rates are $1.50–$5 per bag, per day. Parking is divided into hourly, daily, and long-term lots. Hourly parking is $4 for the first four hours and then $4 per hour after that. Daily parking costs $22 for 24 hours, with a maximum stay of three days. Long-term is the farthest lot from the airport, though there is a free shuttle bus for passengers. Long-term costs $7 per 24 hours.

AIRPORT INFORMATION • **JFK International Airport** (tel. 718/244–4444). **La Guardia Airport** (tel. 718/533–3400). **Newark International Airport** (tel. 201/961–6000).

TRANSFERS

Call the Port Authority's **Air Ride hot line** (tel. 800/247–7433) for detailed, up-to-the-minute recorded info on how to reach your destination from New York's three major airports via car, private bus, shuttle service, or public transportation. The cheapest option is the public transit system, although what you save in dollars you'll pay for with time and effort, since routes can take an hour or more and may involve transferring between bus and subway. Private shuttle services travel between all three airports and many Manhattan hotels. Taxis and car services are the most expensive option, with fares running as high as $35 one-way, plus $3–$4 in bridge tolls. When all is said and done, you'll find that one of the easiest and most reasonable ways to get to the airport is with a bus service—either NJ Transit to Newark or Carey Transportation to La Guardia and JFK (*see* Shuttle Buses, *below*).

JFK INTERNATIONAL • Taxis and Car Service: There is now a flat $30 fee (plus tolls) for travel from JFK to Manhattan (*not* from the city to the airport) for taxis and private car services. On average, car service to JFK costs about $33 plus tax and tip. Taxis cost a bit more.

Shuttle Buses: The private bus line **Carey Airport Express** (tel. 718/632–0500 or 800/678–1569) picks up outside all JFK terminals every 20–30 minutes between 6 AM and midnight and stops in Manhattan at the Port Authority Bus Terminal (W. 42nd St. at 8th Ave.), Grand Central Terminal (E. 42nd St. at Park Ave.), and a few major hotels. The ride costs $13 to or from JFK and takes anywhere from 45 minutes to an hour, depending on traffic. Outbound Carey buses (from Manhattan to JFK) operate 365 days a year. **Gray Line Air Shuttle** (tel. 212/315–3006 or 800/451–0455) is slightly more expensive ($16.50 one-way from JFK) but is also slightly faster and stops at any major hotel between 23rd and 63rd streets. Make reservations at the airport's transportation center.

Public Transport: Taking the subway to JFK is fairly simple and cheap ($1.50). Take the A train to the Howard Beach Station, from where you can catch a free shuttle run by the Port Authority. The shuttle makes the trip to JFK every 10 minutes and takes about 20 minutes to reach the terminals. All told, it's about a 70-minute trip from Midtown.

LA GUARDIA • Taxis and Car Service: On average, taxi and car service to La Guardia costs $20–$25 plus tax and tip.

Shuttle Buses: The **Carey Airport Express** (tel. 718/632–0500 or 800/678–1569) picks up outside all La Guardia terminals every 30 minutes from 6:45 AM to midnight and stops at the Port Authority Bus Terminal (W. 42nd St. at 8th Ave.), Grand Central Terminal (E. 42nd St. at Park Ave.), and many hotels downtown. The ride costs $10 to or from La Guardia and takes anywhere from 20 minutes to an hour, depending on traffic. **Gray Line Air Shuttle** (tel. 212/315–3006 or 800/451–0455) costs $14 one-way from La Guardia but stops at any major hotel between 23rd and 63rd streets. Make reservations at the airport's ground transportation center or use the courtesy phone.

Public Transport: The **Triboro Coach Corp.** (tel. 718/335–1000) runs its Q-33 line from the airport to the Jackson Heights subway stop in Queens every 10 minutes during peak morning and evening hours. Its Q-47 line services the Marine Air Terminal at La Guardia. The ride costs $1.50, and the buses run daily 4 AM–2 AM. The **MTA** runs its M60 line to La Guardia; catch it in Manhattan on 118th Street at Broadway. The route follows 125th Street across town and runs every half hour. The fare is $1.50.

NEWARK • Taxis and Car Service: On average, car or taxi service to Newark is about $28 plus tax and tip.

Shuttle Buses: **Olympia Trails Airport Express** (tel. 212/964–6233, 718/622–7700, or 908/354–3330) picks up every 15–30 minutes, between 6:15 AM and midnight, outside all Newark terminals and stops at Grand Central Terminal, Penn Station, and the World Trade Center. The ride takes 25–45 minutes and costs $10. The **Gray Line Air Shuttle** (tel. 212/315–3006 or 800/451–0455) costs $14 one-way from Newark and stops at any major hotel between 23rd and 63rd streets (the price is $18.50 from Manhattan to Newark). Make reservations at the airport's ground transportation center or use the courtesy phone.

Public Transport: You can take New Jersey Transit's Airlink buses, which leave every 20 minutes from 6:15 AM to 2 AM, to Penn Station in Newark. The ride takes about 20 minutes and costs $4 (exact change). From there, the cheapest option ($1) is a PATH train from Newark to various stops in Manhattan (for more info *see* Regional Train Services *in* Train Travel, *below*).

BUS TRAVEL

All long-distance bus companies depart from the **Port Authority Bus Terminal** (625 8th Ave., at W. 41st St., Midtown, tel. 212/564–8484. Subway: A, C, or E to W. 42nd St.), open 24 hours. This huge terminal, which services more than 35 bus companies and nearly 200,000 people a day, is in a somewhat squalid neighborhood. For New York City buses going uptown, board the M10 on the east side of

8th Avenue; board the downtown M11 on 9th Avenue across the street from the south wing entrance; board the cross-town M42 on 42nd Street at 8th Avenue. You are expected to tip the terminal's Red Caps if they help you haul your 200-pound suitcase to a ticket window.

GREYHOUND

Bus service in North America can be grungy and depressing—but it is cheap. **Greyhound-Trailways** (tel. 212/971–6300 or 800/231–2222) has routes throughout the United States, including service between New York and Boston (4½ hrs, $27), Philadelphia (2½ hrs, $13), Washington, D.C. (4½ hrs, $27), Chicago (18 hrs, $79), Atlanta (21 hrs, $87), San Francisco (2½ days, $128), and Los Angeles (3 days, $125). You can order tickets by mail with a credit card or buy your ticket at the station up to one hour before the bus leaves. Cheapest fares are offered during the low season (January–June). You're allowed two carry-on and two checked pieces of luggage.

GREYHOUND PASSES • Greyhound's **Ameripass,** valid on all U.S. routes, can be purchased in advance in cities throughout the States; spontaneous types can also buy it up to 45 minutes before the bus leaves the terminal. The pass allows purchasers unlimited travel within a limited time period: seven days ($179), 15 days ($289), 30 days ($399), or 60 days ($599). Foreign visitors get slightly lower rates.

REGIONAL BUS SERVICES

For bus travel into and around New Jersey, contact **New Jersey Transit** (tel. 201/762–5100 or 800/772–2222). **East Coast Explorer** (tel. 718/694–9667 or 800/610–2680) runs backroad trips to Boston ($29 one-way) and Washington, D.C. ($32), with stops at places of natural, historical, and cultural interest—like Newport, Rhode Island, and the Pennsylvania Amish country. Buses depart New York for Boston on Monday and for Washington, D.C., on Thursday; returns are on the following day and travel a different route.

IN NEW YORK

Though New York's subway system is amazingly comprehensive and quick, there are a few reasons to venture above ground and onto a city bus. For one thing, it's a good way to sightsee while you travel, and you'll probably feel a great deal more cheery if you're not spending all your time in a dark, dank, subterranean tunnel. Second, buses provide better door-to-door service if you just want to go a few blocks and can't find (or don't want to pay for) a cab. Say you want to skip from the Metropolitan Museum (5th Ave. at 82nd St.) to Sak's Fifth Avenue (5th Ave. at 50th St.) for some shopping; that's a 15-minute bus ride, but it'd be 40 minutes or more of walking and waiting and climbing stairs if you wanted to go by subway. You'll find that in some neighborhoods where subway lines are scarce—like the Upper East Side, Chelsea west of 8th Avenue, and the East Village—you'll be practically forced to grab a bus to quickly move from point A to B. Ditto for crossing Central Park. A final reason, valid only in summer: All buses are air-conditioned (subway cars are air-conditioned, too, but subway platforms are typically sweltering hot). Keep in mind that during rush hours all the nice things we've told you about buses will still make for a pleasant trip—but not if you're in any kind of hurry. Manhattan's snarled traffic makes for slow going weekday mornings and evenings.

In Manhattan, buses run along virtually every north–south avenue, with several lines running up heavily used routes like 5th Avenue, Madison Avenue, and Broadway. Cross-town buses run at least every 10 blocks, and across Central Park at 66th, 72nd, 79th, 86th, and 96th streets. Stops are every two or three blocks on north–south avenues and every block on crosstown streets. Bus stops are indicated by a red, white, and blue sign on a pole, plus a yellow-painted curb. You'll also find a route schedule and map posted at each stop (you can pick up a map detailing *all* of the Manhattan bus routes at any subway station). During rush hours, buses run about every seven minutes (although you may have to let a too-crowded bus go by and wait for the next one), but at other times, and in bad weather, you can easily end up waiting 10–15 minutes or more. At night many bus routes run less frequently (or not at all); check the posted route schedule for info.

Bus fare is $1.50 per person, just like the subway, and buses accept subway tokens. You can also pay the fare with coins—but not pennies or dollar bills. But remember: Drivers will not make change, ever, even if you rend your clothing and weep loudly. Don't forget to ask for your free transfer ticket after you've paid. It's good on one intersecting bus route (from a list on the back of the ticket) and must be used within two hours. You can use the MetroCard (*see* Subway Travel, *below*) on all New York City Transit buses in Manhattan, which now enables you to transfer free from bus to subway, subway to bus, or bus to bus for up to two hours.

For schedule information, *see* Transportation, *below*.

CAR RENTAL

Renting a car in New York might make you think that it's cheaper just to buy one and drive it home. Rates in New York City begin at $46 a day and $205 a week for an economy car with air-conditioning, automatic transmission, and unlimited mileage. This does not include tax on car rentals, which is 13¼%. On summer weekends, cars can be scarce, so reserve one in advance.

CUT COSTS

To get the best deal, **book through a travel agent who is willing to shop around.** When pricing cars, **ask about the location of the rental lot.** Some off-airport locations offer lower rates, and their lots are only minutes from the terminal via complimentary shuttle. You also may want to **price local car-rental companies,** whose rates may be lower still, although their service and maintenance may not be as good as those of a name-brand agency. They sometimes undercut the major agencies on daily or weekly rates, but you may not get unlimited mileage.

Also **ask your travel agent about a company's customer-service record.** How has it responded to late plane arrivals and vehicle mishaps? Are there often lines at the rental counter, and, if you're traveling during a holiday period, does a confirmed reservation guarantee you a car?

No matter who you rent from, remember to **ask about required deposits, cancellation penalties, and drop-off charges** if you're planning to pick up the car in one city and leave it in another.

MAJOR AGENCIES • Avis (tel. 800/331–1212; 800/879–2847 in Canada). **Budget** (tel. 800/527–0700; 0800/181181 in the U.K.). **Dollar** (tel. 800/800–4000; 0990/565656 in the U.K., where it is known as Eurodollar). **Hertz** (tel. 800/654–3131; 800/263–0600 in Canada; 0345/555888 in the U.K.). **National InterRent** (tel. 800/227–7368; 0345/222525 in the U.K., where it is known as Europcar InterRent).

LOCAL AGENCIES • Allstar Rent A Car (325 W. 34th St., between 8th and 9th Aves., Midtown, tel. 212/563–8282), open Monday–Thursday 7:30–6:30, Friday 7:30 AM–8 PM, Saturday 8–6, Sunday 8–2. **Amcar Discount Car Rentals** (315 W. 96th St., between West End Ave. and Riverside Dr., Upper West Side, tel. 212/222–8500), open weekdays 7:30–7:30, weekends 9–5. **Elite Car Rental** (1041 Coney Island Ave., between Foster and 18th Aves., Brooklyn, tel. 718/859–8111), open Monday–Thursday and Sunday 8–7, Friday 8–5). **Rent-A-Wreck** (tel. 800/535–1391) specializes in cheaper, older, and uglier cars, sometimes undercutting the national companies on rates—but make sure the lower cost is not eclipsed by added mileage charges. **Thrifty** (tel. 800/367–2277).

NEED INSURANCE?

When driving a rented car you are generally responsible for any damage to or loss of the vehicle. You also are liable for any property damage or personal injury that you may cause while driving. Before you rent, **see what coverage you already have** under the terms of your personal auto-insurance policy and credit cards.

For about $14 a day, rental companies sell protection, known as a collision- or loss-damage waiver (CDW or LDW), that eliminates your liability for damage to the car; it's always optional and should never be automatically added to your bill. New York has outlawed the sale of CDW and LDW altogether.

In most states you don't need CDW if you have personal auto insurance or other liability insurance. However, **make sure you have enough coverage to pay for the car.** If you do not have auto insurance or an umbrella policy that covers damage to third parties, purchasing CDW or LDW is highly recommended.

BEWARE SURCHARGES

Before you pick up a car in one city and leave it in another, **ask about drop-off charges or one-way service fees,** which can be substantial. Note, too, that some rental agencies charge extra if you return the car before the time specified on your contract. To avoid a hefty refueling fee, **fill the tank just before you turn in the car,** but be aware that gas stations near the rental outlet may overcharge.

MEET THE REQUIREMENTS

In the United States you must be 21 to rent a car, and rates may be higher if you're under 25. You'll pay extra for additional drivers (about $2 per day). Residents of the United Kingdom will need a reservation voucher, a passport, a U.K. driver's license, and a travel policy that covers each driver in order to pick up a car.

CONSUMER PROTECTION

Whenever possible, **pay with a major credit card** so you can cancel payment if there's a problem, provided that you can provide documentation. This is a good idea whether you're buying travel arrangements before your trip or shopping at your destination.

If you're doing business with a particular company for the first time, **contact your local Better Business Bureau and the attorney general's offices** in your state and the company's home state, as well. Have any complaints been filed?

Finally, if you're buying a package, always **consider travel insurance** that includes default coverage (*see* Insurance, *below*).

LOCAL BBBS • Council of Better Business Bureaus (4200 Wilson Blvd., Suite 800, Arlington, VA 22203, tel. 703/276–0100, fax 703/525–8277).

CURRENCY EXCHANGES

You'll have no trouble finding currency-exchange services in Manhattan—**try touristy areas** like the South Street Seaport, World Trade Center, Herald Square, Times Square, or Grand Central Terminal. All three airports also offer currency exchange. Currency-exchange offices are less common in the outer boroughs, so **try a bank**; they have good rates but short hours (they typically close at 3 PM on weekdays and shut down entirely on weekends).

Chase Foreign Currency Department has more than a dozen offices throughout Manhattan, plus branches in Queens and the Bronx. Each offers a multilingual staff. **Chequepoint USA** has four branches in Midtown. The main office is open daily from 8 AM to 11:30 PM. **Thomas Cook Currency Services** has five offices throughout Manhattan, including one at Grand Central Terminal.

EXCHANGE OFFICES • Chase Foreign Currency Department (tel. 212/935–9935). **Chequepoint USA** (Main office: 22 Central Park S, at 5th Ave., tel. 212/750–2400). **Thomas Cook Currency Services** (Main Office: 1590 Broadway, at W. 48th St., tel. 800/287–7362).

CUSTOMS & DUTIES

ENTERING AUSTRALIA

If you're 18 or older, you may bring back A$400 worth of souvenirs and gifts, including jewelry. Your duty-free allowance also includes 250 cigarettes or 250 grams of tobacco and 1,125 milliliters of alcohol, including wine, beer, or spirits. Residents under 18 may bring back A$200 worth of goods.

RESOURCES • Australian Customs Service (Regional Director, Box 8, Sydney, NSW 2001, tel. 02/9213–2000, fax 02/9213–4000).

ENTERING CANADA

If you've been out of Canada for at least seven days you may bring in C$500 worth of goods duty-free. If you've been away for fewer than seven days but more than 48 hours, the duty-free allowance drops to C$200; if your trip lasts 24–48 hours, the allowance is C$50. You may not pool allowances with family members. Goods claimed under the C$500 exemption may follow you by mail; those claimed under the lesser exemptions must accompany you.

Alcohol and tobacco products may be included in the seven-day and 48-hour exemptions but not in the 24-hour exemption. If you meet the age requirements of the province or territory through which you reenter Canada you may bring in, duty-free, 1.14 liters (40 imperial ounces) of wine or liquor *or* 24 12-ounce cans or bottles of beer or ale. If you are 16 or older you may bring in, duty-free, 200 cigarettes and 50 cigars; these items must accompany you.

You may send an unlimited number of gifts worth up to C$60 each duty-free to Canada. Label the package UNSOLICITED GIFT—VALUE UNDER $60. Alcohol and tobacco are excluded.

INFORMATION • Revenue Canada (2265 St. Laurent Blvd. S, Ottawa, Ontario K1G 4K3, tel. 613/993–0534; 800/461–9999 in Canada).

ENTERING NEW ZEALAND

Although greeted with a "Haere Mai" ("Welcome to New Zealand"), homeward-bound travelers with goods to declare must present themselves for inspection. If you're 17 or older, you may bring back NZ$700 worth of souvenirs and gifts. Your duty-free allowance also includes 200 cigarettes or 250 grams of tobacco or 50 cigars or a combo of all three up to 250 grams; 4.5 liters of wine or beer and one 1,125-milliliter bottle of spirits.

RESOURCES • New Zealand Customs (Custom House, 50 Anzac Ave., Box 29, Auckland, New Zealand, tel. 09/359–6655, fax 09/309–2978).

ENTERING THE U.K.

From countries outside the European Union, including the United States, you may import, duty-free, 200 cigarettes or 50 cigars; 1 liter of spirits or 2 liters of fortified or sparkling wine or liqueurs; 2 liters of still table wine; 60 milliliters of perfume; and 250 milliliters of toilet water; plus £136 worth of other goods, including gifts and souvenirs.

INFORMATION • HM Customs and Excise (Dorset House, Stamford St., London SE1 9NG, tel. 0171/ 202–4227).

ENTERING THE U.S.

Visitors age 21 and over may import the following into the United States: 200 cigarettes or 50 cigars or 2 kilograms of tobacco, 1 liter of alcohol, and gifts worth $100. Prohibited items include meat products, seeds, plants, and fruits.

DISABILITIES & ACCESSIBILITY

ACCESS IN NEW YORK

Although New York was largely built decades before the watershed Americans with Disabilities Act, most of the major sights, museums, and parks are accessible to those who use wheelchairs. Hotels, hostels, restaurants, bars, and clubs are a different story: Generally, only the newest and most recently renovated are fully accessible. If you're in doubt about accessibility at a particular destination, your best bet is to call ahead.

LOCAL RESOURCES • Hospital Audiences, Inc., now staffs the **HAI Hotline** (tel. 888/424–4685) weekdays 9–5, offering information on transportation, hotels, restaurants, and cultural venues. **Big Apple Greeters** (1 Center St., Suite 2035, 10007, tel. 212/669–8159) offers tours of New York City tailored to visitors' personal preferences and will provide guides with a knowledge of accessibility in the city, as well as guides for visitors with hearing and vision impairments.

PUBLICATIONS • The bible for New York visitors with disabilities is *Access for All* ($5), published by Hospital Audiences, Inc. (220 W. 42nd St., New York, NY 10036, tel. 212/575–7663, TDD 212/575–7673). It lists theaters, museums, and other cultural institutions that offer wheelchair access and services for people with hearing or vision impairments. The free *I Love New York Travel Guide* and *Big Apple Visitors Guide,* describing access to the city's major sights, is available from the New York State Division of Tourism (1 Commerce Plaza, Albany, NY 12245, tel. 518/474–4116 or 800/225–5697). The Andrew Heiskell Library for the Blind and Physically Handicapped (40 W. 20th St., between 5th and 6th Aves., Midtown, tel. 212/206–5400, TDD 212/206–5458) has a large collection of Braille, large-print, and recorded books, from city history to current fiction.

GETTING AROUND

Of the 469 subway stations in New York, a paltry 23 have elevators—and even those aren't very dependable. City buses are more convenient: All 3,700 buses kneel to the curb, 95% are equipped with wheelchair lifts, and drivers will announce stops for riders with vision impairments. People with disabilities are eligible for reduced fares on public buses and subways with proper ID; call 212/878–7294 for info on obtaining a disability ID card. The Transit Authority's **Accessibility Hotline** (tel. 800/734–6772) has 24-hour recorded info regarding subway elevators and escalators, or you can speak directly to a Transit Authority representative about accessibility by calling 718/596–8585 daily 6 AM–9 PM. Take note: Taxi drivers tend to avoid passengers who might cause them inconvenience or delay, while drivers for car services (which charge a per-trip flat rate) are more accommodating.

TIPS & HINTS

When discussing accessibility with an operator or reservationist, **ask hard questions.** Are there any stairs, inside *or* out? Are there grab bars next to the toilet *and* in the shower/tub? How wide is the doorway to the room? To the bathroom? When possible, **opt for newer accommodations,** more likely to have been designed with access in mind. Older buildings may offer more limited facilities. Be sure to **discuss your needs before booking.**

COMPLAINTS • Disability Rights Section (U.S. Dept. of Justice, Box 66738, Washington, DC 20035–6738, tel. 202/514–0301 or 800/514–0301, fax 202/307–1198, TTY 202/514–0383 or 800/514–0383) for general complaints. **Aviation Consumer Protection Division** (*see* Air Travel, *above*) for airline-related problems. **Civil Rights Office** (U.S. Dept. of Transportation, Departmental Office of Civil Rights, S-30, 400 7th St. SW, Room 10215, Washington, DC 20590, tel. 202/366–4648) for problems with surface transportation.

TRAVEL AGENCIES

Some agencies specialize in travel arrangements for individuals with disabilities.

BEST BETS • Access Adventures (206 Chestnut Ridge Rd., Rochester, NY 14624, tel. 716/889–9096), run by a former physical-rehabilitation counselor. **Hinsdale Travel Service** (201 E. Ogden Ave., Suite 100, Hinsdale, IL 60521, tel. 630/325–1335), which offers advice from wheelchair traveler Janice Perkins. **Wheelchair Journeys** (16979 Redmond Way, Redmond, WA 98052, tel. 206/885–2210 or 800/313–4751), for general travel arrangements.

DISCOUNTS & DEALS

While your travel plans are still in the fantasy stage, start studying the travel sections of major Sunday newspapers: You'll often find listings for good packages and incredibly cheap flights. Surfing on the Internet can also give you some good ideas. Travel agents are another obvious resource; the computer networks to which they have access show the lowest fares before they're even advertised. Agencies on or near college campuses, accustomed to dealing with budget travelers, can be especially helpful.

Always **compare all your options before making a choice.** A plane ticket bought with a promotional coupon may not be cheaper than the least expensive fare from a discount ticket agency. (For more on getting a deal on airfares, *see* Get the Lowest Fare *in* Air Travel, *above*.) When evaluating a package, keep in mind that what you get is just as important as what you save. Just because something is cheap doesn't mean it's a bargain.

CREDIT CARDS & AUTO CLUBS

When you use your credit card to make travel purchases you may get free travel-accident insurance, collision-damage insurance, and medical or legal help, depending on the card and the bank that issued it. So **get a copy of your credit card's travel-benefits policy.** If you are a member of the American Automobile Association (AAA) or an oil-company-sponsored road-assistance plan, always **ask hotel or car-rental reservationists about auto-club discounts.** Some clubs offer additional discounts on admission to attractions. And don't forget that auto-club membership entitles you to free maps and trip-planning services.

DISCOUNTS BY PHONE

Don't be afraid to **check out "1-800" discount reservations services,** which use their buying power to get a better price on hotels, airline tickets, even car rentals. When booking a room, always **call the hotel's local toll-free number** (if one is available) rather than the central reservations number—you'll often get a better price. Always ask about special packages.

CHEAP AIRLINE TICKETS • Tel. 800/FLY–4–LESS. Tel. **800/FLY–ASAP.**

CHEAP HOTEL ROOMS • Accommodations Express (tel. 800/444–7666). **Central Reservation Service (CRS)** (tel. 800/548–3311). **Hotel Reservations Network (HRN)** (tel. 800/964–6835). **Quickbook** (tel. 800/789–9887). **Room Finders USA** (tel. 800/473–7829). **RMC Travel** (tel. 800/245–5738). **Steigenberger Reservation Service** (tel. 800/223–5652).

SAVE ON COMBOS

Packages and guided tours can both save you money, but don't confuse the two. When you buy a package your travel remains independent, just as though you had planned and booked the trip yourself. Fly-drive packages, which combine airfare and car rental, are often a good deal. In cities, ask the local visitors bureau about hotel packages. These often include tickets to major museum exhibits and other special events you'd be going to anyway.

DRINKING

The legal drinking age in New York state is 21. It's unevenly enforced, and corner stores ("bodegas" in New York lingo) are likely to sell beer to anyone who looks like they've graduated junior high. Most bars and clubs do not ask for ID, which translates into lots of college freshmen getting tanked in bars on the weekends. However, if you're underage and you're caught drinking, you may be fined and/or prosecuted. Likewise, despite the fact that people from Wall streeters to derelicts can be seen drinking in public, the punishment—spending a few hours in a holding tank—is not worth the thrill.

DRIVING

The biggest mistake you could make while living in or visiting New York is driving a car—New Yorkers typically only use cars to *leave* the city, not drive around in it. So consider this: If the city's Department of Transportation doesn't get you (with unfilled potholes and outdated signs), a car thief might get your car. Reports of grand larceny (or vehicles stolen when the driver was not around) totaled 12,978 in 1994, for example. Also keep in mind that traffic in New York is simply awful: On a good day, it can take 30 minutes to travel 30 blocks during the rush-hour commute. Though it is possible to see Manhattan by car, you should definitely get to know the city a little before committing to the four-wheel experience.

AUTO CLUBS • In the United States, **American Automobile Association** (tel. 800/564–6222). In the United Kingdom, **Automobile Association** (AA, tel. 0990/500–600), **Royal Automobile Club** (RAC, tel. 0990/722–722 membership; 0345/121–345 insurance).

PARKING

Whether you opt for a garage or take your chances parking on the street, you'll have a few headaches to contend with. The first is price: Parking lot and garage rates vary from neighborhood to neighborhood, but you should expect to pay upwards of $6–$14 per hour or $25–$31 per day. The highest rates are on the Upper East Side and in Midtown around Times Square. Long-term parking in a garage is almost equal to putting up another person, with average monthly costs ($250–$400) equal to half the rent on a studio apartment; the cheapest garages are on the Lower East Side. Or you can make the long trek north on the B or C trains to **WD Lot** (304 W. 135th St., at Amsterdam Ave., Harlem), which offers rock-bottom prices: $3 an hour, $10 a night, or $100 a month.

If you want to conserve cash you can park on the streets for free. Most New York street-parkers tape hand-lettered signs inside their vehicles reading, NO RADIO, NOTHING OF VALUE INSIDE CAR to discourage thieves. It sometimes works. New Yorkers also contend with a boggling number of posted parking restrictions, including the dreaded alternate side of the street system—which means moving your car across the street every morning at 6 AM to make way for street sweepers. The moral here is always read curbside signs, and if you're serious about parking on the street, call 212/225–5368, a 24-hour automated help line, to find out about when alternate side of the street parking is suspended, and to get the skinny on other parking regulations. To speak to a live human being, call between 7 AM and 7 PM.

BRIDGE & TUNNEL TOLLS

New York City has dozens of bridges and tunnels. Manhattan is built on an island, remember? And while we're at it, so are Brooklyn and Queens. Tolls are levied one-way only, usually on traffic headed into Manhattan. Bridges leading into Manhattan and charging a toll are the George Washington Bridge ($4), which connects New York with New Jersey, and the Triboro Bridge ($3.50), which leads from the Bronx and Queens into Harlem. Around a dozen other bridges connect the outer boroughs and charge tolls ranging from $1.50 to $4. Tunnels leading into Manhattan include the Brooklyn Battery Tunnel ($3.50), Holland Tunnel ($4), Lincoln Tunnel ($4), and Queens Midtown Tunnel ($3.50). For more info, contact the Triborough Bridge and Tunnel Authority (tel. 212/360–3000) or the Port Authority of New York and New Jersey (tel. 212/435–7000).

EMERGENCIES & CONSULATES

CONSULATES • **Australia** (630 5th Ave., near 51st St., tel. 212/408–8400). **Canada** (1251 6th Ave., between 49th and 50th Sts., tel. 212/596–1600). **Ireland** (345 Park Ave., at 51st St., 17th floor, tel. 212/

319–2555). **United Kingdom** (845 3rd Ave., near E. 51st St., tel. 212/745–0200). For other consulates, check the New York Yellow Pages.

EMERGENCIES • Dial 911 for **police, fire,** and **ambulance.**

HOSPITALS & DOCTORS

Heaven help you if you should get sick or injured in New York and not have insurance—low-cost care is really hard to come by. Fortunately, most hospitals take credit cards. On the other hand, New York is filled with some of the best hospitals and doctors in the world. If you need health care, call a referral service (*see below*) or try one of the following hospitals.

DENTISTS • The **Dental Referral Service** (tel. 800/917–6453) gives referrals to standard-rate private practices.

HOSPITALS • **Bellevue** (462 1st Ave., at E. 27th St., Gramercy, tel. 212/562–4141 or 212/562–4344 for emergency room). **Cabrini** (227 E. 19th St., between 2nd and 3rd Aves., Gramercy, tel. 212/995–6000). **St. Vincent's** (170 W. 12th St., at 7th Ave., West Village, tel. 212/604–7000).

PHYSICIAN REFERRAL SERVICES • Referral services can usually refer you to doctors offering sliding-scale fees, meaning that you pay based on your ability to pay. To use a referral service is absolutely free, so try calling around to a few of the following hospital referral lines if you're worried about getting a giant doctor's bill: **Beth Israel** (tel. 800/420–4004); **Columbia-Presbyterian** (tel. 212/305–5156); **Cornell** (tel. 800/822–2694); **Lenox Hill** (tel. 212/434–2046); **Mount Sinai** (tel. 800/637–4624); **New York University** (tel. 212/263–5000); or **St. Luke's–Roosevelt** (tel. 212/876–5432).

PHARMACIES

Need drugs? For the legitimate stuff try a **Duane Reade** discount drugstore. Of their 50 stores citywide, several are open 24 hours: 57th Street and Broadway (tel. 212/541–9708), 47th Street and Lexington Avenue (tel. 212/682–5338), 91st Street and Broadway (tel. 212/799–3172), and 74th Street and 3rd Avenue (tel. 212/744–2668). A few pharmacies even deliver; try **Kaufman Pharmacy** (tel. 212/755–2266) or **McKay Drugs** (East Village, tel. 212/254–1454; West Village, tel. 212/255–5054; Upper East Side, tel. 212/794–7000).

HOT LINES • If you are the victim of an assault or rape, call the 24-hour **Sex Crimes Hotline** (tel. 212/267–7273) to report it and get help. The office is staffed by female investigators of the New York Police Department. The 24-hour **Crime Victims Hotline** (tel. 212/577–7777) provides over-the-telephone counseling and referrals. A few other numbers you'll hopefully never need: the **New York City Department of Health AIDS Hotline** (tel. 212/447–8200); **Poison Control Center** (tel. 212/764–7667 or 212/340–4494; 212/836–3667 for Spanish speakers); **Substance Abuse Information Line** (tel. 800/522–5353); and the **Sexually Transmitted Disease Hotline** (tel. 212/788–4415).

GAY & LESBIAN TRAVEL

GAY- & LESBIAN-FRIENDLY TRAVEL AGENCIES • **Advance Damron** (1 Greenway Plaza, Suite 800, Houston, TX 77046, tel. 713/682–2002 or 800/695–0880, fax 713/888–1010). **Club Travel** (8739 Santa Monica Blvd., West Hollywood, CA 90069, tel. 310/358–2200 or 800/429–8747, fax 310/358–2222). **Islanders/Kennedy Travel** (183 W. 10th St., New York, NY 10014, tel. 212/242–3222 or 800/988–1181, fax 212/929–8530). **Now Voyager** (4406 18th St., San Francisco, CA 94114, tel. 415/626–1169 or 800/255–6951, fax 415/626–8626). **Yellowbrick Road** (1500 W. Balmoral Ave., Chicago, IL 60640, tel. 773/561–1800 or 800/642–2488, fax 773/561–4497). **Skylink Women's Travel** (3577 Moorland Ave., Santa Rosa, CA 95407, tel. 707/585–8355 or 800/225–5759, fax 707/584–5637), serving lesbian travelers.

HOLIDAYS

Just about everything—including banks, museums, stores, and some restaurants—close on the following national holidays: **New Year's Day** (January 1), **Martin Luther King Jr.'s Birthday** (third Monday of January), **Presidents' Day** (third Monday of February), **Memorial Day** (last Monday in May), **Independence Day** (July 4), **Labor Day** (first Monday of September), **Columbus Day** (second Monday in October), **Veteran's Day** (November 11), **Thanksgiving** (fourth Thursday in November), and **Christmas** (December 25). Buses and trains follow weekend schedules on holidays.

INSURANCE

It's worth noting that organizations such as STA Travel and the Council on International Educational Exchange (*see* Students, *below*) include health-and-accident coverage when you acquire a student ID.

Citizens of the United Kingdom can buy an annual travel-insurance policy valid for most vacations during the year in which it's purchased. If you are pregnant or have a preexisting medical condition, make sure you're covered. According to the Association of British Insurers, a trade association representing 450 insurance companies, it's wise to buy extra medical coverage when you visit the United States.

TRAVEL INSURERS • In the United States, **Access America** (6600 W. Broad St., Richmond, VA 23230, tel. 804/285–3300 or 800/284–8300), **Carefree Travel Insurance** (Box 9366, 100 Garden City Plaza, Garden City, NY 11530, tel. 516/294–0220 or 800/323–3149), **Travel Guard International** (1145 Clark St., Stevens Point, WI 54481, tel. 715/345–0505 or 800/826–1300), **Travel Insured International** (Box 280568, East Hartford, CT 06128-0568, tel. 860/528–7663 or 800/243–3174). In Canada, **Mutual of Omaha** (Travel Division, 500 University Ave., Toronto, Ontario M5G 1V8, tel. 416/598–4083; 800/268–8825 in Canada). In the United Kingdom, **Association of British Insurers** (51 Gresham St., London EC2V 7HQ, tel. 0171/600–3333).

LAUNDRY

Finding a Laundromat is no problem in New York; they're on practically every block. Self-service machines typically cost $1.50 per wash and 75¢–$1.50 for 10 or 15 minutes of dryer time. Most machines only accept quarters. Drop-off service (where you leave your stinky stuff in the morning and pick it up clean and folded at the end of the day) costs 60¢–$1.50 per pound. Bleach and softener cost an additional 50¢ each. Dry cleaning will set you back $3–$6 per pair of pants, or $4 each for blouses and shirts. At **Ecowash** (72 W. 69th St., between Columbus Ave. and Central Park W, Upper West Side, tel. 212/787–3890) you can clean your clothes without hurting the planet.

MEDIA

New York is a news- and gossip-intensive town—not surprising for this home of international movers and shakers. What other city in the country has three (count 'em quickly, before one goes bankrupt) daily papers? The city also has its own 24-hour cable TV news station, **New York One** (Channel 1), with local and international news announcements around the clock and daily recaps at 6:30, 9:30, 10, and 11 PM. City weather reports are broadcast "on the ones" (1:01, 1:11, 1:21, etc.).

NEWSSTANDS

The best newsstands for browsing include **Hotaling's** (142 W. 42nd St., near 6th Ave., Midtown, tel. 212/840–1868), around since 1905 and great for foreign publications and obscure titles; **Nikos Magazine & Smoke Shop** (462 6th Ave., at W. 11th St., West Village, tel. 212/255–9175), which stocks some 2,500 titles, from scholarly stuff to 'zines like *Paranoia: The Conspiracy Reader*; and **Universal News Ltd.** (676 Lexington Ave., at E. 56th St., Midtown, tel. 212/750–1855), which amasses some 4,000 foreign and domestic rags. The citywide café/newsstand chain **News Bar** (*see* Cafés and Coffee Bars *in* Chapter 4) is also great for a CNN fix or if you want to browse a rack of more than 400 foreign and domestic publications.

NEWSPAPERS

The tabloid-style *New York Daily News* (50¢) bills itself oxymoronically as "New York's Hometown Newspaper." Look for lots of slang and lurid headlines.

New York Observer. The city's peach-colored weekly has some of the better in-depth reporting on New York arts, media, and political scenes, with an often tongue-in-cheek tone. Its "Eight-Day Week" is a quirky listing—equal parts uptown society and downtown hip. *Tel. 212/755–2400. Cost: $1. Published Wed.*

New York Post. World War III–size headlines bark out the "news" in Rupert Murdoch's cheap, gritty tabloid that's way more in line with most New Yorkers than the *Times.* It's got the quick and dirty on local murders and national scandals, plus "Page Six," the city's premier gossip column. *Tel. 800/552–7678. Cost: 50¢. Published Mon.–Sun.*

New York Press. This free weekly rag features some of the most acerbic writing in all of New York. Plus there are comprehensive restaurant, film, art, theater, and music listings. *Tel. 212/941–1130. Published Tues.*

New York Times. The nation's newspaper of record is ultimately a tool of the establishment, and it shows in its high-falutin' business, arts, social, and fashion pages. Still, for quality writing and in-depth reporting you can't beat the Grey Lady. Special sections include Science (Tuesday); Living (Wednesday); Home (Thursday); and Weekend (Friday). The Sunday paper, bigger than a Britannica, is required reading for most New Yorkers. *Tel. 800/631–2500. Cost: Mon.–Sat. 60¢, Sun. $2.50.*

Village Voice. For political coverage that's strongly left of center, arts coverage that tends toward the avant-garde, and personal ads so hot they seem to smoke on the printed page, pick up the weekly bible for the downtown set. Must-reads include "Voice Choices," for unbeatable cinema, music, and club listings, and gifted gossip columnist Michael Musto's "La Dolce Musto." *Tel. 800/875–2997. Cost: Free ($1.25 outside Manhattan). Published Wed.*

Wall Street Journal. This business-only paper (it's published by Dow Jones & Company) won't familiarize you with New York beyond the world of Wall Street mergers and acquisitions. *Tel. 800/778–0840. Cost: 75¢. Published weekdays.*

MAGAZINES

New York. This glossy magazine delivers weekly reports on city politics and endless looks at how the monied "other half" lives. Its "Cue" section is great for arts listings and reviews, its "Best Bets" and "Sales & Bargains" required reading for shopaholics. *Tel. 800/535–1168. Cost: $2.95.*

The New Yorker. The nation's revered literary weekly, founded in 1925, has shaken off its penchant for timeless, quirky ruminations and gotten a hell of a lot more modern under sassy Brit editor-in-chief Tina Brown, once of *Vanity Fair*. Which means a lot more coverage of Roseanne and photos by *Rolling Stone* star Annie Leibovitz and fewer contributions by American humorists like Garrison Keillor and Ian Frazier. Its "Goings On About Town" is a critical listing of theater, gallery shows, readings, dance, film, and classical music concerts. *Tel. 800/825–2510. Cost: $2.95.*

Paper. This monthly ($3) isn't specifically about New York, but it's a great resource for what's happening on the downtown art/music/club scene.

Time Out. A new arrival in New York (other versions thrive in London and Amsterdam), the weekly *Time Out* offers the city's most comprehensive and easy-to-read listings and reviews for theater, music, film, readings, sports, art exhibitions, you name it. It's hip, but not intimidating. *Tel. 212/539–4444 or 800/457–4364. Cost: $1.95.*

RADIO

Here's a sampling of what's going out over the FM airwaves in New York City: WNYU (89.1), whatever's cool at New York University; WKCR (89.9), whatever's cool at Columbia University; New York's infamous "shock jock" Howard Stern broadcasts live weekday mornings from WXRK (92.3); WNYC (93.9), National Public Radio; WQXR (96.3), classical music; WQHT (97.1), the phattest hip-hop jams; WRKS (98.7), soul; WBAI (99.5), cutting-edge music of all sorts; WHTZ (100.3), alternative rock and Top-40; WCBS (101.0), oldies; WNEW (102.7), classic rock; and WAXQ (104.3), lots of '80s rock.

CYBER NEW YORK

A few cool New York–specific sites to browse include the New York Public Library at http://www.nypl.org/; mega–New York dance club Webster Hall at http://www.webster-hall.com; Movielink 777–FILM Online at http://www.777film.com/; and Columbia University's Web Music Archive at http://www.columbia.edu/~hauben/music/.

Of New York's many webcams, the **UpperWestSide Cam** at http://www.zietgeist.com/camera/ and its view of Columbus and 72nd may be the most famous. The **Village Voice** at http://www.villagevoice.com/ and **New York Sidewalk** at http://newyork.sidewalk.com/ offer comprehensive, searchable events listings. The **New York Subway Finder** at http://www.krusch.com/nysf.html/ provides subway directions between any two New York addresses.

MONEY

New York is, was, and will always be one of the most expensive cities in the United States. Stores and restaurants usually accept traveler's checks but prefer cash, and a few turn up their noses at credit cards. At least there are plenty of banks.

ATMS

Virtually all U.S. banks belong to a network of card-slurping, cash-expectorating ATMs. Before leaving home, **make sure that your credit cards have been programmed for ATM use.**

ATM LOCATIONS • Cirrus (tel. 800/424–7787). **Plus** (tel. 800/843–7587).

COSTS

In New York it's easy to get swept up in a debt-inducing cyclone of $50 dinners, $40 theater tickets, $25 club covers, $10 cab rides, and $100 hotel rooms. Don't do it. Get around on the subway, check out Off-Broadway performances, and take advantage of lunch specials at restaurants and no-cover nights at clubs and bars. In this case, you'll have a fabulous time for about $50 per day.

ACCOMMODATIONS • Hostels are the best deal for solo travelers, with dorm beds for $22–$25. Singles and doubles cost $40–$90 at even the cheapest (and, predictably, skankiest) hotels, though groups of three or more can find decent hotels offering triples, quads, and suites for a bargain $75–$125. Note: Temperatures really soar in New York during summer, so you might want to plunk down a few extra dollars to stay at a hotel or hostel that offers rooms with air-conditioning; many (but not all) do.

FOOD • It's easy to gorge yourself at a cool restaurant in the East Village for under $10, but in other neighborhoods you'll probably spend twice that. That said, many restaurants cut prices drastically for their "lunch specials" (typically weekdays 11 AM–6 PM). Hot dogs, falafel sandwiches, tacos, pizza slices, and bagels are easy to find, and all cost under $2. The city's many Greenmarkets (see Chapter 4) also offer inexpensive, fresh produce.

ENTERTAINMENT & NIGHTLIFE • This is where you can go broke fast. Cover charges for nightclubs can hit $20 or more, not including drinks ($2–$5 each). Tickets to Les Miz or Rent are $25–$100 a pop. A beer in a bar usually costs $2–$3.50, though some Manhattan bars serve $1 pints during weekday "happy hours." Movies are a ridiculous $9 most places. Crazy, huh? If you steer clear of the big names you can find live music and dance clubs with covers under $10, Off-Broadway shows with tickets for $5–$25, and, especially in summer, tons of concerts and performances for free.

PACKING FOR NEW YORK

The first thing you may notice when you arrive in New York: Everyone here wears black, lots of black, year-round. This is considered chic. Whether you do the same is up to you, but you should keep in mind that New York is a fashionable city, and residents do not—as Seinfeld would have you believe—wear white Reeboks and windbreakers. Though it's important to pack pragmatically (bring comfortable, easy-to-clean clothes) you may feel awkward if you're always dressing down. It's better to have one decent shirt you can wear every other day than a whole slew of tacky T-shirts. Summers are gruesomely hot, so bring lightweight clothes, as well as a sweater or jacket for overly air-conditioned subway cars and museums. In winter, you'll need a coat and shoes that can handle snow, sleet, and ice, plus a hat, gloves, and a scarf to protect you from those -10° winds. And you should be prepared for rainfall any time of year.

You've heard it a million times. Now you'll hear it once again: Pack light. The heaviness of your luggage is directly proportional to how many days you've been carrying it around. Bring an extra pair of eyeglasses or contact lenses in your carry-on luggage, and if you have a health problem, **pack enough medication** to last the entire trip. It's important that you **don't put prescription drugs, your passport, or other valuables in luggage to be checked**: you don't want to be stuck without it if you luggage gets lost. Use containers that seal tightly and pack them in a separate waterproof bag; the pressure on airplanes can cause lids to pop off and create instant moisturizer slicks inside your luggage. Hostels require that you use a sleep sheet; some include them, and some don't.

Other stuff you might not think to take but will be damn glad to have: a miniature flashlight, good in dark places; a pocket knife for cutting fruit, spreading cheese, and opening wine bottles; a water bottle; sunglasses; several large zip-type plastic bags, useful for wet swimsuits, leaky bottles, and rancid socks; a travel alarm clock; a needle and a small spool of thread; extra batteries; a good book; and a day pack.

LUGGAGE

In general you are entitled to check two bags on flights within the United States. A third piece may be brought on board, but it must fit easily under the seat in front of you or in the overhead compartment. If your bag is too porky, be prepared for the humiliation of rejection and a last-minute baggage check.

Airline liability for baggage is limited to $1,250 per person on flights within the United States. On international flights it amounts to $9.07 per pound or $20 per kilogram for checked baggage (roughly $640 per 70-pound bag) and $400 per passenger for unchecked baggage. Insurance for losses exceeding these amounts can be bought from the airline at check-in for about $10 per $1,000 of coverage; note that this coverage excludes a rather extensive list of items, shown on your airline ticket.

At check-in, **make sure that each bag is correctly tagged** with the destination airport's three-letter code. If your bags arrive damaged or not at all, file a written report with the airline *before* leaving the airport. If you're traveling with a pack, tie all loose straps to each other or onto the pack itself, so that they don't get caught in luggage conveyer belts.

PASSPORTS & VISAS

AUSTRALIAN & NEW ZEALAND CITIZENS

Australian citizens need a valid passport to enter the United States. If you are staying for fewer than 90 days on vacation and have a return or onward ticket, you probably will not need a visa. However, you will need to fill out the Visa Waiver Form, 1-94W, supplied by the airline.

INFORMATION • Passport Office (tel. 008/131–232).

CANADIANS

A passport is not required to enter the United States.

U.K. CITIZENS

British citizens need a valid passport to enter the United States. If you are staying for fewer than 90 days on vacation and have a return or onward ticket, you probably will not need a visa. However, you will need to fill out the Visa Waiver Form, 1-94W, supplied by the airline.

INFORMATION • London Passport Office (tel. 0990/21010) for fees and documentation requirements and to request an emergency passport. **U.S. Embassy Visa Information Line** (tel. 01891/200–290) for U.S. visa information; calls cost 49p per minute or 39p per minute cheap rate. **U.S. Embassy Visa Branch** (5 Upper Grosvenor St., London W1A 2JB) for U.S. visa information; send a self-addressed, stamped envelope. Write the **U.S. Consulate General** (Queen's House, Queen St., Belfast BTI 6EO) if you live in Northern Ireland.

In one scam, a thief will create a distraction as you leave an ATM machine—by "accidentally" breaking an egg or popping a packet of ketchup in your face. Amidst confusion, apologies, and a hasty cleanup, your wallet will mysteriously disappear.

PUBLIC REST ROOMS

For travelers with tiny bladders, New York is a cold and stingy town. In Midtown, there are clean, pleasant rest rooms at **Bryant Park** (W. 42nd St. between 5th and 6th Aves.), decent ones in **Grand Central Terminal** (E. 42nd St. at Park Ave.), and grit-your-teeth options at the **Port Authority Bus Terminal** and **Penn Station.** Downtown near City Hall you'll find a single, high-tech, coin-operated toilet kiosk modeled after those on the streets of Paris. There are rest room facilities in a few subway stations, but you're better off staying away from them. You can discreetly visit the bathrooms in public buildings, diners, cafés, and hotels such as the **St. Regis,** on 55th Street and 5th Avenue; the **Plaza,** on 59th Street and 5th Avenue; or the **Stanhope,** at 81st Street and 5th Avenue. Department stores are also a good bet. The plush, unguarded rest rooms at **Bloomingdale's** (3rd Ave. at E. 59th St.), for example, are no secret to shoppers. If you're looking for the ultimate bathroom read, check out *Where To Go: A Guide to Manhattan's Toilets,* by Vicki Rovere. It's available at most city bookstores. Come to think of it, Barnes & Noble isn't a bad bathroom experience either.

SAFETY

Crime in New York has dropped like a rock in recent years: The New York crime rate of 1995 was ranked 22nd among major U.S. cities, down from 18th in 1993, and continues to fall. And this has a lot to do with the increasing vigilance of New York's cleaned-up cop force. Petty offenses like public drinking or urination or petty drug-peddling won't get the nudge-and-a-wink treatment these days, and the biggies will land you in jail for sure. Drug possession and/or consumption warrants arrest and fines. Stay on the right side of the law unless you want your vacation to include a stay on Riker's Island (you don't).

Money belts may be dorky and bulky, but it's better to be embarrassed than broke. You'd be wise to carry all cash, traveler's checks, credit cards, and your passport there or in some other inaccessible place: front or inner pocket, or a bag that fits underneath your clothes. Waist packs are safe if you keep the pack part in front of your body. Don't take naps on the train, and **never leave your belongings unguarded,** even if you're only planning to be gone for a minute.

PRECAUTIONS FOR WOMEN

Solo women travelers often have to put on a tough and surly facade to avoid unwelcome advances. You can take some comfort in knowing that some 1.1 million single women call New York home, but you'll still need to take some precautions, especially at night. Obviously, **avoid situations where you're alone** with a stranger—in a subway car, for example, or at an ATM machine. On city streets, **walk briskly and with confidence,** even if you're lost; you can duck into a café or shop to discreetly check your map. Your best bet is to hook up with fellow travelers whom you feel you can trust, then enjoy exploring the city together.

RESOURCES • Women's Action Alliance (370 Lexington Ave., tel. 212/532–8330). **Young Women's Christian Association** (YWCA; 610 Lexington Ave., at E. 53rd St., tel. 212/755–4500), which offers social-service programs and accommodation referrals for women. **National Organization for Women** (NOW; 105 E. 22nd St., Suite 307, New York, NY 10010, tel. 212/260–4422), which offers regular meetings, support groups, lectures, and referrals.

STUDENTS

To save money, **look into deals available through student-oriented travel agencies** and the various other organizations involved in helping out student and budget travelers. Typically, you'll find discounted airfares, rail passes, tours, lodgings, or other travel arrangements, and you don't necessarily have to be a student to qualify.

The big names in the field are STA Travel, with some 100 offices worldwide and a useful Web site (http://www.sta-travel.com), and the Council on International Educational Exchange (CIEE or "Council" for short), a private, nonprofit organization that administers work, volunteer, academic, and professional programs worldwide and sells travel arrangements through its own specialist travel agency, Council Travel. Travel CUTS, strictly a travel agency, sells discounted airline tickets to Canadian students from offices on or near college campuses. The Educational Travel Center (ETC) books low-cost flights to destinations within the continental United States and around the world. And Student Flights, Inc., specializes in student and faculty airfares.

Most of these organizations also issue student identity cards, which entitle their bearers to special fares on local transportation and discounts at museums, theaters, sports events, and other attractions, as well as a handful of other benefits, which are listed in the handbook that most provide to their cardholders. Major cards include the International Student Identity Card (ISIC) and Go 25: International Youth Travel Card (GO25), available to nonstudents as well as students age 25 and under; the ISIC, when purchased in the United States, comes with $3,000 in emergency medical coverage and a few related benefits. Both the ISIC and GO25 are issued by Council Travel or STA in the United States, Travel CUTS in Canada, at student unions and student-travel companies in the United Kingdom, and by STA in Australia. The International Student Exchange Card (ISE), issued by Student Flights, Inc., is available to faculty members as well as students, and the International Teacher Identity Card (ITIC), issued by Travel CUTS, provides similar benefits to teachers in all grade levels, from kindergarten through graduate school. All student ID cards cost between $10 and $20.

STUDENT IDS & SERVICES • Council on International Educational Exchange (CIEE; 205 E. 42nd St., 14th floor, New York, NY 10017, tel. 212/822–2600 or 888/268–6245, fax 212/822–2699), for mail orders only, in the United States.

HOSTELS

If you want to scrimp on lodging, **look into hostels.** In some 5,000 locations in more than 70 countries around the world, Hostelling International (HI), the umbrella group for a number of national youth hostel associations, offers single-sex, dorm-style beds and, at many hostels, "couples" rooms and family accommodations. Membership in any HI national hostel association, open to travelers of all ages, allows you to stay in HI-affiliated hostels at member rates (one-year membership about $25 for adults; hostels about $10–$25 per night). Members also have priority if the hostel is full; they're eligible for discounts around the world, even on rail and bus travel in some countries. There are also two international hostel directories, one on Europe and the Mediterranean, the other covering Africa, the Americas, Asia, and the Pacific ($13.95 each).

ORGANIZATIONS • Hostelling International—American Youth Hostels (HI–AYH; 733 15th St. NW, Suite 840, Washington, DC 20005, tel. 202/783–6161, fax 202/783–6171). **Hostelling International—Canada** (HI–C; 400–205 Catherine St., Ottawa, Ontario K2P 1C3, tel. 613/237–7884, fax 613/237–7868). **Youth Hostel Association of England and Wales** (YHA; Trevelyan House, 8 St. Stephen's Hill, St. Albans, Hertfordshire AL1 2DY, tel. 01727/855215 or 01727/845047, fax 01727/844126). **Australian Youth Hostels Association** (YHA; Level 3, 10 Mallett St., Camperdown, New South Wales 2050, tel. 02/565–1699). **Youth Hostels Association of New Zealand** (YHA; Box 436, Christchurch 1, tel. 3/379–9970).

YMCA

Y's Way International is a network of YMCA overnight centers offering low-cost accommodations (average overnight rate of $40) in New York City (224 E. 47th St., New York, NY 10017, tel. 212/308–2899), around the United States, and around the world to travelers of all ages. Its booklet, "The Y's Way," details locations, reservation policies, and package tours.

Anything can happen on New York subways, from meeting the love of your life to being accosted by a some freak claiming to be from Jupiter. The underground network is a city of its own, a place to buy flowers, catch some live music, or have your shoes shined.

SUBWAY TRAVEL

New York's subway system is amazing—it covers Manhattan and the outer boroughs thoroughly, it's quick and easy to use, and it's air-conditioned (on the trains). The city's 714-mi system operates 24 hours a day and is used by over 3.5 million people daily, but it's safest to avoid deserted subway platforms and cars late at night.

Subway fare is $1.50, although reduced fares are available for senior citizens and people with disabilities during nonrush hours. If you're just taking a few trips, you should pay with tokens (available at token booths in the subway). It's better to **buy more than one token at a time to avoid waiting in lines later.** To enter the subway, simply drop a token ($1.50) into the turnstile; you can now ride anywhere you want and transfer as many times as you wish before exiting. For four or more trips, you may find it easier to use the new MetroCard, a plastic card with a magnetic strip; swipe it through the reader on the turnstile, and the cost of the fare is automatically deducted. You can buy a card for a minimum of $3 and a maximum of $80. More than one person can use the same card. The MetroCard also enables you to transfer free from bus to subway, subway to bus, or bus to bus within two hours. But, if you lose your MetroCard, you've lost all the credits you paid for, so keep it in a safe place.

A quick orientation for the first-time straphanger: Express trains only stop at major stations and transfer points, while local trains stop at every station. You can transfer to another subway line free of charge at many express stations—just follow the easy-to-read signs from platform to platform. Also, maps are posted at every subway station and inside every car. Subway station entrances are often specific to uptown or downtown trains; be sure you enter on the correct side. If there's a green globe light outside the station, that means the station is open and there's a transit clerk inside. A red globe means the entrance is closed. All stations have off-hours waiting areas (usually near the staffed booth), designated by bright yellow signs. If you're at all concerned about your safety, wait in one of these areas rather than wandering off alone.

For schedule information, *see* Transportation, *below*.

TAXIS & CAR SERVICES

The only real difference between taxis and car services is that a taxi is yellow and a car-service sedan is not. Taxis run on a meter (charging by the amount of time a trip takes) while car services charge a flat fee based on distance, no matter how long the trip takes. Most of the time, the price ends up being about the same. The only times car services come in handy are when you're going cross-town (which tends to be slower going), when you're traveling during commute-hour traffic (especially to and from the airports), or when you're in the outer boroughs late at night and can't find a taxi.

There are 12,053 yellow cabs and 30,000 private cars (including limos) for hire in the city. The **New York City Taxi and Limousine Commission** (TLC; tel. 212/692–8294) calculates that there are about 30,000 "gypsy" taxi drivers out there as well; these drivers are not licensed by the taxi commission and often do not even have a driver's license, much less insurance. Licensed private cars must display a decal in the shape of a diamond on the right-hand side of their windshields—look for it. There is now a flat $30 fee for travel from JFK to Manhattan (*not* from the city to the airport) for taxis and private car services.

TAXIS

With the exception of rainy days, when everyone wants a cab, all you have to do is stick out your arm and about four taxis should come careening toward you for the fare. (There are fewer free cabs on rainy days.) Taxis cost $2 for the first ⅕ mi, 30¢ for each ⅕ mi thereafter, 30¢ for each 90 seconds in standing traffic, plus a 50¢ surcharge daily 8 PM–6 AM. There is no surcharge for additional people or luggage. Still, taxi fare adds up pretty quickly, so unless you're rich stick with public transportation—unless it's late at night or you don't feel safe in a particular neighborhood. Because a taxi's meter calculates time as well as distance, the meter should click, adding another 30¢ about every four blocks while you're moving at a good clip. In slow traffic, or when you're traveling crosstown, the meter may click as often as every block. Sadly, drivers have been known to manipulate their meters in all kinds of crafty ways to speed them up and stick you with a higher fare—like the one chap who connected his meter to the radio, so that every time he turned up the volume, his meter increased the rate.

Be sure to ask for, and save, your receipt so if you have a complaint about a taxi, or wish to compliment the driver, or if you leave something in the car, the Taxi Commission can locate the car and driver easily.

CAR SERVICES

In order to use a car service, you must call ahead. Most companies have a flat-rate chart they consult for different distances and for different times of the day. The rate per mile is about $2. Some charge extra for large luggage and additional passengers. A few reliable services include **Highbridge Car Service** (tel. 212/927–4600), **Carmel** (tel. 212/666–6666), and **Tel-Aviv** (tel. 212/777–7777).

TELEPHONES

The area code for Manhattan is 212. Any call from Manhattan to another area code must be dialed like so: 1 + (area code) + (seven-digit number). The Bronx, Brooklyn, Queens, and Staten Island are in area code 718. Most cellular phones and pagers in New York City are in area code 917. For local directory assistance, dial 411. For long-distance help, dial the area code plus 555–1212. If you don't know the area code or need help with a local call, dial 0 for the operator; for long-distance or international calls, dial 00. To find out if a particular business has an 800 number, call 800/555–1212.

Calls to Canada can be dialed as regular long-distance calls. To reach any other country, dial 011, the country code, the city code (dropping the initial zero if there is one), then the actual number. The country code for Great Britain is 44, Ireland 353, New Zealand 64, and Australia 61. Rates vary widely, depending on the hour of your call; ask a long-distance operator for exact rates.

Charges for collect calls are higher than for normal long-distance calls, so if you want to keep your friends, give them your number so they can call you back. (Not all pay phones accept incoming calls, so read the fine print on the phone before trying this.) Station-to-station is the standard collect call; anyone answering at the number you dial can accept the charges. Less common, and even more expensive, is a person-to-person call, which authorizes only the person whose name you give to the operator to accept the charges. On the upside, you won't be charged if the person you want to reach is out. Collect calls can be made by dialing 0 + the number or, more cheaply, by dialing 800/COLLECT.

There are more than 58,000 public telephones in New York, which translates to one on almost every street corner. Of those that work (probably about half), most allow you to place international calls and use a calling card. Pay phones cost 25¢ for the first three minutes of a local call (this includes calls between 212 and 718 area codes); an extra deposit is required for each additional minute. Local directory-assistance calls are free.

CALLING LONG DISTANCE

AT&T, MCI, and Sprint long-distance services make calling home relatively convenient and let you avoid hotel surcharges. In the United States, you typically dial an 800 number.

At the **AT&T Public Calling Center,** on the Main Concourse level of Grand Central Terminal (E. 42nd St. and Park Ave., Midtown), you can make long-distance calls in relative quiet using a credit card or calling card. It's open weekdays 7 AM–9 PM.

TIPPING

The customary tipping rate is 15% for taxi drivers and waiters. You can do the math quickly in restaurants by just doubling the tax noted on the check—it's 8¼% of your bill—and rounding up or down. Bartenders should get between 50¢ and $1 per drink, or more if you're sloshed. Hotel maids and porters should be tipped about $1. Tip $1 per coat checked.

TOUR OPERATORS

Buying a vacation package can make your trip to New York less expensive. The tour operators who put them together may handle several hundred thousand travelers per year and can use their purchasing power to give you a good price. Their high volume may also indicate financial stability. But some small companies provide more personalized service; because they tend to specialize, they may also be more knowledgeable about a given area.

A GOOD DEAL?

The more your package includes, the better you can predict the ultimate cost of your vacation. Make sure you know exactly what is covered, and **beware of hidden costs.** Are taxes, tips, and service charges included? Transfers and baggage handling? Entertainment and excursions? These add up.

If the package you are considering is priced lower than in your wildest dreams, **be skeptical.** Ask about the hotel's location, room size, beds, and whether it has a pool, room service, or programs for children, if you care.

BUYER BEWARE

Each year consumers are stranded or lose their money when tour operators—even large ones with excellent reputations—go out of business. So **check out the operator.** Find out how long the company has been in business, and ask for references that you can check. And **don't book unless the firm has a consumer-protection program.**

Members of the National Tour Association and United States Tour Operators Association are required to set aside funds to cover your payments and travel arrangements in case the company defaults. Nonmembers may carry insurance instead. Look for the details, and for the name of an underwriter with a solid reputation, in the operator's brochure. And when it comes to tour operators, **don't trust escrow accounts.** Although there are laws governing charter-flight operators, no governmental body prevents tour operators from raiding the till. For more information, *see* Consumer Protection, *above.*

TOUR-OPERATOR RECOMMENDATIONS • National Tour Association (NTA, 546 E. Main St., Lexington, KY 40508, tel. 606/226–4444 or 800/755–8687). **United States Tour Operators Association** (USTOA, 342 Madison Ave., Suite 1522, New York, NY 10173, tel. 212/599–6599, fax 212/599–6744).

USING AN AGENT

A good travel agent is an excellent resource. When shopping for one, **collect brochures from several sources** and remember that some agents' suggestions may be skewed by promotional relationships with tour and package firms that reward them for volume sales. If you have a special interest, **find an agent with expertise in that area** (*see* Travel Agencies, *below*).

SINGLE TRAVELERS

Remember that prices for vacation packages are usually quoted per person, based on two sharing a room. If traveling solo, you may be required to pay the full double-occupancy rate.

PACKAGES

The companies listed below offer vacation packages in a broad price range.

AIR/HOTEL • Continental Vacations (tel. 800/634–5555). **Delta Dream Vacations** (tel. 800/872–7786, fax 954/357–4687). **United Vacations** (tel. 800/328–6877). **US Airways Vacations** (tel. 800/455–0123). **Amtrak's Great American Vacations** (tel. 800/321–8684).

CUSTOM PACKAGES • Amtrak's Great American Vacations (tel. 800/321–8684).

HOTEL ONLY • SuperCities (139 Main St., Cambridge, MA 02142, tel. 800/333–1234).

FROM THE U.K. • Americana Vacations Ltd. (11 Little Portland St., London W1 5ND, tel. 0171/637–7853). **Jetsave** (Sussex House, London Rd., East Grinstead, West Sussex RH19 1LD, tel. 01342/312033). **Key to America** (1–3 Station Rd., Ashford, Middlesex, TW15 2UW, tel. 01784/248–777). **Premier Holidays** (Westbrook, Milton Rd., Cambridge CB4 1YQ, tel. 01223/516–688). **Trailfinders** (42–50 Earls Court Rd., London W8 6FT, tel. 0171/937–5400; 58 Deansgate, Manchester M3 2FF, tel. 0161/839–6969). **Travelpack** (Clarendon House, Clarendon Rd., Eccles, Manchester M30 9AL, tel. 0990/747–101).

THEME TRIPS

CULTURAL TOURS • IST Cultural Tours (225 W. 34th St., New York, NY 10122-0913, tel. 212/563–1202 or 800/833–2111, fax 212/594–6953).

PERFORMING ARTS • Dailey-Thorp Travel (330 W. 58th St., #610, New York, NY 10019-1817, tel. 212/307–1555 or 800/998–4677, fax 212/974–1420). **Keith Prowse Tours** (234 W. 44th St., #1000, New York, NY 10036, tel. 212/398–1430 or 800/669–8687, fax 212/302–4251). **Sutherland Hit Show Tours** (370 Lexington Ave., #411, New York, NY 10017, tel. 212/532–7732 or 800/221–2442, fax 212/532–7741).

SPAS • Spa-Finders (91 5th Ave., #301, New York, NY 10003-3039, tel. 212/924–6800 or 800/255–7727).

TENNIS • Championship Tennis Tours (7350 E. Stetson Dr., #106, Scottsdale, AZ 85251, tel. 602/990–8760 or 800/468–3664, fax 602/990–8744). **Dan Chavez's Sports Empire** (Box 6169, Lakewood, CA 90714-6169, tel. 310/920–2350 or 800/255–5258). **Esoteric Sports Tours** (2005 Woods River La., Duluth, GA 30155, tel. 770/622–8872 or 800/321–8008, fax 770/622–8866). **Spectacular Sport Specials** (5813 Citrus Blvd., New Orleans, LA 70123-5810, tel. 504/734–9511 or 800/451–5772, fax 504/734–7075). **Steve Furgal's International Tennis Tours** (11828 Rancho Bernardo Rd., #123-305, San Diego, CA 92128, tel. 619/675–3555 or 800/258–3664).

TRAIN TRAVEL

Unlike the rest of this car-obsessed country, people on the East Coast actually rely on trains to get from city to city or commute from home to work. Departures are frequent and fares are cheap. New York City has two major railroad stations: **Pennsylvania Station** (W. 31st–34th Sts. between 7th and 8th Aves.; Subway A, C, E, 1, 2, 3, or 9 to W. 34th St.) and **Grand Central Terminal** (W. 42nd–45th Sts. at Park Ave.; Subway 4, 5, 6, or 7 to Grand Central). Trains bound for Grand Central also stop at the tiny 125th Street Station (125th St. at Park Ave.; Subway 4, 5, or 6 to E. 125th St.).

AMTRAK

Amtrak (tel. 212/582–6875 or 800/875–7245) is the only passenger rail service in the United States. It's also a damn fine way to travel to New York; you get a dining car, a smoking lounge (if you're so inclined), and lots of pretty scenery. Trains arrive daily at Pennsylvania Station (*see above*) from Boston (5 hrs, $43 one-way), Philadelphia (1½ hrs, $36), Washington, D.C. (3½ hrs, $60), Chicago (18 hrs, $141), Seattle (2¾ days, $259), Los Angeles (3 days, $259), and many other American cities. Fares fluctuate according to time of the year and other factors (they're generally higher on Fridays and holidays), so call ahead for the latest ticket info.

RAIL PASSES • Amtrak's All-Aboard America Fare, actually a booklet of tickets, allows riders special rates for three stops made in 45 days of travel. Ticket agents need to know your dates of travel and intended destinations for ticketing, so reserve in advance. Cost is $198–$378, depending on the season and the number of regions traveled. Amtrak's **USARail Pass** is terrific for the foreign budget traveler (it's not available to U.S. or Canadian citizens) because it allows unlimited travel on any of Amtrak's U.S. routes, with no formal itinerary required. A 15-day pass costs $355 ($245 September–May), a 30-day pass $440 ($350). You can buy one at a travel agency in your home country before you leave or from an Amtrak office in the States. A passport and visa are required for purchase, and reservations are recommended several months in advance.

REGIONAL TRAIN SERVICES

Whether you're a freshman at Yale or a visitor crashing at your aunt's house in Greenwich, Connecticut, there's a train to take you into New York City. One-way fares from most destinations cost less than $12; purchase your ticket before you board to avoid a $1–$3 lazy person's surcharge. The **Metro-North Commuter Railroad** (tel. 212/532–4900) serves New York's northern suburbs and southern Connecticut, terminating in New Haven. The **Long Island Railroad** (LIRR; tel. 718/217–5477) runs through Long Island, smarty. **New Jersey Transit** (tel. 201/762–5100) offers service from towns in northern and central New Jersey, including Princeton. In Manhattan, Metro-North trains stop at Grand Central Terminal and at 125th Street; the LIRR and New Jersey Transit lines terminate at Pennsylvania Station.

PATH

The **PATH** (tel. 800/234–7284) trains run between New York City and terminals in New Jersey (including Hoboken, Jersey City, and Newark). In Manhattan, PATH stations are at the World Trade Center; on Christopher Street (at Greenwich Street); and along 6th Avenue at West 9th, 14th, 23rd, and 33rd streets. Trains run 24 hours and depart every 10–30 minutes. The fare is $1.

TRANSPORTATION

The **Metro Transit Authority** (MTA) publishes excellent fold-out maps that show all the subway and bus routes and stops; ask for one in any subway station. You might also want to request the MTA's booklet, "Token Trips: New York City Subway and Bus Travel Guide," which lists every conceivable attraction in the city with easy-to-follow travel directions. The tiny "Transitwise NY Metropolitan Commuter Rail Map" ($6.95) is worth purchasing if you don't want to advertise your tourist status, because it shows all Manhattan subways and buses, but tri-folds to fit in a pocket. It's available at bookstores and newsstands. For general city bus and subway travel info, call the **MTA/New York City Transit hotline** (tel. 718/330–1234), staffed daily 6 AM–9 PM, or the **Multilingual Transit hot line** (tel. 718/330–4847), staffed daily 6 AM–9:30 PM. For info on ferry service to the Statue of Liberty, Ellis Island, and Staten Island, *see* Chapter 2.

TRAVEL AGENCIES

A good travel agent puts your needs first. **Look for an agency that specializes in your destination, has been in business at least five years, and emphasizes customer service.** If you're looking for an agency-organized package, choose an agency that's a member of the National Tour Association or the United States Tour Operator's Association (*see* Tour Operators, *above*).

LOCAL AGENT REFERRALS • American Society of Travel Agents (ASTA; 1101 King St., Suite 200, Alexandria, VA 22314, tel. 703/739–2782, fax 703/684–8319). **Alliance of Canadian Travel Associations** (1729 Bank St., Suite 201, Ottawa, Ontario K1V 7Z5, tel. 613/521–0474, fax 613/521–0805). **Association of British Travel Agents** (55–57 Newman St., London W1P 4AH, tel. 0171/637–2444, fax 0171/637–0713).

TRAVEL GEAR

Travel catalogs specialize in nifty items that can save space when packing.

MAIL-ORDER CATALOGS • Magellan's (tel. 800/962–4943, fax 805/568–5406). **Orvis Travel** (tel. 800/541–3541, fax 540/343–7053). **TravelSmith** (tel. 800/950–1600, fax 800/950–1656).

U.S. GOVERNMENT

The U.S. government can be an excellent source of inexpensive travel information. When planning your trip, **find out what government materials are available.**

ADVISORIES • U.S. Department of State American Citizens Services Office (Room 4811, Washington, DC 20520); enclose a self-addressed, stamped envelope. Interactive hot line (tel. 202/647–5225, fax 202/647–3000). Computer bulletin board (tel. 202/647–9225).

PAMPHLETS • Consumer Information Center (Consumer Information Catalogue, Pueblo, CO 81009, tel. 719/948–3334) for a free catalog that includes travel titles.

VISITOR INFORMATION

Contact the New York City visitors information offices below for brochures, subway and bus maps, a calendar of events, listings of hotels and weekend hotel packages, and discount coupons for Broadway shows. For a free "I Love New York" booklet listing New York City attractions and tour packages, contact the New York State Division of Tourism.

CITY INFORMATION • New York Convention and Visitors Bureau (2 Columbus Circle, New York, NY 10019, tel. 212/484–1200, fax 212/484–1280), weekdays 9–5; **New York City Visitors Information Center** (tel. 212/397–8222).

STATEWIDE INFORMATION • New York State Division of Tourism (1 Commerce Ave., Albany, NY 12245, tel. 518/474–4116 or 800/225–5697).

VOLUNTEERING

A variety of volunteer programs are available. Council (*see* Students, *above*) is a key player, running its own roster of projects and publishing a directory that lists other sponsor organizations, *Volunteer! The Comprehensive Guide to Voluntary Service in the U.S. and Abroad* ($12.95 plus $1.50 postage). Service Civil International (SCI), International Voluntary Service (IVS), and Volunteers for Peace (VFP) run two- and three-week short workcamps; VFP also publishes the *International Workcamp Directory* ($12). WorldTeach programs, run by Harvard University, require that you commit a year to teaching on subjects ranging from English and science to carpentry, forestry, and sports.

RESOURCES • SCI/IVS (5474 Walnut Level Rd., Crozet, VA 22932, tel. 804/823–1826). **VFP** (43 Tiffany Rd., Belmont, VT 05730, tel. 802/259–2759, fax 802/259–2922). **WorldTeach** (1 Eliot St., Cambridge, MA 02138-5705, tel. 617/495–5527 or 800/483–2240, fax 617/495–1599).

WHEN TO GO

CLIMATE

If you don't like the weather in New York, goes the old joke, wait a minute. Temperatures not only fluctuate dramatically from season to season, they often change from balmy to miserable and back again in a single afternoon. In winter, lows can hit 15°F (-9°C), with or without wicked winds and blizzards of snow. Summers bring hotter-than-hell temperatures coupled with 99.9% humidity. Because New York is so awfully hot in summer, many locals get the hell out June–August, when the streets are quieter, the bars are less crowded, and the ratio of tourists to locals jumps way up.

Without a doubt, fall and spring are the best times of year to visit New York, both in terms of the weather and the scenery. In fall the city's parks turn golden, and there's something about the smell of roasting chestnuts carried on a crisp autumn breeze that makes you feel at peace with the world. In spring, usually by early April, the snow melts for good, flowers start blooming, and the birds start singing—ah, sylvan Manhattan. The following chart shows the average highs and lows in Manhattan:

Jan.	41°F	5°C	May	70°F	21°C	Sept.	76°F	24°C
	29	-2		54	12		61	16
Feb.	43°F	6°C	June	81°F	27°C	Oct.	67°F	19°C
	29	-2		63	17		52	11
Mar.	47°F	8°C	July	85°F	29°C	Nov.	56°F	13°C
	34	1		70	21		43	6
Apr.	61°F	16°C	Aug.	83°F	28°C	Dec.	43°F	6°C
	45	7		68	20		31	-1

FORECASTS • Weather Channel Connection (tel. 900/932–8437), 95¢ per minute from a Touch-Tone phone.

FESTIVALS

Every month of the year finds some kind of celebration or happening, whether it's a daylong parade up 5th Avenue or a summer-long series of performances. The huge diversity of people in New York adds plenty of spice to the mix—a wild proliferation of events celebrating different groups and all kinds of ethnic holidays, from the huge St. Patrick's Day parade to the Festival of San Gennaro in Little Italy. For more festival info ask at the NYCVB (*see* Visitor Information, *above*) for a calendar of events or get a copy of the *Village Voice, Time Out, The New Yorker,* or the Friday edition of the *New York Times.* For info on free summer concerts and music festivals, *see* Summer Arts *in* Chapter 7.

JANUARY • For New Year's Eve you have two very different options: Hang out with drunken out-of-towners on Times Square and watch the famous ball drop at midnight, or catch a free midnight fireworks display in Central Park. On New Year's Day the Polar Bear Club takes its annual swim in the frigid Atlantic, at Coney Island.

The **Winter Antiques Show** (tel. 212/665–5250), held near the end of the month at the Seventh Regiment Armory (Park Ave. at E. 67th St.), is one of the nation's largest. It sounds dull, but it's actually pretty cool if you like antiques.

FEBRUARY • In Chinatown the streets crackle with firecrackers, hailing the **Chinese New Year,** on the first full moon after January 21, with processions and a dragon parade. The main parade starts on Mott Street in Chinatown and continues down Canal Street and East Broadway. *Tel. 212/267–5780 or 212/744–8188.*

It's a dog-eat-dog world (not literally) at Madison Square Garden, as Schnauzers, Rottweilers, and Afghan hounds compete for the title of champion at the **Westminster Kennel Club Dog Show.** Believe it or not, this is a big deal in New York. The show is usually held the second Monday and Tuesday of February, but in 1998 it will take place on February 16 and 17. (After 1998 it will resume its normal schedule.) *Tel. 212/682–6852.*

MARCH • The gargantuan **Art Expo** (tel. 216/826–2858 or 800/827–7170), at the Jacob K. Javits Convention Center, includes cultural performances from around the world. For blooms, check out Bronx's New York Botanical Gardens' **Spring Flower Show** (tel. 718/817–8700). The Sunday **Easter Parade** (April 12 in 1998) is all about people in extravagantly odd hats sauntering along 5th Avenue from 49th Street to 59th Street.

The **St. Patrick's Day Parade** is the city's biggest event, held every March 17 on 5th Avenue between 44th and 86th streets. The four-hour parade features lots of beer, green hats, and woozy marchers. In the past few years it's also featured an unsanctioned band of Irish gays and lesbians protesting their exclusion from the official ceremonies. *Tel. 212/484–1200.*

MAY • The **Cherry Blossom Festival,** held at the Brooklyn Botanic Garden, includes haiku readings, taiko drumming, the ancient tea ceremony, and exhibits of Japanese art. *Tel. 718/622–4433. Free with paid admission to garden ($3).*

On the first Sunday after May 17, Brooklyn's thriving Scandinavian community parties down at the annual **Norwegian Constitution Day Parade** in Bay Ridge. The **Loisada Street Fair** takes place on the last weekend in May, celebrating those hip and funky inhabitants of the Loisada (Lower East Side).

The Brooklyn Academy of Music (*see* Arts Centers *in* Chapter 7) hosts the largest annual gathering of African-American dance companies in the States for **Dance Africa.** Accompanying the performances are classes, discussions, and a bazaar with African-American crafts and foods.

Navy ships from the United States and abroad are joined by Coast Guard ships during **Fleet Week** for a parade up the Hudson River, then a docking in Manhattan during which ships are open to the public. It all happens at the *Intrepid* Air, Sea, and Space Museum (*see* Museums and Galleries *in* Chapter 2) during the week before Memorial Day.

Ninth Avenue, site of the most varied ethnic foods in the city, closes to traffic between West 34th and West 57th streets when it hosts the **Ninth Avenue International Food Festival** for an entire weekend so chefs can show off their stuff. *Tel. 212/581–7217 or 212/581–7029.*

New York's Ukrainian community whoops it up at the **Ukrainian Festival,** an East Village affair, held on the weekend between Mother's Day and Memorial Day. *E. 7th St. between 2nd and 3rd Aves., tel. 212/674–1615.*

At the **Washington Square Art Show,** artists display their work around this Village park on Memorial Day weekend and the following weekend, and then again during the first two weekends of September. *5th Ave. at Washington Sq. North, West Village, tel. 212/982–6255.*

JUNE • East Broadway between Rutgers and Montgomery streets is the site of the **Lower East Side Jewish Spring Festival,** held on the second Sunday in June.

New York's **Gay Pride Parade,** held on the last Sunday in June, commemorates the 1969 Stonewall riots—considered by many the birth of the gay rights movement. *Tel. 212/807–7433.*

The wild and wacky **Mermaid Parade** along the Coney Island boardwalk celebrates the summer solstice; marching bands and antique cars share the procession with people dressed like creatures of the sea. *Tel. 718/372–5159.*

During the annual **Museum Mile Festival,** 5th Avenue from 82nd Street to 104th Street is closed to traffic 6–9 PM. Admission to the Mile's museums is either free or greatly reduced. *Tel. 212/606–2296 or 212/397–8222.*

During the raucous **Puerto Rican Day Parade,** flag-waving Puerto Ricans jam the streets for an exuberant celebration of one of New York's biggest immigrant groups. Join the crowds on 5th Avenue between 44th and 86th streets. *Tel. 212/484–1200.*

For two weeks the Italian **St. Anthony of Padua Feast** is held on Sullivan Street from Spring to Houston streets in SoHo; carnival rides, street vendors, and joviality climax in a grand pageant. Hooray! *Tel. 212/777–2755.*

JULY • On American **Independence Day** (July 4), the city explodes with illicit and legit fireworks (the East Village sounds like a war zone). And keep an eye out for the **African Street Festival** in Brooklyn's Bedford-Stuyvesant neighborhood, a weeklong block party celebrating African-American culture.

AUGUST • The **Caribbean Cultural Center** produces Carnival (tel. 212/307–7420), held the first weekend in August and celebrating people of the African diaspora. The last Sunday in August sees **Fiesta Folklorica,** a Latin American festival in Central Park. Harlem celebrates its heritage with **Harlem Week** (tel. 212/427–7200), a weeklong bash of cultural events.

SEPTEMBER • New York's biggest German-American event is the **German-American Steuben Parade** along 5th Avenue from 64th to 86th streets on the third weekend in September (tel. 516/239–0741). Mulberry Street in Little Italy is the site of the hugely popular **Festival of San Gennaro,** an Italian street carnival—the entire street is lined with arcade games, sellers of Italian kitsch, and stands selling greasy snacks or cotton candy.

The three-day **New York is Book Country** festival, in mid-September, celebrates books of all kinds. On one afternoon, 5th Avenue from 48th to 57th streets is closed and handed over to publishers, bookstores, and small presses displaying their wares. *Tel. 212/207–7242.*

The **New York Film Festival,** held late September–early October, is the premier showcase for dozens of films from around the world—and your best bet for seeing directors and actors at the opening of their films. The **New York Video Festival** runs concurrently. *140 W. 65th St., at Broadway, tel. 212/875–5050.*

OCTOBER • The **Columbus Day Parade** (tel. 212/249–9923), the second-largest in New York after St. Paddy's Day, is held around October 12 on 5th Avenue between 44th and 86th streets. The Cathedral of St. John the Divine (Amsterdam Ave. at W. 112th St., tel. 212/316–7540) is the site of the **Feast of St. Francis** on the first Sunday in October, featuring a Blessing of the Animals. The **International Expressions Festival** is a monthlong affair highlighting Caribbean and African-diaspora cultures (tel. 212/307–7420).

NOVEMBER • The **New York City Marathon,** in early November, is one of the world's most prestigious, featuring racers from around the world. Starting at the Verrazano-Narrows Bridge in Staten Island, the race proceeds through Brooklyn, Queens, and the South Bronx before finishing at Tavern on the Green in Central Park. *Tel. 212/860–4455.*

Macy's **Thanksgiving Parade** takes place on Thanksgiving Day, beginning at Central Park West and 77th Street, heading down to Columbus Circle, and then snaking down Broadway to 34th Street. The night before finds many New Yorkers watching the whole shindig being prepared—somebody's gotta blow those balloons up—on Central Park West from 77th to 88th streets. *Tel. 212/695–4400.*

DECEMBER • In late November or early December a Christmas tree is lit up at **Rockefeller Center** (5th Ave. at 50th St., tel. 212/632–3975). The scene is *very* New York. With the annual **Christmas Spec-**

tacular (tel. 212/247–4777), Radio City Music Hall puts on its Christmas bash through January 4; expect rapping elves and lots of lasers. The hyper-consumptive 5th Avenue is closed to traffic on the two Sundays before Christmas so people can go berserk with their credit cards. **Kwanzaa,** an African-American holiday, celebrates the "first fruits of the harvest" (as the name means in Swahili) and includes various cultural events and fairs at the Jacob K. Javitz Convention Center.

EXPLORING NEW YORK CITY

UPDATED BY DAVID LOW, AMY MCCONNELL, JENNIFER PAULL, BRENT PEICH,

HELAYNE SCHIFF, MIRA SCHWIRTZ, JILLIAN STONE

O n returning from a visit, Charles Dickens once described New York City as "a vast amount of good and evil intermixed and jumbled up together." Though he pissed off a great number of his American readers, he made an excellent point. You'll need to endure a bit of evil, whether it's a rude taxi driver or a heavy-breathing guy standing next to you at an ATM, to discover the beauty of this city. Don't be scared by the throngs of tourists lined up to make the trip to the top of the World Trade Center or the Empire State Building—nowhere else on earth can you get views so vertigo-inducing. Though your bladder may rupture before you find one of its hidden rest rooms, the Metropolitan Museum of Art has days' worth of stunning art and artifacts to view, and a stroll over the Brooklyn Bridge at sunset has to be one of the best 1-mi walks anywhere.

Don't forget to stray off the beaten path: Hop on the subway to Fort Tryon Park, get up at 5 in the morning to see the fishmongers close shop at the Fulton Fish Market, or spend the afternoon in a Hell's Kitchen Irish pub drinking Guinness with regulars who probably have been glued to their bar stools for the past four decades. The outer boroughs have major attractions, too: The mammoth Brooklyn Museum, the world-famous Bronx Zoo, and the New York Botanical Gardens are just a few examples, and all are certainly worth day trips.

Wherever you go, you'll find New York's subway system extremely efficient, perfect for those of you engaged in the see-and-flee mode of sightseeing. That said, moving around Manhattan by bus or, better yet, on your own two feet is the ideal way to get a real feel for the city. New York's street life—its glamour, its frenetic pace, even its occasional hints of evil—is an important element of any visit.

GUIDED TOURS

If you were planning to skip this section because you bristle at the thought of being led around by the nose like a show pony, stop and reconsider. Not all guided tours will treat you like you're on a fourth-grade field trip. Indeed, if you're new to New York and unfamiliar with its offerings, doesn't it make sense to turn to an expert? Many of the museums, historical buildings, parks, and other attractions described in this chapter offer guided tours that will give you a rare, behind-the-scenes look at how they operate, or enchant you with historical tidbits and lore. Best of all, many of these tours are absolutely free once you've paid your admission (if any). Some of the most fascinating tours include those at **Lincoln Center,** the **New York Stock Exchange, Carnegie Hall, Times Square,** the **American Museum of Natural History,** the **United Nations,** the **Fulton Fish Market,** the **Steinway & Sons Piano Factory,** the **Brooklyn Botanical Garden,** the **Federal Reserve Bank,** and the **Historic Orchard Street Bargain District,** but of course there are dozens of others. For times and locations, *see below.*

NBC Studio Tour. What could be better for a TV junkie than a one-hour tour ($10) of the sets of NFL Live, Saturday Night Live, Dateline NBC, or the Rosie O'Donnell Show? (Don't set your heart on seeing a particular show's set, however—it may not be available that day.) Plus, you'll peek at behind-the-scenes stuff like tons of technical gizmos, and look at all of NBC's broadcast milestones. There's also a demonstration of the three elements of TV: light, sound, and action. Tours depart weekdays every 15 minutes (during January and February and September and October every half hour) between 9:30 and 4:30, but arrive early because tickets are usually sold out before noon. *30 Rockefeller Plaza, at 6th Ave., Midtown, tel. 212/664–7174. Subway: B, D, F, or Q to W. 47th–50th Sts./Rockefeller Center.*

WALKING TOURS

Walking tours are one of the best ways to learn about New York and make new friends, all at the same time. And they're not just for tourists: Longtime New Yorkers rely on walking tours to get into some of New York's most inaccessible places, and into places they might not feel comfortable going to on their own. For a guide, you'll usually get some sort of expert, like a professor, graduate student, historian, or author. Most walking tours are held on weekends year-round and require reservations. Walking tours are listed in the "Above and Beyond" section of *The New Yorker's* "Goings On About Town" listings, the "Around Town" section of *Time Out,* and *New York's* "Cue" pages.

There are two types of must-see attractions in New York: those that lifelong New Yorkers dismiss with "never been there," and the kind over which they gush, "you must go there first." Do them both.

Several museums offer walking tours focusing on their particular neighborhood or area of expertise. For tours focusing on New York history, check out the **Cooper-Hewitt Museum** (tel. 212/860–6321), which charges $15, or the **Museum of the City of New York** (tel. 212/534–1672, ext. 206), where you can join a tour for $9. The **New-York Historical Society** (tel. 212/873–3400) asks for a donation of $5 for walking tours relating to their exhibits. If you want out of Manhattan, try the **Brooklyn Historical Society** (tel. 718/624–0890), which offers tours of different Brooklyn neighborhoods for about $12 for nonmembers ($5 for members). The $8 tours offered by the **Lower East Side Tenement Museum** (90 Orchard St., tel. 212/431–0233) focus on the history and culture of Lower East Side immigrant groups—Chinese, Latino, Italian, Irish, German, or Jewish. The **New York Transit Museum** (tel. 718/243–3060) offers tours most weekends and Wednesdays through spooky, abandoned New York City subway tunnels. Wednesday tours are $9, weekend tours $15; reservations are required. For more details on each museum, *see* Museums and Galleries, *below.*

92nd Street Y. The Y's excellent tours range from two hours to a full day, and can take in anything from "Chinatown's Herb Markets" and "Hell's Kitchen: A Political History" to a look inside the Harvard Club or a walk through artists' studios. Tickets cost $15–$25. *1395 Lexington Ave., New York, NY 10128, tel. 212/996–1100. Tours given year-round; call for schedule. Reservations recommended.*

Adventure on a Shoestring. For a bargain $5 you get a 1½-hour tour of the city's less-touristed neighborhoods, like Hell's Kitchen; Astoria, Queens; the Carnegie Hill area on the Upper East Side; Chelsea; or Roosevelt Island. Tours of ethnic neighborhoods end with lunch. *300 W. 53rd St., New York, NY 10019, tel. 212/265–2663. Tours given weekends.*

Big Onion Walking Tours. Grad students pursuing degrees in American history are your enthusiastic guides to attractions such as the Brooklyn Bridge or New York's Revolutionary War sites. There's also a multiethnic eating tour of the Lower East Side, taking in Chinatown, Little Italy, and the Jewish East Side. The 2½-hour tours are $9–$12. *Cherokee Station, Box 20561, New York, NY 10021, tel. 212/439–1090. Most tours given weekends at 1 PM.*

Harlem Your Way! These 2½- to three-hour tours explore Harlem's historic districts and landmarks, like Sugar Hill, Hamilton Grange, and the Apollo Theater. On Sundays, the tour takes in a gospel church service. Cost is $25. *129 W. 130th St., near Adam Clayton Powell Jr. Blvd., New York, NY 10027, tel. 212/690–1687. Tours given Mon.–Sat. at 1:30 PM, Sun. at 10:30 AM. Reservations required.*

Municipal Art Society. The Municipal Art Society's "Discover New York Tours" focus on architecture, history, and urban planning, with offerings like "57th Street: Culture and Kitsch" or "New York's Con-

THE FIVE BOROUGHS

Newark International Airport

Goethals Bridge

Bayonne Bridge

Newark Bay

Pulaski Skyway

Kill Van Kull

ST. GEORGE Terminal
Snug Harbor Cultural Center
Jacques Marchais Museum
Ferry
Liberty

STATEN ISLAND

ROSEBANK

Alice Austen House

Verrazano-Narrows Bridge

Ellis I.

Statue of Liberty

Liberty I.

Battery Tunnel

Holland Tunnel

Tunnel

M

Brooklyn-Battery Tunnel

Brooklyn Bridge

Manhattan Bridge

Williamsburg Bridge

East River

GREENPOINT

WILLIAMSBURG

QUEENS

BAY RIDGE

SUNSET PARK

Queens Expwy.

COBBLE HILL

BROOKLYN HEIGHTS

FORT GREENE

BEDFORD-STUYVESANT

PARK SLOPE

Prospect Park

Atlantic Ave.

Eastern Pkwy.

Brooklyn Museum of Art and Botanic Gardens

FLATBUSH

CROWN HEIGHTS

CANARSIE

Belt Pkwy.

BENSONHURST

Ocean Pkwy.

Flatbush Ave.

Linden Blvd.

Jackie Robinson

BROOKLYN

SHEEPSHEAD BAY

MANHATTAN BEACH

Marine Park

BRIGHTON BEACH

CONEY ISLAND

NY Aquarium

Rockaway Inlet

Jacob Riis Park

Floyd Bennett Field

Gateway National Recreation Area

Jamaica Bay Wildlife Refuge

Cross Bay Blvd.

Rockaway Beach

Southern Pkwy.

J.F.K. International Airport

Expwy.

ATLANTIC OCEAN

NEW JERSEY

Meadowlands
Sports Complex

3

17

80

46

4

95

95

Palisades Pkwy.

Hudson River

George
Washington
Bridge

Spuyten
Duyvil

Wave Hill
RIVERDALE

Van Cortlandt
Park

Woodlawn
Cemetery

WESTCHESTER

MANHATTAN

Central
Park

Harlem R.

Fordham
University
Bronx
Park

Grand Concourse

FORDHAM

BELMONT

Bronx Zoo and New York
Botanical Garden

THE BRONX

Pelham Bay
Park

Orchard
Beach

Long Island
Sound

Queensboro
Bridge

LONG
ISLAND
CITY

Grand Central Pkwy.

ASTORIA

Triborough
Bridge

Yankee
Stadium

Bronx Museum
of the Arts

Crotona
Park

95

East

Eastchester
Bay

City I.

JACKSON
HEIGHTS

Northern Blvd.

La Guardia
Airport

Whitestone
Bridge

River

Little Neck
Bay

FOREST
HILLS

Flushing Meadows-
Corona Park

Queens
Museum

Shea
Stadium

Queens
Botanical
Garden

USTA Nat'l
Tennis Center

FLUSHING

Long Island Expwy.

Throgs Neck
Bridge

NASSAU

JAMAICA

Grand Central Pkwy.

Clearview Expwy.

Cross Island Expwy.

Alley
Pond
Park

N

0

0

5 km

5 miles

SIGHTSEEING ON THE CHEAP

If you want a motorized overview of Manhattan but don't want the perky commentary, save some cash by joining New York's cranky commuters on a standard city bus. On a hot summer day, it's particularly pleasant in the air-conditioning. You won't get the tape-recorded rundown on the sights, but you can use a single subway token or $1.50 in change for any of the following routes:

Bus M1: Battery Park, the World Trade Center, Wall Street, SoHo, Union Square, the New York Public Library, Rockefeller Center, Central Park, the Metropolitan Museum of Art, Museum Mile.

Bus M4: Empire State Building, Central Park, Columbia University, Harlem, the Cloisters Museum, and Fort Tryon Park.

Bus M10: Central Park West, the American Museum of Natural History, Times Square, Chelsea, the West Village, and the World Trade Center.

Bus M11: West Village, Chelsea, Hell's Kitchen, Lincoln Center, the Upper West Side, Columbia University, Riverbank State Park.

Bus M101: City Hall, Chinatown, Little Italy, the East Village, Gramercy, Murray Hill, Grand Central Terminal, the Upper East Side, Martin Luther King Jr. Boulevard in Harlem, and Washington Heights.

---

temporary Architecture." Tours are 1½ hours and cost $10–$15. *Tel. 212/935–3960 or 212/439–1049 for recorded information on tours. Tours given year-round. Reservations recommended for some tours.*

Wildman Steve Brill. The Wildman leads four-hour tours of Greater New York's parks, on which you'll learn how to identify, harvest, and prepare edible and medicinal plants, including berries, mushrooms, roots, herbs, seeds, seaweed, and greens. Suggested donation is $10. *143–25 84th Dr., Suite 6C, Jamaica, NY 11435, tel. 718/291–6825. Tours given weekends and holidays Mar.–1st weekend in Dec.; send SASE for schedule. Reservations required.*

BUS TOURS

Bite the bullet, because you're going to be branded a tacky, cheesy tourist the second you board a tour bus. That said, an air-conditioned bus ride is one of the better ways to explore the city during the summer heat (keep in mind that most double-decker buses don't have air-conditioning). Tours generally zip around on one of 10–20 different routes, stopping for a quick look-see from ground level before hustling off to the next big attraction.

Gray Line Tours. Gray Line aims to please: They offer two types of tours. Double-decker buses follow uptown and downtown loops; armed with a two-day pass, you can get on and off at your leisure, stopping at blockbusters like the Metropolitan Museum of Art, Central Park, the Empire State Building, the World Trade Center, and Chinatown. Gray Line also offers six- to nine-hour motor-coach tours. Reservations for either type of tour are unnecessary; just call for the day's schedule and show up at the new Gray Line terminal (in the Port Authority bus terminal, 42nd Street and 8th Avenue, 42nd Street entrance, street level) 30 minutes before departure. They'll also show you New York by helicopter ($44–$79) and Central Park by trolley car. *Port Authority bus terminal, 42nd St. and 8th Ave., Midtown, tel. 212/397–2600; for information and brochures, write to 1740 Broadway, New York, NY*

[handwritten: $33 42 + 8 Ave]

10019. Subway: A, C, E, 1, 2, 3, or 7 to 42nd St. Tickets: Double-decker tours $19–$36, motor-coach tours $41–$54. Tours daily 8:30–6:30.

Harlem Spirituals, Inc. These multilingual tours of Harlem and other uptown neighborhoods include stops at Hamilton Grange, the neighborhood of Sugar Hill, and a Baptist church service. The jazz tour ($69) includes dinner and club cover charge. *1690 8th Ave., at 43rd St., Midtown, tel. 212/391–0900. Tickets: $30–$75.*

New York Apple Tours. Want to ride around New York in an authentic London double-decker? Here's your chance. These big, bright-red buses run daily 9–6 on three loops: uptown, downtown, and along the Hudson River. A two-day pass with unlimited stops is $30 for all three loops and $21 for the downtown route (there is no pass for the river route only). They also offer nighttime "city lights" tours late May through early October. You can pick up buses at 8th Avenue at 50th Street or 7th Avenue at 41st Street. **New York Doubledecker Tours** (Empire State Bldg., 34th St. and 5th Ave., tel. 212/967–6008) offers similar services. *Tel. 212/944–9200.* *[handwritten: 39]* *[handwritten: 9AM – 6PM $35.00]*

BOAT TOURS

One of the best, and cheapest, ways to see New York by boat is aboard the **Staten Island Ferry** (*see* Staten Island *in* the Outer Boroughs, *below*); as of 1997 it's free. From Pier 16 at the South Street Seaport (*see* Lower Manhattan *in* Manhattan Neighborhoods, *below*) you can take a two-hour voyage ($16) to New York's past aboard the 1885 iron cargo schooner **The Pioneer** (tel. 212/669–9400), or one-hour sightseeing tours ($12) of New York Harbor and Lower Manhattan with **Seaport Liberty Cruises** (tel. 212/425–3737). For info on ferry service to the Statue of Liberty and Ellis Island, *see* Major Attractions, *below*.

Circle Line. More than 40 million passengers have steamed around Manhattan on the eight 165-ft Circle Line yachts since the cruises were inaugurated in 1945. It's one of those true New York experiences—Conan O'Brien and crew even taped an episode of *Late Night* from the deck of a moving Circle Line ship in 1995. Once you've finished the three-hour, 35-mi circumnavigation of Manhattan (or the two-hour Express tour), you'll have a good idea of where things are and what you want to see next, and your hair will possess that sought-after windblown quality. *Pier 83, 12th Ave. at W. 42nd St., Midtown, tel. 212/563–3200. Subway: A, C, or E to W. 42nd St. (Port Authority). Fare: $20, Express tour $17. Call for schedule.*

HORSE-DRAWN CARRIAGE TOURS

Whether it's a frosty, crisp winter morning or a warm summer night, one of the most romantic ways to see the city is by horse-drawn cab. Carriages occasionally go as far as Times Square, but a spin through the southern stretch of Central Park is perfect. Carriages line up on Grand Army Plaza (at the corner of 5th Avenue and 59th Street), and along 59th Street between 5th and 7th avenues. The cost is city-regulated at $34 for the first half hour, $10 for each quarter hour after that; the fare is calculated by time, not per passenger. In recent years, PETA (People for the Ethical Treatment of Animals) and other animal-rights groups have agitated for better working conditions for the city's carriage horses. Reforms mean the horses are treated better than they have been in the past, but the question of whether or not to ride is ultimately yours to answer.

MAJOR ATTRACTIONS

It takes months, or even years, to really get to know New York, but if you're only in town for a few days you'll want to check out the city's "bests"—its top museums, tallest skyscrapers, most stirring monuments, and best-loved park. Just don't try to do them all in one afternoon.

EMPIRE STATE BUILDING

The Empire State Building may no longer be the world's tallest building, or even the tallest building in New York, but it's certainly one of the world's most famous skyscrapers. Some 2½ million visitors a year make the trip up to its observatory decks on the 86th and 102nd floors, where they gawk and snap photos and speculate about whether a penny dropped from this height would really bore a hole through the skull of someone on the sidewalk below. So, you ask, what's to love about a 1,250-ft-tall skyscraper? For one, the building's stats are pretty impressive: Approximately 20,000 people fill its offices (which includes the state's largest sperm bank), and its 73 elevators cruise 7 mi of shafts at speeds ranging from 600 to 1,200 ft per minute. In its framework you'll find 60,000 tons of steel, enough to lay tracks from New York City to Baltimore, and on its top you'll find the world's greatest TV tower, which reaches eight million television sets in four states. Then there are the windows, all 6,500 of them, which are continuously being hand-washed by people who we can only presume are unafraid of heights. Beyond size, the Empire State Building, a New York City and National Landmark, is a real beauty: Zoning laws of the 1930s required that its design include numerous setbacks to allow sunlight to reach the street, and this step-like effect is a delight to the eye. With its graceful art deco embellishments, it's 10 times more attractive than the boxy World Trade Center. No wonder the Empire State Building has appeared in over 100 movies during its lifetime, including 1933's unforgettable *King Kong*.

Hard to imagine, isn't it, that the whole thing started with a pencil. Yes, the design of the most imitated building in the world was inspired by a large pencil one of the principal architects noticed sitting on his desk. Construction started in March 1930 and was completed in April 1931 at a cost of $41 million. The framework rose at a rate of 4½ stories per week, making the Empire State Building the fastest-rising major skyscraper ever built. Of course, the Great Depression put a damper on opening day ceremonies, and for the next few decades New Yorkers referred to it as the "Empty State Building." To further sour things, the original plan to make the building into a mammoth blimp mooring pad was a total failure. Two blimps briefly made contact in 1931, but barely. Eventually, the 102nd floor (where the blimps were to moor) and the 86th floor (where the blimp ticket agencies and baggage rooms were to be situated) were turned into observation decks.

The blimp world's loss is a tourist's gain, because the views from the two observation decks are absolutely incredible. The better is on the 86th floor, with amazing *plein air* views of the city and far, far beyond. On a clear day you can see as far as 80 mi, meaning you've got stellar views of not just New York City, but also parts of New Jersey, Pennsylvania, Connecticut, and Massachusetts. Another thing to look for: In certain atmospheric conditions, the 86th floor's outdoor deck experiences enormous buildups of static electricity, and quite a few couples have experienced "shocking" kisses. Unless you're a fiend for high spots, don't bother with the extra wait at the elevators to go up 200 more ft to the smaller, cramped 102nd floor observatory; you really won't see much more, and you'll have to look out through badly vandalized windows at that. Security has been beefed up since the 1997 shooting. Now you have to go through x-ray machines on the second floor before going up. Better safe than sorry. It's worth timing your visit to the Empire State Building for early or late in the day, when the sun is low on the horizon and the shadows are deep across the city. Morning is the least crowded time, while at nighttime the views of the city's lights are absolutely dazzling.

If you're lucky enough to visit the Empire State Building around a major holiday, you'll notice the top 30 floors are lit up at night with seasonal colors. What started in 1976 with red, white, and blue lights for the American bicentennial has grown to include: Christmas (red and green lights); Easter (white and yellow); Thanksgiving (red and orange); Martin Luther King Jr. Day (red, black, and green); Valentine's Day (red and white); Pulaski Day (red and white); Columbus Day (red, white, and green, the colors of the Italian flag); and of course, the Fourth of July (red, white, and blue). *350 5th Ave., at 34th St., Midtown, tel. 212/736–3100. Subway: 6 to E. 33rd St. or B, D, Q, or F to W. 34th St./Herald Sq. Admission $4.50. Open daily 9:30 AM–11:30 PM.*

NEW YORK SKYRIDE • The Empire State Building's brand-new motion simulation ride ain't cheap, but it may be the hairiest eight minutes you'll have in New York outside a cab. After being subjected to a Comedy Central video laced with subliminal messages (e.g., "Buy your kid NY stuff") and a *Blade Runner*–like "pre-flight" briefing in English and Japanese, strap yourself into the cramped flight seats and look up at the two-story-tall movie screens for a bucking, rough ride through New York City. It's not recommended for anyone who has trouble with motion sickness; pregnant women are not admitted. *Tel. 212/279–9777 or 212/564–2224. Admission $11.50 for skyride, $14 for Skyride and Observatory. Open daily 10–10.*

STATUE OF LIBERTY

The Statue of Liberty is one of America's most potent icons—the thing Batman rappelled off in *Batman Forever*, that Charlton Heston viewed with rising dread (well, the crown part, anyway) in *Planet of the*

Apes, and that author David Foster Wallace fancied as a product spokesmodel (holding aloft Tuck's medicated pads and Whoppers instead of a torch) in his epic *Infinite Jest.* Of course, to New Yorkers, this great monument is practically a cliché. But France's gift to America, officially entitled *Liberty Enlightening the World,* still impresses even the most jaded. The only way you could avoid a rush of patriotism as you chug through New York harbor toward this great green toga-covered lady is if you've gotten so seasick you're stuck in the ferry's loo.

Behind every 151-ft-tall, 225-ton woman, of course, stands a much smaller man. For Ms. Liberty that's Frédéric-Auguste Bartholdi, a renowned 19th-century French sculptor. An odd fellow ruled by strong passions (after a trip to the Sphinx and Great Pyramids he became infatuated with the idea of building a Suez Canal colossus, which Egypt's king squelched), Bartholdi executed the statue as a monument to French–American solidarity. During a trip to New York he chose tiny, uninhabited Bedloe Island, where "people get their first view of the New World," as the perfect spot to display his work. Bartholdi made a few sketches with his mother as model, and 15 years later, on October 28, 1886, the statue was unveiled to an adoring public. Of course, the man wasn't acting entirely alone. The framework inside the statue was designed by Alexandre-Gustave Eiffel, of Eiffel Tower fame. The 89-ft-tall pedestal on which the statue stands was completed thanks to the efforts of Joseph Pulitzer, publisher of the *New York World.* In a savvy marketing coup, Pulitzer promised the working poor of New York that he would publish in his paper the name of every contributor, no matter how small the donation. The money for the pedestal was raised and Pulitzer increased the *World's* circulation by 50,000. Inscribed on a bronze plaque attached to the statue's base is the sonnet *The New Colossus* ("Give me your tired, your poor, your huddled masses . . ."), written by the radical socialist Emma Lazarus.

Immigrants who have passed through Ellis Island include Charles Atlas, Irving Berlin, Frank Capra, Claudette Colbert, Marcus Garvey, Samuel Goldwyn, Bob Hope, Al Jolson, Bela Lugosi, Rudolph Valentino, and Maria von Trapp and her singing family.

Once you've strolled around Liberty Island, you have two choices at the ground-floor entrance of the monument: You can take an elevator 10 stories to the top of the pedestal, or, if you've got the cardiovascular strength of a Himalayan sherpa, you can climb 354 steps to the crown (visitors are not allowed to climb into the torch). It usually takes two or three hours to walk up to the crown because of the long lines, and the trip is not recommended for claustrophobes. Exhibits on the ground floor illustrate the statue's history, including videos of the view from the crown for those too wimpy to make the ascent. There's also a model of the statue's face for the blind to feel. *Tel. 212/363–3200. Admission free. Open daily 9–5.*

COMING AND GOING • The ferry to the Statue of Liberty and Ellis Island (*see below*) departs from Castle Clinton in **Battery Park** (*see* Lower Manhattan *in* Manhattan Neighborhoods, *below*), at the southern tip of Manhattan. The ferry ride is one loop; you can get off at Liberty Island, visit the statue, then reboard any ferry and continue on to Ellis Island, boarding another boat once you are ready to return. Ferries depart every 30 minutes 9:30–3:30, with more frequent departures and extended hours in summer. *Tel. 212/269–5755 for ferry info. Subway to Battery Park: 1 or 9 to South Ferry; also 4 or 5 to Bowling Green. Round-trip fare to Statue of Liberty and/or Ellis Island: $7.*

1st two sails 9Am - 5:30pm

ELLIS ISLAND

From 1892 to 1924 some 16 million immigrants—men, women, and children—took their first steps on U.S. soil at Ellis Island in New York harbor. In all, by the time the island's federal immigration facility closed for good in 1954, it had processed the ancestors of more than 40% of Americans living today. Now, after many years of restoration, this 27½-acre island has become a museum devoted to immigration. Even if your ancestors didn't arrive here, the visit leaves a powerful impression. At its heart is the **Registry Room,** where inspectors once attempted to screen out "undesirables," like polygamists, criminals, poor people, and people suffering from contagious diseases. The cavernous **Great Hall,** where immigrants were registered, has amazing tiled arches by Rafael Guastavino; white-tiled dormitory rooms overlook this grand space. The **Railroad Ticket Office** at the back of the main building houses exhibits on the "Peopling of America," recounting 400 years of immigration history, and "Forced Migration," focusing on the slave trade. The old kitchen and laundry building has been stabilized, rather than restored, so that you can see what the whole place looked like just a few years ago.

The most moving exhibit is outdoors to the west of the Main Building: the **American Immigrant Wall of Honor,** a circular wall covered in stainless steel and engraved with the names of 420,000 immigrants of all stripes and colors. The names include Miles Standish, Priscilla Alden, George Washington's grand-father, and Irving Berlin; they include people who came to the South on slave ships, to San Francisco on Chinese junks, and to Plymouth, Massachusetts, on the *Mayflower.* A $100 fee was charged for each name on the wall, to pay for Ellis Island's restoration. Guided 30-minute tours of the island are given daily. For info on ferries to Ellis Island, *see* Coming and Going, *above. Tel. 212/363–3200 for recorded info. Admission free. Open winter, daily 9–5; summer, daily 9–6.*

WORLD TRADE CENTER

In a city where practically everything is described in superlatives like "biggest" and "most," the mam-moth World Trade Center—which boasts the two tallest buildings in the city and the third-tallest in the entire world—is the *maxi-plus-ultra*-most. It's more like a miniature city than an office complex, really, with a daytime population of 130,000 (including 50,000 employees and 80,000 visitors); several train stations; dozens of restaurants; an 800-room hotel; and a huge performance space. Hey, it's even got its own blood bank and the world's largest air-conditioning system. The World Trade Center's "twin" tow-ers are actually different heights. One World Trade Center is 1,368 ft tall, and Two World Trade Center is 1,362 ft tall. Besides those famous twin towers, it has five other buildings arranged around an enormous plaza, modeled after Venice's St. Mark's Square. Below that, you'll find a giant subterranean shopping mall. There's lots to explore, but what you're really here to do is ride one of the warp-speed elevators to the Observation Deck (*see below*) on the 107th floor of Tower Two.

Unlike some of the city's other skyscrapers—the Empire State Building, the Chrysler Building in Mid-town, or the Flatiron Building in Gramercy—the Trade Center towers are more an engineering marvel than architectural masterpiece. Completed in 1976, they've since been criticized as being nothing more than boring glass-and-steel boxes. But something about their brutalist design and sheer magni-tude gives them the beauty of modern sculpture, and at night, when they're lit from within, they dom-inate the Manhattan skyline. Where the towers differ most radically from other office buildings is hidden inside; they were engineered so that each of the nearly 1-acre floors is completely open, free of beams, pillars, and other visible means of support. Think about this for a minute and you might won-der how the whole thing keeps from collapsing like a house of cards. Don't worry. Structurally, the tow-ers are capable of withstanding sustained winds of over 100 mi per hour. It probably would take a nuclear bomb to level them.

Of course, anyone who watches CNN knows that the World Trade Center is not invincible. On February 26, 1993, a Ryder van loaded with explosives detonated in one of the underground parking garages, killing six and injuring thousands. Today, the damage has been fixed and the main suspects are serving life sentences in prison. The only reminders are the metal detectors that all employees and visitors must now pass through before entering the center, and a small, granite **memorial** imbedded in the sidewalk of the outdoor plaza.

VISITOR INFO • The New York Visitor Information Center, on the mezzanine of Two World Trade Cen-ter, is an excellent place to begin your visit. Helpful if eccentric little old ladies will furnish you with an abundance of info on the Trade Center and other Big Apple sights. On the same level, you'll find the ticket booth for the Trade Tower's observation deck and the downtown branch of **TKTS** (*see* Chapter 7), your one-stop shop for cheap theater tickets. *Subway: C or E to World Trade Center; also 1 or 9 to Cort-landt St. Open weekdays 9–5; also Sat. 9–4:30 in summer.*

OBSERVATION DECK • The best views in Manhattan are from the newly renovated 107th-floor Observation Deck at Two World Trade Center. And if you look at the line of tourists waiting to buy tickets at the mezzanine-level office, you'll see that this is no big secret (the line is shortest weekday mornings and evenings). The elevator ride alone is worth the price of admission, as you hurtle a quarter-mile into the sky in only 58 seconds. Once you reach the top you can, if you dare, press your nose to the glass of the floor-to-ceiling windows and look out upon the entire island of Manhattan, or across the New York Bay to the Statue of Liberty and Ellis Island (the view potentially extends 55 mi, although signs at the ticket window disclose how far you can see that day). Brand-new additions include three helicopter sim-ulation theaters with moving seats and a nightly laser-light show. There's a café here as well as a Cen-tral Park–themed dining room. The prices are elevated to correspond with the height. A can of Coke costs $2, sandwiches $7.50. On nice days you can ride up another few floors to the **Rooftop Observa-tory,** the world's highest outdoor observation platform. It's offset 25 ft from the edge of the building and surrounded with a barbed-wire electric fence, to thwart spontaneous hurlers of bowling balls. Notice that planes and helicopters are flying *below* you. *Tel. 212/323–2340. Admission $10. Open June–Sept., daily 9:30 AM–11:30 PM; Oct.–May, daily 9:30 AM–9:30 PM.*

COMMODITIES EXCHANGE • At Four World Trade Center, one of those other, shorter Trade Center buildings, you can spy on the capitalist equivalent of circus clowns: commodities traders, who roll up their sleeves and then sweat, shout, and shove their way through a day handling millions of dollars worth of petroleum, livestock, precious metals, and agricultural products (the exchange started in 1886 as the New York Butter and Cheese Exchange). Pick up a pass (free) from the security checkpoint at the southeast corner of the Trade Center's Mall. Warning: You'll be exposed to an endlessly repeating tape—espousing the glory of the free market—that only a Young Republican could love. *Open weekdays 10:30–3.*

CENTRAL PARK

Central Park is probably America's best-loved and best-known park, an 843-acre rectangle of green smack in the middle of Manhattan. You've probably spied it in Absolut Vodka ads, various episodes of *Seinfeld,* and countless movies old and new. If you care, it's the reason behind "Central Perk," the name of the café in *Friends,* the place where Robin Williams danced nude in *The Fisher King,* and where Holden Caulfied in *Catcher in the Rye* spent his late night driving around in a taxi cab. On the flip side, it's also made national headlines as the place where teenage gangs go "wilding," though these days the park is pretty safe—so long as you don't go wandering around its northern woods after dark.

Enough aluminum was slapped onto the World Trade Center to side 7,000 homes, and enough concrete was poured for the foundations to build a 5-ft-wide sidewalk from New York to D.C.

Conceived in 1853, Central Park was America's first landscaped public park. Wealthy New Yorkers lobbied hard for its creation so that they'd have as pretty a place for carriage rides as their rivals in London and Paris, and also because they felt it would get the working classes out of the saloons. Besides, the stretch of land between 59th and 110th streets was at the time a swampy no-man's-land filled with squatters and roving packs of wild pigs and dogs. Leading the campaign was *New York Post* editor and part-time writer of nature poetry William Cullen Bryant, who later got a fine park named after himself in Midtown (*see* Parks and Gardens, *below*). Ultimately, master landscape architects Frederick Law Olmsted and Calvert Vaux (*see box* They Built This City, *below*) were teamed to draw up its design. The two met at night, walking over every acre of the land as they drew up plans to reconfigure it. What resulted, called the "Greensward Plan," cultivates the impression of rural English countryside, with wide sweeps of forest and lawn interspersed with beautiful cast-iron bridges and elaborate fountains. It took 15 years to mark out the park and another 40 for the trees to grow and fill in the outline. Over the decades the park has continued to grow, and it now includes 22 playgrounds, 26 ball fields, 30 tennis courts, and 58 mi of paved pedestrian paths.

You'll probably want to start your exploration at the south end of the park. Between Center and East Drives is the first of a few small bodies of water in the park, **The Pond** and **Hallett Nature Sanctuary.** The area between 59th and 65th streets is largely devoted to children: The **Conservatory Water** is a small pond usually cluttered with model boats and their child captains. Races and regattas are held here every weekend. On the west end of the basin is a statue of **Hans Christian Andersen** with his pet goose; on the north end, saddling a huge mushroom, sits **Alice in Wonderland** with a few of her eccentric friends. The park's **Children's Zoo** was recently redesigned into a more naturalistic setting for its animal residents. At 79th Street, the landscape jogs upward to the top of **Vista Rock,** which forms the foundation for playful **Belvedere Castle** (*see below*). Just off to the left is the **Shakespeare Garden,** a beautiful plot crammed with flowering plants immortalized by the bard. East of the garden is the **Swedish Cottage,** where the **Marionette Theater** (tel. 212/988–9093) performs year-round Tuesday–Thursday and Saturday at noon and 3 PM. At the edge of the park at 5th Avenue and 82nd Street is the grand **Metropolitan Museum of Art** (*see below*). Above 86th Street things start getting a little wilder, partly due to the original design, which called for footpaths through small rocky gorges and along creek beds, and partly due to lapsed supervision, although this area is undergoing a cleanup. While you're up here, look for the stone **Blockhouse,** the oldest building in the park. It dates from the War of 1812; you can still see gun ports in its decaying walls. Take a breather alongside the recently spruced up **Harlem Meer.** This idyllic, shady spot is usually thronged with Spanish families picnicking and napping in hammocks they truss between trees.

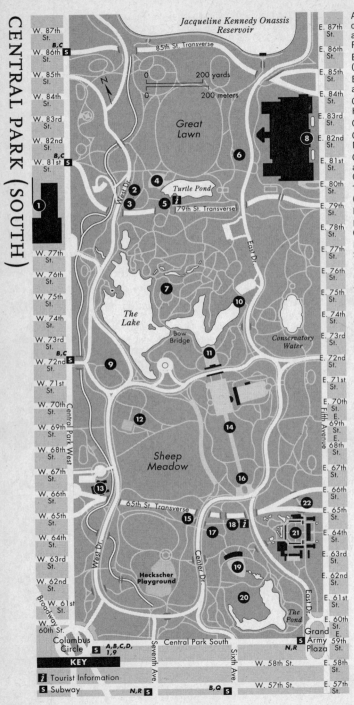

CENTRAL PARK (SOUTH)

Jacqueline Kennedy Onassis Reservoir

W. 87th St.
B,C
W. 86th St. **S**
W. 85th St.
W. 84th St.
W. 83rd St.
W. 82nd St.
B,C
W. 81st St. **S**

85th St. Transverse

N

0   200 yards
0   200 meters

Great Lawn

W. 77th St.
W. 76th St.
W. 75th St.
W. 74th St.
W. 73rd St.
B,C
W. 72nd St. **S**
W. 71st St.
W. 70th St.
W. 69th St.
W. 68th West
W. 67th St.
W. 66th St.
W. 65th St.
W. 64th St.
W. 63rd St.
W. 62nd St.
W. 61st St.
W. 60th St.

West Dr.

Turtle Pond

79th St. Transverse

East Dr.

The Lake

Bow Bridge

Conservatory Water

The Ramble

Central Park West

Sheep Meadow

65th St. Transverse

West Dr.

Center Dr.

Heckscher Playground

The Pond

East Dr.

Broadway

Columbus Circle **S** **A,B,C,D, 1,9**

KEY

i Tourist Information
S Subway

Seventh Ave.

Central Park South

Sixth Ave.

W. 58th St.
W. 57th St.

N,R **S**

B,Q **S**

E. 87th St.
E. 86th St.
E. 85th St.
E. 84th St.
E. 83rd St.
E. 82nd St.
E. 81st St.
E. 80th St.
E. 79th St.
E. 78th St.
E. 77th St.
E. 76th St.
E. 75th St.
E. 74th St.
E. 73rd St.
E. 72nd St.
E. 71st St.
E. 70th St.
E. 69th St.
E. 68th St.
E. 67th St.
E. 66th St.
E. 65th St.
E. 64th St.
E. 63rd St.
E. 62nd St.
E. 61st St.
E. 60th St.
E. 59th St.
E. 58th St.
E. 57th St.

Fifth Avenue

Grand Army Plaza

N,R

American Museum of Natural History and Hayden Planetarium, **1**
Belvedere Castle (tourist info), **5**
Bethesda Fountain and Terrace, **11**
Chess and Checkers House, **17**
Children's Zoo, **22**
Cleopatra's Needle, **6**
Croquet Grounds and Lawn Bowling Greens, **12**
The Dairy (tourist info), **18**
Delacorte Theater, **4**
Friedsam Memorial Carousel, **15**
Hallett Nature Sanctuary, **20**
Literary Walk, **16**
Loeb Boathouse, **10**
The Mall, **14**
Metropolitan Museum of Art, **8**
The Ramble, **7**
Shakespeare Garden, **3**
Strawberry Fields, **9**
Swedish Cottage/ Marionette Theater, **3**
Tavern on the Green, **13**
Wildlife Conservation Center (Zoo), **21**
Wollman Rink, **19**

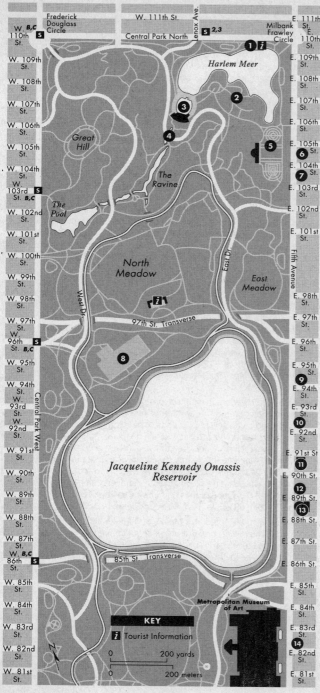

Conservatory Garden, **5**

Huddlestone Bridge, **4**

Charles A. Dana Discovery Center, **1**

Lasker Rink and Pool, **3**

McGowan's Pass, **2**

Tennis Courts, **8**

Museum Mile

Cooper-Hewitt National Design Museum, **11**

El Museo del Barrio, **6**

Goethe House, **14**

Solomon R. Guggenheim Museum, **13**

International Center of Photography (ICP)–Uptown, **9**

The Jewish Museum, **10**

Museum of the City of New York, **7**

National Academy of Design, **12**

Map labels

Frederick Douglass Circle

W. 111th St.

Central Park North

Milbank Frawley Circle

Lenox Ave.

W. 110th St. **S**

E. 111th St.

E. 110th St.

W. 109th St.

E. 109th St.

Harlem Meer

W. 108th St.

E. 108th St.

W. 107th St.

E. 107th St.

W. 106th St.

E. 106th St.

Great Hill

W. 105th St.

E. 105th St.

W. 104th St.

E. 104th St.

W. 103rd St. **S** **B,C**

The Ravine

E. 103rd St.

W. 102nd St.

The Pool

E. 102nd St.

W. 101st St.

E. 101st St.

W. 100th St.

North Meadow

East Dr.

Fifth Avenue

W. 99th St.

W. 98th St.

East Meadow

E. 98th St.

W. 97th St.

97th St. Transverse

E. 97th St.

W. 96th St. **S** **B,C**

E. 96th St.

West Dr.

W. 95th St.

E. 95th St.

W. 94th St.

E. 94th St.

W. 93rd St.

E. 93rd St.

Central Park West

W. 92nd St.

E. 92nd St.

W. 91st St.

Jacqueline Kennedy Onassis Reservoir

E. 91st St

W. 90th St.

E. 90th St.

W. 89th St.

E. 89th St.

W. 88th St.

E. 88th St.

W. 87th St.

E. 87th St.

W. 86th St. **B,C** **S**

85th St. Transverse

E. 86th St.

W. 85th St.

E. 85th St.

W. 84th St.

Metropolitan Museum of Art

E. 84th St.

W. 83rd St.

E. 83rd St.

KEY

i Tourist Information

W. 82nd St.

E. 82nd St.

0   200 yards

W. 81st St.

0   200 meters

E. 81st St.

Public rest rooms are scattered throughout the park: at Bethesda Terrace, the Loeb Boathouse, the North Meadow Recreation Center, the Conservatory Garden, the Charles A. Dana Discovery Center, and north of the Reservoir near the tennis courts. For food, there's a restaurant/café at the Loeb Boathouse and the Ice Cream Café at the Conservatory Water. During summer, the park is home to numerous free arts performances, including the enormously popular **Summerstage** and **New York Shakespeare** festivals; for more info *see* Summer Arts *in* Chapter 7. Year-round, the park draws all sorts of sporting enthusiasts for rock-climbing, tennis, horseback-riding, softball, you name it, including winter ice-skating on its famous **Wollman Rink**; for more info, *see* Ice-Skating and Ice Hockey *in* Chapter 8. *Tel. 212/360–3456 or 800/201–7275 for park events, 212/572–4820 for emergencies, or 800/281–5722 for TDD. Park open daily 30 mins before sunrise–1 AM.*

THE DAIRY • If you're planning to make a day of exploring Central Park, make this charming Victorian-style cottage your first stop. Back in the 19th century, when cows grazed on what's since become an ice-skating rink, the cottage was a dairy selling milk by the glass. It now houses the **Central Park Reception Center,** where you can pick up maps and info on park events, or check out exhibits on the park's history and wildlife. The striped-brick **Chess and Checkers House,** a short walk south of the Dairy, is perched atop a large rock named the *Kinderberg,* or "children's mountain." You'll find plenty of chess tables; with a $20 deposit, you can pick up pieces to play with at the Dairy. *Mid-park at 65th St., tel. 212/794–6564. Subway: N or R to 5th Ave. Open Tues.–Sun. 11–5 (shorter hrs in winter).*

FRIEDSAM MEMORIAL CAROUSEL • This turn-of-the-century carousel was brought to the park from Coney Island (*see* Brooklyn *in* the Outer Boroughs, *below*) in 1951. Its 58 beautiful, hand-carved jumping steeds, three-quarters the size of real horses, go 'round to music by a wheezy but cheerful pipe organ. *Mid-park at 65th St., just west of Center Dr., tel. 212/879–0244. Admission 90¢. Open weekdays 10:30–5, weekends 10:30–6.*

WILDLIFE CONSERVATION CENTER (ZOO) • The Zoo has given itself a snappy new eco-friendly name and labored long and hard to give its small collection of furred and feathered residents more natural habitats, like in the **Tropic Zone,** where birds and reptiles cavort among jungle vines and palm fronds. There's also **Temperate Territory** for monkeys, and **Edge of the Ice Pack** for a flock of penguins. But there's been trouble in the **Polar Circle,** where Gus, the 700-pound polar bear, was diagnosed as suffering from depression; like every other New Yorker, he now has a therapist. Just outside the Zoo's gates look for the **Delacorte Musical Clock.** Every hour its six-animal band circles around and plays a tune while monkeys on the top hammer their bells. *E. 64th St. at 5th Ave., tel. 212/861–6030. Subway: N or R to 5th Ave. Admission $2.50. Open Apr.–Oct., weekdays 10–5, weekends 10:30–5:30; Nov.–Mar., daily 10–4:30.*

SHEEP MEADOW • Look around Sheep Meadow on a sunny summer Sunday and you'll see 15 acres full of sunbathers and Frisbee players. Stick around for an hour or two and you'll eventually meet the genius who walks around in a flapping red cape, selling cold cans of beer out of a paper bag. Unlike at the park's other grassy fields, team sports are prohibited here, so it's the perfect place to picnic or fly a kite. And, as you might have guessed from the name, the meadow was indeed once home-sweet-home to a woolly flock, evicted in 1934. Around that time the nearby sheepfold was turned into a glitzy restaurant, **Tavern on the Green** (Central Park W at W. 67th St., tel. 212/873–3200), which is expensive but just the tiniest bit tacky, with lots of trees wrapped in twinkling lights and deer antlers on the walls. Just north of Sheep Meadow are the manicured **Croquet Grounds** and **Lawn Bowling Greens.** You must have a permit ($30) to play on them; call 212/360–8133 for info. *Mid-park between 65th and 69th Sts.*

THE MALL • Sorry, this isn't the kind of "mall" that has a Macy's and Mrs. Field's Cookies. It's a wide avenue shaded by tall elms and made for strolling; pretend you're in a painting by Seurat. At its southern end is the **Literary Walk,** so named because statues of dead white scribes like William Shakespeare, Robert Burns, and Sir Walter Scott line the path. One welcome addition was **The Indian Hunter,** sculpted in 1869 by John Quincy Adams Ward; this was the first piece of made-in-America sculpture to stand in the park. *Mid-park between 66th and 72nd Sts.*

BETHESDA FOUNTAIN AND TERRACE • Not many New York views are more romantic than the one from the top of the magnificent stone staircase that leads down to Bethesda Fountain. And it makes an excellent place to meet when the weather's nice—you can either sit on the fountain's edge and let preteens soak you with their splashings, or choose one of the benches scattered around the elaborately patterned terrace. The fountain itself was created in 1873 and named for the biblical pool in Jerusalem that was supposedly given healing powers by an angel. The four figures around Bethesda Fountain's base symbolize Temperance, Purity, Health, and Peace. Beyond the terrace stretches the Lake (*see* Loeb Boathouse, *below*), filled with drifting swans and amateur rowboat captains. *Mid-park at 72nd St.*

LOEB BOATHOUSE • At the Loeb Boathouse, on the eastern side of the park's 18-acre **Lake,** you can rent a dinghy (or the one authentic Venetian gondola) for $10 per hour (plus $30 deposit), or pedal off on a bicycle for $8 per hour. There's also an open-air café-bar that's packed with a crowd of tipsy professionals on summer evenings. *Mid-park at 74th St., near East Dr., tel. 212/517–2233 for boat rentals and café or 212/861–4137 for bike rental. Subway: 6 to E. 77th St. Rental shop open daily 11:30–6; café closed fall–spring.*

STRAWBERRY FIELDS • Also known as the International Garden of Peace, Strawberry Fields is a memorial to the late John Lennon, donated by wife Yoko Ono. Every year on December 8, Beatles fans gather around the star-shaped, black-and-white tiled IMAGINE mosaic set into the sidewalk to mourn Lennon's 1980 murder, which took place across the street at the Dakota apartments (*see box* Don't You Wish You Lived Here?, *below*), where he lived. The curving paths, well-tended shrubs, and orderly flower beds of this small garden are supposed to look a bit British. *W. 72nd St. near Central Park W.*

THE RAMBLE • Yearning for romantic, Gothic wilderness? The Ramble comprises 37 acres of narrow footpaths that snake through thickets of trees, wind around a tiny stream, and even lead to a secret cave. It's one of the best parts of the park to wander (or ramble) because you're absolutely, positively guaranteed not to encounter any Rollerbladers. The Ramble is particularly popular with bird-watchers— and among some of the city's gay men, who come here to do something besides looking for titmice and warblers. The **Urban Park Rangers** lead bird-watching tours here; call 212/427–4040 for more info. *Mid-park between 74th and 79th Sts.*

BELVEDERE CASTLE • What park would be complete without a fanciful turreted castle? The Belvedere's a mishmash of styles—Norman, Gothic, Moorish—and deliberately built small so that when it was viewed from across the nearby lake, the lake would seem bigger. Now that the trees have grown you can't see the lake at all. Since 1919 the castle has housed a U.S. Weather Bureau station—look for twirling meteorological instruments on top of its tower. Inside is a **visitor information bureau** and some geology exhibits. *Mid-park at 79th St., tel. 212/772–0210. Subway: B or C to W. 81st St. Open Tues.– Sun. 11–5 (shorter hrs in winter).*

CLEOPATRA'S NEEDLE • Over the centuries this sturdy relic has really racked up the mileage: It began life as a giant obelisk in Heliopolis, Egypt, around 1600 BC, was eventually carted off to Alexandria by the Romans in 12 BC, passed a little time hither and yon, and was ultimately presented to the city of New York by the khedive of Egypt on February 22, 1881. Ironically, a century in New York has done more to ravage the Needle than millennia of globe-trotting, and the hieroglyphics have sadly worn away to a *tabula rasa.* Thank Ra it wasn't the Rosetta Stone. *Mid-park at 81st St., behind Metropolitan Museum of Art.*

JACQUELINE KENNEDY ONASSIS RESERVOIR • This 106-acre reservoir (named for the former First Lady after her death in 1994) takes up most of the center of the park, from 86th to 97th streets. Around its perimeter is a 1.58-mi track popular with runners year-round. Even if you're not training for the New York Marathon, it's worth visiting for the stellar views of surrounding high-rises and the stirring sunsets. *Mid-park between 86th and 97th Sts.*

CONSERVATORY GARDEN • The formal, symmetrical Conservatory Garden (laid out during the Depression as a WPA project) is a nice contrast to the rustic wilderness of the rest of Central Park. It's a favorite with couples and mournful poets. The **Central Garden** is bordered by flowering crab-apple trees (beautiful in spring), and has a reflecting pool and wisteria arbor. The **North Garden,** built around a pleasant fountain, explodes with some 20,000 tulip blossoms in spring and 5,000 chrysanthemums in fall. The **South Garden,** dedicated to *The Secret Garden* author Frances Hodgson Burnett, offers 175 kinds of perennials marshaled into proper British rows. Those impressive wrought-iron gates you passed through to enter the garden from 5th Avenue once graced the mansion of Cornelius Vanderbilt II. *5th Ave. between E. 103rd and 106th Sts. Subway: 6 to E. 103rd St. Open daily 8 AM–dusk.*

HUDDLESTONE BRIDGE • If you're exploring the north end of the park, take a few minutes to look at Huddlestone Bridge, made from boulders weighing up to 100 tons. No mortar was used in its construction—instead, the sheer weight of the rocks "huddling together" keeps it from falling apart. Head southwest on one of the footpaths and you'll pass several small waterfalls before arriving at the **Pool,** a romantic spot surrounded by weeping willows and clusters of tall reeds. *Mid-park at 105th St., just south of Lasker Rink and Pool.*

HARLEM MEER AND THE CHARLES A. DANA DISCOVERY CENTER • First, before you ask: *Meer* is the Dutch word for lake. This particular meer has been recently spruced up and stocked with 50,000 bluegills, largemouth bass, and catfish, which you're allowed to catch and release (what would you do with a dead fish at your hotel anyway?). Pick up fishing poles (free) at the **Charles A. Dana Dis-**

THEY BUILT THIS CITY

FREDERICK LAW OLMSTED (1822–1903), a farmer from Staten Island, and CALVERT VAUX (1824–95), a young architect from England, first teamed up in 1853 to design Central Park. Together the dynamic landscape architects went on to create Morningside Park, Prospect Park, the Eastern Parkway, and many others. Their designs tended to be naturalistic rather than formal, re-creating the look of the English countryside, for example, with rustic stone walls, wide lakes, and scattered groves of trees. Eventually, the partnership dissolved in 1872 as Olmsted became antagonistic toward city politicians he felt were cramping his style; he bitterly opposed city-mandated additions to his parks by McKim, Mead & White (see below). Insanity forced his retirement in 1895. Vaux continued and worked on the Metropolitan Museum of Art and American Museum of Natural History with architect Jacob Wrey Mould. As the years passed he became increasingly bitter over the lack of recognition for what he considered his greatest works—Central Park and Prospect Park—and drowned under mysterious circumstances.

Just about every landmark beaux arts and neo-Renaissance building in town dating from 1880 to 1915 was designed by the architecture firm of McKim, Mead & White. Most notably: the Tiffany showroom, the Plaza Hotel, the Harvard Club, the Brooklyn Museum, J. P. Morgan's private library (now the Pierpont Morgan Library), City Hall's Municipal Building, portions of the Metropolitan Museum of Art, and all of Columbia University. WILLIAM RUTHERFORD MEAD (1846–1928) had a fairly low profile, but STANFORD WHITE (1853–1906) and CHARLES MCKIM (1847–1909) led busy lives outside the firm. White, lover of Italian Renaissance design, was solo designer for the triumphal Washington Square arch, Striver's Row houses in Harlem, and the original Madison Square Garden. He met an ironic end at a party on the roof of the Garden when he was shot point-blank by one Harry K. Shaw. White had been having an affair with Shaw's showgirl wife since she was 16. Meanwhile, White's partner, Charles McKim, was regarded as the most talented and influential architect of his day; he designed many beautiful New York mansions but lived alone in a modest rented flat. He suffered a nervous breakdown when White was shot and died soon after at the home of White's widow.

covery Center (tel. 212/860–1370), disguised as a petite Swiss chalet; the center is closed Mondays. Just south of the meer is **McGowan's Pass,** through which American troops fled from the British on September 15, 1776, and returned victoriously at the end of the Revolutionary War led by General Henry Knox. *Near 5th Ave., between E. 106th and 110th Sts. Subway: 6 to E. 110th St.*

BROOKLYN BRIDGE

"The complete work, when constructed in accordance with my designs, will not only be the greatest bridge in existence, but it will be the greatest engineering work on this continent, and of the age." So wrote John Augustus Roebling, the visionary architect, legendary engineer, metaphysical philosopher, fervid abolitionist, and unabashed egotist who practically willed the Brooklyn Bridge into existence in the mid-1800s. At a length of 6,016 ft, it was four times longer than the longest suspension bridge of its day. Its twin Gothic-arched towers rise 268 ft from the river below, while the roadway is supported by a web of human-size steel cables, hung from the towers and attached to block-long anchorages on either shore. From roadway to water is about 133 ft, high enough to allow the tallest ships to pass. Though it is hardly the longest suspension bridge in the world anymore, the Brooklyn Bridge is still one of New York's noblest landmarks, testimony to the 19th century's potent mix of ambition and technology.

John Roebling first conceived of the bridge on an icy winter's day in 1852, pissed off because he couldn't get to Brooklyn—the East River had frozen solid, and the ferry had as much chance of crossing it as the proverbial snowball in hell. Roebling spent the next 30 years designing, raising money for, and building the bridge. But tragically, two years into construction, a falling timber crushed his foot, and the stubborn

In the Early Dynasty gallery of the Egyptian wing, look for the Met's unofficial mascot, William: a turquoise-colored statuette of a chubby hippo.

visionary died of gangrene a week later. Roebling's son Washington rose valiantly to the task, only to suffer extensive nerve damage during the underwater phase of construction and end up in a wheelchair. Ultimately, the job of foreman fell to another Roebling, Washington's wife. In 1883, under her supervision, the bridge was finally completed. The public was so captivated by the long struggle to build this mighty bridge that it was quickly crowned the "Eighth Wonder of the World."

A walk across the **Great Bridge promenade,** a pedestrian walkway and bike path elevated slightly above the roadway, is a New York experience on par with the Statue of Liberty trip or the Empire State Building ascent. It's a 40-minute walk from Manhattan's civic center to the heart of charming Brooklyn Heights (*see* the Outer Boroughs, *below*). Most days the promenade is quite busy, with camera-toting tourists and a variety of New Yorkers speeding by on foot, bike, or 'blades. (When it comes to bikes, "speeding" hardly does justice to how fast some cyclists zoom across the bridge, so *absolutely* obey the lane markings: pedestrians keep to the north half of the promenade, bicyclists to the south.) At dusk the views of Manhattan's twinkling skyline are a ravishing feast for even the most jaded been-there-done-thatters. A last note: It's fine to zip across on a bike after the sun goes down (provided you're equipped with lights and reflective gear), but if you're on foot, don't plan to linger up here after the dark—especially if you're alone. *Subway: 4, 5, or 6 to Brooklyn Bridge/City Hall (Manhattan); also A or C to High St./Brooklyn Bridge (Brooklyn).*

METROPOLITAN MUSEUM OF ART

The Met, as it's known to New Yorkers, is a gargantuan treasure trove of art from around the world. It's a collection to end all collections (not bad, considering we had a late start). In fact, it's not really a single museum at all, but instead a vast network of many museums all under one roof. In its permanent collections are nearly three million works of art, from a reconstructed Egyptian temple to delicate Han dynasty dishes, spanning time from the good old Paleolithic days right up to the present. At any given time, only a quarter of the Met's permanent collection is on display. This is hardly surprising, considering holdings include thousands of European paintings and drawings, an equal number of American paintings and statues, 4,000 medieval objects, a comparable group of musical instruments, and a million prints. Add to that more than 30 special exhibitions each year and you'll see why even longtime city residents answer evasively when asked if they've seen everything in this 1½-million-square-ft megamuseum.

Despite the size and breadth of its collection, the Met does have its detractors. Its reputation as a bastion of Eurocentrist art was only slightly improved back in 1969, when oil magnate Nelson Rockefeller donated significant cash to improving the collections of art from Africa, Oceania, and the Americas. Lately, however, attempts to diversify the collections have been picking up speed. In early 1996, the new African Gallery opened, with a focus on sculpture from the Kingdom of Benin (Nigeria). The spring of 1997 was especially good for the Chinese art collection; the newly expanded galleries reopened just in time to display a tremendous gift of 11 paintings, including "The Riverbank," a 10th-century silk scroll that is one of the most important landscape paintings in the world. Special exhibitions are also looking farther afield; shows planned for 1998 include collections of Costa Rican jades and classical Indian carpets, as well as European favorites. And as with any time-honored institution, the Met has to fight the fuddy-duddy demon. While it's not going to invest in Jeffrey Koonz anytime soon, it did receive a quick transfusion in late 1995—a major gift of 20th-century art by the likes of Picasso, Modigliani, and Brancusi, not to mention the museum's first Juan Gris painting.

It's hard to believe that the whole thing began in 1870 at a building south of its present location with a modest 174 works of art. The Met moved to its current home along posh 5th Avenue, in Central Park, a decade later, and there it began to grow. The first permanent building was designed by architects Calvert Vaux and Jacob Wrey Mould; most of this has since been swallowed up by additions (if you look just inside the Robert Wood Johnson, Jr., Gallery you can see one of the original pointed Gothic archways). Some of New York's most noted architects have had a hand in the Met's expansion, including R. M. and R. H. Hunt, and McKim, Mead & White. Beginning in the '70s, the museum's separate buildings were unified by bridging the spaces between them with huge glass-and-grid walls and roofs. Unlike most things from that style-challenged decade, this has resulted in some of the museum's most exuberant spaces. Finally, the huge stone steps out front, which had for decades terrorized those wanting in youthful energy (and to some embodied the museum's attitude toward its public), were redesigned to include landings where climbers could stop for rest. These days you'll find the steps crowded with citizens from all over the world, resting their weary feet and watching cabs jockey on 5th Avenue.

The biggest mistake you can make at the Met is to try to see everything (or even most things) in one visit. Unless you're on Rollerblades, you should really focus on two to four sections rather than attempting the whole shebang. Because of reduced funding and ongoing renovations, some galleries are closed on a rotating schedule; inquire at the Information Desk (*see below*) when you pick up your trusty museum map. *1000 5th Ave., at 82nd St., Upper East Side, tel. 212/879–5500. Subway: 4, 5, or 6 to E. 86th St. Open Sun. and Tues.–Thurs. 9:30–5:15, Fri.–Sat. 9:30–8:45.*

PRACTICALITIES

The $8 admission is only a suggested amount, so if you're really broke, you can pay less—do as your conscience tells you. Your admission here also entitles you to a free same-day visit to the Cloisters (*see Museums and Galleries, below*), the Met's annex for medieval art. But that's a hell of a lot of art to absorb in one day.

The museum's **Information Desk** is in the center of the Great Hall—you can't miss it. You'll want to pick up a Floor Plan (without this you'll never make it out alive) and the calendar of special programs. Ask about the scheduled walking tours, usually free with your museum admission. The **International Visitors Desk** (tel. 212/650–2987), also in the Great Hall, assists those speaking Chinese, French, German, Italian, Japanese, or Spanish. For info on **services for visitors with disabilities,** call 212/535–7710 or TDD 212/879–0421.

Self-guided **audio tours** (tel. 212/570–3821) focus on the highlights of a particular wing or gallery, including European paintings, ancient Egypt, Greek and Roman art, and musical instruments, as well as major special exhibitions. The 45-minute tapes rent for $4 from the Audio Tour Desk in the Great Hall.

Special exhibits scheduled for 1998 include "Flowers Underfoot: Indian Carpets of the Mughal Era" from November 1997 through March 1998, a display of extremely rare Paul Strand prints from February 10 to May 3, early Picasso works from May 5 to September 6, the first U.S. retrospective of Napoleonic court painter Pierre-Paul Prud'hon from March 10 to June 7, and "When Silk Was Gold: Central Asian and Chinese Textiles" from March 3 to May 17. Lectures, films, and panel discussions take place almost hourly in the **Grace Rainey Rogers** and **Uris Center** auditoriums on topics as diverse as the collections. Classical music concerts are also regularly scheduled at the Met; *see Music in Chapter 7.*

COLLECTION HIGHLIGHTS

The **20th-Century Art** galleries (first and second floors) span everything from Grant Wood's *The Ride of Paul Revere* to totally abstract stuff like gigantic Clyfford Still canvases of black and red, and Ellsworth

Kelly's *Curve XXXII,* a gigantic slab of Corten steel. In the **Islamic Art** galleries (second floor) you'll find a reconstructed room from an Ottoman Empire upper-class home, complete with a gurgling fountain. Nearby are the **Ancient Near Eastern Art** galleries, where you'll see portions of the Persepolis monument and the famous Assyrian reliefs from the palace of Ashurnasirpal II. A narrow hallway is all that is devoted to **Drawings, Prints, and Photographs**; if you're interested in photography, you're better off heading to the Museum of Modern Art (*see below*).

AMERICAN WING • The American Wing offers room after reconstructed room of early American interiors and some of the museum's best-known paintings. If you enter the wing from the European painting galleries, you'll find yourself in a huge glass-roofed atrium; there's an indoor terrace on the first floor level. Taking up an awful lot of wall space in Gallery 223 is Emanuel Leutze's *Washington Crossing the Delaware,* the size and noble aspect of which should stir a patriotic feeling or two...never mind the glaring historical inaccuracies. A couple of rooms are devoted to the artists of the Hudson River School; in Frederic Edwin Church's 1859 masterwork *The Heart of the Andes,* look for Church's signature "carved" into a tree. Winslow Homer is well represented; his 1866 work *Prisoners from the Front* makes for an interesting character study of a handful of Confederate POWs. Turn-of-the-century paintings range from the pistol-packing cowboys of Frederic Remington to the genteel beauties of John Singer Sargeant portraits. You'll also find a room from one of Frank Lloyd Wright's Prairie-style homes. *1st and 2nd floors.*

Don't miss the Met's collection of vintage baseball cards, on display in the American Wing. They date from the late 1800s to the 1950s.

EUROPEAN SCULPTURE AND DECORATIVE ARTS • This warren of rooms includes sculpture, glass, porcelain, and jewelry that date from the 16th to 20th centuries. There are also scores of reconstructed interiors, including an 18th-century French bedroom that would be at home in Versailles. If all the ormolu is getting to you, look for the plain, carved wooden door with a brass knocker—it's a French storefront from 1775, complete with a small hanging sign. The number and shape of these galleries make it easy to get lost; if you're waking up a guard for directions, ask about the Carroll and Milton Petrie European Sculpture Court while you're at it. The court makes a great rest stop (you can buy a drink near the windows onto the park), and you can see part of the museum's original 1888 carriage entrance facade. *1st floor.*

COSTUME INSTITUTE • One floor below the Great Hall, you'll find the Costume Institute, a relatively small suite of rooms that exhibits a rotating array of items from the Met's huge collection of fashions—everything from 19th-century royal wedding gowns to see-through plastic dresses. *Ground floor.*

LEHMAN PAVILION • The **Robert Lehman Collection** was one of the Met's greatest acquisition coups; the mind-bogglingly large and diverse selection covers 18th-century French furniture, Renaissance paintings, a smattering of Renoirs, even a stained-glass dome from Lehman's home. However, the donation came with a hefty string attached—Lehman insisted the collection be housed together. As the pavilion shows, he got his way; the works are arranged around a skylit courtyard. At the center of the courtyard is a 15th-century Florentine fountain with an unhappy provenance: It was commissioned by a merchant who lost his life trying to snuff out a rival family, and his unhappy heirs ended up hawking it to pay the bills. *1st and ground floors.*

THE EGYPTIAN WING • The Met owns one of the most comprehensive collections of Egyptian Art outside Cairo, with objects from every facet and era of Egyptian life: crumbly yellow household linens, stone tools dating back some 6,000 years, and even a mummified gazelle that was once the pet of a royal court singer. It may be swamped with schoolkids, but it's also got scads of helpful information, from historical and geographical background to hieroglyph translations. Adjacent to the Egyptian Collection is the magnificent **Temple of Dendur,** an ancient temple donated by the Egyptian government. The whole shebang was transported here block by giant block. *1st floor.*

PRIMITIVE ART • In the Michael C. Rockefeller Wing you'll find the somewhat sparse galleries devoted to the **Arts of Africa, Oceania, and the Americas.** The sculptures, ritual objects, and everyday artifacts span 3,000 years. Michael Rockefeller had a special interest in the Asmat people of New Guinea, hence the respectively rich numbers of their artifacts, including shaggy woven body masks and a canoe that's almost 50 ft long. The Jan Mitchell Treasury gallery lures people in with shining gold masks and ornaments from Central and South America. *1st floor.*

ARMS AND ARMOR • The Arms and Armor galleries hold some impressive European armor—for both men and their horses. The decoration of both the weapons and armor is so finely worked it can be hard to keep their grisly purpose in mind. (It brings a whole new meaning to the phrase "going out in style.") To one side of the main hall is a wild collection of Japanese instruments of destruction; to the other are swords, shields, and early guns, including an original Colt percussion revolver (check out the portrait of George Washington on the cartridge cylinder). *1st floor.*

MEDIEVAL ART • The galleries housing art from the Dark Ages are dimly lit, appropriately enough, and home to a towering wrought-iron choir screen from Spain's Cathedral of Valladolid. (The annual museum Christmas tree and crèche are put up in front of the screen.) In the cavernous sculpture hall, built to resemble a church, there's a strikingly natural *Madonna and Child*; the baby is getting his mother's attention by playing with the pages of the book on her lap. *1st floor.*

GUBBIO STUDIOLO • Between the medieval art galleries and the arms and armor exhibit is this phenomenal little room, opened in May 1996 after almost a decade of restoration. One of only two surviving 15th-century *studioli* (private studies), this was originally made for the duke of Urbino. Using tiny pieces of differently colored wood, the artist covered the walls with trompe-l'oeil benches, shelves, and latticed doors; in the "cupboards" are books, musical instruments, even the count's coat of arms. Tear your eyes away from this amazing feat of perspective and look at the polychrome carved ceiling too. *1st floor.*

GREEK AND ROMAN ART • After prolonged renovations, the Greek and Roman art galleries are back with their dazzling displays of gold and silver tableware, ceremonial vessels, and Grecian urns. There's a wonderful series of Roman portrait busts, known for their striking realism, and a display case explaining the uses for various Attic vases. *1st and 2nd floors.*

ASIAN ART GALLERIES • If you enter the Asian Art wing from the Great Hall Balcony, head straight to the newly expanded, much lauded Chinese art galleries. Right up front you'll see the Met's latest serious catch: Dong Yuan's monumental landscape, *The Riverbank*. Done in the 10th century, this giant hanging scroll is the root of the Chinese landscape tradition. The other works aren't too shabby either— silk scrolls and fans covered with didactic illustrations, bird-and-flower paintings, and poetry (almost always translated). The smooth mahogany columns and soft light—thank the renovation team—could almost make you forget you're in the Met. Take an uptight friend up to the third floor rooms and watch them swoon over the infinitesimally detailed lacquer carvings. An unassuming round entryway leads to the Zen-like peace of the Astor Court, modeled on the 16th-century Garden of the Master of the Fishing Nets in Soochow. This in turn leads to the Ming Scholar's Retreat, whose lattices, columns, and roof are all held together by joinery (look ma, no nails!). The exhibits in the Japanese art galleries rotate more frequently than those in the Chinese rooms, but you could see a beautifully spare, re-created *shoin* (study) or a turn-of-the-century sumo wrestler's ceremonial outfit. *2nd floor.*

EUROPEAN PAINTINGS • Straight ahead as you come up the main staircase are the European paintings (pre–19th century, that is). These galleries necessarily cover a lot of art-historical ground, including some crisp, Neoclassical works by Jacques-Louis David, the mercilessly pink cheeks done by Rococo pets Fragonard and Boucher, a few clear-as-a-bell portraits by Hans Holbein the Younger, and the violently lit paintings of El Greco. There are some mesmerizing canvases by Goya, such as *Majas on a Balcony* (who *are* those shady characters in the background?). Sixteenth-century Italian painters are headed by Veronese, Titian, and Bronzino (whose subject in *Portrait of a Young Man* could surely stare down the haughtiest member of New York society). Pieces by Flemish painter Peter Paul Rubens include a portrait of the artist, his second wife, and one of their children—a proverbial May–December marriage, he was 53, she 16. Velázquez's portrait, *Juan de Pareja*, was one of the museum's greatest acquisitions; ever since its creation, it's been compared to truth itself. Galleries 11–15 are devoted to Dutch painters such as Johannes Vermeer, Frans Hals, and Gerard Ter Borch—and there are 19 (count 'em, 19) Rembrandts. *2nd floor.*

MUSICAL INSTRUMENTS • This collection, featuring an extraordinary array of world instruments, is a must-see, even if you failed fifth-grade music class. There are curious (read: obsolete, and often unpronounceable) instruments at every turn: ophicleides, shawms, African lamellaphones, a clavicytherium, a double virginal, and Polynesian courtship instruments. There's even a barrel organ (*sans* monkey). Rent an "Acoustiguide" cassette tape ($4) on your way into the museum, and you can hear how exquisite craftsmanship translates into sound. *2nd floor.*

19TH-CENTURY EUROPEAN PAINTINGS AND SCULPTURE • These beaux arts galleries are one of the glories of New York. They also draw the biggest crowds. The long sculpture hall has an impressive number of Rodin works. Branching off of this are the galleries where you'll find painting after world-famous painting by Corot, Courbet, Millet, Turner, Pissarro, Dégas, Gauguin, Seurat, and many others. There are several flushed-looking Renoirs, some creamy-skinned portraits by Manet, and more than half-a-dozen works by van Gogh, including a double-sided piece (on one side is a self-portrait, on the other a study of a woman peeling potatoes). In the room devoted to Cézanne you can catch hints of the cubist theory. And there's the whole gamut of Monet, from haystacks to Rouen Cathedral to lilypond. During the latter half of every year some of the galleries showcase *TV Guide*--magnate Walter Annenberg's collection of impressionist and postimpressionist masterpieces; upon Annenberg's death the installation becomes permanent. *2nd floor.*

SCULPTURE GARDEN • If you've made it this far, then you owe it to yourself to visit the **Iris and B. Gerald Cantor Roof Garden,** generally open May through October. From atop the museum, you'll have a millionaire's view of Central Park.

MUSEUM OF MODERN ART (MOMA)

The Museum of Modern Art, or MoMA, has long been the world's premier showcase for modern art. Opening on the heels of the 1929 stock-market crash, the museum's first exhibition, *Cézanne, Gauguin, Seurat, van Gogh,* was revolutionary—those now-famous artists were, at the time, unknowns in the United States, and their postimpressionist style had few admirers. Fortunately, scholar and founding director Alfred H. Barr, Jr.'s aesthetic agenda found an enthusiastic audience in New York City, and as the collections grew the museum expanded several times. It moved to its current location in 1939, and its gallery space was doubled in 1984. Then, in early 1996, after years of fractious negotiations, the museum closed a $50-million deal to purchase three adjoining buildings, which will double its present-day gallery space in the next decade. Currently, the museum is able to show only a fraction of its vast collection at any given time—but what a fraction it is. Among its treasures are many pivotal works of the modern era, including a good collection of surrealist works, several huge canvases of Monet's *Water Lilies,* and van Gogh's *Starry Night.* Drawings, prints, books, film, video, and design are also well represented. And you'll find a few surprises, like

The MoMA continues to grapple with questions of relevancy and the true meaning of "modern art" as many of its original pieces turn 100 years old.

a helicopter, lamps, and models of landmarks in modern architecture such as Frank Lloyd Wright's "Falling Water." Photography, too, has long been richly acknowledged by the MoMA, well before it acquired fine-art status, and its collection is one of the best around—for instance, it has the only complete set of *Untitled Film Stills* by Cindy Sherman. Plans for 1998 include major exhibitions on Fernand Léger, Pierre Bonnard, and architect Alvar Aalto. *11 W. 53rd St., near 5th Ave., Midtown, tel. 212/708–9480. Subway: E or F to 5th Ave. Admission $8.50 (pay what you wish Fri. 4:30–8:30). Open Sat.–Tues. and Thurs. 10:30–6, Fri. 10:30–8:30.*

PRACTICALITIES

Brown bag lunch lectures (tel. 212/708–9795 or 212/333–1117) happen Tuesday and Thursday from 12:30 to 1:15; pay the $5 and learn while you eat. **Gallery talks** are conducted daily and are free with admission. Other programs include **Conversations with Contemporary Artists** (Friday at 6:30, entrance $5, free for students) and **Special Exhibition Programs**; for more information call 212/708–9795 or 212/708–9798. **MoMA INFORM** ($4) self-guided audio tours can be used for the painting and sculpture collections. Any galleries may be temporarily closed while new or changing exhibitions are installed.

COLLECTION HIGHLIGHTS

LOWER LEVEL/THEATER LEVEL • The **René d'Harnoncourt Galleries** and the **Theater Gallery** house temporary exhibitions. Films and videos (often related to what's hanging on the museum's walls) are presented in the **Roy and Niuta Titus Theaters 1** and **2.** Tickets (free) are distributed in the main lobby; for more info, *see* Movies and Video *in* Chapter 7.

GROUND FLOOR • Besides the information desk, checkroom, and bookstore, you'll find two galleries showing temporary exhibitions on the ground floor: the **International Council Galleries** and the small **Projects Gallery. Jazz at the MoMA** is live and free on Friday evenings from September through May. Groups play in the **Garden Café** where decent cafeteria food ($3.50–$9.50) is served in a pleasant setting, while **Sette MoMA** (tel. 212/708–9710) serves up really pricey but good Italian food and usually requires reservations. Outside is the serene **Abby Aldrich Rockefeller Sculpture Garden**; this wonderful courtyard was planned by Philip Johnson to be an outdoor "room," with trees, fountains, pools, and (of course) sculpture. Julliard Music School students perform free concerts in the garden during summer; for more info *see* Music *in* Chapter 7.

SECOND FLOOR • Coming up the escalator, you'll be delivered to the foot of Constantin Brancusi's soaring bronze *Bird in Space*—and you haven't even gotten to the galleries yet. The main collection of

painting and sculpture is exhibited in galleries 1–17; it begins with postimpressionism, cuts into Cubism, romps through Dada and Surrealism, and finishes up with Mexican art of the 1930s. Besides the magnet van Gogh, there are gems like Rousseau's *The Sleeping Gypsy,* still lifes by Cézanne, and the glowing colors of Matisse's *The Red Studio* and *Dance,* not to mention *Les Demoiselles d'Avignon,* one of the roots of all the attention Picasso's been getting these days. After an eyeful of the hard angles of Braque cubism, take a look at the smooth-as-a-pebble surfaces of more Brancusi sculptures. And there are over a dozen Mondrian canvases (*Composition* always seems to elicit a chorus of "I could've done that!"). If you need a respite, visit Monet's *Water Lilies,* separated from the rest of the collection in one of the museum's most peaceful interior spaces. The **photography** galleries hold a rotating display of the museum's renowned collection.

THIRD FLOOR • The **painting and sculpture** collection continues on the third floor in galleries 18–26. The art picks up in 1940s Europe, including the attenuated figures of Giacometti, continues through abstract expressionism (Pollock, de Kooning), and finally ends with a rotating selection of contemporary art (Warhol, on cue). The third floor also carries rotating exhibits from the museum's collections of **drawings, prints,** and **illustrated books.**

FOURTH FLOOR • This floor holds the **architecture and design** collection—that is, all the 3-D stuff that doesn't sit flat against the wall. Included is a Formula One race car, some extremely desirable kitchenware, and a Bell-47 helicopter suspended over the escalators.

MANHATTAN NEIGHBORHOODS

Regardless of who you are or what you're after, New York City has a neighborhood to fulfill your every whim. Virtually all of the major "touristy" sights are in **Midtown,** including the Theater District, Rockefeller Center, and Times Square. If museums are what you want, the **Upper East Side**'s Museum Mile has more than enough for even the most energetic art lover, while the **Upper West Side,** home to Lincoln Center, holds all the cards when it comes to the performing arts. If you're looking for a little boho culture, you might want to spend your time in the bar- and café-crowded **East Village** or **Chelsea.** There's great people-watching in the **West Village,** home to New York University students, the city's gay community, and a bunch of aging Beat poets. **SoHo** and **TriBeCa** have long been the haunts of artists and the people who profit from them, and both are packed with art galleries. For a vicarious taste of the good (or at least expensive) life, head to the ritzy blocks of **Gramercy, Union Square,** and up-and-coming **Flatiron District.** The **Lower East Side, Harlem, Little Italy,** and **Chinatown** are miniature cities in their own right, having been settled by Jewish, African, Italian, and Asian immigrants respectively. If you're interested in New York's legal and financial institutions, make your way to **Lower Manhattan.**

UPPER WEST SIDE

If you can believe it, the Upper West Side was actually a bunch of small villages until the late 1860s, an area the Dutch referred to as Bloemendael (Vale of Flowers). In those days wealthy islanders would take sleigh and carriage trips to Bloemendael and crash for the night in mansions converted into guest inns. The main thoroughfare was tree-lined Bloomingdale Road, which connected "urban" Manhattan (that is, everything below 23rd Street) to Bloomingdale Village (around 114th Street). As Central Park West quickly developed into a fashionable address, many of the area's pig farms and slaughterhouses were converted into low-income apartments. And by the end of World War II, the area west of Broadway was a slum ridden with drugs and prostitution. The government poured tons of money into building large plots of low-rent housing during the 1950s and '60s, but it wasn't until the building of Lincoln Center (*see below*) and the Fordham University campus that the area cleaned up its act. Today, famous folk like Ethan Hawke, Madonna, Yoko Ono, Barbra Streisand, Paul Simon, John MacEnroe, and Liam Neeson live in the Upper West's giant luxury apartment buildings. Less hyped are the methadone clinics and soup kitchens between 90th and 110th streets.

In an attempt to confuse you, some streets change their name at 59th Street, the southern boundary of the neighborhood: 8th Avenue becomes **Central Park West,** 9th Avenue becomes **Amsterdam Avenue,**

UPPER WEST SIDE

880 yards
800 meters

West Side Highway

RIVERSIDE

PARK

Riverside Dr.

Hudson River

Cathedral Pkwy.
W. 109th St.
W. 108th St.
W. 107th St.
W. 106th St.
W. 105th St.
W. 104th St.
W. 103rd St.
W. 103rd St.
W. 102nd St.
W. 101st St.
W. 100th St.
W. 99th St.
W. 98th St.
W. 97th St.
W. 96th St.
W. 95th St.
W. 94th St.
W. 93rd St.
W. 92nd St.
W. 91st St.
W. 90th St.
W. 89th St.
W. 88th St.
W. 87th St.
W. 86th St.
W. 85th St.
W. 84th St.
W. 83rd St.
W. 82nd St.
W. 81st St.
W. 80th St.
W. 79th St.
W. 78th St.
W. 77th St.
W. 76th St.
W. 75th St.
W. 74th St.
W. 73rd St.
W. 72nd St.
W. 71st St.
W. 70th St.
W. 69th St.
W. 68th St.
W. 67th St.
W. 66th St.
W. 65th St.
W. 64th St.
W. 63rd St.
W. 62nd St.
W. 61st St.
W. 60th St.
W. 59th St.

Manhattan Ave.
West End Ave.
Amsterdam Ave.
Broadway
Columbus Ave.
Central Park W.
West End Ave.

CENTRAL PARK

Damrosch Park
Columbus Circle

KEY
AE American Express Office
i Tourist Information

1,9   1,2,3,9   B,C   A,B,C,D, 1,9

American
Broadcasting
Company (ABC), **13**

American Museum
of Natural History/
Hayden
Planetarium, **6**

The Ansonia, **8**

Apthorp
Apartments, **5**

Boat Basin, **3**

The Dakota, **10**

Dante Park, **16**

Julliard School, **14**

Lincoln Center for
the Performing
Arts, **17**

Lotus Garden, **2**

Museum of
American Folk
Art, **15**

New-York Historical
Society, **7**

New York
Convention and
Visitors Bureau, **18**

Nicholas Roerich
Museum, **1**

Sherman
Square, **11**

Sony IMAX
Theater, **12**

Verdi Square, **9**

Zabar's, **4**

10th Avenue becomes **Columbus Avenue,** and 11th Avenue becomes **West End Avenue.** The main drag on the Upper West Side is **Broadway,** and the main cross streets are 72nd, 79th, 86th, and 96th streets. Amsterdam, Columbus, and Broadway are crammed with funky bars, restaurants, and boutiques. Near **Riverside Park** (*see* Parks and Gardens, *below*), there's little action or excitement on the primarily residential streets of West End Avenue and Riverside Drive.

COLUMBUS CIRCLE

At all hours of the day and night, traffic zooms around Columbus Circle, where West 59th Street, Broadway, Central Park West, and 8th Avenue intersect. Besides acting as a sort of gateway from Midtown to the Upper West Side, it's home to that miraculous dispenser of bus maps and free TV tickets, the **New York Convention and Visitors Bureau** (*see* Visitor Information *in* Chapter 1). At the center of the circle (atop a marble pillar, gift of the city's Italian Americans) stands an 1894 sculpture of Mr. Round Earth himself, Christopher Columbus. Speaking of the earth, at the north end of the circle, thanks to Donald Trump, there's now a miniature chrome, much-tackier rendition of the 380-ton globe built for the 1939 World's Fair in Queens. *Subway: A, B, C, D, 1, or 9 to W. 59th St./Columbus Circle.*

BROADWAY

Broadway is home to one of the city's greatest food shrines—namely **Zabar's** (*see* Markets and Specialty Shops *in* Chapter 4), which stocks everything from reasonably priced deli items to expensive Belgian chocolates. It's always packed with New Yorkers who shop like they're stocking up for Armageddon. The massive **Sony IMAX Theater** (1998 Broadway, between W. 67th and 68th Sts., tel. 212/336–5000) is a ten-plex movie theater and "urban entertainment center" where you can see 3-D movies on eight-story-high screens (with the aid of heavy plastic viewing helmets), or movies of the usual 2-D variety.

A few "parks" along Broadway offer benches where you can munch sandwiches and rubberneck at careening taxis: Across from Lincoln Center, **Dante Park** is a tiny triangle named for the Italian poet; **Sherman Square** (south of W. 72nd St. subway station) is a tiny triangle named for the Civil War general; **Verdi Square** (north of W. 72nd St. subway station) is a tiny triangle named for the Italian opera composer—but was better known as "Needle Park" during the height of its popularity with drug dealers in the '70s. Really, you're better off heading a few blocks east to Central Park or a few blocks west to Riverside Park.

COLUMBUS AVENUE

Columbus Avenue, once just a street where residents of Central Park West stopped to pick up a few pints of Haagen-Dazs, has blossomed in the last decade as a tony stretch of cafés, boutiques, and restaurants. Watch for your favorite soap star or news anchor from the sidewalk facing the headquarters of the **American Broadcasting Company (ABC)** (56 W. 66th St., between Columbus Ave. and Central Park W); for info on getting tickets to tapings of some of its TV shows, *see box* Your Own 15 Minutes of Fame, *below*. Nearby are two museums: the **Museum of American Folk Art** and the mammoth **American Museum of Natural History** (for both, *see* Museums and Galleries, *below*), which has over 36 million artifacts, including a newly renovated dinosaur exhibit on the cutting edge of exhibition design. If you're around on a Sunday, check out the flea market/greenmarket on the corner of West 77th Street and Columbus Avenue.

CENTRAL PARK WEST

The *real* Central Park West has very little to do with that soapy, sleazy, failed Fox TV series *Central Park West.* It's basically just a quiet residential street bordering Central Park, where multimillionaires raise their families in peace and quiet. Besides the famous **Dakota** (*see box* Don't You Wish You Lived Here?, *below*), there's an abundance of stately apartment buildings dating back to the late 19th century. Also here is the **New-York Historical Society** (*see* Museums and Galleries, *below*).

LINCOLN CENTER FOR THE PERFORMING ARTS

Lincoln Center, the largest performing arts center in the United States, is the year-round home for ballet, opera, musical, and drama performances of all kinds—some are even free. When it was conceived of in the late 1950s to meet "some of the needs of an anxious age," the idea of a single city center for the arts was considered pretty radical; neighbors protested the construction of the $165-million complex as disruptive, while the literati pronounced its design boring and limited. At its completion in the mid-'60s a critic for the *New York Times* sniffed that the halls "are lushly decorated, conservative structures that the public finds pleasing and most professionals consider a failure of nerve, imagination, and talent." Nonetheless, it's responsible for transforming the Upper West Side from urban ghetto to gourmet ghetto. For the complete scoop, consider one of the daily hour-long guided tours ($7.75) led by excitable Carol Channing look-alikes. For more info on various Lincoln Center activities, *see* Walter

DON'T YOU WISH YOU LIVED HERE?

For the last century or so, the Upper West Side has competed with the Upper East Side for that rather limited pool of New Yorkers able to afford apartments equipped with live-in maid's quarters, grand ballrooms, and wall-to-wall priceless antiques. Although recently it was dubbed the Gold Coast, satisfying every Westsider's one-up competitive streak with the always posh East Side. A few of the West's best:

The Ansonia. This beaux arts beauty, built in 1904, has turrets, ornamented balconies, and rooftop gargoyles; live seals once played in the entrance hall's enormous fountain. Soundproof walls have made it especially attractive to musicians, like Enrico Caruso, Igor Stravinsky, and Arturo Toscanini, as well as theater producer Florenz Ziegfeld and writer Theodore Dreiser. More recently it served as the setting for the movie "Single White Female." 2108 Broadway, between W. 73rd and 74th Sts.

The Apthorp Apartments. Designed to look like a pumped-up Italian Renaissance palazzo, this giant complex has shown up in a half-dozen films, including "The Cotton Club" and "The Money Pit." It was built in 1908 by major New York landowner William Waldorf Astor (think Astor Place and Waldorf Astoria Hotel). New Yorkers in the know envy its rent-controlled apartments whereby enormous spaces are still renting for 1920s prices. 2101–2119 Broadway, between W. 78th and 79th Sts.

The Dakota. Most famous of all the apartment buildings along Central Park West is the Dakota. Squint at it and it looks like a dark, spooky castle (although, slightly less so since its incredible cleaning a couple of years ago). The design is by Henry Hardenbergh, who later did the famous Plaza Hotel; Singer sewing-machine heir Edward S. Clark ponied up the cash. When it was finished in 1884 it was so far uptown that it was jokingly described as being "out in the Dakotas." Ha, ha, ha—it rented anyway. A 10-room apartment originally cost $250 per month, which included service by the building's 150-person staff. In December 1980 resident John Lennon was fatally shot by a deranged fan on the sidewalk outside. Yoko Ono still keeps an apartment here, and Lennon is memorialized across the street in Central Park's Strawberry Fields. 1 W. 72nd St., at Central Park W.

Reade Theater, and just about everything in Chapter 7. *W. 62nd to 66th Sts. between Columbus and Amsterdam Aves., tel. 212/546–2656. Subway: 1 or 9 to W. 66th St./Lincoln Center.*

Stand on Columbus Avenue, facing the central court with its huge fountain (where, incidentally, Cher and Nicholas Cage cavorted in *Moonstruck*). The three concert halls on this plaza are all made of pale travertine marble. To your left is the **New York State Theater** (tel. 212/870–5570), home to the New York City Ballet and the New York City Opera. The interior, designed to look like a jewel box, is covered in red plush with diamondlike light fixtures. In the lobby is a $20-million Jasper Johns creation, *Numbers*. Straight ahead, at the rear of the plaza, is the grand **Metropolitan Opera House** (tel. 212/362–6000), where the Metropolitan Opera and American Ballet Theatre perform. Its crystal chandeliers were a gift of the Austrian government; the brilliantly colored tapestries seen through the windows are by Marc Chagall. To your right, abstract bronze sculptures distinguish **Avery Fisher Hall** (tel. 212/875–5030), host to the New York Philharmonic Orchestra. The hall was originally plagued with sound problems; technicians struggled with bizarre makeshift solutions like hanging giant sheets of metal around the stage. In 1976 stereo-maker and philanthropist Avery Fisher donated a large sum and the problem was fixed for good.

Wander through the plaza, then head left past the Opera House into **Damrosch Park,** where summer open-air festivals like "Mostly Mozart" are often accompanied by free concerts at the Guggenheim Bandshell. Walk right from the plaza, between the Opera House and Avery Fisher, and you'll come to the North Plaza and a reflecting pool with a massive reclining sculpture by Henry Moore. To the rear is the **Library and Museum of the Performing Arts.** Visitors can listen to any of their 50,000 records and tapes, or check out its four galleries. Next to the library is the **Vivian Beaumont Theater,** officially considered a Broadway house. Below it is the smaller **Mitzi E. Newhouse Theater,** where many award-winning plays have originated.

On Thanksgiving eve, thousands of New Yorkers crowd the blocks around the American Museum of Natural History to watch giant balloons like Bart Simpson and the Cat in the Hat being inflated for the annual Macy's Thanksgiving Day parade.

An overpass leads from the North Plaza across 65th Street to the world-renowned music and theater school, **The Julliard School** (tel. 212/769–7406), alma mater of Robin Williams, Christopher Reeves, Itzhak Perlman, and other famous folk far too numerous to mention. There's usually something going on at its theater and recital hall. To the left is Lincoln Center's newest venue, the **Walter Reade Theater** (tel. 212/875–5600), screening avant-garde films. Take the elevator down to street level to find **Alice Tully Hall** (tel. 212/875–5050 or 212/875–5788), home to the Chamber Music Society and the New York Film Festival.

COLUMBIA UNIVERSITY AND MORNINGSIDE HEIGHTS

The neighborhood of **Morningside Heights** covers the highest hill in Manhattan. To the east, Harlem sprawls below you; to the west is **Riverside Park** (*see* Parks and Gardens, *below*) and the mighty Hudson River. These days, the neighborhood is 99% geared toward serving the students of Columbia University. The area's main thoroughfares—Broadway and Amsterdam Avenue—are more a conglomeration of résumé services, textbook exchanges, and all-night diners than any kind of community. But before it became a college town, Morningside Heights was the sight of a pivotal victory (1776) for General Washington's forces during the American Revolution, in a buckwheat field since replaced by the all-women Barnard College (*see* Columbia University, *below*).

Besides Columbia University, several theological institutions are based here, as well as the respected **Manhattan School of Music** (*see* Music *in* Chapter 7). Cut into the steep gorge beneath the Morningside cliffs is **Morningside Park** (Morningside Dr. between W. 110th and 123rd Sts.), an overgrown and littered lot that was once a prime piece of greenery designed by Central Park's Frederick Law Olmsted and Calvert Vaux.

COLUMBIA UNIVERSITY

Founded by British royal charter in 1754 as King's College (the name changed after the Revolutionary War), Columbia University is the fifth-oldest institution of higher learning in the United States and the oldest in New York state. It's also wealthy, private, and a member of the Ivy League. Their only blight is

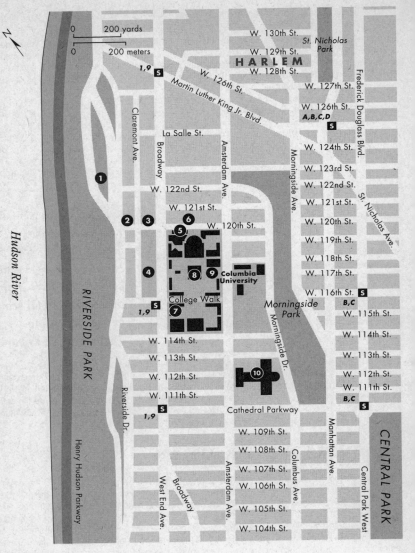

COLUMBIA UNIVERSITY AND MORNINGSIDE HEIGHTS

Hudson River

HARLEM

St. Nicholas Park

W. 130th St.
W. 129th St.
W. 128th St.
W. 127th St.
W. 126th St.
A,B,C,D
W. 124th St.
W. 123rd St.
W. 122nd St.
W. 121st St.
W. 120th St.
W. 119th St.
W. 118th St.
W. 117th St.
W. 116th St.
B,C
W. 115th St.
W. 114th St.
W. 113th St.
W. 112th St.
B,C
W. 111th St.

W. 126th St.
Martin Luther King Jr. Blvd.

1,9 S

La Salle St.

Claremont Ave.
Broadway
Amsterdam Ave.
Morningside Ave.
Frederick Douglass Blvd.
St. Nicholas Ave.

W. 122nd St.
W. 121st St.
W. 120th St.

Columbia University

College Walk

Morningside Park

W. 114th St.
W. 113th St.
W. 112th St.
W. 111th St.

Morningside Dr.

Cathedral Parkway
W. 109th St.
W. 108th St.
W. 107th St.
W. 106th St.
W. 105th St.
W. 104th St.

RIVERSIDE PARK

Riverside Dr.

Henry Hudson Parkway

West End Ave.
Broadway
Amsterdam Ave.
Columbus Ave.
Manhattan Ave.
Central Park West

CENTRAL PARK

0   200 yards
0   200 meters

1,9 S
1,9

Columbia University
Barnard College, **4**
Low Memorial
Library, **8**
Pupin Hall, **5**
St. Paul's Chapel, **9**
School of
Journalism, **7**
Teachers College, **6**

Morningside Heights
Cathedral of St.
John the Divine, **10**
Grant's Tomb, **1**
Manhattan School
of Music, **3**
Riverside Church, **2**

their football team. Original alumni include John Jay, the first Chief Justice of the Supreme Court, and Alexander Hamilton, the first Secretary of the Treasury. The university's current campus was designed by McKim, Mead & White (*see box* They Built This City, *above*) and completed in 1897. Yes, its neo-classical and Renaissance-style buildings are covered with ivy, as you'd expect; they've also got copper roofs, used specifically because they'd turn green with oxidation over the years and create the illusion of vegetation (grass being fairly sparse then, as now). The university's underground tunnel system—third-largest in the world, after the Kremlin and the Massachusetts Institute of Technology—was closed indefinitely, due to "mischievous goings-on."

Start your exploration of Columbia in the central quad at the **Low Memorial Library.** Outside, it's styled to look like the Greek Parthenon; inside is the spectacularly domed, templelike Reading Room. At the visitors center (Room 213, tel. 212/854–4900) you can pick up maps, or hook up with one of the free, student-led campus tours, given at 11 AM and 2 PM daily. Low's steps, presided over by the statue *Alma Mater* (designed by Daniel Chester French, who also did the statue of Abraham Lincoln in Washington, D.C.'s Lincoln Memorial), were a rallying point for students during the riots of '68. East of the library is the exquisite Byzantine-style **St. Paul's Chapel,** with a student-run art gallery (tel. 212/854–1953) on the ground level. Friday and Saturday nights the gallery hosts poetry readings and musical perfor-mances. At the north edge of campus is **Pupin Hall,** where the world's first successful splitting of an uranium atom took place on January 22, 1939—launching the Manhattan Project and ultimately leading to the development of the atom bomb. The university's renowned **School of Journalism,** founded by Joseph Pulitzer, holds classes in the building just south of the campus's west gates.

The ornate stone carvings on the facade of St. John the Divine feature the usual saints and biblical scenes, plus a few modern details—like a tiny Manhattan skyline.

Across Broadway from Columbia is its sister institution, **Barnard College,** established in 1889. One of the former Seven Sisters of women's colleges, Barnard has steadfastly remained a single-sex institution and maintained its independence from Columbia, although its students can take classes there. Follow Broadway north to 120th Street, where you'll see the redbrick Victorian building of Columbia's **Teachers College,** founded in 1887 and today still the world's largest graduate school in the field of education.

CATHEDRAL OF ST. JOHN THE DIVINE

Someday, the Cathedral of St. John the Divine will be the largest cathedral in the world. But first they have to finish it: Construction has been off and on since 1892. Still unbuilt are three towers, the transept, and a "bioshelter," a plant-filled skylight that will create the effect of stained glass. What is done is the mammoth, soaring nave, the length of two football fields and with enough space for 5,000 worshipers. It's bigger than the nave in St. Peter's in Rome. Lining either side of the nave are small chapels dedicated to American history, the arts, people with AIDS, even lawyers. In some of the niches you'll find very unchurchly things like a 2,000-pound quartz crystal, a menorah, and a 100-million-year-old fossilized sea creature. The great front doors, called the Portal of Paradise, are opened only twice a year; once at Easter, and once on the first Sunday in October so that elephants and chihuahuas can walk the main aisle for the Blessing of the Animals. Other festivities include Halloween (with silent hor-ror flicks and ghouls rappelling from the ceiling) and summer solstice (with ringing of a giant bronze gong). Tours ($3) of the cathedral are offered daily, and, on the first and third Saturday of each month, the cathedral offers vertical tours ($10), which allow you to climb around its towers and other tall parts. Next door, the **Children's Sculpture Garden** features a giant statue of a gruesome-looking angel tri-umphing over the devil, with surrounding inscriptions by Georgia O'Keeffe, John Lennon, Ray Charles, and Gandhi. *Amsterdam Ave. and W. 112th St., tel. 212/316–7540 or 212/932–7347 for tour reserva-tions. Subway: 1 or 9 to W. 110th St. Suggested donation $2. Open Mon.–Sat. 7–5, Sun. 8–5.*

RIVERSIDE CHURCH

Riverside Church has a gargoyle-encrusted neo-Gothic exterior modeled after the cathedral in Chartres, France, plus vaulted ceilings and archways so pretty they'll make you weep. Its congregation is nonde-nominational, interracial, extremely political, and socially conscious; live music and theatrical produc-tions are a big thing here year-round (*see* Music *in* Chapter 7). If you're here on Sunday, take the elevator ($2) to the top of the 22-story, 356-ft tower, topped with a 74-bell carillon—the largest in the world. *Riverside Dr. and W. 120th St., tel. 212/870–6700. Subway: 1 or 9 to W. 116th St. Open Mon.–Sat. 9–5, Sun. noon–4.*

GRANT'S TOMB

The final resting place of Ulysses S. Grant, Civil War general and 18th U.S. president, and Julia Dent Grant, his wife, is a white-marble rotunda influenced by the tomb of King Mausolus at Halicarnassus, the tomb of Roman Emperor Hadrian, and Napoleon's tomb in the Hôtel des Invalides. It's the second-largest mausoleum in the western hemisphere (try to imagine what this place would look like if he'd been elected to a second term). Inside are various Civil War artifacts and, of course, his-and-hers black marble sarcophagi. Tours are given on request, and occasionally the staff here wear Civil War costumes. Recently cleaned and restored, the monument is resplendent in fresh paint and buffed statuary. *100 W. 122nd St., at Riverside Park, tel. 212/666–1640. Subway: 1 or 9 to W. 116th St. Open daily 9–5.*

HARLEM

Harlem is the birthplace of what was once a purely American art form—jazz. It's also awash with crack and blighted housing projects. The difficulty is in separating the misconceptions from the reality. Many areas in Harlem, from the main commercial spine of **Martin Luther King Jr. Boulevard** (125th Street) to the residential enclaves along **St. Nicholas Avenue,** are experiencing a commercial and civic renais-sance. Rastafarian and Senegalese restaurants overflowing with customers, Dominican families listen-ing to *musica* on their front stoops—these are some of the sights of Harlem today. Note that the city's numbered north–south avenues acquire different names up here, commemorating heroes of black his-tory: 6th Avenue becomes **Malcolm X Boulevard** (formerly Lenox Avenue); 7th Avenue is **Adam Clayton Powell Jr. Boulevard**; and 8th Avenue is **Frederick Douglass Boulevard.** Many people still use the streets' former names, but street signs (and this book) use only the new names.

Harlem's sights are clustered together, making exploring easy: The majority are along Martin Luther King Jr. Boulevard. Farther north are the historic and affluent neighborhoods of **Sugar Hill** (Edgecomb Ave. between W. 145th and 155th Sts.; Subway: A, B, C, or D to W. 145th St.) and **Striver's Row** (*see below*), and, at **155th Street,** a cluster of museums and a spacious riverside park. East of Park Avenue is the predominantly Puerto Rican neighborhood of **East Harlem** (a.k.a. el barrio).

MARTIN LUTHER KING JR. BOULEVARD

Once a vacant strip, Martin Luther King Jr. Boulevard is fast becoming a lively, engaging street. At its intersection with Malcolm X Boulevard you'll find two worthwhile museums: The **Studio Museum in Harlem** (*see* Museums and Galleries, *below*) features exhibitions on African, Caribbean, and African-American art, while one block to the north, the **Black Fashion Museum** (*see* Museums and Galleries, *below*) has over 3,000 pieces in its collection—including all the costumes from *The Wiz.*

Across Malcolm X Boulevard from the Fashion Museum is the famed **Sylvia's Restaurant** (*see* Chapter 4), a 20-year-old institution run by the self-proclaimed "Queen of Soul Food." Incidentally, the intersec-tion of Malcolm X Boulevard with Martin Luther King Jr. Boulevard is also called **Africa Square.** A block away is the **National Black Theater** (*see* Theater *in* Chapter 7), which produces new works by contem-porary African-American writers.

APOLLO THEATER

When it opened in 1913 this was a burlesque hall for white audiences only, but after 1934 music greats such as Billie Holiday, Ella Fitzgerald, Duke Ellington, Count Basie, James Brown, and Aretha Franklin performed (or even got their first break) here. After falling on hard times in the '70s it roared back to life in 1986 and is now a TV studio. The regular Wednesday "amateur night" (7:30 PM) is as wild and rau-cous as it was in the theater's heyday. Tourists and locals flock to the show every week ($10–$19 for tick-ets). *253 MLK Jr. Blvd., between Adam Clayton Powell Jr. and Frederick Douglass Blvds., tel. 212/749-5838. Subway: A, B, C, or D to MLK Jr. Blvd. (W. 125th St.).*

MARCUS GARVEY PARK

Though this rocky, terraced park has fallen into disrepair, it offers spectacular views of the surrounding old Victorian homes and neoclassical churches, part of a designated historical district. Look for the park (renamed in 1973 for the Jamaica-born black nationalist leader of the 1920s) just south of Martin Luther King Jr. Boulevard. Farther south is the onion-domed **Malcolm Shabazz Mosque** (102 W. 116th St., near Malcolm X Blvd.), a former casino turned Black Muslim temple; in the '60s it rang with the preachings of Malcolm X. Several stores operated by Muslims are nearby.

THE BRONX

SUGAR HILL

HARLEM

EAST HARLEM

MORNINGSIDE HEIGHTS

Morningside Park

Marcus Garvey Park

Africa Square

Metro North Train Station

W. 152nd St.
W. 151st St.
W. 150th St.
W. 149th St.
W. 148th St.
W. 147th St.
W. 146th St.
W. 145th St.
W. 144th St.
W. 143rd St.
W. 142nd St.
W. 141st St.
W. 140th St.
W. 139th St.
W. 138th St.
W. 137th St.
W. 136th St.
W. 135th St.
W. 134th St.
W. 133rd St.
E. 132nd St.
E. 131st St.
W. 130th St.
W. 129th St.
W. 128th St.
W. 127th St.
E. 126th St.
W. 124th St.
W. 123rd St.
W. 122nd St.
W. 121st St.
W. 120th St.
W. 119th St.
W. 118th St.
W. 117th St.
W. 116th St.
E. 116th St.
E. 115th St.
W. 114th St.

Harlem River
Harlem River Drive
Major Deegan Expressway
145th St. Bridge
Madison Ave. Bridge
Third Ave. Bridge
E. 149th St.
E. 138th St.
Grand Blvd.
Third Ave.
Bruckner Blvd.
Martin Luther King Jr. Blvd

Bradhurst Ave.
Edgecombe Ave.
Frederick Douglass Blvd.
St. Nicholas Ave.
St. Nicholas Park
St. Nicholas Terr.
Adam Clayton Powell Jr. Blvd.
Malcolm X Blvd.
Fifth Ave.
Madison Ave.
Park Ave.
Lexington Ave.
Third Ave.
Second Ave.
First Ave.
Manhattan Ave.
St. Nicholas Ave.
Morningside Ave.

Lenox Terr. Pl.
134th St. Terr. Pl.

300 yards
300 meters
0

A,B C,D
2,4,5
4,5
6
3
2,3
2,3
4,5,6
6
B,C
A,B, C,D
B,C
2,3

1
2
3
4
5
6
7
8
9
10
11
12
13

Abyssinian Baptist Church, **4**

Apollo Theater, **9**

Black Fashion Museum, **7**

Harlem Court House, **12**

Malcolm Shabazz Mosque, **11**

National Black Theater, **6**

Riverbank State Park, **1**

St. Nicholas Historic District, **2**

Schomburg Center for Research in Black Culture/ American Negro Theatre, **5**

Striver's Row, **3**

Studio Museum in Harlem, **10**

Sylvia's Restaurant, **8**

Willis Avenue Bridge, **13**

STRIVER'S ROW

The handsome set of town houses known as Striver's Row was designed by powerhouse turn-of-the-century architects like Stanford White, who did the north side of West 139th Street. Since 1919, they've been the homes of African-American professionals and entertainers, including musicians W. C. Handy ("The St. Louis Blues") and Eubie Blake ("I'm Just Wild About Harry"). And that's how they got their name: Less affluent Harlemites felt its residents were "striving" to become well-to-do. The surrounding quiet, tree-lined streets of the **St. Nicholas Historic District** are a remarkable reminder of the Harlem that used to be. *W. 138th and W. 139th Sts., between Adam Clayton Powell Jr. and Frederick Douglass Blvds. Subway: B or C to W. 135th St.*

ABYSSINIAN BAPTIST CHURCH

One block east of Striver's Row is the Gothic-style Abyssinian Baptist Church. Founded in 1808, it's New York's oldest black church. Adam Clayton Powell, Jr., the first black U.S. congressman, once preached here; you'll find a tribute to him (including photos of him with Dwight D. Eisenhower, John F. Kennedy, and Lyndon B. Johnson) on the second floor. Stop in on Sunday at 9 or 11 AM to hear the gospel choir and a fiery sermon. A few blocks farther south is the **Schomburg Center for Research in Black Culture** (*see* Museums and Galleries, *below*). *132 W. 138th St., at Adam Clayton Powell Jr. Blvd., tel. 212/862-7474.*

EAST HARLEM

East of Park Avenue and north of 96th Street, all the way to the East River, is **el barrio,** a district with a radically different past from that of central Harlem. Historically home to some of New York's poorest, East Harlem has never known stately brownstone mansions or drawn wealthy inhabitants. In the 1880s, East Harlem's population was two-fifths foreign born: Working-class Germans, Jews, Irish, and enough Italians to earn it the nickname "Italian Harlem" lived in shoddy tenements in the shadow of the elevated railroads (the "El"). Immigration patterns shifted after World War II; by 1990 half of East Harlem's residents were Latin American, and the neighborhood became known as "Spanish Harlem." Housing projects, empty lots (some converted to carefully tended community gardens), burned-out buildings, and graffiti murals eulogizing victims of crack or gang violence all bear testimony to the neighborhood's struggles with chronic unemployment and capital flight. Even locals claim that many of the corner bodegas survive by peddling drugs. It's not the safest neighborhood in the city, but if you show respect to the residents you'll likely be treated with the same.

Most of el barrio's action is along **East 116th Street,** where tiny Puerto Rican cafés with blaring salsa music do quick business in deep-fried *orejas* (pigs ears), and delicious *jugas tropicales* like *horchata* (a sweet rice drink). Botánicas sell herbs and objects for religious ceremonies. The intersection of East 116th Street with Lexington Avenue was Fiorello La Guardia's "lucky corner," where the beloved progressive mayor (and the first ever Italian-American elected to Congress, in 1923), always held his election-eve rallies. *Subway: 6 to E. 116th St.*

North of 116th Street, the sturdy **Harlem Court House** (170 E. 121st St., between Lexington and 3rd Aves.), built in 1891, is the area's most handsome structure and its only designated landmark. For views of East Harlem and the Bronx, cruise up the pedestrian lane of the **Willis Avenue Bridge** (E. 125th St. at 1st Ave.), spanning the Harlem River.

WASHINGTON HEIGHTS

Washington Heights, a.k.a. "Little Santo Domingo," is a mostly Latino neighborhood at the northern tip of Manhattan; its boundary with Harlem is West 155th Street. While wealthy New Yorkers built fanciful country estates here in the 19th century, in the 20th the area has been plagued with urban woes like poverty and drugs: In 1992 several days of rioting followed the shooting of a drug dealer by the police. In the past century, immigrant Greeks, Irish, Jews, Africans, Puerto Ricans, and Cubans have called the Heights their first American home. Presently, the largest Dominican population in the United States—plus a growing number of Salvadorans—live here. Though it won't win a prize as the nicest neighborhood in Manhattan, it's safe to visit Washington Heights during the day. Wander up **Broadway** and you'll find Spanish music blaring, discount merchandisers hawking cut-rate belts, shoes, or electronics, and random pay phones ringing off the hook.

The main attraction here is **The Cloisters** (*see* Museums and Galleries, *below*), the Metropolitan Museum's amazing collection of medieval European art and artifacts. It's housed in an imposing, atmospheric "castle" at the center of **Fort Tryon Park,** which offers inspiring views of the Hudson River. **Fort**

Washington Park, near the George Washington Bridge, and **Inwood Hill Park,** much farther north, also offer open space and greenery rare in the rest of Manhattan. For more on all three parks, *see* Parks and Gardens, *below.*

The **Audubon Ballroom** (W. 165th St. and Broadway) is where Malcolm X was assassinated February 21, 1965, during a rally of his Organization of Afro-American Unity. It's recently been swallowed up by a Columbia University biotechnology research facility, and only portions of the original facade and ballroom remain. Nearby is the oldest standing house in Manhattan, the **Morris-Jumel Mansion** (*see* Museums and Galleries, *below*). On Broadway at West 178th Street is the 14-lane **George Washington Bridge,** which links Manhattan with New Jersey. When it opened in 1931 it was the longest suspension bridge in the world. *Subway: A to W. 175th St.*

AUDUBON TERRACE

At Harlem's northern boundary stands Audubon Terrace, which houses the underappreciated museums of the **Hispanic Society of America** and the **American Numismatic Society** (for both, *see* Museums and Galleries, *below*). The **American Academy of Arts and Letters** (tel. 212/368–5900), also here, opens its doors to the public three months a year to exhibit sculpture, painting, and prints by promising young American artists; call for dates. The whole beaux arts compound was built on the former game preserve of artist/naturalist John James Audubon by a turn-of-the-century railroad magnate turned student of Hispanic culture. In the courtyard are a bas relief of Don Quixote on his emaciated horse and a monumental sculpture of El Cid on his more muscular steed; both are works of the founder's wife. *W. 155th St. and Broadway. Subway: 1 to W. 157th St. Open Mar., May, and Nov., Thurs.–Sun. 1–4.*

Harlem Renaissance author Langston Hughes lived at 20 E. 127th Street for the last two decades of his life.

TRINITY CEMETERY

Across the street from Audubon Terrace, Trinity Cemetery was established in the 19th century by Wall Street's venerable Trinity Church. Famous long-term residents include fowl-lover John James Audubon; rapacious real-estate magnate John Jacob Astor; and Alfred Dickens, son of the late, great British author. Pick up a free map of famous burial sites at the cemetery office (W. 153rd St. and Broadway; open daily 8 AM–9:30 PM). A bit farther west along the Hudson River, **Riverbank State Park** (*see* Parks and Gardens, *below*) has plenty to offer sports fanatics and view seekers. Who would guess such a gorgeous park and recreation complex was situated above a sewage treatment plant? *W. 153rd–155th Sts. between Amsterdam Ave. and Riverside Dr., tel. 212/368–1600.*

ST. FRANCIS XAVIER CABRINI CHAPEL

This is the final resting place of Mother Cabrini, clothed in her habit and lying in a crystal casket. Her smiling face is a wax replica; her real head is locked away somewhere in Rome. According to legend, a lock of the saint's hair supposedly cured a blind infant who grew up to be a priest in Texas. *Ft. Washington Ave. and W. 190th St. Subway: A to W. 190th St.*

YESHIVA UNIVERSITY

Founded in 1886, Yeshiva University is the oldest and largest Jewish studies center in the country. On campus you'll find a small **museum** displaying Hebrew treasures from around the world. The main building, Tannebaum Hall, has a fun-to-look-at facade combining modernist touches with Middle Eastern fancies like turrets, minarets, and pointy arches. *2520 Amsterdam Ave., at W. 185th St., tel. 212/960–5390. Subway: 1 or 9 to W. 181st St. Museum admission $3. Open Sept.–July, Tues.–Thurs. 10:30–5, Sun. noon–6.*

UPPER EAST SIDE

For most of its recent history the Upper East Side has been the domain of the super-rich, from old-money types, like the Rockefellers, whose names pop up on buildings all over town, to *nouveau riche* types like the Trumps and Hollywood celebrities. Luxury co-ops and condominiums, immaculate fin de siècle mansions and town houses, private schools, posh galleries, world-class museums, five-star restaurants, and international shops fill its blocks. You may find the people who live and work in this neighborhood a bit snobbish compared with other New Yorkers, but take it in stride—they treat everybody that way.

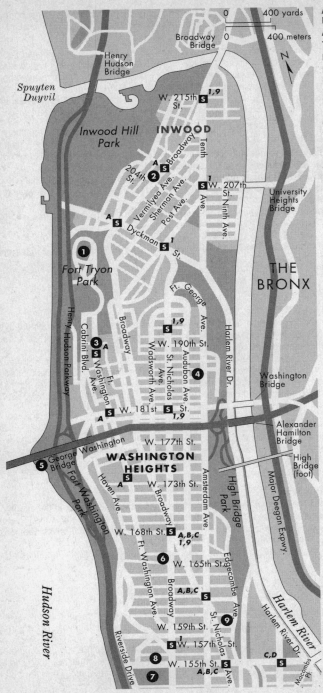

WASHINGTON HEIGHTS

Audubon
Ballroom, **6**
Audubon Terrace, **8**
The Cloisters, **1**
Dyckman House, **2**
Little Red
Lighthouse, **5**
Morris-Jumel
Mansion, **9**
St. Francis Xavier
Cabrini Chapel, **3**
Trinity Cemetery, **7**
Yeshiva
University, **4**

0   400 yards
0   400 meters

N

Broadway
Bridge

Henry
Hudson
Bridge

*Spuyten
Duyvil*

*Inwood Hill
Park*

INWOOD

W. 215th
St.   **S** *1,9*

204th
St.   **A**
    S **2**

Broadway

Tenth Ave.

S *1* W. 207th
St.   **S** *1*

Ninth Ave.

University
Heights
Bridge

Vermilyea Ave.

Sherman Ave.

Post Ave.

A
S   Dyckman   **S** *1*
            St.

*Fort Tryon
Park*

1

**THE
BRONX**

Ft. George Ave.

S *1,9*

Broadway

Henry Hudson Parkway

Cabrini Blvd.

3 **A**
    S

Ft. Washington Ave.

W. 190th St.

Wadsworth Ave.

St. Nicholas Ave.

Audubon Ave.

4

Harlem River Dr.

Washington
Bridge

S W. 181st **S** St.
A   *1,9*

W. 177th St.

Alexander
Hamilton
Bridge

High
Bridge
(foot)

George Washington

5   *Bridge*

**WASHINGTON
HEIGHTS**

S

Haven Ave.

Fort Washington Park

A   W. 173rd St.

Broadway

Amsterdam Ave.

High Bridge Park

Major Deegan Expwy.

W. 168th St. **S** *A,B,C
                    1,9*

6   W. 165th St. **S**

Edgecombe Ave.

Broadway   *A,B,C* **S**

St. Nicholas Ave.

9

W. 159th St.

Harlem River

Hudson River

S W. 157th St.
1

Riverside Drive

8
            W. 155th St. **S**
7   *A,B,C*

C,D

S

Macombs Pl.

Harlem River Dr.

On **5th Avenue** (which borders Central Park) and **Park Avenue** are the homes of the wealthy and beyond wealthy: **998 5th Avenue,** at East 81st Street, was one of the city's first giant luxury apartment buildings, built in 1910. Prior to that, rich folk scraped by in giant mansions like the one that now houses the Polo/Ralph Lauren (*see* New Clothes *in* Chapter 5) store. Quite a few of the grandiose apartment buildings you'll see were designed in the 1920s and '30s by Rosario Candela, a Sicilian-born son of a plasterer; check out the most fantastic ones at 720, 740, 770, and 778 Park Avenue, and 834 and 960 5th Avenue. And if you're around in spring, stop to smell the tulips planted along the median of Park Avenue—the Metro-North Railroad's tracks run underneath it after they dip underground at 96th Street. Sandwiched between Park and 5th avenues is **Madison Avenue,** kingdom of couture, where slews of designer clothes give the *Vogue* editors something to do. For the best of the lot, *see box* Window-Shopping as an Art *in* Chapter 5. Showy reputation aside, between 75th and 83rd Streets there are some great bookstores, such as Crawford Doyle Booksellers (1082 Madison Ave., tel. 212/288–6300) and Archivia (944 Madison Ave., between 74th and 75th Sts., tel. 212/439–9194), where browsing can be as good as hitting a mini-antiquarian book fair.

Fifth Avenue in the Upper East Side as it runs along Central Park, between 59th and 110th streets, is also known as **Museum Mile** for its astounding concentration of, well, museums. In addition to the museums listed below, this area includes the unparalleled **Metropolitan Museum of Art** (*see* Major Attractions, *above*). The **Whitney Museum of American Art** (*see* Museums and Galleries, *below*) is one block east on Madison Avenue, which means it isn't technically part of Museum Mile, but it's easy to include in your afternoon museum orgy. If you're in town in June, check the local listings for the **Museum Mile festival,** when, for three brief hours one weekday evening, the museums along 5th Avenue throw open their doors, and the strip between 82nd and 104th streets becomes a festival for highbrow types.

While the blue bloods and their debutante children dominate the blocks immediately adjoining Central Park, walk east all the way to the river and you'll find squat brownstones, cheap diners, and lots of Rollerbladers on their way to brunch. **Lexington Avenue** tends to show a little grit, while 3rd, 2nd, and 1st avenues are lined with moderately upscale restaurants and bars frequented by missed-the-'80s yuppies.

86TH STREET

A major crosstown artery, 86th Street used to be the center of the neighborhood's German and Austrian immigrant populations. One of the few holdouts in this area, called Yorkville, is **Schaller & Weber** (1654 2nd Ave., at 86th St., tel. 212/879–3047), a German market with a telltale window display of sausages and beer steins. Almost outnumbering the remaining German establishments are the Hungarian markets a few blocks further south on 2nd Avenue; if you see a red-white-and-green awning along this stretch, chances are it's not a pizza parlor. At the east end of 86th Street is **Carl Schurz Park** and the mayor's home, **Gracie Mansion** (for more on both, *see* Parks and Gardens, *below*), where the sounds of birds replace the roar of traffic. It's a sweet place to be, even if the view across the river is of industrial zones. At East End Avenue and 86th Street is **Henderson Place Historic District,** a delightful (but partially amputated) enclave of 1880s brick Queen Anne houses.

ISLAMIC CULTURAL CENTER

This postmodern mosque, built in 1991 on a lawn that looks too good for the likes of Manhattan, was the first Islamic building in New York. If you conform to Islamic dress standards (long pants and shirt for men, neck to ankle *and* hair coverage for women), you can take a short free tour of the interior. Construction has begun on a new cultural center/school, just to the right of the mosque. *E. 96th St. at 3rd Ave., tel. 212/722–5234. Subway: 6 to E. 96th St.*

COOPER—HEWITT NATIONAL DESIGN MUSEUM, SMITHSONIAN INSTITUTION

The former mansion of steel magnate Andrew Carnegie provides the setting for the Cooper–Hewitt, one of few museums in the country dedicated solely to design. Constructed in 1902 when this stretch of 5th Avenue was still all squats and tenements, the mansion—all 64 rooms of it—was built according to Carnegie's simple directive: To have "the most modest, plainest, and most roomy house in New York." OK, so his idea of "modest" is a bit different than yours. In this ornate space (which just underwent major renovations in 1995–96), Smithsonian curators have assembled brilliant exhibitions covering all aspects of design: graphic, industrial, architecture, urban, decorative, etc. In 1997, the museum's centenary, a new design resource center was added, opening up more exhibition space on the second floor. Also not to be missed are the gardens, found by walking straight through the main hall from the

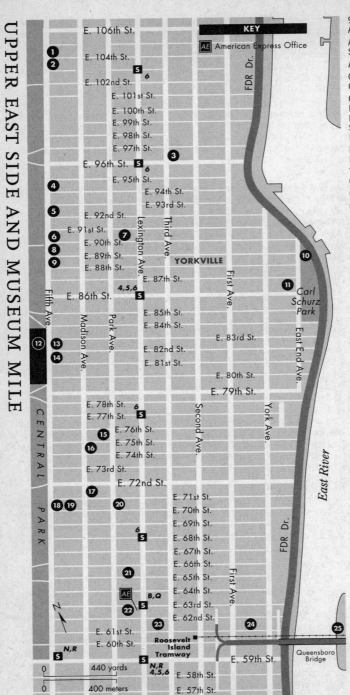

E. 106th St.

E. 104th St.

S 6

E. 102nd St.

E. 101st St.

E. 100th St.

E. 99th St.

E. 98th St.

E. 97th St.

E. 96th St. **S** 6

E. 95th St.

E. 94th St.

E. 93rd St.

E. 92nd St.

E. 91st St.

E. 90th St.

E. 89th St.

E. 88th St.

E. 87th St.

YORKVILLE

E. 86th St. 4,5,6 **S**

E. 85th St.

E. 84th St.

E. 83rd St.

E. 82nd St.

E. 81st St.

E. 80th St.

E. 79th St.

E. 78th St. 6

E. 77th St. **S**

E. 76th St.

E. 75th St.

E. 74th St.

E. 73rd St.

E. 72nd St.

E. 71st St.

E. 70th St.

E. 69th St.

E. 68th St.

E. 67th St.

E. 66th St.

E. 65th St.

E. 64th St.

E. 63rd St.

E. 62nd St.

E. 61st St.

E. 60th St.

E. 59th St.

E. 58th St.

E. 57th St.

Carl Schurz Park

East End Ave.

East River

FDR Dr.

First Ave.

York Ave.

Second Ave.

First Ave.

Third Ave.

Lexington Ave.

Park Ave.

Madison Ave.

Fifth Ave.

CENTRAL PARK

6 **S**

AE B,Q **S**

Roosevelt Island Tramway

Queensboro Bridge

N,R **S**

S **N,R** 4,5,6

KEY

AE American Express Office

0 ——— 440 yards

0 ——— 400 meters

998 Fifth Avenue, **14**

Abigail Adams Smith Museum, **24**

Asia Society, **20**

China House Gallery, **21**

Cooper–Hewitt National Design Museum/ Smithsonian Institution, **6**

El Museo del Barrio, **1**

The Frick Collection, **18**

Goethe House, **13**

Gracie Mansion, **10**

Henderson Place Historic District, **11**

International Center of Photography (ICP)—Uptown, **4**

Islamic Cultural Center, **3**

The Jewish Museum, **5**

Metropolitan Museum of Art, **12**

Museum of American Illustration, **22**

Museum of the City of New York, **2**

National Academy of Design, **8**

Polo/Ralph Lauren, **17**

Roosevelt Island, **25**

Solomon R. Guggenheim Museum, **9**

Whitney Museum of American Art, **16**

Galleries

Bonni Benrubi, **15**

M. Knoedler, **19**

Stone, **7**

Throckmorton, **23**

entrance. If you notice that the benches around the perimeter seem a little mismatched, there's good reason—they're old city park benches from different eras. The Cooper–Hewitt also sponsors a number of educational programs, including tours, lectures, seminars, and workshops; for information call the Education Department at 212/860–6868. *2 E. 91st St., at 5th Ave., tel. 212/860–6868. Subway: 4, 5, or 6 to E. 86th St. Admission $3 (free Tues. 5–9). Open Tues. 10–9, Wed.–Sat. 10–5, Sun. noon–5.*

EL MUSEO DEL BARRIO

The northern outpost of 5th Avenue's Museum Mile is this museum dedicated to the art of Latin America. In a portion of the Heckscher Building (1921), El Museo really *is* in el barrio (*see* Harlem, *above*), which begins at about 96th Street—though el barrio is less evident along 5th Avenue than just a block east. The exhibition space was handsomely renovated in 1994, and now provides over 8,250 square ft of simple white-walled galleries.

When El Museo was founded in 1969, it comprised only a single classroom in East Harlem. Since then, it has shifted locations several times as it assembled a permanent collection that today includes nearly 8,000 pieces of art, from pre-Columbian objects to contemporary videotapes. The museum also produces numerous temporary exhibitions, drawing from its permanent collection as well as borrowed works; several shows are staged each year. Hour-long **gallery tours** are given Wednesdays at 12:30 and Thursdays–Sundays at 1. *1230 5th Ave., at 104th St., tel. 212/831–7272. Subway: 6 to E. 103rd St. Suggested donation $4. Open Wed.–Sun. 11–5 (May–Sept., Thurs. 11–8).*

THE FRICK COLLECTION

How did an uneducated American industrialist who made a million bucks in coke (the kind used for steel manufacturing) by his 30th birthday attain the cultural sophistication of a European aristocrat? He bought it, of course. Henry Clay Frick (1849–1919) began amassing his fabulous personal collection of paintings, sculptures, and decorative arts after his first trip to Europe in the 1890s, and continued up until his death. The elegant 5th Avenue mansion (built in 1914) where he lived was converted to a museum in 1935—yet it still looks like a home. Rather than echoing halls with sterile display cabinets, you get rooms decorated with 18th-century European furnishings, velvet- and wood-paneled walls, and art hung exactly as the industrialist hung it, brazenly mixing styles and schools and times, so that an ancient Chinese vase rests on a 19th-century French cabinet.

Millionaire industrialist Henry Clay Frick sought aesthetic and spiritual harmony in his collection, and apparently he found it—the Frick museum is often cited as one of the most peaceful spaces in New York City.

The collection itself (one-third of which was added by trustees after Frick's death) is a remarkable if Eurocentric sampling from the early Renaissance through the late 19th century: masterworks by Bellini, Constable, Gainsborough, Goya, Holbein, Rembrandt, Renoir, Titian, Turner, Van Dyck, Velázquez, and Whistler, surrounded by exquisite candlesticks, tables, vases, and bronze and marble sculpture. In particular, look for the Vermeers and Fragonards, Hans Holbein the Younger's *Sir Thomas More*, a work of intoxicating luminosity; Rembrandt's *Self-Portrait*, which reveals the artist beaten by age; and the furious *Samson and Two Philistines*, a 16th-century bronze study by Michelangelo Buonarroti. In keeping with the home-rather-than-museum effect, none of the art carries detailed labels, so pick up the *Guide to Works of Art on Exhibition* ($1) before you start exploring; an introductory video shows in the Music Room at half-past the hour from 10:30 to 4:30 Tuesday–Saturday and 1:30 to 4:30 on Sunday. The museum's downstairs galleries house temporary exhibitions. The Frick's also famous for hosting concerts in its Music Room and Garden Court; for more info, *see* Music *in* Chapter 7.

If you're in need of a serious research library, you came to the right place: The **Frick Art Reference Library** (10 E. 71st St., tel. 212/288–8700) is right behind the museum. Open to scholars and art professionals, the Frick library contains an archive of over 800,000 photographs of works of art; 186,000 books, exhibition catalogs, and pamphlets; and 67,000 art-auction sale catalogs. *1 E. 70th St., at 5th Ave., tel. 212/288–0700. Subway: 6 to E. 68th St. Admission $5. Children under 10 not admitted. Open Tues.–Sat. 10–6, Sun. 1–6.*

GOETHE HOUSE

As the home of the German Cultural Center, the Goethe House exhibits art relating to the German experience in its two small galleries. There's also a library open to the public, as well as language, lecture, and film programs. *1014 5th Ave., between 82nd and 83rd Sts., tel. 212/439–8688. Subway: 4, 5, or 6 to E. 86th St. Admission free. Open Tues. and Thurs. noon–7, Wed. and Sat. noon–5.*

READ 'EM AND WEEP

The members of the New York Landmarks Preservation Foundation have their work cut out for them on the Upper East Side. Every half block there's a notable building worth pointing out. Throughout the neighborhood, particularly between Park and 5th avenues, look for maroon signs on the lamposts—these are a sort of Cliff's Notes for the area's architecture and history.

INTERNATIONAL CENTER OF PHOTOGRAPHY (ICP)–UPTOWN

Housed in a 1915 neo-Georgian mansion that was once home-sweet-home to the founder of the *New Republic,* the ICP features photographic installations culled from its collection of 45,000 works, as well as special exhibitions that change on a regular basis. You'll easily work your way through the modest paneled galleries in a few hours. (Don't zip past the small, circular space just to the right as you enter the museum; there are often some astounding pieces inside.) For information about the ICP's photography education programs, call 212/860–1776, ext. 156. *1130 5th Ave., at 94th St., tel. 212/860–1777. Subway: 4, 5, or 6 to E. 86th St. Admission $4 (pay what you wish Tues. 6–8). Open Tues. 11–8, Wed.– Sun. 11–6.*

THE JEWISH MUSEUM

Found in a French Gothic 5th Avenue mansion built in 1908, this museum assembles Jewish art and artifacts in a beautifully designed interior. The wonderfully conceived permanent exhibition, "Culture and Continuity," tracing the 4,000-year history of Judaism, begins on the fourth floor and continues on the third. Also not to be missed is the "audio café," where you can listen to reenacted conversations of Jews confronting modernity in cities such as New York, Fez, and Tel Aviv. The first two floors carry changing exhibitions, displayed amidst the setting of the original mansion's interior. A small kosher café is on the bottom floor. *1109 5th Ave., at 92nd St., tel. 212/423–3230. Subway: 4, 5, or 6 to 86th St. Admission $7 (free Tues. 5–8). Open Sun.–Thurs. 11–5:45 (Tues. until 8).*

MUSEUM OF THE CITY OF NEW YORK

One of the best ways to start any visit to this daunting metropolis is with a visit to the Museum of the City of New York. Set in a Colonial Georgian mansion built in 1930, the museum provides a venue in which the rich history and contemporary events of New York can be viewed and interpreted. The museum— the first in America dedicated to a city's history—was founded in 1923 and was then housed in Gracie Mansion (now the mayor's residence, found in Carl Schurz Park).

Depending on the installation, the galleries occupy four to five spacious floors. The permanent exhibitions include several reconstructed New York residential interiors (sadly, no working-class rooms are shown), toys (with original stickball equipment, and of course, *Eloise* paraphernalia), decorative arts, and a survey of Broadway productions. You can walk along some docklike planking in the **Marine Gallery** to see models, dioramas, and paintings of early New York port life. There's also the **Fire Gallery,** which has one of New York's first water pipes—made from a hollowed-out pine log. In addition, the museum produces nearly a dozen excellent temporary exhibitions every year, which tend to be more intriguing than the permanent installations. The museum has an extensive **program schedule,** including various tours of New York, performances, film screenings, continuing education opportunities, and symposia. *1220 5th Ave., at 103rd St., tel. 212/534–1672. Subway: 6 to 103rd St. Suggested admission $5. Open Wed.–Sat. 10–5, Sun. 1–5.*

NATIONAL ACADEMY OF DESIGN

The Academy has a tradition of art exhibition and instruction that goes back more than 170 years. At its location in a 1914 mansion (which in this case makes the layout occasionally confusing), the Academy shows off its permanent collection of 19th- and 20th-century American art and architecture, including works by Richard Diebenkorn, Mary Cassatt, I. M. Pei, and John Singer Sargent. In addition to changing installations highlighting its permanent collection, the museum also presents loan exhibitions of all sorts, from Old Masters to contemporary artists. The Academy also produces a small number of lectures, tours, and performances; call for information. *1083 5th Ave., at 89th St., tel. 212/369–4880. Subway: 4, 5, or 6 to 86th St. Admission $5 (pay what you wish Fri. 5–8). Open Wed.–Sun. noon–5 (Fri. until 8).*

SOLOMON R. GUGGENHEIM MUSEUM

The Frank Lloyd Wright building housing the Guggenheim (opened in 1959) is a controversial work of architecture—even many who love its assertive six-story spiral rotunda will admit that it does not result in the best space in which to view art. Inside, under a 92-ft-high glass dome, a quarter-mile-long ramp spirals down past changing exhibitions of modern art. The Wright way to see the Guggenheim (if you'll pardon the pun) is to take the elevator to the top floor and walk *down* the spiral. Otherwise, it's quite a hike. The museum, originally conceived as the Museum of Non-Objective Painting, has especially strong holdings in Wassily Kandinsky, Paul Klee, and Pablo Picasso; the oldest pieces are by the French Impressionists. A (non-round) annex called the Tower Galleries opened in June 1992, creating an additional 20,000 square ft of gallery space to display the Panza di Buomo collection of minimalist art, and touching off frenzied yapping among art-world critics. In its defense, the boring 10-story annex was based on Wright's original designs, and accommodates the extraordinarily large art pieces that the Guggenheim owns but previously had no room to display.

The Guggenheim is unlike other museums in that most of its permanent collection is made up of several great private collections, rather than individually selected works. Besides the di Buomo acquisition, one of the museum's major buttresses is the Thannhauser collection, with works by Cézanne, Picasso, and van Gogh. The photography holdings got a late but impressive start with the 1992 gift of over 200 Mapplethorpe pieces from the Robert Mapplethorpe Foundation.

Several **gallery talks and tours** are offered on exhibitions and the building itself. Inquire at the information desk or call 212/423–3600. Recorded **audio tours** are available for most major exhibitions. On Ramp 2, though a keyhole-shaped entrance, is the **reading room,** a good place to relax while perusing museum publications. The small **museum café** is miles ahead of most in both food and decor; sandwiches run about $6–$7 (but we're not talking soggy grilled cheese), and there are City Bakery signature tarts. Stop by if only to view the hung photos of the museum under construction. *1071 5th Ave., at 88th St., tel. 212/423–3500. Subway: 4, 5, or 6 to E. 86th St. Admission $8 (pay what you wish Fri. 6–8). Open Sun.–Wed. 10–6, Fri.–Sat. 10–8.*

ROOSEVELT ISLAND

In the middle of the East River, straddled by the Queensborough Bridge, looms Roosevelt Island. For many years it was called Blackwell Island, after the English farmer who bought the property in the 18th century (and whose 1796 home still stands here). It was renamed Welfare Island in 1921, and finally Roosevelt Island in 1973. For much of its history, the island has been a repository for lunatics, criminals, smallpox victims, the elderly, and studying nurses. New York's first municipal asylum, the Octagon, was built here; with double the allotted number of patients, it was ripe for an exposé by the time newshound Nellie Bly came along in 1887. After going undercover as an inmate, Bly wrote scathing articles that resulted in much-needed reforms. Still, the island was quite a swinging place throughout the early decades of this century; among briefly incarcerated notables were Mae West and Tammany Hall honcho Boss Tweed. Prisoners pretty much ran their own coops and narcotics trafficking was rampant, until a penal crackdown sent the troublemakers off to Riker's Island. For a few decades the island's buildings lay empty; not until the 1970s did savvy developers move in to create one of the most successful high-density areas in the city, one that consciously mixes persons of all incomes in a postmodern idyll. The composition designed by Philip Johnson and John Burgee is strikingly pleasant: The winding, brick-paved **Main Street,** despite being flanked by some rather huge apartments, feels perfectly welcoming. And cars are mercifully kept all in one place, in an attractive parking structure (forgive the oxymoron) near the bridge that connects the island to Queens.

A walk north from the tram stop will lead you through the island's main residential area, past an 1889 Victorian Gothic chapel, and to the island's lighthouse, designed by James Renwick, Jr., the architect who designed St. Patrick's Cathedral. There's also a small, serene park at the north end. To visit Roosevelt Island, take the B or Q subway to Roosevelt Island. Or better yet, pay $1.50 and take the **Roosevelt Island Tram** (tel. 212/832–4543), which runs parallel to the Queensborough Bridge. Board the trams at 2nd Avenue and East 60th Street; they run every 15 minutes. A brochure describing the island and its history is available for 25¢ at the Manhattan tram station, or on the island at 591 Main Street.

THE MUSEUM THAT FRANK BUILT

As much a piece of modern art itself as the works it was designed to house, Frank Lloyd Wright's Guggenheim Museum can be a startling sight to unwary tourists strolling up 5th Avenue toward 88th Street—it's like a huge, bright-white child's spiral top. Wright's design for the museum was more than 15 years in the planning and wasn't fully completed until a few years after the architect's death in 1959. Much later the Guggenheim became the obvious inspiration for the Pavilion of Japanese Art, designed by Bruce Goff, at the Los Angeles County Museum of Art.

MIDTOWN

If Manhattan has a heart, it is in Midtown, where nearly everything you think of as New York is found: the Empire State Building, Times Square, Rockefeller Plaza, the glitzy stretch of 5th Avenue and schmaltzy length of Broadway, the United Nations, and skyscrapers, by God, like you've never seen before. Fifth Avenue in the 50s looks like one obscenely posh mall, where tourists with fat wallets spend up a storm. Sixth Avenue is America's corporate heartland, a menacing tunnel of skyscrapers. Seventh and Eighth avenues in the 50s—and Broadway, which cuts the block between them—is tourist hell, where souvenir shops mix with expensive restaurants where certain visitors are titillated by the possibility of a star sighting.

The west side of Midtown, on the other hand, has long had a dicey reputation. In the 30s and 40s, Hell's Kitchen is an area with little to attract tourists—unless they're in search of an hour's furtive interlude. Here, the history of ethnic poverty and barroom slashings near the docks shows through the current gloss of gentrification. Ninth Avenue, populated by a comfortable mélange of ethnic eateries, shops, and small apartments, is the heart of Hell's Kitchen. For info on the veritable buffet of cheap ethnic restaurants in this area, *see* Midtown West of 5th Avenue *in* Chapter 4.

One last note: Even though they're all in Midtown, we've covered the **Empire State Building** and the **Museum of Modern Art (MoMA)** *above,* in Major Attractions. You'll find reviews of Midtown's myriad museums in Museums and Galleries, *below*: the **American Craft Museum, International Center of Photography–Midtown,** *Intrepid* **Air, Sea, and Space Museum, Japan Society, Museum of Television and Radio, Pierpont Morgan Library,** and **Sony Wonder Technology Lab.** Midtown's only good-sized park, **Bryant Park,** is in Parks and Gardens, *below.*

GRAND ARMY PLAZA

What was once a splendid public plaza, Grand Army Plaza is now the scene of intolerable traffic and tourist trappings—note the drivers of horse-drawn cabs (*see* Guided Tours, *above*) jockeying for potential fares. On the north half of the plaza is a massive gilded statue of Civil War general William Tecumseh Sherman and an unnamed, lithe Nubian; the southern half is dominated by the Pulitzer Memorial Fountain, now in a state of disrepair. Appropriately enough for this ritzy area, the lady on top is *Pomona,* the goddess of abundance. The palatial **Plaza Hotel** (768 5th Ave., at 59th St., tel. 212/759–3000), at the western edge of the plaza, is New York's finest hotel building, home to Frank Lloyd Wright when he was in town building the Guggenheim Museum. It's difficult to believe that the architect who dreamt up the sinister-looking Dakota apartments (*see* Don't You Wish You Lived Here?, *above*), Henry Hardenbergh, could have concocted this confection with white-glazed brick and copper-and-slate roof. The hotel has been featured in notable films like *Plaza Suite* and *North by Northwest,* as well as less notable ones like *Crocodile Dundee* and *Home Alone 2.*

Next to the plaza, the **General Motors Building** (767 5th Ave., between 58th and 59th Sts.) is a much-maligned, 50-story tower of white Georgia marble and glass. Spoil your inner child by going into the building's mammoth **F.A.O. Schwarz** (*see* Specialty Stores *in* Chapter 5) for an $8,000 teddy bear or similarly extravagant toy. Beware of overly enthusiastic employees who feel the need to make you "play," tossing balloons or balls in your direction as you descend the stairs. If your inner grown-up is screaming for attention, don't forget about nearby **Bergdorf Goodman** (754 5th Ave., at 58th St., tel. 212/753–7300), where outrageously expensive clothing and housewares are sold by employees with an attitude. For more info on the shrines to consumerism that start here and stretch to the north, *see* Chapter 5.

CARNEGIE HALL

New York's premier concert hall, Carnegie Hall, has been hosting musical headliners since 1891, when its first concert was conducted by no less than Tchaikovsky. Audiophiles the world over have a lot to say about the hall's acoustics—though no two seem to be saying the same thing: Some have always said that it's a rare example of an acoustically perfect space. Others say that this has been true only since the 1995 discovery and removal of several tons of cement below the stage. Still others say the removal damaged the acoustics. And don't get them started on the effects of the 1990–1991 centennial renovations. Judge for yourself. For info on performances and tickets, *see* Music *in* Chapter 7, or consider taking a one-hour tour ($6) of the building. Tours are given mid-September through mid-June on Mondays, Tuesdays, Thursdays, and Fridays. *57th St. at 7th Ave., tel. 212/247-7800 for tours. Subway: N or R to W. 57th St.*

A block north and worth a look is the **Alwyn Court Apartments** (180 W. 58th St., at 7th Ave.), an example of what happens when architects get ahold of some terra-cotta and cheap labor. Built in 1909, this was the ultimate luxury apartment house of the time, with up to 34 rooms per apartment. Abandoned by the 1930s, it was renovated in 1985 as three- to five-room apartment units.

Diego Rivera's original murals in Rockefeller Center's RCA building were removed because of his sympathetic depiction of socialism.

ROCKEFELLER CENTER

When movies and TV shows are set in Manhattan, they often start with a shot of Rockefeller Center. To many, this glitzy, 19-building complex *is* New York City. Begun during the Great Depression by John D. Rockefeller (who made his fortune in oil by age 26), Rockefeller Center occupies nearly 22 acres of prime real estate between 5th and 7th avenues and 47th and 52nd streets. At the time, it was the largest urban design project ever undertaken in the city. At its center is the 850-ft tall RCA Building—now the **GE Building,** and also called "The Slab"—which borrowed from Le Corbusier's "tower in the park" concept. But the real genius of its design was its intelligent use of public space: plazas, concourses, and street-level shops that create a sense of community for the nearly 250,000 human beings who use it daily. Headquartered here are such giants as NBC, Time-Warner, RCA, Paramount Publishing/Simon & Schuster, General Electric, and the Associated Press (for more info on NBC, *see* Guided Tours, *above,* and *box* Your Own 15 Minutes of Fame, *below*). Ironically, despite the appearance of so much wealth, one of the center's latest owners, Mitsubishi Estate Company, was forced to file bankruptcy in 1995.

You can skip all the fancy, expensive shops here—they're filled with luxury tchotchkes you wouldn't want and can't afford. But take a stroll through the **Channel Gardens** (5th Ave. between 49th and 50th Sts.), so named because they separate the British building to the north from the French building to the south. Artists, floral designers, and sculptors give the flower beds a fab new look monthly. At the foot of the gardens is the center's most famous sight, the gold-leaf statue of **Prometheus** (more familiarly known as "Leaping Louie"), surrounded by 50 jets of water and flags from the United Nations and United States. He's sprawled above a sunken plaza that holds an open-air café in summer and a romantic ice-skating rink (*see* Ice-Skating and Ice Hockey *in* Chapter 9) in winter. Around Christmas, this is where they set up the enormous Christmas tree; the tree-lighting ceremony (tel. 212/632–3975) during the first week of December draws huge crowds. Inside and around all the center's buildings are innumerable art deco flourishes and artwork: The buff bronze *Atlas* stands guard outside the International Building (5th Ave. between 50th and 51st Sts.). Walking-tour brochures and maps for Rockefeller Center are available in the lobby of the GE building (30 Rockefeller Plaza). *Subway: B, D, F, or Q to W. 47th–50th Sts.*

THE RAINBOW ROOM • On the 65th floor of the GE Building is the über-expensive restaurant The Rainbow Room, which routinely gets described as the "Ultimate New York Experience." If you can afford it, congratulations—the new chef gets raves and the views are fantastic. Of course, gents need to wear coat and tie. *30 Rockefeller Plaza, tel. 212/632-5100.*

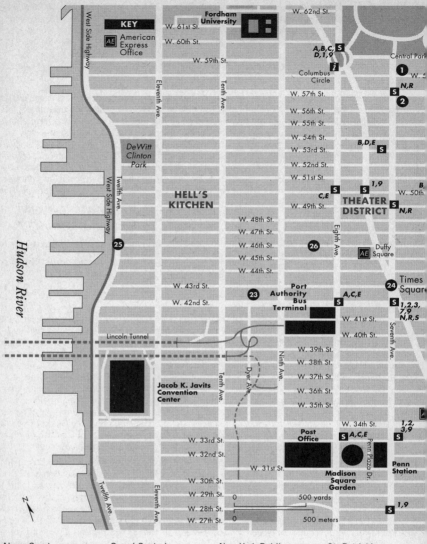

MIDTOWN

KEY

AE American Express Office

Fordham University

Hudson River

West Side Highway

Twelfth Ave.

Eleventh Ave.

Tenth Ave.

DeWitt Clinton Park

HELL'S KITCHEN

Ninth Ave.

Dyer Ave.

Eighth Ave.

Seventh Ave.

Penn Plaza Dr.

W. 62nd St.
W. 61st St.
W. 60th St.
W. 59th St.
W. 57th St.
W. 56th St.
W. 55th St.
W. 54th St.
W. 53rd St.
W. 52nd St.
W. 51st St.
W. 50th St.
W. 49th St.
W. 48th St.
W. 47th St.
W. 46th St.
W. 45th St.
W. 44th St.
W. 43rd St.
W. 42nd St.
W. 39th St.
W. 38th St.
W. 37th St.
W. 36th St.
W. 35th St.
W. 34th St.
W. 33rd St.
W. 32nd St.
W. 31st St.
W. 30th St.
W. 29th St.
W. 28th St.
W. 27th St.

Central Park

Columbus Circle

A,B,C,D,1,9 S
N,R S
B,D,E S
C,E S
1,9 S
N,R S

THEATER DISTRICT

Duffy Square AE

A,C,E S

Times Square

1,2,3,7,9 S
N,R,S

Port Authority Bus Terminal

Lincoln Tunnel

Jacob K. Javits Convention Center

Post Office S A,C,E

Madison Square Garden

Penn Station

1,2,3,9 S

1,9 S

0   500 yards
0   500 meters

25
26
23
24
1
2

Alwyn Court Apartments, **1**

American Craft Museum, **9**

Carnegie Hall, **2**

Chrysler Building, **19**

Empire State Building, **22**

F.A.O. Schwarz, **5**

Grand Army Plaza, **3**

Grand Central Terminal, **18**

Intrepid Air, Sea, and Space Museum, **25**

Japan Society, **16**

Museum of Modern Art (MOMA), **8**

Museum of Television and Radio, **10**

New York Public Library, **20**

Pace Wildenstein, **6**

Pierpont Morgan Library, **21**

Plaza Hotel, **4**

Radio City Music Hall, **12**

Restaurant Row, **26**

Rockefeller Center, **13**

St. Patrick's Cathedral, **14**

Seagram Building, **11**

Sony Wonder Technology Lab, **7**

Theater Row, **23**

Times Square, **24**

United Nations, **17**

Urban Center, **15**

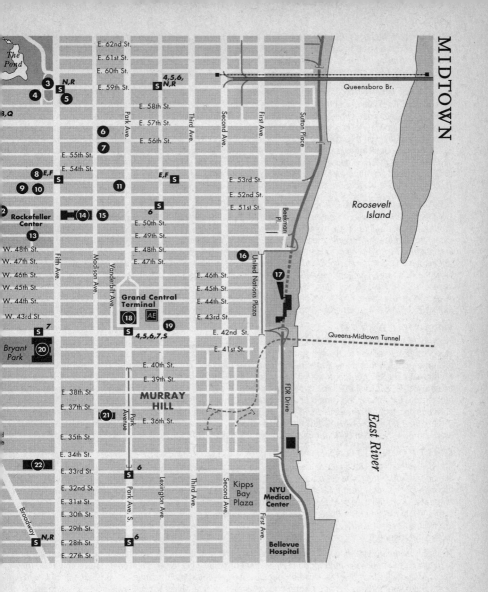

The Pond

E. 62nd St.
E. 61st St.
E. 60th St.
E. 59th St.

3
N,R
4
5

**4,5,6,
N,R**

3,Q

Queensboro Br.

E. 58th St.
E. 57th St.
E. 56th St.

Park Ave.

6
7

Third Ave.

Second Ave.

First Ave.

Sutton Place

E. 55th St.
E. 54th St.

8 **E,F**

9 **10**

E,F

11

E. 53rd St.
E. 52nd St.
E. 51st St.

Roosevelt
Island

Beekman Pl.

2
**Rockefeller
Center**

14 **15**

6

E. 50th St.
E. 49th St.
E. 48th St.
E. 47th St.

13

W. 48th St.
W. 47th St.
W. 46th St.
W. 45th St.
W. 44th St.
W. 43rd St.

Fifth Ave.

Madison Ave.

Vanderbilt Ave.

16

United Nations Plaza

E. 46th St.
E. 45th St.
E. 44th St.
E. 43rd St.

17

7

**Grand Central
Terminal**

18 **AE**

19

4,5,6,7,S

E. 42nd St.
E. 41st St.

Queens-Midtown Tunnel

**Bryant
Park**

20

E. 40th St.
E. 39th St.
E. 38th St.
E. 37th St.
E. 36th St.

**MURRAY
HILL**

FDR Drive

East River

21

Park Avenue

E. 35th St.
E. 34th St.

E. 33rd St.

22

6

Park Ave. S.

Lexington Ave.

Third Ave.

Second Ave.

First Ave.

E. 32nd St.
E. 31st St.
E. 30th St.
E. 29th St.

**Kipps
Bay
Plaza**

**NYU
Medical
Center**

Broadway

N,R

6

E. 28th St.
E. 27th St.

**Bellevue
Hospital**

RADIO CITY MUSIC HALL • This 6,000-seat auditorium was the largest in the world when it was built and is considered one of the art deco jewels of New York City. It's also got singing elves at Christmastime. What more could you want? Behind-the-scenes tours, offered daily, are $13.75. *1260 6th Ave., between W. 50th and 51st Sts., tel. 212/247–4777 for events or 212/632–4041 for tours.*

ST. PATRICK'S CATHEDRAL

Across from Rockefeller Center, St. Patrick's Cathedral is an anatomically incorrect Gothic cathedral of sorts; it's got the ornate white spires, but totally lacks flying buttresses. Even so, as the Roman Catholic Cathedral of New York, it is the site of countless society weddings. If you can get past the limos and Armani-clad throngs, take a spin around the interior. Among the statues in the alcoves around the nave is a striking modern interpretation of the first American-born saint, Mother Elizabeth Seton. The cornerstone was laid in 1858, but the cathedral didn't achieve its present form until 1906, when the Lady Chapel (behind the altar) was built. *5th Ave. between 50th and 51st Sts., tel. 212/753–2261. Subway: B, D, F, or Q to W. 47th–50th Sts.*

SEAGRAM BUILDING

Built in 1958 by Bauhaus founder Mies van der Rohe, the Seagram Building is the high point of high modernism. Its austerity set the tone for dozens of skyscrapers that followed in New York and other cities, though few have come close to the perfection of details in the Seagram. High priest of modern architecture Philip Johnson eats lunch daily at the Four Seasons restaurant (*see box* Serious Splurges *in* Chapter 4) off the main lobby, which he designed. The stark plaza out front—which works around New York's setback zoning laws—became an oft-copied model for high-rise buildings. By setting the base of their building back from the street, architects were free to construct a uniform glass box with sheer, unbroken sides. Free tours of the Seagram Building are given every Tuesday at 3 PM; meet in the lobby. *375 Park Ave., between 52nd and 53rd Sts. Subway: 6 to E. 51st St.*

URBAN CENTER

Housed inside a wing of the Villard Houses, an 1884 complex of some of New York's ritziest brownstones that now serves as the entrance to the New York Palace, the Urban Center acts as the locus of the urban design arts. New York's premier architectural preservation and education organization, the **Municipal Arts Society** (*see* Walking Tours, *above*) has its headquarters here; so too the **Architectural League** (tel. 212/753–1722) and the **Parks Council** (tel. 212/838–9410). The Center has three **galleries** that feature exhibitions focusing on contemporary planning, design, and preservation issues. Panel discussions and lectures are scheduled throughout the year. The Center also houses a library of clippings, leaflets, and books on New York City, open to the public weekdays from 11 to 5 (closed Thurs.). *457 Madison Ave., between 50th and 51st Sts., tel. 212/935–3960. Subway: E or F to 5th Ave./53rd St.*

UNITED NATIONS

The United Nations' site on the East River was an industrial slum district until oil magnate John D. Rockefeller gave $8.5 million to help build the high-modernist complex we know, fronted by the flags of all the member nations, neatly lined up, from Afghanistan to Zimbabwe. The buildings of this "workshop for peace" were finished in 1962, the collaborative product of 11 international architects led by Wallace Harrison. By running FDR Drive underneath the grounds, the architects created one of the most peaceful riverfront portions of Manhattan, including a large grassy expanse from which sunbathers and picnickers are banned.

Though it seems every tourist makes a trip to the U.N., a visit can be disappointing. The main visitor attraction is the hour-long guided tour. On an ideal day, you'll get to see the General Assembly Hall, the Security Council Chamber, the Trustee Council Chamber, and the Economic and Social Council Chamber, though some rooms may be closed on any given day. Still, a visit to one room is like a visit to any of them: They all look more or less like a big auditorium. The **tour,** offered in 20 languages, takes you through several fascinating installations that, unfortunately, are not accessible to those not on a tour. You'll see some terrifying artifacts of the atomic bombing of Hiroshima and Nagasaki, and displays on war, nuclear energy, and refugees, but you'll have little time to absorb it all. The tour guides give you their spiel, hurry you along, and dutifully deposit you in the lower-level gift-shop area. Besides the usual bric-a-brac with the U.N. logo on it, there's the **U.N. Postal Administration** (stamps and postcards bought here *must* be mailed from this post office), a coffee shop, and a bookstore that sells travel books and some of the U.N.'s technical publications.

Even if you decide not to take the tour, you can still visit the shops and the main General Assembly lobby. Its luminous north wall and long curving balconies make it one of New York's great modernist interiors.

In the plaza outside, check out Carl Fredrik Reutersward's twisted gun sculpture, perhaps the best anti-war statement of them all. And if the weather's nice, stroll over to the river for a look at Queens and Roo-sevelt Island. *1st Ave. and E. 46th St., tel. 212/963–7713. Subway: 4, 5, 6, or 7 to Grand Central. Admission free. Tours $7.50. Open weekdays 9–5, weekends 9:15–5.*

CHRYSLER BUILDING

Although the Chrysler Corporation itself moved out a long time ago, the art deco Chrysler Building is a New York icon. The stainless-steel frills, a decorative band emblazoned with cars, and a lobby practi-cally paved in African marble are just a few highlights of William Van Alen's 1930 tour de force. The 480 fluorescent tubes on the spire were added only recently; apparently, technology of the '30s wasn't up to Van Alen's designs for the illumination back then. *405 Lexington Ave., at 42nd St. Subway: 4, 5, 6, or 7 to Grand Central.*

GRAND CENTRAL TERMINAL

More than just a train station, Grand Central Terminal is an architectural jewel, one of the world's great-est public spaces. The disdain with which Isabella Rosellini uttered this name in *Blue Velvet* is unde-served, for it stands as a masterpiece of urban design, a 1913 beaux arts shrine to space and transportation. Its main concourse is a billowing, reverberating hall where the sound of street musicians mixes smoothly with the bustle of commuters taking the Metro-North to Westches-ter County.

Founded in 1945, the U.N. occupies land that is the domain of no nation—when you're there, you aren't really here in New York. Rather, you'll be on land that belongs to the U.N.'s 185 member states and has its own police force and fire department.

Currently Grand Central is undergoing a four-year, $175-mil-lion restoration, scheduled to be completed in 1998. A major cleaning, on par with that given to the Sistine Chapel, will restore the brilliance of the celestial map on the 120-ft ceiling, while part of the lower level will be converted to a food market. The building will also get outfitted with air-conditioning and complete wheelchair access (currently almost nonexistent). Free **tours** of the terminal are given Wednesdays at noon by the Municipal Art Society (*see* Walking Tours, *above*); meet at the Chemical Bank Commuter Express on the main con-course. *E. 42nd St. at Park Ave., tel. 212/439–1049. Subway: 4, 5, 6, or 7 to Grand Central.*

One of the niftier additions to the terminal's Main Concourse is the **New York Transit Museum Gift Shop** (tel. 212/682–7608), adjacent to Vanderbilt Hall, formerly the Main Waiting Room. If you love the sub-ways but can't make it to the New York Transit Museum in Brooklyn (*see* Museums and Galleries, *below*), at least come here to check out the books, T-shirts, and ephemera relating to the magnificent subway system. On the terminal's lower level is the famous, ancient **Oyster Bar and Restaurant** (tel. 212/490–6650), an eatery that seems far too tony to be in a train station. The scallops will set you back a cool $25, the bouillabaisse $26. The interior is cavernous and really cool, except for some nasty 1970s renovations. The take-out counter, found up the ramp from the main entrance, has sandwiches for about $7. Hours are weekdays 11:30–9:30.

Just south of Grand Central Terminal is the perfect al fresco dining area, **Pershing Square Park.** Just show up on the south side of Park Avenue (between E. 41st and 42nd Sts.) on summer weekdays from 11 to 3; the city provides the tables, chairs, umbrellas, and live music, and all you need to bring is the food. As you dine among the suits, get a load of the Park Avenue viaducts routing auto traffic above you—how oddly pleasing.

NEW YORK PUBLIC LIBRARY

A research and exhibition facility rather than a lending library, the **New York Public Library,** built in 1911, is rarely matched in beaux arts splendor anywhere in the city. Surely you've seen those two crouching marble lions—dubbed "Patience" and "Fortitude" by Mayor Fiorella La Guardia—on TV before? Tours of the building, beautifully restored in the 1980s, start in Astor Hall and are given for free Monday through Saturday at 11 AM and 2 PM; sign up in advance at the Information Desk. If you're going it on your own, be sure to peek into the Periodicals Room, decorated with trompe l'oeil paintings by Richard Haas commemorating New York's importance as a publishing center. For information on cur-rent exhibits being shown in the library, call 212/869–8089. If it's a nice day, though, you'd probably just enjoy sitting on the library's steps, an even livelier stage than those at the Metropolitan Museum of Art 40 blocks to the north. For the real scene, though, go behind the library to **Bryant Park** (*see* Parks and

LADIES' MILE

Sixth Avenue, known as Ladies' Mile during its heyday in the gaslight era, was lined with palatial department stores to rival the best in London and Paris. Most relocated to 5th Avenue when their wealthy customers moved uptown, and the buildings stood empty until sharp-eyed developers recently rediscovered them. The fixed-up ones are worth a look: The 1895 Seigel-Cooper Dry Goods Store (6th Ave. at W. 18th St.) is embellished with Corinthian pilasters, Romanesque arches, and lion heads. When it opened it had a fountain, a dental parlor, and an art gallery (and those ho-hum "dry goods") on 18 acres of floor space.

Gardens, *below*). *5th Ave. between 40th and 42nd Sts., tel. 212/930–0800. Subway: B, D, F, or Q to W. 42nd St. Open Mon. and Thurs.–Sat. 10–6, Tues.–Wed. 11–7:30.*

TIMES SQUARE

While it may not exactly be the Crossroads of the World, as it is often called, Times Square is one of New York's white-hot energy centers. Hordes of people, mostly tourists and the pickpockets who prey on them, crowd it day and night to gawk and walk. Though it's called a "square," it's actually a triangle, formed by the angle of Broadway slashing across 7th Avenue at 42nd Street—and the roadways are so wide here that it can be hard to tell where that darned "square" really is. However, the former Times Tower, now clad in white marble and called **One Times Square Plaza,** should be immediately obvious— you may have seen it on TV. When the *New York Times* moved into this, its new headquarters, on December 31, 1904, it publicized the event with a fireworks show at midnight. Fireworks of a different sort have since taken place every New Year's Eve at Times Square. Drunk and rowdy revelers mob the intersection below, and when the 200-pound ball being lowered down the flagpole hits bottom on the stroke of midnight, pandemonium ensues (savvy New Yorkers stay far away). Recently, Times Square promoters have been soliciting ideas for the Year 2000 bash, and a few suggestions include lowering a diapered David Letterman with the ball, painting the ball like an olive and lowering it into a giant martini glass, and inviting the Pope.

Times Square is hardly more sedate on the other 364 nights of the year, mesmerizing visitors with its zillion kilowatts of flashing neon, a mammoth digital display offering world news and stock quotes, a 42-ft-tall bottle of Coke, and the occasional way, way larger-than-life Calvin Klein billboard of a 16-story-tall waif in nothing but panties. Could it get any glitzier? Possibly. The city has made quite an effort in recent years to eradicate Times Square's sex shops, porn palaces, and other elements of XXX sleaze to make the area more palatable to tourists (and maybe even New Yorkers). Times Square's redevelopment has new stores opening up almost every month, replete with blazing neon signs that are required by the city for all new businesses here. The biggest hype surrounded the April 1996 opening of the Virgin Megastore Times Square (*see* Records, Tapes, and CDs *in* Chapter 5), a 75,000-square-ft shrine to pop culture consumerism. There is a Disney Store on 42nd Street and 7th Avenue as well as a state-of-the-art virtual reality and interactive video arcade. Free walking tours of Times Square are given Friday at noon; meet at the Times Square Visitors Center (7th Ave. and W. 42nd St.). *Subway: N, R, 1, 2, 3, 7, or 9 to Times Sq.*

THEATER DISTRICT

Near Times Square, about 30 major Broadway theaters are clustered in an area bounded roughly by 6th and 9th avenues and 41st and 53rd streets. At 47th St. and Broadway you'll find **TKTS** (*see* Chapter 7), where you can pick up half-price tickets on the day of the show. There aren't too many reasons to spend time here, unless you're on your way to a show or looking to buy an inflatable sheep: 42nd Street, especially between 7th and 8th avenues, is still chock-full of porn shops, peep shows, and prostitutes, despite the city's recent renovation efforts. Try to imagine it as a scene out of the movie *Taxi Driver,* lyrical in its squalor.

The bulk of live theater of 42nd Street is provided by a group of thriving Off-Broadway playhouses, called **Theatre Row,** between 9th and 10th avenues. Peek into No. 330, between 8th and 9th avenues, behind the Port Authority Bus Terminal. Originally the McGraw-Hill building, it was designed in 1931 by Raymond Hood, who later worked on Rockefeller Center. The lobby is an art deco wonder of opaque glass and stainless steel. Over 20 restaurants crowd block-long **Restaurant Row** (*see* Midtown West of 5th Avenue *in* Chapter 4) on 46th Street between 8th and 9th avenues, but most are pricey and cater to an upscale theater-going crowd.

CHELSEA

The increasingly hip neighborhood of Chelsea (bounded by 14th Street to the south, 30th Street to the north, 5th Avenue to the east, and the Hudson River to the west) was not named after its equally hip counterpart in London but after the Chelsea Royal Hospital, an old soldiers' home in that British city. The area was at one time the country estate of one very lucky Clement Clarke Moore, a clergyman and classics professor better known for writing *'Twas the Night Before Christmas* in 1822. Moore saw the city moving north and, intuitive urban planner that he was, decided to divide his land into sub-lots in the 1830s. He dictated a pattern of development that ensured street after street of graceful row houses. Manhattan's first elevated railroad was built on 9th Avenue in 1871—look for its remains around 10th Avenue at West 17th Street. The motion picture industry flourished briefly in Chelsea before heading west to Hollywood around World War I. And during the Depression, drama of a different sort flourished on the Chelsea waterfront: Longshoremen and ship owners went head-to-head in some vicious conflicts.

With the 1990s came gentrification: **8th Avenue** between West 14th and 23rd streets now rivals Christopher Street in the Village as the city's main gay street, with a slew of trendy restaurants, bars, cafés, gyms, and shops. The action continues on many side streets, particularly **West 18th Street.** Wander east on 18th Street to the block between 5th and 6th avenues to find a number of new bookstores (*see* Chapter 5). The stretch from **20th to 29th streets** between 10th and 11th avenues is where you'll find galleries displaying art so new the paint is still wet; **Dia Center for the Arts** and the **Paula Cooper Gallery** are among the places worth checking out (*see* Museums and Art Galleries, *below*). Shopaholics should head to **6th Avenue,** between 18th to 22nd streets, where several grand old cast-iron buildings have been transformed into upscale discount stores (*see* Ladies' Mile, *below,* and Chapter 5). Tenth through 12th avenues is the land of warehouses, with a sprinkling of dance clubs; use caution when exploring around here at night. If you're here on a weekend, check out the **Annex Antiques Fair and Flea Market** (*see* Flea Markets *in* Chapter 5), the city's longest-running outdoor market with over 300 vendors of treasure.

CHELSEA PIERS SPORTS AND ENTERTAINMENT COMPLEX

Way back in 1910, the Chelsea Piers was the launching point for a new generation of ocean liners. For the past few decades, the piers were pretty much abandoned, but in 1995 the old pier buildings along the Hudson River were turned into a sports lovers' dream come true: a 1.7-million-square-ft state-of-the-art facility with two year-round indoor ice-skating rinks; a field house for gymnastics, soccer, field hockey, lacrosse, basketball, and batting practice; two outdoor in-line and roller-skating rinks; and the city's only year-round outdoor golf driving range. There's also a huge Sports Center containing the world's longest indoor running track, the largest rock-climbing wall in the Northeast, three basketball courts, and a 25-yard pool. The Maritime Center, the city's largest marina, has a 1.2-mi walking esplanade, and Spirit Cruises, which provides sightseeing around New York Harbor. Consider ending your day at one of Chelsea Piers' several restaurants with river views, including the Crab House and the Chelsea Brewing Company. For more details *see* throughout Chapter 8. *Piers 59–62 on the Hudson River from 17th to 23rd Sts.; entrance at 23rd St., tel. 212/336–6666. Subway: E to W. 23rd St.*

CHELSEA HISTORIC DISTRICT

In Chelsea's historic district—West 19th to 23rd streets between 8th and 10th avenues—you'll find examples of all of Chelsea's architectural periods, dating back to the days of Clement Clarke Moore. The houses of **Cushman Row** (406–418 W. 20th St., at 9th Ave.) are some of the country's most perfect examples of Greek Revival town houses. Look for tiny pineapple decorations on Nos. 416 and 418. **St. Peter's Episcopal Church** (344 W. 20th St., between 9th and 10th Aves.) "welcomes all faiths and uncertain faiths." Its fieldstone building is one of New York's earliest examples of Gothic Revival architecture, and its brick Victorian Gothic parish hall is home to the Atlantic Theater Company. Check out **467 West 21st Street,** at 10th Avenue; its live-in landlord was the late Anthony Perkins, of *Psycho*

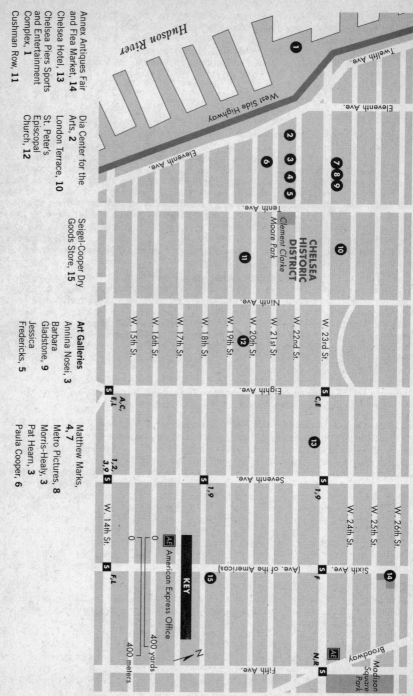

CHELSEA

Annex Antiques Fair
and Flea Market, **14**
Chelsea Hotel, **13**
Chelsea Piers Sports
and Entertainment
Complex, **1**
Cushman Row, **11**

Dia Center for the
Arts, **2**
London Terrace, **10**
St. Peter's
Episcopal
Church, **12**

Seigel-Cooper Dry
Goods Store, **15**

Art Galleries
Annina Nosei, **3**
Barbara
Gladstone, **9**
Jessica
Fredericks, **5**

Matthew Marks,
4, 7
Metro Pictures, **8**
Morris-Healy, **3**
Pat Hearn, **3**
Paula Cooper, **6**

Hudson River

West Side Highway

Twelfth Ave.

Eleventh Ave.

Eleventh Ave.

Tenth Ave.

Ninth Ave.

Eighth Ave.

Seventh Ave.

Ave. of the Americas

Sixth Ave.

Fifth Ave.

Broadway

Madison
Square
Park

**CHELSEA
HISTORIC
DISTRICT**

Clement Clarke
Moore Park

W. 14th St.
W. 15th St.
W. 16th St.
W. 17th St.
W. 18th St.
W. 19th St.
W. 20th St.
W. 21st St.
W. 22nd St.
W. 23rd St.
W. 24th St.
W. 25th St.
W. 26th St.

A.C.
E,L
S

S
C,E

S
1,9

S
F

S
N,R

1,2,
3,9 S

S 1,9

S
F,L

KEY

AE American Express Office

N

0   400 yards
0   400 meters

72

fame. Built in the 1930s, **London Terrace** (W. 23rd and 24th Sts. between 9th and 10th Aves.) is a 1,670-unit apartment complex that isn't revival-anything. It's just big—really, really big. The theme-crazed management used to dress up the doormen as London bobbies.

CHELSEA HOTEL

Chelsea's most famous landmark is the Chelsea Hotel, a slightly seedy redbrick building with lacy wrought-iron balconies. Though the street it stands on is half run down, when the Chelsea opened in 1884 this was the center of New York's theater industry. It has traditionally catered to long-term (and often eccentric) tenants, including Mark Twain, Eugene O'Neill, O. Henry, Thomas Wolfe, Tennessee Williams, Vladimir Nabokov, Mary McCarthy, Arthur Miller, Dylan Thomas, William S. Burroughs, and Arthur C. Clarke (who wrote the script for *2001: A Space Odyssey* while living here). Andy Warhol filmed *The Chelsea Girls* here in 1966; in the '80s, the film *Sid and Nancy* (1986) revisited Sid Vicious's old haunts. *222 W. 23rd St., between 7th and 8th Aves., tel. 212/243–3700. Subway: 1 or 9 to W. 23rd St.*

GRAMERCY AND UNION SQUARE

The wealthy residential neighborhood of Gramercy (roughly defined as everything east of 5th Avenue between 14th and 30th streets) has a few quiet streets near Gramercy Park that allow you to get away momentarily from Manhattan's fast pace. The blocks along **Broadway,** particularly where it meets bustling Union Square, are home to some of New York's most happening bars, shops, and restaurants.

The Union Square Greenmarket (see Chapter 4) is the place where New York's finest chefs come to purchase farm-fresh produce, bread, cheese, and fruit.

Originally, 17th-century Dutch settlers called this part of Man-hattan island *Krom Moerasje* (little crooked swamp), and much of the area remained marshy swampland until developer Sam-uel Ruggles got his hands on it in 1831. Ruggles drained the swamp, replaced it with 66 beautiful town houses, and lured the rich with the promise of a private garden, **Gramercy Park** (E. 20th to 21st Sts. at Lexington Ave.), accessible only with a golden key. Over 150 years later it's still one of the most exclu-sive addresses in New York. And though the keys are no longer golden, the private park is still off-limits and residents fiercely guard this privilege (ironically, the park is frequently empty). Original 19th-century town houses in Greek Revival, Italianate, Gothic Revival, and Victorian Gothic styles still face the west and south sides of the park. The **Players Club** (16 Gramercy Park S) is an exclusive actor's club with notable alumni, including Mark Twain, Lionel Barrymore, Irving Berlin, Winston Churchill, Sir Laurence Olivier, Frank Sinatra, Walter Cronkite, and—the David among these Goliaths—Richard Gere. Next door, the **National Arts Club** (15 Gramercy Park S) was once the home of 19th-century New York governor Samuel Tilden; today this national historic landmark has free art exhibits open to the public and literary readings sponsored by the Poetry Society of America (*see* Spoken Word *in* Chapter 7).

UNION SQUARE

During the Civil War, Union troops paraded around, were reviewed in, and embarked from Union Square. History buffs will also recall that Union Square was the home of America's labor, socialist, and anarchist movements. In fact, a list of Union Square's former tenants reads like a who's who of America's radical left; the newspaper *Socialist Call,* the *Daily Worker,* the ACLU, the International Ladies Garment Workers' Union, and the League for Peace and Democracy all had their headquarters here. If that fails to interest you, at least come to Union Square to pay homage to an event that paved the way for a three-day week-end: On September 21, 1882, the Knights of Labor, a union that even during the 19th century included women and minorities, held a rally here. This rally was later commemorated as Labor Day.

During the early 20th century, demonstrations became increasingly large, and often violent, as city officials started calling in the heavy-handed NYPD to bash heads. At a vigil on the night that scapegoat anarchists Sacco and Venzetti were to be executed, National Guardsmen manned machine guns from the roofs of sur-rounding buildings. If you dropped by the square in the 1940s, you'd find big banners draped across the Communist party headquarters, urging DEMONSTRATE AGAINST IMPERIALIST WAR! FOR DEFENSE OF THE SOVIET UNION!

By mid-century, the left and Union Square became an entertainment center, full of bars and movie houses—a working-class Times Square (back before it became a den of sleaze). During the '60's, Andy Warhol had his famous Factory off Union Square, and Marcel Duchamp, expatriate French dada-ist, lived a block away. Today it's home to some of the city's finest restaurants, including **Union Square Cafe** (*see*

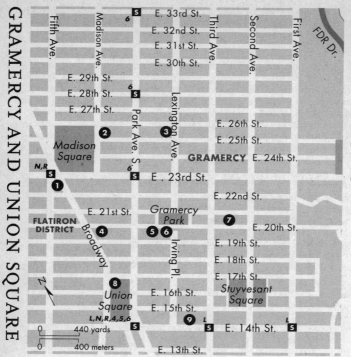

69th Regiment Armory, **3**

Con Edison Energy Museum, **9**

Flatiron Building, **1**

National Arts Club, **5**

New York City Police Museum, **7**

New York State Supreme Court, **2**

Players Club, **6**

Theodore Roosevelt Birthplace, **4**

Union Square Greenmarket, **8**

box Serious Splurges *in* Chapter 4). At the northwest corner of the square, note the statue of Gandhi, surrounded by lovely flowers during spring and summer. Just north of Union Square is a mini-neighborhood, the **Persian Rug District,** where many shops hang richly patterned rugs in their windows. Check out every New Yorker's favorite store, **ABC Carpet and Home** (*see* Chapter 5), which arranges its expensive goodies in big jumbles like in grandma's attic. *Subway: N, R, 4, 5, or 6 to Union Sq.*

FLATIRON BUILDING

Christened the Fuller Building, this dramatic neo-Renaissance building was popularly called the Flatiron Building because of its resemblance to the clothes-pressing device popular at the time. Built on a triangular wedge of land in 1902, it rose 286 ft (20 stories), a height unprecedented at the time; it is often considered the world's first skyscraper. Its internal steel frame structure was revolutionary, allowing for taller and taller buildings (Otis's elevator also helped). Its unusual shape also had the effect of creating unusually strong winds at its tip at 23rd Street. Dirty old men (and young ones, too) would gather to watch the wind raise the ankle-length skirts of passing women. To these men policemen gave the warning "23-skidoo." *175 5th Ave., between 23rd and 24th Sts. Subway: N or R to E. 23rd St.*

South of the Flatiron Building, between 5th Avenue and Park Avenue South, lies the **Flatiron District,** where some of the trendiest higher-priced restaurants and boutiques in New York have recently been popping up.

MADISON SQUARE

Most days this 7-acre park is full of activity: children playing, bums snoozing, and Fox TV execs rushing to lunch (the Fox offices are on the park's northwest corner). Statues in the park include Admiral David G. Farragut, Civil War hero, and one of those patently forgettable presidents, Chester A. Arthur. More important is the park's history: On this spot in 1842, a group of men calling themselves the Knickerbockers started playing a game known as New York ball—which was later to be known as baseball. By 1845, they had codified the rules that were later to become standard across the country. If you're a dog lover, head to the northwest corner of the park, where you'll find beloved pets scampering about in an area called James Dog Run.

Right off the park, between East 26th and 27th streets—where the New York Life Building now stands—was where the original incarnation of **Madison Square Garden** stood (it's since moved a few blocks farther northwest). Designed by Stanford White, an illustrious architect who helped design much of Columbia University, the Garden was the place where New York society gathered for hedonistic post-theater revelries. During a boisterous party at the Garden, White was shot through the head by Harry Thaw, a partner in White's firm. For the sordid details of White's "affairs," *see box* They Built This City, *above. E. 23rd to 26th Sts. between 5th and Madison Aves. Subway: N or R to W. 23rd St.*

Right across the street from Madison Square Park is the Appellate Division of the **New York State Supreme Court** (35 E. 25th St., at Madison Ave.), a gem of a courthouse, built on the heels of the City Beautiful movement in 1900. Flanking the portal are figures representing "Wisdom" and "Force"; among the other figures on the building are "Peace" and "Justice." Go inside to see the exhibitions in glass cases of New York historical ephemera (including a share in the stock of the City Lunatic Asylum) and the attractive murals. If it seems like there's a statue missing from the balustrade, there is: In the 1950s, the statue of Mohammed was removed at the request of local Islamic groups, as Islamic law forbids the representation of humans in sculpture or painting.

69TH REGIMENT ARMORY

Today, the only crowds moving in and out of the ugly, warehouselike 69th Regiment Armory are uniformed National Guardsmen. But over 85,000 New Yorkers caught the controversial 1913 Armory Show, which brought modern art by Picasso, Duchamp, and other artists to the American public for the first time. The stuffy American press roundly criticized the show: The European art was labeled subversive, and the American art too derivative of the European art. *E. 26th St. at Lexington Ave. Subway: 6 to E. 23rd St.*

Just north of the Armory, on Lexington Avenue between 27th and 29th streets, you'll find a number of Indian restaurants and groceries stores, where you can purchase exotic spices.

WEST VILLAGE

The West Village is also known as **Greenwich Village,** or sometimes just **The Village.** Greenwich Village used to encompass everything between 14th Street and Houston Street, from the Hudson to the East River. Nowadays, east of Broadway is considered the East Village, and everything west is the West Village. The Village really did begin life as its own little village, named Grin'wich, in the early 1700s. The people of New York City (who then lived much farther south, at the tip of Manhattan) regarded this as a resort town. When a series of nasty smallpox and yellow fever epidemics struck the city from 1799 to 1822, residents fled north to Grin'wich. Eventually, the area became a neighborhood of bluebloods who built lofty Greek Revival and Italianate style homes (some of which still survive) before continuing their migration north.

By the start of the 20th century, the Village had earned a pretty dicey reputation. The area around **Washington Square** (*see below*) became known as "Frenchtown" and was site of the city's highest concentration of brothels and rough bars. Writers and artists moved into its ornate brownstones anyway, because rent was cheap. Some former Village residents include: in the 19th century, Henry James, Edgar Allan Poe, Mark Twain, Walt Whitman, and Stephen Crane; at the turn of the century, O. Henry, Edith Wharton, Theodore Dreiser, and Hart Crane; and during the 1920s and '30s, John Dos Passos, Norman Rockwell, Sinclair Lewis, Eugene O'Neill, Edward Hopper, Margaret Sanger, and Edna St. Vincent Millay. In the late 1940s and early '50s, the abstract expressionist painters Franz Kline, Jackson Pollock, Mark Rothko, and Willem de Kooning congregated here, as did the Beat writers Jack Kerouac, Allen Ginsberg, and Lawrence Ferlinghetti. The 1960s brought folk musicians and poets, notably Bob "Positively 4th Street" Dylan and Peter, Paul and Mary. In the 1970s a burgeoning gay community helped make this the crucible for a national gay-rights movement. Today the area is still a center for liberal politics and tolerant attitudes, a home to writers, video artists, and AIDS activists (as well as yuppies who wish they were more creative)—and a place where the elderly First Bohemians mingle in cafés with those newly minted at **New York University** (*see below*).

Bleecker Street is one of the Village's main drags. Where it intersects with **MacDougal Street** (*see below*) it's jammed with cafés, jazz clubs, and bars. Between 7th Avenue and Abingdon Square you'll

WEST VILLAGE

KEY

i Tourist Information

0 ——— 200 yards
0 ——— 200 meters

Cherry Lane
Theater, **10**
Christopher
Park, **23**
Chumley's, **5**
Church of St. Luke-
in-the-Fields, **9**

Forbes Magazine
Galleries, **21**
Grace Church, **19**
Hudson River
Park, **2**
Jefferson Market
Library, **22**

Judson Memorial
Church, **13**
75½ Bedford
Street, **8**
Meat-Packing
District, **1**
77 Bedford Street, **7**
Sheridan Square, **3**
The Row, **17**

St. Luke's Place, **11**
Twin Peaks, **4**
Twin Sisters, **6**
Washington
Mews, **18**

New York University
Elmer Holmes Bobst
Library, **15**
Grey Art Gallery, **16**
Loeb Student
Center, **14**

Provincetown
Playhouse, **12**
The Strand
Bookstore, **20**

Hudson River

West Side Highway
West St.

find a more mellow Bleecker Street, with cozy little restaurants and purveyors of everything from Japanese furniture to African art. Consider making a detour off Bleecker Street to visit **18 West 11th Street**; the radical group The Weathermen had their bomb-making factory here until they accidentally blew it up in 1970. (At the time, Dustin Hoffman lived next door—he was seen on TV news coverage frantically trying to rescue his possessions.) Or follow Bleecker Street east of 7th Avenue, to **Leroy Street,** to find an old Italian neighborhood that's a lot livelier than Little Italy these days: Italian butchers, bakers, and pizza-pie makers abound. To the west, Bleecker Street ends at **Hudson Street,** which has a lot of small, slick restaurants and a handful of lesbian bars and clubs. Beyond that, way over on **West Street,** you'll find druggies and prostitutes hanging out by the piers.

In addition to the must-sees listed below, be sure to check out the **Forbes Magazine Galleries** (*see* Museums and Galleries, *below*) and **Hudson River Park** (*see* Parks and Gardens, *below*). The Village is also home to the outrageous **Halloween Parade** and monthlong **Gay Pride** festivities; for more on these, *see* Festivals *in* Chapter 1.

WASHINGTON SQUARE

At the heart of the Village is Washington Square. Before it became a public park in 1827, this was a cemetery for victims of yellow fever, a military parade ground (bad idea—the heavy artillery kept collapsing into old graves), and finally a site of public executions during the late 18th and early 19th centuries. Quite a few citified desperadoes met their maker at the **Hanging Elm,** which stands at the park's northwest corner. These days, the square is a maelstrom of playful activity, shared by a truly bizarre mix of people: earnest-looking NYU students, ruthless chess players, businesslike drug dealers, homeless hippie folk singers, bongo-drum players, joggers, skateboarders, vociferous protesters—and people like you, sitting on benches, witnessing the grand opera of it all. At the center of the square is a perpetually broken and waterless **fountain**: It's the New York City equivalent of Speaker's Corner

The Church of St. Luke-in-the-Fields (487 Hudson St., between Christopher and Barrow Sts.), a simple chapel built in 1821, has a small garden area that is open to the public during the day. It's a pleasant spot for a picnic lunch.

in London, a theater in the round for musicians, magicians, and ranting amateur politicians. Dominating the square's northern end is the triumphal **Washington Arch,** beyond which lies the start of glorious 5th Avenue. Originally, a wood-and-plaster arch was erected in 1889 to celebrate the 100th anniversary of George Washington's presidential inauguration; it proved so popular that a Tuckahoe marble version (designed by the irrepressible Stanford White) was thrown up in 1895. Below it you'll find two pollution-corroded statues of the president who hated to pose for portraits and such because it meant wearing those dreadful wooden teeth: "Washington at Peace," sculpted by Alexander Stirling Calder, and the Ying to Calder's Yang, "Washington at War," by Hermon MacNeil. Bodybuilding legend Charles Atlas was the model for "Peace." *Between Waverly Pl. and W. 4th St. at 5th Ave. Subway: A, B, C, D, E, F, or Q to W. 4th St. (Washington Sq.).*

Most of the striking old buildings bordering Washington Square belong to **New York University** (*see below*). The **Row,** a line of well-preserved, Federal-style town houses lining the north side of the square between 5th Avenue and University Place, now serves as offices and housing for lucky NYU faculty. Ditto for **Washington Mews** (half a block north), a cobblestone private street lined on one side with the former stables of the residences on the Row. Because Washington Square has long been considered tony real estate, it's had its share of famous residents: Author Willa Cather once lived at 60 Washington Square South, and Henry James's grandmother made her home at 18 Washington Square North (now demolished); James used it as the setting for his creatively titled, bodice-ripping novel *Washington Square.* Eugene O'Neill wrote *The Iceman Cometh* between trips to the pub from his home at 38 Washington Square South.

The **Judson Memorial Church,** a Romanesque Revival masterwork built in 1892 by McKim, Mead & White, is known as much for the social activism of its congregation as its impressive stained glass and marble reliefs: The Baptist church has supported AIDS research and abortion rights. The building's 10-story campanile makes it easy to identify. *55 Washington Square S, at Thompson St.*

MACDOUGAL STREET

Pick up MacDougal Street on the west side of Washington Square to watch Village people do their thing. South of the Square, between West 3rd and Bleecker streets, you'll find a row of ancient cafés that all claim to have been the Beats' "favorite" hangout (*see* Cafés *in* Chapter 4). The intersection with

JUSTICE IS DONE

At the corner of Greene Street and East Washington Place, one of New York City's great tragedies took place. Owners of the Triangle Shirtwaist Company, employers of about 500 women, felt the easiest way to keep workers at their sewing machines was to lock all the doors. When a fire broke out on March 25, 1911, there was no escape; 146 women perished, some by leaping to their deaths from the 10th floor. Families of 23 victims sued for damages and won, sort of, when a court ordered the company to pay each $75. The real victory came when the state passed 56 new laws regarding workers' safety.

Bleecker Street is a major bar scene—well, for the bridge-and-tunnel crowd, anyway. North of Washington Square you'll find the **Provincetown Playhouse** (133 MacDougal St.), which helped to start the career of the great playwright Eugene O'Neill; the gracious Federal homes at **127–131 MacDougal Street** were once owned by former vice president and unfortunately accurate marksman Aaron Burr. Fiorello La Guardia, the enormously popular mayor of the 1930s and '40s who passed major social reforms (and also read "Dick Tracy" comic strips over the radio) was born at **177 Sullivan Street,** a block east of MacDougal Street. MacDougal Street ends to the north at **West 8th Street,** a.k.a. "The Shoe Street." It's filled with discount footwear boutiques.

NEW YORK UNIVERSITY

New York University was founded 1831 by a group of prominent citizens fed up with what they saw as a ridiculous infatuation with Greek and Latin among the colleges of their day. NYU, they proclaimed, would cater to the common person. Today, it's the largest private university in the United States, offering over 2,500 courses (including Greek and Latin) and 25 degrees to both graduate and undergraduate students. Almost all of the programs at NYU are among the top in the nation, but its film school—which has graduated the likes of Spike Lee, Martin Scorcese, and Ang Lee—is perhaps the most famous one. Most of the buildings you'll see around Washington Square belong to the school—just look for the purple flags.

The **Elmer Holmes Bobst Library** (70 Washington Sq. S, at La Guardia Pl.) is a repository of some 2.5 million books. In the 1960s, well-intentioned but aesthetically impaired university officials planned (with aid of architects Philip Johnson and Richard Foster) to reface *all* its Washington Square buildings in ugly red sandstone, just like this one. Thankfully, cost proved prohibitive and they soon abandoned the plan. Next door, the **Loeb Student Center** (566 La Guardia Pl., at Washington Sq. S, tel. 212/998–4900) stands on the site of a famous boardinghouse, nicknamed the House of Genius for the talented writers who lived there over the years—Stephen Crane, O. Henry, and Theodore Dreiser, to name a few. Check its North Lobby for flyers about happenings around NYU. Pop by the university's Main Building (entrances at 100 Washington Sq. E and 33 Washington Pl.) to check out the exhibits, usually of contemporary art, at **Grey Art Gallery** (*see* Museums and Galleries, *below*). For maps and such, stop by **NYU information,** on the first floor of Shimkin Hall (50 W. 4th St., at Washington Sq. E, tel. 212/998–4636). It's open weekdays 8:30–8, weekends 10–4. On weekdays during the school year, **free tours** of the university are given several times daily. Tours depart from the Office of Undergraduate Admissions (22 Washington Sq. N, tel. 212/998–4524). Reservations are not necessary. *Subway: N or R to E. 8th St.*

BROADWAY

The Great White Way turns incredibly unglamorous around NYU. It's lined by modern university highrises, fast-food joints, and mallish clothing stores. Two shops are worth checking out: The **Strand** (*see* Used and Rare Books *in* Chapter 5) overflows with some 8 mi of books, and a few steps north on the same block, **Forbidden Planet** (*see* Specialty Bookstores *in* Chapter 5) claims the title of world's largest comic book and sci-fi store. And **Tower Records** (*see* Records, Tapes and CDs *in* Chapter 5) is simply just big.

GRACE CHURCH • Seeing this ornate Gothic church on an undistinguished block of Broadway is a bit like spying a wedding dress in a rack of poly-blend T-shirts. James Renwick, Jr., a parishioner with a very odd hobby (some people collect model trains, he drew cathedrals) designed it for free; when it opened for business 1846, it was the first Gothic-style church in the United States. During the 19th century its flock was incredibly rich. Step inside and admire the glorious English stained-glass windows that bathe the interior in an otherworldly glow. Free brochures at the back of the church point out some of the church's architectural highlights. Classical music concerts (usually around $10–$12) are held here throughout the year. *802 Broadway, between 10th and 11th Sts., tel. 212/254–2000. Admission free. Open weekdays 10–5:30, Sat. noon–4.*

WEST OF 6TH AVENUE

If you've been navigating Manhattan's efficient, numbered grid and just crossed over 6th Avenue into the heart of the Village, you're in for a shock: Its tree-lined streets are short and narrow, and cross each other at unfathomable angles. But don't let this vex you. It's one of the most beautiful neighborhoods in the city, with rows of ivy-covered brick town houses and nary a skyscraper in sight. Spend the afternoon wandering, then park yourself in one of its woodsy taverns (many former speakeasies) for a drink.

JEFFERSON MARKET LIBRARY • The triangle formed by West 10th Street, 6th Avenue, and Greenwich Avenue originally held a meat market, an all-women jail, and the magnificent 1877 courthouse that is now the Jefferson Market Library (a branch of the New York Public Library system). It's another fine design by the ubiquitous Calvert Vaux and Frederick Clarke Withers. A group of architects voted it one of the "ten most beautiful buildings in America" in 1885, but critics often have a hard time describing it. Some say it's "Venetian," others call it "High Victorian Gothic." Villagers, noting the alternating wide bands of red brick and narrow strips of white granite, dubbed it the "Lean Bacon Style." *425 6th Ave., at W. 10th St., tel. 212/243–4334. Subway: 1 or 9 to Christopher St. (Sheridan Sq.). Open Mon. and Thurs. 10–6, Tues. and Fri. noon–6, Wed. noon–8, Sat. 10–5.*

Much to the chagrin of its stuffy parishioners, the February 10, 1863, marriage of "General" Tom Thumb to Lavinia Warren, orchestrated by P. T. Barnum, temporarily turned Grace Church into a circus—literally.

Around the corner you'll find two tiny, charming courtyards, **Patchin Place** (off W. 10th St. between Greenwich Ave. and 6th Ave.) and **Milligan Place** (off 6th Ave., just north of W. 10th St.). Both were built in the 1850s for the waiters (mostly Basques) who worked at posh 5th Avenue hotels. **No. 4 Patchin Place** was the onetime home of e. e. cummings. Also worth a quick look is the gourmet wonderland **Balducci's,** which began decades ago with the lowly vegetable cart of the late Louis Balducci, and **Bigelow's Pharmacy** (414 6th Ave., between W. 8th and 9th Sts., tel. 212/533–2700), which looks the same as the day it opened in 1838, right down to the wooden display cases.

GAY STREET • This short, crooked lane is lined with small row houses circa 1810. It was once a black neighborhood and later a strip of speakeasies. Ruth McKenney wrote *My Sister Eileen* (based on experiences with her sister and her brother-in-law, Nathaniel West) in the basement of **No. 14 Gay Street.** *Between Christopher St. and Waverly Pl., just west of 6th Ave.*

SHERIDAN SQUARE • In 1863 this was the site of one of the nastiest riots in American history; a mob outraged with the Civil War draft turned against the city's freed slaves and some 125 people were killed. You'll find a statue of the mighty and heavily mustached military man for whom the square is named, Civil War general Philip "Little Phil" Sheridan, near the north end. *7th Ave. S at intersection of Christopher, W. 4th, and Grove Sts. Subway: 1 or 9 to Christopher St. (Sheridan Sq.).*

Southwest of Sheridan Square is **Christopher Street,** chock-full of gay bars and shops and strolling gay couples. Whatever your sexual orientation, you should stop by the **Li-Lac Chocolate Shop** (120 Christopher St., tel. 212/242–7374) for homemade chocolate and buttercrunch. The national gay-rights movement was born not far from Sheridan Square in 1969, when riots broke out over a police raid of the now-defunct gay club, **Stonewall Inn,** which was at 51 Christopher St. The Inn is long gone, but a plaque marks the site. In tiny **Christopher Park** (Christopher St., north of Sheridan Sq.) you'll find statues by sculptor George Segal of a lesbian couple sitting on a bench and gay male partners standing nearby.

BEDFORD STREET • The narrowest house in the Village is at **75½ Bedford Street,** a scant 9½ ft wide. It led a fine life as an alley until soaring real-estate prices inspired someone to put it to good use in 1873. Pulitzer-winning poet Edna St. Vincent Millay lived here in the 1920s. Next door, **77 Bedford**

Street is the oldest house in the Village (1799), while **86 Bedford Street** was the site of a Prohibition-era speakeasy. The bar that stands here now, **Chumley's** (*see* Chapter 6), keeps up the tradition by leaving its entrance unmarked; for decades, it was a meeting place for writers, including John Steinbeck, Ernest Hemingway, and Jack Kerouac. At the intersection with Grove Street, look for the chalet-like 1835 house that Villagers call **Twin Peaks** (102 Bedford St.).

COMMERCE STREET • Walk two blocks south of Grove Street on Bedford Street to find the homes of more famous dead folk: Aaron Burr at **17 Commerce Street,** Washington Irving at **11 Commerce Street.** The two identical brick houses separated by a garden are popularly known as the **Twin Sisters** (39–41 Commerce St.). Local legend has it that they were built by an indulgent sea captain for his two spoiled daughters, who loathed each other. The **Cherry Lane Theater** (38 Commerce St., tel. 212/989-2020) is one of the city's very first Off-Broadway houses and site of American premieres of works by O'Neill, Beckett, Ionesco, and Albee.

ST. LUKE'S PLACE • St. Luke's Place (the proper name for Leroy Street between Hudson Street and 7th Avenue South) is *the* place to go to check out classy 1850s town houses with famous pasts: Poet Marianne Moore lived at **No. 14**; Jimmy Walker, mayor of New York during the '20s and one of its most colorful political figures, lived at **No. 6** (the lampposts out front are special "mayor's lamps"); **No. 12** is shown as the Huxtables' home on *The Cosby Show* (although the family ostensibly lived in Brooklyn); and **No. 4** was the setting of the Audrey Hepburn movie *Wait Until Dark. Subway: 1 or 9 to Houston St.*

MEAT-PACKING DISTRICT

Believe it or not, New York City was the largest center of beef production in America during the mid-1800s. But with the advent of refrigeration, most meat packers quit trying to wrangle whole dead heifers into Manhattan and instead moved out West where the cows were. Still, more than a few have stuck around to serve the city's large Jewish community, since kosher meat can be kept only three days after butchering. Wholesale meat markets—fragrant enough to make your nose quiver even if you've never read anything by Upton Sinclair—can still be found sandwiched along the cobblestone streets west of Washington Street and south of 12th Street. (The men you see lingering at corners here work a different kind of meat market.) Photographers love the grit and rawness (no pun intended) of the meat-packing district, and if you stroll around you're bound to see a few fashion shoots in progress. Quite a few late-night restaurants and clubs have sprung up here in recent years. *Subway: A, C, E, or L to W. 14th St.*

EAST VILLAGE AND ALPHABET CITY

The East Village, originally considered part of the Lower East Side, was colonized by the young artists and intellectuals of the 1950s and '60s who'd abandoned Greenwich Village because it was too expensive. Beats like Jack Kerouac, Allen Ginsberg, and William S. Burroughs, jazz greats Charlie Parker and Charles Mingus, and artists like Willem de Kooning and Mark Rothko cruised these streets for inspiration or, sometimes, drugs. Which is not to say the East Village didn't exist before these artists got here: In 1925 George Gershwin penned "I'm Something on Avenue A," and prior to the Civil War rich folks like the Vanderbilts made **Astor Place** (*see below*) one of the city's most exclusive addresses.

While neighborhoods like the West Village, SoHo, and TriBeCa have recently morphed into overpriced yuppielands, the East Village—bounded to the west by 4th Avenue and Lafayette Street, to the north by 14th Street, to the south by Houston Street, and to the east by the East River—has miraculously remained the domain of nihilists, starving artists, and people with lots of dyed hair, pierced body parts, and tattoos. Main drags in the East Village are **St. Marks Place** and **Avenue A,** littered with bars, clubs, cafés, avant-garde galleries, hole-in-the-wall theaters, and purveyors of secondhand kitsch. Along the East River is the blissfully uncrowded **East River Park** (*see* Parks and Gardens, *below*), where the views of the Brooklyn Bridge can't be beat.

Add to the mix a few thriving ethnic enclaves: **Little Ukraine** (1st and 2nd Aves., near E. 7th St.) has a handful of Ukrainian diners, a few Eastern Orthodox churches, the **Ukrainian Museum** (*see* Museums and Galleries, *below*), and a bunch of dives where elderly Ukrainian women tend bar. **Little India** (6th St. between 1st and 2nd Aves.) is jam-packed with restaurants vying to serve you the cheapest tandoori in the most garish surroundings. For more on neighborhood restaurants, *see* Chapter 4.

ASTOR PLACE

At the intersection of 4th Avenue and Lafayette Street, Astor Place is the gateway to the East Village: Teen skateboarders hang out; and the occasional band sets up to grind out a few Eagles oldies. The subway entrance here is a cast-iron replica of the beaux arts original. Next to it is *Alamo*, a huge black steel

EAST VILLAGE AND ALPHABET CITY

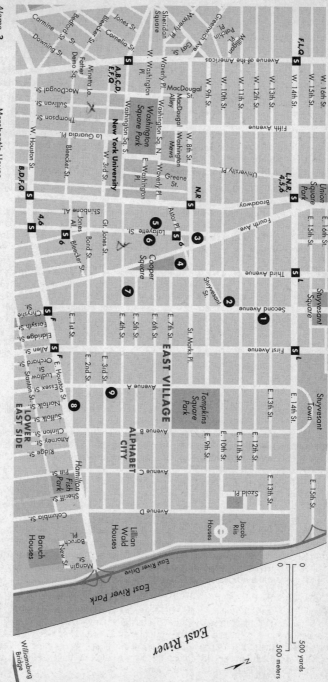

Alamo, **3**
Colonnade Row, **5**
Cooper Union, **4**
First Houses, **9**
Joseph Papp
Public Theater, **6**

Merchant's House
Museum, **7**
Red Square, **8**
St. Mark's-in-the-
Bowery Church, **2**
Ukrainian
Museum, **1**

81

cube sculpted in 1967 by Bernard Rosenthal. It balances on one corner and was designed to pivot, but, alas, pivots no more. *Subway: 6 to Astor Pl.*

The street's namesake, John Jacob Astor, made his first millions by trading furs in the Pacific Northwest (bas-relief beavers on the tiles at the Astor Place subway station are fuzzy little reminders). Once settled in New York City he degenerated into a human Jabba the Hut, amassing enough land and wealth to be considered the richest man in America by 1840—all with a girth too great to get out of bed and on a steady diet of human milk. On his deathbed he expressed the desire to buy every foot of land in Manhattan.

One of the bloodiest riots in New York history occurred on Astor Place in 1849, over a disparaging remark made by Charles Macready, an English tragedian (popular with the city's Anglophilic elite), about the abilities of Edwin Forrest, an American actor worshiped by the working classes. Hundreds of protesters armed with rotten eggs, fruit, and rocks interrupted Macready's performance of *MacBeth* at the Astor Place Opera House. The ensuing riot left 31 dead, over 150 injured, and painfully underscored the chasm between New York's classes.

COLONNADE ROW

These days, Colonnade Row's four remaining town houses resemble Greek ruins more than Greek Revival masterpieces. The original 1833 development of nine homes—named "La Grange Terrace" after the country estate of the Marquis de Lafayette—was derided as tacky by New York elites until bigshots like John Jacob Astor, Cornelius Vanderbilt, and Charles Dickens moved in. Current tenants are much less impressive. On the street level of two of the houses are the popular **Indochine** restaurant and the **Astor Place Theatre,** whose present tenant *Blue Man Group* may run forever. *428–434 Lafayette St., between Astor Pl. and E. 4th St. Subway: 6 to Astor Pl.*

JOSEPH PAPP PUBLIC THEATER • The imposing Italian Renaissance–style building across the street began life as the city's first free library (a gift from the usually miserly John Jacob Astor in 1854), then became offices for the Hebrew Immigrant Aid Society (HIAS) before being renovated in the '60s to serve as the New York Shakespeare Festival's Joseph Papp Public Theater. Under the leadership of the late Joseph Papp, the Public's five playhouses built a reputation for innovative performances: The Aquarian hippie-fest *Hair* started here, as well as *A Chorus Line,* and it helped launch the careers of Meryl Streep, Raul Julia, Kevin Kline, James Earl Jones, and David Mamet. For more information, *see* Chapter 7. Today the Public is overseen by producer-director George Wolfe, who directed the big Broadway hit, *Bring in 'Da Noise, Bring in 'Da Funk. 425 Lafayette St., at Astor Pl., tel. 212/598-7150. Subway: 6 to Astor Pl.*

COOPER UNION AND COOPER SQUARE

If self-made millionaire, railroad industrialist, and inventor Peter Cooper were still alive, every year he'd probably get 1,000 big wet kisses from the engineers, artists, and architects in training at the Cooper Union, a totally *tuition-free* college. Cooper himself came from a poor family and learned to read late in life, so he plowed his big bucks back into an institute of higher learning for working folks, opened in 1859. Lectures in its **Foundation Building** (the city's first internal steel-frame building, which was Cooper's own invention) helped launch the NAACP and catapulted Abraham Lincoln to the presidency—Abe gave his famous "Might Makes Right" speech here in 1860. The building has two free galleries presenting changing art shows during the academic year. Call or check the paper for the current lecture and concert schedule. *41 Cooper Sq., between 3rd and 4th Aves., tel. 212/254-6374. Subway: 6 to Astor Pl.*

Cooper Union stands, logically, on **Cooper Square** (bordered by St. Marks Place, 3rd and 4th Aves., and the Bowery), an immaculate—and locked—park with a regal-looking statue of Peter Cooper at its center. To the west stands **Carl Fisher Music Store** (56–62 Cooper Sq., tel. 212/677–0821), which sells sheet music and, more importantly, keeps a large monthly calendar with the birthdates of every major and minor musician on the planet (Boy George and Burl Ives share a special day, if nothing else). South of Carl Fischer are the **offices of the *Village Voice*** (36 Cooper Sq.).

ST. MARKS PLACE

St. Marks Place, as 8th Street is called between 3rd Avenue and Avenue A, is still one of the liveliest streets in the East Village. Hippies and acid heads tripped here in the '60s, and disco fever found its first NYC outlet here in the '70s at a club called Get Down. Green-haired neo-punks blasting the Boredoms are now making the scene. You can buy just about anything in the string of cluttered shops or at the de facto flea market that appears daily along the sidewalk, from vintage clothes to a new guitar. Unfortunately, there's even a Gap. *Subway: 6 to Astor Pl.*

ST. MARK'S-IN-THE-BOWERY CHURCH

This 1799 fieldstone country church was built over the family chapel of Peter Stuyvesant (who is buried here), and is the city's oldest continually used church. Its liberal clergy has sponsored voter-registration drives, preached for civil rights, and opened the nation's first lesbian health-care clinic. In the '20s, one pastor livened up the boring Episcopalian ceremonies with American Indian chants, Greek folk dancing, and recitation of Eastern mantras. It currently hosts dance, poetry, and musical performances; call for a schedule. *2nd Ave. at E. 10th St., tel. 212/674–8194. Subway: L to 3rd Ave.*

The stretch of 2nd Avenue next to St. Mark's Church was known as the "Jewish Rialto" at the turn of the century because its eight Yiddish theaters presented the best in comedy, melodrama, and musicals from the Old World. On the sidewalk in front of the **Second Avenue Deli** (*see* East Village and Alphabet City *in* Chapter 4) are Hollywood-style squares commemorating luminaries of the Yiddish stage.

TOMPKINS SQUARE

Recently restored Tompkins Square Park is the physical, spiritual, and political heart of the radical East Village. It's a good-size park, and you can always find a drum circle or game of Rollerblade basketball or whatever. Look for two monuments: **Temperance Fountain,** oddly out of place given the number of people drinking beers out of brown bags, and the **General Slocum Memorial,** which commemorates 1,021 German immigrants from the East Village who perished on the way to a church picnic when their ship caught fire and sank.

The square takes its name from four-times governor Daniel Tompkins, an avid abolitionist and vice president under James Monroe who once owned this land from 2nd Avenue to the East River. Its history is long and violent: The 1874 Tompkins Square Riot involved some 7,000 unhappy laborers and 1,600 police. The police gained control by beating bystanders and demonstrators indiscriminately. The 1988 Tompkins Square Riot involved police on horseback charging homeless-rights and anti-gentrification protesters armed with sticks and bottles—Mayor David Dinkins had ordered the square cleared of proliferating refrigerator-box castles and tent mansions. The park did not reopen until 1992, midnight curfew in place. In between the tumultuous events, activist Abbie Hoffman and his New Left Yippies held a few rallies at the square in the '60s. Between 1950–1954, jazz great Charlie Parker lived east of the park at 151 Avenue B. *E. 7th–10th Sts. between Aves. A and B. Subway: 6 to Astor Pl.*

The Corinthian columns fronting the town houses at Colonnade Row were built by talented inmates of Sing Sing Penitentiary.

ALPHABET CITY

As you head toward the East River to the blocks along Avenues A, B, C, and D you enter Alphabet City. It's predominantly a Puerto Rican community, once known as the heroin capital of New York. Gentrification and a police crackdowns on drugs have made it a somewhat safer place—**Avenue A** has been recently annexed by East Village hipsters and is crowded with bars, cafés, and cheap restaurants. But avenues C and D are still places to use caution (or avoid) after dark. On abandoned buildings throughout the neighborhood look for graffiti murals, beautiful and poignant. Many eulogize members of the community who have fallen to gang violence. A towering sculpture built from old motorcycles, hubcaps, 55-gallon drums, half a rowboat, and wound with iridescent pink ribbon stands on Avenue B at E. 2nd Street. A 30-ft-tall sister sculpture, of welded-together children's toys, stands on Avenue C between East 5th and 6th streets. Other landmarks to look for: **Red Square** (Houston St. between Aves. A and B) is a redbrick high-rise with a gloriously beaming statue of Vladimir Lenin (plundered from Russia after the fall of Communism) on its roof. The bland, blocklike **First Houses** (E. 3rd St. at Ave. A), built in 1935, have the dubious distinction of being the first public-housing projects in the entire country.

Despite Alphabet City's economic troubles and bitter on-again, off-again war between police and squatters (who have taken over some of the neighborhood's condemned tenement buildings), there's a sense of community here that many other neighborhoods in the city totally lack. On street corners, elderly Puerto Rican men play dominoes, children chase each other on beat-up banana bikes, and homeless young punks gather together to panhandle for the price of a forty.

LOWER EAST SIDE

In the century before the Beats carved out their own urban utopia, the East Village, for radical politics and experimental art, everything east of Broadway and from 14th Street south to Canal Street was con-

TENEMENT BUILDINGS

Tenements, cheap to build and easy to maintain (or neglect), were considered the perfect solution to the city's 19th-century immigration boom. Early tenements were typically six-story buildings with four tiny, windowless apartments per floor and no indoor plumbing, heating, gas, or electricity. To afford rent, as many as 20 people would cram into each apartment—crowded, dangerous, and depressing. Muckraking journalists like Jacob Riis and Stephen Crane helped expose the squalid conditions of tenement dwellers, leading to reforms in the 1870s and 1900s that mandated basics like ventilation, plumbing, and electricity. You can still see tenement buildings throughout the Lower East Side; notice that the style of the time dictated that even low-cost housing come with ornate Italianate facades.

The Lower East Side Tenement Museum (see Museums and Galleries, below) has two carefully re-created tenement buildings with displays depicting the families that once lived there. The museum also offers weekly neighborhood walking tours for $10–$15, a must if you're into the history of immigrant America.

sidered the "Lower East Side." Today it's roughly confined by Houston Street to the north, the Bowery to the west, and Canal Street to the south. Almost every ethnic group to arrive in America has spent some time here: Italians, Eastern-Europeans, Jews, Russians, Ukrainians, and Poles in the 1880s, and more recently Africans, Puerto Ricans, Chinese, Dominicans, Filipinos, Indians, and Koreans. Wander its streets and you can find octogenarian Sengalese playing dominoes, overhear a heated argument about the meaning of a particular verse in the Talmud, or purchase Spanish-language comics at a corner newsstand.

Although waves of immigrants fresh from Ellis Island made this the most crowded neighborhood in the world around 1915, until recently it had grown nearly deserted. Club kids, Kurt Cobain mourners, and adventurous yuppies have started drifting south from the East Village in search of cheaper rents and bigger thrills; they're responsible for the self-consciously seedy bars and cafés that have sprung up along **Ludlow Street** and **East Houston Street.** Pinch me bubbi, I think I'm in a Calvin Klein ad! Seriously, though: Recent additions aside, the historically minded will enjoy an afternoon stroll though this fascinating neighborhood. *Subway: F to 2nd Ave.*

ESSEX STREET AND THE JEWISH COMMUNITY

In the '20s a half million Jews comprised one of the largest enclaves on the Lower East Side. Many Jewish shops, delis, and temples still line Essex Street, particularly its intersection with **Hester Street.** An unparalleled junk shop, **Israel Wholesale** (21 Essex St., at Hester St., tel. 212/477–2310) supplies the diaspora with menorahs 'n' more. Buy your yarmulkes at **H&M Skullcap Company** (46 Hester St., near Essex St., tel. 212/777–2280) or some hamentaschen (apricot- or prune-filled pastries) at **Gertel's Bakery** (53 Hester St., at Essex St., tel. 212/982–3250). **Guss' Lower Eastside Pickle Corp.** (35 Essex St., between Grand and Hester Sts., tel. 212/254–4477) sells its vinegary delicacies straight from the barrel and is an essential New York experience.

SCHAPIRO'S WINERY • Also worth a visit is America's first kosher winery. Though it's been around since 1899, Schapiro's will never steal the thunder from France's Châteauneuf-du-Pape; the original

Schapiro's slogan was SO THICK YOU CAN CUT IT WITH A KNIFE. The dusty store doles out free samples (Sunday 11–5) and offers free half-hour tours of its cellars on Sundays from September to Passover; call for exact times. *126 Rivington St., between Essex and Norfolk Sts., tel. 212/674–4404. Subway: J, M, or Z to Essex St.*

ELDRIDGE STREET SYNAGOGUE • Built in 1887 for the newly arrived Eastern-European Jewish community, the Eldridge Street Synagogue is one of the Lower East Side's largest and grandest remaining synagogues. Although years of neglect have taken their toll, its intricate carvings and masonry remain intact, as well as its overwhelming sense of history and sanctity. The temple is currently being restored as a cultural heritage center and remains open for guided tours ($4), given every Sunday on the hour noon to 4 and by appointment Tuesday–Thursday. *12–16 Eldridge St., at Canal St., tel. 212/219–0888. Subway: J, M, or Z to Essex St.*

ORCHARD STREET BARGAIN DISTRICT

Orchard Street is lined with old-time mom-and-pop stores selling ersatz leather goods, linens, bootleg tapes, fabrics, "designer" watches, clothing, housewares, and just plain junk. Originally, immigrants came here to hawk buttons or heirloom diamonds or whatever else they owned. Scores of New Yorkers still come for cut-rate prices, or at least to wander: Where else can you hear bargaining in every tongue from Polish to Farsi to Hindi? Most shops are closed Saturday—but that's okay. The big deal is Sunday, when Orchard Street is closed to traffic between Houston and Hester streets and the whole area takes on the air of an exotic bazaar. Between April and December, free **walking and shopping tours** (tel. 212/995–8258) of the district are given on Sunday at 11 AM; meet at Katz's Delicatessen (Ludlow and Houston Sts.). *Subway: F to 2nd Ave.; walk 4 blocks east.*

Around the turn of the century, the few square blocks along Orchard Street could attract as many as 25,000 pushcart salesmen in a single day. Eventually the city declared pushcarts a nuisance and banished them for good.

LITTLE ITALY

Welcome to Little Italy. Did you expect to find Mafiosi chasing down narrow streets, as in Martin Scorcese's *Mean Streets*? Or stoops filled with wizened old women in black, passing the days with talk of the Old Country? Maybe you expected to catch Italian-American actors like Tony Danza, Danny Aiello, and Robert DeNiro slurping down cannolli and espresso at a café? Sorry. All of that went *arrivederci* a long time ago, *bambino*. At the turn of the century, Piedmontese, Neapolitan, Genoan, Sicilian, Tuscan, and Calabrian settlements filled the blocks south of Houston Street; in 1932, an estimated 98% of the area's inhabitants were of Italian birth or heritage. Though technically the neighborhood still occupies a corridor between Lafayette Street and the Bowery, from Houston Street south to Canal Street, in reality, Chinatown's continuing expansion has swallowed most of traditional Little Italy. What's left is confined to the blocks along **Mulberry Street.**

The best time to visit is during the 10-day **Feast of San Gennaro** (tel. 212/226–9546), a rollicking party held every mid-September to honor the patron saint of Naples. Streets are closed to traffic, decorated with tinsel, then packed with game booths and vendors of Italo-snacks. It's officially sponsored by the **San Gennaro Church** (113 Baxter St., near Canal St.). In June is the smaller **Feast of St. Anthony of Padua.** For more on both, *see* Festivals *in* Chapter 1.

What you get on Mulberry Street are souvenir shops sandwiched between tourist-filled trattorias and sidewalk cafés; looming above are the tenement buildings into which immigrant families once crowded. It's a street for strolling, gawking, and inhaling the aroma of garlic and olive oil, but you'll need an appetite to explore. Off Mulberry at 195 Grand Street, **Ferrara's** (tel. 212/226–6150) is a 100-year-old pastry shop. It's a truly wonderful place to eat tiramisu and sip cappuccino, even if you're sitting next to some bloke who thinks the Grand Canal is a sewage treatment plant in the Bronx. Also on Grand Street, the **Alleva Dairy** (188 Grand St., at Mulberry St., tel. 212/226–7990) has been selling its homemade mozzarella for over a century. Finally, **D&G Bakery** (45 Spring St., near Mulberry St., tel. 212/226–6688) is one of the last coal-oven bakeries in the United States. Everyone agrees that their bread is some of the best in the city, and they start selling it daily at 8 AM. *Subway: 6 to Spring St.*

If you want to see a thriving Italian-American community populated by Italian Americans, not tourists, hop a subway to Carroll Gardens in Brooklyn or Arthur Avenue in the Bronx.

Lower East Side

CBGB & OMFUG, **1**

Eldridge Street Synagogue, **15**

Gertel's Bakery, **18**

Guss' Lower Eastside Pickle Corp., **19**

H&M Scullcap Company, **17**

Israel Wholesale, **16**

Lower East Side Tenement Museum, **20**

Orchard Street Bargain District, **22**

Schapiro's Winery, **21**

Little Italy

Alleva Dairy, **4**

Ferrara's, **3**

D&G Bakery, **2**

San Gennaro Church, **6**

Chinatown

Asian American Arts Center, **12**

Church of the Transfiguration, **9**

Confucius Plaza, **13**

First Shearlith Israel graveyard, **10**

Kam Man, **7**

Mahayana Temple, **14**

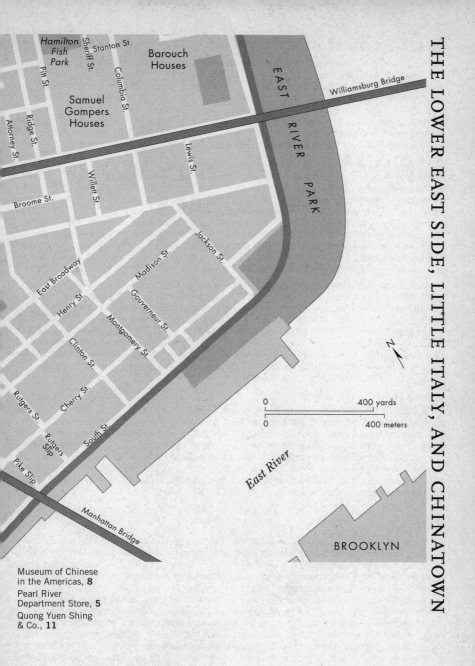

Hamilton Fish Park

Sheriff St.

Stanton St.

Barouch Houses

EAST

Pitt St.

Columbia St.

Samuel Gompers Houses

Ridge St.

Attorney St.

Lewis St.

RIVER

Willett St.

Broome St.

PARK

Williamsburg Bridge

East Broadway

Madison St.

Jackson St.

Henry St.

Gouverneur St.

Clinton St.

Montgomery St.

Cherry St.

Rutgers St.

Rutgers Slip

South St.

Pike Slip

Manhattan Bridge

East River

0   400 yards

0   400 meters

N

BROOKLYN

Museum of Chinese
in the Americas, **8**

Pearl River
Department Store, **5**

Quong Yuen Shing
& Co., **11**

CHINATOWN

When you walk into Chinatown, you may feel like you've been transported from Manhattan to Shanghai. Everywhere its streets are crowded, bustling, and vibrant; many of the shopkeepers' signs and billboards are written in Chinese characters, and sidewalk markets offer buckets of live fish, stacks of alien-looking vegetables, and bundles of refrigerated chicken feet. Even the smells are different, courtesy of street vendors serving up steaming chow mein and conch dumplings. Around half of the city's population of 300,000 Chinese live here; some 55% of its residents speak little or no English. In recent years, a flood of immigrants from Thailand, Korea, Vietnam, Taiwan, and especially Hong Kong have settled beyond the traditional boundaries of Chinatown and swallowed parts of Little Italy and the Lower East Side.

CANAL STREET

Formerly Chinatown's northern barrier, Canal Street (which was once really a canal) is now one of the busiest streets in the neighborhood and lined with interesting shops. Check out the **Pearl River Department Store** (277 Canal St., at Broadway, tel. 212/431–4770) for porcelain tea cups and Maoist postage stamps and **Kam Man** (200 Canal St., between Mulberry and Mott Sts., tel. 212/571–0330) for Chinese food items. Just south of Canal Street on the Bowery, you'll find the **Asian American Arts Centre** (*see* Museums and Galleries, *below*). At the eastern end of Canal, across the Bowery and near the entrance to the Manhattan Bridge, is the Buddhist **Mahayana Temple** (133 Canal St., tel. 212/925–8787), with a bright yellow facade, red columns, and golden dragons at the entrance; inside incongruous crystal chandeliers hang above the 15-ft tall golden Buddha. *Subway: J, M, N, R, Z, or 6 to Canal St.*

Be sure to stop at the **Museum of Chinese in the Americas** (*see* Museums and Galleries, *below*), a block south of Canal Street. Other streets great for wandering include **Mott Street, Pell Street,** and **Bayard Street**; the intersection of Mott and Pell streets is the heart of Chinatown. On Mott Street you can visit the ancient curio shop **Quong Yuen Shing & Co.** (32 Mott St., near Pell St., tel. 212/962–6280); and, across the street, the **Church of the Transfiguration** (25 Mott St., at Mosco St., tel. 212/962–5157), a Georgian structure with Gothic windows and a Chinese Catholic congregation. Mass is said in Cantonese, Mandarin, and English. If you're looking for a place to relax, check out **Columbus Park** (Bayard St. between Baxter and Mulberry Sts.). This tiny, paved park was once the site of a tough, 19th-century slum of Irish and German immigrants.

CHATHAM SQUARE

Eight different roads converge at Chatham Square, causing vehicular and pedestrian nightmares aplenty. On the center island is the **Kim Lau Arch,** a memorial to the Chinese Americans who died defending the United States in foreign wars (good luck getting across the street to take a closer look). The area north of the square, where Bowery and Canal Street come together, is called **Confucius Plaza,** possibly because a spectacular statue of Confucius stands guard. At the statue's base you'll see a long, thought-provoking quote from the 2,000-year-old wise man's treatise, *The Chapter of the Great Harmony (Ta Tung)*. Just south of Chatham Square on St. James Place you'll come upon the **First Shearlith Israel graveyard,** the first Jewish cemetery (1656) in the United States.

SOHO

SoHo (so-named because it's the area SOuth of HOuston Street), formerly industrial and now high-wattage hip, shed its working-class roots not so long ago. In the mid-19th century this was a light-industry district, with makers and sellers of goods like china, furs, textiles, glass, and lace; shops and factories and even sweatshops were housed in grand **cast-iron buildings.** Unfortunately, the overcrowded area caught fire so frequently it was dubbed "Hell's Hundred Acres"; as late as 1962 a City Club of New York study called it "commercial slum number one." In the '70s, the city's restless population of artists—always looking for large, cheap, well-lit spaces—defied zoning laws to move into SoHo's run-down and abandoned warehouses. By the '80s it was all over: Zoning laws changed, art-collecting debutantes moved in, and loft prices soared into the millions. Today the smallish, walkable neighborhood (which encompasses only 40 blocks from Houston Street south to Canal Street and from Lafayette Street west to 6th Avenue) is the epitome of postmodern chic. An amalgam of black-clad art dealers, models, artists, celebrities, and other Beautiful People rush in and out of galleries, bistros, and boutiques all day long. Some New Yorkers have lately taken to referring to the area as "like a shopping mall." This is not a compliment.

WEST
VILLAGE

Leroy St.

Clarkson St.

W. Houston St.

King St.

Downing St.

Ave. of the Americas (Sixth Ave.)

MacDougal St.

Sullivan St.

W. Houston St.

B,D,F,Q

Prince St.

SOHO

Spring St.

Hudson St.

Charlton St.

Vandam St.

Varick St.

Spring St.

Dominick St.

Broome St.

Holland Tunnel
Entrance

Canal St.

Watts St.

Desbrosses St.

Vestry St.

Laight St.

Hubert St.

Greenwich St.

Washington St.

Hudson St.

Holland Tunnel
Exit

Ericsson Pl.

Moore St.

Franklin St.

TRIBECA

Harrison St.

Staple St.

Jay St.

Independence
Plaza

Washington
Market
Park

Chambers St.

West Side Hwy./West St.

Hudson River Park

West Broadway

Thompson St.

Wooster St.

Greene St.

Mercer St.

Broadway

Crosby St.

Lafayette St. Baxter St.

Broome St.

Grand St.

Howard St.

Canal St.

Lispenard St.

Walker St.

White St.

Franklin St.

Leonard St.

Worth St.

Thomas St.

Duane St.

Reade St.

West Broadway

Church St.

Broadway

Lafayette St.

Federal
Plaza

Duane Park

N,R

N,R

C,E

A,C,E

A,C

N,R

City Hall
Park

Warren St.

Murray St.

Alternative Museum, **7**
Ghostbusters'
headquarters, **16**
Guggenheim
Museum SoHo, **4**
Haughwout
Building, **11**
Institute for
Contemporary
Art/Clocktower
Gallery, **19**
King of Greene
Street, **10**

Museum for
African Art, **6**
New Museum of
Contemporary Art, **5**
New York City Fire
Museum, **21**
Queen of Greene
Street, **13**
SoHo Grand, **14**
Tribeca Film
Center, **15**
Tribeca Performing
Arts Center, **20**

Art Galleries
Art in General, **17**
The Drawing
Center, **9**
Franklin Furnace
Archive, Inc., **18**
Holly Solomon, **2**
Howard Greenberg, **8**
Leo Castelli, **3**
New York Earth
Room, **1**

Thread Waxing
Space, **12**

CAST-IRON BUILDINGS

You know how used-car lots put out lots of flags and balloons to attract customers? Well, the shop and factory owners of the 19th century wanted big, showy buildings with large windows for that exact same reason. Between 1860 and 1890 most of these four- to six-story buildings were made of cast iron, which was cheaper, stronger, and easier to work with than brick. Cast iron could be molded to mimic any style—Italianate, Victorian Gothic, neo-Grecian, Second Empire, Star Wars, whatever. Even buildings that housed sweatshops had beautiful facades with fantastic embellishments. Kind of a depressing thought, isn't it?

Some of the finest remaining cast-iron buildings in the world are on Greene Street between Canal and Grand streets: The "Queen of Greene Street" (28–30 Greene St.) is only surpassed by its colossal neighbor the "King of Greene Street" (72–76 Greene St.). The "Parthenon of Cast Iron," the Haughwout Building (488 Broadway), was originally a china and glassware business with an exterior inspired by a Venetian palazzo. Inside, it contained the world's first commercial passenger elevator, a steam-powered device invented by Elisha Graves Otis.

Naturally, SoHo is packed with zillions of galleries (*see* Museums and Galleries, *below*), which look intimidating and in fact sell paintings you will never, ever be able to afford. Relax. No one's going to object to your looking, and much of the art complements whatever's currently on view at the Guggenheim, MoMA, or Met. Here's the best part: The galleries are free. Not surprisingly, artsy SoHo also brims with artsy museums: The **New Museum of Contemporary Art**; the **Guggenheim Museum SoHo**; the **Alternative Museum**; and the **Museum for African Art.** For more information on each, *see* Museums and Galleries, *below*.

In SoHo's shops hang clothing and furnishings and even toothbrushes for sale so beautiful they could qualify as objets d'art, too. Of course they're priced accordingly. Great for wandering and window-shopping are the blocks along **Prince Street, Spring Street, West Broadway, Wooster Street,** and **Greene Street,** where you'll find hip Euro-style boutiques like **Agnès B.** (116 Prince St., tel. 212/925–4649). But don't max out your credit cards just yet: There are a few affordable things to buy in SoHo, provided you find the right corner. On **Broadway** south of Spring Street you'll find vintage- and secondhand-clothing stores, while vendors at the small vacant lot on the corner of Wooster and Spring streets sell cheapie clothes and trinkets. For more information, *see* Chapter 5.

In 1996 the 15-story **SoHo Grand** (310 W. Broadway, at Grand St., tel. 212/965–3000) became the first major hotel to open in the neighborhood since the 1880s. Be sure to take a look at its chicly designed second-floor lobby; after pounding the pavement, you can relax in one of the oversized sofas or chairs and admire all the well-groomed guests; many of them work in the film, fashion, and design industries. The inviting Canal Room restaurant, serving regional American cuisine, is not as pricey as most other hotel restaurants.

TRIBECA

As Manhattan neighborhoods go, TriBeCa (the name that savvy real-estate developers dreamed up for the TRIangle BElow CAnal Street) is fairly laid back. The area's development shares many similarities with nearby SoHo. This was historically a commercial neighborhood, once filled with fish-packing plants and chemical manufacturers. Its warehouses and factories were all but abandoned in the 1960s; they were recolonized as residential lofts by artists in the '70s, grew trendy in the '80s, and are now afford-able only to investment bankers. Like SoHo, TriBeCa still has its share of hip art galleries (see Museums and Galleries, below) and artsy shops, even if many of the artists have moved elsewhere. Unlike SoHo, TriBeCa (bounded to the north by Canal Street, to the east by Broadway, to the south by Chambers Street, and to the west by the Hudson River) has a tendency to shut down entirely on weekends. But you can still have some fun.

You can cover TriBeCa's attractions in an afternoon, really: Along Broadway, White Street, and Thomas Street are cafés, restaurants, and some shops, many housed in charmingly detailed cast-iron buildings from the late 1800s. Follow White Street across West Broadway to Moore Street; the firehouse (114 Moore St.) you'll see was **Ghostbusters' headquarters** in the two movies of the same name. (Do not disturb the firemen.) A bit farther west is Robert DeNiro's **Tribeca Film Center** (375 Greenwich St., at N. Moore St.), a movie-production complex housed in an old coffee-and-tea warehouse. You might even see DeNiro himself dining at his restaurant downstairs, **Tribeca Grill** (see Chapter 4). Farther south, interesting residential areas to explore include **Staple Street** (barely an alley) and **Jay Street.** Nearby **Duane Park** (Duane St. between Staple and Hudson Sts.) has been preserved since 1800 as a calm, shady triangle; it is still surrounded by cheese, butter, and egg warehouses.

Several of SoHo's streets have been spiffed up with quaint Belgian cobblestones, just like Europe. Or Disneyland.

In contrast, **Independence Plaza** (Greenwich St. near Harrison St.) is a bunch of nondescript '70s high-rises. If it weren't for a bunch of building-hugging preservationists, the entire neighborhood would now look like this apartment complex. At the southern edge of TriBeCa on Greenwich Street is **Washington Market Park** (see Parks and Gardens, below). On Saturdays a dozen or so vendors gather to sell fresh flowers, vegetables, fish, and baked goods (see Greenmarkets in Chapter 4). Of course, it's not the same as Bear Market, which flourished around these parts in the early 19th century. Then, you could buy wild game and caviar. Just north of the park off Chambers Street, you can take in a music, dance, or theatrical performance at the **Tribeca Performing Arts Center** (see Arts Centers in Chapter 7) at the Borough of Manhattan Community College. And further north of the arts complex, across the West Side Highway, you can enter **Hudson River Park** (see Parks and Gardens, below).

LOWER MANHATTAN

In Lower Manhattan, behemoth glass-and-steel skyscrapers lie mere blocks from ancient churches and cobblestone alleys. Walk a few blocks and it will seem like every building has a plaque recalling some event from the past quarter of a millennium. It was here, after all, that the Nieuw Amsterdam colony was established by the Dutch in 1625; the city did not really expand much above Canal Street until the middle of the 19th century. Today, this tiny section of Manhattan is a global financial center, and swarms of businesspeople clutching cellular phones crowd its sidewalks on weekdays. You can practically hear the wheels of commerce grinding, and the spirit of the place is pretty infectious—you might get struck with the urge to put on a power tie and renounce socialism if you stay too long. On evenings and weekends, however, the streets are eerily empty of everyone except tourists (and the handful of crazy New Yorkers who come down to Rollerblade the empty streets). Don't expect to find open restaurants, bars, bodegas, or even hot-dog vendors after 5 PM or on weekends.

Streets in Lower Manhattan were laid out back when heavy traffic was defined as a dozen yoked oxen pulling wagons. So, besides **Broadway,** which ends its 17-mi run down the length of Manhattan at **Bowling Green** (see Parks and Gardens, below), there really isn't a main drag. The most famous of lower Manhattan's labyrinthine streets is Wall Street (see box, Wonder Wall, below). **Pearl Street** was actually a shoreline drive before more land was reclaimed from the harbor. **Fulton Street** is named for Robert Fulton, whose steam ferry (the first in the world) carried passengers and cargo between Manhattan and Brooklyn.

At the very tip of Lower Manhattan is **Battery Park** (see Parks and Gardens, below), named for the battery of cannons that was originally placed along the shore to scare off those nasty Brits. It offers awe-inspiring views of the harbor. Stop by the visitors center at **Castle Clinton National Monument** to look at historical exhibits or pick up ferry tickets to Ellis Island and the Statue of Liberty (see Major Attractions,

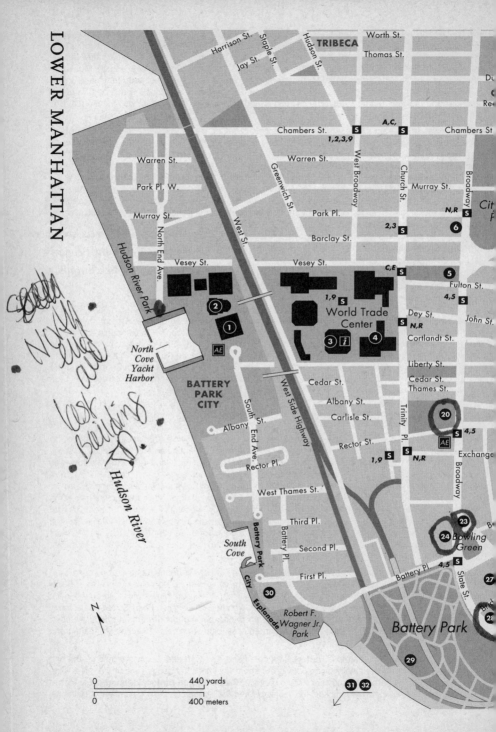

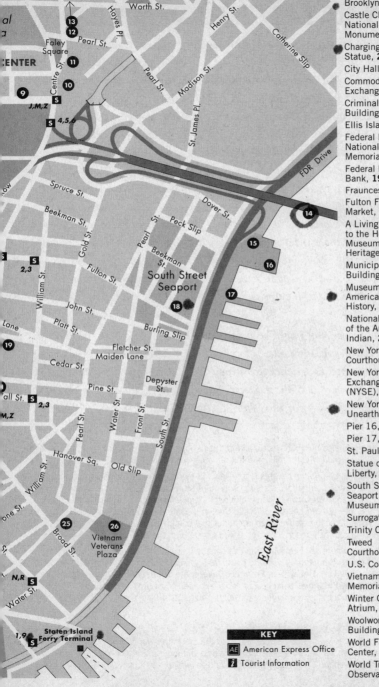

Brooklyn Bridge, **14**

Castle Clinton National Monument, **29**

Charging Bull Statue, **23**

City Hall, **7**

Commodities Exchange, **4**

Criminal Courts Building, **13**

Ellis Island, **31**

Federal Hall National Memorial, **21**

Federal Reserve Bank, **19**

Fraunces Tavern, **25**

Fulton Fish Market, **15**

A Living Memorial to the Holocaust— Museum of Jewish Heritage, **30**

Municipal Building, **10**

Museum of American Financial History, **24**

National Museum of the American Indian, **27**

New York County Courthouse, **12**

New York Stock Exchange (NYSE), **22**

New York Unearthed, **28**

Pier 16, **17**

Pier 17, **16**

St. Paul's Chapel, **5**

Statue of Liberty, **32**

South Street Seaport Museum, **18**

Surrogate's Court, **9**

Trinity Church, **20**

Tweed Courthouse, **8**

U.S. Courthouse, **11**

Vietnam Veterans Memorial, **26**

Winter Garden Atrium, **2**

Woolworth Building, **6**

World Financial Center, **1**

World Trade Center Observation Deck, **3**

KEY

AE American Express Office

i Tourist Information

93

WONDER WALL

Back in the 1640s, when hostile Indian territory started around 40th Street, Dutch settlers built a protective wooden stockade around the northern outskirts of their settlement. The colony grew so quickly they bagged the wall in 1699, but the name stuck to the street that followed. Wall Street is both an actual street and a shorthand name for the vast, powerful financial community that clusters around the New York and American stock exchanges. While captains of industry, robber barons, and social Darwinists have long revered this street, radicals have cursed it as the heart of capitalist wrongdoing. Not surprisingly, when a horse-drawn wagon loaded with explosives detonated on September 16, 1920, in front of what is now Federal Hall, it was quickly blamed on anarchists bent on disrupting world financial markets. The noontime blast killed 30 and wounded 100, making it the deadliest American bombing of the century—until Oklahoma City in 1995. However, several bystanders (perhaps with cooler heads) testified that the wagon belonged to an explosives company who carelessly abandoned it. No culprits were found, and the explosion remains a mystery to this day.

The real Wall Street, you might be surprised to know, is only ⅓ of a mile long and not much wider than an alley. On all sides it's surrounded by unbelievably tall buildings. To best experience this trippy Grand Canyon effect, stand at the corner of Wall Street and William Street. Then look up. Subway: 4 or 5 to Wall St. (at Broadway). Also: 2 or 3 to Wall St. (at William St.).

above). Castle Clinton has also held jobs as an island fort (landfill has now made it part of Manhattan) and an immigration depot (nearly eight million immigrants passed through here).

The best way to see Lower Manhattan's sights is to follow the Heritage Trail. This self-guided tour winds through the streets of Lower Manhattan, passing important stuff like the New York Stock Exchange, Tweed Courthouse, and Castle Clinton. You can pick up the maps and brochures you'll need to start your tour at City Hall, the South Street Seaport, or Castle Clinton in Battery Park; just look for Heritage Trail kiosks. City Hall also offers free interactive video machines that dispense info on Lower Manhattan sights, City Hall history, and mass transit options. For more info on the Heritage Trail, call 212/269–1500.

Besides being the place where Michael Milken types sell their soul to the devil for pocket change and golden parachutes, Lower Manhattan is home to some fascinating museums: the **National Museum of the American Indian, New York Unearthed, Fraunces Tavern,** the **South Street Seaport Museum,** and the **Museum of American Financial History.** For more info, *see* Museums and Galleries, *below.* And don't forget to check out that massive magnet to terrorists and tourists alike, the World Trade Center (*see* Major Attractions, *above*).

NEW YORK STOCK EXCHANGE (NYSE)

This hoary hall of high finance, the largest securities exchange in the world, had humble beginnings: Originally Wall Street traders were not tasseled-loafer types, but local merchants who gathered to buy and sell stocks under the shade of a nearby buttonwood tree (which has long since become firewood).

In its earliest incarnation, stocks were called out and bid on one at a time. These days, the "Big Board" is capable of handling up to one trillion shares of stock per day, and when the NYSE sneezes, prime ministers in far-off countries murmur nervous "bless you"s. The NYSE's current home is a grand 1903 building with an august Corinthian entrance—a fitting temple to the almighty dollar. Don't miss a trip to the glass-enclosed **visitors' gallery** overlooking the immense trading hall, from which you can peer down at the chaos of video monitors and 1,500 madly gesticulating brokers some 50 ft below. (A free multilingual tape explains all the action.) The glass was installed in 1967 after members of Students for a Democratic Society staged a protest here, throwing $1 bills onto the trading floor. Same-day visitors tickets are issued from 9 AM on a first-come, first-served basis; to get one, arrive before 1 PM. *20 Broad St., at Wall St., tel. 212/656–5168. Subway: 4, 5, 1, or 2 to Wall St.; also J, M, or Z to Broad St. Admission free. Open weekdays 9–4:30.*

● TRINITY CHURCH ●

The Trinity Church you're looking at now was built in 1846 on the site of the 1697 original. For 50-odd years it was the tallest building in the city, but today it's like a dollhouse in the shadow of the World Trade Center's towers. Trinity's medieval-looking sanctuary doesn't hold a candle to the dark Gothic ambience of Grace Church (*see* West Village, *above*) or the colossal grandeur of St. Pat's (*see* Midtown, *above*), but the 2-acre graveyard's a fascinating jumble of crumbling headstones. At rest here are notable dead folk like Alexander Hamilton (thanks to Aaron Burr) and Robert Fulton. A free 45-minute tour of the church is given daily at 2 PM. *74 Trinity Pl., at corner of Broadway and Wall St., tel. 212/602–0800. Subway: 4 or 5 to Wall St. Open weekdays 9–11:45 and 1–3:45, Sat. 10–3:45, Sun. 1–3:45.*

Herman Melville was born at 6 Pearl Street and worked as a customs officer on the Gansevoort Street pier while writing "Moby Dick."

ST. PAUL'S CHAPEL

Six blocks north of Trinity Church on Broadway, St. Paul's Chapel is the oldest (1766) surviving church in Manhattan; it was modeled after London's St. Martin-in-the-Fields. George Washington said his prayers here immediately after being sworn in as America's first president (look for his pew in the north aisle). Both Trinity and St. Paul's offer live music at lunchtime (*see* Music *in* Chapter 7). *Broadway at Fulton St., tel. 212/602–0874.*

VIETNAM VETERANS MEMORIAL

On a large brick plaza near the eastern end of Battery Park, you'll find a 70-ft-long, 16-ft-high wall of greenish glass. It's etched with letters, diaries, and poems written by servicemen and servicewomen during the Vietnam War, as well as excerpts from news dispatches and public documents. *Next to 55 Water St., just north of Broad St. Subway: N or R to Whitehall St. (South Ferry).*

FEDERAL HALL NATIONAL MEMORIAL

Federal Hall, built as a Customs House in 1842, is a mishmash of Europe's greatest hits: Its Doric-columned entrance is modeled after the Acropolis in Athens, and its rotunda is modeled after the Panthenon in Rome. Add to that a statue of George Washington (who was sworn in as president on this spot in 1789) that would look more at home in Washington, D.C. Inside, you'll find a few exhibits on New York and Wall Street. The original building served as our nation's great capitol building until the whole bureaucracy packed off to Philadelphia in 1790. *26 Wall St., at Nassau St., tel. 212/825–6888. Subway: 2, 3, 4, or 5 to Wall St.; also J, M, or Z to Broad St. Admission free. Open weekdays 9–5.*

FEDERAL RESERVE BANK

Shakespeare may have said "all that glitters is not gold," but when you're in a room with enough gold to buy most medium-sized nations, you may beg to differ. The Federal Reserve Bank's got over 10,325 tons of the stuff (equal to one-seventh of the gold ever mined) in a vault carved from solid bedrock 80 ft below street level. Most of it belongs to foreign nations, but the United States lets them store it here for free. They won't talk about the recent World War II gold controversy. Yes, this is the bank that Jeremy Irons's character robbed with such ease in *Die Hard with a Vengeance*. No, such a thing would not be possible in real life. You can take the fascinating, free, 40-minute tour, however, if you call for a reservation at least one week in advance. Tours are given weekdays four times daily. *33 Liberty St., between Nassau and William Sts., tel. 212/720–6130. Subway: 2 or 3 to Wall St. Admission free. Reservations required.*

THE CHARGING BULL STATUE

Soon after the stock-market crash of 1987, playful Italian artist Arturo DiModica dumped a 3½-ton bronze statue of a charging bull in front of the New York Stock Exchange under cover of night. It dismayed stock brokers (who didn't need reminding that the bull market of the '80s was over), but it irked city officials even more. So the statue was "temporarily" parked just north of **Bowling Green** (*see* Parks and Gardens, *below*) until a buyer could be found. And there it stands. Facing north, up Broadway, the Bull menacingly crouches, nostrils flared, large enough to gore a city bus. Some feel the city's cool reception to this fine piece of public art has to do with the bull's gargantuan genitals—tourists seem to take more pictures of the rear of the bull than the front. *Broadway near Beaver St. Subway: 4 or 5 to Bowling Green.*

SOUTH STREET SEAPORT

The closest thing Manhattan has to Disneyland is the 11-block South Street Seaport Historic District, with its snapping, brightly colored flags, smartly painted colonial-style buildings, and tethered flock of tall ships festooned with twinkling lights. If you think it looks a bit like Boston's Quincy Market, you're right; the same corporation "restored" them both. Over 12 million tourists from all over the world come to the Seaport annually to find they've been snookered into shopping at mall standards like the Gap, Sharper Image, and J. Crew. That said, there are a few reasons to spend an hour or two here: The **South Street Seaport Museum** (*see* Museums and Galleries, *below*) and the **Fulton Fish Market** (*see below*) both give fascinating glimpses into the area's illustrious past. This was, after all, a throbbing zone of brothels, boarding houses, gambling parlors, and saloons during the era of the clipper ship, and its cobblestone streets were once filled with randy sailors. Now, of course, it's the haunt of pimpled teens looking for the virtual-reality game center (hint: It's at Pier 17). As you walk along Fulton Street—closed to cars east of Water Street—look out for the historic 19th-century buildings of **Cannon's Walk Block** and **Schermerhorn Row.** The tiny white lighthouse you'll notice is the **Titanic Memorial** (Fulton and Water Sts.), commemorating the 1912 sinking of the "unsinkable" ocean liner. Check out **Pier 17** if you have a hankering for souvenir T-shirts and cheese fries, or **Pier 16** to see the tall ships, including the *Peking,* the second-largest sailing ship in existence. For info on boat tours that depart from Pier 16, *see* Guided Tours, *above.* *Tel. 212/732–7678. Subway: J, M, Z, 2, 3, 4, or 5 to Fulton St.; also A or C to Broadway–Nassau St.*

FULTON FISH MARKET

Strolling by, you might think that this is the smelliest place on earth. And you'd almost be right. Opened in 1831, Fulton is the oldest and largest fish market in the United States—but somewhere out there (we won't tell you where) there's a fish market that's *bigger* and *smellier.* Fishmongers at Fulton deal in a pungent 600 species of fish and shellfish, annually hauling in over eight million pounds. You'll need to arrive before 9 AM to catch the action; after that, the whole place shuts down. Behave nicely (i.e., don't gawk or ask fishmongers to take a picture of you with their fish) and you can sometimes score the catch of the day at wholesale prices. During summer, you can also hook up with a fascinating tour ($10). Tour guides will not answer questions about the fish market's alleged ties to the mob, or the recent suspicious fire that crippled some of the market. They suggest you don't wander around alone here before dawn. *South St. between Fulton St. and Peck Slip, tel. 212/748–8600. Subway: J, M, Z, 2, 3, 4, or 5 to Fulton St.; also A or C to Broadway–Nassau St. Market open daily midnight–9 AM. Tours given Apr.–Oct. on 1st and 3rd Thurs. at 6 AM; reservations required.*

CIVIC CENTER

New York City's civic center, just north of the financial district, is so filled with grand buildings it puts most of the nations' *state* capitals to shame, including the one in Albany, New York. But considering most New Yorkers' unshaken belief that their city is vastly superior to all others, does this really surprise you? You can spend a few hours wandering around the stately government and justice buildings, most of which have appeared in countless movies and TV shows like *Wall Street* and "Law and Order." Besides those mentioned below, worth a quick look-see are the **New York County Courthouse** (40 Centre St.), backdrop for Henry Fonda's tirades in *12 Angry Men*; the spectacular beaux arts **Surrogate's Court** (31 Chambers St.); and the towering **U.S. Courthouse** (Foley Sq.). Though these buildings are all crowded together, it's easy to identify each: The U.S. Courthouse has imposing marble steps and a golden pyramid on top. The New York County Courthouse has imposing marble steps and a hexagonal shape (its pediment reads "The true administration of justice is the firmest pillar of good government"). Meanwhile, the grim-looking art deco **Criminal Courts Building** (100 Centre St.) got a bit part in Tom Wolfe's *Bonfire of the Vanities.* This is also where you'll find the entrance to the **Brooklyn Bridge** (*see* Major Attractions, *above*). *Subway: N or R to City Hall; also 4, 5, or 6 to Brooklyn Bridge/City Hall.*

New York's most important federal court, housed in the U.S. Courthouse, is where the creator of the Lone Ranger sued for copyright infringement; where Julius and Ethel Rosenberg were tried for espionage; where the owners of the *Titanic* were sued for gross negligence; where D. H. Lawrence's *Lady Chatterley's Lover* was declared obscene (and James Joyce's *Ulysses* was not); and where hotel queen Leona Helmsley was tried for tax evasion.

CITY HALL • Refreshingly, New York's City Hall looks more like a pastoral New England courthouse than a Politboro. Its exterior columns reflect the classical influence of Greece and Rome, while its crowning statue of Lady Justice seems a nod to positive thinking. The whole thing was built in 1802 and touched up a bit in 1858, after fireworks launched from its roof set the top half aflame. At some point the back side was finished off with nice white limestone—city fathers originally assumed New York would never grow north of Fulton Street and had skimped on the part that wouldn't "show." Inside are the city council chambers and the offices of the mayor. Some rooms, including the Governor's Room, brimming with official tchotchkes, are open to the public. *Broadway, at Park Row. Subway: N or R to City Hall. Admission free. Open weekdays 10–4:30.*

CITY HALL PARK • The triangular park surrounding City Hall started life as the town common and has seen its share of hangings, riots, and demonstrations. Look for the statue of Nathan Hale (hanged as a spy by the visiting Brits) on the Broadway side. **Park Row,** the street bordering the hypotenuse side of the triangle, is itself pretty historic. From the mid-19th to early 20th century it was dubbed "Newspaper Row" because most of the city's 20 or so daily papers had their offices here. A statue of Benjamin Franklin (who was, after all, a printer) stands in tribute across the street from the park near Pace Plaza.

The city's lights are beautiful at night, aren't they? Imagine the sight when the world's first electrical generating station lit up Manhattan like a birthday cake on September 4, 1882. A plaque marks the spot of the former station at 40 Fulton Street.

TWEED COURTHOUSE • The Tweed Courthouse, named after legendary "Boss" William Magear Tweed, stands north of City Hall in City Hall Park (*see above*). The swaggering, 300-pound Tweed, who wore an enormous diamond in his shirtfront and seemed preternaturally disposed to the Lee Atwater school of spin control, was adored by the poor as a do-no-wrong Robin Hood. This while he was apparently embezzling some $10 million of the $14 million budgeted to build the courthouse. The truth eventually caught up with Tweed and he died, ironically, in a jail that had earlier been a pet construction project. Peek inside the courthouse (which now houses municipal offices) to see its magnificent seven-story rotunda. *52 Chambers St., between Broadway and Centre St. Subway: N or R to City Hall. Admission free. Open weekdays 9–4:30.*

WOOLWORTH BUILDING • Rising 792 ft above the street like a Gothic church on steroids, the so-called Cathedral of Commerce was the world's tallest building when it opened in 1913. The finest in Gothic design is what Frank W. Woolworth wanted and got when he ponied up $13.5 million in cash to have architect Cass Gilbert build a suitable headquarters for his Woolworth Company. It's got gargoyles. It's got flying buttresses. It's also got one of the most ornate entryways ever constructed by a perfectly sober man. As you enter, notice on your left the two sculptures set into arches in the ceiling: One is of elderly F. W. Woolworth pinching his pennies, and the other is of Cass Gilbert holding a model of the building you are standing in. *233 Broadway, at Park Pl. Subway: N or R to City Hall.*

MUNICIPAL BUILDING • This was the city government's first skyscraper, and if you've been paying any attention at all to this book, you know something of such monumental importance could only be entrusted to the architectural firm of McKim, Mead & White. And so, in 1914, it was. In the world of *Batman,* the Municipal Building was stunt double for "Gotham City Police Headquarters." In the real world, it's where New Yorkers go to pay parking fines, obtain marriage licenses, and get hitched in civil ceremonies. You can make a quick buck if you hang around on weekdays with a Polaroid camera and offer to capture the moment for ill-prepared newlyweds. *1 Centre St., near entrance to Brooklyn Bridge. Subway: 4, 5, or 6 to Brooklyn Bridge/City Hall.*

BATTERY PARK CITY

Battery Park City is connected to the World Trade Center (*see* Major Attractions, *above*) by a pair of pedestrian walkways spanning West Street. There's another, deeper connection, too: Developers needed someplace to stick all the extra dirt (about 1 million cubic yards of it) they had lying around after they dug the foundation for the World Trade Center's whopping twin towers. Rather than filling a barge and floating it to Jersey, they added landfill to lower Manhattan, and, voilà, Battery Park City was born.

Battery Park City *is* like a separate city, sort of, with over 5,000 residents and 20,000 workers. It's just not a very exciting one to visit. The best thing about it is the ever-growing **Battery Park City Esplanade,** which runs along the Hudson River. It offers those rarest of rare things in lower Manhattan, sunsets, trees, and open space, plus stellar views of the Statue of Liberty and New Jersey's "Gold Coast." The **World Financial Center** (West St. between Vesey and Liberty Sts., tel. 212/945–0505) dominates the rest of the landscape with its five geometric-capped towers, each 16 to 51 stories high. They're some of the least-offensive modern architecture in the city and serve as world headquarters for companies such as American Express, Merrill Lynch, and most recently, The Mercantile Exchange. On the concourse level you'll find shops and restaurants, plus the gorgeous, glass-walled **Winter Garden Atrium** (open daily 7 AM–1 AM). The 120-ft-tall vaulted atrium is filled with giant palms and hosts free concerts, dance recitals, and art exhibits. *Subway: 1 or 9 to Cortlandt St.; also C or E to World Trade Center.*

A LIVING MEMORIAL TO THE HOLOCAUST— MUSEUM OF JEWISH HERITAGE

Moored in one of the city's most enviable waterfront settings, at the north end of Robert F. Wagner Jr. Park just below Battery Park City, this newest of downtown museums focuses on the dynamism of 20th-century Jewish culture around the globe; Hitler's war against the Jews, using firsthand recollections; and Jewish life after the Holocaust. *40 1st Pl., Battery Park City, tel. 212/968–1800. Subway: 1 or 9 to Cortlandt St.; also C or E to World Trade Center.*

THE OUTER BOROUGHS

When most people think of New York, they think of Manhattan as "The City," and Brooklyn, Queens, the Bronx, and Staten Island as one big peripheral blob—the sticky, brown caramel surrounding the real Big Apple. While Manhattan Island admittedly contains most of the sights that the city is known for, it's only one of the five **boroughs** (counties) that comprise New York City. Almost 80% of New York City's population *doesn't* live in Manhattan, and many will assure you that a trip to New York really isn't complete without a trip to the outer boroughs. After all, what could be more indicative of the city's diversity than a morning spent at the high-tech New York Stock Exchange, and an afternoon out in a sleepy Bronx fishing village, where shop owners leave signs saying GONE TO THE BEACH in their windows?

Even if your visit to New York is only a short one, there is no excuse for spending all your time on Manhattan Island: Most sights in Brooklyn, Queens, and the Bronx are less than 40 minutes away by subway, and the 20-minute, free ferry ride to Staten Island is a treat in itself. Even the most distant destinations, like **City Island** in the Bronx (an hour away), are definitely worth the schlep for those interested in expanding their horizons beyond the asphalt grid.

Many museums, parks, and historical sights in the outer boroughs warrant a special trip: the Bronx Zoo, Coney Island, the Brooklyn Museum, the Brooklyn Botanic Garden, Yankee Stadium, and the American Museum of the Moving Image, to name a few. Lesser-known gems include Wave Hill estate (where Franklin Roosevelt, Mark Twain, and Toscanini each lived); the Steinway & Sons Piano Factory (where you can watch a single piece of wood being shaped into a grand piano); the Jacques Marchais Museum (home to the largest private collection of Tibetan art outside Tibet, personally blessed by the Dalai Lama); and the Russian neighborhood of Brighton Beach. Additionally, the outer boroughs are where you'll find New York City's only **beaches**; for more info, *see box* Land of Skyscrapers and Beaches?!, *below.*

BROOKLYN

Hardly Manhattan's wimpy sidekick, Brooklyn is a metropolis in its own right, full of world-class museums, spacious parks, landmark buildings, five-star restaurants, and lively ethnic neighborhoods. In fact, it's the most populous of all the boroughs, with 2.3 million residents; even if it were sheared from the rest of New York, it would still be among the 20 largest cities in the United States. It's no wonder that an intense and long-standing rivalry exists between Brooklyn and Manhattan, a rivalry that recently led Brooklyn-born newspaperman Pete Hamill, now the editor-in-chief of the *New York Daily News*, to refer to the 1898 unification of Brooklyn with the rest of the city as "the Great Mistake."

Not only does Brooklyn boast more residents, but more people visit it than any of the other outer boroughs, particularly the charming 19th-century neighborhoods of Brooklyn Heights, Cobble Hill, and Carroll Gardens. Don't listen to dyed-in-the-wool Manhattanites who think you need a visa to cross the Brooklyn Bridge. Those who know better make the trip to take in the Egyptian treasures in the Brooklyn Museum, cycle or rollerblade around Prospect Park, walk the Celebrity Path at the Botanic Garden, take in the Next Wave Festival or some other can't-see-that-anywhere-in-Manhattan performance at the Brooklyn Academy of Music (a.k.a. BAM), or even head to Coney Island for a stroll along the beach boardwalk and a ride on the Cyclone roller coaster. Its major attractions aren't the only reason to come here, though. Brooklyn is a city of neighborhoods, most of which are more intimate in scale and considerably less frenetic than virtually any of those across the East River, and which will easily reward a few hours of leisurely exploring. For up-to-date listings of Brooklyn's cultural events, museum and gallery exhibits, street fairs and festivals, and walking and bike tours, the quarterly *Meet Me in Brooklyn* (30 Flatbush Ave., Suite 427, New York, NY 11217, tel. 718/855–7882, ext. 51, fax 718/802–9095) can't be beat. Write for a copy, or pick one up at the New York Convention and Visitors Bureau (*see* Visitor Information *in* Chapter 1).

BROOKLYN HEIGHTS

"All the advantages of the country, with most of the conveniences of the city." So ran the ads for a real-estate development that sprang up in the 1820s just across the East River from downtown Manhattan. Brooklyn Heights (named for its enviable hilltop position) was New York's first suburb, linked to the city first by ferry and later by the mighty Brooklyn Bridge. In the 1940s and 1950s, the neighborhood was said to be home to the city's largest number of writers outside the Village. Among the scribes who've lived here then and in the decades since are Carson McCullers, W. H. Auden, Hart Crane, Arthur Miller, Truman Capote, Richard Wright, Alfred Kazin, and Norman Mailer (still a resident). The Heights deteriorated in the 1930s, but thanks to the vigorous efforts of preservationists in the 1960s, much of the neighborhood was designated as New York's first historic district. Today some 600 buildings more than 100 years old, representing a wide range of American building styles, are lovingly preserved on quiet, tree-lined streets, none more than a few blocks from the Heights' best attraction, the **Promenade.**

Wander a few blocks north of Montague Street and you'll encounter unusual street names like Cranberry, Pineapple, and Orange. The names were bestowed by a Miss Sarah Middagh, who objected to the practice of naming streets for the town fathers.

The main thoroughfare in Brooklyn Heights is **Montague Street,** which offers cafés, pubs, and plenty of prosperous-looking real-estate offices. Here you'll find **St. Ann's and the Holy Trinity Church,** which boasts 60 of the first stained-glass windows made in America, installed in 1849. Over half have been restored to date—to see the restoration process up close, call the box office to arrange a visit. In 1980 the church created its own performing arts center, "Arts at St. Ann's," where you can hear a wide variety of non-classical music—jazz, blues, world and new music; musical theater; and experimental opera—March through May and October through December. The church is open only for performances and Sunday at 11 AM for Episcopal services. *157 Montague St., at Clinton St., tel. 718/858–2424. Subway: 2 or 3 to Clark St.; M, N, or R to Court St.; or 2, 3, 4, or 5 to Borough Hall.*

Just north of Brooklyn Heights proper is the up-and-coming Fulton Ferry landing area, where Robert Fulton's steam ferry once arrived carrying passengers from Manhattan. Though the ferry is gone, **Old Fulton Street** is gradually adding new restaurants, cafés, and bars. The area is also dotted with old warehouses and Federal-style row houses, all watched over by the towering Brooklyn Bridge. In the vaults under the bridge look for the **Brooklyn Anchorage** (Hicks and Old Fulton Sts., no phone), a funky art gallery/performance space (Sonic Youth showed up to perform here one night in June 1997) with a medicinal herb garden out front. If you're looking for a place to chill, cruise north to the **Empire Fulton Ferry State Park** (*see* Parks and Gardens, *below*). *Subway: A or C to High St./Brooklyn Bridge.*

BROOKLYN HEIGHTS PROMENADE • From any one of the antique benches along this ⅓-mi, cobbled waterfront promenade, you have spectacular views of the Lower Manhattan skyline, the South Street Seaport, and the majestic Brooklyn Bridge. The small island to your left is Governors Island, a recently deaccessioned military installation, the future of which is being hotly debated (a nine-hole golf course and New York's version of Colonial Williamsburg are among the dozens of plans being floated). If you're the kind of person who hates lovey-dovey, lip-locked couples, stay far away on moonlit summer nights. Mornings are an especially good time to come, when the rising sun's rays reflect off the thou-

BROOKLYN HEIGHTS, COBBLE HILL, AND CARROLL GARDENS

40 Verandah
Place, **5**
197 Amity Street, **6**
Brooklyn
Anchorage, **1**
Brooklyn Heights
Promenade, **2**
Brooklyn Historical
Society, **4**
Cammereri Brothers
Bakery, **8**
New York Transit
Museum, **7**
St. Ann's and the
Holy Trinity
Church, **3**

East River

Brooklyn Bridge

Manhattan Bridge

N

Old Fulton St.

Empire
Fulton Ferry
State Park

Plymouth St.
Water St.

DUMBO

Front St.

Poplar

Cranberry

Middagh St.

Orange

Pineapple St.

St.

Henry St.

Columbia Heights

Willow St.

Hicks St.

Clark St.

HIGH ST./
BROOKLYN
BRIDGE
A,C

Cadman
Plaza

CLARK ST.
2,3

BROOKLYN
HEIGHTS

Tillary St.

Adams St.

Pierrepont
Pl.

Montague
Terrace

Pierrepont St.

Montague St.

Remsen St.

Grace
Ct.

278

Willow
Pl.

Hicks St.

Joralemon St.

Henry St.

Clinton St.

COURT ST.
M,N,R

JAY ST./
BOROUGH HALL
A,C,F

Joy St.

BOROUGH
HALL
2,3,4,5

State St.

Sidney Pl.

Livingston St.

Schermerhorn St.

LAWRENCE ST./
METROTECH
M,N,R

Fulton St.

Atlantic Ave.

Pacific St.

HOYT ST./
FULTON MALL
2,3

Congress St.

Amity St.

Verandah Pl.

Warren St.

Cobble Hill
Park

Court St.

Boerum Pl.

Smith St.

DOWNTOWN
BROOKLYN

Baltic St.

Kane St.

Henry St.

Clinton St.

COBBLE
HILL

Dean St.

Bergen St.

Warren St.

Baltic St.

Kane St.

Douglass St.

DeGraw St.

HOYT/
SCHERMERHORN STS
A,C,G

BERGEN ST.
F,G

Hoyt St.

Bond St.

Sackett St.

Union St.

President St.

Carroll St.

1st Pl.

2nd Pl.

3rd Pl.

Court St.

CARROLL
GARDENS

CARROLL ST.
F,G

0   1/2 mile

0   1/2 km

sands of windows on the skyscrapers opposite. On the 4th of July, fireworks aficionados head here for inimitable views of the annual show over the East River. *Subway: M, N, or R to Court St.; walk 1 block south to Remsen St., then west to waterfront.*

COBBLE HILL AND CARROLL GARDENS

A few blocks south of Brooklyn Heights, Cobble Hill is a slightly less manicured version of its northern neighbor, with equally charming old town houses. Virtually all of the neighborhood's commercial establishments are confined to Court Street, leaving the rest of the tree-lined streets as quiet as you'll find anywhere in the City. **Atlantic Avenue** (which separates Cobble Hill from the Heights) offers interesting window-shopping: It's lined with Middle Eastern spice shops and stores selling dirt-cheap antiques. If you've got a spare hour, you can hunt for **40 Verandah Place,** former home of novelist Thomas Wolfe, and **197 Amity Street,** where Jennie Jerome (Winston Churchill's mother) was born. *Subway: F or G to Bergen St.*

Still farther south, below Degraw Street, is the steadfastly Italian neighborhood of **Carroll Gardens.** Here you'll find octogenarians playing boccie in the parks or smoking and chatting on their stoops. On streets like **First Place, Carroll Street,** and **President Street,** because of how deep the blocks were laid out, the houses have front yards (tiny by suburban standards, but nothing to laugh about in front-yard-deficient New York). They're best seen around Christmas, when everyone puts out glow-in-the-dark nativity scenes and giant, plastic Virgin Marys. Our final stop should be the **Cammereri Brothers Bakery** (502 Henry St., at Sackett St., tel. 718/852–3606), where Nicholas Cage slaved over a hot oven in *Moonstruck. Subway: F or G to Carroll St.*

DUMBO

Dumbo—not Disney's flying pachyderm, but down under the Manhattan Bridge overpass—is the place to go if SoHo's suburbanized atmosphere leaves you cold and broke. Since the mid-1980s this has been a true struggling-artists' community, with turn-of-the-century brick industrial buildings, cobblestone streets crisscrossed with old railroad tracks, and the ever-present rumble of subway cars (the B, the D, and the Q) rattling across the Manhattan Bridge above. Needless to say, TV and film crews come here when they want "atmosphere." The best blocks to explore are north of **Front Street,** between Main Street and Hudson Avenue. Though you won't find any art galleries, there are several groovy art supply stores; check out **Chamber's Paper Fibers** (139 Plymouth St., between Pearl St. and Anchorage Pl., tel. 718/624–8181) and **Pilot Pilot** (47 Pearl St., between Plymouth and Water Sts.). Dumbo is also the international headquarters for the Jehovah's Witnesses—strange bedfellows for bohemian artists. *Subway: F to York St.*

FORT GREENE

Bounded to the north by the East River, to the east by Vanderbilt Avenue, to the south by Atlantic Avenue, and to the west by Flatbush Avenue, Fort Greene is a neighborhood of brownstones and row houses, home to many of the city's African-American professionals, musicians, and artists. Among Fort Greene's residents is director Spike Lee; his store, **Spike's Joint** (1 S. Elliot Pl., at DeKalb Ave., tel. 718/802–1000), is full of clothing and movie memorabilia. In a nearby renovated firehouse you'll find Lee's production company, **40 Acres and a Mule** (256 DeKalb Ave.). To get a firsthand look at Fort Greene's artistic bent, check out **Urban Glass** (647 Fulton St., near Flatbush Ave., tel. 718/625–3685), the only studio/gallery in New York devoted to glassblowing.

Beyond tiny, eclectic galleries, Fort Greene is home to a world-class avant-garde art space, **BAM** (*see* Arts Centers *in* Chapter 7). Adjoining BAM, the **Williamsburgh Savings Bank Tower** (1 Hanson Pl., between Atlantic and Flatbush Aves.) is Brooklyn's tallest building at 512 ft. Completed in 1929, the tower was meant to signal Brooklyn's emergence as a commercial superpower. Of course these plans went down the tube a few months later with the Black Tuesday stock market crash, leaving most floors standing empty for decades. Today the building's spectacular mosaic-tile lobby is an inspiring place to use an ATM. *Subway: D, Q, 2, 3, 4, or 5 to Atlantic Ave.*

PRISON SHIP MARTYR'S MONUMENT • A macabre chapter in Fort Greene's history is forever remembered at this 148-ft-tall monument, the world's tallest freestanding Doric column, which stands in shady **Fort Greene Park** (*see* Parks and Gardens, *below*). During the American Revolution, the Brits crowded their colonial prisoners into cattle ships moored in the bay just north of here; some 11,500 died. The corpses were dumped in trenches and continued, horribly, to wash ashore until 1792. *Subway: D, M, N, Q, or R to DeKalb Ave.*

WILLIAMSBURG

Alternately an Orthodox Jewish neighborhood, a Latino community, and the home of hip young artists, the northern neighborhood of Williamsburg is suffering a bit of an identity crisis that makes it one of New York's most interesting places to visit. To explore this mishmash, start at the **Bedford Avenue** subway station: The neighborhood around this part of Bedford Avenue feels positively small town, with an eclectic mix of organic-food stores, thrift shops, Polish butcher shops, and a few neighborhood bars. One of the more popular watering holes is **Mug's Ale House** (125 Bedford Ave., at N. 10th St.). Just north of Broadway is a cluster of Latino bodegas and cheap Puerto Rican and Mexican restaurants and coffee shops. Take note: Broadway runs underneath the elevated subway line and isn't a very pleasant place at night. *Subway: L to Bedford Ave.*

If you follow Broadway west to the water you'll find signs announcing LOFT FOR RENT, a good indication that you're entering Williamsburg's artist quarter—often called the "**Right Bank.**" Artists and writers who've fled gentrified SoHo have been colonizing the industrial buildings near the water and under the ugly gray Williamsburg Bridge for the last 20-odd years. If you double back to Bedford Avenue and follow it south, you'll come to the heart of the second-largest Orthodox Jewish community in Brooklyn (the largest is farther east, in Crown Heights). **Lee Avenue,** which runs parallel to Bedford Avenue, is Jewish Williamsburg's main street. Here you'll see men wearing identical black suits, prayer shawls, long beards, and black hats, alongside women with colorful but conservative dresses. Stop by the **Southside Kosher Bakery** (454 Bedford Ave., between S. 9th and 10th Sts., tel. 718/218–8512) for a tasty kosher snack.

GREENPOINT

The Polish community of Greenpoint (north of Williamsburg and just a stone's throw south of Queens) is one of the most thriving ethnic enclaves in the city, today home to immigrants not only from Poland but also Puerto Rico, the Dominican Republic, Guyana, Colombia, Pakistan, and China, among elsewhere. Thanks to the Polish, Russian, and Italian immigrants who settled here in the 19th and early 20th centuries, there are lots of beautiful old churches; the 1916 **Cathedral of the Transfiguration of Our Lord** (N. 12th St. and Driggs Ave.), a Russian Orthodox church with five huge copper-clad onion domes, is the finest. The main drag, **Manhattan Avenue,** is lined with Polish bakeries; Polish coffee shops serving up kielbasa, stuffed cabbage, and flan; and even a few Polish curio shops and clothing stores. Drop by **Zakopone** (714 Manhattan Ave., between Nassau and Meserole Sts.) for weird souvenirs and framed photos of the Pope. **Stodycze Wedel** (722 Manhattan Ave., at Meserole St., tel. 718/349–3933) has sparkling clean shelves full of imported Polish candies, crackers, and other gourmet items. *Subway: G to Greenpoint Ave.*

BEDFORD-STUYVESANT

Bed-Stuy, as it's commonly known, is an inland neighborhood lying south of Williamsburg and just east of Fort Greene. Spike Lee fans will recognize it as the place where the shit went down in *Do the Right Thing,* and it's true that drugs and crime have plagued the area since the 1960s. These days, however, a community revival's afoot, and more and more African-American professionals are gentrifying the area. It's worth an afternoon visit to see some of the finest Victorian brownstones in the city, most of which line Chauncey, Dacatuer, MacDonough, and Hancock streets. Other notable sights include the **Billie Holiday Theater** (1368 Fulton St., at New York Ave., tel. 718/636–0918), a showcase for African-American playwrights and actors; and the **Simmons African Arts Museum** (1063 Fulton St., between Classon and Grand Aves., tel. 718/230–0933), with a small collection of contemporary African artwork. If your empty belly takes precedence over cultural endeavors, try the **Carolina Country Kitchen** (1993 Atlantic Ave., at Saratoga Ave., tel. 718/346–4400) for authentic southern cooking. In July, keep an eye out for the **African Street Festival,** a weeklong block party celebrating black culture. *Subway: A or C to Nostrand Ave.*

PARK SLOPE

With street after tree-lined street of gorgeous, meticulously maintained brownstone, limestone, and brick row houses, Park Slope is a little like Brooklyn's Upper East Side (in fact, for a short time in the late 19th century, just as it was coming of age, it was the wealthiest neighborhood in America). Thanks to its handsome infrastructre and its proximity to three of Brooklyn's major assets—**Prospect Park** (*see* Parks and Gardens, *below*), the Brooklyn Museum, and the Brooklyn Botanic Garden—today the Slope is one of Brooklyn's most sought-after places to live for thousands of professionals of all stripes, both straight and gay, married and single.

On weekends the stroller traffic along the sidewalks on **7th Avenue,** the neighborhood's main strip, can be as heavy as the BQE at rush hour, but amid all the real estate agents, churches, dry cleaners, and

9th Street Bandshell, **12**
Beyond Words, **1**
Brooklyn Museum of Art, **7**
Brooklyn Public Library, **6**
Collectionary, **2**
Clay Pot, **3**
Holy Cow, **10**
Wollman Memorial Rink, **14**
Last Exit Books, **9**
Leaf 'n Bean, **4**
Long Meadow, **8**
Scouting Party, **11**
Soldiers' and Sailors' Memorial Arch, **5**
Prospect Park Wildlife Conservation Center, **13**

mediocre restaurants, a number of stores make a stroll down 7th worthwhile. **Leaf 'n Bean** (83 7th Ave., between Union and Berkeley Sts., tel. 718/638–5791) sells lots of hard-to-find tea and coffee accoutrements, plus just what the name promises. The **Clay Pot** (162 7th Ave., between 1st St. and Garfield Pl., tel. 718/788–6564) sells a constantly changing slate of crafts and jewelry handmade by leading American craftspeople. **Holy Cow** (442 9th St., at 7th Ave., tel. 718/788–3631) has plenty of old vinyl and new review copies of CDs—mostly pop, rock, and jazz. **Last Exit Books** (447 6th Ave., at 9th St., tel 718/788–6878), since it opened in April 1997, has quickly established itself as Brooklyn's finest used bookstore, with carefully selected stock at better prices than at comparable Manhattan stores. The funkiest shop in the Slope, **Scouting Party** (349 7th Ave., at 10th St., tel. 718/768–3037) sells a riotous mix of toys and doodads plus jewelry, crafts, cards, and, in case that's not enough to get you out here, some used books.

If you want to experience a less yuppified version of the Slope, head two blocks west to **5th Avenue,** which marks the eastern edge of what area residents affectionately call **Park Slide.** Long the hub of the area's Latino community, 5th Avenue is rapidly developing into the boho version of 7th Avenue, with a hodge-podge of bodegas, tchotchke shops, artsy cafés, and the sorts of other slightly offbeat stores that, here as elsewhere, seem to portend a wave of gentrification. **Collectionary** (219 5th Ave., tel. 718/638–4676), piled high with collectibles of all kinds, is the most established used emporium on the street. Fifth Avenue is also home to a budding mini–lesbian-and-gay zone, with two gay-owned cafés flanking a lesbian/gay/feminist bookstore, **Beyond Words** (186 5th Ave., tel. 718/857–0010). *Subway: D or Q to 7th Ave. (at Flatbush Ave.); F to 7th Ave. (at 9th St.); or N, R, or M to Union St.*

While you're in Park Slope you'll also want to check out **Grand Army Plaza** (Flatbush Ave. at Eastern Pkwy.) for its fantastic 80-ft-tall **Soldiers' and Sailors' Memorial Arch**—Brooklyn's post–Civil War answer to the Arc de Triomphe. On Saturdays New York's second-largest farmers' market (after Union Square's) sets up at its base. Also on the plaza are the stately **Brooklyn Museum of Art** (*see* Museums and Galleries, *below*), the **Brooklyn Public Library** (tel. 718/780–7700), and the entrance to the lovely **Brooklyn Botanic Garden** (*see* Parks and Gardens, *below*), an essential springtime destination. On

LAND OF THE FREE AND THE FAMOUS

Fact: One in seven famous Americans is from Brooklyn. If you're not convinced, consider this (very incomplete) list of famous Brooklynites, past and present:

George Gershwin, Mary Tyler Moore, Truman Capote, Lena Horne, Mae West, Barbara Stanwyck, Spike Lee, Danny Kaye, Shelly Winters, Barbra Streisand, Maurice Sendak, Woody Allen, Richard Dreyfuss, Neil Simon, Max Roach, Joan Rivers, Elliot Gould, Joseph Heller, Mike Tyson, John Steinbeck, Lenny Bruce, Harvey Fierstein, Mickey Rooney, Jackie Gleason, Clarence Birdseye, Buddy Hackett, Eddie Murphy, Dom DeLuise, Thomas Wolfe, Bud Abbot, Philip Glass, Harry Houdini, Woody Guthrie, Barry Manilow, Alan Arkin, Henry Miller, Arthur Miller, Al Capone, Sandy Koufax, Isaac Asimov, Bobby Fisher, Mel Brooks, Neil Diamond, F. W. Woolworth, and W. E. B. DuBois.

weekends and holidays from noon to 5 PM, you can ride for free on the old-fashioned trolley (tel. 718/965–8967) that runs between the Public Library, the Brooklyn Museum, the Botanic Garden, and several points in Prospect Park. *Subway: 2 or 3 to Grand Army Plaza.*

BAY RIDGE

Bay Ridge, just south of Sunset Park, is characterized by posh circa-1915 homes and a large Scandinavian population. Before the subway ruined the neighborhood's exclusivity, Brooklyn's wealthiest lived in Bay Ridge, and a few of their spectacular waterfront mansions remain: the **Gingerbread House** (82nd St., near Narrows Ave.), in the style of a thatch-roofed English cottage, and the **Fontbonne Hall Academy** (9901 Shore Rd., near 99th St.), a huge mansion turned private girls' school. Your best bets for shopping and eating in Bay Ridge are along **3rd Avenue** and **5th Avenue,** between 70th and 90th streets. Try **Nordic Delicacies** (6909 3rd Ave., at 69th St., tel. 718/748–1874) for authentic Scandinavian deli food. On the first Sunday after May 17, the whole 'hood parties down at the annual **Norwegian Constitution Day Parade,** which runs along 5th Avenue between 67th and 90th streets. *Subway: R to 77th St.*

CONEY ISLAND

During the late 1800s the sandy beach of Coney Island (actually not a separate island) was New York City's golden riviera, and the resort hotels lining its 2-mi-long boardwalk were patronized by presidents and captains of industry. With the introduction of the 5¢ elevated line in the early 20th century, fancy hotels were replaced by penny arcades, roller coasters, and oddities like a hotel built in the shape of an elephant. During this period as many as one million people (nearly 20% of New York's population at the time) would flock to Coney Island on hot summer Sundays. After World War II, as more people were able to afford cars and head elsewhere, Coney Island began its decline. In what is now a no-man's-land west of the boardwalk you can catch a glimpse of the park's forgotten past: Look for the looming, vine-covered remains of the Thunderbolt roller coaster and the abandoned Parachute Jump (which once lured patriotic post-war riders with the claim that it was used to train GIs).

Despite its decline, there's still a degree of charm in Coney Island, though it's of the seamy carnival-show variety. Video arcades, go-carts, merry-go-rounds, and kiddie rides dominate the Midway, at the heart of which towers the 70-year-old **Cyclone** (Surf Ave. at W. 10th St., tel. 718/266–3434), a legendary roller coaster ($4) still considered one of the world's scariest. Of course, you could attribute a portion of the fright factor to the fact that the coaster's rickety old wooden tracks seem ready to fall apart with every carload of screaming teenagers. Near the Cyclone, the **Astrotower** ($2) is a Seattle Space Needle wanna-be, providing panoramic views of Coney Island and Brighton Beach. The circa-1920s **Wonder**

Wheel hurls you back and forth, giving you the delicious feeling that you are about to fall to a certain death. For a demolition-derby disco experience, complete with flashing lights and pumping house music, head to the **Eldorado Auto Skeeter** (Surf Ave. between W. 12th and Hendrickson Sts.).

Freak shows are another big attraction along the Midway, and yes, they've all got a "two-headed" baby and the "world's largest" rat. If you're gonna give in to curiosity, the **Coney Island Circus Sideshow** (on boardwalk at W. 12th St., tel. 718/372–5159) gives you the best value for your $3, with acts like the human blockhead and the sword-swallowing bearded lady. Owner Dick D. Zugin (a Yale graduate) also runs the **Coney Island Museum** (99¢; upstairs from the sideshow), with Coney Island memorabilia, a funky hall of mirrors, and a small café. North and west of the boardwalk is quite dodgy after dark, so stick to the well-lit Midway. *Subway: B or F to Coney Island.*

NEW YORK AQUARIUM FOR WILDLIFE CONSERVATION • New York City's only aquarium is Coney Island's major sightseeing attraction, apart from the beach and the boardwalk with its fun and games. Among the things to do here are getting close and personal with sharks and stingrays in their 90,000-gallon habitat; exploring **Sea Cliffs,** a coastal California habitat with playful sea otters; touching your slimy and spiky friends from the sea at **Discovery Cove**; or, at the **Beluga Whales** exhibit, pondering whether these intelligent marine mammals might be a tad pissed off that their entire world is limited to a 400,000-gallon tank. (Probably not, since recently two of the whales got pretty friendly and produced the first Beluga whale born in captivity). *Surf Ave. and W. 8th St., tel. 718/265–3474. Subway: D or F to W. 8th St. Admission $7.75. Open daily 10–5 (Memorial Day–Labor Day, weekends until 6).*

BRIGHTON BEACH

Long before Brighton Beach was immortalized in the Neil Simon play-turned-movie, *Brighton Beach Memoirs,* it was just an old-fashioned Jewish community east of Coney Island, with lots of high-rise retirement towers lining the shore. These days, a flood of Russian, Ukrainian, and Georgian émigrés have earned it the nickname "Little Odessa" (itself the name of a 1995 movie, starring Jodie-Foster-boy-look-alike Edward Furlong, which dramatized the plight of a young Russian gangster). Along **Brighton Beach Avenue** (which runs under the rattling, rusting, elevated 'D' subway line) you'll find Russian merchants hawking fruit, bargain-priced caviar, lingerie, and Russian-language video tapes—it's an amazing scene. Stick around for nightfall, when many of the Russian restaurants (*see* Outer Borough Restaurants *in* Chapter 4) along the avenue and on the boardwalk push their tables to the wall for a frenzied night of dancing and vodka drinking. *Subway: D or Q to Brighton Beach.*

SHEEPSHEAD BAY

While Brighton Beach is Russian, neighboring Sheepshead Bay is an authentic Italian fishing community with a small-town, 1940s flavor. To get a real feel for the place, walk down **Emmons Avenue** (which runs parallel to the bay) and over the Ocean Avenue footbridge. Here you'll find old salts hunched over the sea wall, diligently fishing up tonight's dinner. Head to the north end of the pier to discover dozens of deep-sea fishing boats ready and willing to take you out for the day (if you can rally by around 7 AM) for the absurdly low price of $25, equipment and advice included. If you've literally missed the boat, you can sometimes purchase fish at the end of the day (lucky fishermen sell their catch from their boats). *Subway: D or Q to Sheepshead Bay.*

QUEENS

Most Manhattan residents only set foot in Queens en route to La Guardia or J.F.K. airport, but those who manage to get past the area's dull appearance will discover a few surprises. According to estimates, well over 100 nationalities coexist in Queens (including people from Afghanistan, China, Colombia, the Dominican Republic, the Philippines, India, Pakistan, Bangladesh, Korea, Mexico, Uruguay, Argentina, Peru, Romania, Thailand, and Ireland), and the area's strong ethnic flavor is perhaps its main draw. Named for Queen Catherine of Braganza, wife of Charles II, Queens was an independent British outpost until it joined with New York City in 1898. Today it's the largest of the city's five boroughs, accounting for a full third of the city's entire area. It's also the second most populous, surpassed only by Brooklyn.

Almost all of the sights in Queens are accessible by subway. Train rides take between 15 and 45 minutes from midtown Manhattan; the ride to the Rockaways takes more than an hour. The Greek community of Astoria lies over the Triborough Bridge from Manhattan, at the northwestern tip of Queens. Just south of here is the industrial center of Long Island City, a vital artists' community. To the east is the giant Flushing Meadows–Corona Park, site of two World's Fairs, in 1939 and 1964; you can't miss the

380-ton *Unisphere*—the largest known model of the earth—as you drive to the La Guardia or J.F.K. Flushing, in the northeastern corner of Queens, is predominantly Asian. Near the center of the borough you'll find ritzy residential neighborhoods filled with Tudor-style houses and tree-lined streets, as well as stunning **Forest Park** (*see* Parks and Gardens, *below*). East of the park is the primarily African-American neighborhood of Jamaica, and beyond that is **Alley Pond Park** (*see* Parks and Gardens, *below*). To the south lies the uninhabited Jamaica Bay Islands, site of the 9,155-acre **Jamaica Bay Wildlife Refuge** (*see* Parks and Gardens, *below*), and the narrow, beach-lined Rockaway Peninsula.

ASTORIA

Astoria, home to one of the largest Greek communities this side of the Adriatic, is packed with sidewalk cafés, family-run stores, and Greek tavernas with live music and dancing. Though Colombian greasy spoons and characterless chain stores are now almost as ubiquitous as Greek-owned establishments, the Greek community still thrives in isolated pockets along the old-fashioned blocks between **Broadway** and **Ditmars Boulevard**, from 21st Street to Steinway Street. Stroll along Broadway between 31st and 36th Avenues: Here *xaxaroplasteion* (Greek pastry shops) and coffee houses abound, and the elevated subway brings a constant stream of activity. Further up, 30th Avenue has every kind of food store imaginable; between 35th and 36th Streets alone you'll find a salumeria, a meat market, a bakery, a wholesale international food store, and more. The largest orthodox community outside Greece worships at **St. Demetrios Cathedral** (30-11 30th Dr.), at the corner of 31st Drive. *Subway: N to Broadway.*

You probably won't find the Marx Brothers or Bill Cosby walking down the streets of Astoria today—but in fact they have all done time here, along with many other big names in the American motion-picture industry. Before Hollywood, in the 1920s and '30s, the **Kaufman-Astoria Studios** (36–11 35th Ave., at 36th Ave.) were the hub of American movie-making. The likes of Gloria Swanson, Rudolph Valentino, and Claudette Colbert got their starts here. The studios are still used for major films and television shows—*Scent of a Woman, The Cotton Club, The Cosby Show,* and even *Sesame Street* have all been filmed here. Though the studios are closed to the public, you can visit the excellent **American Museum of the Moving Image** (35th Ave. at 36th St., tel. 718/784–0077), where interactive exhibits give you an in-depth and entertaining view of how movies and television are made. *Subway: N to 36th Ave.*

FLUSHING

Flushing is a curious mix of American history and ethnic diversity. To walk down Main Street today, with its staggering number of Asian restaurants and markets, you'd never guess that this was one of the first settlements of the Dutch, dating back to 1645. But venture north of the subway station into the historic area bounded by Northern and Parsons boulevards, Roosevelt Avenue, and Main Street, and you'll find several remnants of a 17th-century Quaker village. There's a fascinating history here: Having been forbidden to worship in public, the Dutch Quakers of *Vlissingen,* as Flushing was then called, found a loophole in the governing patent that granted all villagers liberty of conscience—a finding that not only ended their plight, but also served as the basis for the religious freedom that is granted in the U.S. Constitution.

THE FLUSHING FREEDOM MILE • The Queens Historical Society does a great job of preserving the area's historical buildings and providing information for curious visitors. Their headquarters are at the **Kingsland Homestead** (143–35 37th Ave., west of Parsons Blvd., tel. 718/939–0647)—a 1785 house where you can pick up maps and a self-guided tour brochure. While you're here, check out the **Weeping Beech Tree** in the garden out back: With a 14-ft-round trunk and an 85-ft branch spread, this hulking green giant planted in 1847 is the granddaddy of all American beech trees and one of two living landmarks in New York. (The other is not Ed Koch, but a magnolia tree in Brooklyn.) The nation's first nursery stood on this site, and today you'll still find rare trees throughout Flushing—golden larch, cedar of Lebanon, sassafras, mulberry, boxwood bush, and more. At the **Bowne House** (*see* Museums and Galleries, *below*), you can get a feel for life in the 1600s and pay homage to John Bowne, the key player in the establishment of freedom of religion. Three blocks away on Northern Boulevard, the shingled **Friends' Meeting House** (137–16 Northern Blvd., tel. 718/358–9636), in service since 1719, is the oldest house of worship in New York City. Across the street, the **Flushing Town Hall** (137–35 Northern Blvd., tel. 718/463–7700) houses a small art gallery/café, with live jazz ($20) on every other Friday night. *Subway: 7 to Main St.*

THE BRONX

Burned-out tenement buildings, drug crimes, and general urban decay are what most people associate with the Bronx. While these images are true to some extent, New York City's northernmost borough is

American Museum
of the Moving
Image/Kaufman–
Astoria Studios, **4**

Institute for
Contemporary Art/
P.S. 1 Museum, **5**

Isamu Noguchi
Garden Museum, **3**

St. Demetrios
Cathedral, **1**

Socrates Sculpture
Park, **2**

23rd Ave.

24th Ave.

S DITMARS
BLVD.
N

Grand Central Pkwy.

21st St.

Astoria Blvd.

S ASTORIA BLVD.
N

Newtown Ave.

31st St.

Steinway St.

A S T O R I A

Main Ave.

30th Ave.

S 30TH AVE.
(GRAND AVE.)
N

1

30th Dr.

31st Ave.

12th St.

14th St.

34th
St.

2

Vernon

Blvd.

Broadway

S

BROADWAY
N

S

STEINWAY ST.
G,R

S

Crescent St.

34th Ave.

38th St.

3

12th St.

35th Ave.

4

Steinway St.

L O N G   I S L A N D
C I T Y

36th Ave.

37th St.

36th St.

S

36TH AVE.
N

Roosevelt
Island
Bridge

S

36TH ST.
G,R

31st St.

Blvd.

S

East River

Crescent St.
27th St.

23d St.

21st St.

S

39TH AVE.
N

Northern

Queensbridge
Park

Vernon

Blvd.

41st Ave.

**QUEENSBORO
PLAZA**
N,7

33RD ST.
7

S

**21ST ST./
QUEENSBRIDGE**
B,Q

S

Queens

**QUEENS
PLAZA**
E,F,G,R

S

Blvd.

Queensboro
Bridge

43rd Rd.

**COURT HOUSE
SQUARE**
G

Thomson Ave.

45th Ave.

**23RD ST./
ELY AVE.**
E,F

S

S

Skillman Ave.

**45TH ST./
COURT HOUSE SQ.**
7

45th Ave.

45th Rd.

S

5

Jackson Ave.

49th Ave.

Vernon

Blvd.

46th Rd.

Long Island Expwy.

N

0 ___ 330 yards

0 ___ 300 meters

also home to some of the grandest mansions and greenest parks around, not to mention the much-loved **Yankee Stadium** (*see* Chapter 9), the famous Bronx Zoo, and the stunning **New York Botanical Gardens** (*see* Parks and Gardens, *below*). The city's only mainland borough (the others are all on islands), the Bronx was first settled by Jonas Bronck, a Dane, in the 17th century. Legend has it that the Bronx got its name because other settlers would say, "Let's go see the Broncks." (In fact, the Bronx River had its name long before the Bronck family came along.) Wealthy New Yorkers maintained rural retreats in the Bronx in the 19th century, when the area consisted of a picturesque patchwork of farms, market villages, and country estates. In the 1920s, the Bronx experienced a short-lived golden age: The new elevated subway line attracted an upwardly mobile population, and the **Grand Concourse** was fashioned as New York City's Champs-Elysées. But the Bronx declined as quickly as it had boomed; today, vestiges of its glory days are few and far between.

Aside from the Grand Concourse and the **Bronx Museum of the Arts** (*see* Museums and Galleries, *below*), the southwestern part of the Bronx is not the best place to be . . . unless, of course, you're a Yankee fan. Major attractions—the zoo, the botanical gardens, and the Italian community of Belmont—are clustered in Central Bronx. Riverdale, in the hilly, northwest corner of Bronx, is a wealthy community of estates, including Wave Hill (*see* Museums and Galleries, *below*). To the east, City Island is a quaint, slightly bohemian fishing community packed with boat-repair shops and fish restaurants. The northern half of the Bronx is dominated by the vast **Van Cortlandt** and **Pelham Bay** parks (for both, *see* Parks and Gardens, *below*). And, if you're a big fan of the man who penned "The Raven," take a peek at the **Edgar Allan Poe Cottage** (*see* Museums and Galleries, *below*). Most Bronx sights are no more than 45 minutes from midtown Manhattan; Yankee Stadium is just a 15-minute ride. Within the Bronx, stick to subways and buses; this is not a place where you'd want to get lost on foot.

BRONX ZOO

With 265 acres and more than 4,000 animals, this is the largest and most interesting of New York City's wildlife conservation centers. Most of the exhibits rely on moats rather than cages to keep animals (and humans) in their proper places, and are landscaped like natural habitats. Be sure to see **Jungle World,** an indoor tropical rain forest complete with five waterfalls; and **Wild Asia,** where tigers, elephants, and rhinos roam freely through 40 acres of open meadows and forest; you can view them from the lofty vantage point of a monorail. Bus and tram tours are also available at certain times of the year. Also don't miss the **World of Birds,** where you can walk among your winged friends, and **World of Darkness,** a windowless building that reverses day and night so that you can see bats, leopard cats, and other nocturnal creatures in action. The zoo is also home to a troupe of around 17 gorillas, each with a unique personality. Free walking tours of the zoo are offered on weekends; call 718/220–5141 for reservations. *Bronx River Pkwy. at Fordham Rd., tel. 718/367–1010. Subway: 2 to Pelham Pkwy., then walk 3 blocks west. Bus: Liberty Lines BXM11 Express Bus from midtown Manhattan; call 718/652–8400 for schedule and fares. Admission $6.75; free Wed. Open Apr.–Oct., weekdays 10–5, weekends 10–5:30; Nov.–Mar., daily 10–4:30.*

BELMONT

Though today's Belmont is populated mostly by African Americans and Hispanics, the short stretch of **Arthur Avenue** between 187th Street and Crescent Avenue remains the heart of an old Italian neighborhood, once home to more than 25,000 Italian Americans. The best time to visit is on a Saturday afternoon (the whole place shuts down Sunday). Arrive hungry because numerous bakeries, trattorias, and cafés (*see* Outer Borough Restaurants *in* Chapter 4) line the streets, and tiny markets sell cured olives and giant slabs of salami. You can atone for your gluttony at the **Church of Our Lady of Mount Carmel** (627 E. 187th St., between Hughes and Belmont Aves.) or drop by the **Catholic Goods Center** (630 E. 187th St., tel. 718/733–0250) for religious statuettes and Bibles in every tongue—Nigerian, Serbian, Albanian, and Creole, to name a few. *Subway: D to Fordham Rd. (20 mins), then walk 1 mi east on E. Fordham Rd. to Arthur Ave., turn right and walk 3 blocks to E. 187th St. Train: Metro-North to Fordham Rd. (10 mins).*

CITY ISLAND

City Island is probably the only place in New York where shop owners hang signs reading GONE TO THE BEACH. This mile-and-a-half long, half-mile-wide spit of land (connected by bridge to the rest of the Bronx) feels like a cross between ye olde New England fishing village and a California hippie commune from the '60s. First settled in the 1760s, the whole place might have dried up and blown away if it weren't for its highly profitable yacht-building industry (the Astors and Vanderbilts have shopped here)

Bronx Zoo, **4**

Church of Our Lady
of Mount Carmel, **2**

Edgar Allan Poe
Cottage, **1**

New York Botanical
Gardens, **3**

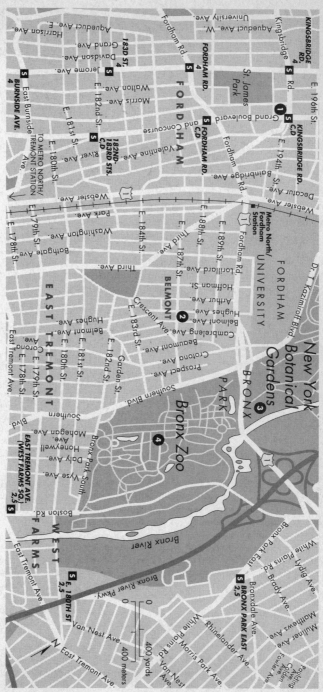

A TRIP TO
THE SOUTH BRONX

The south Bronx, once a well-to-do neighborhood, has a sad history. After World War II industries began drifting out of New York City, forcing the many Bronx residents who depended on high-wage jobs in Manhattan to pick up and haul their possessions elsewhere. By the 1960s and '70s, as immigrants and laborers poured into the city, cheap housing projects were built in the Bronx— a comfortable distance from Manhattan. Crime flourished, buildings rotted, and some landlords even took to torching their empty, run-down apartment buildings to collect the insurance money. Only recently have grass-roots programs started to pull the south Bronx out of its long depression. Today the Grand Concourse (its main drag) shows remnants of its former appeal, with its grand (albeit decaying) Art Deco buildings housing a lively community of immigrant families. At one end of a four-block span (161st to 165th Streets) you'll find the great "House that Babe Ruth Built," better known as Yankee Stadium; at the other is the Bronx Museum of the Arts. On Sunday afternoon, Joyce Kilmer Park (at 162nd Street) fills with salsa dancers and sellers of crafts for the Bronx Sunday Market.

and dozens of boat-repair businesses. Today there's not much else going on here, precisely City Island's charm. Spend the day strolling along the marina, poking around the funky, ramshackle little shops, or feasting on fried seafood at seagull-infested picnic tables. Afterward, take a peek inside the **North Wind Undersea Institute** (610 City Island Ave., tel. 718/885–0701), open weekdays 10–5 and weekends noon–4, whose ragtag collection includes whaling artifacts, scrimshaw art, and deep-sea diving gear (ask to see the video of Physty, the rescued sperm whale). At **Mooncurser Antiques** (229 City Island Ave., tel. 718/885–0302), you'll find a collection of 50,000 used LPs presided over by a bearded old eccentric. At the **Boat Livery** (663 City Island Ave., tel. 718/885–1843) you can grab a beer or bait and tackle (they're sold over the same counter), or rent a four-person dinghy ($20 per day) and row out into Pelham Bay. *Subway: 6 to Pelham Bay Park (45 mins); also Bus BX29 to City Island Ave. (20 mins).*

STATEN ISLAND

It used to be that if you asked a few New Yorkers what's fun to do in the Big Apple for 50¢ or less, they would either shake their heads and tell you to stop dreaming, or they'd brightly mention the ferry ride to Staten Island. Now it's free, of course, but even still, ask them *what's on Staten Island* and they'll stare blankly and shove off. This ignorance is infectious: Every day, hordes of tourists join commuters on the Staten Island Ferry (*see below*) for panoramic views of the Statue of Liberty, Ellis Island, and Lower Manhattan. Once there, most get right back on the next boat to Manhattan.

Staten Island is truly the forgotten borough. Though it's twice the size of Manhattan Island, its claims to fame (if it has any) are as the city's official garbage dump, and as the borough that is perpetually agitating to secede from New York City. The two are not unrelated: Islanders resent being dumped on (literally) and fear the environmental ramifications of having the world's largest landfill in their backyard. In addition, they resent paying New York City taxes, which they feel benefit Manhattan and the other boroughs far more than themselves.

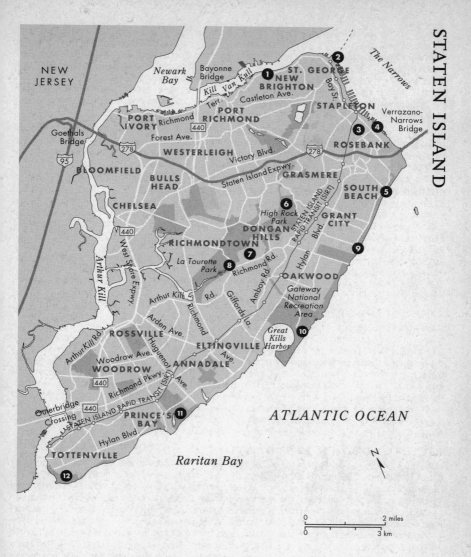

NEW
JERSEY

Newark
Bay

Bayonne
Bridge

The Narrows

Kill Van Kull

ST. GEORGE

1 NEW
BRIGHTON

Boy St.

STAPLETON

Castleton Ave.

Terr.

Richmond

PORT
IVORY

PORT
RICHMOND

Richmond

440

Goethals
Bridge

Forest Ave.

WESTERLEIGH

Victory Blvd.

278

ROSEBANK

Verrazano-
Narrows
Bridge

3 **4**

95

278

BLOOMFIELD

BULLS
HEAD

Staten Island Expwy.

GRASMERE

SOUTH
BEACH

5

CHELSEA

High Rock
Park

6

GRANT
CITY

DONGAN
HILLS

RICHMONDTOWN

7

STATEN ISLAND RAPID TRANSIT (SIRT)

Hylan Blvd.

9

La Tourette
Park

8

Richmond Rd.

OAKWOOD

West Shore Expwy.

440

Richmond Rd.

Amboy Rd.

Gateway
National
Recreation
Area

Arthur Kill

Arthur Kill

Rd.

Giffards La.

Great
Kills
Harbor

10

Arden Ave.

Richmond

ELTINGVILLE

ROSSVILLE

Woodrow Ave.

Huguenot Ave.

Ave.

ANNADALE

WOODROW

440

Richmond Pkwy.

ATLANTIC OCEAN

STATEN ISLAND RAPID TRANSIT (SIRT)

Outerbridge
Crossing

440

PRINCE'S
BAY

11

Hylan Blvd.

Raritan Bay

N

TOTTENVILLE

12

0   2 miles

0   3 km

Alice Austen
House, **4**

Conference
House, **12**

Ferry Terminal, **2**

Garibaldi–Meucci
Museum, **3**

High Rock Park/
Todt Hill, **6**

Jacques Marchais
Museum of Tibetan
Art, **7**

Richmondtown
Restoration/Staten
Island Historical
Society Museum, **8**

Snug Harbor
Cultural Center, **1**

Beaches

Great Kills Park **10**

Midland Beach, **9**

South Beach, **5**

Wolf's Pond
Park, **11**

Garbage dumps notwithstanding, Staten Island can be a lovely place to visit. It has more natural, unpaved areas than any of the other boroughs, including coastline beaches and the hiker's paradise, **High Rock Park** (*see* Parks and Gardens, *below*). It also has a whole lot fewer people: The island's population in the late 1980s was comparable to Manhattan's in 1845. You'll find it's still got an old-time, rural feel, especially in the re-created 18th-century village of Richmondtown and in the 19th-century sailors' haunt of Snug Harbor. Oddly enough, Staten Island is also home to an excellent museum of Tibetan art, the **Jacques Marchais Museum of Tibetan Art,** as well as the **Conference House,** onetime meeting place of Benjamin Franklin and his revolutionary crew (for both, *see* Museums and Galleries, *below*).

If you do disembark the ferry on Staten Island, plan on spending at least half a day there, since the island is vast and the sights spread apart. From the **Ferry Terminal** (*see below*) you can catch a bus directly to Snug Harbor (20 min), Richmondtown (40 min), and most other sights. At the Ferry Terminal you can also pick up the Staten Island Railway (SIRT), which makes limited stops on its way to Totenville, at the south end of the island. Pick up bus maps and train schedules inside the terminal.

COMING AND GOING BY FERRY • The Staten Island Ferry, which used to cost a bargain 50¢ round-trip, just got cheaper—now it's free. Ferries run 24 hours, departing every 15 minutes during morning and evening rush hours, hourly after 11 PM and on weekend mornings, and every 30 minutes most other times; call for current schedules. In Manhattan the ferry departs from the **Staten Island Ferry Terminal** in Battery Park (South St., near State St., Lower Manhattan; Subway: 1 or 9 to South Ferry). Passengers disembark in Staten Island at the Ferry Terminal in St. George, on the northeastern tip of the island (from there it's easy to catch a bus or train to all of the island's attractions). The trip is 20–30 minutes one-way. A tip: The newer boats are super-fast, but try to get a ride on one of the older ones, which have big open-air decks that are great for snapping photos of the Manhattan skyline and the Statue of Liberty. *Tel. 718/727–2508 or 718/390–5253.*

SNUG HARBOR CULTURAL CENTER

Once home to a colony of "aged, decrepit and worn-out sailors," Snug Harbor is now an 83-acre cultural center full of landmark Greek Revival and Victorian buildings, artists' workshops and studios, a pleasant **Botanical Garden** (tel. 718/273–8200; free), a **Children's Museum** (tel. 718/273–2060; $4), the **Newhouse Center for Contemporary Arts** (tel. 718/448–2500; $1); and the **Music Hall,** the second-oldest music hall in New York City—after Carnegie Hall (call the general number, *below,* for performance information). The colony was founded in 1831 at the bequest of wealthy shipowner Robert Richard Randall, and for the next 140 years it served as the nation's first maritime hospital and home for retired seamen. Free weekend tours (departing from the visitor center daily at 2 PM) will fill you in on the history of the colony. *1000 Richmond Terr., tel. 718/448–2500. From Ferry Terminal, take Bus S40 (10–15 mins). Museums open Wed.–Sun. noon–5; grounds open daily dawn–dusk.*

RICHMONDTOWN RESTORATION

Sure, it sounds hokey: A living history museum with a bunch of people dressed in silly costumes and lots of 18th-century buildings. But the Richmondtown Restoration is so well done it's cool. Many of the buildings in this 100-acre village are over 200 years old; one you won't want to miss is the **Guyon-Lake Tysen House,** one of the best surviving examples of Dutch Colonial architecture anywhere in the country (stick around in summer to see folks in period costume whip up snacks in a beehive oven). The **Voorlezer's House,** built in 1695, is thought to be the oldest elementary school in the country. Here the *voorlezer,* or lay minister, conducted church services and taught children how to read the Bible. You can also watch the tinsmith practicing his craft at the **Tinsmith's Shop,** or drop by an old print shop and a restored general store. Also in Richmondtown, the **Staten Island Historical Society Museum** (*see* Museums and Galleries, *below*) is worth a quick stop. Tours of the village depart from the visitors center on the hour. *441 Clarke Ave., tel. 718/351–1611. From Ferry Terminal, take Bus S74 (40 mins). Admission $4. Open Sept.–June, Wed.–Sun. 1–5; July–Aug., Wed.–Fri. 10–5, weekends 1–5.*

ROSEBANK

The Italian community of Rosebank, centered around Tompkins and Bay streets near the Verrazano Bridge, has been around since the late 1800s. Among the well-tended houses you'll find the **Garibaldi–Meucci Museum** (*see* Museums and Galleries, *below*), which commemorates Rosebank's most famous residents; **Alice Austen House** (*see* Museums and Galleries, *below*), full of works by this photographer of the early 20th century; and the fabulously gaudy shrine to **Our Lady of Mount Carmel** (Amity St. at White Plains Ave.), studded with garishly painted plaster statuettes of various saints, strings of light bulbs, and eternally burning candles. Reach it from Tompkins Avenue by following St. Mary's Street to White Plains Avenue and then turning right onto Amity Street. *From Ferry Terminal, take Bus S78 Tompkins Ave. (15 mins).*

MUSEUMS AND GALLERIES

Despite the recent rise of high-art quotients in metropolises like Los Angeles and Chicago, New York City is still the museum capital of the United States. And, New York being New York, overkill is key. Most cities would be ecstatic just to host the likes of the **Metropolitan Museum of Art** or the **MoMA** (*see* Major Attractions, *above*), but that's not nearly enough for New Yorkers. From the unabashedly Eurocentric Pierpont Morgan Library to the downright esoteric Jacques Marchais Museum of Tibetan Art, New York's museums and galleries successfully enshrine every imaginable object of human and nonhuman contrivance. Throw in an aircraft carrier, a preserved early-19th-century tenement, a giant collection of Fabergé eggs, and dozens of other collections large and small, and you'll begin to see why New York can rightly be considered the United States' museum capital. By some estimates, there are more than 150 museums in the city of New York. This chapter covers the best 72 of 'em.

The American Museum of Natural History's fossilized dinosaur embryo on display is thought to be 70 to 80 million years old. Jurassic Park, anyone?

Many of the city's blockbuster museums are conveniently clustered on 5th Avenue between 82nd and 104th streets, also known as **Museum Mile** (*see* Upper East Side *in* Manhattan Neighborhoods, *above*). These include the **Solomon R. Guggenheim Museum, Frick Collection, National Academy of Design, Cooper-Hewitt National Design Museum, El Museo del Barrio, Goethe House, International Center of Photography (ICP)–Uptown, The Jewish Museum,** and the **Museum of the City of New York.**

In addition to pretty pictures and fascinating artifacts, you'll find that museums offer guided tours, lectures, films (*see* Movie Houses *in* Chapter 7), concerts (*see* Music *in* Chapter 7), dance performances, and more. Often, these activities are free with museum admission, a deal that can turn even the most dedicated museum-hater into a true devotee. For info on current shows and events, check listings in one of the city's weeklies, like *The New Yorker* or *Time Out,* or the "Weekend" section of the Friday *New York Times.* In case your cultural pursuits span lunch hour, most major museums have attractive cafeterias and/or cafés, where you may or may not get a decent value for your dollar—the one at the American Museum of Natural History is called the Diner Saurus. If you keep your admission ticket (or button), however, you can always pop outside for a cheap slice of pizza and reenter the museum. Some museums, like the Met, the MoMA, the Frick, and the Cloisters, offer stunning courtyards and gardens to relax in. And, of course, all museums have gift shops.

Almost all of the city's museums are closed on Mondays. Otherwise, museum hours vary greatly; many major ones offer extended hours on Tuesday or Thursday, and further tempt weekday visitors by making admission free after 6 PM on those evenings. As you would expect, museums are closed on New Year's Day, Independence Day, Thanksgiving, and Christmas. If you want to visit a museum on other holidays, you should call ahead and confirm hours. Keep an eye out for copies of *Museums New York* in your hotel lobby or by museum information desks; this glossy not-quite-a-magazine has a great coupon section as well as rundowns on current exhibits.

AMERICAN MUSEUM OF NATURAL HISTORY

The American Museum of Natural History, established by scientist Albert Bickmore in 1868, is one of the largest and most important museums of its kind. All of the "-ologies" are represented here—including zoology, anthropology, vertebrate paleontology, ornithology, and evolutionary biology, to name a few—in a collection of more than 36 million artifacts and specimens enclosed in 40 halls and galleries. If you're expecting just a bunch of dead, stuffed elk displayed in stale, airless rooms, you're in for a big surprise. There's something here for everyone, from the world's largest collection of insects (17 million and counting) to the world's biggest sapphire (563 carats). Of course, there are also plenty of dead, stuffed elk.

But the museum has long been on the cutting edge of research in its fields, and is constantly changing its exhibits to jive with the times: During the first decades of the 20th century, the museum president arranged exhibits in the Hall of the Age of Man to reflect his racist belief in the supremacy of northern Europeans, but curators in the 1960s completely revamped the displays and renamed them the Hall of the Biology of Man. More recently, the museum completed a much-needed $34-million overhaul of its world-famous **dinosaur halls** (*see below*).

The museum and the attached Planetarium (*see below*) dominate a four-block tract on the Upper West Side. Originally, architects Calvert Vaux and Jacob Wrey Mould (who both also designed the Metropolitan Museum of Art) were determined to make this the largest building in the United States. They finished one wing and, from 1892 to 1936, other architects finished the rest. The last and most grandiose section, the work of John Russell Pope, is the neoclassical facade that borders Central Park West. It's quite a striking backdrop for the giant statue of Teddy Roosevelt. *Central Park W at W. 79th St., Upper West Side, tel. 212/769–5100. Subway: B or C to W. 81st St. Suggested donation $8. IMAX or Planetarium tickets, including museum admission, $8–$12. Open daily 10–5:45 (Fri.–Sat. until 8:45).*

PRACTICALITIES

Free tours of the museum's highlights are given daily at 10:15, 11:15, 1:15, 2:15, and 3:15, beginning at the African Mammals Hall on the second floor. They provide an excellent overview if you've never been here before, or if you've only got one afternoon to explore. Year-round, the museum offers a number of special performances, films, and lectures; call for the schedule.

COLLECTION HIGHLIGHTS

If you're pressed for time, skip everything else and head directly to the museum's famed **dinosaur halls** (*see below*). Otherwise, most of the good stuff is on the first floor, including the 94-ft-long (that's actual whale size) fiberglass model of a blue whale, which is suspended from the ceiling of the **Ocean Life Room.** In the **Hall of Minerals and Gems** you'll find the famous 563-carat Star of India sapphire, the largest in the world, while the adjoining **Hall of Meteorites** contains the Cape York Meteorite, smaller than a Volkswagen but so heavy that its supporting pillars go through the museum's floor and straight down into the bedrock below the building. The **Hall of Human Biology and Evolution** is all about man's favorite subject, namely, him- or herself; don't miss the "Visible Woman" hologram, a spooky life-size display that flashes from skeleton to internal organs to veins, arteries, and nerves to flesh-and-blood person, depending on the angle you look at her from. To see what a slice of a 1,300-year-old giant sequoia tree looks like, check out the **Hall of North American Forests.**

On the second and third floors, you'll find rooms devoted to the peoples of the world. Look for the **Chinese Wedding Chair** (Hall of Asian Peoples); the 3,000-year-old giant jade **Kunz Axe** and the silver-and-gold **Royal Llama of the Inka** (Hall of Mexico and Central America); and the amazing model of an **African Spirit Dancer** wearing a costume made of real snail shells (Hall of African Peoples). Sharing these floors are dioramas of animals in their natural habitats, many bagged by wealthy American taxidermist Carl Akeley in the 1920s—it's hard to think of Akeley as a hero while you're staring at a whole herd of stuffed African elephants in the **Akeley Hall of African Mammals.** You'll have to admit, however, that the Hall of Reptiles and Amphibians' display of three **Komodo dragons** eating a large wild boar is a little titilating.

THE DINOSAUR HALLS • In 1995, after four years and $34 million worth of work, the museum opened two spectacular new dinosaur halls: the **Hall of Suarischian Dinosaurs** and the **Hall of Ornithischian Dinosaurs,** both on the fourth floor. Then, in 1996, they opened the **Hall of Vertebrate Origins,** with displays of primitive fishes and pterodactyls. In these halls, interactive computer displays feature animated footage of how these monstrous beasts got around. More to the point, you'll find the single largest collection of real dinosaur fossils in the world: approximately 100 skeletons, 85% of which are real fossils (not that you would ever notice the difference). During the renovation process some of the skeletons were taken apart and rebuilt according to scientists' improved understanding of how the animals moved; for example, the **Apatosaurus,** previously known as Brontosaurus, got a new skull, additional neck bones, and a tail that has been lengthened by 20 ft. Other highlights include the **Warren Mastodon,** which was discovered in a bog less than 100 mi from New York City and is one of the most complete skeletons of the hairy prehistoric elephant ever found; a **Dinosaur Mummy,** important because it shows the skin and other soft tissues of a duck-billed dinosaur; the **Glenn Rose Trackway,** a series of 107-million-year-old fossilized dinosaur footprints; and last but certainly not least, the mighty, meat-eating **Tyrannosaurus Rex,** reset in a stalking (as opposed to a standing) posture. The rest of the museum's dinosaur collection is on the second floor, and has also been recently restored.

HAYDEN PLANETARIUM • The old Hayden Planetarium is undergoing an extensive renovation and will tentatively re-open in 2000 as the Earth and Space Center. It will feature a state-of-the-art Sky Theater for stellar views of the constellations and two new exhibition halls.

IMAX THEATER • Films on the IMAX Theater's 40-ft-high, 66-ft-wide screen are usually about nature, whether it's a jaunt through the Grand Canyon, a safari in the Serengeti, or a journey to the bottom of the sea to the wreck of the *Titanic*. If you've never watched a flick on a giant IMAX screen before, you're in for an awe-inspiring experience. *Tel. 212/769–5650 for show times. Admission $8. Purchase tickets at IMAX ticket counter in museum's W. 77th St. lobby.*

BROOKLYN MUSEUM OF ART

With the Met, MoMA, the Whitney, and a slew of other museums hogging all the attention in Manhattan, is it any wonder that the Brooklyn Museum of Art doesn't make it onto every New York visitor's itinerary? It should—and not only because it's the seventh-largest museum in the United States (and the second-largest in New York), with a 1.5-million item collection that runs the gamut from Egyptian mummy cases to plastic-and-metal Elsa Shiaparelli jewelry, Brooklyn Dodgers uniforms, and Winslow Homer watercolors.

Now housed in an elephantine, turn-of-the-century Beaux Arts monument by McKim, Mead & White, the Brooklyn Museum (the "of Art" in the name was added in 1997) was founded in 1823 as the Brooklyn Apprentices' Library Association (Walt Whitman was one of its first directors). Initial plans made this the largest art museum in the world—larger even than the Louvre in Paris—and although Brooklyn's 1898 annexation to Manhattan thwarted those plans (only five years after the building opened), a hundred years later the museum is in the midst of concerted renewal efforts stemming from an ambitious 1986 renovation master plan: More space, reinstalled galleries, extended Saturday hours, film screenings, readings, and musical performances are all part of the

If you're in town in June, check the local listings for the Museum Mile festival, when, for three brief hours one weekday evening, all the museums on 5th Avenue throw open their doors, and the strip becomes a free block party for highbrow types.

museum's recent efforts to put this at the top of New York's hyper-competitive museum heap. Special exhibits scheduled for 1998 include "Masters of Light and Color," an exhibit of watercolors by two leading practitioners of the genre, Winslow Homer and John Singer Sargent (March 20–July 5), and "The Qajar Epoch: 200 Years of Painting from the Royal Persian Courts" (October 23, 1998–January 24, 1999). *200 Eastern Pkwy., Park Slope, Brooklyn, tel. 718/638–5000. Subway: 2 or 3 to Eastern Pkwy./Brooklyn Museum. Admission $4. Open Wed.–Fri. 10–5, Sat. 11–9, Sun. 11–6.*

COLLECTION HIGHLIGHTS

The Brooklyn Museum pioneered the collection and study of non-Western art, and its **African and Pre-Columbian Art** galleries are outstanding. Make sure you view the 2,000-year-old *Paracas Textile,* which is considered by many to be the most important ancient Andean textile in the world. The museum's collection of **Asian Art** (second floor) includes pieces from Afghanistan, China, Korea, India, the Islamic world, and much more. You'll also find an impressive number of European and American paintings and sculpture here: The galleries of **Old Masters and French impressionists** (fifth floor) show works by Hals, Monet, Degas, Pissarro, Cassatt, Toulouse-Lautrec, and others. On the first floor, the **Grand Lobby installations** feature work created by contemporary artists specifically for this grandiose space.

AMERICAN COLLECTION • This collection, which rivals that of the Met, chronicles American art from its origins to the present with paintings by Copley, John Singer Sargent, William Merritt Chase, Winslow Homer, and Thomas Eakins. Don't miss *Brooklyn Bridge* by Georgia O'Keeffe. *5th floor.*

THE EGYPTIAN GALLERIES • The **Schapiro Wing** houses the museum's Egyptian art, considered the finest collection outside London and Cairo. The galleries, watched over by massive Assyrian wall sculptures, contain incredible treasures from ancient Egyptian tombs and royal cities dating from the Predynastic period (4,000–3,000 BC) to the Muslim conquest (7th century AD). Besides mummies in glorious sarcophagi, you'll see jewelry; pots; tools; solemn statues of queens, kings, cats, and dogs; and lots of small precious objects made from alabaster or ivory. *3rd floor.*

FRIEDA SCHIFF WARBURG MEMORIAL SCULPTURE GARDEN • This zany outdoor garden features relics from the "lost New York," such as a lion's head from Coney Island's old Steeplechase Park and the white goddess that once cradled the Penn Station clock. You'll find lots more cherubs, lions, scrolls, capitals, Medusas, and Greek-looking columns rescued from 19th-century buildings before they were torn down. During August, this is also a cool place to catch Sunday jazz concerts (3 PM).

IRIS AND GERALD CANTOR GALLERY • This attractive gallery showcases 58 sculptures by Auguste Rodin, including works related to *The Gates of Hell, The Burghers of Calais,* and *Balzac. 5th floor.*

PERIOD ROOMS • Impressive are the 28 period rooms—parlors, sitting rooms, and dining rooms, from plantation mansions and New England cottages—that show how New Yorkers lived from 1675 to 1830. Viewing the Jan Martense Schenck House, the oldest, is like stepping into a painting by a Dutch master, and the somber, exotic Moorish Room from John D. Rockefeller's town house is a tycoon's Alhambra. Costume galleries and decorative arts displays complement the period rooms. *4th floor.*

THE CLOISTERS

Perched atop a wooded hill near Manhattan's northernmost tip, the Cloisters houses the medieval collection of the Metropolitan Museum of Art (*see* Major Attractions, *above*) in an appropriately medieval monastery-like setting. Colonnaded walks connect authentic French cloisters, a Spanish Romanesque chapel, a 12th-century chapter house, and a Romanesque apse. The whole complex is spectacularly set overlooking the Hudson River, at the high point of Fort Tryon Park; for more on Fort Tryon Park itself, *see* Parks and Gardens, *below*. The galleries that display the collection are organized chronologically, starting with pieces from AD 1200, continuing through the Gothic period, and ending around 1520. Featured are chalices, altarpieces, sculptures, precious illuminated manuscripts, and works in stained glass, metal, enamel, and ivory. An entire room is devoted to the richly woven and extraordinarily detailed 15th- and 16th-century Unicorn Tapestries—a must-see. Just as noteworthy as the art on the walls are the museum's three **formal gardens**: In the central courtyard you'll find a splashing fountain, flowering plants, and piped-in choir music; the herb garden is full of strangely named greens once employed in medieval cures; and the Unicorn garden blooms with flowers and plants depicted in the famous Unicorn Tapestries. The Cloisters also frequently hosts special concerts of medieval music; for more info, *see* Music *in* Chapter 7. *Fort Tryon Park, Washington Heights, tel. 212/923–3700. Subway: A to 190th St.; also Bus M4 to last stop. Suggested donation $8 (includes same-day admission to Metropolitan Museum of Art). Open Mar.–Oct., Tues.–Sun. 9:30–5:15; Nov.–Feb., Tues.–Sun. 9:30–4:45.*

PIERPONT MORGAN LIBRARY

Both a museum and a center for scholarly research, the Morgan Library was originally built in 1906 as the private library for Pierpont Morgan, an immensely influential banker, philanthropist, and collector. This outstanding treasury has a renowned collection of rare books, manuscripts, and drawings that focus on the history and culture of Western civilization from the Middle Ages to the 20th century. Collection highlights include letters penned by Thomas Jefferson and John Keats; handwritten music by Beethoven and Mozart; a summary of the theory of relativity in Einstein's own elegant handwriting; three Gutenberg Bibles; drawings by Dürer, da Vinci, Rubens, and Degas; and original manuscripts by Charlotte Brontë. The galleries at the museum's main entrance have changing exhibitions; beyond these rooms, you'll find the opulent period rooms of Morgan's original library. The **East Room** (the main library) houses a portion of the Library's collection of rare books. The **West Room,** Morgan's personal study, contains a remarkable selection of mostly Italian Renaissance carvings, furniture, paintings, and other marvels. (The room, however, is so dark and sullen with red damask walls and heavy furniture that you may wonder if Morgan ever actually *read* here.) The **Rotunda,** with its marble columns and Raphael-esque ceiling mosaics, is one of the grandest small spaces in New York. When you get hungry or tired, linger awhile at the museum's delightful glass-roof garden court, which offers salads and sandwiches ($8–$9). Free guided tours of the museum take place weekdays at noon. Since it became a public institution in 1924, the Library has grown to half a city block, including the adjacent 1852 Italianate brownstone that belonged to Morgan's son, J. P. Morgan, Jr. Here you'll find the exceptional Morgan Library Shop. *29 E. 36th St., at Madison Ave., Murray Hill, tel. 212/685–0008. Subway: 6 to E. 33rd St. Suggested donation $5. Open Tues.–Fri. 10:30–5, Sat. 10:30–6, Sun. noon–6.*

WHITNEY MUSEUM OF AMERICAN ART

Gertrude Vanderbilt Whitney founded the Whitney Museum in 1930 with the noble notion of celebrating artists while they were still alive; the result is one of Manhattan's most dynamic institutions. Mrs. Whitney's own collection is the nucleus of the permanent collection of some 12,000 20th-century paintings, sculpture, and works on paper by more than 1,500 artists, including George Bellows, Stuart David, Edward Hopper, Jasper Johns, Willem de Kooning, Alex Katz, Ellsworth Kelly, Roy Lichtenstein, Georgia O'Keeffe, Maurice B. Prendergast, Jackson Pollock, Mark Rothko, John Sloan, Frank Stella, and Andy Warhol. In early 1998 the Whitney will for the first time put part of its collection on permanent display. The collection, works from 1900 to 1950, will fill the galleries on the fifth floor. This is a dry way of covering astounding pieces from the museum's strongest collections, like O'Keeffe's *The White Calico Flower,* Hopper's *Early Sunday Morning,* and his long-in-hiding early work *Soir Bleu.* Other galleries focus on the urban landscape and American social realism.

In addition, there are always lively special exhibits; the 1998 lineup includes Mark Rothko (fall), a study of the "Great American Nude" (summer), and an Arthur Dove retrospective (spring). Pause for a moment before entering the museum and size up this granite-clad building (1966), designed by the great Bauhaus/modernist architect Marcel Breuer. If you peer into the surrounding "moat," you'll see the busy hive of Sarabeth's; East-siders have been known to skip the museum entirely and just come here for brunch. One of the biggest regular events at the Whitney is the **Biennial Exhibition,** which is held in the spring of every odd-numbered year and highlights what the museum considers the greatest creations by American artists during the previous two years. Biennial shows are a blast; they're always wildly controversial and usually generate some wicked banter within the art community. The Whitney also offers a film and video series; dial 212/570–3676 for more info.

At the Whitney Museum, look for artist Charles Simonds's tiny, overlooked model based on an Indian pueblo, tucked into a corner of the stairwell.

If you still haven't had your fill, visit the Whitney's small Midtown outpost, the **Whitney Museum of American Art at Philip Morris** (120 Park Ave., at E. 42nd St., Midtown, tel. 212/878–2550), which has galleries and a sculpture court. *945 Madison Ave., at E. 75th St., Upper East Side, tel. 212/570–3676. Subway: 6 to E. 77th St. Admission $8; free Thurs. 6–8. Open Wed. and Fri.–Sun. 11–6, Thurs. 1–8.*

MORE ART MUSEUMS

Alternative Museum. As the sign outside says, this two-room gallery SEEKS TO EXHIBIT THE WORK OF THOSE ARTISTS WHO HAVE BEEN DISENFRANCHISED BECAUSE OF IDEOLOGY, RACE, GENDER, OR ECONOMIC INEQUALITY. It boasts some of the most interesting and engaging (and occasionally offensive or confrontational) art in SoHo. *594 Broadway, between Houston and Prince Sts., SoHo, tel. 212/966–4444. Subway: N or R to Prince St. Suggested donation: $3. Open Tues.–Sat. 11–6.*

American Craft Museum. Across the street from the famous Museum of Modern Art (MoMA), this small museum showcases contemporary American crafts in clay, fabric, glass, metal, wood, and even chocolate. Stop worrying about the distinction between "crafts" and "high art" while you're here—most of this stuff is just fun to look at. *40 W. 53rd St., between 5th and 6th Aves., Midtown, tel. 212/956–3535. Subway: E or F to 5th Ave. Admission $5. Open Tues.–Sun. 10–6, Thurs. until 8.*

Asian American Arts Centre. This space may not be as slick as galleries further uptown, but it does showcase contemporary works by talented Asian-American artists not easily seen elsewhere in the city. It also hosts annual Chinese folk-art exhibitions during the Chinese New Year and performances by the Asian American Dance Theater. The center sells a small selection of singular art objects from China. There's no sign out front; the door reads "KTV-City"; ring buzzer No. 1. *26 Bowery, between Bayard and Canal Sts., Chinatown, tel. 212/233–2154. Subway: N, R, J, M, or 6 to Canal St.; also B, D, or Q to Grand St. Admission free. Open Tues.–Fri. noon–6, Sat. 3–6.*

Bronx Museum of the Arts. Don't expect pretty paintings in this progressive museum. The exhibits, by artists of African, Asian, and Latin American descent, range from "The Body in Contemporary Photography" (in which striking black-and-white photos depict cultural and religious practices associated with the body) to the architecture of the Bronx and the history of its residents. The museum is in a former synagogue, and the three-story, glass-enclosed atrium gives it an airy, unstuffy feel. *1040 Grand Concourse, at 165th St., Bronx, tel. 718/681–6000. Subway: C, D, or 4 to 161st St./Yankee Stadium. Admission $3; free Wed. Open Wed. 3–9, Thurs.–Fri. 10–5, weekends 1–6.*

Dia Center for the Arts. This facility arrived in Chelsea several years before the most recent gallery craze. Here artists can develop new work or mount an organized exhibit or installation on a full floor for extended periods. Works from Dia's permanent collection may also be on view, including art by Joseph Beuys, Walter De Maria, Dan Flavin, Blinky Palermo, Cy Twombly, and Andy Warhol, among others. Up on the roof there's a coffee bar and an inspired exhibition by Dan Graham—a two-way mirror glass cylinder inside a cube. *548 W. 22nd St., Chelsea, tel. 212/989–5912. Subway: E to W. 23rd St. Suggested donation $4. Open Thurs.–Sun. noon–6.*

Grey Art Gallery. New York University's main building on Washington Square's east side contains this unpretentious street-level museum with changing exhibitions usually concentrating on contemporary artists. The gallery also houses two major art collections: the NYU art collection, which includes a few works by Picasso, Miró, and Matisse; and the Abbey Weed Grey Collection, which showcases contemporary Asian and Middle Eastern art. *100 Washington Sq. E, West Village, tel. 212/998–6780. Subway: N or R to E. 8th St./NYU. Suggested donation $2.50. Open Sept.–July, Tues.–Fri. 11–6:30 (Wed. until 8:30), Sat. 11–5.*

Guggenheim Museum SoHo. The SoHo outpost of the world-renowned Solomon R. Guggenheim Museum (*see* Upper East Side *in* Manhattan Neighborhoods, *above*) has struggled to define itself since its 1992 opening in a landmark redbrick warehouse on one of the city's chicest blocks. It displays contemporary art and works from the permanent collection and, increasingly, cutting-edge multimedia, design, and electronic exhibits. The large gift shop is certainly appealing, but you'll have to look hard to find any bargains. *575 Broadway, at Prince St., SoHo, tel. 212/423–3500. Subway: N or R to Prince St; 6 to Spring St.; or B, D, F, or Q to Broadway/Lafayette St. Admission $6. Open Wed.–Sun. 11–6 (Sat. until 8).*

The Institute for Contemporary Art/Clocktower Gallery. Ride up to the 13th floor to visit this gallery of avant-garde art and sculpture by resident artists (whose studios are closed to the public, except by appointment). The building, which once housed the New York Life Insurance Company, is a 1895 design by McKim, Mead & White. *108 Leonard St., TriBeCa, tel. 212/233–1096. Subway: A or C to Chambers St. or E to Canal St. Suggested donation $2. Open Wed.–Sun. noon–6.*

The Institute for Contemporary Art/P.S. 1 Museum. What do you get when you take an 85,000-square-ft former public school and invite emerging and international artists to fill it up with their avant-garde works? Add to that a gritty location in the midst of the factories and warehouses of Long Island City, and a phenomenal view of the Manhattan skyline, and you have the P.S. 1 Museum. Newly opened after a three-year renovation, P.S. 1 challenges traditional mores about how to present art. You'll find installations in the most unusual spaces—in the attic, the boiler room, the closets—even the bathrooms. If you're in the mood to meditate, look for "Meeting," a room with uniquely colored lights from Sweden and a motorized ceiling that opens to reveal the sky. *46–01 21st St., between 46th Rd. and 46th Ave., Long Island City, Queens, tel. 718/784–2084. Subway: 7 to 45th Rd./Court House Sq. Suggested donation $2. Open Wed.–Sun. noon–6.*

Isamu Noguchi Garden Museum. More than 300 works by the famous late Japanese-American sculptor Isamu Noguchi are on display here, from abstract bronzes inspired by Brancusi (a mentor to Noguchi during the '20s) to traditional Japanese ceramic and cast-iron sculpture to surrealist-inspired works in marble, slate, and wood. The peaceful outdoor garden is graced by a traditional *tsukubai* (fountain). *32–37 Vernon Blvd., between Broadway and 35th Ave., Long Island City, Queens, tel. 718/721–1932. Subway: N to Broadway. Admission $4. Open Apr.–Oct., weekdays 10–5, weekends 11–6.*

Museum for African Art. This is one of only two museums in the United States devoted exclusively to the arts of Africa. Its impressive exhibitions, which change every six months, may include wooden sculptures, masks and headdresses, jewelry, and religious relics; items on display are usually accompanied by printed narratives and photographs showing how the artifact was actually used. The museum shop carries African musical instruments, textiles, pottery, jewelry, and children's books. There's a free guided tour every Saturday at 2. *593 Broadway, between Houston and Prince Sts., SoHo, tel. 212/966–1313. Subway: N or R to Prince St.; also B, D, F, or Q to Broadway/Lafayette St. Admission $5. Open Tues.–Fri. 10:30–5:30, weekends noon–6.*

Museum of American Folk Art. A trip to this museum would be a lot like a foray into your grandmother's attic, assuming she hoarded paintings, quilts, carvings, dolls, wooden decoys, furniture, silver pieces, altars, copper weather vanes, and a beautiful collection of carousel horses. You can read all about how these pieces were made, and which immigrant groups brought them here. *2 Lincoln Sq., on Columbus Ave. between W. 65th and 66th Sts., Upper West Side, tel. 212/595–9533. Subway: 1 or 9 to W. 66th St. Suggested donation $3. Open Tues.–Sun. 11:30–7:30.*

Museum of American Illustration. The Society of Illustrators, founded in 1901, mounts exhibits of the commercial arts, such as children's book illustrations, book and magazine covers, postal stamps, car-

In case you want to see the world.

At American Express, we're here to make your journey a smooth one. So we have over 1,700 travel service locations in over 120 countries ready to help. What else would you expect from the world's largest travel agency?

In case you want to be welcomed there.

We're here to see that you're always welcomed at establishments everywhere. That's why millions of people carry the American Express® Card — for peace of mind, confidence, and security, around the world or just around the corner.

do more ®

Cards

In case you're running low.

We're here to help with more than 118,000 Express Cash locations around the world. In order to enroll, just call American Express before you start your vacation.

do more

Express Cash

And just in case.

We're here with American Express® Travelers Cheques and Cheques *for Two*.® They're the safest way to carry money on your vacation and the surest way to get a refund, practically anywhere, anytime.
Another way we help you...

do more ®

AMERICAN EXPRESS

Travelers Cheques

toons, and print advertisements. The museum's small galleries are in an 1875 carriage house. *128 E. 63rd St., between Park and Lexington Aves., Upper East Side, tel. 212/838–2560. Subway: B or Q to Lexington Ave. Admission free. Open Sept.–July, Tues. 10–8, Wed.–Fri. 10–5, Sat. noon–4.*

New Museum of Contemporary Art. What you'll see here is experimental, often radically innovative work by unrecognized artists—and none of it is usually more than 10 years old. *583 Broadway, between Houston and Prince Sts., SoHo, tel. 212/219–1222. Subway: N or R to Prince St.; also B, D, F, or Q to Broadway/Lafayette St. Admission $4.50; free Sat. 6–8. Open Wed.–Sun. noon–6 (Sat. until 8).*

Nicholas Roerich Museum. Housed in a beautiful Upper West Side town house (built in 1898), this small, eccentric museum displays the work of the prolific Russian artist who was also author, philosopher, explorer, archaeologist, and set designer (he designed sets for Diaghilev ballets). His vast paintings of the Himalayas are suffused with such a trippy mysticism that they give the whole place a cultish appeal. Also displayed are Roerich's books and travel treasures. Drop by on a winter weekend for poetry readings and classical-music performances. *319 W. 107th St., between Broadway and Riverside Dr., Upper West Side, tel. 212/864–7752. Subway: 1 or 9 to W. 110th St. Donations appreciated. Open Tues.–Sun. 2–5.*

Queens Museum of Art. If there's one reason to make the trek to Flushing Meadows–Corona Park, it's to see the knock-your-socks-off **New York City panorama** in the Queens Museum of Art. The 9,335-square-ft model, constructed for the 1964 World's Fair, faithfully replicates all five boroughs of the city, building by building, on a scale of 1 inch per 100 ft. The model's tiny brownstones and skyscrapers are updated periodically to look exactly like the real things. The museum's other exhibits examine the history of the World's Fair, and its

Curators at the New Museum of Contemporary Art feel that art, like fish and house guests, starts to smell if it hangs around too long.

frequent art exhibitions often reflect the cultural diversity of Queens. The park's New York City Building, which houses the museum, was also the site of several United Nations meetings between 1939 and 1964. *Flushing Meadows–Corona Park, tel. 718/592–9700. Subway: 7 to Willets Point/Shea Stadium. Admission $3. Open Wed.–Fri. 10–5, weekends noon–5.*

Studio Museum in Harlem. The museum's extensive collection of artifacts and art from the African diaspora includes sculptures, masks, headdresses, delicately beaded clothing, and religious tokens from Guinea, Tanzania, the Ivory Coast, Nigeria, Zaire, Ghana, Cameroon, Angola, and the Zulu people of South Africa. Also look for works by the Studio Museum's artists-in-residence, who come from all over the world. *144 W. 125th St., between Adam Clayton Powell Jr. and Malcolm X Blvds., Harlem, tel. 212/864–4500. Subway: B, C, D, 2, or 3 to W. 125th St. Admission $5. Open Wed.–Fri. 10–5, weekends 1–6.*

MUSEUMS ABOUT NEW YORK

Brooklyn Historical Society. The Historical Society has been collecting weird and wonderful artifacts about the borough and its citizenry since 1863. Seventeen years later, its elegant redbrick museum and library opened to house it all, and it has been on a collecting spree ever since. The building was the first major structure in New York to feature terra-cotta ornamentation, which includes lifelike busts, capitals, friezes, and string courses. Alas, a major renovation started in 1997; scaffolding will shroud the building through most if not all of 1998, during which time it will be closed. Its exhibits on Brooklyn history and its impressive library will not be accessible during the renovation, but to compensate for the closure the society will be offering frequent Saturday walking tours ($12 nonmembers) of different Brooklyn neighborhoods; reservations are recommended. *128 Pierrepont St., at Clinton St., Brooklyn Heights, tel. 718/624–0890. Subway: 2 or 3 to Clark St. Closed for renovations. Call for information about walking tours.*

Lower East Side Tenement Museum. This is the only museum in the country devoted to re-creating and remembering the urban squalor of the tenements (no-frills apartment buildings that opportunistic landlords constructed on the Lower East Side during the mid-1800's immigration boom). For $2 a month, destitute Jewish, Italian, and Irish immigrants crowded into one-room tenement apartments; they typically lived in dark, cramped, unventilated, and waterless quarters, and shared a single outdoor privy and water pump with up to 400 other residents. At the museum, you can take a fascinating guided tour of four restored apartments in a 19th-century tenement building (97 Orchard St.). If the tour doesn't interest you, you can watch a slide show about the tenement building's history and a video of interviews with Lower East Side natives. The free gallery has displays relating to Lower East Side history. *90 Orchard St., between Delancey and Broome Sts., Lower East Side, tel. 212/431–0233. Subway: F to Delancey St.*

Admission $8; includes tenement tour, slide show, and video. Open Tues.–Fri. noon–5; weekends 11–5. Tenement tours Tues.–Fri. 1, 2, and 3, weekends every 45 mins 11–4:15. Neighborhood walking tours weekends 1:30 and 2:30. Walking tour $8; tenement and walking tour $12.

New York City Fire Museum. It may not be as exciting as a three-alarm blaze, but the nifty collection of ornate old fire carriages and engines is a kick to look at—so are its photos of the horse-drawn fire wagons that once raced around New York, dousing flames and saving babies. There are exhibits devoted to all kinds of lore, including why firehouses have always favored black-and-white-spotted Dalmatians rather than, say, toy poodles. The museum itself is housed in a quaint old fire station that was active from 1904 to 1959. *278 Spring St., between Varick and Hudson Sts., SoHo, tel. 212/691–1303. Subway: C or E to Spring St. Suggested donation $4. Open Tues.–Sun. 10–4.*

New York City Police Museum. *NYPD Blue* this isn't. The city's police museum doesn't celebrate lurid crimes but instead exhibits historical items such as antique firearms, badges, and uniforms. There are intriguing collections of old mug shots—including ones of Al Capone—and drugs and funny money found on New York's mean streets. You'll need to show your photo ID to visit. *235 E. 20th St., between 2nd and 3rd Aves., Gramercy, tel. 212/477–9753. Subway: 6 to E. 23rd St. Admission free. Open weekdays 9–3; groups by appointment only.*

New-York Historical Society. Since its founding in 1804, the Historical Society has collected over one million artifacts of the city's past, including Ben Franklin's glasses; the Louisiana Purchase contract, complete with Napoleon's signature; the first English Bible published in America; hundreds of busts and statues; 250 Tiffany lamps (the largest such collection in the world); and the remains of a leaden King George statue that had been melted down for bullets during the Revolutionary War. Concerts and walking tours are also part of the Society's program. *2 W. 77th St., at Central Park W, Upper West Side, tel. 212/873–3400. Subway: B or C to W. 81st St. Suggested donation $5. Open Wed.–Sun. noon–5.*

New York Transit Museum. You don't have to be enraptured by public transportation to find this museum fascinating. Housed in a restored 1930s subway station, it shows off 20 retired subway cars (some with ceiling fans and fancy seats), a couple of funky elderly city buses, and exhibits on how the subway tunnels were built, or sometimes dynamited. The museum offers a variety of walking tours, including a rotating series of one-hour lunchtime tours on Wednesday at 1 PM that take you through a power control center, a ventilation plant, and the perpetually under-construction Canal Street Station. *Boerum Pl. at Schermerhorn St., Brooklyn Heights, tel. 718/243–3060; 718/243–8601 for tour information. Subway: A, C, or F to Jay St./Borough Hall. Admission $3. Open Tues.–Fri. 10–4, weekends noon–5.*

New York Unearthed. Whenever they start raising a new glass-and-steel monstrosity in Manhattan, New York Unearthed's crack team of urban archaeologists sifts through the dirt. At this museum/laboratory, you'll see artifacts from the prehistoric days right up through the 1950s (interestingly, tobacco pipes seem to be the one artifact common to all eras)—and learn what lies where under New York's pavement. There's some pretty astounding stuff, including 200-year-old oyster shells, each more than a foot long. *17 State St., between Bridge and Pearl Sts., Lower Manhattan, tel. 212/748–8628. Subway: 4 or 5 to Bowling Green. Admission free. Open Jan.–Mar., weekdays noon–6; Apr.–Dec., Mon.–Sat. noon–6.*

South Street Seaport Museum. In the middle of yuppified South Street Seaport stands this great museum, dedicated to New York's early history as an international port. You'll find a working 19th-century printing press, scrimshaw art, model ships, and temporary exhibits on lively topics such as 19th-century sailors' tattoos. Your ticket also lets you board six historic ships, including the *Peking,* a four-masted barque from 1911; the *Wanetree,* an 1885 three-masted tall ship; and the *Ambrose,* a 1908 lightship once used to guide other ships into port. *12–14 Fulton St., between Front and South Sts., Lower Manhattan, tel. 212/748–8600. Subway: J, M, Z, 2, 3, 4, or 5 to Fulton St. Admission $6. Open Wed.–Mon. 10–6, Thurs. 10–8.*

Staten Island Historical Society Museum. Bet you never knew that Crisco, Ivory soap, and dental drills were all made on Staten Island in the 19th century, or that Staten Island was the principal source of New York City's beer in the 1850s. This excellent little museum, in Staten Island's Richmondtown Restoration, displays tools, furniture, toys, photos, fishing paraphernalia, and other objects that shed light on New York's forgotten borough. One room displays a full-size oyster-fishing boat—a reminder of the humble origins of Staten Island's economy. *Tel. 718/351–1611. For directions and admission, see Staten Island in the Outer Boroughs, above. Admission $4. Open June and Sept., Wed.–Sun. 1–5; July–Aug., Wed.–Fri. 10–5, weekends 1–5.*

ETHNIC AND CULTURAL MUSEUMS

The Asia Society. John D. Rockefeller III, great-grandson of the original gajillionaire Rockefeller, founded the Asia Society in 1956 to further the understanding of Asia in America. The Society's modest galleries display art from all reaches of Asia, as well as New Zealand, Australia, and the Pacific Islands; the gift shop has a fantastic book selection. Free gallery talks are given Tuesday–Saturday at 12:30 (also at 6:30 on Thursday) and Sunday at 2:30. Shows change several times a year. *725 Park Ave., at E. 70th St., Upper East Side, tel. 212/288–6400 or 212/517–6397. Subway: 6 to E. 68th St. Admission $3; free Thurs. 6–8. Open Tues.–Sat. 11–6 (Thurs. until 8), Sun. noon–5.*

Black Fashion Museum. The recently renovated Black Fashion Museum has more than 3,000 pieces in its collection, including all the costumes from *The Wiz*, a few Michael Jackson outfits, a slave girl's original gingham dress, and a copy of Mary Todd Lincoln's second inaugural gown. A few of the designers featured include Lenny Varnadoe (creator of a number of Bobby Brown's getups), Anne Lowe (whose credits include Jacqueline Kennedy's wedding dress), and Willi Smith (the creative force behind WilliWear). *157 W. 126th St., between Adam Clayton Powell Jr. and Malcolm X Blvds., Harlem, tel. 212/666–1320. Subway: 2 or 3 to W. 125th St. Admission $3. Open by appointment only.*

China House Gallery. A pair of fierce, fat stone lions guard the doorway to the China Institute. Inside, you'll find galleries where three or four museum-quality shows are mounted yearly, generally on historical topics. The Institute also offers film programs, lectures, and classes in language, calligraphy, cooking, and painting (classes are organized by semester). *125 E. 65th St., between Park and Lexington Aves., Upper East Side, tel. 212/744–8181. Subway: B or Q to Lexington Ave. Suggested donation $5. Open Mon.–Sat. 10–5 (Tues. until 8), Sun. 1–5.*

> *In 1991 the Dalai Lama blessed the Jacques Marchais Museum, and since then, Buddhists have journeyed from around the world to worship here.*

Hispanic Society of America. Relics and paintings from the 10th through the 15th centuries are displayed at this 90-year-old museum, housed in a Spanish-style building. Don't miss the giant wall paintings by Joaquin Sorolla y Bastida, which colorfully depict pain in the 1860s–1920s. You'll also find three giant oil paintings by Spanish masters Goya, El Greco, and Velasquez and a bunch of altars and nifty marble sarcophagi. The library houses more than 200,000 books about (surprise, surprise) Spain and Portugal. *Audubon Terr., Broadway at W. 155th St., Washington Heights, tel. 212/926–2234. Subway: 1 to W. 157th St. Admission free. Open Tues.–Sat. 10–4:30, Sun. 1–4.*

Jacques Marchais Museum of Tibetan Art. Find nirvana among the *bodhisattvas* (religious deities), *tankas* (ritual paintings used to aid meditation), *mani* stones (slates inscribed with Tibetan prayers), and other Tibetan artifacts at this hilltop temple museum, seeming totally out of place in Staten Island. It's the brainchild of Edna Coblentz (a.k.a. Jacques Marchais), an Asian art dealer from the Midwest, who indulged her passion for a country she never visited by building this Tibetan center next door to her home. Outside, you'll find a serene garden filled with ponds, statues, and strings of prayer flags. If you're taking the bus, be prepared for a steep uphill walk to the museum. *338 Lighthouse Ave., Staten Island, tel. 718/987–3500. From Ferry Terminal, take Bus S74 to Lighthouse Ave. Admission $3. Open Wed.–Sun. 1–5 (Dec.–Mar., by appointment only).*

Japan Society. Not far from the United Nations is the headquarters of the Japan Society, which produces a range of cultural events, including occasional gallery exhibits, film series, and lectures. In its lobby you'll find a touch of Kyoto: a pond, bamboo trees, and shoji screens. The gallery is newly opened after a year of renovations. *333 E. 47th St., between 1st and 2nd Aves., Midtown, tel. 212/832–1155. Subway: 4, 5, 6, or 7 to Grand Central. Admission free. Lobby open weekdays 9–7:30; gallery open Tues.–Sun. 11–5.*

Museum of Chinese in the Americas (MCA). In a century-old schoolhouse once attended by Italian-American and Chinese-American children, MCA is the only museum in America devoted to preserving the history of the Chinese people throughout the Western hemisphere. The permanent exhibit—"Where's Home? Chinese in the Americas"—delves into the Chinese-American experience through displays of artists' creations and personal and domestic artifacts alongside of historical commentary. Slippers for binding feet, Chinese musical instruments, and items from a Chinese laundry are just some of the unique objects on view. Changing exhibits fill a second room; recent shows focused on sights around Chinatown and Brooklyn's Sunset Park Chinese community. *70 Mulberry St., 2nd floor, Chinatown, tel. 212/619–4785. Subway: N, R, J, M, or 6 to Canal St.; also B, D, or Q to Grand St. Admission $3. Open Tues.–Sun. 10:30–5.*

National Museum of the American Indian. This incredible museum, a branch of the Washington, D.C.–based Smithsonian Institute, houses George Gustav Heye's collection of more than one million American Indian artifacts. Wealthy and passionate collector Heye spent the first half of the 20th century traveling the world, gathering jade ornaments from the ancient Mayans, stone carvings from the peoples of the Pacific Northwest, and even a shrunken head or two. Whether you consider his activities grossly exploitative, you'll find the artifacts—games, clothing, religious items—displayed intelligently, each accompanied by an explanation written by a member of the tribe or group of its origin. The museum is in the former **Alexander Hamilton U.S. Custom House,** one of the most spectacular examples of beaux arts architecture in New York: The first row of statues atop the pediment represents the various continents, while the second row symbolizes the major trading cities of the world. *1 Bowling Green, between State and Whitehall Sts., Lower Manhattan, tel. 212/668–6624. Subway: 4 or 5 to Bowling Green. Admission free. Open daily 10–5 (Thurs. until 8).*

Schomburg Center for Research in Black Culture. Arturo Alfonso Schomburg, black scholar and bibliophile, dedicated his life to collecting evidence of and denouncing white prejudice. At his death in 1938 he had amassed some 100,000 items, including books, photographs, political cartoons, paintings, oral histories, and even the white robe and hood of a KKK member—it's an amazingly powerful collection. In addition to gallery space, the center (part of the New York Public Library system) holds a research library and the recently renovated **American Negro Theatre,** where Sidney Poitier, Ruby Dee, and Harry Belafonte have performed. *515 Malcolm X Blvd., at W. 136th St., Harlem, tel. 212/491–2265. Subway: 2 or 3 to W. 135th St. Admission free. Open Mon.–Wed. noon–8, Thurs.–Sat. 10–6, Sun. 1–5.*

Ukrainian Museum. The exhibitions in the two small rooms were put together by Ukrainian Americans, obviously with much pride in their rich cultural heritage. On permanent display are Ukrainian ceremonial costumes, jewelry, and footwear. Seasonal exhibits include Christmas decorations and fabulously ornate Easter eggs (the latter are worth a special trip). *203 2nd Ave., between E. 12th and 13th Sts., East Village, tel. 212/228–0110. Subway: 4, 5, 6, N, or R to Union Sq./E. 14th St.; also L to 3rd Ave. Admission $1. Open Wed.–Sun. 1–5.*

HISTORICAL HOUSES

Abigail Adams Smith Museum. Back when the Upper East Side was nothing but farmland, Abigail Adams Smith, daughter of President John Adams, set up a nifty 23-acre estate on the East River. Today, her 1799 house is hemmed in by massive brick buildings and auto shops. Tours show off the *in situ* collection of Federalist and Empire furniture, art, and household implements; in fall 1997, several rooms were reopened, having been restored to their original appearance when the house was the Mount Vernon Hotel, a ritzy resort for downtowners. *421 E. 61st St., between 1st and York Aves., Upper East Side, tel. 212/838–6878. Subway: N, R, 4, 5, or 6 to E. 59th St./Lexington Ave. Admission $3. Open Sept.–May, Tues.–Sun. 11–4; June–July, Tues. 11–9, Wed.–Sun. 11–4.*

Alice Austen House. Whoever said that the Victorians were a repressed lot was not accounting for Alice Austen, a woman who was out photographing city life during an age when most sat around doing needlepoint. Here at "Clear Comfort," the harborfront cottage where Austen lived luxuriously (until she lost her fortune in the 1929 stock market crash), you'll see her striking and vivid photos. Compare those of tennis matches and other scenes of the "larky life" with those of the immigrant street sweepers, ash collectors, Irish policemen, and the many other laborers who flooded turn-of-the-century New York. *2 Hylan Blvd., at Bay St., Rosebank, Staten Island, tel. 718/816–4506. From Ferry Terminal, take Bus S51 to Hylan Blvd. (15 mins). Admission $3. Open Thurs.–Sun. noon–5; grounds open daily until dusk.*

Bowne House. U.S. citizens, thank Mr. John Bowne, the original owner of this 1661 house, for your freedom of religion. The defiant Bowne held Quaker meetings here despite the Dutch governor's ban on the sect, and was eventually thrown in jail. At his trial, Bowne successfully argued that the colony's patent granted its new citizens the right "to have and enjoy liberty of conscience"—a principle that was later consecrated by the Bill of Rights. Besides being incredibly old, this house, with its slanting floors and low ceilings, is also considered one of the finest examples of Dutch–English architecture in the United States. *37–01 Bowne St., Flushing, Queens, tel. 718/359–0528. Subway: 7 to Main St. Admission $2. Open Tues. and weekends 2:30–4:30.*

Conference House. This place couldn't be more out-of-the-way, but if you're up for the long bus ride to the tip of Staten Island, you'll be rewarded with a neat history lesson. On one fateful day in 1776, Benjamin Franklin, John Adams, and Edward Rutledge met at this Staten Island house with British Admiral Lord Howe. The rabble-rousing revolutionaries pooh-poohed the Lord's offer of "clemency and full pardon to all repentant rebels," and the rest, as they say, is history. The Conference House's rooms have been fixed up to look the same as they did when American insurgents used them to talk war over "good claret, good bread, cold ham, tongues, and mutton." Outside, in Conference House Park, the small beach where Franklin allegedly took his post-lunch naps, is a prime spot for watching the sailboats in Raritan Bay. *7455 Hylan Blvd., Tottenville, Staten Island, tel. 718/984–2086. From Ferry Terminal, take Bus S78 to Craig Ave., walk 1 block south. Admission $2. Open May–Nov., Fri.–Sun. 1–4.*

Dyckman House. This 1784 Dutch farmhouse-turned-museum is the only attraction in Inwood, the teeny neighborhood north of Washington Heights. Not surprisingly, Dyckman House is the last farmhouse remaining in Manhattan. Surprisingly, there's more to see here than a few rusty hoes: The Relic Room features a Revolutionary War uniform and musketry. In the garden is a replica of a Revolutionary War military hut. *4881 Broadway, at W. 207th St., Inwood, tel. 212/304–9422. Subway: A to W. 200th St. Admission free, donations accepted. Open Tues.–Sat. 11–4.*

Edgar Allan Poe Cottage. In the hope that the fresh, clean country air of Fordham Village might improve the health of Virginia, his tuberculosis-stricken wife, the 37-year-old Poe moved to this cottage in 1846. Alas, Virginia soon passed away, leaving Poe alone with his mum-in-law until 1849, when he, too, succumbed. Not exactly a happy history, but at least fans of Poe's "Annabel Lee," "Ulalume," and "The Bells" can admire the room in which they were written. There's a small collection of manuscripts, a seedy surrounding park, and no rest rooms. *Grand Concourse and Kingsbridge Rd., Fordham, Bronx, tel. 718/881–8900. Subway: D to Kingsbridge Rd. Admission $2. Open Sat. 10–4, Sun. 1–5.*

> *The bayberry candles you see in Bowne House were sort of like colonial chastity insurance. According to lore, when a bayberry candle burned out, all visiting males were supposed to pick up immediately and leave.*

Fraunces Tavern. So central was Fraunces Tavern to the American Revolution, you'd think the entire insurrection was plotted here over a few pints and tavernkeep Samuel Fraunces's fancy desserts. During the war, the Sons of Liberty met at the tavern, and George Washington bid his officers farewell here in 1783. Later, it housed the fledgling U.S. government's departments of the Treasury, Foreign Affairs, and War. The whole thing was restored in 1904, patched up a bit in 1975 (when it was bombed by a Puerto Rican nationalist organization), and today contains a collection of 18th- and 19th-century paintings, decorative arts, prints, and documents. Downstairs is a re-creation of the original tavern, where you can eat an overpriced meal or down a pint yourself. *54 Pearl St., at Broad St., Lower Manhattan, tel. 212/425–1778. Subway: J, M, or Z to Broad St. Admission $2.50. Open weekdays 10–4:45, weekends noon–4.*

Garibaldi–Meucci Museum. General Giuseppe Garibaldi, the man who established Italy as a nation, took refuge here in 1850 as the guest of Antonio Meucci, argued to be the true inventor of the telephone. This museum is full of informative exhibits about both men—you'll get to see a chair that clever Meucci carved out of tree branches, and the shirt and dagger that Garibaldi used in battle. A guided tour and video tell the sad tale of Meucci's invention of electromagnetism (he died before he was able to renew the costly patent, and Alexander Graham Bell sucked up all the glory). *420 Tompkins Ave., between Vanderbilt and Hylan Aves., Staten Island, tel. 718/442–1608. From Ferry Terminal, take Bus S78 (15 mins) to Tompkins Ave. $3 donation requested. Open Apr.–Nov., Tues.–Sun. 1–5; Dec.–Mar., Tues.–Fri. 1–5; or by appointment.*

Merchant's House Museum. This museum is a fully restored Federal- and Greek revival–style town house, built with red bricks and marble trim in 1831–32. Retired merchant Seabury Treadwell and his descendants lived here from 1835 right up until it became a museum in 1933. All of the family's furniture remains, along with personal items such as clothing, needlepoint, and photographs. Concerts, lectures, readings, and cooking demonstrations are held throughout the year. For a free guided tour, come on Sunday afternoon. *29 E. 4th St., between Bowery and 2nd Ave., East Village, tel. 212/777–1089. Subway: 6 to Astor Pl. Admission $3. Open Sun.–Thurs. 1–4.*

Morris-Jumel Mansion. This Palladian-style mansion, built in 1765, is the oldest standing house in Manhattan, and a lot has happened here in the last 200 years. During the Revolutionary War, it was used by the Brits, the Hessians, and George Washington and troops (not all at once, of course). Eliza Bowen Jumel—a former prostitute who in 1832 became the wealthy widow of French wine merchant Stephen Jumel—lived here during her short (1834–1836), unhappy marriage to former Vice President Aaron Burr. Since 1906, the mansion has been a museum of exquisitely refurbished rooms, some of

Burr's desks, and a chaise rumored to have once belonged to Napoleon. The gorgeous rose garden offers spectacular views of the Harlem River, and the surrounding **Jumel Terrace Historic District** (W. 160th–162nd Sts. between St. Nicholas and Edgecombe Aves.) encompasses blocks of beautiful 19th-century brownstones. *65 Jumel Terr., between W. 160th and 162nd Sts., Washington Heights, tel. 212/923–8008. Subway: B to W. 163rd St./Amsterdam Ave. Admission $3. Open Wed.–Sun. 10–4.*

Theodore Roosevelt Birthplace. The building now standing isn't the actual house where the Bull Moose was born, but instead a brick-by-brick re-creation (1923). The original brownstone was purchased for Teddy's father by Cornelius Roosevelt, who at the time was the fourth-richest man in New York. House tours, spiced up with anecdotes about Teddy's childhood in New York, look at five rooms filled with authentic furniture. Two galleries are filled with the former president's personal effects (the "big stick" is nowhere to be found). From Labor Day to Memorial Day, you can catch concerts Saturday at 2 PM. *28 E. 20th St., between Broadway and Park Ave. S, Gramercy, tel. 212/260–1616. Subway: N or R to W. 23rd St.; also 4, 5, or 6 to E. 23rd St. Admission $2. Open Wed.–Sun. 9–5; tours given on the hr until 4.*

Wave Hill. This lavish estate, in the exclusive Bronx neighborhood of Riverdale, was home at various times to Teddy Roosevelt, Mark Twain, and Arturo Toscanini. It consists of two houses—the 1843 gray-stone Wave Hill House (where you'll find an open-air café) and the newer, neo-Georgian Glyndor House (which has an art gallery)—and 28 acres of beautifully landscaped gardens. The Pergola Overlook, a gazebo with a river view, is the ultimate spot for romance seekers. Garden tours (free) convene Sundays at 2:15 PM. On-site dance performances take place Wednesday and Sunday evenings in July. *675 W. 249th St., at Independence Ave., Bronx, tel. 718/549–3200. Subway: 1 or 9 to W. 231st St. (45 mins), then Bus BX 7 or 10 (10 mins). Train: Metro-North to Riverdale Station (30 mins). Admission $4; free Tues. and before noon Sat. (free Nov. 15–Mar. 14). Open mid-May–mid-Oct., Tues.–Sun. 9–5:30 (Fri. until dusk); mid-Oct.–mid-Mar., Tues.–Sun. 9–4:30.*

MUSEUMS OF MOVIES AND TELEVISION

American Museum of the Moving Image. Housed in the historic Kaufman-Astoria studios, this museum of movies is absolutely worth the trip to Astoria, Queens. You can play with all kinds of high-tech gizmos to create your own special effects; dub your voice over Clint "go ahead, make my day" Eastwood's; produce and play back your own animated shorts; or pose while a camera makes a video flip-book (the same kind that's used in cartoon animation) of you. Check out one of the vintage film serials or shorts shown every hour in Tut's Fever Movie Palace, a garish re-creation of an Egyptian-style picture palace of the 1930s. The museum's **Riklis Theater** shows new and old films, with famous actors and directors as guest speakers. Most films are free with museum admission. *36–11 35th Ave., at 36th St., Astoria, Queens, tel. 718/784–0077. Subway: N to 36th Ave. Admission $5. Open Tues.– Fri. noon–4, weekends noon–6.*

Museum of Television and Radio. In this museum it's okay to lounge in cushy chairs watching old episodes of the *Brady Bunch* instead of traipsing past peeling paintings of Christs-on-the-cross and haloed Madonnas-with-Child. In fact, this museum has *60,000* of the best and most significant television and radio programs—from *Howdy Doody* to CNN broadcasts of Princess Di's wedding. And you're free to fast-forward, pause, rewind, whatever. All you have to do is stroll in, select up to four programs at a time from a computer index, then settle down at one of the unbelievably comfortable state-of-the-art viewing consoles (is this the greatest museum you've ever been to, or what?). The museum, which opened in 1991, also offers gallery exhibitions, lectures, and group screenings. *25 W. 52nd St., between 5th and 6th Aves., Midtown, tel. 212/621–6600 or 212/621–6800. Subway: E or F to 5th Ave. Admission $6. Open Tues.–Sun. noon–6 (Thurs. until 8; screening rooms until 8 on Fri.).*

MUSEUMS OF THE SCIENCES

American Numismatic Society. The study of money is what goes on at this 130-year-old organization. Even if you don't have *mucho dinero* yourself, it's a pretty interesting place. They've got more than one million pieces of currency representing every period of history, from ancient Egypt to the Elizabethan age right up through the present. *Audubon Terr., Broadway at W. 155th St., Washington Heights, tel. 212/234–3130. Subway: 1 to W. 157th St. Admission free. Open Tues.–Sat. 9–4:30, Sun. 1–4.*

Con Edison Energy Museum. If you're yearning to re-create the feeling of going on an elementary-school class trip, then this museum's for you. The emphasis is on Thomas Edison and early electrical power generation in New York City, and all the displays look like they were put together sometime in the

1970s. Still, they're in great shape—presumably because of light traffic. "The Underground World," a five-minute multimedia presentation, is a kitschy pleasure with faux stone walls and funky psychedelic lights; it explains how electric power is generated beneath the streets of Manhattan. *145 E. 14th St., between 3rd and Lexington Aves., Gramercy, tel. 212/460-6244. Subway: L, N, R, 4, 5, or 6 to E. 14th St. Admission free. Open Tues.–Sat. 9–5.*

Sony Wonder Technology Lab. This Sony product–filled place will really wow you, especially if you're one of those who can't program a VCR or considers the microwave oven cutting-edge technology. All the exhibits are interactive and hands-on: Start in the lobby by recording your name, image, and voice on a plastic chip, which acts as your "key" to other exhibits too weird and astounding to describe here. One of the best is the High Definition Theater, where you and other audience members orchestrate a video adventure from your seats—you actually get to determine the outcome of the movie by voting with a futuristic joystick attached to the arm of your chair. *550 Madison Ave., between E. 55th and 56th Sts., Midtown, tel. 212/833–8100. Subway: 4, 5, or 6 to E. 59th St.; also E or F to 5th Ave./53rd St. Admission free. Open Tues.–Sat. 10–6, Thurs. 10–9, Sun. noon–6.*

NONE-OF-THE-ABOVE MUSEUMS

At the Ferry Terminal in Staten Island is a small museum of ferry paraphernalia, including antique ships' wheels, scale models of ferries, and black-and-white vintage photos of commuters from the 1950s. Check it out if you have a few minutes to kill.

Forbes Magazine Galleries. While millionaires Gertrude Vanderbilt Whitney and Henry Clay Frick collected oil paintings, sculpture, and drawings, magazine magnate Malcolm Forbes gathered items that excited his boyhood fancy. On the ground floor of the Forbes Magazine headquarters you'll find his whimsical collections; they include: "Ships Ahoy," a flotilla of over 500 toy boats; "On Parade," an army of more than 12,000 toy soldiers arranged in battle; "Monopoly," with many versions of Forbes's favorite board game; "Presidential Papers," an impressive assembly of presidential correspondence; and "Fabergé," the world's second-largest private collection of the famous jeweled Russian eggs. Exhibits change regularly in the large painting gallery. *62 5th Ave., between 12th and 13th Sts., West Village, tel. 212/206–5548. Subway: F to W. 14th St.; also 4, 5, 6, N, or R to Union Sq./E. 14th St. Admission free. Open Tues.–Wed. and Fri.–Sun. 10–4.*

Intrepid Air, Sea, and Space Museum. Maximum war glorification is yours for the asking at this World War II aircraft carrier–cum–floating museum. More than two dozen warplanes and helicopters are parked on the deck and inside, including a Grumman Avenger painted for World War II pilot George Bush (look for "Barbara" calligraphed near the cockpit window). Other exhibits cover this century's plentiful wars, outer-space exploration, and aircraft and nautical history. The 10- to 40-minute tours explore the *Intrepid*, plus a few other ships and a submarine docked nearby. *12th Ave. and W. 46th St. at the Hudson River, Midtown, tel. 212/245–0072. Subway: A, C, or E to W. 42nd St. Admission $10. Open June–Sept., daily 10–5 (Sun. until 6); Oct.–May, Wed.–Sun. 10–5.*

Museum of American Financial History. In the former Standard Oil Building, the tiny Museum of American Financial History displays odd Wall Street–related memorabilia such as a bond certificate owned by George Washington; "Wall Street" brand cigars from the 19th century; and ticker tape from the day of the crash. The paper's weather reports, which read "SECtional Showers" or "Wet, Followed by Hangover," prove once and for all that some people should keep their day jobs. *28 Broadway, at Bowling Green, Lower Manhattan, tel. 212/908–4110. Subway: 4 or 5 to Bowling Green. Admission free. Open weekdays 11:30–2:30.*

ART GALLERIES

Is New York the capital of the art world? Draw your own conclusions. It's been home to some of the 20th century's most famous and acclaimed artists and photographers, like Andy Warhol, Jackson Pollack, Keith Haring, Jasper Johns, Willem de Kooning, Mark Rothko, Roy Lichtenstein, Cindy Sherman, Alfred Stieglitz, and Diane Arbus to name a few. And it's probably got more art galleries than any other city in America: Approximately 500 fill Manhattan, mainly in SoHo and on 57th Street, but also in the neighborhoods of TriBeCa, the Upper East Side, and increasingly, Chelsea. Uptown galleries tend to be a bit more snobbish, especially to people who aren't looking to buy, while downtown galleries tend to be more laid-back affairs showing experimental art or just stuff that is way out of the mainstream and is happy to be there. That said, keep in mind that many artists and gallery owners have fled SoHo in recent years, claiming it's morphed into one big bland yuppie fantasyland. If you're after art with *real* edge, head to grittier neighborhoods like west Chelsea, or even Long Island City, Queens (*see* the Outer Boroughs, *above*).

Despite the high pretensions of many galleries, they're a great way to see art. First of all, they're free. And many coordinate their shows to complement special exhibitions at the big museums like the Met, MoMA, or the Guggenheim. For work that isn't normally accessible to the public, whether it's masterworks that are in private hands or work by contemporary artists who haven't made it into the museums yet, art galleries are your ticket. Most galleries open between 10 and 11 AM and close by 5 or 6 PM, Tuesday through Saturday. July through early September (the months when their customers leave New York for their summer châteaus), they're typically open by appointment only. On average, shows change every six to eight weeks, often less frequently during summer. For info on current shows, check *Time Out, New York*, or *The New Yorker*; they list many, but hardly all, galleries and their current exhibitions. The *Village Voice* and *New York Press* also list galleries, with an emphasis on downtown and experimental stuff. At galleries and major museums, you can pick up a copy of **Art Now Gallery Guide** (free), the most complete reference to the art scene you'll find. It lists addresses, phone numbers, and open hours of practically all the city's galleries and provides maps for gallery-hoppers.

SOHO AND TRIBECA

SoHo possesses the lion's share of the city's art galleries. Quite a few are clustered along Broadway between Houston and Spring Streets, but you can wander almost anywhere and find dozens lining its blocks. Several of SoHo's newest galleries can be found on or near Grand Street. TriBeCa, just south of Houston, has fewer galleries, but they're also less commercial.

Art in General. This gallery, founded by a group of artists, shows experimental work with a heavy political message. It's got six floors of space and sometimes installs works in the elevator and windows, too. *79 Walker St., between Broadway and Lafayette Sts., TriBeCa, tel. 212/219–0473. Subway: 6 to Canal St.*

The Drawing Center. The Drawing Center, as you may've guessed from the name, shows exclusively drawings—an art form long neglected by the rest of the world. Recent (and fascinating) shows have included tattoos, cartoons, and even drawings by sidewalk artists. *35 Wooster St., between Broome and Grand Sts., SoHo, tel. 212/219–2166. Subway: 1 or 9 to Canal St.*

Holly Solomon. Solomon has been an art-world heavyweight since the '70s, though the gallery moved downtown only recently. Among the artists whose careers got a boost here are Robert Mapplethorpe (this was the first gallery to show his photos) and William Wegman. *172 Mercer St., at Houston St., SoHo, tel. 212/941–5777. Subway: B, D, F, or Q to Broadway/Lafayette St.*

Howard Greenberg. Vintage 19th- and 20th-century photography is the main focus at this stellar gallery, which also showcases contemporary artists. Count on seeing retrospectives of the work of such respected photographers as Walker Evans, Dorothea Lange, Harry Callahan, André Kertész, Roman Vishniac, and Imogen Cunningham. The emphasis tends toward street and documentary photography. *120 Wooster St., 2nd floor, SoHo, tel. 212/334–0010. Subway: N or R to Prince St.*

Leo Castelli. One of the most famous of all New York galleries, Castelli was where many pop-art and abstract-expressionist artists got their start. Jasper Johns's one-man show in 1958 is recognized by many as the birth of pop art and minimalism. *578 Broadway, at Prince St., 3rd floor, SoHo, tel. 212/431–6279. Subway: N or R to Prince St. 420 Broadway, between Prince and Spring Sts., SoHo, tel. 431–5160. Subway: E to Spring St.*

New York Earth Room. Come here for something completely different and oddly comforting. Thanks to avant-garde artist Walter de Maria, 140 tons of sculpted dirt (22 inches deep) take up 3,600 square ft of space of a second-floor gallery. *141 Wooster St., between Houston and Prince Sts., SoHo, tel. 212/473–8072. Subway: N or R to Prince St.; also B, D, F, or Q to Broadway/Lafayette St.*

Thread Waxing Space. Video installations and, occasionally, performance art take place at this esteemed nonprofit gallery. Past artists include Nam June Paik, Hiroshi Teshigahara, and Robert Rauschenberg. *476 Broadway, between Grand and Broome Sts., SoHo, tel. 212/966–9520. Subway: A, C, or E to Canal St.*

57TH STREET

Midtown's 57th Street, between 6th and Park avenues, is chock-a-block with galleries trying to retain a ritzy image while standing next to mall staples like the Warner Brothers Studio Store. A few buildings are devoted entirely to art galleries: **41 East, 20 West, 24 West,** and **50 West 57th Street.**

Pace Wildenstein. One of the city's top galleries, Pace is the place where you'll find all those million-dollar Dubuffets, as well as solo shows by the hottest contemporary artists. Separate fiefdoms under the same roof include **Pace Editions** for prints, **Pace Primitive** for "primitive" art, and **Pace/MacGill** for photography. *32 E. 57th St., at Madison Ave., tel. 212/759–7999. Subway: N or R to W. 57th St.*

UPPER EAST SIDE

With few exceptions, the Upper East Side's galleries are clustered along Madison Avenue between 65th and 86th streets—which makes for convenient gallery-hopping if you're exploring the Museum Mile (*see* Upper East Side *in* Manhattan Neighborhoods, *above*). One of the most venerable galleries in the neighborhood is **M. Knoedler** (19 E. 70th St., between Park and Madison Aves., tel. 212/794–0550), which you can count on for famous contemporary artists from Europe and America. If you're looking for art by someone other than the usual cast of Dead (and Living) White Males, head to **Stone** (113 E. 90th St., between Park and Lexington Aves., tel. 212/988–6870), which offers shows of contemporary African painting and sculpture, or **Throckmorton** (153 E. 61st St., between Lexington and 3rd Aves., tel. 212/223–1059), which specializes in Latin American art and photography (the photographic work is on public display, but to see the tribal art, you'll have to make an appointment). For an excellent selection of contemporary photography, visit **Houk Friedman** (851 Madison Ave., between 70th and 71st Sts., tel. 212/628–5300); many of the names here are also in the ICP or MoMA. They're also the only New York gallery to represent the haunting and controversial work of Sally Mann.

> *Of the approximately 500 galleries in New York, half are in SoHo and one quarter are along 57th Street.*

CHELSEA

Galleries in Chelsea almost uniformly show emerging and on-the-edge art, photography, sculpture, and multimedia work, which makes it one of the best places in the city to get in touch with the current vibe. Stretching from 20th to 29th sreets between 10th and 11th avenues, the Chelsea art scene really took off in late 1996 and 1997. Several of the recent additions to the neighborhood are big and upscale in the contemporary industrial mode: white-painted, columnless open exhibition spaces, concrete floors, and garage-door exteriors. But you can also find some modest off-beat galleries as well. The easiest place to begin your gallery hopping is on 22nd Street, which has the **Dia Center for the Arts** (*see* More Art Museums, *above*) and seven other galleries, including **Jessica Fredericks Gallery** (504 W. 22nd St., tel. 212/633–6555); **Matthew Marks Gallery** (522 W. 22nd St., tel. 212/861–9455); and three spaces at 530 West 22nd Street: **Morris-Healy** (tel. 212/243–3753), **Pat Hearn Gallery** (tel. 212/727–7366), and **Annina Nosei** (tel. 212/741–8695). On 24th Street, you can stop at three major players—**Barbara Gladstone** (515 W. 24th St. tel. 212/206–9300), **Metro Pictures** (519 W. 24th St., tel. 212/206–7100), and **Matthew Marks**'s second Chelsea gallery space (523 W. 24th St., tel. 212/243–0200).

Paula Cooper Gallery. You don't get much more exclusive than this, a gallery revered even by other snobby gallery owners. After 28 years in SoHo, Paula Cooper moved to Chelsea in 1996; this is an awesome 5,000-square-ft exhibition and office space, perfect for multiple exhibitions, large-scale sculpture shows, and site-specific installations. The main gallery has 2,500 square ft of columnless space, a 27-ft-high beamed vaulted ceiling, and skylights; the other, more intimate 500-square-ft space can be opened to the street. Shows here have been devoted to such international artists as Carl Andre and Andres Serrano. *534 W. 21st St., tel. 212/255–1105. Subway: E to W. 23rd St.*

PARKS AND GARDENS

While there's no ignoring New York's soaring skyscrapers, concrete canyons, and yellow-cab pileups, you'll find that the city offers much more than an urban jungle. It's got some 29,000 acres of park land, playgrounds, gardens, forests, nature reserves, and even beaches—in fact, New York boasts the largest urban forest in the nation—no doubt you've already noticed **Central Park** (see Major Attractions, above), the 843-acre wonderland that occupies a large chunk of upper Manhattan. But you probably haven't yet discovered the enormous, pristine parks of Brooklyn, Queens, the Bronx, and Staten Island, where you can hike for miles without seeing another human being. You can get info on all the city's parks by calling the **City Parks Department hot line** (tel. 800/834–3832). Additionally, the city's **Urban Park Rangers** (tel. 212/772–0210 in Manhattan, 718/287–3400 in Brooklyn, 718/548–7070 in the Bronx, 718/353–2460 in Queens, and 718/667–6042 in Staten Island) have a wealth of info on the parks in their home boroughs. They also offer free guided park tours and nature walks.

The **Gateway National Recreation Area** and the **Staten Island Greenbelt** offer some of the best destinations in the city for would-be tree huggers and bird-watchers. Gateway encompasses 26,000 acres of beach, marsh, and woodlands in New Jersey and the New York boroughs of Staten Island and Queens; the most accessible portions are Jacob Riis Park (see box Land of Skyscrapers and Beaches?!, below) and the Jamaica Bay Wildlife Refuge (see below). For info on other parks contact the National Park Service, Fort Tilden, New York, NY 11695, tel. 718/318–4300. The Staten Island Greenbelt is a 2,500-acre expanse of undeveloped land with 28 mi of trails winding through woods, meadows, wetlands, and beachfront. For particulars, contact the main Greenbelt office (200 Nevada Ave., Staten Island, tel. 718/667–2165).

If you're pining for just a few trees and a breath of fresh air, Manhattan has some unusual alternatives. Besides the decent-sized parks listed below, don't overlook the dozens of **"vest-pocket" parks,** less than a city block in size, that pepper its neighborhoods. In Midtown, you'll find these little parks at West 46th Street (between 6th and 7th Aves.), East 53rd Street (between 5th and Madison Aves.), and East 51st Street (between 2nd and 3rd Aves.). Other great places to kick back with a book and a brown-bag lunch are office building **atriums,** products of the 1980s building boom (you see, something good did come out of the Decade of Greed). In exchange for "giving" the public some open space at ground level, developers got to build even taller skyscrapers, from which they could garner more rent. Waterfalls, foliage, abundant benches, and a small café often complement the scene, and keep in mind that these indoor atriums are invariably air-conditioned. Most are open daily 8 AM–6 PM. Some of the most spectacular include the **Harkness Atrium** (Broadway between W. 62nd and 63rd Sts., Upper West Side), **IBM Garden Plaza** (E. 56th St. at Madison Ave., Midtown), and **Olympic Tower** (51st St. at 5th Ave., Midtown). In a class by itself is the 120-ft-tall, glass-walled Winter Garden Atrium at the **World Financial Center** (see Lower Manhattan in Manhattan Neighborhoods, above), which also hosts art exhibits and live music.

MANHATTAN

In addition to the parks listed below, don't forget **Union Square** and **Madison Square** (for both, see Gramercy and Union Square in Manhattan Neighborhoods, above), **Washington Square** (see West Village in Manhattan Neighborhoods, above), **City Hall Park** (see Lower Manhattan in Manhattan Neighborhoods, above), and **Tompkins Square** (see East Village and Alphabet City in Manhattan Neighborhoods, above)—the latter two are arguably the liveliest parks in the city. If you're sick to death of competing for a patch of green with yuppies in Central Park, their newborns strapped on in some expensive papoose, buy a bumper of Bud, lean up against a tree, and watch the zany characters parade by in one of Manhattan's smaller parks. For flower gardens, don't overlook the formal beds at **The Cloisters** (see Museums and Galleries, above).

Battery Park. At the southernmost tip of Manhattan, skyscrapers and taxi-filled streets give way to green fields, trees, and footpaths filled with camera-toting tourists. Battery Park (so named because a battery of 28 cannons was placed along its shore in colonial days to fend off the nasty British) is built on landfill and has gradually grown over the centuries. In fact, its main structure, **Castle Clinton National Monument,** originally stood on an island some 200 ft from shore—like the mountain coming to Mohammed, the island of Manhattan has gradually snuck up and encompassed it. Since its construction around 1810, Castle Clinton has been a defensive fort, entertainment hall (where P. T. Barnum presented the "Swedish Nightingale" Jenny Lind to an enchanted New York audience), immigration depot, and aquarium. It now holds a **visitor center** and the ticket booth for ferries to the Statue of Liberty and Ellis Island (for info on ferry service and tickets, see Statue of Liberty in Major Attractions, above). The park is loaded with various other statues and monuments, some impressive, some downright obscure. The **East Coast Memorial,** a granite structure topped by a fierce-looking eagle, was dedicated by President

Kennedy in 1963 to the American servicemen who died in the Atlantic during World War II. The **Netherlands Memorial Flagpole,** near Castle Clinton, bears a plaque that describes (in English and Dutch) a bead exchange that procured from American Indians the land used to establish Fort Amsterdam in 1626. Also look for a romantic statue of Giovanni da Verrazano, the Florentine merchant who piloted the ship that first sighted New York and its harbor in 1524, and the extraordinary **Hope Garden,** whose 100,000 rosebushes were planted in 1992 as a living memorial to people with AIDS. After wandering past these monuments, head for the waterfront to get unparalleled views of the New York harbor, including Lady Liberty and the onion-domed brick buildings of Ellis Island. *Broadway at Battery Pl., Lower Manhattan. Subway: 4 or 5 to Bowling Green; also 1 or 9 to South Ferry.*

Bowling Green. The benches at this tiny park, just north of Battery Park (*see above*), fill with brown-bagging business types on sunny weekday afternoons. Colonial lawn-bowling enthusiasts once leased this oval of green from the governor for the annual fee of one peppercorn; it became New York's first public park in 1733. Look closely at the iron fence around parts of the Green and you'll notice the height is uneven. That's because rioters stormed the place on July 9, 1776, after learning about the signing of the Declaration of Independence; they toppled a statue of King George III that had occupied the spot for 11 years and then melted most of its lead into bullets. *Lower Manhattan. Subway: 4 or 5 to Bowling Green.*

Bryant Park. For 20 years Bryant Park, Midtown's only major green space, was abandoned to crack addicts and muggers. An incredible $9-million renovation, however, has transformed it into one of the best-loved and most beautiful parks in all the city. (It also boasts New York's cleanest public bathrooms.) Century-old shade trees and formal flower beds line the perimeter of its grassy central square, scattered with hundreds of smart green folding chairs. The chairs aren't bolted down, and no one steals them; like we said, it's a pretty miraculous place. During summer, it draws thousands of lunching office workers; hosts live jazz and comedy concerts; and presents a free, summer-long, outdoor film festival (*see* Movies and Video *in* Chapter 7) on Mondays at dusk. Several times each year giant tents spring up when New York designers hold their fashion shows here (forget trying to sneak in, but you can look for supermodels hailing cabs on 6th Avenue). Year-round it's home to a chic, expensive restaurant, the **Bryant Park Grill** (tel. 212/840–6500); and a semi-affordable restaurant, the **Bryant Park Café** (tel. 212/575–0733; open April 15–October 14). When money is tight, go west to the 6th Avenue edge of the park, where kiosks sell sandwiches and salads for $5–$6. *From W. 40th to 42nd Sts. between 5th and 6th Aves., Midtown. Subway: B, D, F, or Q to W. 42nd St.*

Carl Schurz Park. When Upper East Siders want fresh air and river views, they head for Carl Schurz Park. Once known as East End Park, it was renamed in honor of a German revolutionary and founder of the Republican party, who served as a U.S. senator, cabinet secretary, and editor of *Harper's Weekly* in the late 1800s. Joggers and dog walkers pace along the pleasant **John Finley Walk** (named for an editor of the *New York Times* who was also an avid stroller), while traffic rumbles just below on FDR Drive. The large, fenced-off home near 88th Street is **Gracie Mansion,** the mayor's residence. Built for Scottish merchant Archibald Gracie, the mansion housed the Museum of the City of New York until the early 1940s, when Parks Commissioner Robert Moses commandeered the mansion for political buddy (and mayor) Fiorello La Guardia. Tours ($3) are offered Wednesdays at 10, 11, 1, and 2. Call 212/570–4751 for reservations, which are required. *East River Dr. between E. 82nd and 90th Sts., Upper East Side. Subway: 4, 5, or 6 to E. 86th St.*

Columbus Park. This Chinatown park isn't the nicest in Manhattan, but if you can deal with the somewhat large homeless population, it's one of the best places in the city to people-watch. Mornings bring groups of elderly Chinese practicing the graceful movements of tai chi. During afternoons, the park's tables fill for heated games of mah-jongg; games are so intense that despite crowds, the only sounds you can hear are the clicking of the mah-jongg tiles. *Bayard St. between Baxter and Mulberry Sts., Chinatown. Subway: J, M, N, R, Z, or 6 to Canal St.*

East River Park. This 1½-mi stretch of green is perfect for running, biking, or just watching the garbage scows toil slowly up the East River. For some reason (maybe because you have to walk through a dicey section of the East Village to get here) the park's fields, baseball diamonds, and tennis courts are completely underutilized. What a shame—the views of Brooklyn Heights, Williamsburg, and the Brooklyn Bridge are unparalleled. *East River Dr. between E. 14th St. and Delancey St., Lower East Side. Subway: F to 2nd Ave.*

Fort Tryon Park. This phenomenal 62-acre spread of terraced walks and riotous gardens was another of Olmsted's landscape creations (*see box* They Built This City, *above*). Though it's a long haul north on

MURDER IN RIVERSIDE PARK

While it's true that just about every park in the City has been the scene of a lurid crime at one time or another, the 1944 murder of David Kammerer by Lucien Carr in Riverside Park must be one of the most bizarre. Carr, an original Beat generation member famous for introducing Jack Kerouac and Allen Ginsberg to William Burroughs, murdered his former Boy Scout master after the lovesick older man followed him from Missouri to New York City. The crime made headlines for weeks; at his trial, Carr was found guilty of manslaughter. He served two years of his sentence before receiving a pardon from the governor.

the subway, it's definitely worth the trip. On a hill at the northern end of the park is **The Cloisters** (*see* Museums and Galleries, *above*), which houses the Metropolitan Museum of Art's collection of medieval art. The central plaza honors Revolutionary War heroine Margaret Corbin. Nearby are the remains of Fort Tryon, used during the Revolutionary War. Walk west along its meandering pathways for spectacular views of the Hudson River or take a breather at the Fort Tyron Park Cafe (tel. 212/923–2233) near the park's entrance. *Entrance on Fort Washington Ave. at W. 190th St., Washington Heights. Subway: A to W. 190th St.; also Bus M4 to last stop.*

Fort Washington Park. This northern Manhattan park is difficult to reach, but worth the trouble: From the foot of Washington Bridge (179th St. and Fort Washington Ave.), walk north to 181st Street, then west across a pedestrian overpass. Once across, follow the path through a tunnel and over some railroad tracks to eventually reach a shady, pleasant rest area. Here you'll find the **Little Red Lighthouse** (of storybook fame), which once guided ships away from this rocky outcrop, plus a few desolate remains of the old Fort Washington. You can also stare up into the steel framework of the mighty Washington Bridge. You can follow the footpath south from here to tennis courts a quarter mile away or theoretically hike down to the island's southern tip although you'll probably drop dead from exhaustion first. *Riverside Dr. between 170th and 181st Sts., Washington Heights. Subway: A to W. 181st St.*

Hudson River Park. If you can ignore the blitzkrieg on 'blades and bikes coming at you from all directions, this welcoming park is just right for a stroll along the water. Or grab one of the dozens of benches and enjoy the spectacle of Lycra-clad weekend warriors huffing and puffing up and down the park's length. The northern end of the park is in the West Village, across the West Side Highway; it extends southward for miles along the Hudson River and eventually connects with the 1.2-mi-long Battery Park City Esplanade (*see* Lower Manhattan *in* Manhattan Neighborhoods, *above*). In Lower Manhattan, you can easily reach Hudson River Park from the corner of Chambers and Greenwich streets; if you continue walking west on Chambers Street toward the Hudson River, you'll need to cross the West Side Highway. Behind the Stuyvesant High School building, you'll find the park. *On the Hudson River, from Gansevoort St. to Battery Park City, West Village/SoHo, tel. 212/353–0366. Subway: A, C, E, or L to W. 14th St.; also 1, 2, 3, 9, A, C, or E to Chambers St.*

Inwood Hill Park. The 196-acre Inwood Hill Park covers the northern tip of Manhattan, an area once inexplicably dubbed *Spuyten Duyvil* ("Spitting Devil") by Dutch colonists. The whole place actually looks much as it did centuries ago, its thick forest a tangle of overgrown brambles. The handful of hilly trails provide an afternoon's escape from car horns and exhaust fumes. *Entrance at Dyckman St. and Seaman Ave., Inwood. Subway: A to Dyckman St. (200th St.).*

Lotus Garden. This small garden on the rooftop of an Upper West Side apartment complex has been kept up for over 20 years by a group of dedicated volunteers. It's a flower- and tree-filled oasis in the sky where you can enjoy a few moments of quiet. Look for the iron entrance gate marked LOTUS GARDENS on West 97th Street at Broadway, next to The Wiz music store. *W. 97th St. and Broadway, Upper West Side. Open Sun. 1–4 and by appointment.*

Riverbank State Park. Riverbank is a park with a dark past. In the early 1990s city officials announced plans to build an enormous sewage plant along the Hudson River in Harlem, then flinched in surprise when Harlem residents protested. Then-governor Mario Cuomo brokered a truce by ordering that a park be built atop the sewage plant, and 28-acre Riverbank State Park opened for business in 1993. Amazingly, it's a lovely and stench-free stretch of grass and trees, with striking views of the Hudson River and athletic facilities, including a hockey rink, Olympic-sized pool, weight room, basketball courts, and track. *Riverside Dr. between W. 137th and 145th Sts., Harlem, tel. 212/694–3600. Subway: 1 or 9 to W. 145th St.*

Riverside Park. Stretching along the Hudson River from the heart of the Upper West Side north into Harlem, this narrow cliff-top park is a favorite of runners, dog-walkers, bicyclists, and Rollerbladers. Its picturesque terraces, rustic stone walls, and rambling paths were designed at the turn of the century by Frederick Law Olmsted and Calvert Vaux to look like a snippet of English countryside. The park's **Promenade** begins at 72nd Street—with a newly installed statue of Eleanor Roosevelt—and continues north for more than a mile, past formal gardens, statues, and a few lofty monuments. At 83rd Street, look for **Mt. Tom,** a boulder Edgar Allan Poe often climbed to ponder the passing river scene. You'll also find a memorial to firemen at 100th Street and a **Joan of Arc Statue** at 93rd Street, the first monument in New York dedicated to a woman when it was put up in 1915. At 121st Street is **Grant's Tomb** (if you want to find out who's buried in Grant's Tomb, *see* Columbia University and Morningside Heights *in* Manhattan Neighborhoods, *above*). Just beyond that at 123rd Street is the **Grave of an Amiable Child,** marking the spot where a five-year-old girl fell to her death in 1797. Though the Henry Hudson Parkway runs alongside most of the park, a pedestrian underpass at 79th Street will take you to the **Boat Basin,** where you can walk right along the river's edge. North of 100th Street the park gets a bit wild and woolly (as you might guess from the number of crack vials scattered under park benches), and isn't the best place to linger alone or at dusk. *Riverside Dr. between W. 72nd and 135th Sts. Subway: 1, 2, 3, or 9 to W. 72nd St.; also 1, 2, 3, or 9 to W. 96th St.*

In spring, the Brooklyn Botanic Garden's Daffodil Hill and Cherry Esplanade are each so colorful you'll swear you're seeing the colorized version.

Washington Market Park. TriBeCa's only park is a 1½-acre former vacant lot turned attractive public square, with a luxurious lawn, children's playground, and Victorian gazebo. It's close to some of TriBeCa's best restaurants and the Tribeca Performing Arts Center (*see* Chapter 7). The park is also a great place to stop for a picnic lunch, especially if you time your visit to coincide with the farmer's market (*see* Greenmarkets *in* Chapter 4) held here every Saturday. *Greenwich St. between Chambers and Duane Sts., TriBeCa. Subway: 1, 2, 3, or 9 to Chambers St.*

THE OUTER BOROUGHS

One of the most romantic gardens in the city can be found in the Bronx at **Wave Hill** (*see* Museums and Galleries, *above*), while awesome views of Manhattan can be had from the **Brooklyn Heights Promenade** (*see* Brooklyn Heights *in* the Outer Boroughs, *above*).

Alley Pond Park. In northeast Queens you'll find 635 acres of woodlands, meadows, fresh- and saltwater marshes, and kettle ponds (a type of lake created 21,000 years ago by melting glaciers). Though the park is crisscrossed by several busy expressways, you'll still find quiet, tree-shaded hiking trails that stretch for miles. Pick up free trail maps and check out the hodge-podge collection of wild animals at the Alley Pond **Environmental Center** (228–06 Northern Blvd., Douglaston, tel. 718/229–4000), at the north end of the park near Little Neck Bay. *Douglaston, Queens. Subway: 7 to Main St. (Flushing), then Bus Q12 to Northern Blvd. (25 mins).*

Brooklyn Botanic Garden. At 52 acres, the Brooklyn Botanic Garden is only one-fifth the size of the stunning New York Botanical Garden in the Bronx. Still, its collection of more than 12,000 different plants constitutes one of the finest botanic gardens in the United States and should be at the top of the list of things to do out here, whether you're on your first or your tenth visit. There are a half-dozen not-to-be-missed sights. Eighty plants immortalized by the bard grow in the intimate **Shakespeare Garden.** The beguiling and serene **Japanese Garden** (50¢ on weekends) takes you out of Brooklyn and into Kyoto with winding paths around a lake shaped in the Japanese character for "heart"; its Japanese cherry arbor turns into a heart-stopping cloud of pink every spring. More than 5,000 bushes, representing 1,200 varieties of the thorny plants, grow in the neatly laid-out **Cranford Rose Garden,** one of the most romantic picnic spots in the city. The **Celebrity Path** is Brooklyn's answer to Hollywood's Walk of Fame, with the names of dozens of homegrown stars inscribed on stepping-stones. Placards written in English and Braille identify plants in the **Fragrance Garden,** designed especially for people who are blind. Don't skip a peek into the $25 million **Steinhardt Conservatory,** a greenhouse encompassing 24,000 square ft. Its Trail of Evolution shows how plant life developed from the mosses of billions of years ago to the plants of present-day deserts, temperate lands, and the tropics. In winter the steamy Tropical Pavilion is almost as good as a trip to Hawaii. The **C. V. Starr Bonsai Museum** in the Conservatory exhibits about 80 miniature Japanese specimens. Excellent free tours of the gardens depart weekends at 1 PM from the lily pools in front of the conservatory. *1000 Washington Ave., at Carroll St., Park Slope, Brooklyn, tel. 718/622–4433. Subway: 2 or 3 to Eastern Pkwy./Brooklyn Museum. Admission $3; free Tues. Open Apr.–Sept., Tues.–Fri. 8–6, weekends 10–6; Oct.–Mar., Tues.–Fri. 8–4:30, weekends 10–4:30. Steinhardt Conservatory open Apr.–Sept., Tues.–Sun. 10–5:30; Oct.–Mar., Tues.–Sun. 10–4.*

Empire Fulton Ferry State Park. New York's ultimate waterfront park is between the Brooklyn and Manhattan bridges on the East River. The views of Manhattan are spectacular and the park itself immaculate. Few people venture here besides sculptors from nearby warehouse studios, who bring their works out onto the grass on sunny days. *Water St. west of Washington St., Brooklyn Heights, Brooklyn. Subway: A or C to High St./Brooklyn Bridge.*

Flushing Meadows–Corona Park. Once a city dump so desolate that F. Scott Fitzgerald referred to it as "a valley of ashes" in *The Great Gatsby*—and later the site of two world's fairs—the 1,200-acre park is now a major hub of professional sports and casual recreation. Here, the annual U.S. Open is held at the U.S.T.A. National Tennis Center, and the Mets attract crowds at Shea Stadium (for more on both, *see* Chapter 8). *Subway: 7 to Flushing Meadows/Corona Park.*

Forest Park. The high hills of this 538-acre park in central Queens offer great views of Long Island Sound and the Atlantic Ocean. Its southwestern half has athletic fields, an antique carousel, a golf course, and a band shell that hosts frequent Sunday concerts June through September. The northeastern half of the park has nature trails winding through stands of 150-year-old oaks. You can rent horses ($20 per hour) to explore the park at nearby **Dixie Drew Riding Academy** (70th Rd. and Sybilla St., tel. 718/263–3500). *Forest Hills/Kew Gardens, Queens, tel. 718/520–5911 for summer concert info. Subway: J to Woodhaven Blvd.; also E or F to Union Turnpike/Kew Gardens; take Bus Q37 to Union Turnpike and Park La. (1 hr).*

Fort Greene Park. This large, underutilized park—another fine product of Olmsted and Vaux—is just waiting for your lazy picnics and ultimate Frisbee games. Its towering hill has great views of both Manhattan and Brooklyn and a long, smooth slope, if you want to make use of your trash-can lid after a good snowfall. The two monuments you'll see are the Prison Ship Martyrs Monument (*see* Brooklyn *in* the Outer Boroughs, *above*) and a memorial to the 126 Spanish soldiers who died during the American Revolution and were buried in Brooklyn. *DeKalb Ave., just east of Flatbush Ave., Fort Greene, Brooklyn. Subway: D, M, N, Q, or R to DeKalb Ave.*

High Rock Park. At only 80 acres, High Rock is one of the smallest but prettiest parts of Staten Island's Greenbelt (*see* Staten Island *in* the Outer Boroughs, *above*). Trails meander through hardwood forest and lush wetlands dotted with glacial ponds; check out the ¼-mi loop around Marsh Pond for spring wildflowers, or take the arduous trek up **Todt Hill** for an eagle-eye view of the Greenbelt, the bay, and Sandy Hook, NJ. At the visitor center (open weekdays 9–5, weekends 10–4) you can pick up a trail map or join a ranger-led ecology walk weekends at 2 PM. *200 Nevada Ave., Staten Island, tel. 718/667–2165. From Ferry Terminal, take SIRT to New Dorp. Also Bus S74 to Rockland Ave.*

Jamaica Bay Wildlife Refuge. You might spot any one of 325 bird species, plus butterflies, box turtles, and small mammals like muskrats and raccoons among the salt marshes, fields, woods, and mud flats of this 9,155-acre wildlife preserve just south of JFK International Airport. Spring and fall are the best times to catch migrating birds, and the wildflowers are tremendous in spring. In summer you'll need insect repellent or a giant fly swatter. Pick up a map and mandatory free permit at the **visitor center** (open daily 8:30–5) before hitting the trail. *Queens, tel. 718/318–4340. Subway: A (make sure it's marked "Rockaways" and not "Lefferts Blvd.") to Broad Channel; walk west to Cross Bay Blvd., turn right and walk ¾ mi north.*

New York Botanical Garden (NYBG). Considered one of the world's leading botany centers, this 250-acre botanical garden built around the dramatic gorge of the Bronx River is reason enough to make a trip to the Bronx. The garden's founders, Lord Hawthorne and his wife, Elizabeth, patterned it after Britain's Royal Botanical Gardens in 1891. In the Alfred E. Haupt Conservatory, you can stroll among ferns, tropical flora, and Old and New World deserts. Or step outside and smell the roses—230 different varieties—

in the formal rose garden. The 40-acre tract of virgin hemlock forest—the largest remnant of the forest that once covered New York City—is the perfect place to ponder deep thoughts. Guided forest tours are offered on weekends at 1:30 and 3:30, and bird-watching tours take place Saturdays at 1:30. At the Lorillard Snuff Mill—built in 1840 to power the grinding of tobacco for snuff—you can sit at an outdoor café table and watch the Bronx River churn by. Free guided walking tours depart weekends at 1, 1:30, 3, and 3:30. *200th St. and Southern Blvd., Bronx, tel. 718/817–8500. Subway: D or 4 to Bedford Park Blvd. Train: Metro-North to Botanical Gardens. Admission $3; free Wed. and Sat. 10–noon. Open Apr.–Oct., Tues.–Sun. and Mon. holidays 10–6; Nov.–Mar., Tues.–Sun. and Mon. holidays 10–4.*

Pelham Bay Park. Though the highlight of New York City's largest park is Orchard Beach, this 2,764-acre wooded sprawl has a handful of other attractions, including the **Bartow-Pell Mansion** (895 Shore Rd., tel. 718/885–1461), an elegant 1840s country estate built by Thomas "Lord of Pelham" Pell; two golf courses; miles of hiking trails; and the **Thomas Pell Wildlife Refuge and Sanctuary,** whose wetlands attract thousands of birds in spring and fall. To see the entire park, follow the 6-mi Siwanoy Trail starting on Shore Road at the north side of Pelham Bridge. Or you can rent horses at **Pelham Bit** (tel. 718/885–0551) for $20 per hour. *Bronx, tel. 718/885–3466 or 718/430–1890. Subway: 6 to Pelham Bay Park. Admission to Bartow-Pell Mansion: $2.50 (free 1st Sun. of month).*

Prospect Park. Brooklyn's answer to Central Park, Prospect Park is a 526-acre playground-cum-backyard for the tens of thousands of Brooklyn residents whose neighborhoods abut its periphery. The arrowhead-shape park is regarded by Frederick Law Olmsted aficionados as among his very best creations, superior to Central Park (being completed as work started here in 1866) because no streets divide it and no skyscrapers infringe on its borders. The park is a bit more feral than its more famous Manhattan cousin (fallen trees, overgrown shrubs, untended piles of dirt and woodchips, and uncut grass are everywhere), but a number of restoration projects now planned or in progress should help improve the look of things.

There's something magical about standing in a marsh watching snowy egrets at the Jamaica Bay Wildlife Refuge, the World Trade Center visible in the distance through sepia-hued smog.

The best way to experience the park is to travel its 3.3-mi circular drive and make detours off of it as you like. On summer evenings and weekends year-round the drive is closed to vehicular traffic when a high-energy parade of joggers, skaters, and bicyclists have it to themselves. One of the best places to kick off your shoes is on the 75-acre **Long Meadow,** near the Grand Army Plaza entrance. If you can believe it, this is the largest open space in an urban park in the entire United States. The 60-acre Prospect Lake dominates the opposite (south) end of the park. On weekends and holidays from April through the end of October you can tool around the lake in pedal boats; rentals ($10 per hour) are at the **Wollman Memorial Rink** (tel. 718/282–7789), where in winter you can do the Hamill Camel and your other favorite skating moves ($3 skate rental). The rink is directly across the circular drive from the **Drummers Grove,** an officially recognized gathering spot for Caribbean and African-American musicians, drummers, chanters, dancers, and other revelers who cook up a storm here on Sunday afternoons through all but the coldest months.

Don't be fooled by the PC name of the **Prospect Park Wildlife Conservation Center** (450 Flatbush Ave., tel. 718/399–7339); it's really a zoo, with a tiny collection of sea lions, baboons, prairie dogs, wallabies, and red pandas. Admission is $2.50. The park's antique **carousel,** near the zoo, was created by a Russian immigrant; its 56 horses, chariots, lions, and giraffes gambol in circles in perpetuity. During summer, Prospect Park's 9th Street Bandshell (at Prospect Park West) is home to the wonderful **Celebrate Brooklyn** festival (*see* Summer Arts *in* Chapter 7). *West of Flatbush Ave. and south of Grand Army Plaza, Park Slope, Brooklyn, tel. 718/965–8999. Subway: D or Q to Prospect Park; F to 15th St./Prospect Park; or 2 or 3 to Grand Army Plaza.*

Socrates Sculpture Park. Venture past rows of abandoned factories, and you'll come to this strange but peaceful 4-acre park on the East River. Formerly an illegal dump site, it's now filled with mammoth abstract sculptures made from scrap metal, broken pipes, and used tires—the perfect spot to contemplate weighty themes like Man vs. Nature, Man vs. Machine, and, of course, Art. The views of Manhattan are superb. *Vernon Blvd. at Broadway, Long Island City, Queens, tel. 718/956–1819. Subway: N to Broadway, walk 8 blocks west to river. Open daily 10 AM–sunset.*

Van Cortlandt Park. With 1,146 acres of forest and wetlands, this park offers much more than lots of green space and hiking trails. On the park's Parade Grounds stands the oldest building in the Bronx

LAND OF SKYSCRAPERS AND BEACHES?!

Beaches in New York? It's not as strange as you'd think. Though you'd need to venture out to Long Island to find really great beaches, there are some decent stretches of sand in Brooklyn, the Bronx, Queens, and Staten Island. Just prepare yourself for 48° water, even in June, and lots of crowds.

Brighton Beach. At Brighton Beach, a.k.a. "Odessa by the Sea," boardwalk stands hawk Russian snacks like pierogies alongside popsicles and hot dogs. Waves are small enough to let grandma get in the water. Brooklyn. Subway: D or Q to Brighton Beach; walk 2 blocks south.

Coney Island Beach and Boardwalk. There's nothing quite like Coney Island in summer, with its Cyclone roller coaster, carnival side shows, and savvy entrepreneurs covertly peddling cans of ice-cold beer. Brooklyn. Subway: B, D, or F to Coney Island (Stillwell Ave.); walk 2 blocks south.

Jacob Riis Park. Besides a full mile of beachfront, Jacob Riis Park offers softball fields, paddle ball courts, and a pitch-and-putt golf course, all free. At the eastern end of the park is a gay (and until recently, nude) beach. Gateway National Recreation Area, Queens, tel. 718/318–4300. Subway: 2 or 5 to Flatbush Ave./Brooklyn College, then Bus Q35 (1 hr).

Manhattan Beach. Though less than half a mile long, this is one of the city's nicest beaches for sunning and swimming. It's just east of Brighton Beach, off Oriental Boulevard, Brooklyn. Subway: D or Q to Brighton Beach.

Rockaway Beach and Boardwalk. New York City's longest beach faces the Atlantic Ocean. That means decent-size waves and a minimum of pollution. Of course, this is no secret, and in summer it can be difficult to find a spot to spread your towel. Follow the boardwalk past the last subway stop (116th Street) to the area where wealthy residents have tacked up NO PARKING signs. This spot is actually public and much less crowded than the rest of the strand. Queens, tel. 718/318–4000. Subway: A (make sure it's labeled "Rockaway Park") to Broad Channel, then switch to the C and get off at 105th St./Seaside or 116th St./Rockaway Park.

Staten Island beaches. The entire southeast shore is lined with some of New York City's most undiscovered beaches. There are lifeguards on duty at Wolf's Pond Beach (tel. 718/984–8266), Great Kills Beach (tel. 718/351–6970), South Beach, and Midland Beach (tel. 718/987–0709 for both). For information on transport, see Staten Island in the Outer Boroughs, above.

(1748), the chock-full-of-antiques **Van Cortlandt House Museum** (tel. 718/543–3344). It was twice used by George Washington as headquarters during the Revolutionary War. You can sometimes catch Anglophiles playing cricket on the Parade Grounds. Also here is the country's oldest municipal golf course—people have been putting around these greens since 1885. If you like to hike, follow the forest-lined **Old Croton Aqueduct Trail,** the **Cass Gallagher Nature Trail,** or the tracks of the **Old Putnam Railroad line,** which once linked New York and Boston. The **John Kieran Nature Trail** circles Van Cortlandt Lake—New York City's largest—and offers great bird-watching. *Bronx, tel. 718/430–1890. Subway: 1 or 9 to 242 St./Van Cortlandt Park.*

CHEAP THRILLS

In summer, it's impossible not to stumble across some sort of free concert, play, or dance performance in the course of a day's exploration; check one of the city weeklies like the *New York Press* or *Time Out* to see what's going down, where. For more info, *see* Summer Arts *in* Chapter 7. If you plan visit New York repeatedly, you might want to invest in a yearly subscription of *Free Time* (20 Waterside Plaza, Suite 6F, New York, NY 10010; $13.50), a monthly guide that lists about 450 free concerts, lectures, dance recitals, and plays per issue. You can buy (nope, it's not free) a single copy at most newsstands and some bookstores for $1.

COOL VIEWS
Once you've seen all the obvious cool views—from the **Empire State Building,** the **World Trade Center,** and inside the head of the **Statue of Liberty** (for all, *see* Major Attractions, *above*)—you're ready for the advanced stuff. If you want to work for it, consider the 14-floor climb up the building housing the **Clocktower Gallery** (*see* Museums and Galleries, *above*) in TriBeCa; in Brooklyn, you can climb up the inside of the 80-ft-tall **Soldiers' and Sailors' Memorial Arch** (*see* the Outer Boroughs, *above*); it's open to climbers weekends in warm weather. If you're feeling lazy, take the elevator ($1) to the top of the 22-story, 356-ft tower of **Riverside Church** (*see* Columbia University and Morningside Heights *in* Manhattan Neighborhoods, *above*) to spy on the Hudson River below. If you're just looking to stroll along, sopping up all the New York atmosphere, try one of these less-obvious spots: The 1.2-mi **Battery Park City Esplanade** (*see* Lower Manhattan, *above*) offers stellar views of the Statue of Liberty and New Jersey's "Gold Coast"; the ⅓-mi **Brooklyn Heights Promenade** (*see* the Outer Boroughs, *above*) is packed on summer evenings with New Yorkers whose gaping mouths and reverent stares at the skyline contradict their world-weary cynicism. In the very un-touristy neighborhood of Long Island City, Queens, you'll find breathtaking waterfront views of the Manhattan skyline at the quirky **Socrates Sculpture Park** (*see* the Outer Boroughs *in* Parks and Gardens, *above*).

HIGH CULTURE: THE FINE ARTS
Unless you're planning to buy that Joan Miró instead of just admiring it, visiting **art galleries** is always free (*see* Art Galleries, *above*). For a taste of shopping, museum-going, people-watching, and high drama all rolled into one, New York's famous auction houses **Sotheby's** (1334 York Ave., at 72nd St., Upper East Side, tel. 212/606–7000) and **Christie's** (502 Park Ave., at 59th St., tel. 212/546–1000) are just the ticket. You can attend both the previews (where they display all the stuff about to be sold) and the auctions themselves for free; call for details. The most famous auctions (not counting the Jackie O frenzy in 1996) are those for paintings, which happen in November and May.

Many of the city's churches and museums bring string quartets and such into their courtyards and gardens for free performances. One of the best freebies is at the **Metropolitan Museum of Art,** which holds concerts Friday and Saturday evenings on its Great Hall balcony. For info on all your options, *see* Music *in* Chapter 7. And what could be more civilized than free Shakespeare in Central Park? *See* Summer Arts *in* Chapter 7 for details on finagling free tickets to the yearly **New York Shakespeare Festival.**

LOW CULTURE: MOVIES AND TV
You've a bunch of ways to get your daily fix of Low Culture for little or no cash. During summer, classic flicks are shown at dusk on a giant outdoor screen in **Bryant Park** (*see* Movies and Video *in* Chapter 7), so pack the picnic basket. All shows at all times are only $3 at **Worldwide Cinemas** (*see* Movies and Video *in* Chapter 7). The **Museum of Television and Radio** (*see* Museums and Galleries, *above*) offers *60,000* episodes of radio- and TV-land for your viewing pleasure; admission is $6. To satisfy your TV itch

YOUR OWN 15 MINUTES OF FAME

In New York you can not only watch TV, you can be on it. Numerous shows tape in New York, and they all need studio audiences to laugh, applaud, and answer embarrassing questions. To score a free ticket or two you'll need to plan ahead: Most shows require that you send a postcard (with number of tickets requested) weeks or months in advance. If you missed the boat, you can still land standby tickets if you're willing to spend a morning standing in line.

Fox TV. Fox always has a handful of shows open to studio audiences; call for the latest. Tel. 212/452–3600.

Late Night With Conan O'Brien. Same-day standby tickets are available at the NBC Page Desk in the lobby of 30 Rockefeller Center. NBC Tickets, "Late Night With Conan O'Brien," 30 Rockefeller Plaza, New York, NY 10112, tel. 212/ 664–3055.

The Late Show With David Letterman. Standby tickets are available weekdays at noon in front of the Ed Sullivan Theater. Arrive early. Ed Sullivan Theater, 1697 Broadway, New York, NY 10019, tel. 212/975–1003.

Live With Regis and Kathie Lee. Standby tickets are available at 8 AM weekdays from the ABC headquarters; line up at the corner of 67th Street and Columbus Avenue. Live Tickets, Asonia Station, Box 777, New York, NY 10023, tel. 212/ 456–3537.

Politically Incorrect with Bill Maher. Tapings of this funky and irreverent show are Tuesdays and Thursdays year-round. Tel. 212/512–8959.

Saturday Night Live. Tickets for performances and dress rehearsals are available by lottery, and postcards are accepted only during the month of August. Standby tickets are available at 8 AM on the day of show on the mezzanine of Rockefeller Center (50th Street side). NBC Tickets, "Saturday Night Live," 30 Rockefeller Plaza, New York, NY 10112, tel. 212/664–3055.

with a twist, turn off the tube and go join the studio audience (*see box*, Your Own 15 Minutes of Fame, *below*) for one of the many shows taped in the city.

JOY RIDES

One of the best ways to see the Lower Manhattan skyline and New York Harbor is from the deck of the **Staten Island Ferry** (*see* the Outer Boroughs, *above*), made free in 1997. If you're looking for altitude, climb aboard the **Roosevelt Island Tram** (*see* Upper East Side *in* Manhattan Neighborhoods, *above*), which runs high in the air over the East River, parallel to the Queensborough Bridge. The trip is $1.50. The subway ride to **Rockaway Beach** (*see box*, Land of Skyscrapers and Beaches?!, *above*) is about an hour from mid-Manhattan, and for $1.50 pretty spectacular—the train emerges from below ground to run on elevated tracks through the borough of Queens and finally over the sandy marshes of the Rockaways.

TOTAL KITSCH-O-RAMA

Freak shows are a big thing at the **Coney Island Beach and Boardwalk** (*see* Brooklyn *in* the Outer Boroughs, *above*) and they've all got a "two-headed" baby and the "world's largest" rat. Don't miss the **Coney Island Circus Sideshow**'s ($3) acts like the human blockhead and the sword-swallowing bearded lady.

Chinatown Fair. This sleazy arcade has all your favorite old video games, like PacMan, Galaxian, Frogger, and Space Invaders, plus a smattering of modern ones. Depending on your feelings about animal rights, you can also "play" tic-tac-toe (50¢ per game) against a pathetic-looking chicken. This genius fowl was once featured on *That's Incredible*. *8 Mott St., near Mosco St., Chinatown. Subway: J, M, N, R, Z, or 6 to Canal St.*

THE SPORTING LIFE

Believe it or not, Central Park boasts a lovely public **croquet grounds** (*see* Major Attractions, *above*) where you and your friends can gather together to act out your own version of *Heathers*. You must have a permit ($30) to play, good for an entire year; call 212/360–8133 for more info. If your sport of choice is **disco roller skating,** go to the **Roxy** (*see* Dance Clubs *in* Chapter 6) on Tuesday (gay) or Wednesday (mixed).

Fishing in Central Park. Central Park's Harlem Meer has recently been spruced up and stocked with 50,000 bluegills, largemouth bass, and catfish. You can rent poles for free from the adjacent Charles A. Dana Discovery Center, then catch-and-release to your heart's content. *Near 5th Ave., between E. 106th and 110th Sts., Central Park, tel. 212/860–1370. Subway: 6 to E. 110th St. Open Tues.–Sun. 11–5; shorter hrs in winter.*

Hashing. The New York Hash House Harriers is the club for self-described "drinkers with a running problem." Basically, it's a jolly group of folks who meet weekly to run around the city playing an alcohol-intensive version of the British children's game Hounds and Hares. *Tel. 212/427–4692 for recorded info.*

Moonlight Bike Rides. On the last Friday of each month, **Time's Up** (tel. 212/802–8222) offers moonlight group rides through Central Park; for the October ride everyone's encouraged to come in Halloween costume.

TRIPPING THE LIGHT FANTASTIC

If you've ever had a hankering to swing, waltz, fox-trot, salsa, two-step, lindy, or rumba under the stars, here's your chance. Show up at Lincoln Center's central plaza July 10–August 10 at 6:00 (it starts at 6:30, but the line is long) Wednesday through Saturday for a free hour of instruction; afterwards, you'll have several hours to whirl around practicing your new moves during the **Midsummer Night Swing Dance Extravaganza.** Saturdays the dancing starts at 8:15 (with no prior lesson). Admission is $9. Look for a printed schedule in the Center's concert halls, or call 212/875–5102 for a schedule update. *Lincoln Center, W. 66th St. between Columbus and Amsterdam Aves., tel. 212/875–5400. Subway: 1 or 9 to W. 66th St.*

WHERE
TO SLEEP

UPDATED BY AMY MCCONNELL

There's no way around the fact that lodging in New York City is pricier than a Pentagon hammer. In 1996 the *average* daily hotel room rate was $158, and the ritziest places cost hundreds more. If you can afford spending $100 a night, you won't have a problem finding a room in a modest hotel or bed-and-breakfast; but if you define "splurge" as $50 a night, you'll have to look a bit harder. In fact, if it weren't for hostels (*see* Hostels, YMCAs, and Student Housing, *below*) the lodging situation might force you to skip New York City entirely. Hostels are a big success here and are actually growing in number—and beds in hostels usually cost around $20 a night. Another penny-wise option, especially if you're staying in New York for more than a few weeks during summer, is university dormitory lodging (*see* University Housing, *below*). In any case, be sure to visit the New York Convention and Visitors Bureau (*see* Useful Organizations *in* Chapter 1), since hotels and hostels often offer hefty savings coupons in the NYCVB "Big Apple Visitors Guide." Price categories listed in this book refer to the price of the hotels' least expensive double rooms, excluding the 13½% hotel tax and $2 occupancy tax.

HOTELS

When it comes to hotels, wouldn't you know that the hipper parts of Manhattan—the East and West Village, SoHo, TriBeCa—are devoid of them. In fact, the majority of New York's hotels are in Midtown—which means that to reach the offbeat gems scattered all around the city, you're going to get very familiar with the subways.

Even if you don't want to go with a rock-bottom option, there are plenty of ways to save money. Groups of three or four can opt for triples and quads, always priced lower than singles and doubles. (Even if these larger rooms are not publicized, most hotels have them; just ask.) Rooms without private baths often have at least a sink, which makes shared baths bearable. When checking in or making reservations, ask for a cheaper room than what you were offered; hotels often have some unlisted rooms below the published rates, and you may get one if you pry a bit. And remember that many budget hotels offer major discounts for week-long stays; just talk to the management.

A few final notes: If you're traveling with valuables (never a great idea), stow them in the safe-deposit box at the front desk; virtually all the hotels listed below have them (a few also have in-room safes).

Wherever you stay, reservations are a good idea—especially in summer, around Christmas, and during any of the city's major festivals (*see* Festivals *in* Chapter 1).

UPPER WEST SIDE

Forget about finding a bed on the **Upper East Side**: Chances are slim unless your surname is engraved on a wing in the Met. If you really must stay in this neighborhood, try the funky **Franklin Hotel** (164 E. 87th St., tel. 212/369–1000) or its sister property, the **Hotel Wales** (1295 Madison Ave., tel. 212/876–6000): Both have doubles in the $179–$189 range, and include a lavish breakfast and nightly dessert buffet. Choices on the Upper West Side are few and fairly pricey, but if you can score a room here you'll be able to frolic in Central Park or hop a cross-town bus to the museums on 5th Avenue. The Upper West Side also has an abundance of good bars and restaurants.

UNDER $75 • Broadway American Hotel. The best thing about the aging Broadway American is its location, smack in the middle of the Upper West Side. The handsome gray-toned rooms aren't too shabby, either. If none of the zillion or so cool restaurants in the neighborhood whets your appetite, the hotel has a kitchen for guest use. Singles start at $55 ($80 with private bath), doubles $85 ($110 with bath), triples $105 ($130 with bath). *2178 Broadway, at W. 77th St., Upper West Side, tel. 212/362–1100, fax 212/787–9521. Subway: 1 or 9 to W. 79th St.; walk 2 blocks south on Broadway. 350 rooms, 84 with bath. Kitchen, laundry.*

Over the course of the next five years, there are 10 projects in the works that will add another 4,100 hotel rooms to the city.

Malibu Studios Hotel. This tacky West Coast wanna-be could never be mistaken for Melrose Place, but the young and loud crowd of student interns who summer here would like to think so. Clean, shared-bath singles are $45, doubles $59; for each additional person the rate goes up $10. Rooms with private bath average $20 more; they also have minifridges (shared-bath rooms don't). For longer stays you can usually work a deal. Reservations require a one-night cash deposit. *2688 Broadway, at W. 102nd St., Upper West Side, tel. 212/222–2954 or 800/647–2227, fax 212/678–6842. Subway: 1 or 9 to W. 103rd St. 150 rooms, 75 with bath. Restaurant, air-conditioning, refrigerators, laundry.*

Riverside Tower. If your room's above the sixth floor, you'll enjoy sweeping views of Riverside Park, the mighty Hudson River, and—don't get too excited—the New Jersey skyline. A liberal policy toward smoking (heartily embraced by the European backpackers who flock here) means that singles ($65), doubles ($70), and suites for two, three, or four people ($80, $95, and $105) are not only small and dark, they're also occasionally smoke-singed. But it's cheap, and the staff is young and easy to like. *80 Riverside Dr., at W. 80th St., Upper West Side, tel. 212/877–5200 or 800/724–3136, fax 212/873–1400. Subway: 1 or 9 to W. 79th St. 120 rooms, 116 with bath. Air-conditioning, refrigerators, laundry.*

UNDER $150 • Excelsior Hotel. Its main selling point is location: It's next to Central Park and the Museum of Natural History on a tony street lined with stunning old doorman apartments. An ongoing renovation has given most of the rooms a new, polished look and correspondingly higher prices ($129 for a single or double; $139 for a two-person suite, plus $10 for each additional person); if you're looking to save a buck, request an unrenovated room ($109 for a single or double, $159 for a suite). Rooms at the front of the hotel have a stupendous view of the park. *45 W. 81st St., between Columbus Ave. and Central Park W, Upper West Side, tel. 212/362–9200 or 800/368–4575, fax 212/580–3972. Subway: B or C to W. 81st St. 169 rooms. Coffee shop, air-conditioning.*

Hotel Beacon. With a gold-ceilinged, marble-floored lobby, and spacious, comfortable rooms with huge closets and phones with voice mail, this place is the best deal on the Upper West Side. Singles cost $115, doubles $135–$145; for $40 more you get kitchenettes with coffee makers, full-size refrigerators, and stoves. Best of all, it's three blocks from Central Park and Lincoln Center—what more could you want? *2130 Broadway, at W. 75th St., Upper West Side, tel. 212/787–1100 or 800/572–4969, fax 212/724–0839. Subway: 1, 2, 3, or 9 to W. 72nd St. 198 rooms. Coffee shop, air-conditioning, kitchenettes, laundry.*

The Milburn. Convenient to Lincoln Center and Central Park, this bohemian little hotel has a lobby that looks like a small Bavarian castle. The homey, spacious two-person studios cost $125 ($10 for the second person); suites that accommodate up to four people cost $165 ($10 for the second, third, and fourth guests). All have kitchenettes, a bonus since Zabar's—the ultimate Manhattan food bazaar—is only 5 blocks away. *242 W. 76th St., Upper West Side, tel. 212/362–1006 or 800/833–9622, fax 212/721–5476. Subway: 1, 2, 3, or 9 to W. 72nd St. 102 rooms. Air-conditioning, kitchenettes, laundry.*

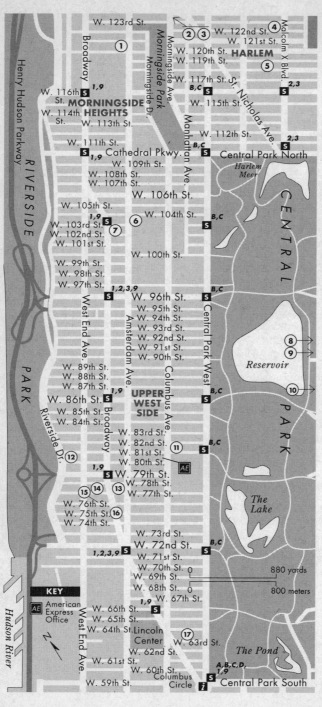

UPTOWN LODGING

HARLEM

MORNINGSIDE HEIGHTS

UPPER WEST SIDE

RIVERSIDE PARK

CENTRAL PARK

Harlem Meer

Reservoir

The Lake

The Pond

Lincoln Center

Columbus Circle

Central Park North

Central Park South

Central Park West

Hudson River

Henry Hudson Parkway

Riverside Dr.

West End Ave.

Broadway

Amsterdam Ave.

Columbus Ave.

Manhattan Ave.

Morningside Ave.

Morningside Dr.

Morningside Park

St. Nicholas Ave.

Malcolm X Blvd.

Cathedral Pkwy.

W. 123rd St.
W. 122nd St.
W. 121st St.
W. 120th St.
W. 119th St.
W. 117th St.
W. 116th St.
W. 115th St.
W. 114th St.
W. 113th St.
W. 112th St.
W. 111th St.
W. 109th St.
W. 108th St.
W. 107th St.
W. 106th St.
W. 105th St.
W. 104th St.
W. 103rd St.
W. 102nd St.
W. 101st St.
W. 100th St.
W. 99th St.
W. 98th St.
W. 97th St.
W. 96th St.
W. 95th St.
W. 94th St.
W. 93rd St.
W. 92nd St.
W. 91st St.
W. 90th St.
W. 89th St.
W. 88th St.
W. 87th St.
W. 86th St.
W. 85th St.
W. 84th St.
W. 83rd St.
W. 82nd St.
W. 81st St.
W. 80th St.
W. 79th St.
W. 78th St.
W. 77th St.
W. 76th St.
W. 75th St.
W. 74th St.
W. 73rd St.
W. 72nd St.
W. 71st St.
W. 70th St.
W. 69th St.
W. 68th St.
W. 67th St.
W. 66th St.
W. 65th St.
W. 64th St.
W. 63rd St.
W. 62nd St.
W. 61st St.
W. 60th St.
W. 59th St.

880 yards
800 meters

KEY
AE American Express Office

Hotels and B&Bs

Broadway American Hotel, **13**

Excelsior Hotel, **11**

Franklin Hotel, **10**

Hotel Beacon, **16**

Hotel Wales, **9**

Malibu Studios Hotel, **7**

The Milburn, **15**

New York Bed-and-Breakfast, **5**

Riverside Tower, **12**

Hostels and Dormitories

Banana Bungalow, **14**

Blue Rabbit International House, **2**

De Hirsch Residence at the 92nd Street YMHA, **8**

Hostelling International–New York, **6**

Sugar Hill International House, **3**

Uptown Hostel, **4**

Columbia University, **1**

YMCA–West Side, **17**

MIDTOWN

Midtown has the largest selection of hotels, and your choices range from grossly opulent to flea-infested, smelly joints. Hotels around **Times Square** and in the **Theater District** will put you in prime tourist territory—meaning lots of ugly souvenir T-shirts and bad, expensive food. You'll also be bombarded with sleaze, sleaze, sleaze, thanks to the XXX storefronts and prostitutes wandering the streets. It goes without saying that these areas have New York's cheapest hotels. On the flip side, **Chelsea** is a hip and happening neighborhood with a few good hotels. In the primarily residential Midtown neighborhood of **Murray Hill** and the no-man's-land around the Empire State Building you'll find another cluster of budget hotels, though you'll want to catch a subway or cab to somewhere more interesting at night.

UNDER $75 • Allerton House. This women-only hotel is an excellent deal. It's extremely secure and clean, and it's near Midtown's museums, art galleries, and ritzy boutiques. Good-sized rooms with shared baths are $35–$50, and spacious top-floor doubles with private baths are $75. There's also a roof deck with views into the heart of Gotham. *130 E. 57th St., between Lexington and Park Aves., Midtown East, tel. 212/753–8841. Subway: N, R, 4, 5, or 6 to E. 59th St. 350 rooms, 30 with bath. Restaurant, bar, laundry.*

Carlton Arms. What do you get when you cross a pack of artists with a down-and-out hotel? You get the decades-old Carlton "It Ain't No Holiday Inn" Arms, where each room is done up with a way funky motif, from Astroturf to tropical to hip-hop to faux Grecian. Shared-bath singles run $54, doubles $68, triples $81, and quads $86. Rooms with bathtubs are $63 (singles), $76 (doubles), $92 (triples), and $97 (quads). Students, foreigners, and those who stay for a week or more get a 5%–10% discount. It's got an international cult following, so reserve far in advance. *160 E. 25th St., near 3rd Ave., Gramercy, tel. 212/679–0680. Subway: 6 to E. 23rd St. 54 rooms, 20 with bath.*

According to a sign at the Allerton House's registration desk, men found above the third floor are promptly arrested.

Hotel Wolcott. This place has a gilded lobby to rival Versaille's Hall of Mirrors, though the medium-sized rooms are sterile as a rest·hospital. Downstairs is the Blues Supply jazz club (*see* Live Music *in* Chapter 6), the most exciting thing within a stone's throw of the Empire State Building. Singles and doubles cost $65 ($90 with bath). *4 W. 31st St., between 5th Ave. and Broadway, Midtown West, tel. 212/268–2900, fax 212/563–0096. Subway: B, D, F, N, Q, or R to W. 34th St. (Herald Sq.); also 6 to E. 33rd St. 200 rooms, 190 with bath. Air-conditioning, laundry.*

Martha Washington. Renovations have brought flowery wallpaper and dainty furniture to this ancient, women-only hotel. Many of the guests are long-term residents in their 50s and 60s who appreciate the extra security and low rates. Singles are $45 (weekly $165), doubles $65 (weekly $260). The cheapest rooms share a bath. *30 E. 30th St., between Park Ave. S and Madison Ave., Murray Hill, tel. 212/689–1900, fax 212/689–0023. Subway: 6 to E. 28th St. 450 rooms, 225 with bath. Air-conditioning, kitchenettes, laundry.*

Park Savoy. This inexpensive hotel is just a block south of Central Park and only a few blocks from the Museum of Modern Art—and if you think that's no big deal, try strolling into the glittering lobby of the Plaza Hotel and asking for something "budget." Needless to say, the Park Savoy is a good find, even if the clean rooms are miniscule and lack TVs. Singles run $60, doubles $75, triples $110, quads $130—*and* you get a 10% discount at the Italian restaurant next door. There's no safe-deposit box here, so don't bring valuables. *158 W. 58th St., between 6th and 7th Aves., Midtown West, tel. 212/245–5755, fax 212/765–0668. Subway: B, Q, N, or R to W. 57th St. 98 rooms. Restaurant.*

UNDER $100 • Arlington Hotel. The Arlington has signs in both English and Chinese, plus mediocre Asian art on the walls—a bow to the Chinese businesspeople who frequent the place on trips to Chelsea's warehouses. The rooms themselves are large but unspectacular; singles are $79, doubles $89, triples $99, suites $105. International students get a 10% discount. *18 W. 25th St., between Broadway and 6th Ave., Chelsea, tel. 212/645–3990, fax 212/633–8952. Subway: F, N, or R to W. 23rd St. 96 rooms. Air-conditioning.*

Chelsea Inn. This quaint old brownstone is just a couple blocks from the Union Square farmer's market and surrounded by tempting restaurants. Rooms ($99, $119 with bath) are clean and inviting, with dark-wood furniture, country-style quilts, big TVs, sinks, refrigerators, and hot plates; the white-tiled bathrooms are spic-and-span. Foursomes should ask for the 4-person suite ($169). Those who stay 7 days or more get $10 taken off each additional day. *46 W. 17th St., between 5th and 6th Aves., tel. 212/*

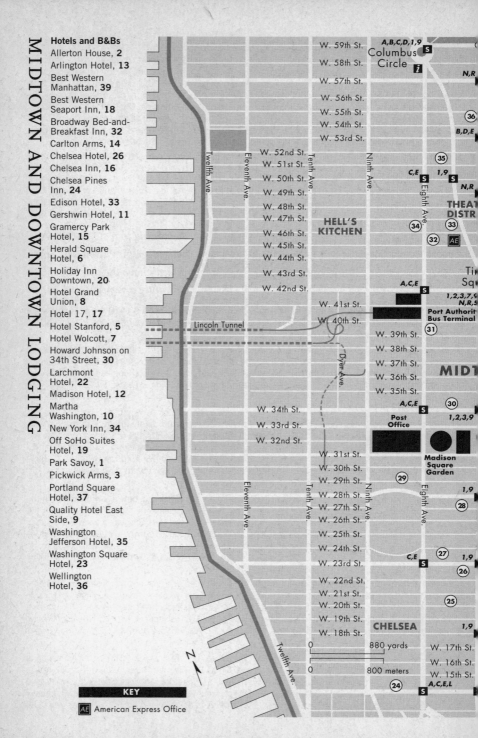

MIDTOWN AND DOWNTOWN LODGING

Hotels and B&Bs
Allerton House, **2**
Arlington Hotel, **13**
Best Western Manhattan, **39**
Best Western Seaport Inn, **18**
Broadway Bed-and-Breakfast Inn, **32**
Carlton Arms, **14**
Chelsea Hotel, **26**
Chelsea Inn, **16**
Chelsea Pines Inn, **24**
Edison Hotel, **33**
Gershwin Hotel, **11**
Gramercy Park Hotel, **15**
Herald Square Hotel, **6**
Holiday Inn Downtown, **20**
Hotel Grand Union, **8**
Hotel 17, **17**
Hotel Stanford, **5**
Hotel Wolcott, **7**
Howard Johnson on 34th Street, **30**
Larchmont Hotel, **22**
Madison Hotel, **12**
Martha Washington, **10**
New York Inn, **34**
Off SoHo Suites Hotel, **19**
Park Savoy, **1**
Pickwick Arms, **3**
Portland Square Hotel, **37**
Quality Hotel East Side, **9**
Washington Jefferson Hotel, **35**
Washington Square Hotel, **23**
Wellington Hotel, **36**

KEY

AE American Express Office

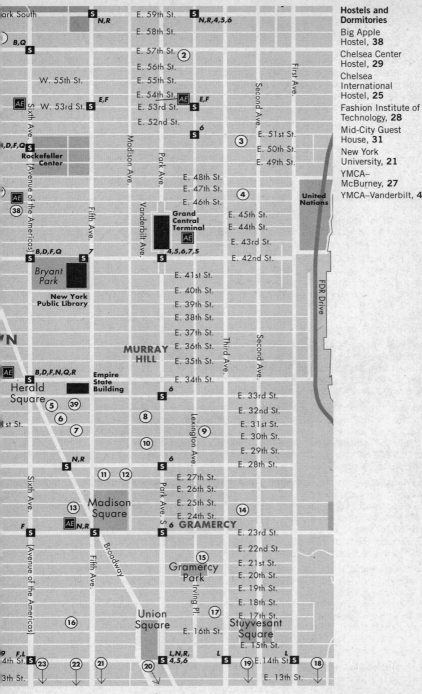

Hostels and Dormitories

Big Apple Hostel, **38**

Chelsea Center Hostel, **29**

Chelsea International Hostel, **25**

Fashion Institute of Technology, **28**

Mid-City Guest House, **31**

New York University, **21**

YMCA–McBurney, **27**

YMCA–Vanderbilt, **4**

645–8989, fax 212/645–1903. Subway: F to 14th St.; 1 or 9 to 14th St. or 18th St.; 4, 5, 6 to Union Sq. 24 rooms, 3 with bath. Air-conditioning, refrigerators.

Gershwin Hotel. This place caters to a younger and more cosmopolitan clientele than most budget places, offering impromptu barbecues and occasional live music. You can schmooze with fellow Gen-Xers at the rooftop wine and beer bar, or over lattes in the hip little café. A bed in one of the sparkling four- to eight-person dorm rooms costs $22. Standard doubles are $80, triples $90. A handful of superior rooms (with phones and TVs) are $110 (double) or $120 (triple). Lockers are often available ($1). 7 E. 27th St., between Madison and 5th Aves., Gramercy, tel. 212/545–8000, fax 212/684–5546. Subway: 6 to E. 28th St.; or N or R to W. 28th St. 350 beds. Coffee shop, bar.

Herald Square Hotel. This hotel, in the former Life magazine building, pays homage to the pre-MTV era with lots of framed Life covers. Rooms are bright, clean, and even equipped with telephone voice mail. Singles are $75–$95, doubles $95–$105, triples and quads $115–$125. Singles with shared bath are $50. Lockers are available ($1). 19 W. 31st St., between 5th Ave. and Broadway, Midtown West, tel. 212/279–4017 or 800/727–1888, fax 212/643–9208. Subway: B, D, F, N, Q, or R to W. 34th St. (Herald Sq.). 120 rooms, 109 with bath. Air-conditioning, in-room safes.

Hotel Grand Union. Though little distinguishes this hotel from others in Murray Hill, at least the newly renovated rooms are clean and spacious. Singles and doubles run $83–$95, triples and quads $95–$110. Students with an ISIC card get a 10% discount. 34 E. 32nd St., between Park Ave. S and Madison Ave., Murray Hill, tel. 212/683–5890, fax 212/689–7397. Subway: 6 to E. 33rd St. 95 rooms. Coffee shop, air-conditioning, refrigerators.

Hotel 17. This trendy Euro-style hotel—with its colorful mélange of slackers, club kids, and European funksters—is reason enough to visit New York. Most rooms are small and share a bath, but there's plenty of space to ogle fashion victims or the parade of fabulous guests (among them, Madonna and David Bowie). Be prepared to look pouty and glamorous, and be sure to reserve far in advance. Doubles cost $75 (shared bath) or $95 (private bath). 225 E. 17th St., near 3rd Ave., Gramercy Park, tel. 212/475–2845, fax 212/677–8178. Subway: L, N, R, 4, 5, or 6 to E. 14th St. (Union Sq.). 200 rooms, 12 with bath. Air-conditioning, laundry.

Madison Hotel. The no-frills Madison adds a little touch of its own: An amazing reproduction of Jasper Johns's Three Flags hangs behind the bulletproof reception counter. Rooms are dingy but big and all have private baths. Singles run $80, doubles $90, triples and quads $110. Telephones are available with a deposit ($40). 27 E. 27th St., at Madison Ave., Gramercy, tel. 212/532–7373, fax 212/799–5179. Subway: 6 to E. 28th St. 75 rooms. Air-conditioning, refrigerators.

New York Inn. This small, shabby hotel straddles an uncomfortable corner—one where the ersatz glamour of Restaurant Row meets sleazy, porn-spangled 8th Avenue. Rooms are decent but nothing more, and to reach them you need to deal with creaky, narrow stairs (there's no elevator). Singles cost $70, doubles $80. Continental breakfast is free. 765 8th Ave., between W. 46th and 47th Sts., Theater District, tel. 212/247–5400 or 800/777–6933, fax 212/586–6201. Subway: A, C, or E to W. 42nd St. 50 rooms. Restaurant, air-conditioning.

Pickwick Arms. The Pickwick's homogenized rooms are clean and reasonably spacious, and when you tire of watching Mork and Mindy reruns on TV you can chill on the rooftop patio. Shared-bath singles cost $50–$65, private singles $85, and doubles $105. Studios with double beds and sofas are a good deal at $125, plus $15 for each additional person. The small café next door puts out a phenomenal Middle Eastern buffet spread: $6 for all you can eat. 230 E. 51st St., between 2nd and 3rd Aves., Midtown East, tel. 212/355–0300, fax 212/755–5029. Subway: 6 to E. 51st St.; E or F to E. 53rd St./3rd Ave. 370 rooms, 320 with bath. Restaurant (no dinner), air-conditioning.

Portland Square Hotel. Though the lobby of this renovated 1904 hotel has the besieged feel of a Tel Aviv airport, the Portland's small, antiseptic rooms offer welcome extras such as in-room safes and phones with voice mail. Guests also have access to a small laundry room and a closet-size exercise room. A final bonus: You're not too far from the Theater District's bars and restaurants. Shared-bath singles run $50, private singles $80, doubles $94–$104, triples $109, quads $125. Small and large lockers are available ($1–$2). 132 W. 47th St., between 6th and 7th Aves., Theater District, tel. 212/382–0600 or 800/388–8988, fax 212/382–0684. Subway: N or R to W. 49th St. 144 rooms, 112 with bath. Air-conditioning, laundry.

Quality Hotel East Side. American-eagle wallpaper trumpets the theme of this New York City newcomer. Rooms, which cost $119–$149, or $79–$99 with shared bath, are stocked with phones, TVs, hairdryers, and irons and ironing boards. Checkered curtains and prints of American quilts add to the Americana motif. *161 Lexington Ave., at E. 30th St., Murray Hill, tel. 212/532–2255, fax 212/481–7270. Subway: 6 to E. 28th St. or E. 33rd St. 110 rooms, 85 with bath. Air-conditioning.*

Washington Jefferson Hotel. If you love the color pink, you'll feel right at home in the tiny rooms here. Narrow beds are shoved up against walls and the windows look out over the street—but rooms are spotless and you can get cable TV and minirefrigerators (in half the rooms only). Plus you can't beat this place for low prices: $75 for a single, $50 for a double with shared bath, $85 for a double with a teacupsize, black-and-white tile bath. *318 W. 51st St., between 8th and 9th Aves., Midtown, tel. 212/246–7550, fax 212/246–7622. Subway: E or C to W. 50th St.; also N or R to W. 51st St. 260 rooms, 130 with bath. Air-conditioning.*

UNDER $150 • Best Western Manhattan. Rooms here are decorated in one of three themes: 5th Avenue (ritzy), Central Park (lots of florals), or SoHo (dramatic colors). Whether you find this corny or cool, at least they're brand new and equipped with coffee makers. There's even a tiny exercise room with a couple of aerobic machines and some weights. And you're just south of the Empire State Building in a bustling Korean neighborhood, near lots of shops and restaurants. Singles are $85, doubles $95, triples $100, quads $110. *17 W. 32nd St., between 5th Ave. and Broadway, Midtown, tel. 212/ 736–1600 or 800/567–7720, fax 212/695–1813. Subway: B, D, F, or Q to W. 34th St. (Herald Sq.). 150 rooms. Restaurant, bar, air-conditioning.*

The Gershwin Hotel keeps a Campbell's Soup can in the lobby, but it's not for emergency snacking—this one is signed by Andy Warhol.

Chelsea Hotel. The Victorian-era Chelsea is one of the city's most famous residential hotels, home to innumerable artists and other creative folk over the last century: Thomas Wolfe, Arthur Miller, Sarah Bernhardt, Robert Mapplethorpe, Christo, Bob Dylan, Dylan Thomas, Leonard Cohen, Eugene O'Neill, and the late Willem de Koonig. Some of the artists who called the Chelsea Hotel home left paintings and sculpture in lieu of paying their bills; there's a gallery of their work in the lobby. Its giant rooms vary widely in personality; some are regal and others are time capsules from the shag-carpet '70s. Per night, singles cost $110–$175, doubles $125–$185, suites $275–$375. Naturally, the people who've lived here for decades pay a lot less. *222 W. 23rd St., between 7th and 8th Aves., Chelsea, tel. and fax 212/243–3700. Subway: 1 or 9 to W. 23rd St. (7th Ave.); also C or E to W. 23rd St. (8th Ave.). 330 rooms, 310 with bath. Air-conditioning, kitchenettes.*

Edison Hotel. This mondo Art Deco hotel gets major business from big (and big-haired) tour groups. A relic from the Roaring '20s, it's got some over-the-top extras like a cool hotel bar, a dramatic mural-filled lobby, and a pink-plaster coffee shop that attracts show-business types. Rooms aren't cheap, but they are plush. Singles are $105, doubles $115, triples $125, and quads $135. *228 W. 47th St., between Broadway and 8th Ave., Theater District, tel. 212/840–5000 or 800/637–7070, fax 212/596–6850. Subway: 1 or 9 to W. 50th St.; also C or E to W. 50th St. 1,000 rooms. Restaurant, coffee shop, bar, airconditioning.*

Gramercy Park Hotel. The grand old Gramercy may be showing its age (e.g., worn carpets, peeling walls, and bathrooms clamoring for Tilex), but it's still an elite address. More to the point, it also has keys to the city's only private, locked park; grab a key, head across the street, and spend a day lounging in one of Manhattan's finest sylvan sanctuaries. Another plus: The suites ($180 for two, plus $10 for each additional person) are big enough to fit you, your backpack, your friends, and, say, the entire Italian men's soccer team. Singles cost $135, doubles $145. Additional guests pay $10 each. At this rate, you can afford to order room service (it's available). *2 Lexington Ave., at E. 21st St., Gramercy Park, tel. 212/ 475–4320 or 800/221–4083, fax 212/505–0535. Subway: 6 to E. 23rd St. 500 rooms. Restaurant, bar, air-conditioning, in-room safes, refrigerators, laundry.*

Hotel Stanford. The impeccably renovated Stanford is in the center of Midtown's dynamic Korean enclave, its three lobby clocks set for London, New York, and Seoul/Tokyo time. The tidy rooms range from mini to monstrous: Singles are $85, doubles $100–$130, suites $180. And your craving for a little karaoke can be satisfied, thanks to the hotel cocktail bar. *43 W. 32nd St., between 5th Ave. and Broadway, Midtown West, tel. 212/563–1500, fax 212/629–0043. Subway: B, D, F, N, Q, or R to W. 34th St. (Herald Sq.). 130 rooms. Bar, air-conditioning.*

Howard Johnson on 34th Street. A major rehab by HoJo hoteliers turned the dumpy Penn Plaza Hotel into a spiffy business hotel, complete with modem hookups on all telephones. Singles cost $109, doubles $129, plus $15 for each additional person. Students get a 10% discount. *215 W. 34th St., between*

7th and 8th Aves., Midtown, tel. 212/947–5050 or 800/446–4656, fax 212/268–4829. Subway: A, C, E, 1, 2, 3, or 9 to W. 34th St. (Penn Station). 111 rooms. Air-conditioning.

Wellington Hotel. This large, old-fashioned property's main advantage is its location near Carnegie Hall—a big draw for budget-conscious Europeans. Rooms are small but clean. Singles cost $135; doubles that accommodate up to 4 people with no extra charge are a bargain at $145. *871 7th Ave., at 55th St., Midtown, tel. 212/247–3900 or 800/652–1212, fax 212/581–1719. Subway: N or R to W. 57th St. 700 rooms. Restaurant, coffee shop, air-conditioning.*

DOWNTOWN

Super-cheap or super-glitzy, hotels of any sort are hard to find below 14th Street. Need proof? When the World Trade Center opened a hotel in 1982, it was Lower Manhattan's first new lodging in over a century. Village-bound hipsters are better off finding a bed in one of the dozens of cheap hotels filling Midtown. One relative bargain is the **Holiday Inn Downtown** (138 Lafayette St., near Canal St., tel. 212/966–3933), just outside Chinatown: Doubles cost $155, suites are just a bit more.

UNDER $100 • Larchmont Hotel. This West Village newcomer is hard to beat for location and price—and it even occupies an atmospheric Beaux Arts brownstone complete with geranium-filled window boxes. Inside there's a funky safari theme: Rooms have rattan furniture, ceiling fans, and framed animal or botanical prints. Singles run $60–$80, doubles $85–$99. There are two bathrooms on each floor (six rooms per floor), but every room has its own private sink. Continental breakfast is included, and there's also a communal kitchen for guests. *27 W. 11th St., West Village, tel. 212/989–9333, fax 212/989–9496. Subway: E or F to W. 4th St. 55 rooms, all with shared bath.*

Off SoHo Suites Hotel. Amidst the urban decay of the Bowery, this self-described "European" hotel couldn't stand out more if it had been wrapped by Christo. The two-person suites ($89) share a kitchen and bath, while the four-person suites ($149) are completely private. All are extremely clean, if totally generic. Because of its small size, reserve well in advance. *11 Rivington St., between Chrystie St. and Bowery, Lower East Side, tel. 212/979–9808 or 800/633–7646, fax 212/979–9801. Subway: J or M to Bowery. 40 suites, 28 with bath. Air-conditioning, kitchenettes.*

UNDER $150 • Best Western Seaport Inn. If you're set on staying near the South Street Seaport and willing to shell out the bucks, head for this chain hotel with the feel of a Colonial sea captain's home. You can spend as little as $104 (for a standard room with no view) or as much as $164 and up (for a room with a terrace and whirlpool tub and a view of the Brooklyn Bridge); both types of rooms have VCRs. Rates are significantly lower on weekends. *33 Peck Slip, at South St. Seaport, Lower Manhattan, tel. 212/766–6600 or 800/468–3569, fax 212/766–6615. Subway: 2, 3, or A to Fulton St. 72 rooms. Air-conditioning, in-room safes, refrigerators.*

Washington Square Hotel. This turn-of-the-century hotel has a prime West Village location and an irresistible bohemian mood—especially in the tiny lobby, where wrought-iron benches and gleaming brass conjure up old New York. A 1996–97 renovation has spruced up the small rooms: Singles now cost $90, doubles $115–$122, and king-size quads $144. Extras include complimentary beer or wine on arrival, free breakfast at the C3 restaurant, use of the small gym, and unlimited jazz tips from the savvy manager (catch a set at the nearby Blue Note). Lockers can be rented for $1 per day. *103 Waverly Pl., at MacDougal St., West Village, tel. 212/777–9515 or 800/222–0418, fax 212/979–8373. Subway: A, B, C, D, E, F, or Q to W. 4th St. (Washington Sq.). 170 rooms. Restaurant, bar, air-conditioning.*

BED-AND-BREAKFASTS

Most of the bed-and-breakfast establishments in New York City are residential apartments with some (or all) of their rooms reserved for guests. These are booked through reservation services that charge no fee but often require a deposit equal to 25% of the total cost. (Ask about weekly rates if you plan to stay for awhile.) There are also a handful of independent B&Bs where you book directly. These places are more likely to have the traditional comforts, such as a complimentary (and often gourmet) breakfast, and a desirable location—quite a few are in Brooklyn, near Prospect Park and other scenic neighborhoods. Wherever you stay, rates average $100 a night. But be warned: Not all places do serve breakfast, and many do not accept credit cards.

B&B RESERVATION SERVICES

You have two options when you use a B&B reservation service: a hosted or an unhosted apartment. A **hosted apartment** is simply an extra room or two in someone's apartment. Your host or hostess will probably feed you a continental breakfast, let you come and go as you please, and give you access to amenities such as a TV, phone, and private bath. Best of all, hosts are happy to offer the lowdown on where to dine, shop, or drink, and what to see. The more expensive **unhosted apartment** is unoccupied (but furnished), often with an owner out of town. Here you'll have the run of the place, including full kitchen privileges. Apartments range in size from tiny walk-up studios to expensive penthouses with full-time doormen. Reservation services list hundreds of apartments, so they can set you up in almost any neighborhood. Make reservations as far in advance as possible; refunds (minus a $25 service charge) are given up to 10 days before arrival.

Abode Bed-and-Breakfast. These 30 or so unhosted apartments throughout Manhattan start at $110. Minimum stay is three nights. *Box 20022, New York, NY 10021, tel. 212/472–2000 or 800/835–8880.*

All Around the Town. This service has only six hosted singles ($65–$75) and doubles ($80–$90)—which means all the properties are carefully selected. Unhosted apartments start at $110; all are in Manhattan. *150 5th Ave., Suite 711, New York, NY 10011, tel. 212/675–5600, fax 212/675–6366.*

Bed-and-Breakfast in Manhattan. The friendly woman who runs this service has hosted singles and doubles for $80–$100, and unhosted apartments for $100–$250. *Box 533, New York, NY 10150, tel. 212/472–2528, fax 212/988–9818.*

Bed-and-Breakfast Network of New York. This service lists more than 300 apartments throughout Manhattan and Brooklyn. Hosted singles run $60–$80, doubles $90–$100. Unhosted apartments start at $100. *134 W. 32nd St., Suite 602, New York, NY 10001, tel. 212/645–8134 or 800/900–8134.*

City Lights Bed-and-Breakfast. Many of this service's hosts are gay friendly. Hosted doubles are $85–$110. Unhosted studios and one-bedrooms are $110–$160. *Box 20355, Cherokee Station, New York, NY 10021, tel. 212/737–7049, fax 212/535–2755.*

Urban Ventures. The oldest of the reservation services, Urban Ventures lists around 800 locations throughout Manhattan and the outer boroughs. Hosted doubles cost $75–$125. Unhosted apartments start at $95. Full payment by credit card is required at least 10 days in advance. *38 W. 32nd, Suite 1412, New York, NY 10001, tel. 212/594–5650, fax 212/947–9320.*

INDEPENDENT B&BS

MANHATTAN

Broadway Bed-and-Breakfast Inn. This cozy inn, opened in 1995, musters country charm in the middle of Manhattan's Theater District. Rooms are small but immaculate, and the lobby—with brick walls and stocked bookshelves—is the setting for your Continental breakfast. The staff is too friendly and helpful to be native New Yorkers. The ground-floor restaurant gives Broadway guests a 20% discount. Singles run $85–$95, doubles $105–$140. *264 W. 46th St., between Broadway and 8th Ave., Theater District, tel. 212/997–9200 or 800/826–6300, fax 212/768–2807. Subway: N, R, 1, 2, 3, 7, or 9 to W. 42nd St. (Times Sq.); also A, C, or E to W. 42nd St. (Port Authority). 40 rooms. Air-conditioning.*

Chelsea Pines Inn. It may not be Aspen or even Fire Island, but for many gay and lesbian couples the Chelsea Pines ranks among the best B&Bs anywhere (straights are welcome, too). The tidy rooms are filled with kitsch items and vintage movie posters. The delicious breakfasts include fresh fruit and homemade bread. Doubles range from $75–$89 (shared bath) to $89–$99 (private bath). Each extra person pays $20. In summer and fall you should reserve at least a month in advance, especially for the less-expensive rooms. *317 W. 14th St., between 8th and 9th Aves., Chelsea, tel. 212/929–1023, fax 212/645–9497. Subway: A, C, E, or L to W. 14th St. 23 rooms, 7 with bath. Air-conditioning, refrigerators.*

New York Bed-and-Breakfast. This beautiful old Harlem brownstone is owned by Gisele, a friendly Canadian who also runs the Uptown Hostel (*see* Hostels, YMCAs, and Student Housing, *below*). It's got an ardent fan club of French and German tourists who return annually to enjoy its five rooms with one shared bath. Singles cost $35, doubles $45. There's a Continental breakfast to boot. *134 W. 119th St., between Lenox Ave./Malcolm X and Adam Clayton Powell Jr. Blvds., Harlem, tel. 212/666–0559. Subway: 2 or 3 to W. 116th St. 5 rooms, all with shared bath. Cash only.*

BROOKLYN

Bed-and-Breakfast on the Park. This spectacular brownstone is a great reason to leave Manhattan. Every detail is exquisite, from the rooms appointed with 19th-century antiques and oil paintings to the gourmet breakfasts. And if you ever manage to leave your bedroom, there's a kitchen open to guests. Two shared-bath doubles cost $100 and $125; doubles with private bath start at $170. *113 Prospect Park W, between 6th and 7th Sts., Park Slope, tel. 718/499–6115, fax 718/499–1385. Subway: F to 7th Ave. (Park Slope). 9 rooms, 7 with bath. Cash only.*

HOSTELS AND YMCAS

On the whole, hostels are most popular with students and foreign backpackers and are great for hooking up with other travelers. But you'll need to be able to tolerate lots of noise. Independent hostels and those affiliated with **Hostelling International (HI)** (*see* Students *in* Chapter 1) are similar in price and style: They almost always have private rooms as well as dorms that sleep four to 12 people. The three private hostels in Harlem charge $14–$16 per dorm bed, while Midtown joints generally cost $20 or more. From this, clever readers may draw the conclusion that the farther uptown a hostel is, the cheaper the rates. There are no hostels south of 14th Street. Unlike hotels, not all hostels have lockers or safety-deposit boxes—when in doubt, leave your gems at home. All the hostels listed below provide free linens.

Contrary to popular belief, **YMCA**s (it stands for Young Men's Christian Association, though these places are not religious) are not always cheaper than hotels. They do offer one big bonus, however: free use of their usually extensive gym facilities with a night's stay. And the atmosphere at most is fairly subdued, thanks to the preponderance of families, older single travelers, and long-term elderly residents. All the Ys listed below have safety-deposit boxes.

The general rule about reservations is to make them at least two weeks in advance (more around Christmas and in late summer). Both hostels and YMCAs often charge a $5–$10 key deposit, so be sure to carry some extra cash. One final note for Americans only: Many private hostels (like Banana Bungalow) have an unadvertised policy of refusing Americans. Why? Well, it seems that Americans have an ugly reputation for being demanding and for destroying hostel property. If you can politely convince a private hostel that you're an exception, they may let you in.

UPTOWN

The hostels in **Harlem** are usually the least crowded, and the cheapest, of any type of lodging in New York City. Contrary to a somewhat popular belief, Harlem can be a perfectly safe place to stay, as long as you stick to the better neighborhoods such as Sugar Hill. Though, if you plan on coming and going late at night, be sure to travel with company. Hostels on the **Upper West Side** are more expensive but are within walking distance of more snazzy restaurants, lots of bars, Central Park, the Museum of Natural History, Lincoln Center, and more. Hostels throughout upper Manhattan are usually only a block or two from a subway station; from Harlem it's a 20- to 30-minute subway ride to downtown (the same trip's shorter by taxi but also costs $10–$20—as opposed to $3 round-trip by subway).

Banana Bungalow. A foreign passport is your E-ticket to the magic Banana kingdom, where a bed in one of the six-person coed dorms costs $18 ($1 off with an ISIC card). You have easy access to Upper West Side sights, plus all the beer you can drink at the hostel's Friday-night parties held on its fabulous rooftop garden: Pay $4 for a stein, then keep refilling. *250 W. 77th St., between Broadway and West End Ave., Upper West Side, tel. 212/362–7700 or 800/646–7835, fax 212/877–5733. Subway: 1 or 9 to W. 79th St. 100 beds. Reception open 24 hrs, check-in anytime, checkout 11 AM. Kitchen.*

Blue Rabbit International House. Ride the C train to its end in the well-to-do Sugar Hill section of Harlem to this clean, comfortable, recently refurbished hostel, under the same management as the adjacent Sugar Hill International House (*see below*). Coed and women-only dormitory-style rooms sleep four to eight and cost $16 per night; giant doubles are $18 per person. There's a rooftop terrace, friendly pet cats (and a barking dog), a communal kitchen, and European tourists galore (a passport is required for check-in). Reservations are essential in summer and fall. *730 St. Nicholas Ave., between W. 145th and 146th Sts., Harlem, tel. 212/491–3892 or 800/610–2030, fax 212/283–0108. Subway: A, B, C, or D to 145th St. 25 beds. Reception open 24 hrs, check-in 9 AM–5 PM, checkout 9–11 AM. Kitchen. Cash only.*

De Hirsch Residence at the 92nd Street YMHA. Stay in the Upper East Side's only affordable lodging and you'll be able to see every Degas, Arbus, and Giacometti on Museum Mile, no prob. Despite the name (Young Men's Hebrew Association), this is a non-sectarian hostel with immaculate dorms and a kitchen, laundry, and shared bath on every floor. You'll also have access to the superb fitness facilities, library, community room, and all sorts of cultural and social events. Here's the catch: You must fill out an application at least three weeks in advance, and you must stay a minimum of three nights. Singles cost $49, doubles $70. *1395 Lexington Ave., at 92nd St., Upper East Side, tel. 212/415–5650 or 800/858–4692, fax 212/415–5578. Subway: 4, 5, or 6 to E. 86th St. 350 beds. Reception open Mon.–Thurs. 9 AM–7 PM, Fri. 9 AM–5 PM, Sun. 10 AM–5 PM, check-in 1 PM, checkout noon. Air-conditioning, laundry.*

Hostelling International–New York. Despite the barbed wire, this monstrous landmark building (designed by big-deal 19th-century architect Richard Morris Hunt) is the largest youth hostel in North America. The neighborhood is safe and filled with great bars, and the Big House itself boasts an entire city block's worth of clean, airy rooms, a garden, and an upper-level outdoor terrace. Beds in four- to 12-person dorms run $25–$28 ($27–$30 in summer), while a handful of private rooms that accommodate up to 4 people (with bath) cost $75. Flash an Hostelling International card for a $3 discount. If you plan on coming in summer, reserve far, far in advance. *891 Amsterdam Ave., at W. 103rd St., Upper West Side, tel. 212/932–2300, fax 212/932–2574. Subway: 1 or 9 to W. 103rd St. 540 beds. Reception open 24 hrs, check-in anytime, checkout 11 AM. Air-conditioning, kitchen, laundry.*

Clubs and bars advertise cheap happy hours and theme parties at hostels, so stay on the lookout.

Sugar Hill International House. This hostel, brought to you by the same cheery folks as the Blue Rabbit International House (*see above*), is clean, comfortable, and friendly, with easy subway access and a sunny communal kitchen. Coed and women-only dorms (four to eight beds each) are $16. Or try to score the Sugar Hill's only double ($18 per person). *722 St. Nicholas Ave., at W. 146th St., Harlem, tel. 212/926–7030, fax 212/283–0108. Subway: A, B, C, or D to 145th St. 20 beds. Reception open 9 AM–10 PM, check-in 9 AM–6 PM, checkout 9–11 AM. Kitchen. Cash only.*

Uptown Hostel. Sure, you're a traveler and you're tired, but think of poor Gisele: The hardworking owner of this beautiful brownstone has labored for months to refurbish it, so don't go messing it up with your smelly ol' socks and sad lack of personal hygiene. Coed dorms (four to six beds) are $14 per night. A private double is $18 per person. Gisele also operates the slightly more expensive New York Bed-and-Breakfast (*see above*), about three blocks away. *239 Lenox Ave./Malcolm X Blvd., at W. 122nd St., Harlem, tel. 212/666–0559. Subway: 2 or 3 to W. 125th St.; walk 3 blocks south on Lenox Ave./Malcolm X Blvd. 30 beds. Reception open 9 AM–8 PM, check-in 10 AM–8 PM, checkout anytime. Kitchen. Cash only.*

YMCA–West Side. Live like a sultan in this attractive, vaguely Middle-Eastern style building mere blocks from Lincoln Center. Clean, comfortable doubles are $90 with bath or $65 without—and this princely sum entitles you to use the Y's gym, sauna, pool, indoor track, and squash courts (you packed your racquet, right?). If you get hungry, there's a cafeteria. There's also an airport shuttle to J.F.K. airport ($13). Now the caveats: You must be at least 18 years old and can stay no longer than 25 days. Reservations (credit-card number required) are best made two weeks in advance. *5 W. 63rd St., between Central Park W and Broadway, Upper West Side, tel. 212/787–4400, fax 212/875–1334. Subway: A, B, C, D, 1, or 9 to W. 59th St. (Columbus Circle). 550 rooms, 100 with bath. Reception open 24 hrs, check-in after 2 PM, checkout noon. Air-conditioning, laundry.*

MIDTOWN

Conveniently, several hostels are in the heart (or at least on the fringe) of the myriad Midtown tourist attractions. Of them, the **Chelsea International Hostel** (*see below*) is the most "downtown"—in other words, it's the closest to good bars and restaurants and is only a short walk to the West Village. Another good option is the $22 dorms at the hip **Gershwin Hotel** (*see Midtown in Hotels, above*).

Big Apple Hostel. The Big Apple takes up seven floors of an old hotel with not a single air conditioner in sight—but who cares when you've got all of Times Square lying at your feet like a lathered, drooling beast? You'll also get brisk service, bathrooms that sparkle, and a big outdoor patio where you can sip free coffee with lots of overstimulated Europeans. Four-person dorms are $22, private doubles $58. The management prefers not to host locals: You must show an out-of-New York City driver's license or foreign passport to stay. *119 W. 45th St., between 6th and 7th Aves., Theater District, tel. 212/302–2603, fax 212/302–2605. Subway: N, R, 1, 2, 3, 7, or 9 to W. 42nd St. (Times Sq.). 106 beds. Reception open 24 hrs, check-in anytime, checkout 11 AM. Kitchen, laundry.*

Chelsea Center Hostel. You can take your shower in the bathroom or you can take your shower in the kitchen at this compact, homey hostel on the northern edge of Chelsea. They've also got two coed dorms and a lush back patio to enjoy. The multilingual staff prefers foreigners but will accept Americans during the off-season. Beds are $20 ($22 in summer); Continental breakfast is included. Behave yourself, or you'll be shipped 10 blocks south to the hostel's annex. *313 W. 29th St., between 8th and 9th Aves., Chelsea, tel. 212/643–0214, fax 212/473–3945. Subway: A, C, or E to W. 34th St. (Penn Station). 22 beds. Reception and check-in 8:30 AM–11:30 PM, checkout 11 AM. Kitchen. Cash only.*

Chelsea International Hostel. This hostel compensates for cramped rooms with a decent Midtown location, comfortable bedding, and free pizza 'n' beer parties Wednesday nights (plus free beer Sundays). It's a favorite with boisterous young Europeans. Space in a four-person dorm costs $20, doubles are $40; a $10 deposit and international passport are required for a check-in. Flash your HI or ISIC card for a $1-per-day discount. *251 W. 20th St., between 7th and 8th Aves., Chelsea, tel. 212/647–0010, fax 212/727–7289. Subway: C or E to W. 23rd St.; also 1 or 9 to W. 23rd St., walk 3 blocks south on 7th Ave. then ½ block west. 200 beds. Reception open 8 AM–9 PM, check-in anytime, checkout 1 PM. Kitchen.*

Mid-City Guest House. Despite its sleazy XXX locale near Port Authority, this hostel has a super-friendly staff and a few nice touches, like fireplaces and brick walls. The coed dorms have wimpy foam mattresses and an original soundtrack performed by the traffic on 8th Avenue. There's no sign, so find the address and then go up two flights of stairs. Beds are $18 ($20 in summer), and include Continental breakfast. You must brandish a passport and/or a backpack to stay. *608 8th Ave., between W. 39th and 40th Sts., Midtown West, tel. 212/704–0562. Subway: A, C, or E to W. 42nd St. (Port Authority). 24 beds. Midnight curfew (Fri. and Sat. 1 AM), lockout noon–6 PM. Reception open 8 AM–midnight, check-in anytime, checkout noon. Kitchen. Cash only.*

YMCA–McBurney. Many of McBurney's residents are long-term and mildly unsavory. And, depending on your point of view, the security guard and glassed-in reception are either reassuring or depressing. Still, you get free use of the Y's gym, a small but decent bedroom, and a bathroom down the hall. Singles cost $40 ($47 with TV), doubles $56, triples $70, quads $88; all 270 rooms share two big communal bathrooms. A $40 deposit is required unless you arrive before 6 PM. *206 W. 24th St., between 7th and 8th Aves., Chelsea, tel. 212/741–9226, fax 212/741–8724. Subway: C or E to W. 23rd St.; also 1 or 9 to W. 23rd St.; walk 1 block north on 7th Ave. 270 rooms, none with bath. Reception open weekdays 7 AM–11 PM (weekends from 8 AM), check-in anytime, checkout noon. Air-conditioning.*

YMCA–Vanderbilt. This popular Y packs in backpackers like the 42nd Street Shuttle at rush hour. The tiny and linoleum-floored rooms share bathrooms; the immaculate building itself is mere blocks from Grand Central Station. Best of all, a stay here entitles you to free use of the vast health facilities (pools, cardiovascular equipment, Nautilus machines, even a roving trainer) and airport shuttle service ($12 to La Guardia, $15 to J.F.K.). Singles start at $52, doubles at $63, and quads at $82. *224 E. 47th St., between 2nd and 3rd Aves., Midtown East, tel. 212/756–9600, fax 212/752–0210. Subway: 6 to E. 51st St.; also E or F to Lexington/3rd Aves. 377 rooms, none with bath. Reception open 24 hrs, check-in 1 PM, checkout noon. Air-conditioning.*

UNIVERSITY HOUSING

For those who need longer-term budget housing, a handful of colleges and universities open their dormitories to non-students during summer. The catch: You must call or send away for an application far in advance (usually during spring), then wait for a reply—which may come as much as a week or two later. The best choice is **New York University (NYU)** (New York University Summer Housing Office, 14A Washington Pl., NY 10003, tel. 212/998–4621, fax 212/995–4097), whose dormitories are ideally situated in the East and West Village, smack in the middle of the city's coolest clubs, bars, cheap restaurants, and cafés. Housing is available mid-May through mid-August; weekly rates are $70–$175, and the *minimum* stay is three weeks.

Other options: From mid-May through mid-August, **Columbia University** (Residential Life Office, 525 W. 120th St., Morningside Heights, Box 312, NY 10027, tel. 212/678–3235, fax 212/678–3222) offers small, clean single rooms at one of two Upper West Side/Morningside Heights dormitories for $24–$35, depending on length of stay (the lowest rates go to those spending 30 days or more). Nicer rooms with kitchen and bath are $25–$55. Year-round there are also a few shared-bath rooms at a nightly rate of $35 (single) or $45 (double), and private-bath rooms with kitchens at $55; maximum stay for these is six nights.

FOOD

BY AMY MCCONNELL, MIRA SCHWIRTZ, AND TOM STEELE,

WITH ANTO HOWARD, MATTHEW LORE, AND BRENT PEICH

ining out is an intensely important part of experiencing New York City. If you need proof, consider this: Ruth Reichl, the restaurant critic for the *New York Times,* spends around $350,000 a year reviewing restaurants. True, that's a lot more money than most people would spend on chow in an entire lifetime, but then again, there are more good restaurants here than in any other city in the world. Besides the high-end experiences like Le Cirque 2000, Chanterelle, La Côte Basque, Gramercy Tavern, and Union Square Cafe with five-star chefs and waiters so utterly obsequious they'd probably take a bullet for you, there are many thousands of humbler establishments serving affordable and highly imaginative fare, as well as New York staples like pizza-by-the-slice and bagels—old-world creations perfected over the centuries in America's numero uno melting pot. It's impossible not to be impressed by the city's countless immigrant groups—Irish, Latin American, Eastern European, Italian, Asian, and more—who've proudly introduced their respective culinary secrets to New York: pub grub, burritos, pierogi, dim sum, pad thai, tandoori chicken, and killer cannoli. Live a little while you're here; if you don't know what *feijoada* is, or have never tasted Burmese cuisine before, this is the only place in the world where you can give both a try merely by crossing the right street.

The recession of the early 1990s caused restaurant owners to lower prices and improve the quality of their food and often the size of their portions in order to win back the hearts of jaded diners. Happily, you'll find that this trend has continued unabated—as long as you know where to look. For here, you can easily spend $100 for mediocre food in a trendy restaurant; you could also spend $15 on the best meal of your life in some totally obscure family-run joint. And another important tip: You should try to sample some of New York's finer restaurants during the week, when most offer reduced-price lunch specials. This is especially true in Midtown, where a $15 lunch entrée could easily fetch $50 at dinner.

Throughout New York, it's difficult to define a place strictly as a bar, café, or restaurant—many spots tend to function as all three. Cafés often pour beer and mix cocktails, while plenty of restaurants have very popular bars. Likewise, lots of bars have extremely active kitchens. The point is that you're never far from a decent meal in New York City. And you'll often find that the cheaper the establishment, the longer the hours. In fact, many places that charge less than $10 for a filling feast stay open until the wee hours—good news for bar crawlers who need a food fix after the bars close at 4 AM.

So after you've exhausted the reviews in this book, you're still left with those 15,917 other restaurants to explore—and well over 8,000 of those are in Manhattan alone. Zealous New Yorkers who dine out often refer to **The Zagat Survey** ($11.95), an annual guide to some 1,800 restaurants in all price ranges, mostly in Manhattan. Look for its slim, rectangular, maroon cover at all bookstores and most newsstands. And there is an extremely useful Web site—menusonline.com/cities/new_york—that provides very complete menus and vital statistics for hundreds of restaurants in New York. The site is definitely worth a visit before you set out for the city; you can download a dozen menus and drool all the way in. And remember that, because of the city's uniquely plentiful foot traffic, virtually every restaurant in Manhattan posts its menu(s) in the front window, near the entrance, where you'll occasionally encounter a gathered crowd. A poorly kept secret: This is a splendid place to meet people, if only to get or share sage gustatory advice. But you might also find a lunch or dinner companion by lingering near an enticing menu and smiling carefully.

The allegedly make-or-break restaurant reviews in the **New York Times** are worth considering, especially since their beats more regularly include affordable places. The **Village Voice** and the **New York Press** tend to review and list restaurants that are affordable, and even include places of interest in the outer boroughs. Strict vegetarians visiting New York should invest in **The Vegan Guide to New York City**, available for $4.75 from Rynn Berry (159 Eastern Parkway, Apt. 2H, Brooklyn, NY 11238). If you're still not sure where to eat, your best bet is to cruise the streets of the East or West Village, 8th Avenue between 14th and 30th streets, or one of the city's many ethnic enclaves, and seek out a place overflowing with locals.

Some final notes: The price categories in this chapter refer to the cost of a main course, including a non-alcoholic drink. If you insist on drinking lots of wine or finishing your meal with a flaming bananas Foster, all bets are off. Also, in our reviews we won't mention a restaurant's credit-card acceptance policy unless it doesn't accept credit cards at all, in which case we'll say "Cash only"; otherwise, you can assume that the establishment takes some or all major cards. Likewise, unless otherwise indicated, all establishments are open seven days a week.

MANHATTAN RESTAURANTS

UPPER WEST SIDE

Restaurants are plentiful along the Upper West Side's three main north–south avenues: **Columbus Avenue, Amsterdam Avenue,** and **Broadway.** All three (and their surrounding side streets) offer just about anything your stomach might desire. Columbus Avenue has the most swank, expensive options, while Amsterdam Avenue draws a crowd that's semi-hip. On Broadway you'll discover an awful lot of nondescript diners offering cheapie Greek gyros and Italian hero sandwiches. If you're looking to dine before catching a performance at **Lincoln Center** (see Chapter 7), be warned: The restaurants in this area are pricey. After all, they're catering to people who think nothing of paying $115 for a single opera ticket.

UNDER $5 • Good Earth Natural Foods Inc. Everything here seems to contain brown rice or tabbouleh. But given the name, did you expect cubed Spam? The half-dozen tables upstairs draw a crowd that looks more familiar with fluorescent lighting and cigarettes than organic gardening and soy milk. *167 Amsterdam Ave., between W. 66th and 67th Sts., tel. 212/496–1616. Subway: 1 or 9 to W. 66th St. Other location: 1330 1st Ave., between E. 71st and 72nd Sts., Upper East Side, tel. 212/472–9055.*

Gray's Papaya. In this enlightened city the natural accompaniment to a couple of dogs is a big frothy cup of papaya juice. Total cost for two hot dogs, a drink, and a taste of a New York institution: $1.95. *2090 Broadway, at W. 72nd St., tel. 212/799–0243. Subway: 1, 2, 3, or 9 to W. 72nd St. Open 24 hrs. Other location: 402 6th Ave., at W. 8th St., West Village, tel. 212/260–3532. Cash only.*

New York City Bagels. Top your circular sandwich with a stunning variety of shmears, including chocolate chip, raisin-carrot, and three flavors of tofu cream cheese. For lunch, try a bagel with tuna salad or salami. *164 Amsterdam Ave., at W. 67th St., tel. 212/799–0700. Subway: 1 or 9 to W. 66th St. Cash only.*

Zabar's. The Zabar's cafeteria, part of the city's famous gourmet food emporium (see Markets and Specialty Shops, below), dispenses quality eats at everyman prices: Bagels with lox, salmon chowder, and sandwiches are all about $4. Counter service is quick, though you'll suffer a long line of cranky New Yorkers. *2245 Broadway, at W. 80th St., tel. 212/787–2004. Subway: 1 or 9 to W. 79th St.*

UNDER $10 • Big Nick's Burger/Pizza Joint. Customers are urged to "confide their ultimate pizza fantasy," and the menu features hard-to-swallow combinations like Gyromania (gyro strips, onions, tomatoes, and cheese), Farmer's Pizza (fresh tomatoes and hard-boiled eggs), and Reuben, Reuben (pastrami, sauerkraut, cheese, and tomato sauce). Of course, there are burgers, too. *2175 Broadway, at W. 77th St., tel. 212/362–9238 or 212/724–2010. Subway: 1 or 9 to W. 79th St. Open 24 hrs. Other location: 70 W. 71st St., at Columbus Ave., tel. 212/799–4444. Cash only.*

Café con Leche. This cheery restaurant blends Dominican, Cuban, and Spanish cuisines to produce wildly popular dishes like *arroz con pollo y chorizo* (rice, chicken, and Spanish sausage), *camarones en salsa de coco* (shrimp in coconut sauce), and *filete de pollo al ron* (sautéed chicken in spicy red sauce). Their paella features the special Spanish stew of rice, chicken, sausage, and seafood. *424 Amsterdam Ave., between W. 80th and 81st Sts., tel. 212/595–7000. Subway: 1 or 9 to W. 79th St.*

The Cottage. This ancient, dark-paneled Chinese restaurant has a loyal following among young Upper West Siders, mainly because of its reasonably priced chef's specialties and the "all the wine you can drink—free" policy at dinner. *360 Amsterdam Ave., at W. 77th St., tel. 212/595–7450. Subway: 1 or 9 to W. 79th St.*

La Caridad. The crowds keep coming back to this Creole/Chinese eatery—despite the high grease factor—because portions are huge and prices cheap. A small roasted chicken or side of beef with a mountain of fried rice is $5–$7; seafood dishes are $5 and up. Expect to wait hours for a table (or show some initiative and snag a counter seat). *2199 Broadway, at W. 78th St., tel. 212/874–2780. Subway: 1 or 9 to W. 79th St. Cash only.*

Monsoon. Join Upper West Siders casually dining on skillfully prepared Vietnamese delicacies like *bun xao* (stir-fried noodles with shrimp, egg, and chopped peanuts), spicy curries, and vegetarian dishes. Though large portions make an appetizer unnecessary, the *cha gio chay* (spring rolls) are first class. *435 Amsterdam Ave., at W. 81st St., tel. 212/580–8686. Subway: 1 or 9 to W. 79th St.*

New Yorkers have a staggering 16,000 restaurants to choose from. Do three a day and you'd finish in around 14 years—at which point you'd have to start all over, because by then, thousands of new restaurants will have flung open their doors.

UNDER $15 • Gabriela's. An authentic *taquería* cherished for its huge portions and zesty *mole* (that famous spicy chocolate sauce), Gabriela's is about as good as it gets in a town where Mexican cuisine is still angling for a foothold. The tamales are fresh and cheap (only $2.95 for chicken or pork) or get a traditional platter-size dish like the *Pozole*, or meat stew, for $7. *685 Amsterdam Ave., at W. 93rd St., tel. 212/961–0574. Subway: 1, 2, 3, or 9 to W. 96th St.*

Gennaro. Gennaro Picone, the former chef at downtown hot spot Barolo, has opened his own restaurant-in-miniature in the heart of uptown Amsterdam Avenue funk. Small it may be (tables for two are best) but the remarkable food would overshadow any setting: The grilled Italian sausage is delectable while the handmade potato gnocchi won accolades from tough critics. *665 Amsterdam Ave., at W. 92nd St., tel. 212/665–5348. Subway: 1, 2, 3, or 9 to W. 96th St.*

Josie's. This hip, earth-friendly restaurant does hearty food the organic way. We really like the sweet-potato ravioli with gulf shrimp, the grilled-chicken salad with hearts of palm and mango, and the free-range hamburger on focaccia bread. Wash it down with a kiwi-strawberry lemonade. *300 Amsterdam Ave., at W. 74th St., tel. 212/769–1212. Subway: 1, 2, 3, or 9 to W. 72nd St.*

Luzia's. Your gregarious hosts Luzia and Murray serve up filling Portuguese-influenced fare like white-bean salad, baked ham with pineapple glaze, and salmon poached in champagne, all accompanied by (heavenly) fresh Portuguese bread. The brunch menu includes omelets and Portuguese sausage. *429 Amsterdam Ave., between W. 80th and 81st Sts., tel. 212/595–2000. Subway: 1 or 9 to W. 79th St. Closed Mon.*

UNDER $20 • City Grill. As befitting the now-gentrified Upper West Side, its greasy-spoon diners of yore have been reborn as "grills" serving cholestrol-conscious burgers and sandwiches laden with arugula. So it is with this place, which made room for wok charred tuna next to Mom's Meatloaf, and scored just about every patron imaginable. The dozen salad options are unusually fresh and ample. *269 Columbus Ave., between 72nd and 73rd Sts., tel. 212/873–9400. Subway: B or C to 72nd St.*

Fujiyama Mama's. This slick, loud sushi hot spot rocks nightly with young professionals doing the groove-and-food thing while a DJ spins tunes. Sushi à la carte averages $4.25; a variety of entrées are $16–$22. *467 Columbus Ave., between W. 82nd and 83rd Sts., tel. 212/769–1144. Subway: 1 or 9 to W. 79th St.*

DINNER,
FAMILY STYLE

The family-style Italian restaurant is a special New York institution—it's the perfect setting for celebrating a birthday, graduation, suspended sentence, whatever. If you've got a big, hungry group of people who want lots of vino and garlicky food in a festive atmosphere, reserve a table at one of the following: Carmine's (2450 Broadway, between W. 90th and 91st Sts., Upper West Side, tel. 212/362–2200; 200 W. 44th St., between Broadway and 8th Ave., Midtown, tel. 212/221–3800), Sambuca (20 W. 72nd St., between Columbus Ave. and Central Park W, Upper West Side, tel. 212/787–5656), or Osso Buco (88 University Pl., between E. 11th and 12th Sts., East Village, tel. 212/645–4525).

Good Enough to Eat. On weekends, Volvo-deprived West Side couples pack this Manhattan substitute for a rustic Vermont farmhouse to feast on delicious blueberry pancakes, Mexican scrambled eggs with tortillas, or the formidable Lumber Jack special (two eggs, two strips of bacon, and two giant pancakes). Hearty dinners include roast chicken, meat loaf, or stuffed brook trout. Just up the street, **Popover Cafe** (551 Amsterdam Ave., at W. 87th St., tel. 212/595–8555) also does a mouthwatering country brunch with fantastic popovers, of course. *483 Amsterdam Ave., between W. 83rd and 84th Sts., tel. 212/496–0215. Subway: 1 or 9 to W. 86th St.*

Les Routiers. The name means "truck stop" in French, but you won't find any local teamsters inside. The new chef has shot up the usual bistro fare with some Indochine flavor, resulting in such delicacies as marinated flank steak with wasabi horseradish mashed potatoes and pan-seared sea scallops with sweet-pea sauce and curry oil. *568 Amsterdam Ave., between W. 87th and 88th Sts., tel. 212/874–2742. Subway: 1 or 9 to W. 86th St.*

Perretti Italian Cafe. Well known for its wood-oven-baked pizza, this restaurant recently upgraded from typical noodles-and-sauce Italian fare to inspired Mediterranean cuisine. Now we're talking grilled tuna with orange zest and fresh tomato or chicken breast Parmigiana baked in a fresh bread crumb crust. But nothing can replace the pizzas: Choose from six varieties ranging from $8.50 to $11.95. *270 Columbus Ave., between 72nd and 73rd Sts., tel. 212/362–3939. Subway: B or C to W. 72nd St.*

Rain. With its wicker furniture, Oriental rugs, and Asian vases, you might think you've retreated into colonial Saigon when stepping into this beautiful restaurant. This kind of attention to detail is conspicuous in such dishes as *kanom jeab,* dumplings filled with pork and shrimp, and the *pla bing,* roasted salmon with pepper and garlic served in a banana leaf. The friendly service is a bonus. *100 W. 82nd St., at Columbus Ave., tel. 212/501–0776. Subway: B or C to W. 81st St.*

COLUMBIA UNIVERSITY AND
MORNINGSIDE HEIGHTS

Morningside Heights, the neighborhood surrounding **Columbia University** and **Barnard College,** caters to students who love to eat but hate spending all their hard-earned loan money on food. You'll find dozens of cheap snack shops and 24-hour diners on **Broadway** and **Amsterdam Avenue,** between West 110th and 116th streets. When that gets boring, head north along Broadway to the blocks around 125th Street (a.k.a. Martin Luther King Jr. Boulevard) to find some terrific West African eateries.

UNDER $5 • Amir's Falafel. Everything at this relaxed student hangout is pretty darn cheap. For less than $4 you can eat your fill of falafel, stuffed grape leaves, and baba ghanoush. Sandwiches, loaded with tahini and marinated chicken or beef, are also a steal. *2911-A Broadway, between W. 113th and 114th Sts., tel. 212/749–7500. Subway: 1 or 9 to W. 116th St. Cash only.*

Bread Shop Cafe. Come to this hole-in-the-wall pizza shop–bakery to scarf down heavenly hot 'n' greasy slices or any one of the dozens of exotic delicacies like Chilean potato cake or chocolate-covered rum balls. *3139 Broadway, at La Salle St., tel. 212/666–4343. Subway: 1 or 9 to W. 125th St. Cash only.*

Tamarind Seed Health Food Store. If you don't mind being surrounded by vitamin bottles and cans of soy milk, you'll learn to love this health-food store/deli. Sandwiches (tuna, tabbouleh, soy corned beef) are $3.50, and everything at the bountiful salad bar (chow mein, tofu, pasta, plenty of raw vegetables) is $3.59 per pound. *2935 Broadway, between W. 114th and 115th Sts., tel. 212/864–3360. Subway: 1 or 9 to W. 116th St.*

UNDER $10 • Bengal Cafe. Count on this classy, little restaurant for delicious Indian dishes like shrimp curry, chicken tandoori masala, beef vindaloo, and *aloo gobi motar* (sautéed cauliflower with tomatoes and onion), accompanied by big helpings of basmati rice, cabbage, and a half dozen other relishes. *1028 Amsterdam Ave., between W. 110th and 111th Sts., tel. 212/662–7191. Subway: 1 or 9 to Cathedral Pkwy. (W. 110th St.).*

Hunan Garden. It's been in business for more than two decades, thanks largely to hungry, tightfisted Columbia students who crave giant portions of hand-pulled noodles with shredded pork, beef, or vegetables. Diversify with chef's specialties like Peking fried shrimp, orange beef, and the Royal Vegetarian platter. *2850 Broadway, between W. 110th and 111th Sts., tel. 212/866–6900. Subway: 1 or 9 to Cathedral Pkwy. (W. 110th St.).*

For those who worship at the house of Jerry (Seinfeld, not Garcia), Tom's Restaurant is a sacred place; its neon sign is featured at some point in every show.

La Rosita. This Cuban joint's breakfast specials (rice, beans, eggs, juice, and toast) are served around-the-clock, along with *chuletas* (pork chops) and Cuban sandwiches ($2.75–$3.95). The crowd, all cab drivers and unemployed intellectuals, stream in for the tasty (and cheap: $1.10) cafe con leche. *2809 Broadway, at W. 108th St., tel. 212/663–7804. Subway: 1 or 9 to Cathedral Pkwy. (W. 110th St.). Cash only.*

Obaa Koryoe. Tease your senses with African techno music and West African cuisine. The traditional chicken, tripe, fish, cow foot, oxtail, and lamb dishes come with *wachey* (rice and black-eyed peas) or *jolloff* (rice with tomato sauce); both are delicious. Recently picked as a "top ten" choice by the *Village Voice*. *3143 Broadway, at 125th St., tel. 212/316–2950. Subway: 1 or 9 to W. 125th St. Cash only.*

Riverside Church Cafeteria. Students from the Manhattan School of Music, Columbia University, and Riverside Church's own theological school flock here for the $5.50 lunch platter (chicken, meat loaf, or fish, with greens and bread or potatoes). Breakfast costs even less. *490 Riverside Dr., at W. 120th St., tel. 212/222–5900. Subway: 1 or 9 to W. 125th St. Cash only. Closed weekends.*

Selam Cafe. An addition to Harlem's burgeoning trend toward African cuisine is this simple Ethiopian restaurant. Its significant staple is the *berbere* sauce (a blend of natural herbs and spices that can be made mild or hot), which is added to lamb, chicken, or beef dishes. There's also good live jazz on Friday nights. *3161 Broadway, near W. 125th St., tel. 212/749–4449. Subway: 1 or 9 to W. 125th St.*

Tom's Restaurant. A mixed crowd of old-timers and Columbia students come here to chow on cheeseburgers ($2.75), salads ($5), triple-decker sandwiches ($5), and thick brain-freezing milk shakes. Curious *Seinfeld* fans just come in to gawk at the blown-up photo of the gang, complete with their signatures. *2880 Broadway, at W. 112th St., tel. 212/864–6137. Subway: 1 or 9 to Cathedral Pkwy. (W. 110th St.). Open Thurs.–Sat. 24 hrs. Cash only.*

UNDER $15 • The Mill. It's the side of *kimchee* (spicy pickled cabbage and hot pepper sauce) that adds a little peppery tingle to Korean dishes like *dak bokum* (stir-fried chicken), *haemul dolsott bibimbob* (seafood and rice in hot earthen bowl), and *bulgogi* (barbecued beef). The decor is upscale and understated; you're more likely to see a Ph.D. holder here than a starving student. *2895 Broadway, between W. 112th and 113th Sts., tel. 212/666–7653. Subway: 1 or 9 to Cathedral Pkwy. (W. 110th St.).*

HARLEM

You'll find East African, West African, Creole, Caribbean, and Southern restaurants aplenty along Harlem's main commercial arteries: **Malcolm X Boulevard** (Lenox Avenue), **Adam Clayton Powell Jr. Boulevard** (7th Avenue), **Martin Luther King Jr. Boulevard** (125th Street), and **138th Street.** Many of the West African restaurants double as community centers for African immigrants—you can enjoy a really good meal while soaking up a little foreign culture. In **East Harlem** there are dozens of Latino restaurants on Lexington Avenue between East 116th and 125th streets that serve pupusas and tacos for a few bucks apiece. As a tourist, you'll have no problem visiting Harlem or East Harlem during the day. At night use caution and stay on main thoroughfares or take a cab.

UNDER $5 • Joseph's Food Basket. Everything here is free of additives, preservatives, and chemicals (and sometimes free of dairy, wheat, and cholesterol). Breakfast is an unbelievable $2.50, while lasagna, stir-fried vegetables, macaroni pie, and savory stews are all $1.50–$3. There's also a wide selection of gourmet coffees and fresh organic juices. *471 Malcolm X Blvd., between W. 133rd and 134th Sts., tel. 212/368–7663. Subway: 2 or 3 to W. 135th St. Cash only. Closed Sun.*

UNDER $10 • Darou Minan. The only conversation you'll hear in English at this friendly Senegalese restaurant will probably be your own. For $5–$6 fill up on spicy entrées like *yassa ganaar* (lemon chicken with rice), vegetarian *mafe* (vegetables in peanut sauce), or *thiebou dieun* (stewed fish with rice and vegetables in tomato sauce). For dessert go with the *tiacri* (sour cream, couscous, and milk). *1943 Adam Clayton Powell Jr. Blvd., between W. 117th and 118th Sts., tel. 212/665–4711. Subway: 2 or 3 to W. 116th St. Open 24 hrs. Cash only.*

Ethel's Southern Quarters (ESQ). Hospitable Ethel and her daughters really know how to whip up superb home-cooked catfish and shrimp, fried chicken, and buffalo wings and ribs. For breakfast try a gut-buster of bacon, eggs, grits, and home fries for only $3. *747 St. Nicholas Ave., between W. 147th and 148th Sts., tel. 212/694–1686. Subway: A, B, C, or D to W. 145th St. Cash only. Closed Mon.*

Mandingo Restaurant. Mandingo's easygoing waitstaff serves traditional West African dishes by night and soul food by day. For dinner try the palm oil sauce with rice or lamb sauce with mashed yams. For lunch, choose between oxtail soup and smothered chicken. *353 Malcolm X Blvd., between W. 127th and 128th Sts., tel. 212/932–2524. Subway: 2 or 3 to W. 125th St.*

The Reliable. This ramshackle Sugar Hill favorite serves some fine, authentic Southern food: smothered chicken, barbecued ribs, sweet curried chicken, and salmon cakes, served with tasty cooked greens and corn bread. Next door and under the same ownership, **Copeland's** (547 W. 145th St., tel. 212/234–2356) is a bit more upscale, with great Southern breakfasts and brunch. *547 W. 145th St., between Broadway and Amsterdam Ave., tel. 212/234–2357. Subway: 1 or 9 to W. 145th St. Cash only.*

Singleton's Bar-B-Que. Singleton's claims to have the only brick-oven barbecue in the entire city, and the product is outstanding soul food. Try the hickory-smoked chicken slathered with barbecue sauce and paired with collard greens or yams. The $5 breakfast includes omelets, pancakes, and plenty of meat. *525 Malcolm X Blvd., between W. 136 and 137th Sts., tel. 212/694–9442. Subway: 2 or 3 to W. 135th St. Cash only.*

UNDER $15 • Sylvia's. The most famous soul-food restaurant in New York remains popular with locals, despite having fed celebs like Dan "potatoe" Quayle. Dinner favorites are deep-fried fish, smothered steak, and barbecued ribs. On Sunday there's a gospel brunch with live music. Look for matronly Sylvia presiding over the two large dining rooms and outdoor seating area. *328 Malcolm X Blvd., at W. 126th St., tel. 212/996–0660. Subway: 2 or 3 to W. 125th St.*

WASHINGTON HEIGHTS

Washington Heights, at the very northern tip of Manhattan, is so far from most tourist attractions that you wouldn't want to make the trip just to get something to eat. But if you're in the neighborhood you can enjoy kosher bagels and lox, Salvadoran fried plantains, or a cup of syrupy Cuban coffee—at prices far lower than in the rest of Manhattan. The main thoroughfares—**St. Nicholas Avenue** and **Broadway**—are chockablock full of street carts and cheap, divey eateries offering Dominican, Salvadoran, Cuban, and other Latin fare. (It helps if you speak Spanish, though you'll find most places serve familiar stuff like tostadas and burritos. And you can always point.) The blocks around **Yeshiva University** (Audubon Ave., near 186th St.) cater to the Jewish student population with dozens of kosher restaurants. Another cluster of diners and bodegas lies a few blocks from **Fort Tryon Park,** around 204th Street. Remember, this isn't the most heavily touristed of neighborhoods, so use your street smarts and don't wander the streets alone after dark.

UNDER $10 • La Cabaña Salvadoreña. At $1.25 apiece, it's easy to fill up on à la carte Salvadoran snacks like *pupusas con queso* (fried tortillas, folded and filled with cheese), enchiladas, and tacos. Or get a combination plate of *carne asada* (grilled steak) or *chuletas de cerdo* (pork chops); both come with fries or rice and beans. *4384 Broadway, at W. 187th St., tel. 212/928–7872. Subway: A to W. 181st St. Cash only.*

Caridad IV Restaurant. If you're a monolingual American, this place can be bewilderingly foreign; the waitstaff speaks *solamente español*. It's worth bridging the language barrier, though, because the food is excellent, especially the paella marinera ($32.95 for two), *filete pescado* (fried fish with bananas), and omelets. The coffee, brewed Latin American–style, is strong enough to melt your spoon. *554 W. 181st St., between St. Nicholas and Audubon Aves., tel. 212/927–9729. Subway: 1 or 9 to W. 181st St. Open 24 hrs. Cash only.*

Wilson's Bakery and Restaurant. Wilson's Bakery began serving soul and diner food when *Howdy Doody* was a cool new TV show. Nearly 40 years later, breakfast still means eggs any style plus your choice of ham, bacon, sausage, smothered pork chops, beef bologna, grits, pancakes, and french toast. Weekend brunch is popular with neighborhood churchgoers, and seats get scarce after 11 AM. *1980 Amsterdam Ave., at W. 158th St., tel. 212/923–9821. Subway: A, B, or C to W. 155th St. Cash only.*

UPPER EAST SIDE

Upper East Siders have a lot of money to blow on grub, and it shows. For what you'd pay to eat in one of the schmancy restaurants lining 5th and Madison avenues (where, naturally, all the museums are), you could probably buy one of the smaller OPEC countries. That said, there are plenty of affordable options east of Lexington Avenue, along **3rd Avenue** and **2nd Avenue**.

If you don't want to be branded a tourist in Washington Heights, eat your Salvadoran "pupusas" (fried, filled tortillas) with your hands.

UNDER $5 • Soup Burg. A few mirror tricks and a long counter constitute this tiny coffee shop, the quintessential greasy spoon. Order a fat chunk of cow meat with fries (the beef burger de luxe) and an old-fashioned milk shake and don't worry about tomorrow. *1150 Lexington Ave., between E. 79th and 80th Sts., tel. 212/737–0095. Subway: 6 to E. 77th St. Cash only.*

UNDER $10 • Candle Cafe. Earth-friendly dining (at least an upscale version of it) means low-on-the-food-chain vegetarian and macrobiotic dishes. If you need a roughage boost, try a Harvest Salad (romaine lettuce, vegetables, sprouts, and sesame seeds). Wash it down with a glass of wheat-grass juice or some organic coffee. *1307 3rd Ave., between E. 74th and 75th Sts., tel. 212/472–0970. Subway: 6 to E. 77th St.*

EJ's Luncheonette. Good comfort food beckons at this amped-up '90s diner, where the young and the restless love to snuggle into its leather booths, especially for weekend brunch. Flapjacks and waffles are done 14 ways, and the milk shakes are the good, old-fashioned kind. Expect a wait. *1271 3rd Ave., at E. 73rd St., tel. 212/472–0600. Subway: 6 to E. 77th St. Other location: 447 Amsterdam Ave., between W. 81st and 82nd Sts., Upper West Side, tel. 212/873–3444.*

El Pollo. Head here for killer Peruvian-style chicken—grilled, roasted, on a sandwich, or in a mammoth mixed vegetable salad—accompanied by potatoes or fried plantains. Don't let the tiny storefront awning fool you: Inside it's warm and inviting, with brick walls and colorful oil paintings of folk scenes. Pick up a six-pack beforehand at New York Beverage Wholesale, just up the road (428 E. 91st St., tel. 212/831–4000). *1746 1st Ave., between E. 90th and 91st Sts., tel. 212/996–7810. Subway: 4, 5, or 6 to E. 86th St. BYOB.*

Patsy's Pizzeria. The Upper East Side branch of this classic Manhattan pizzeria is much more than a place to grab a slice. Sit at the spiffy polished-wood booths and enjoy some of the city's best brick-oven-fired pizzas, along with massive family-size salads packed with everything but the kitchen sink. *1312 2nd Ave., tel. 212/639–1000. Subway: 6 to E. 68th St. Other locations: 61 W. 74th St., Upper West Side, tel. 212/579–3000; 509 3rd Ave., Upper East Side, tel. 212/689–7500; 67 University Pl., East Village, tel. 212/533–3500.*

Pintaile's Pizza. If you like designer pizza, this is the place for you. No heavy sauce, no goopy cheese—just paper-thin crust topped with fresh ingredients. Go the traditional route, with tomatoes and mozzarella, try Cajun spice pizza (with sausage), shiitake-mushroom, or pesto. *1443 York Ave., between 76th and 77th Sts., tel. 212/717–4990. Subway: 6 to E. 77th St. 1577 York Ave., between 84th and 85th Sts., tel. 212/396–3479. Subway: 4, 5, or 6 to E. 86th St. 26 E. 91st St., between 5th and Madison Aves., tel. 212/722–1967. Subway: 4, 5, or 6 to E. 96th St.*

Samalita's. There's nothing factorylike about this colorful Cal-Mex hole-in-the-wall squeezed among the Upper East Side's chichi restaurants. The soft tacos and burritos are subtly spiced, and so is the decor. *1429 3rd Ave., between E. 80th and 81st Sts., tel. 212/737–5070. Subway: 6 to E. 77th St. Cash only.*

PARK IT

On a sunny day, the best place to eat lunch in midtown Manhattan is in beautiful Bryant Park (see Parks and Gardens in Chapter 2). The charming folding chairs sprinkled across its startlingly green, flower-trimmed lawn are free for you to use—if you can snag a few before legions of pallid office types monopolize them. It also frequently hosts free noontime concerts, poetry readings, and comedy performances.

Taco Taco. One of the few outposts of authentic Mexican food in Manhattan, this festive little taquería is decked out with piñatas and candles everywhere. As the name implies, soft tacos are the specialty: Try a few different kinds, since they're less than $3. Or go for a house special—pork loin with smoked jalapeños and cabbage, or shrimp marinated in garlic and lemon heaped with flavorful beans and rice. *1726 2nd Ave., between E. 89th and 90th Sts., tel. 212/289–8226. Subway: 4, 5, or 6 to E. 86th St. Cash only.*

UNDER $15 • Bangkok House. Bring someone special to swoon over at this quiet Thai restaurant— the lighting is soft and the music exotic. The pad thai and other noodle dishes are tasty. Order a fruit cocktail and you'll get a little paper umbrella in your glass. *1485 1st Ave., between E. 77th and 78th Sts., tel. 212/249–5700. Subway: 6 to E. 77th St.*

Barking Dog Luncheonette. The snazzy tiled dog bar (filled with water) out front is only a precursor to what lies inside. At this retro diner with a twist, the waitstaff wears shirts that say "Sit. Stay." The menu is as silly: There are hefty and inventive salads and sandwiches, and classic hot plates with gussied-up gourmet touches—try Atlantic salmon with black-sesame crust. *1678 3rd Ave., at E. 94th St., tel. 212/831–1800. Subway: 4, 5, or 6 to E. 96th St. Cash only.*

Caffé Buon Gusto. Head and shoulders above the other trattorias on the Upper East Side, this unpretentious place on a cheerful little side street is always crowded at night and on weekends. Warm foccacia to dip in pepper-infused olive oil starts your meal of homemade pastas and nightly specials like swordfish livornese (with black olives and tomatoes). *236 E. 77th St., between 2nd and 3rd Aves., tel. 212/535–6884. Subway: 6 to 77th St. Cash only.*

Eli's Vinegar Factory. Though the Vinegar Factory is notoriously expensive, it's worth making the trip here to check out what some think is New York's highest-quality market, housed in what was once a vinegar factory. Best of all, on weekends only, you can feast on a huge selection of the store's best prepared dishes—all you can eat for less than $15—while peering down at the shoppers. *431 E. 91st St., at York Ave., tel. 212/987–0885. Subway: 4, 5, or 6 to E. 86th or 96th St. No dinner. Closed weekdays.*

Good Health Cafe. If you don't mind eating in a health-food store, you'll get a bang for your buck here— and a healthy one at that. If it's available, get the bento box special: $13.50 for salmon teriyaki (or chicken or shrimp) with cold soba noodles, carrot salad, and various other side dishes arranged neatly in a compartmentalized box. For weekend brunch (11–4), there are wild-rice pancakes, blue-corn waffles, and hefty vegetarian omelets. And there's a juice bar to boot. *324 E. 86th St., between 1st and 2nd Aves., tel. 212/439–9680. Subway: 4, 5, or 6 to E. 86th St.*

MIDTOWN WEST OF 5TH AVENUE

West of 5th Avenue, Midtown sometimes seems as charmless as an armpit. This is where cabs pile up, where skyscrapers tower, and where hundreds of hole-in-the-wall diners and delis feed working stiffs as cheaply and unoriginally as possible. Though it's a bit gritty, the neighborhood of **Hell's Kitchen** is where you should go to seek relief: 9th Avenue in the 40s and 50s is loaded with ethnic restaurants offering some of the cheapest meals in Manhattan. One weekend every May, Hell's Kitchen is also home to an **International Food Festival** (*see* When to Go *in* Chapter 1). **West 32nd Street** between 5th Avenue and Broadway is sometimes referred to as "Korean Restaurant Row," thanks to its cheap Korean and Japanese diners: Try **Won Jo** (23 W. 32nd St., between Broadway and 6th Ave., tel. 212/695–5815), open 24 hours. **West 46th Street** around Broadway boasts a cluster of Brazilian restaurants, cafés, and markets.

Sadly, the **Theater District** is heavy on tourist traps boasting overpriced and often mediocre food. Consider this: Do you really want to blow $20 or more on a substandard pre-theater dinner, especially if you've already paid $35 for restricted-view seats? **Virgil's Real BBQ** (152 W. 44th St., between Broadway and 6th Ave., tel. 212/921–9494) or the Midtown branch of **Carmine's** (*see box* Dinner, Family Style, *above*) aren't particularly cheap, but the food at both is good and the size of the entrées obscene. The district's ritzy **Restaurant Row**—West 46th Street between 8th and 9th avenues—gets a lot of hoopla, and you can eat here without breaking the bank, particularly at a place like tiny **Hourglass Tavern** (373 W. 46th St., tel. 212/265–2060). Its prix-fixe meals are $12.75, after your table's 59-minute hourglass has run out, you are asked to move on.

Finally, there's **West 57th Street** between 5th and 8th avenues. Over the last few years it's undergone a Kafkaesque transmogrification—from plain ol' thoroughfare to one embraced by Disney and bland theme restaurants. As a tourist you may feel obliged to check it out, although real New Yorkers prefer to ignore **Planet Hollywood** (140 W. 57th St., tel. 212/333–7827), **Hard Rock Cafe** (221 W. 57th St., tel. 212/459–9320), **Jekyll and Hyde Club** (1409 6th Ave., at W. 57th St., tel. 212/541–9505), **Motown Cafe** (104 W. 57th St., tel. 212/581–8030), **Brooklyn Diner U.S.A.** (212 W. 57th St., tel. 212/581–8900), and **Harley-Davidson Cafe** (1370 6th Ave., at W. 56th St., tel. 212/245–6000). The point to all these places is never the food (typically $7–$20), but rather the stuff on the walls. Jekyll and Hyde has an electronically animated Great Sphinx and flapping gargoyles, Motown Cafe has its

What do Madonna and Martha Stewart have in common? They both love cakes from the Cupcake Cafe.

Motown Moments quartet singing Four Tops and Temptations songs, while Harley-Davidson has a revvable motorcycle upon which you can get your picture taken ($7). And though it's not exactly on 57th Street, it's hard to ignore the **Fashion Cafe** (51 Rockefeller Center, W. 51st St., between 5th and 6th Aves., tel. 212/765–3131), owned in part by supermodels Naomi Campbell, Claudia Schiffer, and Elle Macpherson.

UNDER $5 • Manganaro's Hero-Boy. Come for fast-food Italian dishes, most notably the biggest and best sub sandwiches in the entire city. *492 9th Ave., between W. 37th and 38th Sts., tel. 212/947–7325. Subway: A, C, or E to W. 34th St. (Penn Station).*

Tachigui-Soba. A large Japanese lantern hangs in front of this Times Square nosh spot, the only indication of the cheap cafeteria-style food that lies within (there's no sign in English). Chicken tempura is $3, chicken teriyaki $4, and *udon* and *soba* soups $3–$5.50. Seating is upstairs in a zero-decor room. *732 7th Ave., between W. 48th and 49th Sts., tel. 212/265–8181. Subway: N or R to W. 49th St.; also 1 or 9 to W. 50th St. Cash only.*

UNDER $10 • Chantale's Cajun Kitchen. Looking weirdly out of place (it's next door to the Port Authority Bus Terminal), this homey New Orleans eatery serves authentic Cajun and Creole dishes as well as meal-size salads. The house special, Chantale's Gumbo, is a stew of shrimp, sausage, scallops, fish, and chicken served in small and large portions. *510 9th Ave., between W. 38th and 39th Sts., tel. 212/967–2623. Subway: A, C, or E to W. 42nd St. (Port Authority). Cash only. Closed Sun.*

Cupcake Cafe. The Cupcake seems trapped in one of those sleepy Twilight Zones where things never seem to age, where pert wanna-be actresses pick daintily at their sandwiches, and where Billie Holiday drifts from the scratchy stereo. Indulge in lusciously frosted baked goods or fill up on decent dinner fare. *522 9th Ave., at W. 39th St., tel. 212/465–1530. Subway: A, C, or E to W. 42nd St. (Port Authority). Cash only.*

Sapporo. At Sapporo, a big bowl of *hiyashi chuka* (cold noodle soup) is perfect on hot summer days. Or try any of the filling ramen noodle and teriyaki dishes that keep this place packed with a mostly Japanese clientele. *152 W. 49th St., between 6th and 7th Aves., tel. 212/869–8972. Subway: N or R to W. 49th St.; also B, D, F, or Q to Rockefeller Center (W. 47th–50th Sts.). Cash only.*

Soul Fixin's. This small restaurant cranks out an enormous, outstanding Country Lunch: your choice of barbecued, fried, baked, or smothered chicken; barbecued spare ribs or fried whiting fish; plus corn bread and two side dishes, such as candied yams or black-eyed peas. Vegetarians can get four meatless side dishes. *371 W. 34th St., near 9th Ave., tel. 212/736–1345. Subway: A, C, or E to Penn Station (W. 34th St.). Cash only. Closed weekends.*

PRIX-FIXE MADNESS

When you're on a shoestring budget, a $70 meal at a world-class restaurant might seem like a sick joke. Happily, impoverished gourmets can score big-time at more than 100 of New York's top restaurants during the annual New York Restaurant Week (mid-June). It all started with $19.92 meals offered during the 1992 Democratic National Convention, which the city hosted. This year, participating restaurants will sell prix-fixe lunches for $19.98—still a bang-up deal. Some restaurants now offer these prices through Labor Day, or even year-round. Past participants have included such way-outta-your-league joints as Lutèce, the Rainbow Room, and the Four Seasons; for more info, check the city's weekly magazines in June. And make reservations far in advance.

Soup Kitchen International. Soup Man Al Yeganeh, who came to the States to study physics, probably never could have guessed that Jerry Seinfeld would be his rocket ride to fame. New Yorkers and tourists alike now line up willingly for a take-out taste (small $6, large $8, or extra large $13) of his excellent vegetable, bean, nut, seafood, or meat soups (about 15 daily varieties, both hot and cold). If you hope to get bread and fruit with your seafood bisque, you've gotta move: Know what you want (ask no questions and speak quickly) and have your money ready. Don't loiter and *don't* call him the Soup Nazi. *259-A W. 55th St., near 8th Ave., tel. 212/757–7730. Subway: A, C, D, or 1 to 59th St./Columbus Circle; also C or E to 50th St. Cash only. Closed Sun.*

Westside Cottage II. The Westside Cottage's menu could be considered the Good Book of Asian food, because it lists more than 200 Hunan, Szechuan, and Cantonese dishes. On top of this are about 50 three-course lunch specials and, at dinner, several dozen chef's specials. *689 9th Ave., between W. 47th and 48th Sts., tel. 212/245–0800. Subway: C or E to W. 50th St.*

UNDER $15 • Arroz y Feijão. White or yellow rice? Black or red beans? Once you've decided, sit back and enjoy a Brazilian feast. Try *feijoada*, a stew of black beans, pork loin, sausage, bacon, and spare ribs, or the *peixe amazonas*, a fish stew with onions, tomatoes, green peppers, and coconut milk. For dessert, the Romeo & Juliet (guava paste and cheese) is a mere $2.50. *744 9th Ave., between W. 50th and 51st Sts., tel. 212/265–4444. Subway: C or E to W. 50th St.*

MIDTOWN EAST OF 5TH AVENUE

Unless you have an AmEx Corporate Card, the food situation is fairly grim east of 5th Avenue. Most of Midtown East is prime big-business country, and nearly all its restaurants are slavishly devoted to the power lunch. On the upside, even the "nice" restaurants offer cheap weekday lunch specials—a good way to sample some of Manhattan's finer eateries without paying $45 for a dinner entrée. If you've absolutely gotta eat in Midtown East, check out the row of Indian and Pakistani restaurants along **Lexington Avenue** between East 27th and 28th streets. Though it's not as vibrant as the East Village's Little India (*see below*), you should be able to suss out a few all-you-can-eat buffets.

UNDER $5 • Fresco Tortilla Grill. Despite its ghastly resemblance to Mickey D's, this place produces fresh, wholesome, tasty Cal-Mex food. Big burritos in homemade tortillas, tostada salads, and steak tacos are all fresh and free of nasty additives. *546 3rd Ave., near E. 36th St., tel. 212/685–3886. Subway: 6 to E. 33rd St. Cash only.*

UNDER $10 • Madras Mahal. A letter posted outside this kosher and 100% vegetarian Indian restaurant—part of Lexington Avenue's "Little India"—informs doubting customers that VEGETABLES ARE CLEANED UNDER SUPERVISION. NO BUGS OR INSECTS. How reassuring. Curries and such are, but the real deal is the all-you-can-eat lunch ($7). *104 Lexington Ave., between E. 27th and 28th Sts., tel. 212/684–4010. Subway: 6 to E. 28th St.*

Sam's Noodle Shop & Grill Bar. Attitude and atmosphere are minimal here; at least you get plenty of well-priced food like Mandarin noodle soups and sizzling platters like pan-fried tofu with vegetables. You can also pick your own vegetables, meat, or seafood to skewer and grill. *411 3rd Ave., at E. 29th St., tel. 212/213–2288. Subway: 6 to E. 28th St.*

UNDER $15 • Tivoli. Stolid and weathered, the Tivoli looks like it's been around for centuries. In reality, it's no older than Donald Trump, with typical coffee-shop fare (sandwiches, salads, and pastas) for both lunch and dinner. *515 3rd Ave., between E. 34th and 35th Sts., tel. 212/532–3300. Subway: 6 to E. 33rd St.*

CHELSEA

Chelsea was not long ago a warehouse wasteland; nowadays it's truly trendy, rivaling the East Village as a magnet for hip twentysomethings and the hangout of choice among gays and lesbians. As a result, **8th Avenue,** between West 30th and 14th streets, and **West 18th Street,** between 6th and 9th avenues, are crammed with stylish bistros, cafés, revamped diners, natural-food restaurants, bakeries, and juice bars. A good morning jumping-off place is the very inexpensive and friendly **Taylor's** (228 W. 18th St., between 7th and 8th Aves., tel. 212/378–2895; West and East Village branches: 523 Hudson St., between W. 10th and Charles Sts., tel. 212/378–2890; 175 2nd Ave., between E. 11th and 12th Sts., tel. 212/674–9501)—scope out the scene from the front porch while enjoying a mouth-watering muffin or donut, three dozen types of salads, or sandwiches. This is also the only living home (other than yours) of giant, jawbreaking, buttery Rice Krispie/marshmallow "treats."

UNDER $10 • Bendix Diner. The menu here is exotic, to say the least, blending American comfort food with Thai dishes. Translation: You can have meat loaf while your date chows on *yaki meshi* (stir-fried chicken teriyaki with soybean sprouts, broccoli, zucchini, and brown rice). The crowd is hip and gay, the servings are huge, and the music kicks. The East Village location needs work on its hygiene. *219 8th Ave., at W. 21st St., tel. 212/366–0560. Subway: C or E to W. 23rd St. BYOB. New Bendix Diner, with the same menu: 167 1st Ave., between E. 10th and 11th Sts., West Village, tel. 212/260–4220.*

Uncle Mo's. A family of Sasquatches could feed for a week on one of Uncle Mo's monstrous burritos, stuffed with *barbacoa* (slow-cooked shredded beef), *pollo verde* (chicken in a mild green chile sauce), or *carne asada* (marinated steak). Less massive but still filling are the tacos and quesadillas. This is best for a late lunch, when you're famished: In friendly weather, do it take-out and skibble over to Union Square to dine on a bench. *14 W. 19th St., between 5th and 6th Aves., tel. 212/727–9400. Subway: F to W. 23rd St.; also N or R to W. 23rd St. Cash only. Closed Sun.*

UNDER $15 • Regional Thai Taste. The cool thing about this funky Thai joint is that instead of serving the same old pad thai, it explores recipes from around the country: Try *kow pad rot fie* (fried rice with shrimp and chicken), traditionally sold on Thai trains; *yum ta lay* (marinated seafood salad), from the island of Phuket; or the Bangkok favorite *kow mun som tum* (shredded beef with coconut rice and green papaya). Big silly drinks, too. Prices are $2–$4 cheaper before 4 PM. *208 7th Ave., at W. 22nd St., tel. 212/807–9872. Subway: 1 or 9 to W. 23rd St.*

UNDER $20 • Mesa Grill. Not to be missed, though you can easily drop more than $20. But chef Bobby Flay remains on the cutting edge of American cooking, and you'll find out exactly why. The food can be spicy, but never overwhelmingly so. Whatever you do, get that day's special quesadilla, and then dive in virtually to rediscover seafood. And these really are the best margaritas in town. *102 5th Ave., between W. 15th and 16th Sts., tel. 212/807–7400. Subway: 4, 5, 6, N, or R to Union Sq.*

Trois Canards. Charming, comfortably elegant, and relaxingly eccentric, this scrupulous bistro does some of the best duck you'll find at the moment: Each part of the fresh halved duck is prepared according to its precise needs. Homemade ravioli is smashing, service is gracious, desserts leave you panting. *184 8th Ave., between W. 19th and 20th Sts., tel. 212/929–4320. Subway: A, C, or E to 14th St.; also 1 to 18th St.*

GRAMERCY AND UNION SQUARE

Some of New York's finest five-star restaurants are tucked between the million-dollar town houses that line the blocks surrounding Gramercy Park and Union Square. If you have money to burn, get thee to the enormously and justifiably popular **Union Square Cafe** or **Gramercy Tavern** (*see box* Serious Splurges, *below*), which enjoy the same ownership and management. Both are truly New York experiences. Don't have the cash? Then meander over to the amiable **Union Square Greenmarket** (*see* Greenmarkets, *below*), a great place to pick up snacks and fresh produce—delightfully packed on summer and fall Saturdays.

Your best bet for cheap eats is along **3rd Avenue,** lined with no-frills ethnic restaurants and pubs, pizzerias, bagel shops, and delis. **Irving Place** between East 19th and 14th streets is lined with moderately priced restaurants and sweet shops like **Mio Pane, Mio Dulce Bakery** (77 Irving Pl., at 19th St., tel. 212/677–1905). **Park Avenue South** in the East 20s and 30s has a hyperactive dinner scene. The hot spots of the moment include **Patria** (250 Park Ave. S, at E. 20th St., tel. 212/777–6211), which brandishes Miami/Cuban cuisine at its very finest and most whimsical, and **Lemon** (230 Park Ave. S, between E. 18th and 19th Sts., tel. 212/614–1200), which boasts some of the hottest looking people on the strip, possibly because its investors include the Ford modeling agency and David Lee Roth.

UNDER $5 • City Bakery. In this very high-tech, minimalist space, you'll encounter simply the best croissants, lemon tarts, hot chocolate (in season), gazpacho (likewise), and lemonade (ditto) you'll find. The proprietor, Maury Rubin, is the author of the all-important *Book of Tarts,* and he's usually on hand to autograph a copy for you, when he isn't too busy flaming the tops of his crème brûlée tartelettes. Savvy New Yorkers come here often, as well they should. *22 E. 17th St., between 5th Ave. and Broadway, tel. 212/366–1414. Subway: L, N, R, 4, 5, or 6 to Union Sq. Closed Sun.*

Ess-a-Bagel. Pretty much everyone agrees that these are the best bagels in Manhattan—fighting words, to be sure, but the lines at peak hours attest. Just ask for a shmear of cream cheese on whatever bulging bagel is freshest, and you'll never really be the same. Believe it. Then get back on line and try an onion bagel with cream cheese and Nova. The accommodations are slightly grubby, but the bagels are so good you wouldn't mind eating them sitting outside on the curb. *359 1st Ave., between E. 20th and 21st Sts., tel. 212/260–2252. Subway: 6 to 23rd St. Other location: 831 3rd Ave., between 50th and 51st Sts., Midtown East, tel. 212/980–1010.*

UNDER $10 • America. Been inside Madison Square Garden yet? This noisy restaurant seems just as vast, and the food is better (but no Knicks). Dishes are painstakingly regional, and named accordingly. Try one of 25 salads—we like the Omaha, which comes with warm bacon and spinach—or one of about 20 sandwiches; our fave is the Berkeley, with avocado, sprouts, and cucumber. *9 E. 18th St., between 5th Ave. and Broadway, tel. 212/505–2110. Subway: L, N, R, 4, 5, or 6 to Union Sq.*

Friend of a Farmer. New Yorkers willingly endure Friend of a Farmer's ultra-cute gingerbread decor to indulge their hankerings for country cooking (even though they can look unusually sheepish doing so). Entrées are steamed or broiled, never fried. Menu highlights include the old-fashioned chicken pot pie and the hefty Farmer's Sandwich. *77 Irving Pl., between E. 18th and 19th Sts., tel. 212/477–2188. Subway: L, N, R, 4, 5, or 6 to Union Sq.*

Galaxy. This smallish, loopy, friendly place with its throwback (1967) decor and eclectic menu will win you over the moment you taste Deb Stanton's new, utterly unpretentious take on fusion cuisine, always served with a smile. Thai'd Pizza is actually a huge trisected handroll of grilled chicken, turkey bacon, mozzarella, Thai peanut paste, and tomatoes that will leave you swooning. She's also found several ways to cook with, well, hemp—from hemp-blackened catfish to hemp-crusted peach cobbler. You simply won't find anyplace like this anywhere else. Nothing on the menu is over $9.95, and most of the offerings are a good deal cheaper. Hit it! *15 Irving Pl., corner of E. 15th St., tel. 212/777–3631. Subway: L, N, R, 4, 5, or 6 to Union Sq.*

Heartland Brewery. Heartland is one of the city's most popular microbreweries, which means it's the latest watering hole for big, meaty Wall Street guys and their pulchritudinous ilk. There are six microbrews ($4.25 per pint) on tap and a menu full of inventive pub grub, especially an eight-item "pu-pu platter" for two that features jalapeño poppers, buffalo wings, and enough other beerish flotsam and jetsam to keep you happy for about 45 minutes. *35 Union Sq. W, between E. 16th and 17th Sts., tel. 212/645–3400. Subway: L, N, R, 4, 5, or 6 to Union Sq.*

Old Town Bar. A zillion people—from cops to picky newspaper food critics to David Letterman—claim that this 1892 saloon serves some of the best burgers in the city. Just beware the weekend crowds. Salads and fancy grilled sandwiches are about $7. *45 E. 18th St., between Broadway and Park Ave. S, tel. 212/529–6732. Subway: L, N, R, 4, 5, or 6 to Union Sq.*

Pete's Tavern. (*see above*) A zillion other people—from tipsy Irish regulars to families of ten to O. Henry, who wrote one of his most famous stories here, no doubt with the hiccups—claim that this even older saloon serves the best burgers in town. There are also nightly special offerings, and prime rib night (currently Tuesday) will quicken your heartbeat sure, and put quite a bounce in your step. *129 E. 18th St., at Irving Pl., tel. 212/473–7676. Subway: L, N, R, 4, 5, or 6 to Union Sq.*

UNDER $15 • Chat 'n' Chew. Simply put: sassy home cookin' with no sense of propriety. Gorge yourself on Roseanne-size portions of macaroni and cheese "with the crunchy top," Not Your Mother's Meatloaf, or Thanksgiving on a Roll (roast turkey, stuffing, cranberry sauce, and mayo on ciabatta bread). And enjoy that trailer-park milieu. *10 E. 16th St., between 5th Ave. and Union Sq. W, tel. 212/243–1616. Subway: L, N, R, 4, 5, or 6 to Union Sq.*

Park Avalon. From the outside, the Avalon looks like all the other overpriced restaurants on Park Avenue South. Happily, its New American/Mediterranean cuisine is surprisingly affordable. And the startlingly beautiful clientele is included at no extra charge. *225 Park Ave. S, between E. 18th and 19th Sts., tel. 212/533–2500. Subway: L, N, R, 4, 5, or 6 to Union Sq.*

Zen Palate. You're more likely to see a banker than a Buddhist in this starkly beautiful restaurant. The tone is set with Asian-influenced, strictly vegetarian dishes like the Oceanic Treasure (veggie "squid" sautéed with peppers), Harvest Delight (vegetables in sesame sauce), and Sweet and Sour Sensation (fried soy protein and steamed broccoli). Note that there is a café on the street level, and a fancier dining room upstairs (enter on E. 16th Street). *34 Union Sq. E, at E. 16th St., tel. 212/614–9345. Subway: L, N, R, 4, 5, or 6 to Union Sq. BYOB. Other locations: 663 9th Ave., at W. 46th St., Midtown West, tel. 212/582–1669; 2170 Broadway, between W. 76th and 77th Sts., Upper West Side, tel. 212/501–7768.*

> *Add a Ted Danson look-alike to the Old Town Bar and you'd have "Cheers."*

WEST VILLAGE

The restaurants on the West Village's narrow tree-lined streets can be so tiny that their tables often spill onto sidewalks or into tranquil back gardens. If you think that's romantic, you're absolutely right. While the scene in the West Village proper has gotten a bit stale in recent years (gays prefer Chelsea, and hipsters have drifted over to the East Village), the neighborhood has plenty of reasonably priced options, especially on noisy **6th Avenue** and **7th Avenue South.** The cheapest eats, though, tend to be on the blocks around **New York University (NYU),** and in regions further east. If you want "charming" and "romantic," try wandering along **West 4th Street, Bleecker Street,** or **Greenwich Avenue.** To sample a few of the cool crowd's hangouts, check out the **meat-packing district,** way off to the west by the Hudson River. If you find you need an oasis, you can linger at **Anglers and Writers** (420 Hudson St., at St. Luke's Pl., tel. 212/675–0810). Also, on **Washington Street,** south of West 12th Street, trendy bistros exist alongside refrigerated meat lockers. This can be a fairly rough area, so use caution at night.

UNDER $10 • Aggie's and **Aggie's Too.** The great Aggie herself says the AA fresh eggs are the main reason why breakfasts taste so good at this hip double-diner. Order those unbelievably wonderful eggs (and any other breakfast food) daily until 3 PM. Or maybe you'd like one of the scrumptious sandwiches. Or, well, Aggie has something for everyone, you'll see. *146 W. Houston St., at MacDougal St., tel. 212/673–8994. Subway: 1 or 9 to Houston St.; also C or E to Spring St. Cash only.*

Benny's Burritos. Hip Benny's makes Cal-Mex tacos, enchiladas, and, above all, burritos the size of a beefy infant's arm. If you must, you can request non-dairy tofu sour cream and whole-wheat tortillas, but what fun is that? Nearby, **Harry's Burritos** (76 W. 3rd St., at Thompson St., tel. 212/260–5588) does practically the same thing with a little less flair. *113 Greenwich Ave., between Jane and W. 12th Sts., tel. 212/633–9210. Subway: 1, 2, 3, or 9 to W. 14th St. Other (original) location: 93 Ave. A, at E. 6th St., East Village, tel. 212/254–2054. Cash only.*

Chez Brigitte. Charming chef and owner Rose Santos freely draws on her Spanish/French heritage, creating some deliciously spiced sandwiches as well as savory entrées like beef bourguignonne. Save room for a slice of homemade pie. *77 Greenwich Ave., at 11th St., tel. 212/929–6736. Subway: 1, 2, 3, or 9 to W. 14th St. Cash only. Closed Sun.*

John's Pizzeria. You should probably sample New York's Finest, and by hotly debated general consensus, this is it: If you live for thin-crusted pizza, topped by only the finest ingredients and blazed by a brick oven that's stoked up hours before the first pie goes in, get thee hence to John's, and accept no substi-

SERIOUS SPLURGES

When your rich uncle and aunt accompany you to town with an empty stomach and a fat wallet, suggest one of the following restaurants, but make reservations well (did we say well?) in advance. What you're getting isn't just fancy food, but a piece of the True New York Experience: stunning decor, impeccable service, and true elbow rubs with the rich-and-famous. Such pampering costs about $65. Per person.

Chanterelle. One of the most enchanting dining experiences in America: contemporary French cuisine at its very finest and freshest, truly elegant service, and a magnificent room to enjoy it in. 2 Harrison St., at Hudson St., TriBeCa, tel. 212/966–6960.

Four Seasons. Its Grill Room has been the deal makers' power-lunch destination for decades. The Pool Room is relentlessly fabulous. 99 E. 52nd St., between Lexington and Park Aves., Midtown East, tel. 212/754–9494.

Gramercy Tavern. Unsurpassedly reliable new American cuisine, from watchfully sautéed foie gras with roasted spring onions, mission figs, and a balsamic reduction to roasted monkfish with pancetta, braised red cabbage, caraway, Jerusalem artichokes, and truffle vinaigrette to, well, you get the idea. 42 E. 20th St., between Broadway and Park Ave. S, Gramercy, tel. 212/477–0777.

Le Cirque 2000. The decor of the new setting is cirque de soleil on LSD, and some complain about blatant favoritism in the way you're treated. Reservations are snapped up faster than tenth-row center seats for "Rent," but the succulent French cuisine and celebrity-ogling justify it all. 455 Madison Ave., between E. 50th and 51st Sts., Midtown East, tel. 212/794–9292.

Nobu. TriBeCa Japanese, and most agree that it's the best in America. Certainly it's the most imaginative. Practice saying "Omikase" before you go—it means you're ordering the chef's pick of the day. 105 Hudson St., at Franklin St., TriBeCa, tel. 212/219–0500.

Peter Luger Steak House. Though it's in a sketchy neighborhood, this is widely and justifiably regarded as the best steak house in the country. 178 Broadway, at Driggs Ave., Brooklyn, tel. 718/387–7400.

Union Square Cafe. The new American cuisine is somewhat less expensive than at other five-star restaurants, but it's no less thrilling—and every bit as popular—and the service is universally rated the very best in Manhattan. 21 E. 16th St., between 5th Ave. and Union Square W, Union Sq., tel. 212/243–4020.

tutes. *278 Bleecker St., between 6th Ave. and 7th Ave. S, tel. 212/243–1680. Subway: A, B, C, D, E, F, or Q to Washington Sq./W. 4th St.*

Moustache. You'll find some excellent Middle Eastern fusion food at this very busy, tiny restaurant on a beautiful residential street. Try the house specialty, *pitzza,* a large pita bread dressed up like a pizza for one, with mushrooms, chicken, lamb, capers, artichokes, eggplant, and other toppings. *90 Bedford St., at Grove St., tel. 212/229–2220. Subway: 1 or 9 to Christopher St. (Sheridan Sq.).*

Taquería de México. This small eatery proudly gives you a $5 lunch special: soup, mixed salad, and rice and beans; or a chicken burrito, rice and beans, and Mexican rice pudding. The regular menu won't break the bank, either. The emphasis on authenticity is unusual and most welcome. *93 Greenwich Ave., between Bank and W. 12th Sts., tel. 212/255–5212. Subway: 1, 2, 3, or 9 to W. 14th St. Cash only.*

UNDER $15 • Home. This appropriately named little treasure features comfort food: chicken dumplings, fresh grilled trout, and hearty french toast breakfasts. Inside it's cozy and warm, and the garden patio out back is glorious. *20 Cornelia St., between W. 4th and Bleecker Sts., tel. 212/243–9579. Subway: A, B, C, D, E, F, or Q to Washington Sq./W. 4th St.*

Kun Paw. Let candlelight and reggae music put you in the mood for good lovin' and good Thai food at Kun Paw. The friendly young staff can help you select from the dozens of inexpensive house specialties; our pick is the *pla katheam* (fried snapper and garlic sauce) with sticky rice. In summer, the tables on Greenwich Avenue offer great people-watching. *39 Greenwich Ave., at Charles St., tel. 212/989–4100. Subway: 1, 2, 3, or 9 to W. 14th St.*

Pink Tea Cup. Fans of Southern diner food will appreciate this shameless emporium, which will whip up the best smothered pork chops in town. Dinner entrées come with a pride of two vegetables, soup, salad, hot bread, and dessert. Breakfasts (from 8 AM) are just as good as you'd expect. And yes, the decor is quite pink. *42 Grove St., between Bedford and Bleecker Sts., tel. 212/807–6755. Subway: 1 or 9 to Christopher St. (Sheridan Sq.). Cash only.*

Rio Mar. One reason to make the trek into the meat-packing district is Rio Mar's giant portions of traditional Spanish dishes, such as paella or *mariscade en salsa verde* (seafood in green sauce); another is the potent sangria and lively bar scene. When the meal is over, head upstairs to the dance floor and salsa till the wee hours. *7 9th Ave., at Little W. 12th St., tel. 212/243–9015. Subway: A, C, E, or L to W. 14th St.*

Tartine. Delicious dishes with a vaguely French accent, like *bouchée à la reine* (chicken pot pie), quiche, and grilled polenta provençale are served with a bit of French surliness at this tiny, attractive restaurant. Local hipsters don't mind waiting up to an hour for a table, especially for weekend brunch. *253 W. 11th St., at W. 4th St., tel. 212/229–2611. Subway: 1 or 9 to Christopher St. (Sheridan Sq.). BYOB. Cash only. Closed Mon.*

Tortilla Flats. Come play some bingo or take the hula hoop for a spin at this loco diner. It's loud, tipsy fun (the pitchers of margaritas don't hurt). Filling the menu are basic enchiladas, tacos, burritos, and tostadas, not to mention shrimp fajitas and chicken mole. Plastic fruit garlands and Elvis paintings clutter the walls. *767 Washington St., at W. 12th St., tel. 212/243–1053. Subway: A, C, E, or L to W. 14th St.*

Universal Grill. If you're up for a big, gay party, complete with tambourines and sing-alongs and plenty of down-home food, come right on in! There's never less than two birthday songs sung in an evening. This place is one very big smile. *44 Bedford St., at Carmine St. and 7th Ave. S, tel. 212/989–5621. Subway: 1 or 9 to Christopher St. (Sheridan Sq.).*

Village Natural Health Food Restaurant. Everything about the Village Natural is simple, from the wood furnishings to the organic, unprocessed entrées (many of which are dairy- and wheat-free). Try spaghetti with "wheatballs" or shiitake mushrooms sautéed with tofu. Omelets are served weekdays 11–2:30. *46 Greenwich Ave., between Charles and Perry Sts., tel. 212/727–0968. Subway: 1, 2, 3, or 9 to W. 14th St.*

UNDER $20 • Florent. This endlessly hip meat-packing-district bistro with a mind of its very own remains the late-night favorite of a surreal mix of drag queens, truckers, club kids, and stray couples from Jersey. Maps (some of non-existent places) and French flags cover the walls while reasonably priced French–American food fills the menu. For the true Fellini-esque experience, arrive after midnight; Florent is open around the clock on weekends. *69 Gansevoort St., between Washington and Greenwich Sts., tel. 212/989–5779. Subway: A, C, E, or L to W. 14th St. Cash only.*

BEYOND MICKEY D'S

A number of citywide chains keep New Yorkers coming back for great, reliable, affordable eats. At the places listed below (many of which have additional locations) you can eat well for less than $10.

Burritoville. Some of the best burritos in town—including tons of veggie options. 451 Amsterdam Ave., between W. 81st and 82nd Sts., Upper West Side, tel. 212/787–8181. 141 2nd Ave., between E. 8th and 9th Sts., East Village, tel. 212/260–3300. 144 Chambers St., at Hudson St., TriBeCa, tel. 212/571–1144. 36 Water St., at Broad St., Lower Manhattan, tel. 212/747–1100.

Daikichi Sushi. These take-out shops serve some of the freshest and cheapest sushi in town. 2345 Broadway, between W. 85th and 86th Sts., Upper West Side, tel. 212/362–4283. 1156 6th Ave., at 45th St., Midtown West, tel. 212/719–0576. 45 E. 45th St., between Madison and Vanderbilt Aves., Midtown East, tel. 212/953–2468. 35 E. 8th St., at University Pl., West Village, tel. 212/254–1987. 32 Broadway, between Beaver St. and Exchange Pl., Lower Manhattan, tel. 212/747–0994.

Dallas BBQ. Hungry carnivores come here to gorge on heaping plates of cheap barbecue and warm corn bread. 27 W. 72nd St., between Columbus Ave. and Central Park W, Upper West Side, tel. 212/873–2004. 21 University Pl., at E. 8th St., West Village, tel. 212/674–4450. 132 2nd Ave., at St. Marks Pl., East Village, tel. 212/777–5574.

John's Pizzeria. Many New Yorkers claim John's makes the best pizzas in the city, bar none. 48 W. 65th St., between Columbus Ave. and Central Park W, Upper West Side, tel. 212/721–7001. 278 Bleecker St., between 6th Ave. and 7th Ave. S, West Village, tel. 212/243–1680.

Mary Ann's. The "especials de la casa" (house specials) at these kitschy Mexican joints are excellent. 2452 Broadway, at W. 91st St., Upper West Side, tel. 212/877–0132. 116 8th Ave., at W. 16th St., Chelsea, tel. 212/633–0877. 80 2nd Ave., at E. 5th St., East Village, tel. 212/475–5939.

Royal Canadian Pancake House. They make pancakes the size of tractor tires here. Think we're kidding? 2286 Broadway, between 82nd and 83rd Sts., Upper West Side, tel. 212/873–6052. 1004 2nd Ave., at E. 53rd St., Midtown East, tel. 212/980–4131. 180 3rd Ave., at E. 17th St., Gramercy, tel. 212/777–9288.

Pò. By all means, treat yourself to a meal at this airy Northern Italian bistro. The people are pretty and the food is scrumptious, under the watchful eye of TV Food Network star (Molto) Mario Batali. Go hearty with grilled boar sausage and sautéed calamari with tomatoes and garlic, or keep it light with white-bean ravioli tossed with balsamic vinegar. The menu changes constantly, but everything works. *31 Cornelia St., between Bleecker and W. 4th Sts., tel. 212/645–2189. Subway: A, B, C, D, E, F, or Q to Washington Sq./W. 4th St. Closed Mon.*

EAST VILLAGE AND ALPHABET CITY

Budget diners, this is your Shangri-la: Nowhere in the city will you find as many funky and cheap restaurants as in the East Village, be they Italian, Middle Eastern, Cambodian, Tibetan, Korean, Mexican, Filipino, Cuban, Burmese, Jewish, Creole, Japanese, Spanish, or plain old American. Even better, most places stay open until the wee hours of the morning, especially in summer when the sidewalks are packed at all hours.

East 6th Street between 1st and 2nd avenues is known as "Little India" for its dozens of savory Indian, Bangladeshi, and Pakistani joints—many of which offer live, free traditional music in the evenings. Walk down the block and you'll score a handful of coupons worth up to 30% off your next meal. Most places here allow you to bring your own beer or wine, though a couple will charge a small corkage fee—even if you're drinking King Cobra. Eastern European (particularly Ukrainian) coffee shops are plentiful on **2nd Avenue** from East 7th to 9th streets. **Avenue A** overflows with all sorts of interesting options, including a number of sushi bars just north of Houston Street. For superior people-watching, pick one of the sidewalk cafés lining **Tompkins Square Park**—try Café Pick Me Up or Life Cafe (*see below*). One practical note: The East Village is not easy to reach on the subway unless you take the L line to 1st or 3rd

A food critic once described the Ukrainian borscht soup at 24-hour Veselka (144 2nd Ave., at E. 9th St., tel. 212/228–9682) as "tasting like something your grandmother would make if you came home with a black eye."

avenues, or the F to 2nd Avenue and Houston. You're better off riding a bus or catching a cab, especially late at night.

UNDER $5 • Dojo. The hordes of East Villagers who favor this snack shack don't seem to mind that most of the burgers and salads arrive smothered in "Japanese-style tahini" dressing (actually a carrot-based vinaigrette with not a hint of tahini). Neither should you: You can definitely chow here for less than $5. *24 St. Marks Pl., between 2nd and 3rd Aves., tel. 212/674–9821. Subway: 6 to Astor Pl. Cash only.*

Elvie's Turo-Turo. Get in line at this tiny Filipino cafeteria and "turo" (point) to whatever looks good, from *lumpia* (a cousin to the Chinese egg roll) to *ginisang gulay* (shrimp and pork stir-fried with seasonal vegetables) to *adobo* (grilled meat marinated in soy sauce, vinegar, garlic, and bay leaves). It's $3.75 for one entrée, $5 for two. *214 1st Ave., between E. 12th and 13th Sts., tel. 212/473–7785. Subway: L to 1st Ave. Cash only.*

Odessa. Sure, they've got omelets and cheeseburgers at this Eastern European diner. But what really make this place famous are the *latkes* (potato pancakes), *pierogi* (dumplings stuffed with a combination of meat, cheese, cabbage, and mushrooms), and giant cheese- or fruit-filled blintzes. The new decor looks like an airport lounge, but the food never changes. Just down the street, **Leshko's Coffee Shop** (111 Ave. A, at E. 7th St., tel. 212/473–9208) serves up similar, but not quite as gratifying, gut-busting Eastern European home-cooking. *117 Ave. A, between St. Marks Pl. and E. 9th St., tel. 212/473–8916. Subway: 6 to Astor Pl. Open 24 hrs. Cash only.*

UNDER $10 • ACME Bar and Grill. A self-proclaimed "okay place to eat," ACME serves Southern faves like chicken-fried steak, fried chicken, and po'boy sandwiches—all better than "okay." Spice things up with the house hot sauce, labeled ALMOST FLAMMABLE. The rock venue Under ACME (*see* Live Music *in* Chapter 6) lies—surprise—under ACME. *9 Great Jones St., between Broadway and Lafayette St., tel. 212/420–1934. Subway: 6 to Bleecker St.*

Angelica Kitchen. What's the vegan definition of heaven? Probably a place like this, where the food is 100% organic and free of animal products. They even serve a funky barley brew in place of regular coffee. Try the Dragon Bowl, a plate of steamed seasonal veggies with rice, beans, and tofu. *300 E. 12th St., between 1st and 2nd Aves., tel. 212/228–2909. Subway: 6 to Astor Pl.; also L to 3rd Ave. Cash only.*

Baby Jakes. Even people who help old ladies across the street may lie, cheat, and steal to get more of the melt-in-your-mouth corn bread served with dinner at this cool Cajun eatery. Try the Jake Burger (with pepper jack cheese and maple barbecue sauce) or the blackened catfish po-boy, or both. *14 1st Ave., at E. 1st St., tel. 212/254–2229. Subway: F to 2nd Ave. Other location: 170 Orchard St., between Houston and Stanton Sts., Lower East Side, tel. 212/982–2229.*

Esashi. At Esashi, visibly excited East Villagers sit next to visiting Japanese businessmen for superb and inexpensive sushi à la carte, both nigiri and in rolls. Dinner specials (5–8 PM) include udon noodle soups ($7) and big sushi combos ($8.50). It's not very fancy, but then neither is a Zen garden. *32 Ave. A, between E. 2nd and 3rd Sts., tel. 212/505–8726. Subway: F to 2nd Ave.*

Frutti de Mare. Savvy New Yorkers usually pass on the *frutti de mare* (seafood) in favor of tasty terrestrial entrées, notably the chicken with balsamic sauce and the homemade pumpkin ravioli in pesto cream sauce. Though the decor is classy, the attitude is very low-key. *84 E. 4th St., at 2nd Ave., tel. 212/979–2034. Subway: 6 to Astor Pl. Cash only.*

Kiev. According to a rough-and-tumble crew of regulars, Kiev's got the best Eastern European cooking west of the Volga. It serves breakfast round-the-clock and has a veggie dinner special (potato pancake, kasha varnishkes, and steamed vegetables) that's bigger than a Yugo. *117 E. 7th St., at 2nd Ave., tel. 212/674–4040 or 212/674–4041. Subway: 6 to Astor Pl. Open 24 hrs. Cash only.*

Life Cafe. On Sunday, slip on your shades and stumble over to Life Cafe for the huge breakfast, coffee and mimosa or Bloody Mary included. Even on days when you don't feel like hell, their Tex-Mex grub tastes pretty damn good. The outdoor tables are great for pondering the action in adjacent Tompkins Square Park. *343 E. 10th St., at Ave. B, tel. 212/477–8791. Subway: 6 to Astor Pl.; also L to 1st Ave. Other location: 1 Sheridan Sq., between W. 4th St. and Washington Pl., West Village.*

Panna. It's a toss-up between most of the homogeneous Indian restaurants on 6th Street, but the humorous, helpful staff in brightly decorated Panna inch it ahead of the pack. They won't moan if you mix and match your order, varying a little from the set menu of classic tandoori and curry dishes. The Bombay chicken sautéed in the chef's secret spices is the owner's favorite. They even have a separate room for smokers, a rarity in the big brother apple these days, and you can bring in your own beer or wine to complete a triumvirate of simple vices. *330 E. 6th St., between 1st and 2nd Aves., tel. 212/475–9274. Subway: 6 to Astor Pl.*

Sahara East. If you think couscous can only be bought in small cardboard boxes marked "instant," you'll sit up and slap yourself after a spoonful from this upscale Middle Eastern restaurant. It's fluffy, soft, and delicious, and it comes with vegetables, grilled lamb, chicken, or fish. *184 1st Ave., between E. 11th and 12th Sts., tel. 212/353–9000. Subway: L to 1st Ave. Cash only.*

Village Mingala. You're greeted with the words *min ga la ba* ("pleasant day") at this Burmese restaurant, then served succulent southeast Asian specialties like squid salad, duck with green and hot red peppers, or Burmese chicken curry with potatoes. The wood-paneled dining room is a bit dark, but not unpleasantly so. *21–23 E. 7th St., between 2nd and 3rd Aves., tel. 212/529–3656 or 212/260–0457. Subway: 6 to Astor Pl.*

Yaffa Café. If you've been given only one meal on Planet Earth, and you happen to be in the East Village, eat it here. The kitschy decor is cool, the patrons are cool, and the waiters and waitresses bedecked in black are just too cool. Filling the five-page menu are cool foods like Berber chicken (with spicy lemon-basil sauce) and the prodigious Yaffa Salad. In summer, grab a seat in the huge, leafy back garden. *97 St. Marks Pl., between 1st Ave. and Ave. A, tel. 212/674–9302. Subway: 6 to Astor Pl. Open 24 hrs.*

UNDER $15 • Avenue A. This is not your typical sushi joint. In addition to the standard Japanese tempura and teriyaki dishes, it's got whacked-out sushi rolls like the Panic (softshell crab tempura and plum paste) and the Dragon (eel, roe, and avocado). Best of all, it sports the ambience of a Tokyo nightclub, including black walls, a DJ spinning house music, and an achingly hip crowd. *103 Ave. A, between E. 6th and 7th Sts., tel. 212/982–8109. Subway: 6 to Astor Pl.*

Great Jones Cafe. It's got a jukebox with one of the best selections in the world and only 10 tables, so you can bet your weight in okra that this Cajun diner is always crowded. A summer favorite is the Crayfish Boil, a pound of the spicy crustaceans that you shell yourself. *54 Great Jones St., between Lafayette St. and Bowery, tel. 212/674–9304. Subway: 6 to Bleecker St. Cash only.*

John's. Possibly the best cheap Italian food outside of Italy, this classy eatery has been around since 1908, when the Belgium mosaic floor and delicate wall murals were finished. Specials like the Portobello mushrooms marinated and grilled and the rollintina of veal and chicken stuffed with a multiple-cheese sauce look and taste great. The elegant, candlelit white-linen tables make you feel like you must be spending a ton of money, until you get your bill, that is. *302 E. 12th St., between 1st and 2nd Aves., tel. 212/475–9531. Subway: L to 1st Ave.*

La Paella. If you're unfamiliar with Spanish cuisine, here's what you need to do: (1) Arrive with a large group of friends; (2) drink several pitchers of sangria; (3) order up a mess of hot or cold tapas; and (4) come back another day for paella (smallest serving feeds two for $20–$32), a traditional stew of rice, saffron, garlic, sausage, and seafood. *214 E. 9th St., between 2nd and 3rd Aves., tel. 212/598–4321. Subway: 6 to Astor Pl.*

Second Avenue Deli. Though it's completely charmless, this has long been one of the city's premier spots for kosher noshes. Try Jewish favorites like gefilte fish and Chicken in the Pot (noodles, carrots, and a matzoh ball), or sink your teeth into a mammoth pastrami sandwich. *156 2nd Ave., at E. 10th St., tel. 212/677–0606. Subway: 6 to Astor Pl.*

St. Dymphna's. Part of the Irish renaissance on St. Marks, this welcoming nouvelle-Gaelic eatery with a sun-splashed garden and full bar is rapidly becoming a top spot on the ever-popular strip. The beef-and-Guinness casserole, with vegetables and mashed potatoes, is a perfect panacea for the New York snows. In summertime, try the crab cakes with vegetable succotash and green pepper sauce. The huge, fry-up Irish breakfast is just right to kickstart your morning. By the way, Dymphna was the patron saint of mental illness; perfect for the Village. *118 St. Marks Pl., between Ave. A and 1st Ave., tel. 212/254–6636. Subway: 6 to Astor Pl.*

Telephone Bar and Grill. Once a very trendy spot with adventurous, budget-conscious uptowners, this quality restaurant, with its unique facade (it consists of three British telephone boxes complete with working phones), still draws in the crowds. The fish-and-chips and shepherd's pie are old English favorites, and the Stilton cheese fritters are a jolly good starter. Colm, the Irish bartender, is a gentleman. *149 2nd Ave., between 9th and 10th Sts., tel. 212/529–5000. Subway: L to 1st Ave.*

Two Boots. This popular village spot has a new, bigger home but still mixes Cajun and Italian cuisines to produce delicious dishes like pizza with andouille sausage and barbecued shrimp ($18 for large) or Linguine Dominique (blackened chicken with spinach linguine). It's popular with families as well as with cool Village types; arrive early on weekend nights. The "boots" in question are Louisiana and Italy, if you hadn't already guessed. *37 Ave. A, between E. 2nd and 3rd Sts., tel. 212/505–2276. Subway: F to 2nd Ave. For take-out-only locations, see box Beyond Mickey D's, above.*

LOWER EAST SIDE

The Lower East Side is an awkward mix of old and new, of kosher eateries unchanged for decades and conspicuously trendy bars and cafes. Some areas have remained largely unchanged since the first Jewish immigrants settled here around the turn of the century, though bagel shops and delis are becoming scarce. **Ludlow** and **Houston streets** represent the epicenter of the Lower East Side, as a parade of East Village colonialists expand their drinking and posing territory. Fortunately, **Moishe's** (181 E. Houston St., tel. 212/475–9629), an old-world Jewish bakery, is still turning out delicious bagels and bialys. The Puerto Rican community has a Lower East Side toehold, a cluster of super-cheap take-out stands near the intersection of **Delancey** and **Clinton streets.** If you crave doner at 4 AM, **Bereket** (187 E. Houston St., at Orchard St., tel. 212/475–7700) sells kebabs and other Turkish goodies "just like the ones in Istanbul" for less than $5.

UNDER $5 • F. Restaurant. This is the most popular of the Puerto Rican take-out stands crammed onto the corner of Clinton and Delancey streets. Everything (except roasted cow tongue and blood sausage) is deep fried and costs $1. And even if you have no idea what *alcapurria* or *pastellito* are, you'll find them mighty tasty. *105 Clinton St., at Delancey St., tel. 212/475–3029. Subway: F to Delancey St.; also J, M, or Z to Essex St. Cash only.*

Yonah Shimmel's Knishery. The Shimmel family has been making knishes (fried or baked turnovers; $1.35) for more than 100 years; some even claim that they invented 'em. Choose from 12 varieties, including potato, mushroom, kasha, and chocolate cream cheese. *Fressers* (Yiddish for "gluttons") should start with a bowl of cold borscht (85¢) and a half-dozen latkes (potato pancakes; $1 each). *137 E. Houston St., at 2nd Ave., tel. 212/477–2858. Subway: F to 2nd Ave. Cash only.*

BAGELS:
THE HOLE STORY

Most cafés and corner stores sell plastic-wrapped bagels, but these are usually too tough or just plain stale. For the real deal, visit one of the popular bagel bakeries listed below. Just don't ask which one is best—no two New Yorkers can agree on how to eat a bagel or where to buy one.

TRADITIONAL BAGELS: H&H Bagels (2239 Broadway, at W. 80th St., Upper West Side, tel. 212/595–8003 or 800/692–2435 for U.S. deliveries; 639 W. 46th St., tel. 212/595–8000).

BIGGEST BAGELS: Ess-a-Bagel (831 3rd Ave., at E. 50th St., Midtown, tel. 212/980–1010; 359 1st Ave., at E. 21st St., Gramercy, tel. 212/260–2252).

24-HOUR BAGELS: Columbia Hot Bagels (2836 Broadway, between W. 110th and 111th Sts., Morningside Heights, tel. 212/222–3200).

BAGELS OF MANY FLAVORS: Bagels on the Square (7 Carmine St., between Bleecker St. and 6th Ave., West Village, tel. 212/691–3041).

LARGEST SELECTION OF SHMEARS: Bagels on Amsterdam (see Upper West Side, above).

BEST SHOP NAME: Kossar's Bialystoker Kuchen Bakery (367 Grand St., between Essex and Norfolk Sts., Lower East Side, tel. 212/473–4810).

UNDER $10 • El Sombrero (The Hat). In the days before the great East Village migration, The Hat existed as a beloved neighborhood dive. Times change, though: not only has The Hat attracted the young and the pierced, but it's now a magnet for fun-seekers from the entire tri-state area. However, it serves some of the best Mexican-style food on the Lower East Side. Try a burrito and wash it down with a pedestrian-yet-potent margarita. *108 Ludlow St., at Stanton St., tel. 212/254–4188. Subway: F to 2nd Ave. Cash only.*

Festival Mexicana. A more sedate alternative to its Ludlow St. neighbor, The Hat, this authentic, above-average bean slinger serves Mexican favorites like chile rellenos, quesadillas, and burritos, plus novelties like lamb tacos (3 for $5.50). *120 Rivington St., between Essex and Suffolk Sts., tel. 212/995–0154. Subway: F to Delancey St.; also J, M, or Z to Essex St. Cash only.*

Katz's Delicatessen. Katz's has been serving knishes and hefty deli sandwiches to Lower East Siders—including magician Harry Houdini, a regular—since 1888. You'll need to shout your order, since the staff is usually bickering behind the counter in thick New Yawk accents. *205 E. Houston St., at Ludlow St., tel. 212/254–2246. Subway: F to 2nd Ave. or Delancey St.; also J, M, or Z to Essex St.*

Ratner's. This dairy (no meat) kosher restaurant is a Lower East Side institution. It's got some of the best blintzes and vegetarian noshes in town. Ratner's recently opened a bar in the back of its dining area called **Lansky Lounge,** in honor of depression-era gangster and Ratner's patron Meyer Lansky; it opens at 8 PM. *138 Delancey St., between Suffolk and Norfolk Sts., tel. 212/677–5588. Subway: F to Delancey St.; also J, M, or Z to Essex St. Closed Fri. 3 PM–Sat. sundown.*

LITTLE ITALY

If you think that Little Italy is the best place in town for Italian food, you need to wake up, stop reading Mario Puzo, and smell the garlic. True, the *ristoranti* here serve authentic—if often pricey—Italian food. It's just that you're paying to sit with a bunch of tourists gushing about how "Olde Worlde" Little Italy is—when, actually, it isn't. Chinatown continues to boom and encroach, and Little Italy has shrunken to just one lonely little avenue, **Mulberry Street.** Walk its length and you'll be accosted by a jacket-wearing waiter at the door of every virtually interchangeable restaurant, bidding you *buon giorno* and tempting you inside with discounts or unbelievably cheap lunch specials—which, come to think of it, is precisely what you'd encounter all over Italy. At some point you'll probably give in, and suck down a plate of spaghetti, order a cappuccino and tiramisu, squint your eyes, and imagine you're in Rome. A couple of glasses of Chianti will certainly help. For something a tad cheaper, try one of Little Italy's many coffeehouses (*see* Cafés and Coffee Bars, *below*).

UNDER $10 • Il Fornaio. This is just about the only place in Little Italy where you can dine like a Mafia don without needing the fortune of a Carlo Ponti. Dive into a generous plate of chicken parmesan or *rigatoni con zucchini. 132A Mulberry St., between Hester and Grand Sts., tel. 212/226–8306. Subway: J, M, N, R, Z, or 6 to Canal St.*

Luna's. The peeling murals of Sicily and the sagging floorboards make it clear this ain't Brunelleschi's Duomo. Despite all that, the food is good and the line often snakes out the door and around the corner. Come early or wait it out. *112 Mulberry St., near Canal St., tel. 212/226–8657. Subway: J, M, N, R, Z, or 6 to Canal St.*

> *The waiters at Luna's are famously rude: Don't be startled if you're greeted with a snarl and told to "quit fooling around and order some food."*

Puglia. People come to Puglia in large groups for two reasons: to gorge on decent pastas and to drink prodigious quantities of vino at one of the communal tables. By the end of the night, most folks are sloshed and singing along with Jorge (a man with a serious Elvis fixation), who croons in Italian while noodling on a cheesy Casio keyboard. *189 Hester St., between Mott and Mulberry Sts., tel. 212/966–6006. Subway: J, M, N, R, Z, or 6 to Canal St.*

UNDER $15 • Umberto's Clam House. Umberto's is famous for being the place where mobster Joey "Crazy" Gallo had his last supper in 1973: He was whacked by the mob while eating a birthday dinner of scungili. Pastas are pricey, all things considered, but good. *129 Mulberry St., at Hester St., tel. 212/431–7545. Subway: J, M, N, R, Z, or 6 to Canal St.*

CHINATOWN

Ask 100 New Yorkers what their favorite Chinatown restaurant is, and you'll get 100 different answers. This is a crowded, bustling, vibrant neighborhood, and restaurants come and go at a manic pace. But don't be deterred: Hit the streets, ponder the boxes of dried what-have-you stationed outside the live-fish markets, and search out your very own favorite pork-bun bakery. And know that Chinatown is more diverse than the name suggests: You'll find dishes from Hong Kong, Shanghai, Bangkok, Seoul, and Taipei, all within walking distance of one another. Whatever else you can say about it, Chinatown ain't dull.

Though Chinatown's restaurants often aren't much to look at and rarely cater to tourists, they do offer phenomenally cheap lunch specials. Most are clustered around the intersection of **Bayard** and **Mott streets.** For a quick snack (like yummy coconut rolls), try bakeries **New Lung Fung** (41 Mott St., between Pell and Bayard Sts., tel. 212/233–7447) or **Manna 2** (87 E. Broadway, near Forsyth St., tel. 212/267–6200). Both offer a dizzying array of delectable Chinese pastries, cakes, and sweet breads for under $1. The **Chinatown Ice Cream Factory** (65 Bayard St., between Mott and Elizabeth Sts., tel. 212/608–4170) has old standbys like vanilla and chocolate, as well as more exotic flavors like red bean, lychee, ginger, green tea, and taro.

UNDER $5 • Bo Ky. At this spartan joint you can select from over 25 Vietnamese and Chinese soups, all loaded with tasty morsels like shrimp balls, squid, roast duck, and various noodles. Service is speedy and polite. *80 Bayard St., between Mulberry and Mott Sts., tel. 212/406–2292. Subway: J, M, N, E, Z, or 6 to Canal St. Cash only.*

Excellent Dumpling House. The green tile walls give it the look of a public rest room, but get over it—the dumplings really are excellent. So are the Shanghai-style noodle soups and stir-frys. At lunchtime

ACT LOCALLY, ~~EAT GLOBALLY~~
EAT GLOBALLY

AFGHANI: Afghan Kebab House (764 9th Ave., between W. 51st and 52nd Sts., Hell's Kitchen, tel. 212/307–1612). ARGENTINEAN: La Portena (7425 37th Ave., between 74th and 75th Sts., Jackson Heights, Queens, tel. 718/458–8111). CAMBODIAN: Cambodian Cuisine (87 S. Elliot Pl., between Fulton St. and Lafayette Ave., Fort Greene, Brooklyn, tel. 718/858–3262). CHILEAN: Pomaire (371 W. 46th St., between 8th and 9th Aves., Theater District, tel. 212/956–3056). HUNGARIAN: Mocca Hungarian (see Upper East Side, above). PERSIAN: Kabul Cafe (265 W. 54th St., between Broadway and 8th Ave., Midtown, tel. 212/757–2037). ROMANIAN: Sammy's Roumanian (157 Chrystie St., at Delancey St., Lower East Side, tel. 212/673–0330). SRI LANKAN: Taprobane (234 W. 56th St., between Broadway and 8th Ave., Midtown, tel. 212/333–4203). TUNISIAN: La Baraka (255–09 Northern Blvd., at Little Neck Pkwy., Queens, tel. 718/428–1461). TURKISH: Bereket (187 E. Houston St., at Orchard St., tel. 212/475–7700).

the place is packed, with good reason. *111 Lafayette St., between Canal and Walker Sts., tel. 212/219–0212. Subway: J, M, N, R, Z, or 6 to Canal St. Cash only.*

Sweet 'n' Tart Cafe. Restore your inner harmony at this crowded snack shop with a few *tong shui* (Chinese sweets believed to have healing properties). The most popular are double-boiled Chinese pears with almonds, licorice-infused gelatin, and walnut broth. The delicious dumplings and noodle soups have no curative properties; they simply taste great. *76 Mott St., at Canal St., tel. 212/334–8088. Subway: J, M, N, R, Z, or 6 to Canal St. Cash only.*

UNDER $10 • 31 Division Dim Sum House. You need to be sociable at this spartan dim sum diner: Waiters will lead you to the first open seat, often at an already occupied table. On weekend afternoons expect long lines of locals eager for *har gow* (steamed shrimp dumplings). Dim sum is served daily 7:30–4. *31 Division St., between Bowery and E. Broadway, tel. 212/431–9063. Subway: B, D, or Q to Grand St.*

House of Vegetarian. The devilish chefs here concoct faux animal flesh out of vegetable gluten, which allows vegetarians to keep their karma intact while tearing into Chinese dishes like lemon "chicken" or Peking "spareribs." Most entrées are $7–$9. *68 Mott St., between Canal and Bayard Sts., tel. 212/226–6572. Subway: J, M, N, R, Z, or 6 to Canal St. Cash only.*

Nha Trang. You can make a complete meal from Nha Trang's Vietnamese rice-noodle soups, called *pho*. But then you'd miss out on all the zesty, unusual entrées made with barbecued beef, pork, curry chicken, or frogs' legs. *87 Baxter St., between Bayard and Canal and Sts., tel. 212/233–5948. Subway: J, M, N, R, Z, or 6 to Canal St. Cash only.*

Thailand Restaurant. Why bother flying to Bangkok when the chef right here is a genius, producing authentic Thai curries, and prodigiously seasoned noodle and rice dishes? The dining room—decorated with dolls and masks from Thailand—is one of the most elegant in Chinatown. *106 Bayard St., at Baxter St., tel. 212/349–3132. Subway: J, M, N, R, Z, or 6 to Canal St.*

Triple Eight Palace. Chinatown's most popular place for dim sum is a chaotic restaurant the size of a football field, crowded from 8 AM on with Cantonese-speaking customers. Rolling by on squeaky carts are 45 varieties of dim sum, from which you'll select *without* the aid of an English menu (just smile and nod and point politely). Only tourists come here for dinner. Dim sum served daily 8–4. *88 E. Broadway, near Market St., tel. 212/941–8886. Subway: F to E. Broadway.*

UNDER $15 • Pho Viet Huong. The *bo la nho* (barbecued beef wrapped in grape leaves) at this Vietnamese restaurant is extraordinarily delicious. Entrées like *com tom cari dau que* (curry shrimp and rice) or *ca chien chua ngot* (sweet-and-sour fish) are equally succulent. Save room for guava ice cream. *73 Mulberry St., between Bayard and Canal Sts., tel. 212/233–8988. Subway: J, M, N, R, Z, or 6 to Canal St.*

SOHO

Many of the restaurants in glamorous, gallery-filled SoHo are too expensive for budget travelers. After all, if you're closing a deal on a $85,000 Stella, you'd look gauche taking your prospective buyer to a greasy spoon. Your options? You can join the Beautiful People and damn the costs. Or you can forsake ambience for a good feed at the smattering of delis and health-food stores in SoHo, notably **Whole Foods** (117 Prince St., between Greene and Wooster Sts., tel. 212/982–1000). SoHo also has two of the city's favorite fancy marketplaces—**Gourmet Garage** (453 Broome St., at Mercer St., tel. 212/941–5850), open daily 8 AM–8:30 PM, and **Dean & Deluca** (*see* Markets and Specialty Shops, *below*)—which offer affordable take-out sandwiches. The most cogent SoHo scene is found along **West Broadway,** especially on late-summer evenings: A sophisticated, often European crowd packs every sidewalk table between Houston and Canal streets.

Stock up on heavenly fresh bread ($2) at SoHo's charming, 75-year-old Vesuvio Bakery (160 Prince St., between Thompson St. and W. Broadway, tel. 212/925–8248), a favorite backdrop of fashion photographers.

UNDER $5 • Spring Street Market and Deli. When they're not busy catering to movie crews and MTV stars, darling, the folks at Spring Street will feed you sandwiches, salads, and gourmet pizzas, all priced around $5. You can eat at one of the back tables or get takeout. *111 Spring St., between Greene and Mercer Sts., tel. 212/226–4410. Subway: C or E to Spring St.*

UNDER $10 • Bell Caffe. Many people describe Bell Caffe as "relaxed." After all, the couches sag and the tables are battered—and it's one of few places in SoHo where you can simply hang out. But ever since Drew "Firestarter" Barrymore was spotted here recently, it's been in danger of being upgraded to "trendy." Besides serving an eclectic menu of steamed mussels, gazpacho, and chicken dumplings, it's got live music nightly, cover-free. *See also* Bars *in* Chapter 6. *310 Spring St., between Hudson and Greenwich St., tel. 212/334–2355. Subway: C or E to Spring St.*

Fanelli's Cafe. This 1872 relic couldn't be more British, with its dark wood, chummy barflies, and permanent reek of spilled ale. Join the crowd with a brew and a burger or a snack: chicken wings, stuffed potato skins, or Cuban black-bean salad. *94 Prince St., at Mercer St., tel. 212/226–9412. Subway: N or R to Prince St. $50 minimum on credit cards.*

Jerry's. At lunch, loudly dressed art connoisseurs and upwardly nubile teenage models nibble tuna salad on greens or sliced chicken breast with roasted-tomato mayonnaise. The decor—red vinyl booths, zebra-striped walls, and glaring green-framed mirrors—exudes as much attitude as the patrons. *101 Prince St., between Greene and Mercer Sts., tel. 212/966–9464. Subway: N or R to Prince St.; also 6 to Spring St.*

Kelley and Ping. All day long, black-clad artists and vintage-clothing store clerks pop into this chaotic noodle house/Asian grocery/tea shop for stir-fry, spring rolls, and Vietnamese, Japanese, Cantonese, or Thai noodles. Stacked sacks of Thai black rice and huge jars of tea enhance the *feng shui. 127 Greene St., between Houston and Prince Sts., tel. 212/228–1212. Subway: N or R to Prince St.; also B, D, F, or Q to Broadway–Lafayette St.*

Lupe's East L.A. Kitchen. Okay, so it's no longer a secret—but this laid-back, divey little Mexican joint is still an un-SoHo haven for luscious quesadillas with rice, beans, and salad or large burritos, all served with killer salsa. *110 6th Ave., at Watts St., tel. 212/966–1326. Subway: A, C, or E to Canal St.; also 1 or 9 to Canal St. Cash only.*

Moondance Diner. Rod Serling could have filmed a *Twilight Zone* in this renovated railroad car on a desolate block. Inside is a 1950s diner with sparkly, blue plastic booths and a big selection of glorious greasy food. Thick milk shakes and root-beer floats complete matters. *80 6th Ave., at Grand St., tel. 212/226–1191. Subway: A, C, E, 1, or 9 to Canal St.*

UNDER $15 • Abyssinia. At this Ethiopian restaurant, adventurous patrons sit on traditional tiny woven stools and enjoy authentic dishes like *ye'beg alitcha* (lamb in ginger-garlic sauce), which you scoop up with sweet and spongy *injera* bread. Combination plates are made for two or more to share. *35 Grand St., at Thompson St., tel. 212/226–5959. Subway: A, C, or E to Canal St.*

Chez Bernard. Bernard is no common butcher but rather an artiste, a man in a spotless smock who saws sides of beef into perfect sculpture. His restaurant serves everything from basic sandwiches to magnificent pâtés and full-blown French meals. *323 W. Broadway, between Grant Ave. and Canal St., tel. 212/343–2583. Subway: A, C, E, 1, or 9 to Canal St.*

Helianthus Vegetarian. Tuck into that Lamb of Happiness or Sweet and Sour Delight without guilt, because all the food at this happy, happy, happy vegetarian café is 100% meat-free. Amazing what you can do with soy protein, wheat gluten, a Chinese wok, and considerable ingenuity. *48 MacDougal St., between W. Houston and Prince Sts., tel. 212/598–0387. Subway: C or E to Spring St.*

Jean Claude. It's smaller than a Left Bank apartment, but somehow this elegant bistro puts out affordable platefuls of truly inspired French cooking. Check out the Atlantic salmon in fennel broth; pan-seared monkfish with potato purée and eggplant rounds; or roast Cornish game hen with herb risotto. *137 Sullivan St., between Prince and Houston Sts., tel. 212/475–9232. Subway: C or E to Spring St. Cash only.*

SoHo Kitchen and Bar. People don't come here for the gourmet pizzas with toppings like Thai chicken, or even for the salads and grilled specialties. The main draw is wine: 110 vintages sold by the glass ($4.50 and up). *103 Greene St., between Prince and Spring Sts., tel. 212/925–1866. Subway: B, D, F, or Q to Broadway–Lafayette St.; also 6 to Spring St.*

UNDER $20 • Balthazar. This is the restaurant of the moment, for celebrities and peasants alike: At two weeks old, the city's major celebs already had special tables assigned them. Fittingly, lofty cathedral ceilings (befitting 10-ft-tall model types) and gigantic mirrors (obvious enough) set the mood in the huge and extremely loud room. Unlike most of the other hot restaurants that arose in the last decade, Balthazar is quite affordable. The utterly superb wine list even offers $16 bottles. The haut bistro fare includes braised rabbit, steak frites, and mouth-watering seafood. Be cool and don't point at Madonna that way! *80 Spring St., at Crosby St., tel. 212/965-1414. Subway: N or R to Prince St.; also 4, 5, or 6 to Spring St.*

L'Ecole. You're dying for a grossly extravagant French meal. You can't afford Lutèce or Chantarelle (where dinner will run you a good $75). Luckily there's L'Ecole, the 100% student-run restaurant at the French Culinary Institute, where aspiring chefs are taught by masters from New York's top restaurants. L'Ecole's prix-fixe lunches (three courses; $16) and dinners (four courses; $22) are worth every penny. And New Yorkers have figured that out: Note that same-day reservations are required Monday–Thursday; for Friday and Saturday reserve at least one week in advance. *462 Broadway, at Grand St., tel. 212/219–3300. Subway: J, M, N, R, Z, or 6 to Canal St. Closed Sun.*

Penang. This place follows a simple recipe: Take traditional Malaysian dishes—from *tuland gunung api* (fried pork ribs) to *ikan bakar* (sea bass wrapped in banana leaves)—and combine them with over-the-top ding-dong Tiki decor, including a waterfall and waving palm fronds. Then stir in a hip crowd that's heavy on drag queens. *109 Spring St., between Greene and Mercer Sts., tel. 212/274–8883. Subway: C or E to Spring St. Other location: 240 Columbus Ave., at 71st St., tel. 212/769–8889. Subway: 1, 2, 3, 9, C, E, B, or D to W. 72nd St.*

TRIBECA

TriBeCa residents have conflicting feelings about their neighborhood's paucity of restaurants: After all, there are only so many times you can eat in Bob DeNiro's posh **Tribeca Grill** (375 Greenwich St., at Franklin St., tel. 212/941–3900). On the other hand, people here don't want SoHo's trendy bistros and high prices. The end result is that on nights and weekends, TriBeCa's streets are empty and . . . even a little creepy. **Broadway** is the place to go if you're looking for fast food. For snacks and such, **Greenwich Street** offers some interesting options, notably **Bazzini's** (339 Greenwich St., at Jay St., tel. 212/334–1280), which has been selling mixed nuts, candy, and ice cream since 1886. The **Pennsylvania Pretzel Co.** (295 Greenwich St., at Chambers St., tel. 212/587–5938) does nothing but hot pretzels, topped with garlic, cinnamon, cheese, or chocolate.

UNDER $10 • Bubby's. If you can overlook the trendiness and the ridiculous name, Bubby's offers great people-watching and an eclectic menu of fine food. It's totally laid-back in a stylish (read: Gen-X) way and the price is right. *120 Hudson St., at N. Moore St., tel. 212/219–0666. Subway: 1 or 9 to Franklin St.*

Yaffa's Bar and Restaurant. At this sprawling boho lair—furnished with vintage couches and weird abstract sculptures, rather like a Southern whorehouse—the food is a multi-ethnic medley of Spanish tapas, sandwiches, and Mediterranean entrées. They offer a big and highly popular bargain brunch ($10) on weekends. Next door, **Yaffa's Tea Room** (tel. 212/966–0577) serves the same fare in addition to high tea ($15 per person) weekdays 2–5; for this treat, reservations are required a day in advance. *353 Greenwich St., at Harrison St., tel. 212/274–9403. Subway: 1, 2, 3, or 9 to Chambers St.*

UNDER $15 • Franklin Station Cafe. Nothing in the name would lead you to expect a warehouse-turned-bistro that plays French rock, pours café au lait, and serves Malaysian dishes like satay chicken and eggplant curry fish, along with more prosaic sandwiches. For breakfast, go ahead and try a curry chicken puff and mango milk shake to get your day off to a peculiar start. *222 W. Broadway, between Franklin and White Sts., tel. 212/274–8525. Subway: 1 or 9 to Franklin St. BYOB.*

LOWER MANHATTAN

This is Manhattan's mighty financial district, and something about its skyscrapers and canyonlike streets makes good restaurants wither and die (either it's the lack of sun or the superabundance of bond traders). While high-rolling types motor uptown for their two-martini lunches, regular working stiffs simply saunter over to **Broadway** between Pine and Liberty streets to pick up a $1.25 hot dog or $2.75 take-out carton of chow mein from the weekday-only jumble of street carts. There's an amazing variety of cuisines represented, and all the chefs are pretty talented with their mobile steam trays. When the weather is fair, take your lunch

Fans of Ronald McDonald and his hamburger friends will of course want a McDonald's tie ($15–$30), T-shirt, or stuffed animal from the Wall Street branch gift boutique.

over to **Liberty Park** (Liberty St., between Trinity Pl. and Broadway). Keep in mind that most people flee Lower Manhattan right after work, and that restaurants tend to close early.

UNDER $5 • McDonald's. If you're enthused because the McDonald's at the Spanish Steps in Rome has a waterfall and salad bar, you're gonna flip when you check out this Wall Street branch. It's got a tuxedoed doorman, table service, a coffee bar, an orchid-filled dining room, and even a pianist at a baby grand. You'd think that all this swank would make your Happy Meal taste like steak frites. *160 Broadway, at Liberty St., tel. 212/385–2063. Subway: N or R to Cortlandt St.; also 4 or 5 to Wall St. Cash only.*

Seaport Soup Company. One of the best kept secrets downtown is this wondrous little place on Fulton Street. You won't find a cleaner restaurant in the area, with quiet jazz and a slender counter that runs under sparkling picture windows that gaze onto a busy corner. This place has a repertoire of 60 soups, and they serve 8–10 of them daily, all of which come with beautiful homemade bread and seasonal fruit. Best shrimp bisque you'll ever taste. *76 Fulton St., at Gold St., tel. 212/693–1371. Subway: N or R to City Hall; also 1, 2, 3, 4, 5 or 6 to Fulton St. Cash only. Closed Sun.*

UNDER $10 • Pearl Street Diner. Professionals who fiddle around with other people's millions but don't want to waste a penny of their own come here for tasty and cheap diner food. You'll pay less than $6 for charbroiled burgers and big breakfast specials. *212 Pearl St., near Maiden La., tel. 212/344–6620. Subway: 2 or 3 to Wall St.*

UNDER $15 • Carmine's. Whatever wriggling fresh seafood they're hawking at the historic Fulton Fish Market (just around the corner) will probably show up as dinner at Carmine's, which has been offering Italian seafood specialties since 1903. The service is rude and the food average, but locals still prefer it to the touristy restaurants at South Street Seaport. *140 Beekman St., at Front St., tel. 212/962–8606. Subway: J, M, Z, 2, 3, 4, or 5 to Fulton St.*

UNDER $20 • Bridge Café. This cozy bistro in a 19th-century town house is in the very shadow of the majestic Brooklyn Bridge. Seasonal entrées include fresh black squid-ink linguine with shrimp ($16) and roast duck in red-wine sauce ($17). *279 Water St., at Dover St., tel. 212/227–3344. Subway: J, M, Z, 2, 3, 4, or 5 to Fulton St.*

OUTER BOROUGH RESTAURANTS

BROOKLYN

The neighborhoods of **Brooklyn Heights, Cobble Hill,** and **Park Slope** cater to people who think they still live in Manhattan. They're packed with all kinds of eateries, from dirt-cheap falafel stands to pricey French bistros. Also in Brooklyn Heights, on **Atlantic Avenue,** you'll find dozens of Middle Eastern and Moroccan restaurants. Just south of that begins the very Italian neighborhood of **Carroll Gardens.** Farther afield, **Williamsburg** has lots of Kosher bakeries and a number of cheap, natural-food joints catering to its growing artist community. When in **Sheepshead Bay,** think "clam bars" and "pasta shops." Meanwhile, **Greenpoint** is rife with Polish coffee shops serving very cheap kielbasa and borscht, and **Brighton Beach** supports a thriving community of Jewish/Russian immigrants.

BROOKLYN HEIGHTS, COBBLE HILL, CARROLL GARDENS, AND DOWNTOWN

UNDER $10 • Fatoosh Barbecue. This Syrian joint serves two things, both of which taste terrific: barbecued meats ($4.50) and *meze* ($3), a vegetarian appetizer made with pita bread and your choice of hummus, baba ghanoush, or puréed red pepper with walnuts. *311 Henry St., between State St. and Atlantic Ave., tel. 718/596–0030. Subway: M, N, or R to Court St.; also 2, 3, 4, or 5 to Borough Hall. Cash only.*

Moroccan Star. If you stayed awake during history class, you would know that the French gave Moroccans a fondness for seafood crepes and their pesky, difficult-to-speak Romance language. But for a taste of something truly Moroccan, try the *patella* (spicy chicken pie) or *glaba* (sautéed lamb with okra), both big enough for two. Be warned: This family-run place looks more like a Kansas City pool hall than anything from *Casablanca*. *205 Atlantic Ave., between Clinton and Court Sts., tel. 718/643–0800. Subway: 2, 3, 4, or 5 to Borough Hall. BYOB.*

Mr. Souvlaki. Don't confuse *souvlaki* ($5), a tasty Greek sandwich of grilled meats, with *Soulvaki,* an album by the Slowdives. *147 Montague St., between Henry and Clinton Sts., tel. 718/858–8997. Subway: M, N, or R to Court St.; also 2, 3, 4, or 5 to Borough Hall. Cash only.*

UNDER $15 • Ozzie's Coffee and Tea. While nestled in a deep wicker chair beneath the bay windows of this posh Brooklyn Heights café, you can discreetly place hexes on the yuppies strolling by outside. There's a second Ozzie's in Park Slope (57 7th Ave., at Lincoln Pl., tel. 718/398–6695). *136 Montague St., between Henry and Clinton Sts., Brooklyn, tel. 718/852–1553. Subway: M, N, or R to Court St.*

Patsy Grimaldi's Pizza. While all those cheesy pizza joints in Manhattan scramble to call themselves "the original" and "number one," Patsy's keeps pulling the crispiest, best-tasting pizza pies in New York City out of their coal-fired oven. It's in a weird no-man's-land below the Brooklyn Bridge, but don't let that stop you. *19 Old Fulton St., between Water and Front Sts., tel. 718/858–4300. Subway: A or C to High St. (Brooklyn Bridge). Cash only. Closed Tues.*

Tripoli Restaurant. Bring some friends to Tripoli if you're going to order *maza* ($42), a traditional Lebanese feast with 20 different entrées or authentic dishes such as *azhi* (an omelet with herbs, onions, pine nuts, and lamb) and *ma'ani* (a spicy sausage). *156 Atlantic Ave., at Clinton St., tel. 718/596–5800. Subway: 2, 3, 4, or 5 to Borough Hall.*

UNDER $20 • Harvest. A 3-ft-high red neon sign proclaims EATS from the brick wall, just what you'll want to do when you're not drawing on the brown butcher paper that covers the dozen tables (crayons supplied). Chef David Schneider has been dishing up Southern comfort food here since late 1996, including crab cakes with tarragon tartar sauce and a grilled marinated trout with sautéed broccoli rabe and sweet potato pancakes. In fair weather you can eat in the garden out back. *218 Court St., between Baltic and Warren Sts., tel. 718/624–9267. Subway: F to Bergen St. Closed Mon.*

La Bouillabaisse. Devotees of this tiny restaurant put up with waits that sometimes extend an hour or more. The crowds return again and again for the eponymous signature dish, prepared in modestly different ways but always chockablock with a half-dozen different fish, including lobster, flounder, snapper, and shrimp. If your idea of a fine time has never included gorging yourself for less than $17, wine included (provided that you bring a bottle from the liquor store up the street), stay away from here. *145*

Atlantic Ave., between Henry and Clinton Sts., tel. 718/522–8275. Subway: 2, 3, 4, or 5 to Borough Hall. BYOB. Cash only.

New City Café. Most people come to this très chic bistro before a performance at the nearby Brooklyn Academy of Music (*see* Arts Centers *in* Chapter 7). Lunch is $6.50–$10, while fancy dinner entrées run $16–$20. *246 DeKalb Ave., at Vanderbilt Ave., tel. 718/622–5607. Subway: G to Clinton–Washington Aves. Closed Mon.*

PARK SLOPE

UNDER $10 • Lemongrass Grill. There's always a line of folks outside this plain little restaurant, waiting to do battle with the sweat-inducing Thai spices. Menu highlights here include *gaiton krai* (Siam chicken), *kae-panang* (lamb with green curry sauce), and the lemongrass pork chops. *61A 7th Ave., at Lincoln Pl., tel. 718/399–7100. Subway: D or Q to 7th Ave; also 2 or 3 to Grand Army Plaza. Other locations in Manhattan: 37 Barrow St., West Village; 80 University Pl., East Village; 2534 Broadway, Upper West Side; 200 W. 84th St., Upper West Side.*

Nam. This fashionable addition to "restaurant row" (7th Avenue) serves fiery and authentic Vietnamese dishes. The menu is heavy on vegetarian and noodle entrées. *222 7th Ave., between 3rd and 4th Sts., tel. 718/788–5036. Subway: F to 7th Ave.*

Park Slope Brewing Company. A dozen brews ($4 a pint), four of which change seasonally, are the main event at this spot on a quiet residential stretch a short walk from the neighborhood's main commercial streets. Standard brew-pub fare is on the menu—fries, buffalo wings, and the like—but you can add a variety of toppings to your burger (both beef and veggie). There's a second branch in Brooklyn Heights (62 Henry St., tel. 718/522–4801). *356 6th Ave., at 5th St., tel. 718/788–1756. Subway: F to 4th Ave.*

Egg-cream sodas have brought Park Luncheonette fame and fortune for more than 50 years.

UNDER $15 • Two Boots. Artsy types and slumming professionals come to drink copiously over a plate of cheap Cajun/Italian food. It's got the same menu as the Two Boots in the East Village (*see above*), plus live music on Tuesday, Thursday, Friday, and Saturday nights. *514 2nd St., between 7th and 8th Aves., tel. 718/499–3253. Subway: F to 7th Ave.*

UNDER $20 • Cucina. Cucina's airy, elegant dining room, with its painted tin ceiling, warm Tuscan colors, and comfortable armchairs, is easily one of Brooklyn's loveliest. Gourmet Italian cuisine is beautifully prepared and presented (especially the small antipasto plates), but it's not cheap. The lobster ravioli with saffron, roast garlic chicken, and brick-oven pizza are all terrific, but if you're on a shoestring, the half portions of the pasta ($9–$11) are a good deal. Others must think so too, so reservations are required. *256 5th Ave., between Carroll St. and Garfield Pl., tel. 718/230–0711. Subway: M, N, or R to Union St. Closed Mon.*

WILLIAMSBURG AND GREENPOINT

UNDER $10 • bean. California transplants usually get very tense and huffy when New York restaurants claim to serve "authentic" Cal-Mex food. But it's not so bad at bean, a funky Williamsburg eatery that serves huge, delicious burritos, enchiladas, and quesadillas. Most dishes are vegetarian and cost $6–$11. *172 N. 8th St., near Bedford Ave., tel. 718/387–8222. Subway: L to Bedford Ave. Cash only.*

Park Luncheonette. At the Park Luncheonette they don't want to hear your sob stories about high cholesterol, because they make their living with fried-egg sandwiches, frankfurters with sauerkraut and chili, and pork chops. *334 Driggs Ave., at Lorimer St., no phone. Subway: G to Nassau Ave. Cash only.*

RBBQ. A barbecue pit, bar, and art gallery—just what you'd expect in wacky Williamsburg. Baby-back ribs, half-pound hamburgers, and shrimp ($6 a dozen) are all cooked on the outdoor grill during the spring and summer; in winter the menu changes to heartier baked dishes. You can also stop in for breakfast. *409 Kent Ave., at Broadway, tel. 718/388–3929. Subway: J, M, or Z to Marcy Ave. Cash only.*

UNDER $15 • Oznot's Dish. By day locals hang out in this café on a quiet corner in Williamsburg, sipping coffee and tea amid the flea-market furniture. In the evening, they come in for large portions of Mediterranean and Middle Eastern fare. Curried chickpea soup and *brik* (baked phyllo with seasonal fillings) make good appetizers. Entrées tend to be less traditionally Middle Eastern, like the grilled polenta atop red split peas with garlicky spinach and grilled eggplant, or the salmon with lemon-sumac butter, basmati rice, and roasted root vegetables. *79 Berry St., at North 9th St., tel. 718/599–6596. Subway: L to Bedford Ave. Cash only.*

CONEY ISLAND, BRIGHTON BEACH, AND SHEEPSHEAD BAY

UNDER $5 • Nathan's Famous. Yup, these are the same Nathan's Famous Hot Dogs that live in the freezer at your local supermarket. Nathan Handwerker started selling these franks back in 1916 for 5¢ each (undercutting competitors who charged a dime); today they're $1.85. And the menu now includes cheese fries and frogs' legs. Best of all, you can satisfy your hot dog craving virtually around the clock. *Surf and Stillwell Aves., Coney Island, tel. 718/946–2202. Subway: B, D, or F to Coney Island (Stillwell Ave.).*

UNDER $10 • Aiello's. This family-run Italian eatery whips up unbelievable pizzas with homemade mozzarella cheese and imported Italian tomato sauce. Also try the hearty pastas and hero sandwiches. *1406 Neptune Ave., at Stillwell Ave., tel. 718/373–1155. Subway: B, D, or F to Coney Island (Stillwell Ave.). Cash only. Closed Sun.*

Cafe Tatiana. Look beyond the Coney Island rides and you might mistake this boardwalk café for part of an exclusive Russian resort on the Black Sea: Everyone is speaking Russian, eating Russian food (heavy on the sausage, potatoes, and onions), and drinking from large carafes of iced vodka. Full meals run $5–$10—now that's a bargain. *On Boardwalk, near Brighton 3 St., no phone. Subway: D or Q to Brighton Beach.*

UNDER $15 • Primorski. Hordes of Russian immigrants flock to this restaurant/nightclub to feast on food from the Motherland, toss back some ice-cold vodka, and dance to a big band fronted by a Russian Sinatra. Entrées like *salyanka* (lamb stew) are great, but those in the know just fill up on appetizers. *282 Brighton Beach Ave., between Brighton 2 and Brighton 3 Sts., tel. 718/891–3111. Subway: D or Q to Brighton Beach.*

Randazzo's Clam Bar. The best Italian seafood restaurant in Sheepshead Bay serves monster-size oysters on the half shell (6 for $7), not to mention Little Neck clams ($11 per dozen) so fresh they were probably living off the coast of Long Island only hours before hitting your plate. Pastas are also available. *2017–2023 Emmons Ave., 1 block from Ocean Ave., tel. 718/615–0010. Subway: D or Q to Sheepshead Bay.*

QUEENS

If you're committed to finding authentic ethnic food, chances are you'll be much happier in Queens than Manhattan, where thriving local immigrant communities support a staggering variety of Chinese noodle shops, Latin American taquerías, and everything in between. Though you can find exotic eating adventures virtually anywhere in Queens, a handful of neighborhoods are especially visitor-friendly: Try **Astoria,** known for its Greek tavernas and cafés as well as an increasing number of Latin American eateries; **Flushing,** a virtual mini-Asia; or **Jackson Heights,** where South American, Caribbean, and East Indian cooking reign supreme.

ASTORIA

Walk down **Broadway** or **30th Avenue** between 31st and 36th streets and you'll find more Greek restaurants, cafés, and food stores than you can count on two hands and an abacus.

UNDER $5 • La Espiga. This tiny grocer/bakery churns out some of the best Mexican food north of the Rio Grande. Beside the usual tacos and burritos, they make *huaraches* (giant tacos) and *tortas* (grilled sandwiches made with sliced jalapeños, avocados, beans, and your choice of 13 different fillings—including fried pork and head cheese). Eat at the counter and watch Spanish TV, or take your grub to go. *32–44 31st St., at Broadway, tel. 718/777–1993. Subway: N to Broadway. Cash only.*

UNDER $10 • La Fonda Antioqueña. A mere $7.50 buys you a big plate of broiled beef, cornmeal cakes, rice-and-beans, fried pork, fried plantains, and fried egg at this tiny Colombian restaurant. If that makes your arteries shriek, plunk down $5 for a bowl of oxtail, chicken, vegetable, or tripe soup, served with rice and avocado. *32–25 Steinway St., at Broadway, tel. 718/726–9857. Subway: R to Steinway St.*

Omonia. In the center of Astoria's Greek community, Omonia always has a crowd lingering over its sweet coffee drinks and authentic Greek pastries—try *kadaifi* (shredded wheat with nuts and honey), or sticky, sweet baklava. (You can also get light meals here, but they're nothing special.) Sit by the glassed-in wall and watch the street life of Broadway. *32–20 Broadway, at 33rd St., tel. 718/274–6650. Subway: N to Broadway.*

Uncle George's. Legs of lamb, chicken, and suckling pigs turn slowly on spits near the door at this 24-hour Greek diner, where locals sit elbow-to-elbow with wide-eyed tourists at family-style tables. The menu runs the gamut from authentic Greek entrées—like the juicy roast lamb with lemon-drizzled potatoes, or octopus sautéed with lemon, vinegar, and oil—to lamb burgers and "Greek-style" spaghetti with meatballs. *33–19 Broadway, at 34th St., tel. 718/626–0593. Subway: N to Broadway. Cash only.*

UNDER $15 • Zenon. On a quiet side street, this place attracts many Greek-speaking locals. Make that annoying friend of yours, the one who always agonizes over the menu for hours, order *meze*, a $14 sampler with 16 different salads, cheeses, and grilled meats. If you're not in the mood to gorge, try the more-manageable Cyprus meatballs or spinach pie. On Wednesdays, Greek singers and dancers entertain with traditional folk tunes on electric guitar. *34–10 31st Ave., between 34th and 35th Sts., tel. 718/956–0133. Subway: N to 30th Ave. Cash only.*

FLUSHING

The blocks around the **Main Street** subway station are crowded with wall-to-wall Asian restaurants, including Hunan, Szechuan, Cantonese, Japanese, Korean, Taiwanese, Vietnamese, and Malaysian. Farther south on Main Street (near the Queens Botanical Gardens), a handful of cheap Indian restaurants rounds out the cultural stew.

UNDER $15 • Joe's Shanghai. This place did so well in Queens that a Manhattan branch has since opened in Chinatown, where it's now all the rage. If you want the more authentic experience, make the trek out to Flushing, where you'll be packed like sardines at family-style tables and hustled through an incredible sequence of hearty dishes such as crispy pork chops with "salt-and-pepper" sauce, sautéed shredded beef, and smoked fish coated with a sugary varnish. Start with the famous soup dumplings—yes, dumplings with soup inside; they're Joe's claim to fame. *136–21 37th Ave., between Main and 138th Sts., tel. 718/539–3838. Subway: 7 to Main St. Cash only.*

On Jackson Heights streets, look for East Indian stands selling "pan" (rhymes with lawn), a mystery concoction of seeds and herbs rolled in a beetlenut leaf. Locals swear the stuff aids digestion; some folks claim it's psychoactive.

Penang. Long before the pan-Asian craze started in Manhattan, this Malaysian mecca had a loyal following in Flushing. Now there are two more ultra-trendy branches in Manhattan, but the Flushing original has by far the best Malaysian food: Its flavors and cooking styles are a melting pot of Chinese, Thai, and Indian influences, all combined in a menu that reads like exotic poetry. Best dishes: *roti cani* (flat bread served with a chicken-and-meat curry sauce), Buddhist yam pot (an actual pot made of fried taro root and filled with chicken, cashews, and vegetables in a savory sauce), and clay-pot noodles with baby corn, black mushrooms, and bean sprouts. *38–04 Prince St., between Main St. and Roosevelt Ave., tel. 718/321–2078. Subway: 7 to Main St. Cash only.*

JACKSON HEIGHTS

Around **Roosevelt Avenue** and **82nd Street,** Colombian, Cuban, Brazilian, Puerto Rican, Argentinean, and Peruvian restaurants churn out chorizo, tripe stew, and other South American fare. Just a few blocks down, at **74th Street,** chile peppers give way to cumin and curry, and cheap Indian food abounds.

UNDER $10 • Jackson Diner. Order tandoori or anything cooked in a *kadai* (a type of earthenware pan) and you will understand how a restaurant with pink walls and fake crystal chandeliers can do such booming business. Go for the lunch buffet ($5–$7) weekdays from 11:30 to 4. *37–03 74th St., at 37th Ave., tel. 718/672–1232. Subway: 7 to 74th St. BYOB. Cash only.*

Tierras Colombianas. Arrive hungry if you're planning to tackle a "mountain plate" of South American staples like stewed beef, fried pork, rice-and-beans, plantains, or cassava. Finish up with a thick, sweet tropical juice. *82–18 Roosevelt Ave., near 82nd St., tel. 718/426–8868. Subway: 7 to 82nd St./Jackson Heights. Cash only.*

LONG ISLAND CITY

UNDER $15 • Pearson's Texas Barbecue. Authentic Texas barbecue devotees gladly make the trek out to this bare-bones joint on a lonely street in Long Island City, where beef brisket and other fleshy delights are slowly smoked on a real barbecue pit outside. Pick your poison in the form of a sandwich, or pay per pound ($13–$14)—and don't forget the hot sauce. *5–16 51st Ave., between Vernon Blvd. and the East River, tel. 718/937–3030. Subway: 7 to Vernon Blvd./Jackson Ave. Cash only.*

THE BRONX

Not many Bronx-bound tourists get beyond the zoo, but those who do will find some rewarding restaurant choices. In the Italian-American neighborhood of **Belmont,** trattorias, pizzerias, caffès, pastry shops, salumerias, fish markets, and cheese stores line the streets. Across the Long Island Sound on **City Island,** you can gorge yourself to the gills on deep-fried seafood—and worry about your health later.

BELMONT

For a truly gluttonous experience, stroll Bronx's "Little Italy" around **Arthur Avenue** and **187th Street,** stopping at **Madonia Brothers Bakery** (2348 Arthur Ave., tel. 718/295-5573), where uncountable loaves of fresh bread have been baked since 1918. **Cosenza's Fish Market** (2354 Arthur Ave., tel. 718/364-8510) has an outdoor fish stand that sells six clams on the half shell for $3. At **Calabria Pork Store** (2338 Arthur Ave., tel. 718/367-5145), dried meats hang from the ceiling and huge blocks of cheese chill on the sidelines.

UNDER $10 • Dominick's. This place is about as unpretentious as it gets, with communal tables, jugs of wine, and a point-and-shout approach to ordering. Locals love it, and on weekends the line stretches out the door. A big Italian dinner costs $8–$15. *2335 Arthur Ave., near 187th St., tel. 718/733-2807. Subway: C or D to Fordham Rd. Train: Metro-North to Fordham station. Closed Tues.*

Ristorante Egidio. Everything at this snazzy lunch spot costs less than $10, so indulge in one of the hearty pastas, soups, or sandwiches. For dessert and espresso, head next door to **Caffè Egidio** (tel. 718/295-6077), which has outlasted two World Wars and the Great Depression and is still Belmont's favorite Italian café. Dig into the gelato or one of 55 kinds of pastries. *622 E. 187th St., at Hughes Ave., tel. 718/364-3157. Subway: D to Fordham Rd. Train: Metro-North to Fordham station.*

UNDER $15 • Ann and Tony's. They've been making mean plates of spaghetti carbonara, veal Parmesan, and chicken marsala at this family-owned restaurant since 1927. Students get a 10%, cash-only discount. *2407 Arthur Ave., at E. 187th St., tel. 718/933-1469. Subway: C or D to Fordham Rd. Train: Metro-North to Fordham station. No dinner Mon.*

CITY ISLAND

UNDER $10 • Johnny's Reef Restaurant. This simple chant will help you through a meal at Johnny's: FRIED FOODS ARE MY FRIEND, FRIED FOODS WILL NOT HURT ME. And, really, the delicious fried shrimp, oysters, and other sea critters are virtually greaseless. *2 City Island Ave., tel. 718/885-2086. Subway: 6 to Pelham Bay (25 mins), then Bus BX12 to end of City Island Ave. (25 mins). Cash only.*

Rhodes. Around the turn of the century, Rhodes was a sailors' home, inn, and whorehouse. Now it's a pub with live music, good burgers, and pub grub. There's even a moose head on the wall. *288 City Island Ave., at Fordham Rd., tel. 718/885-1538. Subway: 6 to Pelham Bay, then Bus BX12 to City Island Ave.*

RIVERDALE, WILLIAMSBRIDGE, AND MORRIS HEIGHTS

UNDER $10 • African and American Restaurant. Ever had Ghanian food? If not, here's the scoop: Ghanian mashes are bricklike blocks of steamed *fufu* (mashed cassava), *gari* (fermented cassava), or *emu-tuw* (kneaded glutinous rice), spiced with toasted melon seeds, peanut, ginger, or garlic and eaten with the right hand. Get in line and point to whatever looks good: There's southern-style grub for the less brazen palate. *1987 University Ave., at Burnside Ave., Morris Heights, tel. 718/731-8595. Subway: 4 to Burnside Ave. BYOB. Open 24 hrs. Cash only.*

An Bēal Bocht. This Irish pub ("The Poor Mouth" in Gaelic) has a funky, bohemian spirit and hosts poetry readings (Tuesday) and live Irish bands (Wednesday–Saturday). The crowd's a cool mix of Irish folk and students from nearby Manhattan College. Foodwise, fill up on Irish stew and soda bread or chicken potpie. Pints of Guinness and Harp are $4. On Sunday they serve a traditional Irish breakfast for $7, with black-and-white pudding, sausage, rashers, eggs, and fried tomatoes. *445 W. 238th St., between Greystone and Waldo Aves., Riverdale, tel. 718/884-7127. Subway: 1 or 9 to 238th St.; walk up 238th St. to steep flight of stairs and start climbing.*

Harry's Jerk Center. The neighborhood's sketchy and the place is a dive, but the Jamaican jerked chicken served here qualifies as Food of the Gods. Harry himself (probably under divine guidance) marinates this stuff for *eight days* in garlic, curry, Scotch bonnet peppers, pimientos, allspice, and whatever else is lying around. The bold among us may want to skip directly to the cow cod soup ("cod" being a code word for "testicles") or the mannish water (translation: goat's head soup). *1296 E. Gun Hill Rd., at Burke Ave., Williamsbridge, tel. 718/798-4966. Subway: 5 to Gun Hill Rd. Closed Sun. Cash only.*

STATEN ISLAND

Though you won't find crowds rushing across the Verrazano-Narrows bridge to dine in Staten Island, there's decent food to be had near Snug Harbor and Richmondtown. At Snug Harbor, **Melville's Cafe** (no phone) puts out a spread of tasty cafeteria grub weekdays from 11 to 2. At Richmondtown, **the Parsonage** (74 Arthur Kill Rd., tel. 718/351–7879) serves sophisticated Continental cuisine in a historic home from 1885 (entrées cost $13–$20).

UNDER $15 • Adobe Blues. There are plenty of reasons to come to this Southwestern hangout three blocks from Snug Harbor: good food (try the chili con carne or Drunken Mexican Shrimp, made with tequila and lime juice), a huge beer selection (200-plus), and a cozy setting—there's even a fireplace. If you happen to be on the Island at night, stop by for live blues on Wednesday. From Snug Harbor, walk three blocks on Fillmore Street to Lafayette. *63 Lafayette St., New Brighton, tel. 718/720–2583. From ferry terminal, take Bus S40 to Lafayette Ave. (5 mins).*

CAFES AND COFFEE BARS

Excluding the West Village and Little Italy, decent coffee—much less café au lait and triple cappuccinos—didn't exist in Manhattan until the early '90s. Around that time a few New Yorkers noticed they'd missed the boat on the whole Seattle coffee craze, and imitation Left-Coast cafés started cropping up like pay-per-view wrestling matches. By 1994, the *New York Times* was moved to explain to its poor, confused readers that these new **coffee bars** were not to be confused with the old **coffee shops.** The distinction is subtle but real, so keep this axiom in mind: At coffee shops the grease is on your plate, while at coffee bars the grease is in the hair of the slacker employees.

While it's now impossible to go a single block without bumping into some sort of espresso bar (or three), not all are the kind of place you'd want to hole up with a pack of smokes and a David Foster Wallace novel. Some, the Type-A cafés, are sterile outlets where the furniture is uncomfortable and the lighting fluorescent. These are sadly common in Midtown. The others, more common in the East Village and Chelsea, are cool and funky and often furnished with comfy thrift-store couches. Many do a lot more than just crank out coffee, like displaying the works of neighborhood artists, holding poetry and fiction readings, hosting live music, or providing access to the Internet. And unlike the Type A's, they won't go ballistic if you decide to linger all afternoon over your $1 purchase. You can count on either kind of café to fill you up with a menu of sandwiches, salads, soups, and desserts when you're down to your last $5. Some even serve beer or wine. Typically, a regular coffee costs $1, fancy caffeine brews $2–$4.

COFFEE-BAR CHAINS

A few coffee-bar chains are worth checking out. If you need a CNN fix or want to browse a rack of 450 (yes, 450) foreign and domestic publications, try **News Bar** (2 W. 19th St., near 5th Ave., Chelsea, tel. 212/255–3996; 107 University Pl., between 12th and 13th Sts., West Village, tel. 212/260–4192). The ubiquitous **Barnes and Noble** (4 Astor Pl., between Broadway and Lafayette St., East Village, tel. 212/420–1322) has cafés in all its Manhattan superstores; they've become legendary cruising zones for literary types who feel most glib and chatty when they're clutching a copy of *Sansho the Bailiff*. And finally, the Seattle chain that started it all is regarded by many as having New York's Best-Tasting Cuppa Joe: **Starbucks** (2379 Broadway, at 87th St., Upper West Side, tel. 212/875–8470; Waverly Pl., at E. 6th St., East Village, tel. 212/477–7776; and many, many more).

UPTOWN

Café Mozart. Pound out your own *Requiem* on this funky café's baby grand piano, right beneath an incredibly ugly framed likeness of its Austrian namesake. The café is a hangout for foreign journalists and literary types who enjoy decent sandwiches. *154 W. 70th St., between Broadway and Columbus Ave., tel. 212/595–9797. Subway: 1, 2, 3, or 9 to W. 72nd St.*

Drip. Eyes are roving as twenty-somethings scan the questionnaire-filled binders strewn about the couches and tables for a potential blind date. If you can't chat up someone actually sitting next to you, Drip provides a free dating service by arranging meetings for people interested in each other's write-ups. The music is hip, the crowd clean-cut, and the atmosphere charged. *489 Amsterdam, between 83rd and 84th Sts., Upper West Side, tel. 212/875–1032. Subway: 1 or 9 to W. 86th St.*

The Hungarian Pastry Shop. Columbia University's alternative crowd comes here to think Deep Thoughts while refueling their physical beings with a selection of sugary confections. *1030 Amsterdam Ave., between W. 110th and 111th Sts., tel. 212/866–4230. Subway: 1 or 9 to W. 110th St. Cash only.*

Muffin Man. On warm days they throw the French doors wide open at the popular Muffin Man. Besides sandwiches ($3–$5) and cheap breakfasts ($3), they have a vast array of sinful baked goodies. *1638 3rd Ave., between E. 91st and 92nd Sts., tel. 212/987–2404. Subway: 6 to E. 96th St. Cash only.*

Positively 104th Street. This place is whatever you want it to be: gourmet coffee emporium, art gallery, or café. And they offer free coffee refills—try finding that anywhere else in Manhattan. *2725 Broadway, at W. 104th St., tel. 212/316–0372. Subway: 1 or 9 to W. 103rd St.*

CHELSEA

Big Cup Tea & Coffeehouse. Sip coffee or slam a triple cappuccino with a hip, gay crowd. Lavender flowers blossom with psychedelic radiance on the Big Cup's lime-green walls—very Alice in Wonderland. *228 8th Ave., between W. 21st and 22nd Sts., tel. 212/206–0059. Subway: C or E to W. 23rd St. Cash only.*

Eureka Joe. Part dentist's office, part Pee Wee's Playhouse, Eureka Joe has gigantic stuffed chairs and couches strewn randomly around a characterless room. Literary hipsters come for the usual café fare as well as beer and wine. *168 5th Ave., at 22nd St., tel. 212/741–7500. Subway: N or R to W. 23rd St. Cash only.*

Paradise Cafe. Hip Chelseans crowd Paradise—while their pooches wait dutifully outside. Try the mysterious Euro-Ice Nutrition Drink ($1.50), which could prolong your life and make you enjoy house music. *139 8th Ave., at W. 17th St., tel. 212/647–0066. Subway: A, C, E, or L to W. 14th St. Cash only.*

WEST VILLAGE

Bleecker Street Pastry Shop. This Italian bakery and café, opened in 1966, doubles as a social club for Sicilian matriarchs. Try the Lobster Tail, an Italian sweet with rum-flavored filling. *245 Bleecker St., at Carmine St., tel. 212/242–4959. Subway: A, B, C, D, E, F, or Q to W. 4th St. (Washington Sq.). Cash only.*

Cafe Borgia. The students of New York University come here in droves for delicious Italian desserts and free-flowing cappuccinos. *185 Bleecker St., at MacDougal St., tel. 212/674–9589. Subway: A, B, C, D, E, F, or Q to W. 4th St. (Washington Sq.).*

Cafe Mona Lisa. You may wish your date were as gorgeous as this café. Arrive in the evening, when the lights are low and some singer's rich baritone is turned on high. *282 Bleecker St., between Jones St. and 7th Ave. S, tel. 212/929–1262 or 212/929–1347. Subway: 1 or 9 to Christopher St. (Sheridan Sq.).*

Cafe Reggio. In the '50s this was a favorite hangout of the Beats (at the time, it had the only espresso machine in the Village). Today it's a great place to watch tourists dorking along MacDougal Street. *119 MacDougal St., between W. 3rd and Bleecker Sts., tel. 212/475–9557. Subway: A, B, C, D, E, F, or Q to W. 4th St. (Washington Sq.).*

Caffe Dell Artista. Caffe Dell Artista is a terrific place for a tête-à-tête—if you don't mind shouting a bit to be heard over the French show tunes. Salads, sandwiches, and delicious desserts are less than $6. *46 Greenwich Ave., between Charles St. and 7th Ave., tel. 212/645–4431. Subway: 1, 2, 3, or 9 to W. 14th St. Cash only.*

Caffe Lucca. Notice something? All the people here are *Italian* tourists, which should tell you a thing or two about how good the cappuccinos and gelatos taste. *228 Bleecker St., between Carmine St. and 6th Ave., tel. 212/243–8385. Subway: A, B, C, D, E, F, or Q to W. 4th St. (Washington Sq.).*

The Peacock. The Peacock—like every other Italian coffeehouse on MacDougal Street—claims it was the first in the Village to serve cappuccino. The excellence of their rum cake and tiramisù, however, is undisputed. *24 Greenwich Ave., at W. 10th St., tel. 212/242–9395. Subway: 1 or 9 to Christopher St. (Sheridan Sq.). Cash only.*

EAST VILLAGE AND THE LOWER EAST SIDE

Café Pick Me Up. What could be better than slurping coffee while watching the skate punks, flannel-clad nihilists, hippies, and vinyl fetishists do their thing in Tompkins Square Park? Well, perhaps a $2.25 breakfast that's served until noon. *145 Ave. A, at E. 9th St., tel. 212/673–7231. Subway: L to 1st Ave.; also 6 to Astor Pl. Cash only.*

First Street Cafe. In size it's somewhere between "closet" and "shoe box," but this is the café of choice for East Village slackers looking to ponder life's meaning over coffee and cheap, tasty eats. Check out the Elvis bathroom. *72 1st St., between 1st and 2nd Aves., tel. 212/420–0701. Subway: F to 2nd Ave. Cash only.*

Internet Cafe. E-mail an Armenian bass-fishing expert or chat with foot worshipers from around the globe while sipping espresso. Computers here cost $4 per half hour ($75 for 10 hours). The café even sponsors classes; peruse the listings at their Web site (www.bigmagic.com). *82 E. 3rd St., between 1st and 2nd Aves., tel. 212/614–0747. Subway: F to 2nd Ave.*

Limbo. All-black-clad intellectuals smirk, smoke, and drink cappuccino at the city's most hyped café, run by Vassar grads and founded by a Bergdorf-Goodman heiress. Daytime is for book reading, night-time for loud conversations about Flaubert and cybersex. On Wednesday evening big-name and upcoming writers alike read their prose and poetry. *47 Ave. A, between E. 3rd and 4th Sts., tel. 212/477–5271. Subway: F to 2nd Ave. Cash only.*

LITTLE ITALY

Caffé Roma. More Italian than Michelangelo or World Cup soccer, this Old World transplant has marble-topped tables, an ancient brass espresso machine, and killer cannoli. *385 Broome St., at Mulberry St., tel. 212/226–8413. Subway: 6 to Spring St. Cash only.*

Ferrara. Your plan of attack at this century-old institution is simple: Keep eating desserts. We recommend the *tartufo* (chocolate-covered Bavarian cream puff) and cannoli (fried pastry roll with sweet cream filling). In fact, actor Tony Danza (think "Taxi") liked the cannoli so much that in return he left a few nice framed photos of himself. *195 Grand St., between Mott and Mulberry Sts., tel. 212/226–6150. Subway: B, D, or Q to Grand St.*

SOHO AND TRIBECA

Basset Coffee and Tea Co. A genuinely relaxed atmosphere and pleasant outdoor patio make this TriBeCa coffee and tea emporium a fine place to enjoy a light sandwich or salad. *123 W. Broadway, at Duane St., tel. 212/349–1662. Subway: 1, 2, 3, or 9 to Chambers St.*

Cyber Café. SoHo's Cyber Café, spacious and slick, offers organic foods, gourmet coffees, and all-fruit "Cyber Shakes," plus full Internet access, e-mail, and Web surfing ($12 per hour). Their Web address is www.cyber-cafe.com. *273A Lafayette St., at Prince St., tel. 212/334–5140. Subway: N or R to Prince St.; also 6 to Spring St.*

Duane Park Patisserie. Hidden among TriBeCa's warehouses is a bakery/café selling the kind of cheesecakes, chocolate tortes, and custard tarts for which you'd gladly hock your trousers. *179 Duane St., between Greenwich and Hudson Sts., tel. 212/274–8447. Subway: 1, 2, 3, or 9 to Chambers St. Closed Mon.*

In the Black. Come to this lushly appointed café to confirm all those clichés about SoHo people . . . like their fondness for all-black clothing, neatly clipped goatees, and incisive comments about art. *180 Varick St., between King and Charlton Sts., tel. 212/807–8322. Subway: 1 or 9 to Houston St. Closed Sun.*

Le Gamin. Just as you'd expect from a French café, Le Gamin serves superb crepes and magnificent crème brûlée. And the café au lait comes European-style, in a great big bowl. *50 MacDougal St., between Houston and Prince Sts., tel. 212/254–4678. Subway: C or E to Spring St. Other location: 183 9th Ave., at W. 21st St., Chelsea, tel. 212/243–8864.*

Ninth Street Market. The best thing about this tiny spot is the fireplace. Also, on weekends they serve a fine prix-fixe brunch for $7.25. And did we mention that they have a fireplace? *337 E. 9th St., between 1st and 2nd Aves., tel. 212/473–0242. Subway: 6 to Astor Pl. Closed Mon.*

Scharmann's. This spacious, loftlike café is decorated with mismatched Victorian furniture and populated by well-manicured SoHoers. *386 W. Broadway, between Spring and Broome Sts., tel. 212/219–2561. Subway: C or E to Spring St.*

MARKETS AND SPECIALTY SHOPS

Most New Yorkers treat their kitchens with the same sort of kindly, solicitous dread that St. Augustine extended to leper colonies. They really don't like to deal with cooking, and why should they? The pizza and Thai guys will always deliver—even in a blizzard at 4 AM. That said, there are tons of places to buy the fixings for a do-it-yourself gourmet meal or a glorious but hassle-free picnic. If the selection below leaves you wanting, pick up *New York Eats* by Ed Levine (St. Martin's Press, $16.95); it lists every lox shop and knishery in the five boroughs, and more.

GENERAL MARKETS

Dean & Deluca. SoHo's epicurean fantasyland isn't really a market—it's an art gallery for food. They sell the best in produce, fresh fish, breads, cheeses, desserts, candies, and strangely beautiful kitchen utensils. *560 Broadway, at Prince St., SoHo, tel. 212/431–1691. Subway: N or R to Prince St.*

Fairway. This suburban-style warehouse/megamarket (complete with a 200-car parking lot) is a one-stop shopper's dream. In addition to a large, cheap selection of produce and baked goods, it abounds with fresh meats, poultry, fish, and dairy products—all displayed in a 38°F former meat-packing room. They even supply jackets so you won't catch cold while picking out the perfect flank steak. The other location, at 74th and Broadway, is practically a night out on the town for Upper West Siders. *2328 12th Ave., between 132nd and 133rd Sts., Harlem, tel. 212/234–3883. Subway: 1 to 125th St. Other location: 2127 Broadway, at W. 74th St., Upper West Side, tel. 212/595–1888. Subway: 1, 2, or 3 to 72nd St.*

Russ and Daughters. Although many neighboring stores are run down or boarded up, Russ and Daughters is spit-shined and orderly. Just about everything is made on the premises, from barrels of pickled cucumbers, onions, tomatoes, and peppers to the variety of smoked fishes and spreads. *179 E. Houston St., between Orchard and Allen Sts., Lower East Side, tel. 212/475–4880 or 800/787–7229. Subway: F to 2nd Ave.*

Zabar's. A real New York institution, Zabar's is a crowded and popular food emporium with, among other things, delicious fresh breads, meats, smoked fish, and candy. If you're shopping for housewares, browse the huge selection upstairs. Prices are surprisingly good and often downright cheap. Next door is Zabar's café (*see* Manhattan Restaurants, *above*). *2245 Broadway, at W. 80th St., Upper West Side, tel. 212/787–2000. Subway: 1 or 9 to W. 79th St.*

ETHNIC FOODS

Italian Food Center. They have Italian flags on the walls and a great selection of olive oils, salamis, prosciuttos, focaccia breads, and hero sandwiches. The food here is delizioso, but not exactly low-cal—notice that the employees are prone to overindulgence, too. *186 Grand St., at Mulberry St., Little Italy, tel. 212/925–2954. Subway: B, D, or Q to Grand St.*

Kam Man. This Chinese food and housewares emporium is unparalleled in the city. The main floor has foodstuffs—from ginseng to dried eel to hard candies—while downstairs there's a wide variety of teas, porcelain, noodles, and pots and pans. *200 Canal St., at Elizabeth St., Chinatown, tel. 212/571–0330. Subway: J, M, N, R, Z, or 6 to Canal St.*

M & I International. This is the Brighton Beach community's equivalent to Zabar's—a gourmet store and supermarket with a decidedly Russian flavor (note the jaunty Russian pop blaring from the P.A. system). Browse the vast deli cases filled with sausages, salads, and smoked fish and have lunch on the nearby beach. *249 Brighton Beach Ave., between Brighton 2 and Brighton 3 Sts., tel. 718/615–1011. Subway: D to Ocean Pkwy.*

Sahadi Importing Company. This is New York's best Middle Eastern market. In addition to exotic spices, Sahadi's sells grains, olives (nearly two dozen varieties), dates, dried apricots, nuts, and standbys like hummus and leban. *187 Atlantic Ave., between Court and Clinton Sts., Brooklyn Heights, tel. 718/624–4550. Subway: M, N, or R to Court St. Closed Sun.*

SPECIALTY SHOPS

East Village Cheese. Signs proclaiming ROCK-BOTTOM PRICES cover the entire front window of this dairy mecca. The gimmick is low prices on more cheese than you can shake a stick at, including Camembert and fontina for $2.99 per pound. It also sells fresh breads and low-cost pâtés ($5.99 per lb). *40 3rd Ave., between 9th and 10th Sts., tel. 212/477–2601. Subway: 6 to Astor Pl.*

Essex Street Pickles. If you can't imagine why anyone would trek to the sticks of the Lower East Side for a pickle, you've never been to this 80-year-old institution, which regulars still call Guss Pickles (its original name). Coming here is a quintessential New York experience—you can watch old men stand about gabbing in the doorway while you browse the pickles, sauerkraut, and other vinegar-cured treasures all displayed in brawny wooden barrels. *35 Essex St., between Hester and Grand Sts., Lower East Side, tel. 212/254–4477. Subway: F to E. Broadway. Closed Fri. 2 PM–Sat.*

Joe's Dairy. Pungent wafts of smoked mozzarella lure unsuspecting passersby into Joe's, an old-world emporium packed floor to ceiling with wheels of cheese. *156 Sullivan St., between Prince St. and Houston St., tel. 212/677–8780. Subway: C or E to Spring St.; also 1 or 9 to Houston St. Closed Sun.–Mon.*

WINE AND SPIRITS

Astor Wines & Spirits. A wide selection of wines, spirits, liqueurs, and sake at very nice prices. Astor stocks "good" wines for less than $10, and the prices on hard liquor are some of the best in the city. There's little reason to shop anywhere else. *12 Astor Pl., at Lafayette St., East Village, tel. 212/674–7500. Subway: 6 to Astor Pl.; also N or R to E. 8th St. Closed Sun.*

The lox at Russ and Daughters routinely wins praises as "best in New York." Which is nothing to sneeze at in a city where smoked salmon is, to some, more important than national defense.

GREENMARKETS

Open-air farmers' markets in New York City? Though it sounds like an oxymoron, it's true. And it comes as no surprise that they are the best places to stock up on organic vegetables and fruit, baked goods, fresh fish, flowers, and wine—all sold by real, honest-to-goodness farmers from New Jersey and upstate New York. A few of the best and most centrally located greenmarkets are listed below; unless indicated otherwise, their hours are 8 AM–5 PM rain or shine. For more info contact the city's **Greenmarket Program** (130 E. 16th St., NY 10003, tel. 212/477–3220).

MANHATTAN MARKETS

Union Square. This is the largest of New York's greenmarkets, a place where epicurians (including some of Manhattan's best chefs) swarm around stalls filled with fresh fruit, vegetables, meat, fish, bread, and flowers. Look for **Tweefontein Herb Farm** (Saturday), which makes sorbets from lavender, lemon verbeno, and rosemary. On Saturday afternoon between June and December, star chefs sign copies of their cookbooks, give cooking demonstrations, and dispense free samples. *E. 17th St. at Broadway. Subway: L, N, R, 4, 5, or 6 to Union Sq. (E. 14th St.). Open Mon., Wed., Fri., and Sat.*

Abingdon Square. *W. 12th St. at 8th Ave., West Village. Subway: A, C, E, or L to W. 14th St. (8th Ave.). Open May–Dec., Sat. 8–3.*

City Hall. *Chambers St. at Centre St., Lower Manhattan. Subway: 4, 5, or 6 to Brooklyn Bridge–City Hall. Open Tues. and Fri. 8–3.*

I. S. 44. *W. 77th St. at Columbus Ave., Upper West Side. Subway: B or C to W. 72nd St.; also 1, 2, 3, or 9 to W. 72nd St. Open Sun. 10–5.*

Minisink Townhouse. *W. 143rd St. at Lenox Ave., Harlem. Subway: 3 to W. 145th St. Open mid-July–Oct., Tues. 8–4:30.*

St. Mark's Church. *E. 10th St. at 2nd Ave., East Village. Subway: 6 to Astor Pl.; also L to 3rd Ave. Open June–Nov., Tues. 8–5.*

Sheffield Plaza. *W. 57th St. at 9th Ave., Midtown. Subway: A, B, C, D, 1, or 9 to Columbus Circle (W. 59th St.). Open Wed. and Sat.*

Washington Market Park. *Greenwich St. at Reade St., TriBeCa. Subway: 1, 2, 3, or 9 to Chambers St. Open Sat.*

World Trade Center. *Church St. at Fulton St., Lower Manhattan. Subway: C or E to World Trade Center. Open Thurs. (also Tues. June–Nov.).*

OUTER BOROUGH MARKETS

Albee Square. *Fulton St. and De Kalb Ave., Downtown Brooklyn. Subway: D, Q, M, N, or R to De Kalb Ave. Open Wed. July–Oct.*

Borough Hall. *Court St. at Remsen St., Brooklyn Heights. Subway: 2, 3, 4, or 5 to Borough Hall. Open Tues. and Sat.*

Grand Army Plaza. *At entrance to Prospect Park, Park Slope, Brooklyn. Subway: 2 or 3 to Grand Army Plaza. Open Sat.*

Poe Park. *E. 192nd St. at Grand Concourse, Bronx. Subway: C or D to Fordham Rd. Open mid-July–Nov., Tues. 8–3.*

St. George. *St. Marks Pl. at Hyatt St., St. George, Staten Island. From ferry terminal, walk 3 blocks inland on Hyatt St. Open June–Nov., Sat. 8–2.*

Williamsburg. *Havemeyer St. and Broadway, Williamsburg, Brooklyn. Subway: J, M, or Z to Marcy Ave. Open Thurs. mid-July–Oct.*

Windsor Terrace. *Prospect Park W. and 15th St., Windsor Terrace, Brooklyn. Subway: F to 15th St. Open Wed. July–Nov.*

REFERENCE LISTINGS

BY TYPE OF CUISINE

AFRICAN

Under $10

African and American Restaurant (*Bronx*)

Darou Minan (*Harlem*)

Mandigo Restaurant (*Harlem*)

Moroccan Star (*Brooklyn*)

Obaa Koryoe (*Columbia University*)

Selam Cafe (*Columbia University*)

Sahara East (*East Village*)

Under $15

Abyssinia (*SoHo*)

AMERICAN/DINER FOOD

Under $5

Dojo (*East Village*)

Gray's Papaya (*Upper West Side*)

Joseph's Food Basket (*Harlem*)

McDonald's (*Lower Manhattan*)

Nathan's Famous (*Brooklyn*)

Park Luncheonette (*Brooklyn*)

Seaport Soup Company (*Lower Manhattan*)

Soup Burg (*Upper East Side*)

Spring Street Market and Deli (*SoHo*)

Zabar's (*Upper West Side*)

Under $10

Aggie's and Aggie's Too (*West Village*)

America (*Gramercy*)

Bell Caffe (*SoHo*)

Bendix Diner (*Chelsea and East Village*)

Big Nick's Burger/Pizza Joint (*Upper West Side*)

Cupcake Cafe (*Midtown West*)

EJ's Luncheonette (*Upper East Side*)

Jerry's (*SoHo*)

Johnny's Reef Restaurant (*Bronx*)

Moondance Diner (*SoHo*)

Pearl Street Diner (*Lower Manhattan*)

Riverside Church Cafeteria (*Columbia University*)

Soup Kitchen International (*Midtown West*)

Tom's Restaurant (*Columbia University*)

Wilson's Bakery and Restaurant (*Washington Heights*)

Under $15

Barking Dog Luncheonette (*Upper East Side*)

The Pink Tea Cup (*West Village*)

Tivoli (*Midtown East*)

Universal Grill (*West Village*)

Under $20

City Grill (*Upper West Side*)

Florent (*West Village*)

Good Enough to Eat (*Upper West Side*)

CARIBBEAN/CUBAN

Under $5

F. Restaurant (*Lower East Side*)

Under $10

Café con Leche (*Upper West Side*)

Harry's Jerk Center (*Bronx*)

La Rosita (*Columbia University*)

National Café (*East Village*)

One City Café (*Chelsea*)

CHINESE

Under $5

Bo Ky (*Chinatown*)

Excellent Dumpling House (*Chinatown*)

Sweet 'n' Tart Cafe (*Chinatown*)

Under $10

31 Division Dim Sum House (*Chinatown*)

La Caridad (*Upper West Side*)

The Cottage (*Upper West Side*)

Hunan Garden (*Columbia University*)

House of Vegetarian (*Chinatown*)

Joe's Shanghai (*Queens*)

Sam's Noodle Shop & Grill Bar (*Midtown East*)

Triple Eight Palace (*Chinatown*)

Westside Cottage II (*Midtown West*)

Under $15

Helianthus Vegetarian (*SoHo*)

Penang (*Queens*)

CONTINENTAL

Under $10

Bubby's (*TriBeCa*)

Chez Brigitte (*West Village*)

Frutti de Mare (*East Village*)

Yaffa Café (*East Village*)

Yaffa's Bar and Restaurant (*TriBeCa*)

Under $15

Park Avalon (*Gramercy*)

SoHo Kitchen and Bar (*SoHo*)

Under $20

Balthazar (*SoHo*)

Bridge Café (*Lower Manhattan*)

New City Café (*Brooklyn*)

EAST EUROPEAN

Under $5

Odessa (*East Village*)

Under $10

Cafe Tatiana (*Brooklyn*)
Kiev (*East Village*)
Primorski (*Brooklyn*)

FRENCH

Under $15

Chez Bernard (*SoHo*)
Jean Claude (*SoHo*)
La Bouillabaisse (*Brooklyn*)
Tartine (*West Village*)

Under $20

Florent (*West Village*)
L'Ecole (*SoHo*)
Les Routiers (*Upper West Side*)
Trois Canards (*Chelsea*)

GREEK

Under $10

Mr. Souvlaki (*Brooklyn*)
Uncle George's (*Queens*)

Under $15

Zenon (*Queens*)

HEALTH FOOD

Under $5

Fresco Tortilla Grill (*Midtown East*)
Good Earth Natural Foods Inc. (*Upper West Side*)
Tamarind Seed Health Food Store (*Columbia University*)

Under $10

Angelica Kitchen (*East Village*)
Candle Cafe (*Upper East Side*)
Friend of a Farmer (*Gramercy*)

Under $15

Josie's (*Upper West Side*)
Village Natural Health Food Restaurant (*West Village*)

HOME COOKIN'

Under $10

Aggie's and Aggie's Too (*West Village*)

Friend of a Farmer (*Gramercy*)

Under $15

Chat 'n' Chew (*Gramercy*)
Home (*West Village*)

Under $20

Good Enough to Eat (*Upper West Side*)

INDIAN

Under $10

Bengal Cafe (*Columbia University*)
Jackson Diner (*Queens*)
Madras Mahal (*Midtown East*)
Panna (*West Village*)

ITALIAN/PIZZA

Under $5

The Bread Shop Cafe (*Columbia University*)
Manganaro's Hero Boy (*Midtown West*)

Under $10

Aiello's (*Brooklyn*)
Big Nick's Burger/Pizza Joint (*Upper West Side*)
Dominick's (*Bronx*)
Gennaro (*Upper West Side*)
Il Fornaio (*Little Italy*)
John's Pizzeria (*West Village*)
Luna's (*Little Italy*)
Puglia (*Little Italy*)
Ristorante Egidio (*Bronx*)

Under $15

Ann and Tony's (*Bronx*)
Caffe Buon Gusto (*Upper East Side*)
Carmine's (*Lower Manhattan*)
John's (*East Village*)
Patsy's Pizzeria (*Upper East Side*)
Patsy Grimaldi's Pizza (*Brooklyn*)
Randazzo's Clam Bar (*Brooklyn*)
Two Boots (*East Village and Brooklyn*)

Umberto's Clam House (*Little Italy*)

Under $20

Cucina (*Brooklyn*)
Perretti Italian Cafe (*Upper West Side*)
Pò (*West Village*)

JAPANESE/KOREAN

Under $5

Tachigui-Soba (*Midtown West*)

Under $10

Esashi (*East Village*)
Sapporo (*Midtown West*)

Under $15

Avenue A (*East Village*)
The Mill (*Columbia University*)

Under $20

Fujiyama Mama's (*Upper West Side*)

KOSHER/JEWISH

Under $5

Ess-a-Bagel (*Gramercy and Midtown East*)
New York City Bagels (*Upper West Side*)
Yonah Schimmel's Knishery (*Lower East Side*)

Under $10

Katz's Delicatessen (*Lower East Side*)
Madras Mahal (*Midtown East*)
Ratners (*Lower East Side*)
Vegetarian Heaven (*Midtown West*)

Under $15

Second Avenue Deli (*East Village*)

LATIN AND SOUTH AMERICAN

Under $10

El Pollo (*Upper East Side*)
La Cabaña Salvadoreña (*Washington Heights*)

La Fonda Antioqueña
(*Queens*)

Tierras Colombianas (*Queens*)

Under $15

Arroz y Feijão (*Midtown West*)

MEXICAN/TEX-MEX

Under $5

Fresco Tortilla Grill (*Midtown East*)

La Espiga (*Queens*)

Under $10

bean (*Brooklyn*)

Benny's Burritos (*West Village*)

Bertha's Burritos (*Upper West Side*)

El Sombrero (The Hat) (*Lower East Side*)

Festival Mexicana (*Lower East Side*)

Life Cafe (*East Village*)

Lupe's East L.A. Kitchen (*SoHo*)

Samalita's (*Upper East Side*)

Taco Taco (*Upper East Side*)

Taquería de México (*West Village*)

Uncle Mo's (*Chelsea*)

Under $15

Adobe Blues (*Staten Island*)

Gabriela's (*Upper West Side*)

Tortilla Flats (*West Village*)

Under $20

Mesa Grill (*Chelsea*)

MIDDLE EASTERN

Under $5

Amir's Falafel (*Columbia University*)

Fatoosh Barbecue (*Brooklyn*)

Mamoun's (*West Village*)

Under $10

Al Dewan (*Queens*)

Moroccan Star (*Brooklyn*)

Moustache (*West Village*)

Sahara East (*East Village*)

Under $15

Oznot's Dish (*Brooklyn*)

Tripoli Restaurant (*Brooklyn*)

PUB GRUB

Under $10

An Béal Bocht (*Bronx*)

Fanelli's Cafe (*SoHo*)

Heartland Brewery (*Gramercy*)

Old Town Bar (*Gramercy*)

Park Slope Brewing Company (*Brooklyn*)

Pete's Tavern (*Gramercy*)

Rhodes (*Bronx*)

Under $15

St. Dymphna's (*East Village*)

Telephone Bar and Grill (*East Village*)

SEAFOOD

Under $10

Frutti de Mare (*East Village*)

Under $15

Carmine's (*Lower Manhattan*)

Johnny's Reef Restaurant (*Bronx*)

Randazzo's Clam Bar (*Brooklyn*)

SOUTHEAST ASIAN

Under $5

Bo Ky (*Chinatown*)

Elvie's Turo-Turo (*East Village*)

Under $10

Bendix Diner (*Chelsea and East Village*)

Galaxy (*Gramercy*)

Kelley and Ping (*SoHo*)

Lemongrass Grill (*Brooklyn*)

Marnie's Noodle Shop (*West Village*)

Monsoon (*Upper West Side*)

Nam (*Brooklyn*)

Nha Trang (*Chinatown*)

Thailand Restaurant (*Chinatown*)

Village Mingala (*East Village*)

Under $15

Bangkok House (*Upper East Side*)

Franklin Station Cafe (*TriBeCa*)

Kun Paw (*West Village*)

Penang (*Queens*)

Pho Viet Huong (*Chinatown*)

Regional Thai Taste (*Chelsea*)

Zen Palate (*Gramercy, Midtown West, Upper West Side*)

Under $20

Rain (*Upper West Side*)

Penang (*SoHo*)

SOUTHERN AND BBQ

Under $10

ACME Bar and Grill (*East Village*)

Baby Jake's (*East Village and Lower East Side*)

La Caridad (*Upper West Side*)

Chantale's Cajun Kitchen (*Midtown West*)

Ethel's Southern Quarters (*Harlem*)

RBBQ (*Brooklyn*)

The Reliable (*Harlem*)

Singleton's Bar-B-Que (*Harlem*)

Soul Fixin's (*Midtown West*)

Wilson's Bakery and Restaurant (*Washington Heights*)

Under $15

Great Jones Cafe (*East Village*)

Pearson's Texas Barbecue (*Queens*)

Sylvia's (*Harlem*)

Two Boots (*East Village and Brooklyn*)

Under $20

Harvest (*Brooklyn*)

SPANISH/PORTUGUESE

Under $10

Café con Leche (*Upper West Side*)

Yaffa's Bar and Restaurant
(*TriBeCa*)

Under $15

La Paella (*East Village*)

Luzia's (*Upper West Side*)

Rio Mar (*West Village*)

VEGETARIAN

Under $5

Good Earth Natural Foods
Inc. (*Upper West Side*)

Joseph's Food Basket
(*Harlem*)

Tamarind Seed Health Food
Store (*Columbia University*)

Under $10

Angelica Kitchen (*East
Village*)

bean (*Brooklyn*)

Candle Cafe (*Upper East
Side*)

House of Vegetarian (*Chinatown*)

Madras Mahal (*Midtown East*)

Nam (*Brooklyn*)

Ratner's (*Lower East Side*)

Stacy's (*Brooklyn*)

Under $15

Good Health Cafe (*Upper East
Side*)

Helianthus Vegetarian (*SoHo*)

Village Natural Health Food
Restaurant (*West Village*)

Zen Palate (*Gramercy*)

SPECIAL FEATURES

ALL YOU CAN EAT

Under $5

Beit Eddine (*Midtown East*)

Madras Mahal (*Midtown East*)

BRUNCH

Under $10

31 Division Dim Sum House
(*Chinatown*)

Aggie's (*West Village*)

An Bēal Bocht (*Bromx*)

Bubby's (*TriBeCa*)

Life Cafe (*East Village*)

Ludlow Street Cafe (*Lower
East Side*)

Triple Eight Palace (*Chinatown*)

Wilson's Bakery and Restaurant (*Washington Heights*)

Under $15

Good Enough to Eat (*Upper
West Side*)

Good Health Cafe (*Upper East
Side*)

Home (*West Village*)

Eli's Vinegar Factory (*Upper
East Side*)

Sylvia's (*Harlem*)

Tartine (*West Village*)

EATING AT 4 AM

Under $5

Gray's Papaya (*Upper West
Side*)

Odessa (*East Village*)

Under $10

African and American Restaurant (*Bronx*)

Bell Caffe (*SoHo*)

Big Nick's Burger/Pizza Joint
(*Upper West Side*)

Darou Minan (*Harlem*)

Kiev (*East Village*)

Moondance Diner (*SoHo*)

Singleton's Bar-B-Que
(*Harlem*)

Tom's Restaurant (*Columbia
University*)

Uncle George's (*Queens*)

Under $15

SoHo Kitchen and Bar (*SoHo*)

Tivoli (*Midtown East*)

Under $20

Florent (*West Village*)

MUSIC WITH YOUR MEAL

Under $10

ACME Bar and Grill (*East Village*)

An Bēal Bocht (*Bronx*)

Bell Caffe (*SoHo*)

Puglia (*Little Italy*)

Primorski (*Brooklyn*)

Rhodes (*Bronx*)

Two Boots (*Brooklyn*)

Under $15

Avenue A (*East Village*)

Rio Mar (*West Village*)

Sylvia's (*Harlem*)

Zenon (*Queens*)

Under $20

Fujiyama Mama's (*Upper
West Side*)

**TWIST AND SHOUT
(CROWDED, CAMPY, AND
LOUD)**

Under $15

Tortilla Flats (*West Village*)

Universal Grill (*West Village*)

Under $20

Florent (*West Village*)

NOODLE BARS

Under $5

Excellent Dumpling House
(*Chinatown*)

Sweet 'n' Tart Cafe (*Chinatown*)

Under $10

Hunan Garden (*Columbia
University*)

Kelley and Ping (*SoHo*)

Nam (*Brooklyn*)

Nha Trang (*Chinatown*)

Sam's Noodle Shop and Grill Bar (*Midtown East*)

Sapporo (*Midtown West*)

Under $15

Esashi (*East Village*)

OUTDOOR SEATING

Under $10

Bell Caffe (*SoHo*)

Life Cafe (*East Village*)

St. Dymphna's (*East Village*)

Yaffa Café (*East Village*)

Under $15

Home (*West Village*)

Kun Paw (*West Village*)

Sylvia's (*Harlem*)

Under $20

Harvest (*Brooklyn*)

SWEETS AND DESSERTS

Under $5

The Bread Shop Cafe (*Columbia University*)

City Bakery (*Gramercy*)

Omonia (*Queens*)

Sweet 'n' Tart Cafe (*Chinatown*)

Under $10

Cupcake Cafe (*Midtown West*)

Ozzie's Coffee and Tea (*Brooklyn*)

VERY NEW YORK

Under $10

Luna's (*Little Italy*)

One City Cafe (*Chelsea*)

RBBQ (*Brooklyn*)

Soup Kitchen International (*Midtown West*)

Tom's Restaurant (*Columbia University*)

Under $15

Avenue A (*East Village*)

Barking Dog Luncheonette (*Upper East Side*)

Tortilla Flats (*West Village*)

Under $20

Florent (*West Village*)

Fujiyama Mama's (*Upper West Side*)

Penang (*SoHo*)

SHOPPING

UPDATED BY JENNIFER PAULL

The thrill of a New York shopping experience lies mainly in the pursuit. New Yorkers simultaneously grumble and boast about the miles of sidewalk covered on an average shopping day—and they'll hotly defend their ability to do so. Witness the strong resistance to Mayor Giuliani's rezoning plan to allow more superstores into the city. After all, having everything under one roof would be much too easy.

But there's also a new kind of experience slinking to the fore—the total sensory experience. In newcomer stores like NikeTown or Giorgio Armani, the merchandise seems to play second fiddle to the event of just *being there*. Atmospheres, potent cocktails of music, special displays, atriums, and videos are becoming the new sales tool—as *New York Times Magazine* noted, shopping at Calvin Klein "is like being thrust into an Obsession commercial."

Despite the inroads of such hypnotic environments, the small, neighborhood-defining store is far from extinct. And to find that elusive jazz vinyl or out-of-print Pynchon novel, you'll need to be ready, willing, and able to travel the length and breadth of Manhattan. Don't worry—everybody does it.

Some of the more famous shopping neighborhoods include the **Flower District** (6th and 7th Aves. between W. 25th and 30th Sts.), where shops sell everything from tiny cacti to 20-ft-tall ficus trees; the **Garment District** (*see* Clothes, *below*); the **lamp district** (Bowery between Spring and Hester Sts.); the **restaurant equipment neighborhood** (Bowery between Houston and Delancey Sts.), with great buys on knives and cookware; the **Shoe Street** (*see* Shoes, *below*); the historic **Orchard Street bargain district** (*see* the Lower East Side *in* Chapter 2); the **semicheap antiques street** (Bond St. around Lafayette St.); and the **even cheaper antiques street** (Atlantic Ave. between Clinton and Smith Sts., Brooklyn), where prices average 10% less than in Manhattan boutiques.

Tired yet? There's more: **Madison Avenue** between East 57th and 92nd streets is lined with an ever-expanding range of gleaming "flagship" stores of major designers like Giorgio Armani and Prada. This couture phalanx is matched only by that of **East 57th Street** between 5th and Lexington avenues—but lately the snootier stores here have to compete with megacomplexes like the Warner Bros. Studio Store and NikeTown. **East 7th Street** between 2nd Avenue and Avenue A is crawling with vintage-clothing stores worthy of a stop by. **SoHo** has become increasingly mallified, with chain stores like Victoria's Secret eating away at the galleries, but there are still plenty of distinctive boutiques, especially for fashion and housewares. A bit further east is the up-and-coming home-accessory haven, **Elizabeth Street.** **Chelsea** is newly aswarm with huge discount emporiums like Old Navy; Bed, Bath & Beyond; and

Loehmann's. And don't forget the rich ethnic neighborhoods of **Chinatown, Harlem,** and the **Lower East Side** (*see* Chapter 2).

Of course, you'll have to deal with crowds during the holiday season, skirt chain stores threatening to bring the suburbs to Manhattan streets, and put up with prices that are almost always higher than other American cities (and don't forget to add in that 8¼% sales tax). Nobody said this was going to be easy. So what are you waiting for? Start shopping, already.

DEPARTMENT STORES

New York City's department stores rival the best in Paris. And they leave those of London, Rome, and Tokyo in the dust. At no other stores in the world can you find window displays more overwhelming, perfume sprayers more determined, or customers (and mannequins) more lavishly dressed. It all began around the time when R. H. Macy opened a shop on 6th Avenue at 14th Street in 1858. By the end of the century, the stretch of 6th Avenue between 14th and 23rd streets, called **Ladies' Mile,** was lined with huge department stores in beautiful cast-iron buildings. Fifteen years later most stores had moved uptown, with Macy's (*see below*) landing at 34th Street and most of the higher-fashion stores drifting up 5th Avenue, but the concept was here to stay.

It's easy to treat an afternoon in the department stores like a visit to the museums. They're excellent for an afternoon of harmless fawning, especially around the holiday season, when most don outrageous and whimsical window displays—Barneys is especially notorious for these. Year-round, most department stores offer fancy cafés that are great for latte-drinking and people-watching—just like at the Met and MoMA.

Funniest bathroom in the city: Moschino's Lego-walled "Toy-lette" (803 Madison Ave., between 67th and 68th Sts., Upper East Side).

Barneys New York (660 Madison Ave., at 61st St., Upper East Side; World Financial Center, Lower Manhattan). The glamour-shield Barneys has been using to hide its financial woes is crumbling fast. The original Chelsea space, going way back to 1923, was fed to the bankruptcy lions, after being trimmed down (to make way for the discounter Loehmann's, no less!) in the fall of 1996. Despite the havoc downtown, though, the Madison Avenue store maintains its sangfroid. The men's and women's departments stock labels from the designing world's stratosphere; the women's department in particular will pick up some truly gawk-worthy pieces. (Comme des Garçons body bump, anyone?) Even seasonal sales here are far from cheap, so New Yorkers line up around the block for the semiannual warehouse sales (late August and January).

Bergdorf Goodman (754 5th Ave., between 57th and 58th Sts., Midtown). This pair of stores has the hushed atmosphere of Money (the women's and men's stores face each other across 5th Avenue)—but there's a buzz on the fifth floor of the women's store, where plenty of casual clothes have red slashes on their price tags. ("Casual" in this setting indicates linen trousers, not jeans.)

Bloomingdale's (1000 3rd Ave., at E. 59th St., Midtown). Occupying an entire city block, Bloomingdale's is an institution—as evinced by the high percentage of out-of-towners clutching Bloomie's shopping bags.

Henri Bendel (712 5th Ave., between 55th and 56th Sts., Midtown). Chic Henri Bendel is filled with whimsical, expensive clothing. Somehow the dizzying layout of small rooms around a swirling staircase adds to the gracious atmosphere—thank the daylight coming in from the Lalique windows.

Macy's (Herald Sq., Broadway at 34th St., Midtown). Macy's at Herald Square claims to be the largest department store on earth, and who's going to argue? They've got 2.1 million square ft of selling space on nine floors; fashionwise, they go the middle road. On the Balcony level, you'll find a visitors center where you can get oriented (and even buy theater tickets). Don't leave before descending to the Cellar marketplace, where the cookware and edibles rival those at Zabar's. The store recently embarked on a three-year renovation program that is sprucing up departments one by one; a new restaurant will also be added.

Saks Fifth Avenue (611 5th Ave., between 49th and 50th Sts., Midtown). In addition to excellent people-watching, courtly service, and acres of haute couture, you'll find surprisingly good bargains on just-out-of-season clothes.

WINDOW-SHOPPING AS AN ART

Madison Avenue, 5th Avenue, and 57th Street are reportedly three of the 10 most expensive shopping streets in the world. A half-hour here might be a good time to do as the French do: "lécher les vitrines" (literally, lick the windows). Just consider it part of your aesthetic education. For glittering gems, sidle up to Cartier (2 E. 52nd St., at 5th Ave.) and Tiffany & Co. (727 5th Ave., at E. 57th St.). See what you think of the sleek new Chanel address (5 E. 57th St., at 5th Ave.). Or, on the rowdier side of the coin, there's the neon-striped Gianni Versace (647 5th Ave., between 51st and 52nd Sts.). Calvin Klein (654 Madison Ave., between E. 60th and 61st Sts.) and Giorgio Armani (760 Madison Ave., between 65th and 66th Sts.) seem to be locked in a kind of minimalist one-upsmanship, while Prada (841 Madison Ave., at 70th St.) bathes itself in sea-green light. The new Dolce & Gabbana (825 Madison Ave., between 68th and 69th Sts.) is all that Isabella Rossellini could desire. And for a bit of levity, head for Moschino (803 Madison Ave., between 67th and 68th Sts.) with its fabulously creative window displays.

Takashimaya New York (693 5th Ave., between 54th and 55th Sts., Midtown). This pristine branch of Japan's largest department store somehow casts a spell of Zen-like peace on its customers; even when the store is crowded, everyone seems preternaturally well-behaved. Look in the gardening section–cum–front window display for a little Something transformed by serene design—glazed pots start around $15.

CLOTHES

Not surprisingly for a city that calls itself the fashion capital of the country, New York has a lot of places to buy clothes. And we're not just talking Jack Kerouac's khakis, here, either; how many cities have stores with "Cross Dressers Welcome" signs in the window?

One way to buy clothes cheaply in New York is to head to the **Garment District** (7th Avenue and Broadway, from 34th to 42nd streets), where you can sometimes hit a few **sample sales.** Besides selling the samples (worn by models) of next year's fashion hopefuls, they usually offer overstock of stuff already in the stores. The best times for sample sales are April–June and November–December; look for men handing out flyers on Garment District streetcorners. Just keep in mind that most sales are cash only, no returns and no exchanges, and that not every designer is the next Miuccia Prada.

NEW CLOTHES

New York has all the same chain stores as your hometown mall, and a few are actually worth checking out: Midtown's über **Gap** (60 W. 34th St., at Broadway) is gargantuan—it covers 53,000 square ft. **Banana Republic,** a sort of Gap-goes-to-the-office, has nabbed storefronts in some prime locations (552 Broadway, between Prince and Spring Sts., SoHo; 655 5th Ave., at E. 52nd St., Midtown; 1136 Madison Ave., at E. 85th St., Upper East Side). **Polo/Ralph Lauren** (867 Madison Ave., at E. 72nd St., Upper East Side), Madison's first "life style" store, occupies a former mansion; across the street the **Polo Sport** store flogs "activewear," plus some good-old-boy accessories, like antique pocket watches. At a few branches of the **Original Levi's Stores** (1492 3rd Ave., at E. 84th St., Upper East Side; 750 Lexington Ave., between E. 59th and 60th Sts., Midtown; 3 E. 57th St., at 5th Ave., Midtown), women can order personally tailored jeans, which cost about $15 more than a regular pair. They're ready in three weeks, and Levi's will even ship them to your home.

Canal Jeans (504 Broadway, between Spring and Broome Sts., SoHo). If you can wear it, it's here—and it's cheap. Besides cheap T-shirts ($6) and baggy jeans ($25), Canal offers discounts on some brands like French Connection, plus military surplus stuff and a ton of used Levi's ($5–$29).

Diesel Superstore (770 Lexington Ave., at 60th St., Upper East Side). The display windows styled like washing machines will tip you off as to Diesel's industrial edge. Skip the $100 jeans and browse through the more interesting (and slightly cheaper) spins on waitress dresses or techno-sport zip-up jackets.

J. Crew (99 Prince St., at Mercer St., SoHo; 203 Front St., at South Street Seaport, Lower Manhattan; 91 5th Ave., between 16th and 17th Sts., Chelsea). You'll never lack for a rollneck sweater at these clean-as-a-whistle showcases for East Coast chic. The 14 labels for men and women range from flannels to the Collection, a Calvin Klein–ish women's line.

Label (265 Lafayette St., between Prince and Spring Sts., SoHo). Familiar logos take on very different meanings after a scalding-wit treatment by designer Laura Whitcomb.

Shops in New York City that close early on weekdays often stay open until 7 or 8 PM on Thursday night.

New Republic (93 Spring St., between Mercer St. and Broadway, SoHo). Men who want to look sharp but are allergic to business-as-usual suits and ties can shop here without fear. The fine fabrics and styles translate into steepish prices, so watch for sales.

Old Navy (610 6th Ave., at 18th St., Chelsea). This is a prime example of the new Chelsea phenomenon: a gleaming discount superstore, complete with café. Things cotton are very reasonable; if you need a rib knit, you'll find it here.

O.M.G. (546 Broadway, between Prince and Spring Sts., SoHo). The laid-back atmosphere makes this a great place to shop for those clothes fashion wags call "wardrobe basics." They've got some of the lowest prices in town on Levi's and other jeans.

Patricia Field (10 E. 8th St., between 5th Ave. and University Pl., West Village). This is the essence of the downtown clubkid look—lots of marabou, techno-fabrics, and humor. Beware, the clothes aren't as cheap as you might hope; look upstairs for (relative) bargains.

DISCOUNT CLOTHES

Discount outlets are the bottom of the city's fashion food chain, the final resting place for three-armed jackets and other designer bombs. To find that little $25 Calvin Klein dress takes patience and luck; serious discount hounds arrive early and shop often.

Century 21 (22 Cortlandt St., at Trinity Pl., Lower Manhattan). Who knows if Century 21 will still claim to be "New York's best kept secret," since *Vogue*'s ecstatic article on it. You'll find three vast floors of in-season name-brand and designer fashions for men and women, like beautiful blouses by Paul Smith for $65 (originally $130), or a perfect Calvin Klein men's coat for $300 (originally $900). They also offer shoes, bedding, and cosmetics.

Loehmann's (101 7th Ave., at 16th St., Chelsea). Bargain hunters throughout Manhattan rejoiced when the legendary discounter Loehmann's finally opened a branch downtown. The highest fashion is concentrated in the "Back Room," and there are both communal and private dressing rooms. There's an especially good selection of winter coats.

Moe Ginsberg (162 5th Ave., at 21st St., Chelsea). Moe has multiple floors of men's suits, sport jackets, trousers, and formal wear that will make you look very respectable, at prices that won't kill you. An even-deeper-discount floor opened in 1997.

Syms (400 Park Ave., at 54th St., Midtown; 42 Trinity Pl., at Rector St., Lower Manhattan). Syms is educating a lot more consumers these days; a Park Avenue store opened not too long ago. The emphasis is on suits and other work-appropriate clothes.

SECONDHAND CLOTHING

In this city, secondhand and vintage clothing options go way, way beyond grubby pairs of corduroys. Many of the to-die-for numbers you'll see on passersby are far from new, and finding them is an art. Of course, the older the clothes the higher the price tag: If it's vintage stuff from the '20s and '40s you covet, expect to pay a pretty penny. If you're visiting in early spring, call the Seventh Regement Armory (Park Ave. at 67th St., tel. 212/821–9300) about the Posh on Park benefit sale. The racks of donated high-end clothes at incredibly low prices make this one of the prime events of the year.

Housing Works (143 W. 17th St., between 6th and 7th Aves., Chelsea; 202 E. 77th St., at 3rd Ave., Upper East Side; 307 Columbus Ave., at 75th St., Upper West Side). The darling of New York thrift stores recently spawned a third branch. Separate designer sections can divulge a $20 Calvin Klein button-down—but don't overlook the cheaper racks or the housewares and books sections. The shops benefit housing services for people with AIDS.

The 1909 Company (63 Thompson St., between Spring and Broome Sts., SoHo). Revel in luxe items like vintage cashmere sweaters ($60 and up) and genteel ladies' suits. The sale rack is not to be sniffed at.

Resurrection (123 E. 7th St., between 1st Ave. and Ave. A, East Village). This is the sweet spot of quietly Mod-ish shoes—and just to keep you on your toes, one or two pairs of outrageous boots. The dress selection is particularly good; keep your eyes on the saucy numbers hanging on the walls.

Rose is Vintage (145 1st Ave., at E. 9th St., East Village; 96 E. 7th St., between 1st Ave. and Ave. A, Alphabet City). The impatient among us will love these stores' promise of new merchandise daily. Would you say no to a short faux-Persian lamb coat for $30? Peer into corners and you may find something smashingly retro, like frilly, dainty, '50s-housewife aprons.

Screaming Mimi's (382 Lafayette St., at E. 4th St., East Village). Mimi's is stocked with cool stuff from the '60s and '70s, like plaid kilt skirts ($25 and up) and party dresses ($30 and up). Clamber upstairs to a narrow landing for lost-in-time housewares.

Smylonylon (222-B Lafayette St., between Spring and Broome Sts., SoHo). Polyvinyl and pleather have found more than a home here; they've found a shrine. It's wall-to-wall man-made fibers, with lots of groovy skintight shirts, slinky skirts, and wide pants. Prices start around $10.

Tokio 7 (64 E. 7th St., between 1st and 2nd Aves., East Village). Japanese Kewpie dolls and videos of Euroglam runway shows somehow coexist in this store's window display. Inside, you'll find clothes from Cynthia Rowley and Betsey Johnson for under $40 (albeit a few seasons old). Some of the highest price tags are attached to the shimmering, voluminous kimonos far in the back.

SHOES

West 8th Street between University Place and 6th Avenue is the city's **Shoe Street,** with more than 20 shops selling every kind of footwear from sedate heels to thigh-high glitter platform boots. Prices are pretty cheap. Try **Bootéro** (10 5th Ave., at W. 8th St., West Village), **Wheels of London** (55 E. 8th St., between Broadway and University St., East Village), or **Here & Now** (56 W. 8th St., between 5th and 6th Aves., West Village).

John Fluevog Shoes (104 Prince St., between Mercer and Greene Sts., SoHo). Inventor of the Angelic sole (protects against water, acid . . . and "Satan"), Fluevog designs chunky shoes and boots that are much more than Doc Marten knockoffs. You'll also find the occasional pair of Mod-style pumps. Scramble if you see a sale sign; prices often get cut in half.

Maraolo (782 Lexington Ave., between 60th and 61st Sts., Upper East Side; 551 Madison Ave., at 55th St., Midtown; 835 Madison Ave., at 69th St., Upper East Side). Clothing designers' footwear (Armani, Donna Karan) fills these shelves. Luckily, sales are lengthy affairs. Even better is the factory outlet (131 W. 72nd St., between Columbus and Amsterdam Aves., Upper West Side), which carries mostly Maraolo's own shoe line, with a smattering of other name brands. Prices start at $19 and top out at $99.

99X (84 E. 10th St., between 3rd and 4th Aves., East Village). Brit-owned 99X hasn't messed with a good punk thing. Check out the biggest and best selection of Doc Martens and creepers in the city (sale prices go below $50). You'll also find hipster clothes like Fred Perry shirts and sharp suits.

Omari (132 Prince St., between Wooster St. and W. Broadway, SoHo). The men's and women's shoes here can be discreet and classy or sleekly funky. And expensive—but in the back of the store, on the left side, there's a well-stocked sale rack (bless them!). Prices there dip below three digits, though items tend to be women's styles.

Tootsie Plohound (137 5th Ave., between 20th and 21st Sts., Gramercy; 413 W. Broadway, between Prince and Spring Sts., SoHo; 1116 3rd Ave., between 65th and 66th Sts., Upper East Side). This shop's all about groovy shoes. Most cost about $100, but sale stuff lurks at half that price.

BOOKS

Books are a big deal in New York City. Quite a few residents write them, and even more read them. Many of the bookstores hold regular **author appearances** and **readings** (listed in city weeklies like *Time Out* and *The New Yorker*), kindly tolerate magazine browsing, and even offer in-store cafés. Practically the only time you need to leave anymore is to change your underwear.

In Chelsea, a half-dozen or so bookstores on West 18th Street between 5th and 6th avenues constitute the city's new **Book Row.** Elsewhere, along busy stretches like Prince Street or 86th Street near the subway, look for folks hawking brand-spanking-new hardbacks (usually publishers' overstock) for a few measly bucks. The whole island of Manhattan becomes one big book-lover's paradise during the three-day **New York is Book Country** fair (*see* Festivals and Annual Events *in* Chapter 1), held every September.

Time your shopping sprees to coincide with end-of-season-sales, which most department stores and clothing shops hold July–August and again January–February, and you'll save 30%–50%.

NEW BOOKS

Mega-chain store **Barnes & Noble** (4 Astor Pl., at Lafayette St., East Village; 33 E. 17th St., between Broadway and Park Ave. S, Union Sq.; 1972 Broadway at 66th St. [Lincoln Triangle], Upper West Side; 2289 Broadway, at W. 82nd St., Upper West Side; and an exponentially increasing number of other locations) has made its cookie-cutter presence known in Manhattan (though the hard-cover discount has been cut to 10%). **Borders Books & Music** (5 World Trade Center, Northeast Building, Lower Manhattan; 461 Park Ave., at 57th St., Midtown) is equally overwhelming when it comes to sheer merchandise volume. But be sure to stray from the superstore path—there may not be as many couches, and you might pay a few dollars more, but you'll find some gems and get a little ambiance to boot.

Coliseum (1771 Broadway, at W. 57th St., Midtown). Scant blocks from the book-free zone of Planet Hollywood and the Hard Rock Cafe is this great bookstore with a helpful staff and wide selection of literature, nonfiction (including lots of music, travel, and gift books), and paperbacks.

Rizzoli (31 W. 57th St., between 5th and 6th Aves., Midtown; 454 W. Broadway, near Prince St., SoHo; World Financial Center, Lower Manhattan). Rizzoli stores mercifully avoid the sterile feel and florescent lighting that comes with chaindom. The uptown branch is especially classy, with a marble entrance and chandeliers; the SoHo location has a quirky gift shop. All have a great selection of books on the fine arts, architecture, and travel, plus fiction and nonfiction.

St. Mark's Bookshop (31 3rd Ave., at E. 9th St., East Village). Neo-beatniks will love the great selection of avant-garde and popular works on art, literature, and history. Young intellectuals should check out the exhaustive criticism and philosophy sections.

Shakespeare & Co. (716 Broadway, at Washington Pl., East Village; 939 Lexington Ave., between 68th and 69th Sts., Upper East Side). At these pleasant shops, book displays are always thoughtfully selected from the latest in literature, poetry, and nonfiction. And the staff (full of moonlighting writers and junior editors) has probably even read them.

Tower Books (383 Lafayette St., at E. 4th St., East Village). Around the corner from Tower Records (*see* Records, Tapes, and CDs, *below*) and just as overwhelming, Tower Books carries tons of books, 'zines, and other word-oriented things. For the insatiable, it's open daily until midnight.

USED AND RARE BOOKS

There's nothing quite like that enticing, mildly musty smell of a used-book shop. Many of the stores listed below will be happy to buy any used books you've got laying around, though the prices they pay

BIDDING FOR FUN AND FURNITURE

For an extra adrenaline rush, try New York's auction houses. Sales are advertised in Friday's "Weekend" and Sunday's "Arts & Leisure" sections of the "New York Times"; most houses hold auctions several times a month. Check out the goods during the preview (a few days before the sale) and set a limit for yourself (in case bidding gets hairy). When bidding, be aggressive, as the pace can be very quick.

Tepper Galleries (110 E. 25th St., near Park Ave. S, Midtown). This no-frills house deals in "anonymous estate liquidation." Translation: everything from furs to wincingly ugly sculpture. Lots can go for under $30.

William Doyle Galleries (175 E. 87th St., near Lexington Ave., Upper East Side). In Doyle's "Treasure Auction" room you can score quality sofas for $50 and '50s dresses for $20.

Christie's East and Sotheby's Arcade (Christie's East: 219 E. 67th St., between 2nd and 3rd Aves., Upper East Side; Sotheby's Arcade: 1334 York Ave., at E. 72nd St., Upper East Side). The second-string divisions of the city's two famous auction houses still have paddles and catalogs, you bring your expert eye and good taste; furniture and decorative arts start around $200.

are ridiculously low. Call ahead for buyers' hours—and try not to draw from the experience any general ideas about the State of Literature Today. Several dozen sellers of used and rare books are set up on the ninth floor of the **Chelsea Antiques Building** (*see* Flea Markets, *below*).

Academy (10 W. 18th St., between 5th and 6th Aves., Chelsea). Academy is packed with cheap, interesting books about art, philosophy, history, and psychology. There's a long-hair feeding frenzy here whenever they open a new shipment. Across the street, **Skyline** (13 W. 18th St.) deals in literature, poetry, and used LPs.

Argosy (116 E. 59th St., between Park and Lexington Aves., Midtown). At this tony establishment you'll find an extensive stock of used and rare books, some beautiful prints and maps, and a friendly, helpful staff. The cheap stuff's stacked outside.

Gotham Book Mart (41 W. 47th St., between 5th and 6th Aves., Midtown). Gotham's held the title as New York's most literary bookstore for decades; the late Frances Steloff opened this store years ago with just $200 in her pocket, half of it on loan. She went on to help launch James Joyce's *Ulysses*, D. H. Lawrence, and Henry Miller. Check out the stacks of used literature, poetry, drama, and film books, and don't be afraid to ask for a second opinion.

Gryphon (2246 Broadway, between 80th and 81st Sts., Upper West Side). Practically the width of *War and Peace*, this slip of a bookstore has an unbeatable combination—inexpensive books of all sorts and Mozart on the radio. There are some great first and rare editions as well, and if they don't have the one you're pining for, they'll do a free search. It's open 'til midnight seven days a week. Now that's generosity.

Strand (828 Broadway, at E. 12th St., West Village). The Strand boasts 8 miles of books, but sometimes it feels like 80. In addition to rare books, first editions, and just-plain-old-used books, they carry reviewers' copies of hot-off-the-presses stuff for 50% off retail. The carts outside offer selections weird and wonderful, like a 1930s Balzac translation for $2.50.

SPECIALTY BOOKSTORES

The city has several excellent shops for foreign-language books: **Kinokuniya Bookstore** (10 W. 49th St., at 5th Ave.) stocks books in Japanese; the **Librairie de France** and **Libreria Hispanica** (610 5th Ave., in Rockefeller Center) stock books in French and Spanish. For works on fine art, architecture, and photography, **museum bookstores** (particularly those at the Met and MoMA) can't be beat; *see* Major Attractions *in* Chapter 2.

Biography Bookstore (400 Bleecker St., at W. 11th St., West Village). Famous artists, rock stars, politicians, dictators, ballerinas, religious figures, and TV-show hosts just love to publish their fascinating life stories. This shop sells them.

Books of Wonder (132 7th Ave., at W. 18th St., Chelsea). This is the perfect place to buy that copy of *Eloise.* They've also got a wonderful selection of classic and rare children's literature.

The Drama Bookshop (723 7th Ave., at W. 48th St., Midtown). At this little Theater-District shop, you'll find books on drama, TV, film, and dance, and more unemployed actors than you can shake a *Playbill* at.

Partners & Crime (44 Greenwich Ave., near W. 10th St., West Village). Offering both new and out-of-print mysteries (and loads of British imports), this bright little shop also has a rental library and spooky fireplace. There's a "radio mystery hour" on Saturday evenings; call ahead for reservations.

Printed Matter (77 Wooster St., between Spring and Broome Sts., SoHo). Maybe it's not a gallery, but a lot of the stuff here could qualify as art: handmade and small-press books, text-based objets d'art, and art-related magazines.

You know that X-Large (267 Lafayette St., at Prince St., SoHo) and x-girl (248 Lafayette St., btw Prince and Spring Sts., SoHo) have cool clothes, 'cuz they're fronted by Beastie Boy Mike D, while Sonic Youth bassist Kim Gordon helps design the threads.

RECORDS, TAPES, AND CDS

New York's club scene supports an endless number of 12″ shops, and the city's legions of hipsters and rockers and assorted hangers-on keep CD shops stocked with every imaginable American and European release. On **Bleecker Street** in the West Village and **St. Marks Place** in the East Village you'll find plenty of shops competing to offer the lowest prices and largest selection for stuff new and used. In a pinch, try one of the numerous **HMV**s (57 W. 34th St., at 6th Ave., Midtown; 2081 Broadway, at W. 72nd St., Upper West Side; 565 5th Ave., at 46th St., Midtown).

Academy (10 W. 18th St., between 5th and 6th Aves., Chelsea). In Academy's well-organized bins of used records and CDs you'll find tons of bargains on classical music, rock, and jazz. Almost everything is less than $10.

Bleecker Bob's (118 W. 3rd St., at MacDougal St., West Village). A legendary New York record store, this place is cluttered with nasty rock and roll and punk (including some rare older stuff) and rock junk like stickers and T-shirts. On Friday and Saturday nights it's open until 3 AM.

Dance Tracks (91 E. 3rd St., at 1st Ave., East Village). The music from this store can make the sidewalk vibrate. There's often quite a crush around the DJ, but you can turn to the turntables and sample the wares: 12″ house, plus some hip-hop, soul, and ambient.

Footlight (113 E. 12th St., between 3rd and 4th Aves., East Village). Movie and Broadway soundtracks, R&B, jazz, big band, and early rock and roll await at this used vinyl/new CD shop. The good stuff's more than $10. The rest is $2.

Generation (210 Thompson St., between Bleecker and W. Houston Sts., West Village). This astounding collection of high-quality bootlegs ranges from easy-on-the-ears bands like Counting Crows to more abrasive groups, like the Lunachicks.

Gryphon (251 W. 72nd St., Suite 2F, between West End Ave. and Broadway, Upper West Side). You might, understandably, find a room packed with 90,000 LPs (mostly classical) overwhelming. But give the staff a few minutes and they'll unearth that rare recording you've been pining for.

Kim's Underground/Kim's Video & Audio/Mondo Kim's (Underground: 144 Bleecker St., at La Guardia Pl., West Village; Video & Audio: 350 Bleecker St., at W. 10th St., West Village; Mondo: 6 St. Marks Pl., between 2nd and 3rd Aves., East Village). These three shops (attached to the Village's favorite video-rental stores) stock well-priced indie rock CDs, LPs, and 7"s. Don't think your taste's too obscure—if you've heard it, they have it.

Other Music (15 E. 4th St., between Broadway and Lafayette St., East Village). As if to drive the point home, Other Music is found right across the street from a Tower Records branch. Browse through sections like "La Decadanse" (lots of Serge Gainsbourg), and rows of various alternatives. Roughly half the music is new, the other used.

Sounds (20 St. Marks Pl., between 2nd and 3rd Aves., East Village). Sounds is heavy on hipster rock, jazz, hip-hop, and dance; new releases are always priced $2–$3 below the competition. They only accept cash.

Tower Records and Video (692 Broadway, at 4th St., East Village; 1961 Broadway, at 66th St., Lincoln Center; 725 5th Ave., basement level of Trump Tower, Midtown). This is just like the Tower Records in your hometown, except it's bigger and more crowded. The Lincoln Center branch has expanded, and now includes a café so you can rest your weary, CD-flipping fingertips. If you get lucky, you can catch a free live performance at any of the branches, as bands come through on promo appearances. The uptown stores mostly have classical or jazz artists, while the downtown store hosts the rock groups. Check the papers for a tip-off.

Virgin Megastore Times Square (1540 Broadway, between 45th and 46th Sts., Midtown). Touted as the largest music-entertainment complex in the world (big enough for 938 taxis), this glitzy emporium has a 50-ft DJ tower slicing through three levels of consumer frenzy. There's a café, a travel shop, an interactive game wall, and an excellent bookstore.

HOUSEHOLD FURNISHINGS

The stores listed below are just a smattering of what New York has to offer in the way of beautiful furniture, linens, and accessories for your home (or crowded apartment). Should none of these tickle your fancy, wander around East 9th Street in the East Village—or just about anywhere in SoHo—where cool new purveyors of knickknacks are always setting up shop.

For peddlers of homey stuff cheap and used, New York City has several options: Many secondhand clothing places like **Housing Works** (*see above*) and the **Salvation Army** (536 W. 46th St., between 10th and 11th Aves., Midtown) also stock housewares. Flea markets (*see below*) are another excellent source; get to the 26th Street market before 6 AM and cross discerning glances with some of SoHo's hippest furniture dealers. You could also try your luck at an auction (*see box, above*).

ABC Carpet & Home (888 Broadway, at E. 19th St., Gramercy). Exquisite (and expensive) new and antique furniture, lamps, linens, rugs, and bric-a-brac are displayed in heaps and jumbles at this vast household emporium masquerading as a dowager queen's attic.

Ad Hoc Softwares (410 W. Broadway, at Spring St., SoHo). You'll feel very SoHo as you browse here—natural fibers and nubbly textures abound. The merchandise continues to expand into the home-accessory arena.

Crate & Barrel (650 Madison Ave., at 59th St., Midtown). This is the tried-and-true center for moderately priced glassware, kitchen and bath items, and won't-rock-the-boat furniture. The coordination-impaired should look to the displays to see how everything matches in that blond-wood way. The sales are more than acceptable.

Fish's Eddy (889 Broadway, at E. 19th St., Gramercy; 2176 Broadway, at W. 77th St., Upper West Side). Fish's Eddy resells china from all walks of crockery life—from big corporations to gone-under restaurants. There are also some very cheap new wares, and lots of oddball pieces like finger bowls and porcelain glove molds.

Williams-Sonoma Outlet Center (231 10th Ave., between W. 23rd and 24th Sts., Chelsea). Seconds, returns, and overstocks from Williams-Sonoma, Pottery Barn, Hold Everything, Gardener's Eden, and Chambers include essentials like glassware, dishes, and cookware at 30%–70% off original prices. They occasionally get furniture and linens, too.

Zona (97 Greene St., between Prince and Spring Sts., SoHo). From wrought-iron candlesticks to dining tables, the housewares, furniture, and (suitcase-friendly) accessories at Zona are simply beautiful. You'll buy them even if you don't need them.

SPECIALTY STORES

COSMETICS AND BODY PRODUCTS

Kiehl's (109 3rd Ave., between E. 13th and 14th Sts., East Village). Makeup artists and fashion editors swear by Kiehl's shampoos, soaps, and cosmetics. Try not to choke at the prices; shampoo can easily run $25.

MAC (113 Spring St., between Mercer and Greene Sts., SoHo; 14 Christopher St., between 6th and 7th Aves., West Village). The ballooning popularity of this line of makeup, championed by the likes of RuPaul and k.d. lang, has spawned a pair of exclusive stores. Don't be surprised if the staff has more piercings than they know what to do with.

KITSCH-O-RAMA

Forbidden Planet (840 Broadway, at E. 13th St., East Village). Come here ye fantasy fans and Star Wars addicts, to the mother of all sci-fi stores. They've got new, used, and foreign comics, plus plenty of sci-fi paperbacks.

For a cool souvenir, pop into the black-and-white photo booth at Little Rickie. For $2 you get four pictures of you 'n' your buds.

Little Rickie (49½ 1st Ave., at E. 3rd St., East Village). Little Rickie is all about weird toys and kitsch items like Elvis air fresheners, magnetic poetry kits (great for composing odes on the refrigerator door), and St. Theresa commemorative spoons.

Love Saves the Day (119 2nd Ave., at E. 7th St., East Village). Some of these lunchboxes may look very, very familiar, not to mention the *Charlie's Angels* board game ($39), the Bionic Woman, and '60s Barbie dolls ($1.95 and up).

PAPER, CARDS, AND STATIONERY

Kate's Paperie (561 Broadway, at Prince St., SoHo; 8 W. 13th St., at 5th Ave., West Village). If this store doesn't breed collage fantasies, nothing will. Beautiful handmade papers, from stationery to wrapping, are surrounded by fountain pens, blank books, and other like-minded items.

TOYS AND GAMES

F.A.O. Schwarz (767 5th Ave., at 58th St., Midtown). The constant tinkle of "Welcome to Our World of Toys" may make adult customers bug-eyed, but this store is an undeniable toy fantasyland.

Enchanted Forest (85 Mercer St., between Spring and Broome Sts., SoHo). The antidote to too much Mattel, this store has old-fashioned tin toys, gizmos, and a small, choice selection of children's books. Dozens of stuffed animals peer out from the stairway to the small overhead loft.

ONE-OF-A-KINDS

Kate Spade (454 Broome St., at Mercer St., SoHo). In Kate Spade's only boutique, you'll find a full range of her spare, status-symbol handbags. (These are what started all those knockoffs.) Prices start at a steep $70. Or melt some plastic for adorable clothes and pajamas.

New York Transit Museum Gift Shop (Boerum Pl. and Schermerhorn St., Brooklyn Heights). If Statue of Liberty salt-and-pepper shakers aren't doing it for you, consider this as an alternate souvenir stop. Everything is somehow linked to the MTA, from "straphanger" ties to the solid old subway tokens. And it's authentic from the ground up; the shop was built mostly by transit employees.

NikeTown (6 E. 57th St., between 5th and Madison Aves., Midtown). With its high technology and architecture reminiscent of a school gym, Nike's "motivational retail environment" knows how to push your buttons. The latest in Nike footwear and wick-away fabrics are given the full museum treatment. To evoke that consumer—er, competitive spirit, there are inspirational quotes in the flooring, computer-driven NGAGE foot sizers, and a heart-pumping movie shown every 20 minutes on an enormous screen in the entry atrium.

The Pop Shop (292 Lafayette St., near E. Houston St., East Village). World-famous artist Keith Haring had close ties to New York, ever since his days spray-painting subway cars; images from his unmistakable pop-art pieces cover all sorts of paraphernalia.

FLEA MARKETS

The city's **flea markets,** which are good things, are not to be confused with its street fairs, mostly the domain of sausage-and-onions vendors. Flea markets are held in established locations (usually vacant lots) almost year-round. They're full of stuff that's weird, old, cool, and kitschy. Street fairs pop up randomly all over town during the summer and fall, and no matter where they are, they sell the same old things—block after predictable block of tired houseplants and flimsy T-shirts. Believe us, the pickings are richer almost anywhere else.

MOSTLY ANTIQUES

Every weekend several hundred vendors from as far away as Pennsylvania unpack their wares around the intersection of **West 26th Street and 6th Avenue** for the mammoth Annex Flea Market (*see below*). This is where Andy Warhol used to show up in his black limousine. This is where people like Ralph Lauren and Martha Stewart send their lackeys to find all those old saddles and romantic black-and-white photos they use as props. What started out as a single parking lot has at last count grown to four lots plus three buildings.

Annex Antiques Fair and Flea Market (6th Ave. between W. 24th and 27th Sts., Chelsea; open weekends). The mother of all New York City flea markets now takes up two lots on Saturday and four lots on Sunday. More than 400 dealers display wares ranging from vintage wallpaper and Fiestaware to chandeliers and mismatched spoons.

Chelsea Antiques Building (110 W. 25th St., at 6th Ave., Chelsea; open daily). Looking for World War II photographs? Russian cookie jars? Or out-of-print Austrian poetry books? This 12-story building is filled with specialized dealers, though prices can be steep. The best bargaining happens on weekends.

Grand Street Antiques Fair (Grand St. at Broadway, SoHo; open weekends). Good deals and a great SoHo location are what make this smallish flea market so popular. It's heavy on household items, records, old toys, and vintage clothes.

OTHER SOCIAL DETRITUS

Coney Island Fair (Surf Ave. at Stillwell Ave., Brooklyn; open weekends). About 45 minutes from Manhattan by subway, Russians and other immigrants set up shop every weekend in the shadow of the Cyclone roller coaster. The record selection here is fantastic—but you'll also find true junk like acrylic socks and signed photos of Hulk Hogan.

I.S. 44 Market (Columbus Ave. between W. 76th and 77th Sts., Upper West Side; open Sun.). Over 300 dealers of handmade jewelry, vintage clothing, and bric-a-brac (plus a farmer's market) jam this Upper West Side schoolyard and gym.

Rural connection
west village

www.ruralconnection.com

AFTER DARK

BY MIRA SCHWIRTZ

Manhattan's nightlife is the most garish, brazen, and brilliant show on Planet Earth—and true to every cliché, it never stops. Bars stay open until 4 AM, dance clubs wind down around dawn, and the concept of "weeknight" just doesn't exist. The scene varies by neighborhood. On the **Upper West Side** and **East Side,** you'll find Ivy League grads drinking off another market-driven day. The **West Village** is a center for gay nightlife—even if Bleecker Street near Washington Square is typically saturated with straight, horny, beer-guzzling NYU students. **SoHo** is a Beautiful People brew of dance clubs and funky bars, while the **East Village** and **Lower East Side** are populated by less pretentious packs of the young, pierced, and hip. Whether it's jazz in a basement dive, a crowded club throbbing with a house-happy beat, or a spoken-word show in a smoky bar, New York is where it's at.

If you're new in town, get off your butt and grab a weekly events magazine: *Time Out New York* ($1.95), the *Village Voice* (free), *New York* magazine ($2.95), *The New Yorker* ($2.95), the *New York Press* (free), and the *New York Observer* ($1) all have listings. The most thorough is *Time Out,* though the *Voice* has long been considered the bible of the downtown scene. The *Observer*'s "Eight-Day Week" captures quirky society, fashion, and arts stuff. Note that clubs and bars can draw hugely different crowds on different nights: dykes one day, dweebs the next. To add to the confusion, many bars function as clubs, with live bands and dancing one or two nights a week. And dance clubs frequently showcase live bands. But who's complaining? It sure beats navel-gazing in suburbia. A final note: Wherever you go at night, walk on main streets and use designated off-hour subway platforms, especially if you're alone. Or, better yet, catch a cab.

BARS

In Seattle it may be chic to make coffee into a social event, but this Starbuck's-fueled trend has yet to subvert nightlife in the Big Apple. Whether you're going out with friends, a blind date, business associates, or even your family, you're bound to end up at one of New York's bars—especially since they're legally allowed to serve alcohol until 4 AM. Throughout New York you can have a cocktail with glorious drag queens, drink single-malt with exiled IRA supporters, or just have an anonymous beer in a dark corner. If your idea of good drinking company is the cast of *Friends,* try the **Upper West Side.** Stop by the **Upper East Side** if you want memories of college drinking games to haunt you again. If Smashing Pumpkins or Sonic Youth are more your style, try the **East Village** or **Chelsea**; if you'd rather hang with a slightly more sophisticated (read: moneyed) crowd, try **SoHo**; a more multicultural version of the same mixes in with the gay scene in the **West Village**; nearby Bleecker Street is the place to be if you want to experience New York's version of Collegetown U.S.A.

UPPER WEST SIDE AND AROUND COLUMBIA UNIVERSITY

Theme bars are big with the Upper West Side's post-college crowd. Take a happy-hour crawl along Broadway in the 70s and 80s and you'll visit plenty of alcohol-serving jungle huts, hunting lodges, and surf shacks. Much farther north, the blocks around Columbia University naturally support a number of cheap and divey undergrad and grad student hangouts.

511 Lounge. This swank den has several floors full of upscale types in wire-rimmed glasses. When conversation falters, reach for one of the backgammon boards—there's one at every table. *511 Amsterdam Ave., between W. 84th and 85th Sts., tel. 212/799–4643. Subway: 1 or 9 to W. 86th St.*

1020 Amsterdam. The snip, snip, snip of scissors has been replaced by the thwock of billiard balls at this barbershop turned watering hole (a few old salon chairs remain). Don't lose your shirt to the grad students who shoot pool here; they play to win. *1020 Amsterdam Ave., at 110th St., tel. 212/961–9224. Subway: 1 or 9 to Cathedral Pkwy.*

Hi-Life Bar & Grill. This restaurant-bar may be a little rough on the decor (a few kitsch items and a fish tank near the door are the standouts), but the padded black vinyl walls create a pleasant semblance of a big-band-era cocktail den. Its outdoor seating makes it the anchor of Upper West Side nightlife in summer. A DJ spins '70s hits on weekends. *477 Amsterdam Ave., at W. 83rd St., tel. 212/787–7199. Subway: 1 or 9 to 86th St.*

Jake's Dilemma. While this Jake fellow wrestles his inner demons, join the throng having a fabulous time rehashing favorite *Melrose* episodes in the roomy bar. On Monday, drafts are $1, pitchers $6. *430 Amsterdam Ave., at W. 80th St., tel. 212/580–0556. Subway: 1 or 9 to W. 79th St.*

Raccoon Lodge. Come to observe wild, rugby-striped Upper West Siders who drink beer, think beer-induced romantic thoughts, and drink more beer. The bar itself is an Elks Club knockoff with all the trimmings: stuffed moose head, fireplace, and plenty of scrimmaging for the seats at the bar. *480 Amsterdam Ave., at W. 83rd St., tel. 212/874–9984. Subway: 1 or 9 to W. 86th St.*

UPPER EAST SIDE

Here single yuppies troll for Mr. and Ms. Right–Now in the sanitized Irish bars of 2nd and 3rd avenues, like the eternally popular **Pat O'Brien's** (1497 3rd Ave., between E. 84th and 85th Sts., tel. 212/628–7242). West of Lexington Avenue is the land of the $15 martini—don't say we didn't warn you. Also note that during summer the entire Upper East Side shuts down, mostly because everyone is socializing at their beach houses in the Hamptons. So grab a can of malt liquor and pretend.

American Trash. Though true bikers would rather eat asphalt than party on the Upper East Side, this thrashed bar at least *looks* like a Hell's Angel hangout. Happy hour (daily 4–7 PM) gets you $2 pints and other cheap drinks. *1471 1st Ave., between E. 76th and 77th Sts., tel. 212/988–9008. Subway: 6 to E. 77th St.*

Ruby's Taphouse. The two frat brothers who got together and opened this joint are proud to be your buds. They've got 26 microbrews on tap and decent pub grub. *1754 2nd Ave., between E. 91st and 92nd Sts., tel. 212/987–8179. Subway: 4, 5, or 6 to E. 86th St.*

MIDTOWN

Midtown bars are a weird (and occasionally overwhelming) mix of sleazy Times Square XXX dives, swank hotel bars, and cheesy tourist traps. One small comfort: Virtually every Irish pub you'll see is a winner.

44. You may not be wearing Armani, but the waiter probably is at the Royalton Hotel's outrageously chic cocktail lounge. Must-sees include the padded circular bar and the too-fabulous bathrooms. *44 W. 44th St., between 5th and 6th Aves., tel. 212/869–4400. Subway: B, D, F, or Q to W. 42nd St.*

Full Moon Saloon. This tiny Theater District dive boasts a 100% country-and-western video jukebox, which most customers treat as if it were a dispenser of bubonic plague. A laid-back attitude and lotsa local color make it a worth a visit, despite the country tunes. *735 8th Ave., between W. 46th and 47th Sts., no phone. Subway: A, C, or E to W. 42nd St. (Port Authority).*

Howard Johnson's. The HoJo cocktail lounge, surrounded by Times Square sleaze, is so tacky it's beautiful. There is no place better to sip highballs with complimentary egg-salad sandwiches. The daily happy hour is 4–7. *1551 Broadway, at W. 46th St., tel. 212/354–1445. Subway: 1 or 9 to W. 50th St.*

Monkey Bar. Take a peek at how the other half drinks at the posh Monkey Bar, which has a big, hairless ape at the door. Jungle murals inside don't bring out much barbarism in the mannered banker-types shooting back Scotch. *60 E. 54th St., between Park and Madison Aves., tel. 212/838–2600. Subway: 6 to E. 51st St.*

Morgan's Bar. Supermodels and their kin tuck themselves into this handsome little bar, all gilt mirrors and candles, housed in the basement of Morgan's Hotel. Drinks are pricey. *237 Madison Ave., between E. 37th and 38th Sts., tel. 212/686–0300. Subway: B, D, F, N, Q, or R to 34th St.*

Pen Top Bar and Terrace. Atop the 23rd floor of the Peninsula Hotel you'll find indoor and outdoor seating with fab views of 5th Avenue. It's patronized by a youngish cocktail-drinking crowd. *700 5th Ave., between 54th and 55th Sts., tel. 212/903–3902. Subway: E or F to 5th Ave./53rd St.*

On alternate Wednesday evenings, the New York Beer Appreciation Club convenes at Ruby's Taphouse to swill new brews.

Sardi's. Come to this landmark spot if you want to be a tourist in the Theater District: The walls are covered with caricatures of past and present Broadway stars. Sometimes celebs even occupy Sardi's red-leather booths. *234 W. 44th St., near 8th Ave., tel. 212/221–8440. Subway: A, C, or E to W. 42nd St. (Port Authority).*

Whiskey Bar. With the purchase of an expensive drink you get hours of people-watching at this hyper-trendy bar in the swank Paramount Hotel. *235 W. 46th St., between Broadway and 8th Ave., tel. 212/764–5500. Subway: C or E to W. 50th St.*

CHELSEA AND UNION SQUARE

Take a look at the crowds on **8th Avenue,** particularly around **East 18th Street,** and you'll see that this once blah neighborhood is newly hip—especially among gays. The action spills over into the Union Square area, though things here tend to get pricey. At revamped warehouses on Chelsea's western fringe, bawdy crowds keep things going past 3 AM.

Chelsea Commons. Construction workers mingle with Chelsea dandies at this longtime neighborhood fave. It's got a lamplit brick courtyard straight out of olde London, as well as live music on Saturday. *242 10th Ave., at W. 24th St., tel. 212/929–9424. Subway: C or E to W. 23rd St.*

Ciel Rouge. Sip titillating cocktails like Lady Love Fizz and Bitches Brew in a wicked all-red room straight out of *Amityville Horror.* Don't miss cool happenings like live jazz and piano evenings Tuesday nights. *176 7th Ave., between W. 20th and 21st Sts., tel. 212/929–5542. Subway: 1 or 9 to W. 23rd St.*

Coffee Shop. Arrive way, way, way after midnight to catch the action at this hip, model-owned bar and diner. Attendance is mandatory for club crawlers. *29 Union Sq. W, at E. 16th St., tel. 212/243–7969. Subway: L, N, R, 4, 5, or 6 to Union Sq.*

Flower's. This pitch-dark bar and rooftop patio is crowded with rich and beautiful people. A plus are the jazz and tango bands that play weekly free of charge. *21 W. 17th St., between 5th and 6th Aves., tel. 212/691–8888. Subway: F to W. 14th St.; also L to 6th Ave.*

Rebar. Rebar offers every kind of entertainment except ice-skating polar bears: open-mike nights, stand-up comedy, live bands, and a DJ spinning house and salsa on weekends. *127 8th Ave., at W. 16th St., tel. 212/627–1680. Subway: A, C, E, or L to W. 14th St.*

WEST VILLAGE

Gays and straights, drag queens and rockers, and just plain folks all mix in the West Village's myriad bars and clubs. **Christopher Street** is a center for gay nightlife, while **Hudson Street** is leather-and-

RACK 'EM

The city that never sleeps has a couple of pool halls that never close (literally). It's great for a low-key night out, a low-cost date, or if you find yourself restless at a strange hour. Tables cost $10–$15 per hour and are usually cheaper before 5 PM.

Chelsea Billiards. This classy, crowded joint has 43 pool tables, eight snooker tables, and two billiard tables, all spread over two floors. 54 W. 21st St., between 5th and 6th Aves., Chelsea, tel. 212/989–0096. Subway: N or R to W. 23rd St.

Julian's Famous Poolroom. Look familiar? This smoky joint (with 28 tables plus a few of the Ping-Pong variety) was the setting for "The Hustler" and dozens of music videos. 138 E. 14th St., 2nd floor, between 3rd and 4th Aves., East Village, tel. 212/598–9884 or 800/585–4267. Subway: L, N, R, 4, 5, or 6 to Union Sq.

Le Q. It has 32 tables and some of the lowest rates in town: $3 per person per hour, any time of day. 36 E. 12th St., near University Pl., East Village, tel. 212/995–8512. Subway: L, N, R, 4, 5, or 6 to Union Sq.

---

chains territory. On **West 4th** and **Bleecker streets** there are scores of cheesy, tourist-filled bars—great if you just wanna have fun with buffalo wings and cheap beer. Otherwise, avoid them.

Art Bar. Sip your scotch-and-soda on one of the plush couches by the fireplace at this popular Village bar. It's a great place for a romantic cocktail during the week; on weekends it's really, really crowded. *52 8th Ave., between Horatio and Jane Sts., tel. 212/727–0244. Subway: A, C, E, or L to W. 14th St.*

Bar D'O. At this dimly lit lounge, a friendly, gay and straight crowd cradle large martinis and get cozy on the low-slung couches. On Saturday night top-notch cabaret singers in drag entertain for a $5 cover. *29 Bedford St., at Downing St., tel. 212/627–1580. Subway: 1 or 9 to W. Houston St.*

Bar Six. An idyllic stop for a soft, summer night, with French doors opening on to the street, this elegant bar and restaurant has all the trappings of a New York hot spot without the attitude. Late Sunday the blinds are rolled down to usher in a casual hip-hop and acid jazz dance hour. *502 6th Ave., between W. 12th and 13th Sts., tel. 212/691–1363. Subway: 1, 2, 3, or 9 to 14th St.*

Chumley's. Once a speakeasy, this still-secret pub is great for a civilized pint of ale or a debauched night with old chums. To find the unmarked wooden doorway, listen for boisterous conversation and peals of laughter as you walk past Bedford Street's brick row houses. *86 Bedford St., at Barrow St., tel. 212/675–4449. Subway: 1 or 9 to Christopher St. (Sheridan Sq.).*

Corner Bistro. Founded in 1966, this pub-and-grub-style bar has finally come into its own. The cozy place is so inviting, and the young, professional crowd so friendly, you might think you ducked into a small-town place (if it weren't for the sirens outside). *331 W. 4th St., between Jane St. and 8th Ave., tel. 212/242–9502. Subway: A, C, E, 1, 2, 3, or 9 to 14th St.*

Hogs and Heifers. Sure, this roughneck bar has seen a few fistfights. But most of the time its crew of wanna-be Harley-riding hardasses is just having a damn good, hard-rockin', Pabst-drinkin' time. *859 Washington St., between W. 13th and 14th Sts., tel. 212/929–0655. Subway: A, C, E, or L to W. 14th St.*

Hudson Bar and Books. Satisfy your hankering for brandy and a big fat stogie at this cigar bar, done up like a billionaire's library. Cigars range from $9 (merely stinky) to $16 (Dominican Allone). *636 Hudson St., between Horatio and Jane Sts., tel. 212/229–2642. Subway: A, C, E, or L to W. 14th St.*

Peculier Pub. From Aass Amber to Żywiec, the Peculier Pub stocks more than 500 beers representing 43 countries, including Vietnam, Nicaragua, and the Ivory Coast. The besotted crowd is half as interesting. *145 Bleecker St., between Thompson St. and La Guardia Pl., tel. 212/353–1327. Subway: 6 to Bleecker St.*

Rio Mar. This throwback to Spain sits hidden on a corner in the meat-packing district. Though they stop serving tapas around 6 PM, the bar stays open (and packed) into the wee hours. If you're really hungry, check out the adjoining dining room (*see* Chapter 4). *7 9th Ave., at Little W. 12th St., tel. 212/243–9015. Subway: A, C, E, or L to W. 14th St.*

Tortilla Flats. This haven of kitsch (streamers and tacky movie posters plastered to every possible inch) is a popular, after-hours munch fest and party when the 1–4—that's AM—Saturday-night happy hour kicks into gear. There's outdoor seating and killer margaritas. *767 Washington St., at W. 12th St., tel. 212/243–1053. Subway: A, C, or E to 14th St.*

White Horse Tavern. Go gentle into this good pub, where Dylan Thomas drank himself to death in 1953. A mix of mournful poets and uncaring yuppies carry on the wake at this historic 110-year-old tavern. But unless you want to booze with Jerseyites, come weeknights for a more authentic feel. *560 Hudson St., between W. 11th and Perry Sts., tel. 212/243–9260. Subway: 1 or 9 to Christopher St. (Sheridan Sq.).*

EAST VILLAGE, ALPHABET CITY, AND THE LOWER EAST SIDE

On cold, wintry evenings cozy up to the Art Bar's fireplace and luxuriate in the plushness of it all.

The East Village and Alphabet City are the most bar-dense areas of a city that generally likes to drink. And whether you wear cowboy boots, wing tips, Doc Martens, platform shoes, or go-go boots, you'll have no problem finding something suitable. The big new scene is currently in the Lower East Side, on **East Houston** and **Ludlow streets.** Bars here are hip and nearly unpretentious, frequented by Gen X-ers with lots of style and little cash. If you fall into this category, two mandatory Alphabet City stops are **7B** (E. 7th St. at Ave. B, no phone) for cheap Genesee beer on tap, and **Sophie's** (507 E. 5th St., between Aves. A and B, tel. 212/228–5680) for pinball machines, a jukebox heavy into alternative music, and endless cheap beer—not to mention major crowds on weekend nights.

2A. A mishmash of boozers, pretty young things, and thinker types in heavy glasses patronize this dark, arty bar. If you get tired of the cruising single scene downstairs, relax on one of the comfy couches upstairs. *25 Ave. A, at E. 2nd St., no phone. Subway: F to 2nd Ave.*

Bowery Bar. The celebrities and general scenesters who habitually appear on the *Post's* "Page Six" hold court at this revamped gas station, though its reputation is cooling—a recent drug bust yielded six arrestees, *none* of them famous. *40 E. 4th St., between Bowery and Lafayette St., tel. 212/475–2220. Subway: 6 to Astor Pl.*

Cafe Tabac. Madonna, Drew Barrymore, Francis Coppola, and Keith Richards have been known to drink at this chic boîte. Drinks are weak and cost a fortune. The in-crowd sits upstairs. *232 E. 9th St., between 2nd and 3rd Aves., tel. 212/674–7072. Subway: 6 to Astor Pl.*

d.b.a. The name means "doing business as," a legal term that reflects the owners' inability to choose a name when filing the bar's paperwork at city hall. Employees say it means "don't bother asking" and "drink beer always." Which is easy to do with 60 beers in bottles and 15 on tap. It also has one of the largest collections of single-malt whiskeys outside Scotland. *41 1st Ave., between E. 2nd and 3rd Sts., tel. 212/475–5097. Subway: F to 2nd Ave.*

Decibel Sake Bar. Decibel takes care of business with a small sign outside announcing NO SUSHI, NO KARAOKE. Instead, you'll find 40 kinds of sake and dozens of delicious Japanese appetizers. *210 E. 9th St., between 2nd and 3rd Aves., tel. 212/473–3327. Subway: 6 to Astor Pl.*

Fez. Brass tables, pillow-strewn divans, and gorgeous Arabic tiles fill this dark and smoky room beneath Time Cafe. Nightly events include everything from big band to hip-hop to spoken word. For big-name bands you should make reservations in advance. *380 Lafayette St., at Great Jones St., tel. 212/533–2680. Subway: 6 to Astor Pl.*

K.G.B. East Villagers saddened by the fall of the Wall (Berlin's, not Pink Floyd's) boozily discuss the state of the Revolution in this crimson room hung with old CCCP posters. It's a favorite hangout of literary

RED DEATH AND BUFFALO SWEAT

Did you know that cocktails were invented in New York? Well, according to legend, an 18th-century New York tavern keeper used the tail feather from a rooster to stir drinks, inspiring the name. Two hundred years later, even bars that qualify as "dives" know how to make martinis, Cosmopolitans, and Manhattans. Yet when you need something more exotic and perhaps downright toxic, try one of the following at your own risk.

SoHo's MERCBAR (151 Mercer St., between Houston and Prince Sts., tel. 212/966–2727) specializes in Cement Mixers, a combo of Bailey's Irish Cream and Rose's Lime Juice that solidifies after you swish it around in your mouth for a few seconds.

Also in SoHo, NAKED LUNCH (17 Thompson St., at Grand St., tel. 212/ 343–0828) makes a mean Red Death: vodka, Rose's Lime Juice, Triple Sec, Southern Comfort, Amaretto, sloe gin, and orange juice, topped with Sambuca.

In the East Village, at MARION'S CONTINENTAL LOUNGE (354 Bowery, between Great Jones and W. 4th Sts., tel. 212/475–7621), dive into a Lime Ricky (vodka, club soda, and lime juice), sweet enough to curl your tongue, but big enough so that after a while you won't notice.

types and frequently hosts readings. *85 E. 4th St., between 1st and 2nd Aves., tel. 212/505–3360. Subway: F to 2nd Ave.*

Lucky Cheng's. Drag queens (and the men and women who love them) fill this gay bathhouse turned trendy Chinese bar-restaurant. On weekends, a house DJ takes over the lower level while a glossy drag promenade takes the floor. *24 1st Ave., between E. 1st and 2nd Sts., tel. 212/473–0516. Subway: F to 2nd Ave.*

Ludlow Bar. Part rock club, part dance den, pure funk dive, Ludlow is a bare-bones East Village basement bar favored by a diverse crowd of lesbian pool players and struggling actors. Live bands play during the week, DJs spin soul and acid jazz on weekends. *165 Ludlow St., between E. Houston and Stanton Sts., tel. 212/353–0536. Subway: F to 2nd Ave.*

M & R Bar. You can't find a friendlier place for a chat and a bit of scene than at this comfortable little bar and restaurant favored by a conscientiously understated crowd that'll still talk to you even if you *are* from Wichita. *264 Elizabeth St., between Houston and Prince Sts., tel. 212/226–0559. Subway: 6 to Bleecker St.*

Marion's Continental Restaurant and Lounge. Discover the meaning of *swank* in this fabulous '60s-style cocktail lounge, a onetime fave of Gable and Sinatra. There's also a signed photo from John F. Kennedy. Marion's is still ideal for celeb-watching over a cosmopolitan or Stoli Gibson. The food is tip-top. *354 Bowery, at E. 4th St., tel. 212/475–7621. Subway: 6 to Astor Pl.*

Max Fish. One of the Lower East Side's trendiest bars is always ultracrowded with black-clad slackers, seemingly underaged skaters, and the odd raving bum or two. There's no place to sit, so everyone mills around like it's a junior-high dance. If you want a scene, Max Fish is fine; if you want a quiet drink, go elsewhere. *178 Ludlow St., between E. Houston and Stanton Sts., tel. 212/529–3959. Subway: F to 2nd Ave.*

McSorley's Old Ale House. Not much has changed at this sawdust-carpeted saloon since it opened in 1854. By 11 AM on any given day there's a long line of grizzled regulars and curious tourists waiting to doublefist mugs of McSorley's own brew (two mugs for $3). *15 E. 7th St., between 2nd and 3rd Aves., tel. 212/473–9148. Subway: 6 to Astor Pl.*

Mona's. The Ultimate Neighborhood Dive Bar is the place to drink and play pool with low-key East Villagers. Crowds show for live Irish folk music (Monday), and $2.75 pints of Guinness (Thursday). The neighborhood isn't the greatest, so don't go wandering alone at 4 AM. *224 Ave. B, between E. 13th and 14th Sts., tel. 212/353–3780. Subway: L to 1st Ave.*

Sidewalk Café. Most people come here to fight over a barstool, down a few beers, and leave, though the kitchen's open 24 hours. East Village barhoppers roll through around 10 PM and again at dawn. *94 Ave. A, at E. 6th St., tel. 212/473–7373. Subway: L to 1st Ave.*

CHINATOWN AND LITTLE ITALY

If you're looking for an Italian-American watering hole à la *Goodfellas,* rent the movie—you won't find it in Little Italy. Opium dens are likewise scarce in Chinatown. Sorry, kids.

Marechiaro Tavern. Sometimes known as Tony's, this gruff no-nonsense bar is Little Italy's only authentic spot for a drink. Note the mural-size photo of Frank Sinatra and the barkeep, looking swell together. *176½ Mulberry St., between Broome and Grand Sts., no phone. Subway: 6 to Spring St.*

Diehard geezers at McSorley's Old Ale House still complain about the decision (under court order) to admit women in 1971.

Spring Lounge. Nurse a glass of beer with elderly Italian men reminiscing about the way things used to be. Some people know this place as the "Shark Bar" because of the awning out front. *48 Spring St., at Mulberry St., tel. 212/226–9347. Subway: 6 to Spring St.*

SOHO AND TRIBECA

SoHo is the center of glam New York nightlife, and **West Broadway**'s bars and bistros are always packed, especially when they set up outdoor tables in summer. Along **Greenwich** and **Hudson streets** there are some fine places that happily don't charge the steep prices you'll find at bars in SoHo's center (i.e., along Spring and Mercer streets). TriBeCa has more restaurants than bars, though you will find a few watering holes off Broadway above **Chambers Street.**

Bell Caffe. If any struggling artists still lived in SoHo, they would drown their sorrows in this funky pub filled with lumpy couches and weird kitsch items. Sit outside on summer nights or dive on in for some free live music: sitar on Tuesday, acid jazz on Friday, acid funk on Sunday. *310 Spring St., between Hudson and Greenwich Sts., tel. 212/334–2355. Subway: C or E to Spring St.*

Café Noir. You'll wonder if you're still in SoHo at this chic French-Moroccan oasis: The waiters, waitresses, and bartenders all speak French (and not much English). *32 Grand St., at Thompson St., tel. 212/431–7910. Subway: A, C, or E to Canal St.*

Ear Inn. Rumor has it that this used to be the Bear Inn, until the B fell off the sign. Regardless, this self-described "dump with dignity" draws a crowd of friendly folk to its long, old-fashioned bar for leisurely pints of stout. If it's crowded, head across the way to Bell Caffe (*see above*). *326 Spring St., at Greenwich St., tel. 212/226–9060. Subway: C or E to Spring St.*

Lucky Strike. This über-cool bistro has started quieting down now that the supermodels party elsewhere. Even so, its weekend dance parties are still crowded affairs, with DJs playing funky tunes for the young Euro types boozing it up at the cozy back tables. *59 Grand St., between Wooster St. and West Broadway, tel. 212/941–0479. Subway: A, C, or E to Canal St.*

Match. A hip crowd checks in at this beautifully understated restaurant/bar in between gallery openings, AIDS benefits, loft parties, spoken-word performances, sexual dalliances, etc., etc., etc. *160 Mercer St., between Houston and Prince Sts., tel. 212/343–0020. Subway: N or R to Prince St.; also B, D, F, or Q to Broadway/Lafayette St.*

Mercbar. Always crowded, Merc is a staple SoHo scene, with an eclectic clientele of tourists, bankers, actors, and artists lolling on cushy couches at the front. The hostesses are Gestapo recruits: Don't take

DISCO BOWL

Years ago, there used to be many more lanes to chose from, but bowling is a dying pastime (and cheap date idea) in the city. At one point, many places were replaced with the increasingly popular sanitized pool hall (another cheap date idea). Ah, progress. These two have stuck it out and in the process have moved into "institution" status.

BOWLMOR LANES. A cool Village crowd plays on Bowlmor's busy 44 lanes (try not to think about how many feet have been in your bowling shoes before you); grab a beer at the bar while you wait. The best night is Monday, when you get disco lights, a DJ, and bowling until 4 AM—all for $10. 110 University Pl., between E. 12th and 13th Sts., East Village, tel. 212/255–8188. Subway: L, N, R, 4, 5, or 6 to Union Sq. Open daily 10 AM–1 AM (Mon., Fri., and Sat. until 4 AM).

LEISURE TIME. While you're waiting for a bus outta town, catch a game ($4 per person) at the Port Authority Bus Terminal's 30-lane bowling alley. Once a month (usually on Saturday) they host a "Moonlight Bowl" ($20), which includes food, cheap beer, raffle prizes, a DJ, disco lights, and as many games as you can play until 4 AM. W. 42nd St. and 9th Ave., Midtown, tel. 212/268–6909. Subway: A, C, or E to W. 42nd St. Open daily 10 AM–11 PM (Fri. and Sat. until 2 AM).

it personally, they order everybody around. Look for tall French doors; in SoHo fashion, there's no sign outside. *151 Mercer St., between W. Houston and Prince Sts., tel. 212/966–2727. Subway: N or R to Prince St.*

Novecento. A lively crowd and good music (usually acid jazz or salsa) make this Argentinean café-bar an adventure any night of the week. The downstairs is spacious and airy; upstairs it's intimate, with deep couches and dim lighting. *343 W. Broadway, between Broome and Grand Sts., tel. 212/925–4706. Subway: A, C, E, 1, or 9 to Canal St.*

Pravda. Capitalism may be struggling in the home country, but it's flourishing at this pricey Russian-themed restaurant and bar. A truly beautiful space, you had better be beautiful yourself to get in, or go before 10 PM to slide past the stern bouncers. *281 Lafayette St., between Prince and Houston Sts., tel. 212/226–4696. Subway: 6 to Spring St.*

Red Bench. SoHo's trendiest (and tiniest) late-night bar draws downtown scenesters, stockbrokers, street artists, and nouvelle hippie chicks. Definitely a place to be seen. *107 Sullivan St., between Prince and Spring Sts., tel. 212/274–9120. Subway: C or E to Spring St.*

WaxBar. One of the trendiest hangouts in Manhattan's trendy heart, this mausoleumlike space packs in a lot of people you guess are good looking, but you can barely see them it's so dark. Cleans up on the clamoring masses turned down by Spy (just down the street if you're masochistic), so hot, *no one* gets in. *113 Mercer St., between Spring and Prince Sts., tel. 212/226–6082. Subway: N or R to Prince St.*

Zinc Bar. A perennial favorite in the downtown social scene, this subterranean space oozes sexy ambience (gilt mirrors, flickering candles, and velvet-curtained walls). Catch live jazz Thursday–Saturday and Brazilian music on Sunday. *90 W. Houston St., between W. Broadway and Thompson St., tel. 212/477–8337. Subway: 1 or 9 to Houston St.*

LOWER MANHATTAN

New Yorkers who work on Wall Street don't stick around Lower Manhattan much past 6 PM. As a result, most bars here cater to tourists (and hard-core drunks), close early on weeknights, and shut down completely on weekends. That said, pubs around the **South Street Seaport** keep their doors open relatively late to accommodate the Nikon-toting hordes.

Jeremy's Ale House. Enjoy two-pint styrofoam "buckets" of beer and the ultimate in frat-party ambience (e.g., stacked kegs and bras in the rafters). The crowd is heavy on tourists from the Seaport, with a few Wall Streeters nostalgic for their Ivy days. *254 Front St., at Dover St., tel. 212/964–3537. Subway: J, M, Z, 2, 3, 4, or 5 to Fulton St.*

North Star Pub. This snug London-style pub is one of the only places at the South Street Seaport not completely overrun by tourists. Have an Imperial (20-ounce) pint of Guinness, but skip the greasy, expensive bar food. *93 South St., at Fulton St., tel. 212/509–6757. Subway: J, M, Z, 2, 3, 4, or 5 to Fulton St.*

OUTER BOROUGHS

BROOKLYN

Those comedians you're paying to watch will seem much funnier if you've cut the cost of the cover charge by checking for coupons in the "Village Voice."

Henry's End. Here's a cozy little spot to take a pint after a day's exploration in Brooklyn Heights. They serve a good dinner, too, with entrées around $8. *44 Henry St., at Cranberry St., tel. 718/834–1776. Subway: A or C to High St./Brooklyn Bridge.*

Peter's Waterfront Alehouse. It's not exactly on the waterfront, but the cozy booths, mellow atmosphere, and fine selection of ice-cold beers—50 in bottles, 12 on tap—merit a trip across the East River. *136 Atlantic Ave., between Henry and Clinton Sts., Cobble Hill, tel. 718/522–3794. Subway: 2, 3, 4, or 5 to Borough Hall.*

Primorski. Come to this Brighton Beach joint to toss back iced vodka with old Russian men. *282 Brighton Beach Ave., between Brighton 2 and Brighton 3 Sts., tel. 718/891–3111. Subway: D or Q to Brighton Beach.*

RBBQ. This is where Williamsburg artists, too smart and too poor to pay Manhattan rents, get together to talk abstract expressionism. They serve barbecued everything (*see* Chapter 4). *409 Kent Ave., at Broadway, tel. 718/388–3929. Subway: J, M, or Z to Marcy Ave.*

BRONX

An Bēal Bocht. The crowd at this authentic Irish pub (the name means "The Poor Mouth" in Gaelic) is a cool mix of Irish immigrants and students from nearby Manhattan College. Offerings include poetry readings (Tuesday) and live Irish bands (Wednesday–Sunday). *445 W. 238th St., between Greystone and Waldo Aves., Riverdale, tel. 718/884–7127. Subway: 1 or 9 to 238th St.; walk up 238th St. to steep flight of stairs and climb 'em.*

QUEENS

Amnesia. Local bohemians gather at this lavender-lit, artsy café-bar for live music (European and house) and loud conversation. During summer its outdoor tables are *the* place to scope out Astoria's streetlife. *32–02 Broadway, at 31st St., Astoria, tel. 718/721–1969. Subway: N to Broadway.*

STATEN ISLAND

Adobe Blues. Choose from more than 200 international beers and 33 kinds of tequila at this kitschy but cozy Old West–style bar. On Wednesday, Friday, and Saturday nights you also get live jazz and blues free of charge. The adjoining dining room serves up southwestern and Mexican fare (*see* Chapter 4). *63 Lafayette Ave., at Fillmore St., New Brighton, tel. 718/720–2583. From Ferry Terminal, take Bus S40 to Lafayette Ave. (10 mins).*

COMEDY

There's something sad and a little desperate about forcing people to pay upwards of $17 (and don't forget that two-drink minimum!) for a few hours of yuks. But that's the state of comedy in most New York clubs today, so consider yourself warned. Luckily, "alternative comedy" clubs keep the scene from being a total wash. Comics at these clubs perform a manic mix of stand-up comedy, sketch comedy, and performance art, sometimes to hilarious effect, and sometimes, well, not. Best of all, alternative comedy clubs usually impose little or no cover charge and practically never have a drink minimum. Most clubs (unless otherwise noted) offer one show nightly Sunday–Thursday and two or more shows Friday and Saturday nights.

The "Sunday Night Improv" show (7 PM) at **West End Gate Café** (2911 Broadway, between W. 113th and 114 Sts., Morningside Heights, tel. 212/662–8830) draws funny groups like Chicago City Limits (*see below*) and Ms. Dee's Comedy Ice Tea. If you don't laugh at the jokes, you'll laugh at the price: Cover is $5, with no drink minimum.

Boston Comedy Club. The young and the raunchy bring their gags to this NYU favorite. (It's named the Boston because the owner likes Boston. Funny, huh?) Monday is open-mike amateur night. *82 W. 3rd St., between Thompson and Sullivan Sts., West Village, tel. 212/477–1000. Subway: A, B, C, D, E, F, or Q to W. 4th St. (Washington Sq.). Cover: $5 Sun.–Thurs.; $10 Fri. and Sat. 2-drink minimum.*

Caroline's Comedy Club. Manhattan's high-profile comedy venue has showcased well-known funny people for years; Margaret Cho, Jon Stewart, Sandra Bernhard, and Gilbert Gottfried have all held the stage here. *1626 Broadway, between 49th and 50th Sts., Midtown, tel. 212/757–4100. Subway: C, E, 1, or 9 to W. 50th St.; B, D, or E to 7th Ave.; N or R to W. 49th St. Cover: $12–$15 Sun.–Thurs.; $15–$17 Fri. and Sat. 2-drink minimum.*

Catch a Rising Star. Up-and-coming comics (or as the ad says, "freshly squeezed talent") and established headliners such as Janeane Garafalo and Denis Leary both make appearances at this slick West Chelsea venue with an American bistro. *253 W. 28th St., between 7th and 8th Aves., Chelsea, tel. 212/244–3005. Subway: 1 or 9 to 28th St. Cover: $8 Tues.–Thurs; $12.50–$15 Fri. and Sat. 2-item minimum.*

Chicago City Limits. The oldest comedy and improvisational theater company in the city busts out with outrageous off-the-cuff skits and skewering of celebrities, based entirely on *your* insane suggestions. Okay, they do pre-write some of their material—but it doesn't make it any less funny. *1105 1st Ave., at E. 61st St., Upper East Side, tel. 212/888–5233. Subway: 4, 5, or 6 to E. 59th St.; also N or R to Lexington Ave. Cover: $10 Mon., $20 Wed.–Sat.*

Comedy Cellar. Beneath the Olive Tree Café is this dim and smoky throwback to the Village coffeehouses of the '60s. The nightly lineup features pros from *Letterman*, HBO, and *Conan O'Brien*. Newer talent slinks in after midnight. *117 MacDougal St., between W. 3rd and Bleecker Sts., West Village, tel. 212/254–3480. Subway: A, B, C, D, E, F, or Q to W. 4th St. (Washington Sq.). Cover: $5 Sun.–Thurs., $12 Fri. and Sat. 2-drink minimum.*

Dangerfield's. Rodney "No Respect" Dangerfield and pal opened this kitschy Vegas-style club in '69 so Rodney could become famous. And somehow (don't ask us), he did. It's also served as a springboard to stardom for guys like Jay Leno, Jim Carrey, Andrew Dice Clay, and Sam Kinison (R.I.P.). *1118 1st Ave., between E. 61st and 62nd Sts., Upper East Side, tel. 212/593–1650. Subway: 4, 5, or 6 to E. 59th St.; also N or R to Lexington Ave. Cover: $12.50 Sun.–Thurs., $15 Fri. and Sat.*

Gotham Comedy Club. This relative newcomer to the Flatiron district in Chelsea, housed in a landmark historic building, is certainly snazzier than the usual club; there's a turn-of-the-century chandelier, custom copper bars, and mahogany furnishings (as well as clean bathrooms). Come here for classic stand-up performed by the likes of Chris Rock and David Brenner. A Latino comedy show happens once a month. *34 W. 22nd St., between 5th and 6th Aves., Chelsea, tel. 212/367–9000. Subway: F, N, R, 1, or 9 to 23rd St. Cover: $8 Sun.–Thurs., $12 Fri. and Sat. 2-drink minimum.*

Luna Lounge. On Monday comics both recognizable and obscure try out performance-art comedy skits at this hip club. Expect experimental material that's uproarious or just plain strange. *171 Ludlow St., at Houston St., Lower East Side, tel. 212/260–2323. Subway: F to 2nd Ave. Free.*

New York Comedy Club. Friday puts the spotlight on new talent and more seasoned headliners; the late show brings together "New York's Best African-American and Latino Comics." Wednesday and Thursday expect traditional stand-up. *241 E. 24th St., between 2nd and 3rd Aves., Gramercy, tel. 212/696–5233. Subway: 6 to E. 23rd St. Cover: $5 Sun.–Thurs., $10 Fri. and Sat. 2-drink minimum.*

Stand-up New York. Robin Williams is known to drop by this swank joint to warm up for his *Letterman* appearances. Unannounced. Maybe you'll get lucky. Otherwise, look for young faces you may have seen on TV. *236 W. 78th St., at Broadway, Upper West Side, tel. 212/595–0850. Subway: 1 or 9 to W. 79th St. Cover: $7 Sun.–Thurs., $12 Fri. and Sat. 2-drink minimum.*

DANCE CLUBS

The city's myriad dance clubs encompass every type of music, fashion, sexual preference, ego, and bank account. Biggies, like **Webster Hall** and **Twilo** (*see below*), are fantasylands with thousands of dollars' worth of strobe lights, lasers, and smoke machines and a cast of characters dressed like space men and dominatrixes. House, techno, and ambient are currently in vogue, although plenty of clubs stick to soul, hip-hop, dance hall reggae, and acid jazz.

To visitors with small-town sensibilities, the city's dance scene might seem more shocking than glamorous: Cover for an A-list club costs up to $20 (even more for men). At many clubs you'll encounter the cursed Velvet Rope, cordoning off the rabble from celebrities and hard-core club kids; keep in mind that flashy up-to-the-minute style is what really matters here. Age limits and dress codes may be selectively enforced to keep out those whom the bouncer deems undesirable. If you get rejected, don't take it personally.

New York's dance scene is notoriously fickle, and this week's hottest club may get boarded up a month later. Likewise, a place can host completely different crowds depending on night of the week—drag ball on Tuesday, punk "battle of the bands" on Wednesday—or even shut its doors temporarily to throw a private party. And many places are only open one or two (rotating) nights a week. Call ahead to avoid any nasty surprises. Or check the huge stacks of flyers at one of the city's several dance record stores for upcoming events and—this is key—big discounts (*see* Records, Tapes, and CDs *in* Chapter 5). DJs Junior Vasquez and Danny Tenaglia guarantee a massive, throbbing crowd wherever they spin. Finally, turn to the *New York Press*, **Urb**, or **Project X** for decent (but selective) listings and reviews; the *Village Voice* and *Time Out New York* are the most comprehensive.

If Latin and American ballroom dancing is your thing, come to Roseland on Thursday ($8 for DJ music) or Sunday ($11 for live bands).

The Bank. Wear black—lots and lots of black—to New York's premier industrial and Gothic club. It's the best place in the city to see Trent Reznor look-alikes getting sweaty in a former bank lobby. *225 E. Houston St., at Essex St., Lower East Side, tel. 212/505–5033. Subway: J, M, or Z to Essex St. Cover: $4–$10.*

Buddha Bar. It's SoHo-on-the-Bosphorus at this glam Turkish nightspot peopled with leggy hostesses and a hip, multiracial crowd. *150 Varick St., at Vandam St., SoHo, tel. 212/255–4433. Subway: 1 or 9 to W. Houston St. Cover: $10.*

Den of Thieves. They spin everything from new wave to reggae to trip-hop to acid jazz at this tiny, sleazy club. Most nights it's bathed in red lights and filled with East Villagers with lurid pasts. *145 E. Houston St., between Eldridge and Forsyth Sts., Lower East Side, tel. 212/388–7966. Subway: F to 2nd Ave. Cover: $5 or less.*

Don Hill's. This old warehouse has been converted into a hangout for go-go trash; come for one of the cool weekend dance parties. *511 Greenwich St., at Spring St., SoHo, tel. 212/219–2850. Subway: C or E to Spring St. Cover: $10.*

Expo. At this former theater, scantily clad go-go girls do their thing on stage while a crowd fresh from New Jersey stands around waiting for something to happen. Check out the giant pillows on the upper balcony. *124 W. 43rd St., between 6th Ave. and Broadway, Theater District, tel. 212/819–0377. Subway: N, R, 1, 2, 3, 7, or 9 to Times Sq. Cover: $15 ($20 on Fri. and Sat.).*

Jackie 60. This party, held at the club Mother, is the famous domain of drag queens who strut their stuff for an appreciative crowd of gays and straights. Expect glitter and spectacle with undercurrents of fetish and bondage. *432 W. 14th St., at Washington St., West Village, tel. 212/677–6060. Subway: A, C, E, or L to W. 14th St. Cover: $10. Open Tues. only.*

Jet Lounge. One of the best clubs in New York, but unfortunately, everyone knows it. Expect a 45-minute wait to (maybe) get in. The interior, decorated with millions of glass shards stuck in the plaster walls, and the funky groove are worth it. *286 Spring St., between Varick and Hudson Sts., West Village, tel. 212/675–2277. Subway: 1, 2, 3, or 9 to Houston St.*

Les Poulets. Stylish latinos and latinas come to this spacious supper club to dance to salsa, hip-hop, and disco. *16 W. 22nd St., between 5th and 6th Aves., Chelsea, tel. 212/229–2000. Subway: N or R to W. 23rd St. Cover: $5–$15.*

Life. The most recent aspirant to the title of hottest New York club attracts the usual masses crying to get in. Once you elbow your way past the velvet rope, however, it's a bit of a disappointment. The cavernous, throbbing dance hall is so bare of decor there's little to differentiate it from a community center. The VIP room is upstairs and so is the real action. *158 Bleecker St., between Sullivan and Thompson Sts., West Village, tel. 212/420–1999. Subway: A, B, C, D, E, F, or Q to W. 4th St.*

Nell's. Years ago, this dark and elegant club was *the* haunt of the demimonde. Although it's looking a little shabbier these days, it retains a chic, multiethnic following. *246 W. 14th St., between 7th and 8th Aves., West Village, tel. 212/675–1567. Subway: 1, 2, 3, or 9 to W. 14th St. Cover: $10–$15.*

Roxy. Cavernous Roxy has cool raves and occasional live bands—and don't miss the roller-skating dance fest on Tuesday (gay) and Wednesday (mixed). Rental skates are $5, blades $10. A DJ spins house music on the weekends. *515 W. 18th St., between 10th and 11th Aves., Chelsea, tel. 212/645–5156. Subway: A, C, E, or L to W. 14th St. Cover: $12.*

System. For house and techno, this is the best club in New York. Be prepared to look *very* trendy to get in. *76 E. 13th St., between Broadway and 4th Ave., Union Sq., tel. 212/388–1060. Subway: L, N, R, 4, 5, or 6 to E. 14th St. (Union Sq.). Cover: $20.*

Tunnel. For a long time, the Tunnel had achieved the impossible in clubland: perpetual coolness. Fading now, it still manages to attract a hearty ultra-diverse crowd almost every night. The party ends around, oh, 10 or 11 AM the next day. *220 12th Ave., at W. 27th St., Chelsea, tel. 212/695–4682. Subway: C or E to W. 23rd St. Cover: $20. Ages 18 and over.*

Twilo. Gay muscle boys, hip heteros, post ravers, and club kids fill the wide open dance floor at Twilo. Music is mostly progressive house with some trance in the wee hours. Danny Tenaglia and visiting European DJs spin occasionally. *530 W. 27th St., between 10th and 11th Aves., Chelsea, tel. 212/268–1600. Subway: C or E to W. 23rd St. Cover: $20.*

Vertigo. Hip-hop and house rattle bones at this low-grade disco, favored by crowds in XXXXL baggy pants and baseball caps. Special bonus: a full-body frisk upon entry, under the gaze of bouncer-thugs. *27 W. 20th St., between 5th and 6th Aves., Chelsea, tel. 212/366–4181. Subway: N or R to W. 23rd St. Cover: $10–$20. Ages 18 and over on Sun.*

Webster Hall. Even the truly jaded will find something to do at this 40,000-square-ft megaclub. All kinds, from rastas to transvestites, hang at Webster Hall's four diversion-filled dance floors. *125 E. 11th St., between 3rd and 4th Aves., East Village, tel. 212/353–1600. Subway: 6 to Astor Pl. Cover: $20.*

LIVE MUSIC

Strike up a conversation with most New Yorkers, and they'll tell you about the time when Bono or Eddie Vedder or Sean McGowan, then totally obscure, cruised into their favorite dump and jammed for six hours straight. This is New York City, and you can see the best of everything here, be it cutting-edge indie bands or arena rockers. Bars also host live bands, usually on weekends, sometimes for a cover and sometimes for free. If you're broke, check the *Village Voice* for listings of free shows. To find out what's going on at venues like Central Park's Summerstage, Madison Square Garden, Shea Stadium, Giants Stadium, and Roseland, call the **Concert Hotline** (tel. 212/249–8870).

Summer is the perfect time for free concerts. Central Park offers its **SummerStage** series (tel. 212/360–2777) from June through August, featuring opera performances, rock, world music, and spoken word by some big names. Past performers have included Patti Smith, the Indigo Girls, Steel Pulse, and Paul Simon. For more on Summerstage, *see* Summer Arts *in* Chapter 7. Coney Island offers its own indie-rock version of these events every Friday night in summer at **Steeplechase Park**; for information contact the New York City Parks & Recreation Department (tel. 718/946–1350). The best of jazz is showcased at two big festivals, the prestigious **JVC Jazz Festival** (tel. 212/501–1390), held for 10 days in late June at larger venues (with free shows in Bryant Park) and during the **Jazz at Lincoln Center** series (tel. 212/875–5299 or 212/875–5299), which runs from September through May.

Two gigantic annual music festivals give you a chance to scope up-and-comers in every genre. The **Macintosh Music Festival** (July), playing at clubs around Manhattan, features rock and blues by both little-known and signed bands. Two or three computers are placed at each club so patrons can access the festival Web site on the Internet for a schedule of performances, as well as constantly updated visuals of the action. The **College Music Journal** hosts a major festival every September, featuring college talent with forums for students and industry people. If you're in town during one of these fests, grab a city weekly for more info.

For big events, purchase tickets in advance from one of two agencies—if you don't mind paying a service charge (a big "if"). **Tele-Charge** (tel. 212/239–6200) deals with most shows and charges $4.75 per ticket. Corporate monster **Ticketmaster** (tel. 212/307–7171) has outlets all over the city and charges $3–$5 per ticket (depending on the show and venue), plus an additional $1.50 if you charge by phone. The moral: Avoid ticket agencies (and their service charges) by purchasing tickets in cash at the venue itself or a record store.

MAJOR VENUES

Beacon. Built in 1928 as a vaudeville theater, the Beacon has an interior to rival Radio City Music Hall. It seats around 3,000 and usually hosts big-name music acts from Steve Allman Band to the Indigo Girls. *2124 Broadway, between W. 74th and 75th Sts., Upper West Side, tel. 212/496–7070. Subway: 1, 2, 3, or 9 to W. 72nd St.*

Carnegie Hall. This landmark music hall, built in 1891, features mostly classical and jazz (October–June). Occasionally, major pop and rock acts like Natalie Merchant or Crosby, Stills, and Nash also fill the hall's 2,800 seats. *154 W. 57th St., at 7th Ave., Midtown, tel. 212/247–7800. Subway: N or R to W. 57th St.; B, D, or E to 7th Ave.; also A, C, 1, or 9 to 59th St./Columbus Circle. Closed Aug.*

At Tunnel, top DJs spin techno on a dance floor the size of a bus terminal, and the bar inside the coed bathroom is its own nonstop scene.

Madison Square Garden. This giant 20,000-seat indoor arena hosts mega-major rock and pop concerts, not to mention Knicks and Rangers games (*see* Spectator Sports *in* Chapter 8). *7th Ave. between W. 31st and 33rd Sts., Midtown, tel. 212/465–6741. Subway: A, C, or E to W. 34th St. (Penn Station).*

Paramount. It's adjacent to Madison Square Garden and handles slightly smaller affairs: Capacity is 5,600. *7th Ave. between W. 31st and 33rd Sts., Midtown, tel. 212/465–6741. Subway: A, C, or E to W. 34th St. (Penn Station).*

Radio City Music Hall. Besides the hokey annual "Christmas Spectacular" and the "Easter Show," Rockefeller Center's stylish music hall puts on national music acts of all kinds. Seating capacity is 6,000. *1260 6th Ave., between W. 50th and 51st Sts., Midtown, tel. 212/247–4777. Subway: B, D, F, or Q to W. 47th–50th Sts. (Rockefeller Center).*

Roseland. Tickets for touring rock shows average $15–$30 at this stellar open-floor hall. Seating capacity is 3,200. *239 W. 52nd St., between Broadway and 8th Ave., Midtown, tel. 212/247–0200. Subway: 1 or 9 to W. 50th St.*

Town Hall. This landmark 1921 auditorium seats 1,500 for every imaginable kind of show, from classical to rock to spoken word. *123 W. 43rd St., between 6th and 7th Aves., Midtown, tel. 212/840–2824. Subway: N, R, 1, 2, 3, 7, or 9 to W. 42nd St. (Times Sq.).*

Tramps. Tramps's spacious, table-filled floor is one of the better places in the city to catch live bands. Shows range from record-company freebies to big-name, ticketed items ($10–$30). Some shows are all ages, some are 21 and over; call for details. Seating capacity is 700. *51 W. 21st St., between 5th and 6th Aves., Chelsea, tel. 212/727–7788. Subway: N or R to W. 23rd St.*

CLUBS AND OTHER VENUES

MUSIC MIX

Brownies. Every night there seems to be a different group of people lined up outside this East Village favorite: sometimes grunge kids and New Jersey skate rats, sometimes NYU freshmen, sometimes drunken punks smoking cloves. Needless to say, the music varies from night to night. *169 Ave. A, between E. 10th and 11th Sts., East Village, tel. 212/420–8392. Subway: L to 1st Ave. Cover: $6–$8.*

Knitting Factory. What started as a crude '80s punk venue has grown to include two slick bars and three stages. Shows include everything from jazz to punk to Gothic/industrial, with both big names and local talent. In the front room, pick up a calendar of events or buy a CD of whomever or whatever the hell you just heard. The **AlterKnit Theatre,** downstairs, books folksier artists and cool spoken-word stuff. *74 Leonard St., between Broadway and Church St., TriBeCa, tel. 212/219–3055. Subway: 1 or 9 to Franklin St. Cover: $7–$20.*

Mercury Lounge. Yet another reason to head to the Lower East Side for music. The Mercury's reputation has been built on its eclectic music and great sound system. *217 E. Houston St., at Essex St., Lower East Side, tel. 212/260–4700. Subway: F to Delancey St.; also J, M, or Z to Essex St. Cover: $6–$12.*

Rainy Days Cafe. Come here because nobody else does. This crash-pad café has mellow live music (reggae, acoustic folk, whatever) almost every night, plus a limited health-food menu. Tuesday is "musical chairs night," with poetry reading and a band. *149 W. 21st St., between 6th and 7th Aves., Chelsea, tel. 212/620–4101. Subway: F to W. 23rd St. Cover: $5 or less. Closed Sun.*

ROCK, PUNK, AND ALTERNATIVE

CBGB's & OMFUG. CBGB's may be the most famous rock club in the world. During the 1970s and early '80s, it *was* American Punk and post-Punk, with alumni including the Ramones, Blondie, the Talking Heads, and Sonic Youth. It still is a great—if smoky and seriously crowded—place to see a show; there are usually about four or five bands a night. Not to be missed is the graffiti-covered bathroom, which has never, ever been painted. Next door is **CB's 313 Gallery** (313 Bowery, tel. 212/677–0455), serving up more folksy musical offerings. *315 Bowery, at Bleecker St., East Village, tel. 212/982–4052. Subway: 6 to Bleecker St.; also F to 2nd Ave. Cover: $3–$10.*

Coney Island High. This is the kind of place that your mama warned you about: sleazy crowds listening to alternative bands singing songs about debauchery and destitution. But how can you not love a club whose bar is called the Detention Lounge? *15 St. Marks Pl., between 2nd and 3rd Aves., East Village, tel. 212/674–7959. Subway: 6 to Astor Pl. Cover: $5–$20.*

The Cooler. This former meat locker (look for stray hooks on the walls, once used to hang sides of beef) has become a slick, black-and-stainless-steel club. It draws a hip and tattooed crowd for punk, spoken word, and the occasional dance party. *416 W. 14th St., between 9th and 10th Aves., West Village, tel. 212/229–0785. Subway: A, C, E, or L to W. 14th St. Cover: $10 (free Mon.). Advance tickets ($8–$10) available at Kim's Underground (144 Bleecker St., tel. 212/387–8250).*

Downtime. There are live bands downstairs, a pool room on the second floor, and a steamy industrial dance floor on top. A big drawback: a crowd that takes Goth far too seriously. *251 W. 30th St., between 7th and 8th Aves., Chelsea, tel. 212/695–2747. Subway: 1 or 9 to W. 28th St. Cover: $5–$15.*

Lion's Den. The Den is a great place to catch a ton of rock bands. It's cheap, and the cavernous space means good views and plenty of room for dancing. *214 Sullivan St., between W. 3rd and Bleecker Sts., West Village, tel. 212/477–0192. Subway: A, B, C, D, E, F, or Q to W. 4th St. (Washington Sq.). Cover: $3 and up.*

Under ACME. This basement club is slowly building a reputation as one of the city's great alternative-rock venues. The cover is never more than $6, so you can afford to splurge upstairs at the trendy ACME restaurant (*see* Chapter 4). *9 Great Jones St., between Broadway and Lafayette St., East Village, tel. 212/420–1934. Subway: 6 to Bleecker St.*

Wetlands. This joint rock venue and environmental action center has helped launch big names like Phish, Blues Traveler, the Spin Doctors, and Hootie and the Blowfish. "Save the Rainforest" info is posted on an old VW hippie bus parked next to the dance floor. *161 Hudson St., at Laight St., TriBeCa, tel. 212/966–4225. Subway: 1 or 9 to Franklin St. Cover: $5–$15 (free Tues.). Ages 18 and over.*

FUNK, BLUES, AND REGGAE

The Bitter End. This prominent blues joint draws a cool, mixed-aged crowd. During the '70s it was the place to see folks like Billy Joel, Linda Ronstadt, and Stevie Wonder. *147 Bleecker St., between Thompson St. and La Guardia Pl., West Village, tel. 212/673–7030. Subway: A, B, C, D, E, F, or Q to W. 4th St. (Washington Sq.). Cover: $5.*

Manny's Car Wash. Manny's is your crowded, grungy outpost for blues on the Upper East Side. It's heavy on bridge-and-tunnel types too meek to tackle the downtown scene. *1558 3rd Ave., between E. 87th and 88th Sts., Upper East Side, tel. 212/369–2583. Subway: 4, 5, or 6 to E. 86th St. Cover: $12 or less.*

Mondo Perso. Every night of the week there's a different sound at this sweaty, smoke-filled West Village club. Monday is world beat, Tuesday is reggae, Wednesday is blues, and Thursday is funk/blues. Weekend shows are predominantly blues. In lieu of a cover Mondo Perso has a two-drink minimum per set. *167 Bleecker St., between Thompson and Sullivan Sts., West Village, tel. 212/477–3770. Subway: A, B, C, D, E, F, or Q to W. 4th St. (Washington Sq.).*

S.O.B.'s (Sounds of Brazil). Now 15 years old, S.O.B.'s brings in bands playing African, reggae, Caribbean, Latin, jazz, funk, and soul. *200 Varick St., at W. Houston St., SoHo, tel. 212/243–4940. Subway: 1 or 9 to W. Houston St. Cover: $10–$25.*

JAZZ

Arthur's Tavern. This tiny club, once the stomping ground of Charlie Parker, has been hosting Dixieland jazz for almost 50 years. The stage is so small that patrons can mill around right next to the performers. Best of all, there's rarely a cover. *57 Grove St., at 7th Ave. S, West Village, tel. 212/675–6879. Subway: 1 or 9 to Christopher St. (Sheridan Sq.).*

The Blue Note. Without a doubt, this is one of New York's most famous jazz clubs (Charlie Parker and Duke Ellington have played here), showcasing local and big-name talent almost every night of the week. Now the bad news: The cover charge can be as high as $40. *131 W. 3rd St., between MacDougal St. and 6th Ave., West Village, tel. 212/475–8592. Subway: A, B, C, D, E, F, or Q to West 4th St. (Washington Sq.).*

Take note: Many jazz clubs are not late-night affairs, and bands typically play from 8 PM to around midnight.

Blues Supply. The Wolcott Hotel's posh Louis XVI ballroom is the setting for this jazz supper club, in an otherwise dead part of Midtown. Bands play Monday–Saturday. *4 W. 31st St., between 5th Ave. and Broadway, Midtown, tel. 212/631–0100. Subway: B, D, F, N, Q, or R to W. 34th St. (Herald Sq.). Cover: $10–$15.*

Red Blazer Too. Among the uppity eateries on Restaurant Row, this jazz club is a genuine find. Every night of the week, combos play New Orleans or Chicago Dixieland, swing, and traditional jazz to an older audience in the mood for a post-*Phantom* party. *349 W. 46th St., between 8th and 9th Aves., Theater District, tel. 212/262–3112. Subway: A, C, or E to W. 42nd St. (Port Authority). Cover: $5 with a two-drink minimum per person (free Mon.).*

Smalls. Owner Mitchell Borden (a jazz man from San Francisco, and no relation to Lizzie) keeps the coolest joint in the city: Non-alcoholic beverages are free (BYO stronger stuff), and you get two smokin' sets followed by a jam session stretching into the wee hours of the morning. *183 W. 10th St., at 7th Ave. S, West Village, tel. 212/929–7565. Subway: 1 or 9 to Christopher St. (Sheridan Sq.). Cover: $10.*

Sweet Basil. For almost 20 years, Sweet Basil has been winning praises as one of the city's top spots for jazz. Just don't do any talking: Patrons here want to listen to the *music*, okay? Friday and Saturday feature three shows; on other nights there are two. *88 7th Ave. S, between Bleecker and Grove Sts., West Village, tel. 212/242–1785. Subway: 1 or 9 to Christopher St. (Sheridan Sq.). Cover: $17.50 with a $10 minimum food or drink charge.*

Village Vanguard. The Vanguard isn't a jazz club, it's a jazz institution, presided over by owner Max Gordon. Some of the biggest names in the business have played here since it opened in 1935—Miles Davis, John Coltrane, Sonny Rollins, Charlie Mingus, Dexter Gordon, and Thelonious Monk. *178 7th Ave. S, at W. 11th St., West Village, tel. 212/255–4037. Subway: 1 or 9 to Christopher St. (Sheridan Sq.). Cover: $15 (Mon. $12) with a $10 minimum drink charge.*

THE ARTS

UPDATED BY DAVID LOW

From Eric Bogosian to the Metropolitan Opera, New York City is like no other when it comes to the performing arts, be it name-brand or cutting-edge dance, theater, music, or opera: It's got all the big names and about a million small ones. On any given night you'll wrestle to choose among the world-famous American Ballet Theatre, the renowned New York Philharmonic, and maybe a few Tony- or Pulitzer Prize–winning plays. Or you can chuck it all to cruise the alternative arts scene downtown, maybe take in a poetry slam at the Nuyorican, or catch an outrageous new performance artist at P.S. 122. Sounds fabulous, right? Can't wait to see it all? Reality check: These days, a pair of tickets to a Broadway show can cost you up to $150. That's right, *$150*. Major concerts and recitals don't come so cheap, either. And of course ticket agencies like **Tele-Charge** (tel. 212/239–6200 or 800/233–3123) and **Ticketmaster** (tel. 212/307–4100), which handle most of the city's big theaters and concert halls, slap a hefty $4–$6 per-ticket surcharge on top of that (and sometimes a $2–$3 per-order fee).

Off- and Off-Off-Broadway theaters have their own joint box office called **Ticket Central** (416 W. 42nd St., tel. 212/279–4200). It's open daily between 1 and 8 PM. You won't find discounts here, but tickets to performances in these theaters are usually less expensive than on Broadway. Ticket Central carries a cornucopia of events, including legitimate theater, performance art, and dance.

There are, thankfully, a few ways to beat high ticket prices (*see below*). And lots of the arts centers downtown (particularly on the Lower East Side, in TriBeCa, and the East and West Village) will charge you around $10 to $15 for a full night's entertainment.

PUBLICATIONS

To find out who or what's playing where, your first stop should be a newsstand. Consult *Time Out,* the *New York Times* (particularly Friday's "Weekend" section), the "Goings on About Town" section of *The New Yorker,* the "Cue" listings at the back of *New York* magazine, and the *Village Voice,* which is free. The most thorough is *Time Out,* though the *Voice* has long been considered the bible of the downtown scene.

HOT LINES

You can get updated info by phone from the **NYC/ON STAGE Hotline** (tel. 212/768–1818), the Theatre Development Fund's (TDF) 24-hour performing arts information service. For wheelchair accessibility information, call Tele-Charge or Ticketmaster (*see above*). Additionally, the TDF runs a **Theatre Access**

Project (tel. 212/221–1103) for city residents and tourists with disabilities. Membership (free) gives you access to special seating and discount tickets for some of the city's hottest shows.

FINDING A CHEAP SEAT

Getting a good deal on performance tickets doesn't have to be painful. The best plan, of course, is to buy your tickets at the theater's or concert hall's own box office, where they'll help you choose the best seats and, thankfully, won't stick you with a service charge. You can go the day of the performance, or you can go a few days earlier to avoid crushing disappointment. Some Broadway shows have tickets at a reduced price (about $20) the day of the performance; these seats are usually in the front rows of the orchestra. Occasionally, box offices offer same-day standing-room tickets ($10–$20) for sold-out shows; check with the particular theater for more information. A few Off-Broadway theaters offer discounts the day of the show (*see* Off-Broadway *in* Theater, *below*).

TICKET AGENCIES • The city's two **TKTS** booths offer day-of-performance tickets for selected Broadway and Off-Broadway shows at 25%–50% off (cash or traveler's checks only), plus a $2.50 per-ticket service charge. TKTS also carries tickets for some opera, symphony, and dance performances, though not every day. The **Times Square** TKTS booth (W. 47th St. and Broadway) is open Monday–Saturday 3–8 and Sunday noon–8, with additional hours Wednesday and Saturday 10–2. Expect lines to form an hour before the booth opens; during the week, the lines are usually shorter after 4:30 until closing time; on weekends, lines can be long for most of the day, especially when the weather's warm. The TKTS booth at the **World Trade Center** (Mezzanine Level, 2 World Trade Center), open weekdays 11–5:30 and Saturday 11–3:30, is worth the trek downtown: It's indoors, it's rarely crowded, and (unlike the Times Square booth) it sells matinee and Sunday tickets one day in advance. For more info, call the NYC/ON STAGE Hotline (*see above*).

The annual Workshop Performances of the School of American Ballet (tel. 212/877–0600), whose students eventually graduate into the New York City Ballet's prestigious corps de ballet, are held the first week in June. Tickets are $25–$45.

COUPONS AND VOUCHERS • Look for **"two-fer"** coupons—which offer two tickets for the price of one, or at least some sort of discount—at the New York Visitors and Convention Bureau, and in bookstores, department stores, banks, restaurants, and hotel lobbies. Unfortunately, they're generally available only for the long-running Broadway extravaganzas that probably came to your hometown several years ago. Another option is a **Theatre Development Fund (TDF)** voucher, sold in sets of four ($28) and redeemable at Off- and Off-Off-Broadway theaters as well as at many music and dance spaces. They're available to union members and students (and other limited-income types) only. For an application to see if you qualify, send a SASE to: TDF, 1501 Broadway, Suite 2110, NY 10036, and allow six to eight weeks for processing. For more information, call the TDF's 24-hour information line (tel. 212/221–0013) or the NYC/ON STAGE Hotline (*see above*).

ARTS CENTERS

At the city's arts centers you can catch performance art, classical and new music, serious drama, modern dance, or a literary reading. Whether you're in the mood to see David Byrne or Kathleen Battle, you can probably find the performance you're looking for at one of these cultural clearinghouses.

LINCOLN CENTER

From the moment it opened on the Upper West Side some 30 years ago, the 14-acre Lincoln Center for the Performing Arts has been the undisputed heart of the city's arts scene. This is where you'll find **Alice Tully Hall** (*see* Concert Halls, *below*), home to the Chamber Music Society; **Avery Fisher Hall** (*see* Concert Halls, *below*), home to the New York Philharmonic; the acclaimed **Julliard School** (*see* Music Schools, *below*), which frequently puts on free concerts, theatrical performances, and operas; the grand **Metropolitan Opera House** (tel. 212/362–6000), home to the Metropolitan Opera (*see* Opera, *below*) and the American Ballet Theatre (*see* Dance, *below*); the **New York State Theater** (tel. 212/870–5570), home to the New York City Opera (*see* Opera, *below*) and New York City Ballet (*see* Dance, *below*); and two theaters, the **Vivian Beaumont** and **Mitzi Newhouse.** The Center's outdoor **Damrosch Park and Bandshell** are frequently incorporated into Lincoln Center's many festivals and concerts, such as the **Lincoln Center Festival, Mostly Mozart,** and **Lincoln Center Out-of-Doors** (for more information, *see* Summer Arts, *below*). Its year-round series, **Great Performers at Lincoln Center,** features visits from the

MODERN DANCE:
TRY IT, YOU'LL LIKE IT

If you're at all interested in modern dance, New York City is a great place to broaden your horizons: Its resident companies are some of the most innovative in the world (and many, like the Dance Theatre of Harlem, are also facing budget crunches and could really use your help). Companies perform for a few weeks or months each year at one of the city's dance theaters.

Alvin Ailey American Dance Theater. One of the city's most gorgeous dance troupes carries on the work of the late Alvin Ailey, a brilliant choreographer who blended ballet, modern dance, and jazz (Duke Ellington composed "Les trois rois noirs" for him in 1970). Many of his works, including the well-known "Revelations" and "Blues Suite," pay homage to black culture. Tel. 212/767-0590.

Ballet Hispanico of New York. The nation's leading Latin-influenced modern dance company has been delighting New York audiences for a quarter-century with works inspired by the cultures of the Caribbean, Latin America, and the land of the flamenco, Spain. Tel. 212/362-6710.

Dance Theatre of Harlem. The Dance Theatre of Harlem is famous for taking a traditionally all-white art and standing it on its ear. Led by Arthur Mitchell, the first African-American principal dancer in the New York City Ballet, the company has reworked classics ("Giselle" in a Creole setting, for example) and trained several generations of black dancers and choreographers. Tel. 212/690-2800.

Mark Morris Dance Group. Mark Morris, one of the most creative choreographers alive today, draws on everything from Roland Barthes and Indian ragas to Yoko Ono and 18th-century opera to create pieces blending humor with serious social commentary. Tel. 212/219-3660.

Martha Graham Dance Company. For most of its 65 years, this revered company was headed by the founder of modern dance herself, Martha Graham. It continues to perform some 200 of Graham's works, while former dancers like Alvin Ailey and Merce Cunningham have gone on to form troupes of their own. Tel. 212/838-5886 or 212/832-9166.

Merce Cunningham Dance Company. The unfailingly avant-garde works of Merce Cunningham have included collaborations with John Cage, David Tudor, Paul Taylor, Jasper Johns, Robert Rauschenberg, and Andy Warhol. Tel. 212/255-8240.

world's greatest talents, such as Luciano Pavarotti, the Vienna Philharmonic, and the Boston Symphony. For more on Lincoln Center, including tours of the grounds, *see* Upper West Side *in* Chapter 2. *Mailing address: 70 Lincoln Center Plaza, NY 10023-6583, tel. 212/875–5000 for general info and daily calendar. Subway: 1 or 9 to W. 66th St. (Lincoln Center).*

OTHER VENUES

92nd Street Y. The Y's Kaufmann Hall, the city's most prestigious site for readings and lectures by poets, artists, writers, and scholars, also has a lively menu of music and dance. At its Unterberg Poetry Center are tapes dating back to the 1940s of some of the finest writers of this century reading their work for Y audiences. *1395 Lexington Ave., at E. 92nd St., Upper East Side, tel. 212/996–1100. Subway: 4, 5, or 6 to E. 86th St. Ticket prices vary.*

Brooklyn Academy of Music (BAM). America's oldest performing arts center (opened in 1859) has a reputation for daring and innovative dance, music, opera, performance art, and theater productions. Its fall festival of new music, theater, and dance, **Next Wave,** brings artists from around the globe. The main performance halls are the 2,000-seat Opera House and the more intimate, 900-seat Majestic Theatre (651 Fulton St.). Thanks to a $20-million renovation that began in late 1996 (to be completed by early 1998), BAM gained a café, a bookstore, and a multiplex movie theater. Student rush tickets ($10) are available for some BAM shows; call on the day of performance for information. *30 Lafayette Ave., between Ashland Pl. and St. Felix St., Fort Greene, Brooklyn, tel. 718/636–4100. Subway: D, Q, 2, 3, 4, or 5 to Atlantic Ave.; walk 2 blocks north to Fulton St. and turn left. Tickets: $15–$50.*

Brothers Lee, JJ, and Sam Shubert ruled Broadway in the early 1900s. Now they have to share one lousy theater named after them.

City Center. Under City Center's exotic Spanish dome (built in 1923 by the Ancient and Accepted Order of the Mystic Shrine) you'll find the Manhattan Theatre Club, where you can see innovative new dramas, modern dance troupes such as the Alvin Ailey American Dance Theater and the Paul Taylor Dance Company, and concert versions of American musicals. *131 W. 55th St., between 6th and 7th Aves., Midtown, tel. 212/581–1212. Subway: N or R to W. 57th St. Tickets: $15–$50.*

The Kitchen. This is *the* Manhattan center for performance art, although video, dance, and music have their moments here, too. It's where unclassifiable artists like Philip Glass, Meredith Monk, and Laurie Anderson got their start. *512 W. 19th St., between 10th and 11th Aves., Chelsea, tel. 212/255–5793. Subway: A, C, E, or L to W. 14th St. Tickets: $12–$15.*

New Victory. After a stint as a burlesque theater, the New Victory reopened in 1995 as New York City's first performing-arts center for children. The ornate 500-seat venue underwent $11 million worth of restoration before groups like the Metropolitan Opera Guild, Mabou Mines, and the Flying Karamazov Brothers took the stage. *209 W. 42nd St., between 7th and 8th Aves., Midtown, tel. 212/564–4222. Subway: N, R, 1, 2, 3, 7, or 9 to Times Sq.; also A, C, or E to W. 42nd St. (8th Ave.). Tickets: $10–$25.*

The Performing Garage. This small space has an uncompromising program of performance art, dance, and experimental theater, often by up-and-comers. Alumni of the Performing Garage's resident company, Wooster Grove, include actor Willem Dafoe, director Elizabeth LeCompte, and monologuist nonpareil Spalding Grey. *33 Wooster St., between Broome and Grand Sts., SoHo, tel. 212/966–9796. Subway: A, C, or E to Canal St. Tickets: $15–$25.*

P.S. 122. Performances here are so cutting-edge that the *Village Voice* once called it "the petri dish of downtown culture." Plays, concerts, and exhibits all breed here, especially during their February marathon. *150 1st Ave., at E. 9th St., East Village, tel. 212/477–5288. Subway: L to 1st Ave., 6 to Astor Pl., F to 2nd Ave. Tickets: $12–$15.*

Sylvia and Danny Kaye Playhouse. A pearl of a concert hall, this low-profile venue has a varied calendar of music, dance, opera, and theater events. *Hunter College, 68th St. between Park and Lexington Aves., Upper East Side, tel. 212/772–4448. Subway: 6 to E. 68th St.–Hunter College. Tickets: $20–$35, students $5–$10.*

Town Hall. This Georgian Revival structure, built from 1919–1921, hosts a diverse program of chamber and popular music, cabaret performances, and stand-up comedy at reasonable prices. *123 W. 43rd St., Midtown, tel. 212/840–2824. Subway: B, D, F, or Q to W. 42nd St.; also 1, 2, 3, or 9 to Times Sq. Tickets: $20–$45.*

Tribeca Performing Arts Center. Steps away from several of TriBeCa's trendiest restaurants, this modern complex presents a lively and eclectic program of theater, dance, and music events. *Manhattan Community College, 199 Chambers St., TriBeCa, tel. 212/346–8510. Subway: 1, 2, 3, 9, A, C, or E to Chambers St. Tickets: $12–$15.*

DANCE

Naysayers will tell you that dance in New York City is dead—or at least seriously ailing. But despite the disheartening 1995 relocation of the revered Joffrey Ballet Company (founded here in 1956) to the more dance-friendly city of Chicago, some 140 dance troupes, classic and modern, soldier on. Of those, the New York City Ballet, the American Ballet Theatre, and the Dance Theatre of Harlem are the most celebrated. And, as if that weren't enough, New York continuously attracts troupes from around the globe: the Bolshoi, the Kirov, the Royal Danish, the Stuttgart. See; there must be New Yorkers out there somewhere who will gladly pay to watch men gamboling in tights.

If you're not a by-the-books balletomane, a few venues that feature up-and-coming dance companies and dance/performance art are worth checking out: **Brooklyn Academy of Music, P.S. 122, Sylvia and Danny Kaye Playhouse** (*see* Arts Centers, *above*), and the **Merce Cunningham Studio** (55 Bethune St., near Washington St., West Village, tel. 212/691–9751).

American Ballet Theatre. In its 50-plus years, the American Ballet has included some of the greatest dancers of the century: Mikhail Baryshnikov, Natalia Makarova, Rudolf Nureyev, and Cynthia Gregory. It's famous for its dazzling productions of the great 19th-century classics—*Swan Lake, Giselle, The Sleeping Beauty*—and increasingly for its eclectic repertoire of works by 20th-century masters like Balanchine, Robbins, and de Mille. Two of its newest members, Angel Corella (from Spain) and Vladimir Malakhov (from Russia) have wowed audiences with their spirit and grace. *Metropolitan Opera House at Lincoln Center, tel: 212/362–6000* (see *Arts Centers,* above). *Tickets: $15–$65. Season Apr.–June.*

Danspace Project. This admirable organization sponsors a series of contemporary choreography on the pristine wood floor of a church sanctuary; the season runs every year from September through June. *St. Mark's-in-the-Bowery Church, 10th St. and 2nd Ave., East Village, tel. 212/674–8194. Subway: 6 to Astor Pl.; also N or R to 8th St. Tickets: $12.*

Dance Theater Workshop. The Workshop, on the second floor of a converted warehouse, began in 1965 as a choreographers' cooperative. It now showcases some of the city's freshest dance talent, as well as contemporary music, video, theater, and readings. *219 W. 19th St., between 7th and 8th Aves., Chelsea, tel. 212/924–0077. Subway: 1 or 9 to W. 18th St. Tickets: $12–$15.*

Joyce Theater. This art deco former movie theater has become a major dance center. It's the "unofficial" permanent home of the Feld Ballet Company (founded in 1974 by Elliot Feld, an upstart American Ballet Theatre dancer), which performs during the spring and summer, and a favorite for visiting companies. The eclectic year-round program also includes tap, jazz, ballroom, and ethnic dance. Don't miss the fringe dance hotshots during the "Altogether Different" festival. *175 8th Ave., at W. 19th St., Chelsea, tel. 212/242–0800. Subway: C or E to W. 23rd St. Tickets: $12–$35.*

New York City Ballet. The stellar troupe of more than 80 dancers, started in 1948 by Lincoln Kirstein and George Balanchine, has become one of the most highly praised ballet companies in the world. Its repertoire of 20th-century works is unmatched anywhere, and several of its dancers—Kyra Nichols, Darci Kistler, Damian Woetzel, and Jock Soto—have become stars in their own right. Currently under the leadership of Peter Martins (formerly one of Balanchine's best dancers), the company presents a wide range of works, from the brand-new to the classics. The beloved production of *George Balanchine's The Nutcracker* plays to sellout crowds every holiday season. *New York State Theater, at Lincoln Center* (see *Arts Centers,* above), *tel. 212/870–5570. Tickets: $14–$65. Season mid-Nov.–Feb. and late Apr.–June.*

92nd St. Y Harkness Dance Project. The thoughtful program here focuses on emerging dance troupes with discussion following performances. *Playhouse 91, 316 E. 91st St., Upper East Side, tel. 212/996–1100. Subway: 4, 5, or 6 to E. 86th St. Tickets: $15.*

MOVIES AND VIDEO

New York City is a movie town, and when New Yorkers aren't watching movies, they're making them. Remember that this is where greats such as Spike Lee, Ang Lee, and Martin Scorsese went to school (at New York University) and where dozens of other filmmakers come each year to shoot their next big release. Walk around Manhattan and you'll eventually stumble upon a camera crew, particularly in the summer. Not surprisingly, film aficionados will find quite a few small movie houses and museums devoted exclusively to screening independent and foreign films, both new and classic. For philistines, there's a multiplex showing the latest Jim Carrey flick in just about every neighborhood. The going rate for a first-run film is a sky-high $8.50, though the **Cineplex Odeon Worldwide Cinemas** (340 W. 50th St., between 8th and 9th Aves., Midtown, tel. 212/504–0960) shows second-run and non-blockbuster movies on six screens for $3.

ALTERNATIVE VENUES

Beyond theaters, you've got a few exotic options for movie-watching: Ever seen a 3-D IMAX film? Even if the $9 films are sometimes hokey, the space-age 3-D headsets are hard to resist; check one out at the **Sony Theaters Lincoln Square** (*see* Major Venues, *below*). For experimental (and sometimes incomprehensible) films and videos, head for the **Whitney Museum of American Art** (*see* Museums and Galleries *in* Chapter 2). The **American Museum of Natural History** screens science and nature films in its IMAX theater ($12), while the **Museum of Television and Radio** hosts regular screenings of vintage TV programs (for both, *see* Museums and Galleries *in* Chapter 2). On Sunday evening, **A Different Light Bookstore** (151 W. 19th St., Chelsea, tel. 212/989–4850) shows a free movie with a gay or lesbian angle. Finally, during summer, you can bring a picnic and blankets to **Bryant Park** (6th Ave. at W. 42nd St., Midtown, tel. 212/512–5700) on Mondays just after sunset, when classics like *On the Waterfront, The Sound of Music,* and *King Kong* are shown for free. There's always a crowd, so arrive early.

> Call *MovieFone* (tel. 212/777–FILM) to get theater locations, previews, and current schedules, or to make an advance purchase with a credit card—a good idea, since recent releases often sell out quickly.

FILM FESTIVALS

If you're in town in late September and early October don't miss the annual **New York Film Festival,** held at Lincoln Center, which acts as the premier showcase for dozens of feature films and shorts from around the world; it's also one of your best bets for spotting famous directors and actors. The **New York Video Festival,** founded in 1995, runs simultaneously and features video premiers. For either, check listings in local papers and buy tickets a few days in advance. In March, the often provocative **New Directors/New Films** series at the Museum of Modern Art showcases up-and-coming directors. Additionally, dozens of smaller festivals—like the Human Rights Film Festival, the Asian American International Film Festival, and presentations by film-school students at Columbia and New York universities—pop up year-round.

MAJOR VENUES

American Museum of the Moving Image. The museum itself is housed in the historic Kaufman-Astoria studios in Queens. The theater screens Hollywood classics, experimental videos, documentaries, and major retrospectives of artists' works (sometimes with personal appearances). *Tel. 718/784–0077. For hrs and directions,* see *Museums and Galleries in Chapter 2.*

Angelika Film Center. The Angelika is revered among hip New York movie buffs as a mecca of exceptional independent and foreign films (cult classics screen weekends at midnight). The six screens (some tiny) and austere lobby café inspire lines around the block. *18 W. Houston St., at Mercer St., SoHo, tel. 212/995–2000. Subway: B, D, F, or Q to Broadway–Lafayette St.*

Anthology Film Archives. Anthology's vaults hold more than 10,000 experimental and avant garde films by artists like Cocteau, Flaherty, Eisenstein, and all those other directors whose movies you can't see elsewhere. Its varied, eclectic schedule may include tributes to "auteur" directors like Mike Leigh and Luis Bunuel and thematic programs such as "100 Years of Japanese Cinema." *32 2nd Ave., at E. 2nd St., East Village, tel. 212/505–5181. Subway: F to 2nd Ave.*

Cinema Village. This aging theater shows movies outside the mainstream—independent features, documentaries, and animation. It's home to the annual NY Gay and Lesbian Film Festival and a wildly popular annual tribute to the films of Hong Kong. *22 E. 12th St., between 5th Ave. and University Pl., East Village, tel. 212/924–3363. Subway: L, N, R, 4, 5, or 6 to Union Sq.*

The Film Forum. The Film Forum can't be beat for recent independents, cult classics, and rare uncut versions of old favorites. There's always some sort of tribute on one of the three screens. *209 W. Houston St., at 6th Ave., SoHo, tel. 212/727–8110. Subway: 1 or 9 to Houston St.*

Lincoln Plaza Cinemas. One of the first art-house multiplexes to open in Manhattan, this six-screen underground theater attracts large numbers of extremely serious film-goers who can't seem to get enough of its award-winning, challenging, and often subtitled fare. *30 Lincoln Plaza, Broadway, between 62nd and 63rd Sts., Upper West Side, tel. 212/757–2280. Subway: A, B, C, D, 1, or 9 to W. 59th St./Columbus Circle.*

Museum of Modern Art (MoMA). The MoMA is a treasure house of films dating from cinema's earliest days and covering just about every country that makes 'em. They have screenings almost daily, and your ticket is free once you've paid admission to the museum. Complimentary tickets are available at the main desk beginning at 11 AM for the afternoon show and at 1 PM for the evening show, and they disappear quickly. *11 W. 53rd St., between 5th and 6th Aves., Midtown, tel. 212/708–9480. For hrs and directions,* see *Major Attractions* in *Chapter 2.*

Sony Theatres Lincoln Square. This impressive multiplex has 12 state-of-the-art theaters with huge screens as well as an eight-story IMAX Theater. Though the projection and sound system here can't be beat, the weekend crowds can be exasperating. *1998 Broadway, at W. 68th St., Upper West Side, tel. 212/336–5000. Subway: 1 or 9 to W. 66th St.*

Quad Cinema. Count on unusual choices like blaxploitation revivals and French works on sexual politics on the Quad's four very small screens. Where else can you see a film about phone sex by Vincent van Gogh's great-grandnephew, Theo? *34 W. 13th St., near 5th Ave., West Village, tel. 212/255–8800. Subway: L, N, R, 4, 5, or 6 to E. 14th St.*

Walter Reade Theater. This gem is part of Lincoln Center, specializing in foreign films and often highlighting the work of a single director. *70 Lincoln Center Plaza, at W. 65th St. and Broadway, Upper West Side, tel. 212/875–5600. Subway: 1 or 9 to W. 66th St.*

Ziegfeld. One of the few Manhattan theaters reminiscent of the old movie palaces, the Ziegfeld has a grand screen, bright-red decor, and a sometimes overwhelmingly loud sound system; it's the place to go if you're planning to see a Star Wars revival, the latest Steven Spielberg extravaganza, or a restored widescreen classic such as *Vertigo. 141 W. 54th St., west of 6th Ave., Midtown, tel. 212/765–7600. Subway: B, D, F, or Q to W. 47th–50th Sts.*

MUSIC

Even if you're not a big fan of classical music, you've probably seen *Live at Lincoln Center* on PBS, know that Julliard is the world's most prestigious music school, and have heard the lame joke about "practice" being the only way to get to Carnegie Hall. If these three institutions were all that New York had going for it, its music scene would still surpass the combined efforts of most major U.S. cities. Luckily, though, they represent only the tip of the iceberg. New York City is home to several major orchestras and three of the country's finest music schools; it's also a favorite stop for touring musicians from all over the world. And if this all smacks of too much big money for your taste, perhaps you should scout out the city's museums, churches, and other small venues, which frequently host musical performances both traditional and avant-garde. At these spaces concerts are often free.

CONCERT HALLS

New York concert halls are constantly filled with world-class musicians. Lincoln Center's 2,700-seat Avery Fisher Hall (*see below*) is one of the grandest venues in the city, though nitpickers will tell you that the 1976 renovations didn't entirely repair the hall's dreadful acoustics. In addition to those listed below, venues noted for classical music include the Brooklyn Academy of Music, City Center, The Kitchen, the 92nd Street Y, and P.S. 122 (*see* Arts Centers, *above*).

Aaron Davis Hall. The World Music Institute stages a wide variety of contemporary and classical concerts and theater productions, including a number of events designed for children. One of their theaters holds 750, another 250. Tickets start at $3 for children's shows and run between $8–$20 for other performances. *City College, W. 133rd St. at Convent Ave., Harlem, tel. 212/650–6900. Subway: 1 or 9 to 137th St./City College.*

Alice Tully Hall. The Chamber Music Society of Lincoln Center performs at this intimate, acoustically perfect space, along with promising Julliard students, small ensembles such as the Guarneri and Kronos quartets, musicians using period instruments, famous soloists, and choirs. Seats for the Chamber Music Society's performances are $22–$30. *Lincoln Center (see Arts Centers, above), tel. 212/875–5050 for box office or 212/721–6500 for CenterCharge. Ticket prices vary.*

Avery Fisher Hall. Playing at Avery Fisher is the 150-year-old New York Philharmonic, considered one of the world's premiere symphony orchestras. It's currently led by Kurt Masur; the great Leonard Bernstein was musical director from 1958 to 1970. Weeknight "Rush Hour" Concerts (6:45 PM) and "Casual Saturday" Concerts (2 PM) last one hour and are less expensive than regular concerts. Occasional seats in the orchestra ($25) are available 30 minutes before performances. Weekday rehearsals at 9:45 AM are open to the public for a bargain $10. *Lincoln Center (see Arts Centers, above), tel. 212/875–5030 for box office, 212/721–6500 for CenterCharge, or 212/875–5656 for info on rehearsals. Tickets: $15–$65. Season Sept.–early June.*

More than half of the New York Philharmonic's musicians graduated from the Julliard School.

Bargemusic. This 102-ft former Erie Lackawanna coffee barge, now tethered along the East River, holds a concert hall that seats 125. Bargemusic's resident artists recruit wonderful soloists from around the world and bring them together to make impromptu chamber groups. Tickets are $23. *Fulton Ferry Landing, Brooklyn, tel. 718/624–4061. Subway: A to High St.*

Carnegie Hall. This granddaddy of concert halls has hosted some of the 20th century's greatest orchestras and musicians, including Isaac Stern, Leonard Bernstein, Yo-Yo Ma, Frank Sinatra, Tchaikovsky, and the Beatles (not all at the same time). Though the emphasis is on classical music, it also hosts jazz, cabaret, and folk-music series. The Opera Orchestra of New York puts on concerts of rarely performed works here, and the city's music schools debut their star students in its Weill Recital Hall. Acoustics in the main auditorium are sounding better than ever, thanks to a 1995 renovation. *881 7th Ave., at W. 57th St., Midtown, tel. 212/247–7800. Subway: N or R to W. 57th St. Ticket prices vary.*

Merkin Concert Hall. This relatively new concert hall is doing an admirable job of keeping up with the Joneses, especially considering that the Joneses are the Merkin's near neighbor, Lincoln Center. Lots of famous soloists and chamber groups perform at this 457-seat hall, which also occasionally hosts the New York Philharmonic Ensemble and the Mendelssohn String Quartet. *Abraham Goodman House, 129 W. 67th St., between Broadway and Amsterdam Ave., Upper West Side, tel. 212/501–3330. Subway: 1 or 9 to W. 66th St. (Lincoln Center). Tickets: $10–$20.*

OTHER SPACES

Stray outside the city's concert halls and you'll find venues where the sight lines may be imperfect or the acoustics may be less than ideal, but where the experience is still somehow grand. Nothing can rival a summer evening's concert in the Metropolitan Museum's rooftop garden. And you can't complain about the cost (often free) of performances at the city's top-ranked music schools.

CHURCHES

Musical offerings at churches take place during worship services and afternoon vespers, or frequently as separate concerts. During the Christmas holidays every church and cathedral in the city breaks out the Bach.

Cathedral of St. John the Divine. Mammoth St. John has a lively arts calendar, including music and drama. *1047 Amsterdam Ave., at W. 112th St., Morningside Heights, tel. 212/662–2133. Subway: 1 or 9 to W. 110th St. Ticket prices vary.*

St. Paul's Chapel. Together with nearby **Trinity Church** (Broadway at Wall St., tel. 212/602–0800), St. Paul's offers free lunchtime concerts (starting at noon, Mondays at St. Paul's; Thursdays at Trinity) of everything from Beethoven's symphonies to the traditional music of Zimbabwe. *Broadway, at Fulton St., Lower Manhattan, tel. 212/602–0874. Subway: 4 or 5 to Fulton St. Admission: $2 (suggested).*

Theater at Riverside Church. Chamber music concerts, dance productions, drama, and one of the largest organs in the country make this a great place to catch a performance. *490 Riverside Dr., at W. 122 St., Morningside Heights, tel. 212/870–6700 or 212/870–6784. Subway: 1 or 9 to W. 125th St. Tickets: $10–$20.*

MUSEUMS

For open hours, subway directions, and other info on the museums mentioned below, *see* Museums and Galleries *in* Chapter 2.

The Cloisters Museum. Well-known early music groups perform most Sunday afternoons in the museum's fabulously atmospheric medieval chapel. For tickets send a SASE to: Concerts at the Cloisters, Fort Tryon Park, NY 10040, or call to order by credit card. Traditional Christmas concerts performed by the Waverly Consort sell out fast, so plan ahead. *Fort Tryon Park, tel. 212/923–3700 or 212/650–2290 to order tickets. Tickets: $20–$35.*

The Frick Collection. Sundays bring classical concerts, from Norwegian violinists playing Brahms to quartets performing 16th-century Spanish works. For tickets, send a SASE several weeks in advance to: Concerts Dept., The Frick Collection, 1 E. 70th St., NY 10021. *1 E. 70th St., at 5th Ave., tel. 212/288–0700. Tickets free.*

Metropolitan Museum of Art. The Met offers a wide variety of classical music concerts weekends at its Grace Rainey Rogers Auditorium, priced $15–$40. Standing-room tickets are available 30 minutes before most performances and are half price. Additionally, Friday and Saturday evening concerts on its Great Hall Balcony are free (you pay for the wine). On warm summer evenings, head to the museum's roof, where classical guitar accompanies the view. *5th Ave., at E. 82nd St., tel. 212/570–3949.*

Museum of Modern Art. The MoMA's Summergarden concert series takes place in its beautiful sculpture garden among the Picassos and Rodins. Performances (free) are Friday and Saturday evenings, July–August. *11 W. 53rd St., between 5th and 6th Aves., tel. 212/708–9480.*

MUSIC SCHOOLS

If student recitals make you think of 20 third-graders hacking away at "Chopsticks," think again. New York City's three major music schools are the launching pads for many of the nation's most respected musicians. Best of all, performances by the schools' celebrity wanna-bes are usually inexpensive or free.

The Julliard School. Julliard offers exceptional orchestral, opera, dance, and theater performances in Lincoln Center's Avery Fisher and Alice Tully halls, as well as in its own Paul Recital Hall (also at Lincoln Center). Many performances are free; those that aren't generally cost $15. *Lincoln Center* (see *Arts Centers, above), tel. 212/769–7406.*

Manhattan School of Music. Four concert spaces mean hundreds of classical and jazz performances (most free) throughout the year. *120 Claremont Ave., at W. 122nd St., Morningside Heights, tel. 212/749–2802, ext. 428, or 212/749–3300 for concert hot line. Subway: 1 or 9 to W. 116th St. Tickets: $5–$20.*

OPERA

If you can't consider your trip to New York over until you've heard the fat lady belt out a few arias, you've got a plethora of options—and for an art pegged as highbrow the prices are shockingly plebian. Small and ethnic opera groups are constantly forming in New York, performing cutting-edge and classical operas for a song (sorry). Check out the **National Opera Ebony** (Aaron Davis Hall, City College, W. 133th St. at Convent Ave., Harlem, tel. 212/650–6900) for performances by up-and-coming African-American, Hispanic, and Asian singers. The students of the Julliard American Opera Center, the Manhattan School of Music, and the Mannes College of Music (*see* Music Schools, *above*) perform operas—often for free—on a par with the pros in other cities. At the other end of the spectrum, even the upscale Metropolitan Opera Company will squeeze you in for as little as $12.

Two additional venues for opera are **Carnegie Hall** (*see* Concert Halls, *above*), where the Opera Orchestra of New York performs, and the **Brooklyn Academy of Music** (*see* Arts Centers, *above*). During summer, you can catch an opera under the stars for free (*see* Summer Arts, *below*).

Amato Opera Theater. You've never seen *The Marriage of Figaro* performed more passionately than at the Amato, where up to 70 performers at a time (most of them young, unpaid, and yearning to be discovered) have been known to squeeze onto its 20-ft-wide stage. *319 Bowery, at E. 2nd St., East Village, tel. 212/228–8200. Subway: 6 to Bleecker St.; also B, D, F, or Q to Broadway–Lafayette St. Tickets: $20.*

American Opera Projects. Come to this minuscule (75-seat) SoHo loft/theater to hear short, experimental new operas by American composers. *463 Broome St., between Greene and Mercer Sts., SoHo, tel. 212/431–8102. Subway: N or R to Prince St. Tickets: $12–$15.*

Metropolitan Opera Company. One of the most lauded opera companies in the world performs on a stage the size of a football field. Since 1883, it's given over 16,000 performances of 235 different works, and it continues to crank out four major new productions (with extravagant touches like live horses and falling snow) each season. It attracts the finest singers, like Jessye Norman and Marilyn Horne—and plenty of criticism for a tendency to stick with opera's greatest hits rather than trying anything adventurous. Although tickets can cost more than $100, many less-expensive seats (including 600 sold at $23) and standing room ($12–$15) are available. Weekday prices are lower than weekend prices. Standing-room tickets for the week's performances go on sale (cash only) on Saturday at 10 AM. *The Metropolitan Opera House, at Lincoln Center* (see *Arts Centers*, above), *tel. 212/362–6000. Tickets: $12–$145. Season Oct.–mid-Apr.*

One unorthodox, but very popular, stage is the World Trade Center Plaza, where classical, jazz, oldies, and R&B are staged at least three days a week at 12:15 and 1:15 during the summer.

New York City Opera. In addition to classics like *Carmen, Madama Butterfly,* and *The Magic Flute,* the renowned New York City Opera has a penchant for unusual and rarely performed works like *The Times of Harvey Milk* and *The Most Happy Fella.* It was one of the first opera houses in the country to introduce "supertitling" (line-by-line English translation displayed electronically over the stage) and has helped start the careers of some of the world's finest singers, including Placido Domingo, Frederica von Stade, and Beverly Sills. Tickets are much cheaper than those at the Met, ranging from $20 to $85. Student-rush ($10) and standing-room tickets ($7) are sold on the day of performance starting at 10 AM, cash only. *New York State Theater, at Lincoln Center* (see *Arts Centers*, above), *tel. 212/870–5570. Tickets: $7–$85. Season Sept.–Nov. and Mar.–Apr.*

SPOKEN WORD

Only in New York City do novelists, poets, historians, journalists, and other intellectuals get treated with the sort of adulation and respect normally reserved for American sports heroes. Dozens of readings, workshops, and lectures take place nightly at bookstores, museums, universities, galleries, theaters, and cafés around the city; check one of the weeklies for listings or the ***Poetry Calendar*** (611 Broadway, Suite 905, 10012, tel. 212/260–7097), published monthly September through June, and available by subscription or for free at several Manhattan bookstores.

The city's two most distinguished venues for readings and lectures are the **92nd Street Y** (*see* Arts Centers, *above*) and **Symphony Space** (2537 Broadway, at W. 95th St., Upper West Side, tel. 212/864–5400), which hosts the National Public Radio program "Selected Shorts" (short-story readings by notable authors and actors) twice monthly. **Manhattan Theatre Club** (131 W. 55th St., Midtown, tel. 212/645–5848) hosts "Writers in Performance," a program of readings and discussions with American and foreign writers.

Biblio's (317 Church St., Tribeca, tel. 212/334–6690) and the **Cornelia Street Café** (29 Cornelia St., West Village, tel. 212/989–9319) both schedule readings on a regular basis. The Alterknit Theater at the **Knitting Factory** (74 Leonard St., TriBeCa, tel. 212/219–3006) holds a weekly poetry series and open mike Friday ($5). For odes and sonnets and such, look for events at **Dia Center for the Arts** (548 W. 22nd St., Chelsea, tel. 212/989–5566), the **Poetry Project** (St. Mark's-in-the-Bowery Church, 131 E. 10th St., at 2nd Ave., East Village, tel. 212/674–0910), **Poetry Society of America** (15 Gramercy Park S, Gramercy, tel. 212/254–9628), and **Poets House** (72 Spring St., between Crosby and Lafayette Sts., SoHo, tel. 212/431–7920).

Nuyorican Poets Cafe (236 E. 3rd St., between Aves. B and C, Alphabet City, tel. 212/505–8183) is home of the "poetry slam," ground zero for the whole '90s urban poetry *thing*. Nuyorican poets—not your typical mush-mouthed, whey-faced spewers of wispy sonnets—have even busted rhyme on MTV. A typical night is packed with in-your-face urban rap and hip-hop jams; performing bards are scored by a panel of judges.

Dixon Place (258 Bowery, between Houston and Prince Sts., Lower East Side, tel. 212/219–3088) and the **Kitchen** (*see* Arts Centers, *above*) both sponsor readings regularly, several of which border on performance art. At **SummerStage** (*see* Summer Arts, *below*), the Central Park arts festival, big-time authors read from their latest and greatest works.

SUMMER ARTS

As faithfully as the swallows of San Juan Capistrano, theater groups, orchestras, and opera companies alight in the city's parks come summer for various festivals and freebie concerts. Those noted for their musical offerings include **Bryant Park, Hudson River Park, Washington Square Park, Riverside Park,** the **World Trade Center Plaza,** the **World Financial Center,** and, of course, sprawling **Central Park.** Additionally, many museums, like the **Cooper-Hewitt Museum** and the **Museum of Modern Art,** hold summertime concerts in their gardens and courtyards. For more info on parks and museums, *see* Chapter 2, or check the city weeklies. To find out about concerts and other goings-on in the city's parks, you can also call the **Parks and Recreation Special Events Hotline** (tel. 212/360–3456). For information on the city's summer **jazz festivals,** *see* Live Music *in* Chapter 6.

A hint for the uninitiated: Getting a swatch of lawn at a free summer concert—particularly performances by the New York Philharmonic, which are followed by fireworks—can be as fun and easy as scoring a cab on 42nd Street in rush hour during a snowstorm. Arrive at least an hour before curtain time with a bottle of wine and a blanket and you'll do just fine.

Celebrate Brooklyn. The free Shakespeare, opera, and dance productions and all kinds of concerts at Prospect Park bring Manhattanites across the Brooklyn Bridge in droves. A performance here on a glorious summer evening is *the* best way to enjoy the park and the Slope at their finest. *9th St. Bandshell, Prospect Park, Park Slope, Brooklyn, tel. 718/965–8969. Subway: F to 7th Ave.; also 2 or 3 to Grand Army Plaza. Season June–Sept.*

Central Park SummerStage. Central Park's free performing arts mega-festival features something different just about every day of the week: Verdi operas performed by the New York Grand Opera; readings and performances by novelists and poets like Tom Robbins, Dorothy Allison, and Walter Mosley; modern dance performances; and concerts of just about every sort, including blues, country, folk, jazz, polka, indie rock, and world music. *Rumsey Playfield, mid-park at 72nd St., tel. 212/360–2777 or 800/201–7275. Subway: B or C to W. 72nd St. Season mid-June–early Aug.*

Lincoln Center Festival. In 1996 Lincoln Center inaugurated this international summer performance program, including classical music concerts, contemporary music and dance presentations, stage works, and non-Western arts. The festival makes use of the entire complex, indoors and out. Tickets range from $32 to a wopping $120. *At Lincoln Center, (see Arts Centers, above). Season July.*

Lincoln Center Out-of-Doors. During summer, as many as 300,000 people attend some 100 events at stages set up in Lincoln Center's plaza. Offerings include free performances of theater, modern dance and ballet, symphonic and chamber music, jazz and blues, and even clowns and mimes. *At Lincoln Center, tel. 212/875–5108 (see Arts Centers, above). Season Aug.*

Mostly Mozart. At this indoor festival it's Mozart, Mozart, Mozart, and when you think you've heard it all, more Mozart, by the world's best music groups as well as the finest solo performers and opera singers. *At Lincoln Center's Avery Fisher Hall, tel. 212/875–5030 (see Concert Halls, above). Season late July–3rd wk in Aug.*

New York Shakespeare Festival. Each summer brings two plays by you-know-who, outdoors and under the stars. Pick up tickets (free, limit two per person) from 1 PM onwards the day of the show at the Delacorte Theater in Central Park, or from 1 to 3 PM the day of the show at the Joseph Papp Public Theater box office (425 Lafayette St., at Astor Pl., tel. 212/260–2400). *Delacorte Theater, mid-park at 80th St., tel. 212/861–7277. Subway: B or C to W. 81st St.*

THEATER

There are roughly 250 legitimate theaters in New York, and many more ad hoc venues—lofts, galleries, streets, rooftops—where performances ranging from Shakespeare to sword-dancing take place. Theaters can be divided into three categories, **Broadway, Off-Broadway,** and **Off-Off-Broadway,** based on size, price, and attitude. Count on Broadway theaters for long-running, flashy shows with big casts, big budgets, and big hair—several shows these days are recycled Golden Age musicals. Off-Broadway and Off-Off-Broadway theaters stage performances that can be pretentious, incendiary, or obscure, but rarely boring. Theaters with fewer than 100 seats are Off-Off; those with 100–500 seats are considered Off-Broadway. More seats than that and it's big-time Broadway, no two ways about it. Most theaters are dark on Mondays. Matinees (afternoon shows) are typically staged on Wednesdays, Saturdays, and Sundays. A few Off-Broadway productions have two shows Saturday evenings.

You can get the latest information on Broadway and Off-Broadway shows with one of the arts hot lines or city weeklies, or by phoning **The Broadway Show Line** (tel. 212/563–2929). For extensive reviews and listings of Off-Broadway and Off-Off-Broadway, your best bets are the *Village Voice* and *Time Out*.

BROADWAY

Dozens of magnificent theaters sprang up around Times Square between 1899 and 1925, drawing actors and audiences like no other place on earth. Many were eventually gutted or converted to porn palaces, but those that survived are gathered in a section of Midtown known as the **Theater District** (West 42nd–53rd streets, between 6th and 9th avenues). It's the heart and soul of that state of mind, Broadway. Come here to find marquees emblazoned with Hollywood names like Julie Andrews, Matthew Broderick, Lou Diamond Phillips, and Glenn Close. And carry plenty of cash, since seats regularly cost $15–$75 and continue to inch even higher as the millennium approaches. Broadway theaters typically don't have telephones (possibly to avoid flak about those ticket prices), so for up-to-date show times call a ticket agency, check magazine listings, or visit the box office. Some prominent Broadway theaters are listed below. Call 212/239–6200 for information about specific shows.

Booth. One of Broadway's most intimate theaters, the Booth has hosted four Pulitzer prize–winning productions over the last few decades, including *The Time of Your Life* and Stephen Sondheim's innovative *Sunday in the Park with George. 222 W. 45th St., between Broadway and 8th Ave. Subway: N, R, 1, 2, 3, 7, or 9 to Times Sq.; also A, C, or E to W. 42nd St. (8th Ave.).*

Broadhurst. Opened in 1917 and named for forgotten playwright George Broadhurst, this charmer has been home to several Tony winners, including *Cabaret, Amadeus,* and *Kiss of the Spider Woman* as well as to one of Stephen Sondheim's biggest flops, *Getting Away with Murder. 235 W. 44th St., between Broadway and 8th Ave. Subway: N, R, 1, 2, 3, 7, or 9 to Times Sq.; also A, C, or E to W. 42nd St. (8th Ave.).*

Broadway. *Miss Saigon,* a regurgitation of Puccini's *Madama Butterfly,* is currently parked at this gargantuan theater, which tends to book large-scale musicals; it began as a movie house in 1924. *1681 Broadway, at W. 53rd St. Subway: 1 or 9 to W. 50th St.*

Cort. Some of the most daring shows on Broadway have turned up here, including Anna Deavere Smith's one-woman show *Twilight Los Angeles, 1992,* and the Pulitzer prize–winning *Diary of Anne Frank.* Katharine Hepburn had her debut here in *These Days* (1928), a flop. *138 W. 48th St., between Broadway and 6th Ave. Subway: N or R to W. 49th St.*

Ethel Barrymore. Marlon Brando and Jessica Tandy started their careers here in *A Streetcar Named Desire,* and Sidney Poitier started his in Lorraine Hansberry's *Raisin in the Sun. 243 W. 47th St., between Broadway and 8th Ave. Subway: C, E, 1, or 9 to W. 50th St.; also N or R to W. 49th St.*

Eugene O'Neill. Neil Simon premiered a half dozen of his plays here in the '60s and '70s, when he was its owner. *230 W. 49th St., between Broadway and 8th Ave. Subway: C, E, 1, or 9 to W. 50th St.*

Ford Center for the Performing Arts. Built by the Canadian production company Livent Inc. on the site of two classic 42nd Street legitimate theaters, the Lyric (1903) and the Apollo (1910), this spectacular $22.5 million 1,839-seat theater was scheduled at press time to open at the end of December 1997 with a musical production of E. L. Doctorow's novel *Ragtime.* The design incorporates a landmark 43rd Street exterior wall from the Lyric and architectural elements from the Apollo, including its stage, proscenium, and dome. In the early part of this century, the Lyric and the Apollo attracted such top talents to their stages as the Marx Brothers, Fred Astaire, Ethel Merman, and W. C. Fields. *213–215 42nd St. Subway: N, R, 1, 2, 3, 7, or 9 to Times Sq.; also A, C, or E to W. 42nd St. (8th Ave.).*

Gershwin. This is one of the newest and largest theaters (1972) on Broadway; avoid sitting in seats upstairs, which are fairly far from the stage and not worth the ticket price. The Gershwin has already had scores of hits—including *Sweeney Todd,* Stephen Sondheim's romp about a serial killer, and the acclaimed revival of *Show Boat,* directed by Harold Prince. *222 W. 51st St. Subway: 1 or 9 to W. 50th St.*

Imperial. Shows at the grand Imperial (*Peter Pan, Fiddler on the Roof, Annie Get Your Gun*) rarely flop, earning it the nickname "The Lucky House." *Les Misérables,* currently playing here, celebrated its 10th anniversary in 1997. *249 W. 45th St., between Broadway and 8th Ave. Subway: N, R, 1, 2, 3, 7, or 9 to Times Sq.; also A, C, or E to W. 42nd St. (8th Ave.).*

Majestic. The Majestic is famous for having premiered Rodgers and Hammerstein musicals like *Carousel* and *South Pacific.* Its current tenant, *The Phantom of the Opera,* may play here forever. *245 W. 44th St., between Broadway and 8th Ave. Subway: N, R, 1, 2, 3, 7, or 9 to Times Sq.; also A, C, or E to W. 42nd St. (8th Ave.).*

Neil Simon. It's not just about Neil Simon here. Other playwrights can use the theater, too. *250 W. 52nd St., between Broadway and 8th Ave. Subway: C, E, 1, or 9 to W. 50th St; also N or R to W. 49th St.*

New Amsterdam. Starting in 1903, the likes of Eddie Cantor, Will Rogers, Fanny Brice, and the Ziegfeld Follies packed the crowds into this wonderful Art Nouveau theater. The unlikely new tenant here is the Walt Disney Company, which completely renovated the remarkable theater to serve as a venue for its own productions. The New Amsterdam reopened in May 1997 with the concert premiere of *King David,* a biblical musical by Alan Menken and Tim Rice, who both worked previously on the scores of Disney animated films. *214 W. 42nd St. Subway: N, R, 1, 2, 3, 7, or 9 to Times Sq.; also A, C, or E to W. 42nd St. (8th Ave.).*

Shubert. *A Chorus Line* had its record-breaking 15-year (1975–1990) run here. This is also where Barbra Streisand made her 1962 Broadway debut, and where *Big,* the musical, flopped big time. *225 W. 44th St., between Broadway and 8th Ave. Subway: N, R, 1, 2, 3, 7, or 9 to Times Sq.; also A, C, or E to W. 42nd St. (8th Ave.).*

Walter Kerr. August Wilson's prize-winning *The Piano Lesson* and Tony Kushner's moving two-part epic about gay life, *Angels in America: Millennium Approaches* and *Perestroika,* have played at this lovely theater, renovated and renamed in 1990 for the respected drama critic. *219 W. 48th St., between Broadway and 8th Ave. Subway: C, E, 1, or 9 to W. 50th St.*

Winter Garden. In the Roaring '20s this was *the* place to catch vaudeville extravaganzas by the Shubert brothers. Many hit musicals have played here, including *Funny Girl* and *Mame.* For the last decade it's been inhabited by singing, dancing, jellicle *Cats. 1634 Broadway, at W. 50th St. Subway: C, E, 1, or 9 to W. 50th St.; also N or R to W. 49th St.*

OFF-BROADWAY

Off-Broadway is a good place to catch Broadway smashes in the making—like *A Chorus Line,* which opened at the Public Theater, or Wendy Wasserstein's *The Heidi Chronicles,* which first appeared at Playwrights Horizons—before they relocate to the Great White Way and ticket prices hit the stratosphere. The biggest clusters of Off-Broadway theaters can be found in the West Village (around Sheridan Square) and in Midtown on **Theater Row** (42nd Street, between 9th and 10th avenues).

Off-Off-Broadway, which came of age in the '60s, offers an in-your-face, the-hell-with-it alternative to everything else. Depending on which night you show up, you'll find everything from cabaret and comedy to serious drama at Off-Off-Broadway theaters. They're also the birthplace of **performance art** (a mix of dance, drama, music, and video, usually expressing Very Deep Thoughts). Catch a performance-art piece in New York and you'll really impress those snooty friends of yours back home. Of the theaters listed below, **La MaMa E.T.C.** is known for its devotion to performance art. So are the **Brooklyn Academy of Music,** the **Joseph Papp Public Theater, The Kitchen,** and **P.S. 122** (*see* Arts Centers, *above*). Ticket prices for Off-Broadway shows typically run $15–$45, for Off-Off-Broadway $10–$25.

Actor's Studio. This respected drama school has productions open to the public. Tickets are free ($5 donation suggested), but reservations are required. The Actors Studio M.F.A. Program also has a free repertory season performed by graduate students (tel. 212/229–5488) at the downtown Circle in the Square. *432 W. 44th St., between 9th and 10th Aves., Midtown, tel. 212/757–0870. Subway: A, C, or E to W. 42nd St. (Port Authority).*

American Jewish Theatre Contemporary plays and revivals of musicals, usually with a Jewish theme, are staged at this tiny theater-in-the-round. *307 W. 26th St., Chelsea, tel. 212/633–9797. Subway: C or E to W. 28th St.*

Atlantic Theater Company. Founded by playwright David Mamet and actor William H. Macy, this troupe has productions of challenging new plays by up-and-coming writers. *307 W. 26th St., Chelsea, tel. 212/633–9797. Subway: C or E to W. 28th St.; also A, C, or E to W. 23rd St.*

Classic Stage Company (CSC). Here's a lively showcase for the classics—some arcane, others European—in new translations and adaptations. Rush tickets at $15 are available a half-hour before the performance. *136 E. 13th St., East Village, tel. 212/677–4210. Subway: 4, 5, 6, N, or R to Union Sq.*

Drama Dept. Although it doesn't have a permanent home, this energetic company of young actors, playwrights, and other theater artists has won high acclaim for its imaginative revivals of overlooked plays. *Administrative office: 450 W. 42nd St., tel. 212/629–3014.*

Jean Cocteau Repertory. The company's specialty is the sort of obscure plays that drama geeks rave about. *Bouwerie Lane Theatre, 330 Bowery, at Bond St., East Village, tel. 212/677–0060. Subway: 6 to Bleecker St.*

Joseph Papp Public Theater. The Joseph Papp Public Theater, a complex of five theaters, is the year-round home of the New York Shakespeare Festival. Despite the name, performances are not limited to the bard and are anything but staid: *Bring In 'Da Noise, Bring in 'Da Funk* premiered here in 1995. Each summer, the financially challenged wait for hours at its box office to catch their free Shakespeare performances in Central Park (*see* Summer Arts, *above*). Quiktix at $15 are available a half-hour before curtain time when plays are not sold out. *425 Lafayette St., at Astor Pl., East Village, tel. 212/260–2400. Subway: 6 to Astor Pl.*

> *Don't overlook tomorrow's hits and today's flops—there's something special about seeing a show in previews or seeing an already-panned play before it bites the dust.*

La MaMa E.T.C. Famous alumni of this "MGM of experimental theater" include Sam Shepard, Bette Midler, Andy Warhol, Nick Nolte, and Meatloaf. In its three performance spaces you can find everything from African fables to new wave operas. *74 E. 4th St., between 2nd and 3rd Aves., East Village, tel. 212/475–7710. Subway: 6 to Astor Pl. or F to 2nd Ave.*

Manhattan Theatre Club. Some of the most talked-about new plays and musicals in town are presented here by such major talents as Terrence McNally, Athol Fugard, and John Patrick Shanley. *City Center, 131 W. 55th St., Midtown, tel. 212/581–1212. Subway: N or R to W. 57th St.*

National Black Theater. Come here for new works by contemporary African-American writers. *2033 5th Ave., Harlem, tel. 212/722–3800. Subway: 2, 3, or 4 to 125th St.*

New Dramatists. Playwrights bring their shows here to iron out kinks before moving to Broadway. Tickets are free, so reserve far in advance. Readings, too, are popular here. *424 W. 44th St., between 9th and 10th Aves., Midtown, tel. 212/757–6960. Subway: A, C, or E to W. 42nd St. (Port Authority).*

New York Theater Workshop. The mega-hit musical *Rent* started at this small venue, which produces controversial new theater works by American and international playwrights such as David Rabe, Tony Kushner, and Caryl Churchill. *79 E. 4th St., East Village, tel. 212/460–5475. Subway: 6 to Astor Pl. or F to 2nd Ave.*

Pan-Asian Repertory Theatre. This forum for Asian-American actors and artists presents new work and adaptations of Western plays. *St. Clement's Church, 423 W. 46th St., Midtown, tel. 212/245–2660. Subway: C or E to W. 50th St.*

Pearl Theatre Company. A troupe of resident players concentrates on classics from around the globe; the works of such masters as Molière, Ibsen, Shakespeare, Shaw, and Sophocles find a new life here. *80 St. Marks Pl., East Village, tel. 212/598–9802. Subway: 6 to Astor Pl.*

Playwrights Horizons. This theater is dedicated to developing the talents of new playwrights. *Falsettos* and *The Heidi Chronicles* both began here. *416 W. 42nd St., between 9th and 10th Aves., Midtown, tel. 212/279–4200. Subway: A, C, or E to W. 42nd St. (Port Authority).*

Primary Stages. The spotlight is on new creations by American playwrights such as Charles Busch, David Ives, and Donald Margulies. *354 W. 45th St., Midtown, tel. 212/333–4052. Subway: N, R, 1, 2, 3, 7, or 9 to Times Sq.; also A, C, or E to W. 42nd St. (8th Ave.).*

Repertorio Español. Those who can't follow the action in Spanish can often listen to a simultaneous translation though a nifty cordless headset. *Gramercy Arts Theatre, 138 E. 27th St., between Lexington and 3rd Aves., Gramercy, tel. 212/889–2850. Subway: 6 to E. 28th St.*

Signature Theatre Company. Each season, this company devotes its time to the works of one American playwright; past seasons have reexamined the plays of Edward Albee, Horton Foote, Adrienne Kennedy, and Sam Shepard. In 1998 Arthur Miller's plays will be staged. *424 W. 42nd St., tel. 212/967–1913.*

Sullivan Street Playhouse. Here's the home of *The Fantasticks,* the world's longest-running musical. *181 Sullivan St., between Houston and Bleecker Sts., West Village, tel. 212/674–3838. Subway: A, B, C, D, E, F, or Q to W. 4th St. (Washington Sq.).*

Vineyard Theater. Innovative new plays and musicals by established and emerging artists are given stellar productions. Edward Albee's Pulitzer Prize winner *Three Tall Woman* had its New York premiere here. *108 E. 15th St., Gramercy, tel. 212/353–3366. Subway: 4, 5, 6, N, or R to Union Sq.*

York Theatre Company. If you like musicals, check out the well-received revivals and new works presented by this admirable group. *Theatre at St. Peter's Church, 54th St. at Lexington Ave., Midtown, tel. 212/935–5820. Subway: E or F to Lexington Ave. or 6 to E. 51st St.*

SPORTS AND OUTDOOR ACTIVITIES

UPDATED BY MIRA SCHWIRTZ

New Yorkers may love dining out, drinking cocktails, and smoking—but during summer you'll see a flood of rippled hardbodies on bikes and 'blades, slackers whacking around tennis and soccer balls, and old folks speed-walking through Central Park. Many more fill stadiums and line the streets during major annual events like the U.S. Open, New York Marathon, and Gay Games, and to cheer on the city's pro sports teams. If you feel like joining in, *Time Out New York* ($1.95), available at most newsstands, is a great resource: Its "Sports" section lists upcoming events, times, dates, and ticket info. The *TripBuilder's Sports Guide* ($5), available at bookstores, also has up-to-date info on city sports leagues and places to play.

GYMS AND REC CENTERS

There are plenty of private health clubs in town that charge thousands of dollars for the privilege of sweating your extra flesh off on their StairMasters. Thankfully, **Crunch Fitness** (tel. 212/475–2018) has five locations in Manhattan and only charges $20 for the day. That entitles you to as many yoga, kick boxing, aerobics, and karate classes as you can stand. Crunch Fitness also has a reputation as one of the most gay- and lesbian-friendly gyms in the city. **Equinox** (tel. 212/721–4200), also with five locations, charges $26 per day for use of their upscale facilities, including the gym and steam room, as well as yoga and aerobics classes.

PRIVATE GYMS

Asphalt Green. This 5-acre, state-of-the-art facility features an Olympic-size indoor pool (with special features for swimmers with disabilities), indoor and outdoor tracks, basketball courts, an Astroturf field, and all kinds of exercise equipment and classes. The drop-in fee for the pool or gym is $15 ($25 for both). *1750 York Ave., at E. 91st St., Upper East Side, tel. 212/369–8890. Subway: 4, 5, or 6 to E. 86th St. Open weekdays 5:30 AM–10 PM, weekends 8–8. Pool closed to nonmembers weekdays 3–8.*

Chelsea Piers Sports Center. In this gym the size of three football fields, you'll find the city's longest indoor running track (¼ mi), a boxing ring, indoor sand volleyball courts, a rock-climbing wall, an indoor swimming pool, and just about everything else a sports fiend could want. A day pass ($31) gives you access to everything at the Sports Center (except the rock wall, which is $20 extra) but you can purchase only six day passes per year. Also at Chelsea Piers are an ice-skating rink and roller rink (*see* Participant Sports, *below*); a golf driving range; and indoor soccer, field hockey, and lacrosse fields. All of them operate on different piers next door to the sports center and cost extra. *W. 23rd St., at Hudson River, Chelsea, tel. 212/336–6000 or 212/336–6666 for recorded info. Subway: C or E to W. 23rd St.; walk 3 long blocks or catch a crosstown bus. Open weekdays 6 AM–11 PM, weekends 8 AM–9 PM.*

PUBLIC GYMS

City-operated rec centers are an excellent deal. Pay the $25 annual membership fee at one and you have access to all 12 Manhattan locations. Offerings include swimming pools (outdoor pools are free in summer), basketball and volleyball courts, weight-training equipment, all sorts of exercise bicycles and Nautilus machines, even salsa aerobics and classes in African martial arts; contact the **NYC Parks & Recreation Department** (tel. 212/360–8111 or 800/201–7275 in NYC) for more info. Two of the best are:

Carmine Street. Here you'll find indoor and outdoor pools, an indoor track, indoor volleyball and basketball courts, two gyms, a dance studio, and weight rooms. Classes include yoga, aerobics, fencing, and self-defense. *3 Carmine St., at 7th Ave. S, West Village, tel. 212/242–5228. Subway: 1 or 9 to W. Houston St. Open weekdays 7 AM–10 PM, Sat. 9–5. Hrs vary for courts and pool.*

West 59th Street. Facilities here include an indoor pool, fitness rooms, a gym, and an indoor climbing wall. Classes are held in weight-training and climbing. *533 W. 59th St., between 10th and 11th Aves., Upper West Side, tel. 212/397–3166. Subway: A, B, C, D, 1, or 9 to W. 59th St. Open weekdays 11–10:30. Sat. 10–5 (hrs for recreational swimming vary).*

PARTICIPANT SPORTS

There is no lack of sports activities to do in New York, be it ice-skating at Rockefeller Center or mountain biking on Staten Island. No matter what you're into—jogging, biking, in-line skating, football, soccer, ultimate Frisbee, snoozing by a shady tree—the best place to start is **Central Park** (*see* Major Attractions *in* Chapter 2). Most sports activities are free if you do it yourself or join a pickup game, though for only a few bucks you can also join a fairly organized local team. For info on participant sporting events throughout the city, call the **NYC Parks & Recreation Department** (tel. 212/360–8111 or 800/201–7275 in NYC) and dial your way through their recorded choices.

BASKETBALL

For serious team players, the **New York Urban Professional Athletic League** (tel. 212/877–3614) sponsors two seasons of league games from June through August and November through March. **Yorkville Sports** (tel. 212/645–6488) holds open gym starting at 6:30 PM every Friday night from September through March at High School of Fashion (24th St. between 7th and 8th Aves., 3rd floor gym) for $10 per person. Both leagues have separate divisions for men and women, hold open tryouts, and charge $95–$137 per person. It's a hefty investment, but worth it if you're heavy into hoops. Call a month or two before the season starts to register.

PICKUP GAMES • There are hundreds of outdoor courts all over the city, where competition ranges from inept to life-threatening. Most players are men. Female hoopsters tend to gather at **Tompkins Square Park** (Ave. A at St. Marks Pl., East Village), while the courts on **West 4th Street** at 6th Avenue draw hotshots from around the city (and even an audience). Lively play also takes place on the six half-courts at **West 76th Street** at Columbus Avenue and at two courts in **Central Park**, near the Metropolitan Museum. On the Upper East Side, easygoing players fill three half-courts at **Carl Schurz Park** (E. 84th St. at East End Ave.) and the courts at the **Armory Building** (E. 94th St. at Madison Ave., Upper East Side). If you're looking to be absolutely humiliated, try **Riverbank State Park** (W. 145th St. at Riverside Dr., Harlem).

BIKING

You won't get killed exploring the city by bike, but you'd be smarter to stick to cruising around Central Park, **Riverside Park** (Riverside Dr., between W. 72nd and 135th Sts., Upper West Side), or the **Battery Park City Esplanade** (on the Hudson River between Chambers St. and Battery Pl., Lower Manhattan). Outside Manhattan, the best spots to explore on two wheels are **Forest Park,** Queens, fantastic for BMXers, and **High Rock Park,** in Staten Island, which has a pleasant trail along the beach (for more on both, *see* Parks and Gardens *in* Chapter 2). If you're into racing, you can join the **Century Road Club Association** (tel. 212/222–8062), which meets Saturday mornings (6 AM) in Central Park for three- to eight-lap races around its 6-mi circular drive. If you prefer to pedal for pleasure, join **Time's Up** (*see* Cheap Thrills *in* Chapter 2) for one of their moonlight rides.

BIKE RENTALS AND REPAIRS • Plenty of bike shops in the city will rent you a pair of wheels on which to cruise around. Try **Bicycle Habitat** (244 Lafayette St., between Prince and Spring Sts., SoHo, tel. 212/431–3315), which rents mountain bikes and hybrids for $25 per day (plus $250 deposit); **Bicycles Plus** (1690 2nd Ave., between E. 87th and 88th Sts., Upper East Side, tel. 212/722–2201), which rents the same for $7 per hour ($25 per day), with a $100–$150 deposit; or **Metro Bicycles** (332 E. 14th St., between 1st and 2nd Aves., Gramercy Park, tel. 212/228–4344; and six other locations citywide) rents hybrids for $6 per hour or $25 per day ($35 to keep bike overnight), plus a $150 deposit. In summer you can rent bikes ($6–$12 per hr, $32–$40 per day) inside Central Park at **AAA Bikes** (Loeb Boathouse, mid-park at 74th St., tel. 212/861–4137). Bike owners and would-be owners can't do better than **Frank's Bike Shop** (553 Grand St., between Jackson and Lewis Sts., Lower East Side, tel. 212/533–6332), which charges $20 for a basic tune-up.

CLIMBING

Rock climbers intent on climbing in Manhattan, but not ready to scale the Empire State Building, can test their mettle in a converted racquetball court at the **Manhattan Plaza Health Club** (482 W. 43rd St., between 9th and 10th Aves., Midtown, tel. 212/563–7001). Day access is $10 plus $5 for equipment rental. In Central Park, the **North Meadow Rec Center** (mid-park at 97th St., tel. 212/348–4867) has a 13-ft indoor wall and a 25-ft outdoor wall. Their single-day introductory class is $75; the four-day comprehensive course costs $200. They'll also show you the two places you can climb in Central Park, **Rat Rock** and **Chess Rock,** or take you out to the 50-ft rock in **Fort Tryon Park** (*see* Parks and Gardens *in* Chapter 2). **Extravertical Climbing Club** (Broadway between 62nd and 63rd Sts., tel. 212/586–5718) has a 50-ft and a 30-ft wall within the Harmony Atrium. A day pass is $12 and an evening one is $16; equipment rental is $8. Your horizontally inclined friends can admire you from the adjacent coffee bar. **Chelsea Piers** and the **West 59th Street** rec centers (*see* Gyms and Rec Centers, *above*) also offer indoor climbing walls and instruction for beginners.

If you've never been on Rollerblades before, proceed slowly and cautiously to one of the Central Park Skate Patrol's "Stopping Clinics." From April to October, these quick, free, knee-saving seminars are held daily 12:30–5:30 at the East and West 72nd Street park entrances.

CROSS-COUNTRY SKIING

When a heavy snowfall hits New York, Central Park's bridle paths and roadways make for spectacular treks, particularly in the woodsy wonderland above 86th Street. **Scandinavian Ski and Sports Shop** (40 W. 57th St., between 5th and 6th Aves., Midtown West, tel. 212/757–8524) can set you up with boots, poles, and skis for $16 per half-day, though you'll need to move swiftly to score a pair.

FOOTBALL

You can let Fox TV get under your helmet, or you can do what Jack Kennedy did (and what JFK, Jr., still does) every weekend in Manhattan: Grab family and friends and go play some touch football. Central Park's **Great Lawn** (mid-park, at 83rd St.) and **Sheep Meadow** (near Central Park W, at 66th St.) are the land of pickup games. Most start on weekends by 9 AM, year-round, and there's also action on weeknights in summer.

HIKING

Though hiking in New York City seems an odd concept, there are plenty of nearby places to worship Mother Nature and hug a tree. The obvious choice is Central Park—there are literally hundreds of trails crisscrossing its length, most of which are rarely crowded. In the outer boroughs, enormous parks like **Alley Pond Park, Forest Park, Pelham Bay Park, Van Cortlandt Park,** Staten Island's **High Rock Park,** and the **Jamaica Bay Wildlife Refuge** each offer acres of wilderness and plenty of picnic tables; *see* Parks and Gardens *in* Chapter 2, for more info on each.

The **Urban Park Rangers** (tel. 212/427–4040 or 718/438–0100) organize guided walks throughout the New York area; they can also recommend the best spots for bird-watching, dog walking, jogging, you name it. The **Gateway National Recreation Area** (tel. 718/338–3338) in Brooklyn offers moonlight walks, wildflower walks, and dune hikes, all for under $20 per person (often for free). The **Central Park Conservancy** (tel. 212/360–2734), in Central Park, organizes park hikes, bird-watching expeditions, and other nature programs. **Shorewalkers** (tel. 212/330–7686) leads weekend tours of New York–area shorelines.

HORSEBACK RIDING

Claremont Riding Academy is a 100-year-old institution and the only stable in Manhattan. Experienced English riders can rent horses to explore 6 mi of bridle paths in nearby Central Park for $33 per hour. Claremont also offers classes in riding and jumping for all experience levels. *175 W. 89th St., at Amsterdam Ave., Upper West Side, tel. 212/724–5100. Open weekdays 6 AM–10 PM, weekends 8–5.*

ICE-SKATING AND ICE HOCKEY

If you want to play hockey, the Sky Rink (*see below*) at Chelsea Piers sponsors several year-round leagues, from beginner to expert. Games are $15 for members, $40 for nonmembers. On winter weekends, you can also drop in on a hockey game at Lasker Rink (*see below*) for $4. All ice-skating rinks offer skate rentals, lockers, tacky music, and snack bars serving steaming cups of cocoa. Hockey players need to bring their own gear.

Lasker Rink. This newly revamped rink, at the northern end of Central Park near 110th Street, offers crowd-free skating late October–March. Skate rentals are $3.50. *Tel. 212/534–7639. Subway: 2 or 3 to W. 110th St. (Central Park North). Admission: $3. Open Sun.–Mon. 10–3, Tues.–Wed. 10–3:30, Thurs. 10–3, Fri. 10–4, weekends 11:15–10.*

Rockefeller Center Ice-Skating Rink. The rink isn't huge, but there's still something amazing about skating in the heart of Manhattan on a crisp winter evening. Kids love this place. Skate rentals are $4. *601 5th Ave., between W. 49th and 50th Sts., Midtown, tel. 212/332–7654. Subway: B, D, F, or Q to W. 47th–50th Sts. (Rockefeller Center). Admission: $7–$8.50. Open Oct.–Apr., Mon.–Thurs. 9 AM–10 PM, Fri.–Sat. 8:30 AM–midnight, Sun. 8:30 AM–10 PM.*

Sky Rink. This deluxe indoor rink (the size of Alaska) is in the brand-new Chelsea Piers. It's open year-round. Rentals are $4. Drop-in hockey play is offered weekdays noon–1:20 at a cost of $15, but players must bring their own equipment. They also offer lessons in hockey, speed skating, and figure skating. *W. 23rd St. at the Hudson River, Chelsea, tel. 212/336–6100. Subway: A, C, or E to W. 23rd St. Admission: $9. Open Mon. noon–6:20 and 8–9:20, Tues. noon–6:20, Wed.–Thurs. noon–9:20, Fri. noon–6 and 8–midnight, Sat. 11:45–4:45 and 8–midnight, Sun. 12:30–5:30.*

Wollman Memorial Rink. Ice-skaters pack this famously beautiful Central Park rink, near 59th Street, from November through March. Skate rentals are $3.50. *Tel. 212/396–1010. Subway: B or Q to W. 57th St.; also N or R to 5th Ave. Admission: $7. Open Mon. 10–4, Tues.–Thurs. 10–9:30, Fri.–Sat. 10–11, Sun. 10–9.*

IN-LINE SKATING

On weekends, city parks and roadways swarm with 'bladers oblivious to everything but their Walkmans. Evel Knieval types set up obstacle courses and jumps near **Tavern on the Green** (near Central Park W, at 66th St.) in Central Park. During warm months, the park's **Wollman Memorial Rink** (*see* Ice-Skating and Ice Hockey, *above*) becomes a roller disco on weekends; rentals are $15 (2 hrs) or $25 (all day). Other popular outdoor spots include Hudson River Park, Riverside Park, and the concrete canyons and wide-open plazas of **Wall Street** (nearly car-free on weekends). The brand-new **Chelsea Piers** (W. 23rd St. at the Hudson River, Chelsea, tel. 212/336–6200) has a giant indoor roller rink, which offers classes ($15) for beginner, expert, and hip-hop 'bladers; general skating ($4); and, on Saturday nights, DJ'd dance parties ($8). Rentals are $10 with a credit-card deposit. The **Empire Skate Club of New York** (tel. 212/592–3674) holds instructional sessions and organizes group skates to New Jersey, Long Island, and around Manhattan.

If you need to rent, head to one of the **Blades** branches. Full-day rentals (pads included) are $15 on weekdays, $25 on weekends, plus a credit-card deposit of $300. *120 W. 72nd St., between Columbus Ave. and Broadway, Upper West Side, tel. 212/787–3911. Subway: 1, 2, 3, or 9 to W. 72nd St. Open daily 10–8 (Sun. until 6). Other locations: 160 E. 86th St., between Lexington and 3rd Aves., Upper East Side, tel. 212/996–1644; Westside Hwy. and W. 23rd St., Chelsea, tel. 212/336–6299; 659 Broadway, between Bleecker and W. 3rd Sts., West Village, tel. 212/477–7350.*

IN-LINE SPORTS • Chelsea Piers (*see above*) offers several levels of league play, year-round. If hockey isn't your fancy, the **National In-line Basketball League** (tel. 212/539–1132) sponsors *basketball* games on 'blades. Who'd have thunk it? Members pay $35 to compete three times a week at city parks but drop-ins are welcome for free.

New Yorkers aren't afraid to cross-check, so arrive well-padded wherever you go. The best place to play street in-line hockey is **Robert Moses Playground** (E. 41st St. at 1st Ave., Midtown), where the competition is pretty fierce. In summer you'll also find pickup games at **Riverbank State Park** (W. 145th St. at Riverside Dr., Harlem). Throughout the year on weekends, there are also games at **Tompkins Square Park** (Ave. A, at St. Marks Pl., East Village) and, on Sunday afternoons, at the north end of **Union Square** (E. 17th St. at Broadway, Gramercy).

RUNNING

Though Manhattan streets are crowded with pedestrians, bicycle messengers, city buses, and curb-jumping taxis, there are plenty of places where you can run safely in New York. Most popular is the **Central Park Reservoir** (mid-park, between 85th and 96th Sts.); tenacious people in Lycra orbit its 1½-mi track in every kind of weather. Roads within the park all have designated runners' lanes and close completely to traffic weekdays 10–3 and 7–10 and from Friday at 7 PM until Monday at 6 AM. The entire loop of the park—from 59th Street to 110th Street and back again—is 6 mi.

Other favorite Manhattan circuits are: **Riverside Park** (4½ mi), **Washington Square Park** (½ mi), **East River Park** (¼-mi track), the **Battery Park City Esplanade** (2 mi), and the **Hudson River Esplanade** (1½ mi). In Brooklyn, try either the **Brooklyn Heights Promenade** (1 mi), which offers stunning views of the lower Manhattan skyline, or the loop in **Prospect Park** (6 mi), closed to traffic Sunday. For park locations, *see* Parks and Gardens *in* Chapter 2.

Use caution wherever you run or jog, and don't go out alone in deserted areas or after dark. The New York Road Runners Club (tel. 212/860–4455) can match you with a running partner if you're new in town.

RUNNING CLUBS • New York has almost a dozen clubs geared exclusively toward runners; most organize group runs, provide safety info, plan races, and sponsor events throughout the year. Most clubs meet weekly in Central Park and welcome drop-in participants. The **Achilles Track Club** (tel. 212/354–0300) is primarily for wheelchair racers and runners with disabilities. **Front Runners** (tel. 212/724–9700) is New York's main gay and lesbian running group. **Moving Comfort** (tel. 212/222–7216) is a highly competitive all-women team. The **Warren Street Social and Athletic Club** (tel. 212/807–7422) is known for its friendly attitude toward less-than-Olympic-caliber athletes.

The **New York Road Runners Club** holds free group runs of various distances and paces weekdays at 6:30 PM, Saturday at 10 AM, all starting near Central Park at the club headquarters. They also sponsor classes, races, and "fun runs" year-round, and help to coordinate the annual New York Marathon. *9 E. 89th St., at 5th Ave., Upper East Side, tel. 212/860–4455, fax 212/860–9754. Subway: 4, 5, or 6 to E. 86th St.*

SOCCER

Alexi Lalas aspirants should cruise over to **Soccer Sport Supply** (1745 1st Ave., at E. 90th St., Upper East Side, tel. 212/427–6050), which can outfit you with cleats and Umbro shorts and get you up-to-date on soccer activities around the city.

PICKUP GAMES • You may have noticed that Manhattan isn't blessed with acres of open fields. Your best bet is to join a weekend game at Central Park's **North Meadow** (mid-park, at 97th St.), which has three soccer fields. The softball fields at **Riverside Park** (mid-park, at 103 St.) are the dominion of hot Latino and South American players, but anyone with stamina plays. Downtown diehards play on the narrow strips of grass and asphalt that constitute **Washington Square Park** (Waverly Pl. at University Pl.) and **Tompkins Square Park** (Ave. A at St. Marks Pl.), though the latter is really too small to have a serious game.

SOFTBALL AND BASEBALL

Between April and mid-September, softball dominates the city's parks on weekends and weekday evenings. Most games are sponsored by a league, either men's, women's, or coed and either fast- or slow-pitch. Most people hook up with a league through their employer or with an organization like **Corporate Sports** (tel. 212/245–4738), **Manhattan Indoor/Outdoor Sports** (tel. 718/712–0342), or **Yorkville Sports** (tel. 212/645–6488). It generally costs around $100 per person to join a private league. Otherwise, if you and your friends are all self- or unemployed, or you happen to be traveling with a dozen people who brought mitts, you'll need to buy a permit ($8 for 2 hrs) from the **NYC Parks & Recreation Permit Office** (tel. 212/408–0234) to use one of the city's hundreds of baseball diamonds, even for a single game. Sorry.

RUN FOR YOUR LIFE

New York's marathon is one of city's most celebrated civic events, a 26.2-mi party that passes through all five boroughs before ending in front of Tavern on the Green in Central Park. In a single Sunday in early November, over 27,000 runners from 99 foreign countries and all 50 states will have passed 18,000 yards of barricade tape; 2 million spectators will have whizzed in 550 portable toilets; and 642 tubes of K-Y Jelly will keep the whole thing running smoothly.

SWIMMING

If you're too poor to escape to the Italian Riviera—or even the south shore of Long Island—at least you can keep your cool at a city pool or nearby beach (*see box*, New York City, Land of Skyscrapers and Sunny Beaches?!, *in* Chapter 2). The pools at public rec centers (*see* Gyms and Rec Centers, *above*) are free during summer—and crammed with splashing preteens. You're better off at a private pool: The five-lane indoor pool at **John Jay College of Criminal Justice** (899 10th Ave., at W. 58th St., Midtown, tel. 212/237–8371) is open to the public weekdays until 5 PM; a single visit costs $3. The eight-lane, 50-meter Olympic pool at **Asphalt Green** (*see* Gyms and Rec Centers, *above*) is members-only weekdays 3–8 PM; otherwise it's open to the public for $15 per visit. A $55 annual membership (plus a $6 fee per half hour or $8 for nonmembers) gives you access to the **Midtown YWCA**'s (610 Lexington Ave., at E. 53rd St., Midtown, tel. 212/735–9770) large six-lane pool, perfect for rigorous workouts. Your cheapest option is **Lasker Rink** (tel. 212/534–7639) in Central Park. In summer this skating rink becomes a swimming pool; a full day of splashing around is entirely free. To reach Lasker Rink, enter the park at 110th Street and Lenox Avenue.

TENNIS

Whenever the weather is good, you'll find hundreds of people on the 24 public courts in Central Park. Though pickup games are possible, most people arrive in pairs and aren't in the mood to share their courts with anyone. Reservations are a good idea. Also, you must get a permit to play on a city-owned court from April through November: $5 for a single-play permit or $50 for a full-season permit that's valid in all five boroughs. Call the **NYC Parks & Recreation Permit Office** (tel. 212/360–8133) for more info. Or pick up your permit in person at Room 1 in the Arsenal Building (5th Ave., at E. 64th St., Upper East Side). The courts at **East River Park** (East River Dr. at Delancey St., Lower East Side, tel. 212/529–7185) are available on a first-come, first-served basis; they're never as busy as the courts in Central Park. If you have money to spare and don't mind the trek to Queens, reserve one of 38 outdoor/indoor courts at the **U.S.T.A. National Tennis Center** (Flushing Meadows–Corona Park, Queens, tel. 718/760–6200), site of the U.S. Open. You can make reservations two days to an hour in advance; courts cost $28–$40 depending on the time of day. For directions to Flushing Meadow–Corona Park, *see* Queens *in* Chapter 2.

VOLLEYBALL

League volleyball is half sport and half social: Teams are coed and usually celebrate wins (and losses) with a postgame trip to a bar. The **Big City Volleyball League** (tel. 212/288–4240) fields over 120 teams at seven skill levels. The cost is $8–$9.50 per person for a 10-week season starting in January, April, July, or October. The group also sponsors pick-up games at high-school gyms for advanced- and recreational-level players. The smaller **New York Urban Professional League** (tel. 212/877–3614) has similar schedules and prices. **Yorkville Sports** (tel. 212/645–6488) starts its league games in mid-September; membership is $70. You can drop in on any Friday night at La Guardia High School (65th St. and Amsterdam Ave.) for pick-up games. The cost is $10 and includes beer at a local bar afterwards. If you want to hone that killer serve, try the three nets in Central Park or in one of New York's public rec centers (*see above*).

SPECTATOR SPORTS

Even though they lost their beloved Dodgers to Los Angeles in 1958, sports-crazy New Yorkers still have great pro teams like the Yankees, Mets, Knicks, Islanders, and Rangers. Sure, the *Post* and *Daily News* seem to find more excitement chronicling off-field antics—like Yankee owner George Steinbrenner's bullying (and unending) threats to move his team to New Jersey or Spike Lee's latest courtside outburst—but, hey, a sunny day hanging in the House that Ruth Built (New Yorkers' pet name for Yankee Stadium) while drinking beer with rowdy fans is still a singular New York experience.

The main venues for New York's pro teams are: **Giants Stadium** (*see* Football, *below*); **Meadowlands** (Rte. 3, East Rutherford, NJ, tel. 201/935–3900), accessible by bus from Port Authority; and **Madison Square Garden** (7th Ave. between W. 31st and 33rd Sts., Midtown, tel. 212/465–6000) near the Penn Station subway stop (A, C, E, 1, 2, 3, or 9). In addition to hosting the Knicks and Rangers, the Garden is the place to catch an endless parade of wrestling, boxing, rodeo, and monster-truck shows. Purchase tickets at a team's box office or through **Ticketmaster** (tel. 212/307–4100), which slaps a service charge (usually about $5 per ticket, depending on the game) on whatever you buy.

BASEBALL

Nothing's better than hot dogs, beer, and baseball—except all of that *plus* a free pair of plastic Yanks sunglasses. Annual freebie fests include the Mets' Beach Towel Night and Jersey (shirts, not cows) Day, and the Yankees' Sunglasses and Bat (the baseball-hitting kind, not the flying rodents) days. Regular baseball season runs April–October.

During the big weeks of the U.S. Open, shy guy Andre Agassi has been known to sneak off to the courts of Central Park for a little extra practice.

New York Yankees. In years past, greats like Babe Ruth, Joe DiMaggio, and Lou Gehrig led the Bronx Bombers to championship after championship. These days you never know what to expect, though rowdy bleacher bums guarantee a good time. Bleachers cost $6, reserved seating is $12–$21. *Yankee Stadium, Bronx, tel. 718/293–4300 or 718/293–6000 for automated tickets. Subway: C, D, or 4 to 161st St. (Yankee Stadium). Box office open weekdays 9–5 and during home games.*

New York Mets. The current team has youth and talent. So why have they suffered a losing streak for most of this decade? Tickets cost $7–$19. *Shea Stadium, 123–01 Roosevelt Ave., at 126th St., Flushing, Queens, tel. 718/507–8499. Subway: 7 to Willets Point (Shea Stadium).*

BASKETBALL

The **New York Knickerbockers** (Madison Square Garden, Midtown, tel. 212/465–5867) suffered through several humiliating runs for the championship under Armani-clad coach and personality Pat Reily. Don Nelson (of Golden State Warriors fame) tried his hand as coach from 1995 until he got canned in early 1996, when finally Jeff Van Gundy took over the talented but geriatric crew that includes Patrick Ewing and John Starks. Tickets start at $18 and peak at $1,000. The **New Jersey Nets** (Meadowlands Arena, tel. 201/935–3900), who migrated from NY to NJ in 1977, perennially rank as one of the NBA's worst teams—despite star players like Jimmy Jackson and Kendall Gill. Tickets sell for $16–$55. In the spring, Madison Square Garden hosts the Big East and National Invitational college tournaments, both worth checking out. The pro-basketball season runs late October–April.

FOOTBALL

If you've come to town expecting to see some football, try a sports bar. Tickets for both New York pro teams are almost impossible to get: You can scramble for single **New York Jets** (tel. 516/560–8200) tickets when they go on sale in August, join the waiting list for **New York Giants** (tel. 201/935–8222) tix, or hand a scalper your life savings. Both teams play in New Jersey at **Giants Stadium** (Meadowlands Complex on Rte. 3 in East Rutherford, NJ); catch a bus from Port Authority to reach the stadium. Big college matchups like Army–Navy (tel. 201/935–3900 for games scheduled) occasionally come to Giants Stadium, too. Football season runs September–December.

As an alternative of sorts, check out the **Columbia Lions,** the Ivy League's perpetual doormat. Their losing streaks have hit 40-plus in a row, but they're not gonna dwell on it, OK? The Lions play at Columbia

University's **Baker Field** (200 W. 218th St., Inwood, tel. 212/854–2546) September–November. Tickets cost $13–$14.

ICE HOCKEY

Fast paced, brutal, and full of fights, ice hockey is just like the subway at rush hour—no wonder New Yorkers love it. All three pro teams play in the notorious Atlantic Division, and recent triumphs have made tickets (typically $20–$115) pretty scarce by game time. The season runs October–April.

Though they're wimps compared to their rabid fans, the **New York Rangers** (Madison Square Garden, Midtown, tel. 212/465–6000) did manage to end a 54-year championship drought with a Stanley Cup win in 1994. The **New Jersey Devils** (Meadowlands Arena, New Jersey, tel. 201/935–3900) won the Stanley Cup in 1995 after enduring a lifetime as league losers (Wayne Gretzky once dissed them as "Mickey Mouse"). And the **New York Islanders** won four consecutive Stanley Cups in the early '80s, but unless new tough-guy coach Rick Bowness works a miracle, at least you won't have trouble getting tickets. The Islanders play at Nassau Coliseum (Hempstead Turnpike, Uniondale, Long Island, tel. 516/794–4100), accessible by train from Penn Station.

TENNIS

The prestigious **United States Open Tennis Tournament** (tel. 718/760–6200) takes place late August–early September at the U.S.T.A. National Tennis Center (*see* Tennis *in* Participant Sports, *above*). It's a hugely popular event with New Yorkers, and tickets ($28–$66) to the exciting matches go fast. You can purchase tickets by phone through **TeleCharge** (tel. 212/239–6250 or 800/524–8440) for a $5-per-ticket service fee. The **WTA Tour Championships** (tel. 212/465–6500) sponsored by Chase Bank (it was formerly brought to you by Virginia Slims) brings together the top 16 women's singles and top eight women's doubles for over a million dollars in prizes. It's held at Madison Square Garden in mid-November, and tickets cost $25–$45.

INDEX

A

Aaron Davis Hall, *225*
ABC Carpet & Home, *200*
Abigail Adams Smith Museum, *122*
Abyssinia (restaurant), *173–174*
Abyssinian Baptist Church, *56*
Academy (shop), *198, 199*
ACME Bar and Grill, *167*
Actor's Studio (theater), *230*
Ad Hoc Softwares (shop), *200*
Adobe Blues (restaurant), *181, 211*
African and American Restaurant, *180*
African Street Festival, *24, 102*
Aggie's (restaurant), *163*
Aiello's (restaurant), *178*
Airports and transfers, *3–4*
Air travel, *1–3*
  luggage, *15*
Alcohol, *10*
Alexander Hamilton U.S. Custom House, *122*
Alice Austen House, *122*
Alice Tully Hall, *51, 225*
Allerton House (hotel), *141*
Alley Pond Park, *131*
Alphabet City. *See* East Village and Alphabet City
Alternative Museum, *117*
Alvin Ailey American Dance Theater, *220*
Alwyn Court Apartments, *65*
Amato Opera Theater, *227*
America (restaurant), *162*
American Ballet Theatre, *222*
American Craft Museum, *117*
American Jewish Theatre, *231*

American Museum of Natural History, *113–115*
American Museum of the Moving Image, *124, 223*
American Negro Theatre, *122*
American Numismatic Society, *124*
American Opera Projects, *227*
American Trash (bar), *204*
Amir's Falafel, *154*
Amnesia (bar), *211*
Amtrak, *20–21*
Amusement parks, *104–105*
An Béal Bocht (restaurant), *180, 211*
Angelica Kitchen, *167*
Angelika Film Center, *223*
Anglers & Writers (restaurant), *163*
Ann and Tony's (restaurant), *180*
Annex Antiques Fair and Flea Market, *202*
Annina Nosie (gallery), *127*
Ansonia apartment building, *50*
Anthology Film Archives, *223*
Apollo Theater, *54*
Apthorp Apartments, *50*
Aquariums, *105*
Architecture, *40*
Argosy (shop), *198*
Arlington Hotel, *141*
Arroz y Feijão (restaurant), *160*
Art Bar, *206*
Art Expo, *23*
Art galleries, *125–127*
Arthur's Tavern, *217*
Art in General (gallery), *126*
Art museums, *59, 61, 62–63, 117–119*
  Brooklyn Museum, *115–116*
  The Cloisters, *116, 226*

  Metropolitan Museum of Art, *41–45, 226*
  Museum of Modern Art, *45–46, 224, 226*
  musical performances, *226*
  Whitney Museum of American Art, *116–117*
Arts centers, *219, 221–222*
Asian American Arts Centre, *117*
Asia Society, *121*
Asphalt Green (gym), *233*
Astoria, *106, 178–179*
Astor Place, *80, 82*
Astor Wines & Spirits, *185*
Atlantic Theater Company, *231*
ATMs (automated teller machines), *14*
Auction houses, *198*
Audubon Terrace, *57*
Avenue A (restaurant), *168*
Avery Fisher Hall, *51, 225*

B

Baby Jakes (restaurant), *168*
Bagel bakeries, *170*
Ballet Hispanico, *220*
Balthazar (restaurant), *174*
Banana Bungalow (hostel), *148*
Bangkok House (restaurant), *158*
Bank (dance club), *213*
Barbara Gladstone (gallery), *127*
Bar D'O, *206*
Bargemusic, *225*
Barking Dog Luncheonette, *158*
Barnard College, *53*
Barnes and Noble (shop), *181, 197*

Barneys New York (department store), *193*
Bars, *203–211*
Bar Six, *206*
Bartow-Pell Mansion, *133*
Baseball
participant, *237*
spectator, *239*
Basketball
participant, *234*
spectator, *239*
Basset Coffee and Tea Co., *183*
Battery Park, *128–129*
Battery Park City, *97–98*
Bay Ridge, *104*
Bazzini's (restaurant), *174*
Beaches, *134*
Beacon (theater), *215*
bean (restaurant), *177*
Bed-and-Breakfast on the Park, *148*
Bed-and-breakfasts, *146–148*
Bedford Street, *79–80*
Bedford-Stuyvesant, *102*
Bell Caffe, *173, 209*
Belmont, *108, 180*
Belvedere Castle, *39*
Bendix Diner, *161*
Bengal Cafe, *155*
Benny's Burritos, *163*
Bereket (restaurant), *169*
Bergdorf Goodman (department store), *193*
Best Western Manhattan, *145*
Best Western Seaport Inn, *146*
Bethesda Fountain and Terrace, *38*
Bicycling, *137, 234–235*
Big Apple Hostel, *149*
Big Cup Tea and Coffeehouse, *182*
Big Nick's Burger/Pizza Joint, *152–153*
Billie Holiday Theater, *102*
Biography Bookstore, *199*
Bitter End (club), *216*
Black Fashion Museum, *121*
Bleecker Bob's (shop), *199*
Bleecker Street Pastry Shop, *182*
Bloomingdale's (department store), *193*
Blue Note (club), *217*
Blue Rabbit International House, *148*
Blues clubs, *216–217*
Blues Supply (club), *217*
Boat tours, *31*

Bo Ky (restaurant), *171*
Book shops, *197–199*
Books of Wonder, *199*
Booth (theater), *229*
Borders Books & Music, *197*
Boston Comedy Club, *212*
Bowery Bar, *207*
Bowling, *210*
Bowling Green, *129*
Bowlmor Lanes, *210*
Bowne House, *122*
Bread Shop Cafe, *155*
Breweries, *162*
Bridge Café, *175*
Brighton Beach, *105, 134, 178*
Broadhurst (theater), *229*
Broadway (theater), *229*
Broadway American Hotel, *139*
Broadway Bed-and-Breakfast Inn, *147*
Broadway theaters, *229–230*
The Bronx
bars, *211*
exploring, *106, 108, 110*
restaurants, *180*
Bronx Museum of the Arts, *117*
Bronx Zoo, *108*
Brooklyn
bars, *211*
bed-and-breakfasts, *148*
exploring, *98–99, 101–105*
restaurants, *176–178*
Brooklyn Academy of Music (BAM), *221*
Brooklyn Anchorage, *99*
Brooklyn Botanical Garden, *131–132*
Brooklyn Bridge, *41*
Brooklyn Diner U.S.A., *159*
Brooklyn Heights, *99, 101, 176–177*
Brooklyn Heights Promenade, *99, 101*
Brooklyn Historical Society, *119*
Brooklyn Museum, *115–116*
Brownies (club), *215*
Bryant Park, *129, 158*
Bubby's (restaurant), *174*
Buddha Bar, *213*
Buddhist Temple, *88*
Burritoville, *166*
Bus tours, *30–31*
Bus travel
travelers with disabilities, *8*
to New York, *4–5*
in New York, *5, 21*

C
Cafe Borgia, *182*
Café con Leche, *153*
Cafe Mona Lisa, *182*
Café Mozart, *181*
Café Noir, *209*
Café Pick Me Up, *183*
Cafe Reggio, *182*
Cafés, *181–184*
Cafe Tabac, *207*
Cafe Tatiana, *178*
Caffé Buon Gusto, *158*
Caffe Dell Artista, *182*
Caffè Egidio, *180*
Caffe Lucca, *182*
Caffé Roma, *183*
Calabria Pork Store, *180*
Canal Jeans (shop), *195*
Canal Street, *88*
Candle Cafe, *157*
Caribbean Cultural Center, *24*
Caridad IV Restaurant, *157*
Carl Fisher Music Publishers, *82*
Carl Schurz Park, *129*
Carlton Arms (hotel), *141*
Carmine's (restaurant— downtown), *175*
Carmine's (restaurant— uptown), *154*
Carnegie Hall, *65, 215, 225*
Carnival, *24*
Caroline's Comedy Club, *212*
Carousel (Central Park), *38*
Car rental, *6*
Carroll Gardens, *101, 176–177*
Car services, *18*
Car travel, *10*
Cash machines, *14*
Cast-iron buildings, *88, 90*
Castle Clinton National Monument, *128*
Catch a Rising Star (comedy club), *212*
Cathedral of St. John the Divine, *53, 225*
CBGB's & OMFUG (club), *216*
Celebrate Brooklyn, *228*
Celebrity Path, *131–132*
Cemeteries, *57, 88*
Central Park, *35, 38–39, 41, 137*
Central Park Summerstage, *228*
Central Park West, *49*
Century 21 (shop), *195*
Chantale's Cajun Kitchen, *159*
Chanterelle (restaurant), *164*
Charging Bull Statue, *96*

Charles A. Dana Discovery Center, *39, 41*
Chatham Square, *88*
Chat 'n' Chew (restaurant), *163*
Cheap thrills, *135–137*
Chelsea
art galleries, *127*
bars, *205*
cafés and coffee bars, *182*
exploring, *71, 73*
hotels, *73*
restaurants, *161*
Chelsea Antiques Building, *202*
Chelsea Billiards, *206*
Chelsea Center Hostel, *150*
Chelsea Commons (bar), *205*
Chelsea Historic District, *71, 73*
Chelsea Hotel, *73, 145*
Chelsea Inn, *141, 144*
Chelsea International Hostel, *150*
Chelsea Piers Sports and Entertainment Complex, *71, 233–234*
Chelsea Pines Inn, *147*
Cherry Blossom Festival, *23*
Cherry Lane Theater, *80*
Chess and Checkers House, *38*
Chez Bernard (restaurant), *174*
Chez Brigitte (restaurant), *163*
Chicago City Limits (comedy club), *212*
China House Gallery, *121*
Chinatown
bars, *209*
exploring, *88*
restaurants, *171–173*
Chinatown Fair, *137*
Chinatown Ice Cream Factory, *171*
Chinese New Year, *23*
Christie's East (auction house), *198*
Christmas events, *24–25*
Chrysler Building, *69*
Chumley's (bar), *206*
Churches
Brooklyn, *99, 102*
Chelsea, *71*
Chinatown, *88*
East Village, *83*
Harlem, *56*
Lower Manhattan, *95*
Midtown, *68*
Morningside Heights, *53*
musical performances, *225–226*
Queens, *106*

Staten Island, *112–113*
Washington Heights, *57*
West Village, *77, 79*
Church of St. Luke-in-the-Fields, *77*
Church of the Transfiguration, *88*
Ciel Rouge (bar), *205*
Cinema Village, *224*
City Bakery, *162*
City Center, *221*
City Grill, *153*
City Hall, *97*
City Hall Park, *97*
City Island, *108, 110, 180*
Civic Center, *96–97*
Classic Stage Company, *231*
Cleopatra's Needle, *39*
Climbing, *235*
The Cloisters, *116, 226*
Clothing for the trip, *14*
Clothing shops, *194–196*
Cobble Hill, *101, 176–177*
Coffee bars, *181–184*
Coffee Shop (bar), *205*
Coliseum (shop), *197*
Colleges and universities
Barnard, *53*
Columbia, *51, 53, 150*
Cooper Union, *82*
NYU, *78, 150*
student housing, *150*
Yeshiva, *57*
Colonnade Row, *82*
Columbia University, *51, 53, 150, 154–155, 239–240*
Columbus Circle, *49*
Columbus Day Parade, *24*
Columbus Park, *129*
Comedy Cellar, *212*
Comedy clubs, *211–213*
Commerce Street, *80*
Commodities Exchange, *35*
Con Edison Energy Museum, *124–125*
Coney Island, *104–105, 134, 178*
Coney Island Fair, *202*
Coney Island High (club), *216*
Conference House, *122–123*
Confucius Plaza, *88*
Conservatory Garden, *39*
Consulates, *10–11*
Consumer protection, *7*
Cooler (club), *216*
Cooper-Hewitt National Design Museum, *59, 61*
Cooper Square, *82*
Cooper Union, *82*

Corner Bistro, *206*
Cort (theater), *229*
Cosenza's Fish Market, *180*
Costs, *14*
Cottage (restaurant), *153*
Cranford Rose Garden, *131*
Crate & Barrel (shop), *200*
Credit cards, *14*
Croquet, *38*
Cross-country skiing, *235*
Cucina (restaurant), *177*
Cupcake Cafe, *159*
Currency exchange, *7*
Cushman Row, *71*
Customs and duties, *7–8*
C.V. Starr Bonsai Museum, *132*
Cyber Café, *183*
Cyber services, *13*

D
Daikichi Sushi, *166*
The Dairy, *38*
Dakota apartment building, *50*
Dallas BBQ, *166*
Dance, classical and modern, *220, 222*
Dance Africa, *23*
Dance clubs, *213–214*
Dance instruction, *137*
Dance Theater Workshop, *222*
Dance Theatre of Harlem, *220*
Dance Tracks (shop), *199*
Dangerfield's (comedy club), *212*
Danspace Project, *222*
Darou Minan (restaurant), *156*
d.b.a. (bar), *207*
Dean & Deluca (market), *173, 184*
Decibel Sake Bar, *207*
De Hirsch Residence at the 92nd Street YMHA, *149*
Den of Thieves (dance club), *213*
Dentists, *11*
Department stores, *193–194*
Dia Center for the Arts, *117–118*
Diesel Superstore, *195*
Disabilities and accessibility, *8–9*
Discounts and deals, *9–10*
Dixie Drew Riding Academy, *132*
Doctors, *11*
Dojo (restaurant), *167*
Dominick's (restaurant), *180*

Don Hill's (dance club), *213*
Downtime (club), *216*
Drama Bookshop, *199*
Drama Dept. (theater
company), *231*
Drawing Center, *126*
Drinking age, *10*
Drip (coffee bar), *181*
Driving, *10*
Drugs, prescription, *11*
Duane Park Patisserie, *183*
DUMBO (Down Under the
Manhattan Bridge
Overpass), *101*
Duties. *See* Customs and duties
Dyckman House, *123*

E

Ear Inn, *209*
East Coast Memorial, *128–129*
Easter Parade, *23*
East Harlem (el barrio), *56*
East River Park, *129*
East Village and Alphabet City
bars, *207–209*
cafés and coffee bars, *183*
exploring, *80, 82–83*
restaurants, *167–169*
East Village Cheese, *185*
Edgar Allan Poe Cottage, *123*
Edison Hotel, *145*
EJ's Luncheonette, *157*
Eldridge Street Synagogue, *85*
Eli's Vinegar Factory
(restaurant), *158*
Ellis Island, *33–34*
El Museo del Barrio, *61*
El Pollo (restaurant), *157*
El Sombrero (The Hat)
(restaurant), *170*
Elvie's Turo-Turo (restaurant),
167
Emergencies, *10–11*
Empire Fulton Ferry State
Park, *132*
Empire State Building, *31–32*
Enchanted Forest (shop), *201*
Esashi (restaurant), *168*
Ess-a-Bagel (restaurant), *162*
Essex Street, *84–85*
Essex Street Pickles, *185*
Ethel Barrymore (theater), *229*
Ethel's Southern Quarters
(restaurant), *156*
Eugene O'Neill (theater), *229*
Eureka Joe (café), *182*
Excellent Dumpling House,
171–172

Excelsior Hotel, *139*
Expo (dance club), *213*

F

Fairway (market), *184*
Fanelli's Cafe, *173*
F.A.O. Schwarz (shop), *201*
Farmers' markets, *185–186*
Fashion Cafe, *159*
Fatoosh Barbecue, *176*
Feast of St. Francis, *24*
Federal Hall National
Memorial, *95*
Federal Reserve Bank, *95*
Ferrara (café), *183*
Festival Mexicana (restaurant),
170
Festival of San Gennaro, *24*
Festivals, *23–25, 223*
Fez (bar), *207*
Fiesta Folklorica, *24*
Film festivals, *223*
Film Forum, *224*
First Shearlith Israel
graveyard, *88*
First Street Cafe, *183*
Fishing, *137*
Fish's Eddy (shop), *200*
511 Lounge, *204*
Flatiron Building, *74*
Flea markets, *202*
Fleet Week, *23*
Florent (restaurant), *165*
Flower's (bar), *205*
Flushing, *106, 179*
Flushing Freedom Mile, *106*
Flushing Meadows-Corona
Park, *132*
Fontbonne Hall Academy,
104
Football
participant, *235*
spectator, *239–240*
Footlight (shop), *199*
Forbes Magazine Galleries,
125
Forbidden Planet (shop), *201*
Ford Center for the Performing
Arts, *229–230*
Forest Park, *132*
Fort Greene, *101*
Fort Greene Park, *132*
Fort Tryon Park, *129–130*
Fort Washington Park, *130*
44 (bar), *204*
Four Seasons (restaurant),
164
Fragrance Garden, *132*

Franklin Hotel, *139*
Franklin Station Cafe, *175*
Fraunces Tavern, *123*
Fresco Tortilla Grill, *160*
F. Restaurant, *169*
Frick Collection, *61, 226*
Friend of a Farmer (restaurant),
162
Friends' Meeting House, *106*
Frutti de Mare (restaurant),
168
Fujiyama Mama's (restaurant),
153
Full Moon Saloon, *205*
Fulton Fish Market, *96*

G

Gabriela's (restaurant), *153*
Galaxy (restaurant), *162*
Gardens, *127–128*
Central Park, *39*
Manhattan, *129–130*
outer boroughs, *131–133*
Garibaldi-Meucci Museum,
123
Gay Pride Parade, *24*
Gay Street, *79*
General Motors Building,
64–65
Generation (shop), *199*
Gennaro (restaurant), *153*
German-American Steuben
Parade, *24*
Gershwin (theater), *230*
Gershwin Hotel, *144*
Ghostbusters' headquarters,
91
Gingerbread House, *104*
Goethe House, *61*
Good Earth Natural Foods Inc.
(restaurant), *152*
Good Enough to Eat
(restaurant), *154*
Good Health Cafe, *158*
Gotham Book Mart, *198*
Gotham Comedy Club, *212*
Gourmet Garage (restaurant),
173
Grace Church, *79*
Gracie Mansion, *129*
Gramercy and Union Square
bars, *205*
exploring, *73–75*
restaurants, *162–163*
Gramercy Park Hotel, *145*
Gramercy Tavern, *164*
Grand Army Plaza, *64–65*
Grand Central Terminal, *69*

Grand Street Antiques Fair, *202*
Grant's Tomb, *54*
Grave of an Amiable Child, *131*
Gray's Papaya (restaurant), *152*
Great Jones Cafe, *168*
Greenmarkets, *185–186*
Greenpoint, *102, 177*
Greenwich Village. *See* West Village
Grey Art Gallery, *118*
Greyhound bus service, *5*
Gryphon (shop), *198, 199*
Guggenheim Museum, *63, 64*
Guggenheim Museum SoHo, *118*
Guided tours, *26–27, 30–31*
Guyon-Lake Tysen House, *112*
Gyms and rec centers, *233–240*

H
Hard Rock Cafe, *159*
Harlem
exploring, *54, 56*
restaurants, *155–156*
Harlem Meer, *39, 41*
Harlem Week, *24*
Harley-Davidson Cafe, *159*
Harry's Burritos, *163*
Harry's Jerk Center (restaurant), *180*
Harvest (restaurant), *176*
Hashing, *137*
Heartland Brewery, *162*
Helianthus (restaurant), *174*
Henri Bendel (department store), *193*
Henry's End (bar), *211*
Herald Square Hotel, *144*
High Rock Park, *132*
Hiking, *235–236*
Hi-Life Bar & Grill, *204*
Hispanic Society of America, *121*
Hockey
participant, *236*
spectator, *240*
Hogs and Heifers (bar), *206*
Holiday Inn Downtown, *146*
Holidays, *11*
Holly Solomon (gallery), *126*
Home (restaurant), *165*
Hope Garden, *129*
Horseback riding, *132, 133, 236*
Horse-drawn carriages, *31*

Hospitals, *11*
Hosteling International-New York, *149*
Hostelling organizations, *17*
Hostels, *148*
costs, *17*
Midtown, *149–150*
Uptown, *148–149*
Hotel Beacon, *139*
Hotel Grand Union, *144*
Hotels, *138–139*
Downtown, *146*
Midtown, *141, 144–146*
Upper East Side, *139*
Upper West Side, *139*
Hotel 17, *144*
Hotel Stanford, *145*
Hotel Wales, *139*
Hotel Wolcott, *141*
Hot lines, *11, 218–219*
Houk Friedman (gallery), *127*
Hourglass Tavern, *159*
Household furnishings, *200–201*
House of Vegetarian, *172*
Houses, historic, *112, 122–124*
Housing Works (shop), *196*
Howard Greenberg (gallery), *126*
Howard Johnson hotels
34th St., *145–146*
46th St., *205*
Huddleston Bridge, *39*
Hudson Bar and Books, *206*
Hudson River Park, *130*
Hunan Garden (restaurant), *155*
Hungarian Pastry Shop, *182*

I
Ice-skating and ice hockey, *236, 240*
Il Fornaio (restaurant), *171*
Imperial (theater), *230*
Independence Day, *24*
Independence Plaza, *91*
In-line skating, *236–237*
Institute for Contemporary Art/ Clocktower Gallery, *118*
Institute for Contemporary Art/P.S. 1 Museum, *118*
Insurance, *12*
International Center of Photography (ICP), *62*
International Expressions Festival, *24*
Internet Cafe, *183*
In the Black (café), *183*

Intrepid Air, Sea, and Space Museum, *125*
Inwood Hill Park, *130*
Isamu Noguchi Garden Museum, *118*
I.S. 44 Market, *202*
Islamic Cultural Center, *59*
Italian Food Center, *184*

J
Jackie 60 (dance club), *213*
Jackson Diner, *179*
Jackson Heights, *179*
Jacob Riis Park, *134*
Jacqueline Kennedy Onassis Reservoir, *39*
Jacques Marchais Museum of Tibetan Art, *121*
Jake's Dilemma (bar), *204*
Jamaica Bay Wildlife Refuge, *132*
Japanese Garden, *131*
Japan Society, *121*
Jazz clubs, *217*
J. Crew (shop), *195*
Jean Claude (restaurant), *174*
Jean Cocteau Repertory (theater), *231*
Jefferson Market Library, *79*
Jekyll and Hyde Club, *159*
Jeremy's Ale House, *211*
Jerry's (restaurant), *173*
Jessica Fredericks Gallery, *127*
Jet Lounge, *213*
Jewish community, *84–85*
Jewish Museum, *62*
JFK International Airport, *3–4*
Joan of Arc Statue, *131*
Joe's Dairy, *185*
Joe's Shanghai (restaurant), *179*
John Fluevog Shoes, *196*
Johnny's Reef Restaurant, *180*
John's (restaurant), *168–169*
John's Pizzeria, *163, 165, 166*
Joseph Papp Public Theater, *82, 231*
Joseph's Food Basket, *156*
Josie's (restaurant), *153*
Joyce Theater, *222*
Judson Memorial Church, *77*
Julian's Famous Poolroom, *206*
Julliard School, *51, 226*

K
Kam Man (market), *184*
Kate Spade (shop), *201*

Kate's Paperie (shop), *201*
Katz's Delicatessen, *170*
Kaufman-Astoria Studios, *106*
Kelley and Ping (restaurant), *173*
K.G.B. (bar), *207–208*
Kiehl's (shop), *201*
Kiev (restaurant), *168*
Kim Lau Arch, *88*
Kim's Underground (shop), *200*
Kingsland Homestead, *106*
Kitchen (arts center), *221*
Knitting Factory (club), *216*
Kun Paw (restaurant), *165*
Kwanzaa, *25*

L

Label (shop), *195*
La Bouillabaisse (restaurant), *176–177*
La Cabaña Salvadoreña (restaurant), *156*
La Caridad (restaurant), *153*
Ladies' Mile, *70*
La Espiga (restaurant), *178*
La Fonda Antioqueña (restaurant), *178*
La Guardia Airport, *3–4*
La MaMa E.T.C. (theater), *231*
La Paella (restaurant), *169*
Larchmont Hotel, *146*
La Rosita (restaurant), *155*
Laundry, *12*
Le Cirque 2000 (restaurant), *164*
L'Ecole (restaurant), *174*
Le Gamin (café), *183*
Leisure Time (bowling alley), *210*
Lemon (restaurant), *162*
Lemongrass Grill, *177*
Leo Castelli (gallery), *126*
Le Q (pool hall), *206*
Leshko's Coffee Shop, *167*
Les Poulets (dance club), *214*
Les Routiers (restaurant), *154*
Libraries, *53, 69, 79, 116*
Library and Museum of the Performing Arts, *51*
Life (dance club), *214*
Life Cafe, *168*
Lighthouses, *130*
Limbo (café), *183*
Lincoln Center, *49, 51, 219, 221, 225*
Lincoln Center Out-of-Doors, *228*

Lincoln Center Festival, *228*
Lincoln Plaza Cinemas, *224*
Lion's Den (club), *216*
Little India, *80*
Little Italy
  bars, *209*
  cafés and coffee bars, *183*
  exploring, *85*
  restaurants, *171*
Little Red Lighthouse, *130*
Little Rickie (shop), *201*
Little Ukraine, *80*
Loeb Boathouse, *39*
Loehmann's (shop), *195*
Loisada Street Fair, *23*
Long Island City, *179*
Lotus Garden, *130*
Love Saves the Day (shop), *201*
Lower East Side
  bars, *207–209*
  cafés and coffee bars, *183*
  exploring, *83–85*
  restaurants, *169–170*
Lower East Side Jewish Spring Festival, *24*
Lower East Side Tenement Museum, *119–120*
Lower Manhattan
  bars, *211*
  exploring, *91, 94–98*
  restaurants, *175*
Lucky Cheng's (bar), *208*
Lucky Strike (bar), *209*
Ludlow Bar, *208*
Luggage, *15*
Luna Lounge (comedy club), *212*
Luna's (restaurant), *171*
Lupe's East L.A. Kitchen, *173*
Luzia's (restaurant), *153*

M

MAC (shop), *201*
MacDougal Street, *77–78*
Macy's (department store), *193*
Madison Hotel, *144*
Madison Square, *74–75*
Madison Square Garden, *215*
Madonia Brothers Bakery, *180*
Madras Mahal (restaurant), *160*
Magazines, *13*
Majestic (theater), *230*
Malcolm Shabazz Mosque, *54*
Malibu Studios Hotel, *139*
The Mall, *38*
Mandingo Restaurant, *156*
M & I International (market), *184*

M & R Bar, *208*
Manganaro's Hero-Boy (restaurant), *159*
Manhattan. *See specific neighborhoods*
Manhattan Beach, *134*
Manhattan School of Music, *226*
Manhattan Theatre Club, *231*
Manna 2 (restaurant), *171*
Manny's Car Wash (club), *216*
Maraolo (shop), *196*
Marcus Garvey Park, *54*
Marechiaro Tavern, *209*
Marion's Continental Restaurant and Lounge, *208*
Markets, *184–186*
Mark Morris Dance Group, *220*
Martha Graham Dance Company, *220*
Martha Washington (hotel), *141*
Mary Ann's (restaurant), *166*
Match (bar), *209*
Matthew Marks (gallery), *127*
Max Fish (bar), *208*
McDonald's (Wall Street branch), *175*
McSorley's Old Ale House, *209*
Meat-packing District, *80*
Media, *12–13*
Medical aid. *See* Emergencies
Melville's Cafe, *181*
Mercbar, *208, 209–210*
Merce Cunningham Dance Company, *220*
Merchant's House Museum, *123*
Mercury Lounge, *216*
Merkin Concert Hall, *225*
Mermaid Parade, *24*
Mesa Grill, *161*
Metro Pictures (gallery), *127*
Metropolitan Museum of Art, *41–45, 226*
Metropolitan Opera Company, *227*
Metropolitan Opera House, *51, 219*
Mid-City Guest House, *150*
Midsummer Night Swing Dance Extravaganza, *137*
Midtown
  bars, *204–205*
  exploring, *64–65, 68–71*
  hotels, *141, 144–146*
  restaurants, *158–161*
Milburn (hotel), *139*

Mill (restaurant), *155*
Mio Pane, Mio Dulce Bakery, *162*
Mr. Souvlaki (restaurant), *176*
M. Knoedler (gallery), *127*
Moe Ginsberg (shop), *195*
Moishe's (restaurant), *169*
Mona's (bar), *209*
Mondo Perso (club), *217*
Money, *14*
Monkey Bar, *205*
Monsoon (restaurant), *153*
Moondance Diner, *173*
Morgan's Bar, *205*
Morningside Heights
exploring, *51, 53–54*
restaurants, *154–155*
Moroccan Star (restaurant), *176*
Morris-Healy (gallery), *127*
Morris Heights, *180*
Morris-Jumel Mansion, *123–124*
Mosques, *54, 59*
Mostly Mozart (festival), *228*
Motown Cafe, *159*
Mt. Tom, *131*
Movie houses, *55, 223–224*
Movie museums, *124*
Movie studios, *106*
Muffin Man (café), *182*
Municipal Building, *97*
Museum for African Art, *118*
Museum Mile Festival, *24*
Museum of American Financial History, *125*
Museum of American Folk Art, *118*
Museum of American Illustration, *118–119*
Museum of Chinese in the Americas, *121*
Museum of Jewish Heritage, *98*
Museum of Modern Art (MoMA), *45–46, 224, 226*
Museum of Television and Radio, *124*
Museum of the City of New York, *62*
Museums, *113, 125. See also* Art museums
American Museum of Natural History, *113–115*
ethnic and cultural, *62, 98, 121–122*
historic houses, *122–124*
movies and television, *124*

New York history, *62, 119–120*
Pierpont Morgan Library, *116*
science, *124–125*
Music, classical, *224–227*
Music, popular, *214–217*

N

Naked Lunch (bar), *208*
Nam (restaurant), *177*
Nathan's Famous (restaurant), *178*
National Academy of Design, *62–63*
National Black Theater, *231*
National Museum of the American Indian, *122*
NBC Studio Tour, *27*
Neil Simon (theater), *230*
Nell's (dance club), *214*
Netherlands Memorial Flagpole, *129*
New Amsterdam (theater), *230*
Newark International Airport, *3–4*
New City Café, *177*
New Dramatists (theater), *231*
New Jersey Devils, *240*
New Jersey Nets, *239*
New Lung Fung (restaurant), *171*
New Museum of Contemporary Art, *119*
New Republic (shop), *195*
News Bar, *181*
Newspapers, *12–13*
Newsstands, *12*
New Victory (arts center), *221*
New Year's Eve, *23*
New York Aquarium for Wildlife Conservation, *105*
New York Bed-and-Breakfast, *147*
New York Botanical Garden (NYBG), *132–133*
New York City Bagels (restaurant), *152*
New York City Ballet, *222*
New York City Fire Museum, *120*
New York City Marathon, *24*
New York City Opera, *227*
New York City Police Museum, *120*
New York Comedy Club, *212*
New York Earth Room (gallery), *126*
New York Film Festival, *24*
New York Giants, *239*

New-York Historical Society, *120*
New York Inn, *144*
New York Is Book Country fair, *24*
New York Islanders, *240*
New York Jets, *239*
New York Knickerbockers, *239*
New York Marathon, *238*
New York Mets, *239*
New York Public Library, *69–70*
New York Rangers, *240*
New York Shakespeare Festival, *228*
New York Skyride, *32*
New York State Supreme Court, *75*
New York State Theater, *51, 219*
New York Stock Exchange, *94–95*
New York Theater Workshop, *231*
New York Transit Museum, *120, 201*
New York Unearthed (museum), *120*
New York University, *78, 150*
New York Video Festival, *24*
New York Yankees, *239*
Nha Trang (restaurant), *172*
Nicholas Roerich Museum, *119*
NikeTown (shop), *201*
92nd Street Y, *221, 222*
99X (shop), *196*
1909 Company (shop), *196*
Ninth Avenue International Food Festival, *23*
Ninth Street Market (café), *183*
Nobu (restaurant), *164*
North Star Pub, *211*
Norwegian Constitution Day Parade, *23, 104*
Novecento (bar), *210*
Nuyorican Poets Cafe, *228*

O

Obaa Koryoe (restaurant), *155*
Odessa (restaurant), *167*
Off-Broadway theaters, *230–232*
Off SoHo Suites, *146*
Old Navy (shop), *195*
Old Town Bar, *162*
Omari (shop), *196–197*
O.M.G. (shop), *195*
Omonia (restaurant), *178*

Opera, *226–227*
Orchard Street Bargain District, *85*
Osso Buco (restaurant), *154*
Other Music (shop), *200*
Our Lady of Mount Carmel, *112–113*
Oyster Bar and Restaurant, *69*
Oznot's Dish (restaurant), *177*
Ozzie's Coffee and Tea, *176*

P

Pace Wildenstein (gallery), *127*
Packing for New York, *14–15*
Pan-Asian Repertory Theatre, *231*
Panna (restaurant), *168*
Paradise Cafe, *182*
Paramount (theater), *215*
Park Avalon (restaurant), *163*
Parking, *10*
Park Luncheonette, *177*
Parks, *127–135*
Central Park, *35, 38–39, 41, 137*
East Village, *83*
Gramercy and Union Square, *73–75*
Harlem, *54*
Lower Manhattan, *97*
Midtown, *69–70*
Queens, *106*
TriBeCa, *91*
West Village, *77*
Park Savoy (hotel), *141*
Park Slope, *102–104, 177*
Park Slope Brewing Company (restaurant), *177*
Parsonage (restaurant), *181*
Partners & Crime (shop), *199*
Passports and visas, *15*
Pat Hearn Gallery, *127*
Pat O'Brien's (bar), *204*
Patria (restaurant), *162*
Patricia Field (shop), *195*
Patsy Grimaldi's Pizza, *176*
Patsy's Pizzeria, *157*
Paula Cooper Gallery, *127*
Peacock (café), *182*
Pearl Street Diner, *175*
Pearl Theatre Company, *231*
Pearson's Texas Barbecue, *179*
Peculier Pub, *207*
Pelham Bay Park, *133*
Penang (restaurant—SoHo), *174*
Penang (restaurant—Queens), *179*
Pennsylvania Pretzel Co., *174*

Pen Top Bar and Terrace, *205*
Performing Garage, *221*
Perretti Italian Cafe, *154*
Pershing Square Park, *69*
Peter Luger Steak House, *164*
Peter's Waterfront Alehouse, *211*
Pete's Tavern, *163*
Pharmacies, *11*
Pho Viet Huong (restaurant), *173*
Pickwick Arms Hotel, *144*
Pierpont Morgan Library, *116*
Pink Tea Cup (restaurant), *165*
Pintaile's Pizza, *157*
Planet Hollywood (restaurant), *159*
Plane travel. *See* Air travel
Playwrights Horizons (theater), *231*
Plaza Hotel, *64*
Pò (restaurant), *167*
Pool halls, *206*
Pop Shop, *202*
Portland Square Hotel, *144*
Positively 104th Street (café), *182*
Pravda (bar), *210*
Primary Stages (theater), *232*
Primorski (restaurant), *178, 211*
Printed Matter (shop), *199*
Prison Ship Martyr's Monument, *101*
Prospect Park, *133*
Provincetown Playhouse, *78*
P.S. 122 (arts center), *221*
Puerto Rican Day Parade, *24*
Puglia (restaurant), *171*

Q

Quad Cinema, *224*
Quality Hotel East Side, *144–145*
Queens
bars, *211*
exploring, *105–106*
restaurants, *178–179*
Queens Museum of Art, *119*

R

Raccoon Lodge (bar), *204*
Radio City Music Hall, *68, 215*
Radio stations, *13*
Rain (restaurant), *154*
Rainbow Room, *65*
Rainy Days Cafe, *216*
The Ramble, *39*
Randazzo's Clam Bar, *178*

Ratner's (restaurant), *170*
RBBQ (restaurant), *177, 211*
Rebar (bar), *205*
Record, tape, and CD shops, *199–200*
Red Bench (bar), *210*
Red Blazer Too (club), *217*
Reggae clubs, *216–217*
Regional Thai Taste (restaurant), *161*
Reliable (restaurant), *156*
Repertorio Español (theater), *232*
Restaurants, *14, 151–152*
The Bronx, *180*
Brooklyn, *176–178*
cuisine listings, *172, 187–190*
Manhattan, *152–175*
Queens, *178–179*
special features listing, *190–191*
Staten Island, *181*
Rest rooms, *15*
Resurrection (shop), *196*
Rhodes (restaurant), *180*
Richmondtown Restoration, *112*
Rio Mar (restaurant), *165, 207*
Ristorante Egidio, *180*
Riverbank State Park, *131*
Riverdale, *180*
Riverside Church, *53, 226*
Riverside Church Cafeteria, *155*
Riverside Park, *130, 131*
Riverside Tower (hotel), *139*
Rizzoli (shop), *197*
Rockaway Beach, *134*
Rock clubs, *216*
Rockefeller Center, *65, 68*
Roosevelt Island, *63*
Rosebank, *112–113*
Rose is Vintage (shop), *196*
Roseland (theater), *215*
Roxy (dance club), *214*
Royal Canadian Pancake House, *166*
Ruby's Taphouse, *204*
Running and jogging, *237*
Russ and Daughters (market), *184*

S

Safety, *16*
Sahadi Importing Company, *184*
Sahara East (restaurant), *168*
St. Ann's and the Holy Trinity Church, *99*
St. Anthony of Padua Feast, *24*

St. Demetrios Cathedral, *106*
St. Dymphna's (restaurant), *169*
St. Francis Xavier Cabrini Chapel, *57*
St. Luke's Place, *80*
St. Mark's Bookshop, *197*
St. Mark's-in-the-Bowery Church, *83*
St. Marks Place, *82*
St. Patrick's Cathedral, *68*
St. Patrick's Day Parade, *23*
St. Paul's Chapel, *95, 225–226*
St. Peter's Episcopal Church, *71*
Saks Fifth Avenue (department store), *193*
Samalita's (restaurant), *157*
Sambuca (restaurant), *154*
Sam's Noodle Shop & Grill Bar, *161*
Sapporo (restaurant), *159*
Sardi's (bar), *205*
Schapiro's Winery, *84–85*
Scharmann's (café), *184*
Schomburg Center for Research in Black Culture, *122*
Screaming Mimi's (shop), *196*
Seagram Building, *68*
Seaport Soup Company (restaurant), *175*
Second Avenue Deli, *169*
Selam Cafe, *155*
7B (bar), *207*
Shakespeare & Co. (shop), *197*
Shakespeare Garden, *131*
Sheep Meadow, *38*
Sheepshead Bay, *105, 178*
Sheridan Square, *79*
Shoe shops, *196–197*
Shopping, *192–193*
book shops, *197–199*
clothing shops, *194–196*
department stores, *193–194*
flea markets, *202*
food markets, *184–186*
household furnishings, *200–201*
record, tape, and CD shops, *199–200*
shoe shops, *196–197*
specialty stores, *201–202*
Shubert (theater), *230*
Sidewalk Café, *209*
Signature Theatre Company, *232*
Simmons African Arts Museum, *102*
Singleton's Bar-B-Que, *156*
69th Regiment Armory, *75*
Skiing, *235*

Smalls (club), *217*
Smylonylon (shop), *196*
Snug Harbor Cultural Center, *112*
S.O.B.'s (Sounds of Brazil) (club), *217*
Soccer, *237*
Socrates Sculpture Park, *133*
Softball, *237*
SoHo
art galleries, *126*
bars, *209–210*
cafés and coffee bars, *183–184*
exploring, *88, 90*
restaurants, *173–174*
SoHo Kitchen and Bar, *174*
Soldiers' and Sailors' Memorial Arch, *103*
Sony Theatres Lincoln Square, *224*
Sony Wonder Technology Lab, *125*
Sophie's (bar), *207*
Sotheby's Arcade (auction house), *198*
Soul Fixin's (restaurant), *159*
Sounds (shop), *200*
Soup Burg (restaurant), *157*
Soup Kitchen International, *160*
South Bronx, *110*
South Street Seaport, *96*
South Street Seaport Museum, *120*
Spoken word venues, *227–228*
Sports and outdoor activities, *233–240*
Spring Flower Show, *23*
Spring Lounge, *209*
Spring Street Market and Deli, *173*
Stand-up New York (comedy club), *212–213*
Starbucks coffee bars, *181*
Staten Island
bars, *211*
beaches, *134*
exploring, *110, 112–113*
restaurants, *181*
Staten Island Ferry, *112*
Staten Island Historical Society Museum, *120*
Statue of Liberty, *32–33*
Steinhardt Conservatory, *132*
Stone (gallery), *127*
Strand (shop), *198*
Strawberry Fields, *39*
Striver's Row, *56*
Student housing, *17, 150*

Student travel tips, *16–17*
Studio Museum in Harlem, *119*
Subway system, *17, 21*
travelers with disabilities, *8*
Sugar Hill International House, *149*
Sullivan Street Playhouse, *232*
Summer arts, *228*
Sweet Basil (club), *217*
Sweet 'n' Tart Cafe, *172*
Swimming, *238*
Sylvia and Danny Kaye Playhouse, *221*
Sylvia's (restaurant), *156*
Syms (shop), *195*
Synagogues, *85*
System (dance club), *214*

T

Tachigui-Soba (restaurant), *159*
Taco Taco (restaurant), *158*
Takashimaya New York (department store), *194*
Tamarind Seed Health Food Store, *155*
Taquería de México (restaurant), *165*
Tartine (restaurant), *165*
Taxis, *18*
Taylor's (restaurant), *161*
Telephone Bar and Grill, *169*
Telephone service, *18–19*
Tenement buildings, *84*
Tennis
participant, *238*
spectator, *240*
1020 Amsterdam (bar), *204*
Tepper Galleries, *198*
Thailand Restaurant, *172*
Thanksgiving Parade, *24*
Theater, *229–232*
Theater District, *70–71*
Theodore Roosevelt Birthplace, *124*
31 Division Dim Sum House, *172*
Thomas Pell Wildlife Refuge and Sanctuary, *133*
Thread Waxing Space (gallery), *126*
Throckmorton (gallery), *127*
Ticket services, *219*
Tierras Colombianas (restaurant), *179*
Times Square, *70*
Timing the trip, *22–25*
Tipping, *19*
Tivoli (restaurant), *161*

Tokio 7 (shop), *190*
Tolls, *10*
Tompkins Square Park, *83*
Tom's Restaurant, *155*
Tortilla Flats (restaurant), *165, 207*
Tour operators, *19–20*
Tower Books, *197*
Tower Records and Video, *200*
Town Hall (theater), *215, 221*
Train travel, *20–21*
Tramps (theater), *215*
Transportation, *21*
Travel agencies, *21*
gay and lesbian travelers, *11*
travelers with disabilities, *9*
Travel gear, *21*
TriBeCa
art galleries, *126*
bars, *209–210*
cafés and coffee bars, *183–184*
exploring, *90–91*
restaurants, *174–175*
TriBeCa Film Center, *98*
Tribeca Grill, *174*
Tribeca Performing Arts Center, *222*
Trinity Cemetery, *57*
Trinity Church, *95, 225–226*
Triple Eight Palace (restaurant), *172*
Tripoli Restaurant, *176*
Trois Canards (restaurant), *161*
Tunnel (dance club), *214*
TV museums, *124*
TV studio audiences, *136*
TV studio tours, *27*
Tweed Courthouse, *97*
Twilo (dance club), *214*
2A (bar), *207*
Two Boots restaurants
Brooklyn, *177*
East Village, *169*

U

Ukrainian Festival, *23*
Ukrainian Museum, *122*
Umberto's Clam House, *171*
Uncle George's (restaurant), *179*
Uncle Mo's (restaurant), *161*
Under ACME (club), *216*
Union Square. *See* Gramercy and Union Square
Union Square Cafe, *164*
United Nations, *68–69*
United States Open Tennis Tournament, *240*

Universal Grill, *165*
Upper East Side
art galleries, *127*
bars, *204*
exploring, *57, 59, 61–63*
restaurants, *157–158*
Upper West Side
bars, *204*
exploring, *46, 49–51*
hotels, *139*
restaurants, *152–154*
Uptown Hostel, *149*
Urban Center, *68*
U.S. Government, *21–22*

V

Van Cortlandt Park, *133, 135*
Vertigo (dance club), *214*
Veselka (restaurant), *167*
Vietnam Veterans Memorial, *95*
Views of New York, *135*
Village Mingala (restaurant), *168*
Village Natural Health Food Restaurant, *165*
Village Vanguard (club), *217*
Vineyard Theater, *232*
Virgil's Real BBQ, *159*
Virgin Megastore Times Square, *200*
Visas. *See* Passports and visas
Visitor information, *22*
Volleyball, *238*
Voorlezer's House, *112*

W

Walking tours, *27, 30*
Wall Street, *94*
Walter Kerr (theater), *230*
Walter Reade Theater, *224*
Washington Arch, *77*
Washington Heights
exploring, *56–57*
restaurants, *156–157*
Washington Jefferson Hotel, *145*
Washington Market Park, *131*
Washington Square, *77*
Washington Square Art Show, *24*
Washington Square Hotel, *146*
Wave Hill estate, *124*
WaxBar, *210*
Weather, *22–23*
Webster Hall (dance club), *214*
Weeping Beech Tree, *106*
Wellington Hotel, *146*
West End Gate Café, *212*

Westminster Kennel Club Dog Show, *23*
Westside Cottage II (restaurant), *160*
West Village
bars, *205–207*
cafés and coffee bars, *182*
exploring, *75, 77–80*
restaurants, *163, 165, 167*
Wetlands (club), *216*
Whiskey Bar, *205*
White Horse Tavern, *207*
Whitney Museum of American Art, *116–117*
Whole Foods (restaurant), *173*
Wildlife Conservation Center (Zoo), *38*
Wildlife refuges, *133*
William Doyle Galleries, *198*
Williamsbridge, *180*
Williamsburg, *102, 177*
Williamsburgh Savings Bank Tower, *101*
Williams-Sonoma Outlet Center, *200*
Wilson's Bakery and Restaurant, *157*
Wineries, *84–85*
Winter Antiques Show, *23*
Winter Garden (theater), *230*
Women travelers, *16*
Won Jo (restaurant), *159*
Woolworth Building, *97*
World Financial Center, *98*
World Trade Center, *34–35*

Y

Yaffa Café, *168*
Yaffa's Bar and Restaurant, *175*
Yeshiva University, *57*
YMCA-McBurney, *150*
YMCA overnight centers, *17*
YMCA-Vanderbilt, *150*
YMCA-West Side, *149*
Yonah Schimmel's Knishery, *169*
York Theatre Company, *232*

Z

Zabar's (market), *152, 184*
Zenon (restaurant), *179*
Zen Palate (restaurant), *163*
Ziegfeld (movie theater), *224*
Zinc Bar, *210*
Zona (shop), *201*
Zoos, *38, 108*